Technology Management

Text and International Cases

Technology Management
Text and International Cases

Norma Harrison
Macquarie University, Australia

Danny Samson
University of Melbourne, Australia

Boston Burr Ridge, IL Dubuque, IA Madison, WI New York
San Francisco St. Louis Bangkok Bogotá Caracas Kuala Lumpur
Lisbon London Madrid Mexico City Milan Montreal New Delhi
Santiago Seoul Singapore Sydney Taipei Toronto

McGraw-Hill Higher Education

A Division of The **McGraw-Hill** Companies

TECHNOLOGY MANAGEMENT: TEXT AND INTERNATIONAL CASES

Published by McGraw-Hill, an imprint of The McGraw-Hill Companies, Inc. 1221 Avenue of the Americas, New York, NY, 10020. Copyright © 2002, by The McGraw-Hill Companies, Inc. All rights reserved. No part of this publication may be reproduced or distributed in any form or by any means, or stored in a data base or retrieval system, without the prior written consent of The McGraw-Hill Companies, Inc., including, but not limited to, in any network or other electronic storage or transmission, or broadcast for distance learning.

Some ancillaries, including electronic and print components, may not be available to customers outside the United States.

This book is printed on acid-free paper.

domestic   1 2 3 4 5 6 7 8 9 0 DOC/DOC 0 9 8 7 6 5 4 3 2 1
international 1 2 3 4 5 6 7 8 9 0 DOC/DOC 0 9 8 7 6 5 4 3 2 1

ISBN   0-07-238355-0

Publisher: *Robin J. Zwettler*
Executive sponsoring editor: *Richard T. Hercher, Jr.*
Developmental editor: *Lee Stone*
Marketing manager: *Zina Craft*
Project manager: *Natalie Ruffatto*
Production supervisor: *Rose Hepburn*
Media producer: *Greg Bates*
Designer: *Artemio Ortiz Jr.*
Supplement producer: *Nathan Perry*
Cover design: *Artemio Ortiz Jr.*
Interior design: *Artemio Ortiz Jr.*
Typeface: *10/12 Times Roman*
Compositor: *Lachina Publishing Services*
Printer: *R. R. Donnelley & Sons Company*

Library of Congress Cataloging-in-Publication Data

Harrison, Norma.
    Technology management : text and international cases / Norma Harrison, Danny Samson.
        p. cm.
    Includes index.
    ISBN 0-07-238355-0 (alk. paper)
    1. Technology—Management. 2. Technology—Management—Case studies. I. Samson,
Danny. II. Title.
T49.5 .H37 2002

                                                                    2001034238

INTERNATIONAL EDITION ISBN 0-07-112125-0
Copyright © 2002. Exclusive rights by The McGraw-Hill Companies, Inc. for manufacture and export.
This book cannot be re-exported from the country to which it is sold by McGraw-Hill.
The International Edition is not available in North America.

www.mhhe.com

Brief Contents

Contents

Cases

Preface

This book focuses on two themes. The first theme is that technology and its management are becoming increasingly important and pervasive in businesses and the community. The second core theme is that managers of the future will need to be globally oriented in every respect, and hence need to understand technology and all other aspects of management and leadership in an international context.

Consider briefly the history of technology. Since the origin of the human species, our distinguishing feature has been our ability to use our intellect to build and use tools to leverage our efforts to gain control within and over our environment. From early hunting tools, through the wheel, the steam engine, electricity, and more recently manufacturing automation and the Internet, new technologies have given people, individually and collectively, increasing power to accomplish goals.

In the modern organisation, three key variables are thought to drive competitiveness:

1. Strategic leadership, meaning that the firm is set on a path and well led towards doing the right thing in terms of products, markets, etc.
2. A motivated and committed workforce, achieving the "high performance" work culture
3. Effective use of technology in driving effective and competitive outcomes for the organisation

This book focuses on the third of these factors, but cannot and does not ignore the first two. The first element of business strategy and leadership is in a general sense assumed as a given when we address technology and its management, although the technological opportunities should themselves be an input to strategy formulation.

In respect of employee motivation, it is difficult to implement anything success-fully if the workforce is not committed, but we observe that in many workplaces around the world, "people management" in organisations has improved over the past two decades, even though there is always room for improvement. Once a company or set of companies achieves and sustains high levels of motivation within its workforce, where is the next major competitive battlefield to be found? The answer lies in the field of technology and its management, and more specifically in how well these firms can cap-ture or develop technology, then use that technology to drive their market power and operational effectiveness forward.

Consider the competitive battles that are fought each day in marketplaces in every region of the world between Ford, GM, and Toyota; IBM, Toshiba, Compaq, and Dell; Microsoft, Netscape, and Apple; Deutsche Bank and Citigroup; and many thousands of other companies, from gigantic multinationals to small businesses. They compete on the value that their products and services offer to customers, including the benefits based on the technical features of these, and the cost effectiveness that allows them to competitively price these offerings. The effectiveness through which technology can be developed, introduced, and managed is a major consideration in these competitiveness factors, and hence in determining which companies will be the winners and losers in every market. Indeed, we believe that as business leaders and government policymakers become better at formulating policy and strategy, and as managers and supervisors improve their people-management skills, technology-based, competitive advantage increases in relative importance in most corporate environments.

Some key factors that are explored in this book are expressed as questions below:

- How can companies best source technology in terms of both their products' technical content and features, and their organisations' productive processes?
- When introducing new technology into an organisation, what lessons have been learned by companies around the world in terms of what works?
- What "soft" organisational or cultural and leadership factors relate to success in introducing and implementing new technology?
- What processes, routines, and disciplines tend to lead to success in implementing new technology?
- How do these key success factors vary across different cultures in the world, and what generic elements of success might exist that managers could use in implementing technological change?

These questions are addressed in both the text and cases in this book. Further, this is done through addressing the cultural differences that exist in companies in a variety of industries throughout the world, and across a vast range of technologies, from prod-uct to process, from hard to soft technologies, and from manufacturing through services to Internet-based technologies. The issues are examined in case studies drawn from large multinational companies to smaller single site businesses.

We want to thank the many case study contributors who worked with us in devel-oping the many new cases in this book and who formed a great global team:

Gayle Avery (Institute for International Business Studies, Germany; now Macquarie University, Australia)

Jim Barker, Robert Klassen and Paul Beamish (University of Western Ontario, Canada)

Michael Bommer (Clarkson University, USA), Manuel V. Heitor and Conceicao Vedovello (Instituto Superior Tecnico, Portugal) and Pedro de Noronha Pissarra (BIOTECNOL, Portugal)

Alan Brown and Marc Saupin (Edith Cowan University, Australia)

Karen Brown (Seattle University, USA), Kavasseri V. Ramanathan (University of Washington, USA)

Mark Frohlich (Boston University, USA; now London Business School)

Rebecca Grant (University of Western Ontario, Canada)

John J. Kanet (Clemson University, USA)

Kee Young Kim (Yonsei University, Korea)

Jinichiro Nakane (Waseda University, Japan)

Paul Richardson and Peter Weill (University of Melbourne, Australia)

Peter J. Sackett (Cranfield University, UK)

Graeme Sheather (University of Technology Sydney, Australia)

Thomas G. Schmitt (University of Washington, USA)

Christopher A. Voss and Pär Ahlström (London Business School)

More recently, Simon Poon, Frederique Balard, Scott Cameron, and Jenny Pangas were instrumental in reviewing, updating, and rewriting a number of the cases. We thank them for their generosity of time and care taken in this difficult task.

Acknowledgment is made to Jeffery Miller and Steve Rosenthal of Boston University (USA) for arranging the production of the Hewlett-Packard case; Stuart Romm, Managing Director of HPM (Australia) in the production of the HPM case; and Ivey Publishing in the Richard Evey School of Business, The University of Western Ontario (Canada) for the release of the International Decorative Glass and Advanced Book Exchange, Inc. cases.

We would like to convey our sincere appreciation to the reviewers of this book's proposal and manuscript and thank them for their useful comments and suggestions:

Timothy W. Edlund (Morgan State University)

Sarvanan Devaraj (University of Notre Dame)

Phillip C. Frey (Boise State University)

Richard Goodman (UCLA)

James H. Patterson (Indiana University)

Jeffrey L. Rummel (University of Connecticut)

Marc J. Schniederjans (University of Nebraska)

Bruce M. Smackey (Lehigh University)

We also thank and acknowledge the Australian Government, and particularly Mr. Joe Williams, who supported this project from the start. In 1996–97, we were members of a team that reviewed the adoption and implementation of new technology for the federal government's Department of Industry, Science and Resources. The Department funded the production of a number of the cases included in this book.

Dick Hercher, Lee Stone, Natalie Ruffatto, and the team at McGraw-Hill USA were instrumental in bringing this book to fruition from its beginnings as an applied research project. We certainly appreciate their patience and support through this project.

Finally we thank our respective institutions, Macquarie University and the University of Melbourne as well as the Australian Research Council, for the resources and support that made this work possible.

This book has been designed for courses in the management of technology that combine both the conceptual frameworks and foundations of the field with the practical, real issues that are best highlighted via the case study method.

Norma Harrison
Macquarie University

Danny Samson
University of Melbourne

A Review of Technology Management

Technology management and its subfields are relevant to the needs of government policymakers, industry leaders, and business management students. The subfields covered in this book, which collectively define the field of technology management, include:

- Technology strategy.
- Development of technological capability.
- Innovation management.
- Technological forecasting.
- Technology management, manufacturing strategy, and business competitiveness interfaces.
- Barriers to the adoption of technology.
- Technology and manufacturing flexibility.
- E-business, a rapidly developing field of new technology.

An acute awareness of the issues and complexities associated with managing technology, on behalf of all stakeholders—including policymakers and industry leaders in particular—is a prerequisite for successfully managing wealth creation. We begin this text with a general introduction to the open questions in this field, followed by specific coverage of each of the subfields listed above.

What constitutes technology management and why is it important in the new millennium? We address the first part of this question in Chapter 1, which examines the key issues and the existing knowledge base of the "management of technology" field, both in concept and in practice. This chapter aims to highlight a series of questions and issues about the management of technology, each of which can be further explored in the other chapters of this book. In addition, this book's case studies, taken from most corners of the globe, offer another avenue for exploration in an applied setting.

Why are these fields of technical knowledge and technology management practice important? The answer is simple and demonstrates the power inherent in the field of technology management:

> Technology management is the ultimate battleground that will determine which companies and owners will be the winners and losers in the wealth creation game.

Technology has always been the mechanism through which humankind has leveraged its efforts, both individually and collectively, to improve its quality of life. Early forms of "technology," broadly defined, included simple tools such as the axe, the spear, bows and arrows, and other similar implements that helped people to survive many thousands of years ago. Later came the wheel, the steam engine, electricity, the telegraph, the automated combine harvester, the steam engine, the internal combustion engine, the automobile, penicillin, nuclear power, aircraft, computers, the Internet, automated manufacturing equipment, biotechnologies, and so on. Each of these inventions either provided new technology or used technology as a lever of control over the natural environment to improve the quality of life for people. Technology can be conceived of as artificial or human-devised tools or aids for accomplishing tasks that have a goal or purpose. Control over the natural environment, usually enabled or enhanced through technologies, can be thought of as defining the difference that sets apart the human race from other species such as chimpanzees.

Technology has become a key factor in defining competitive advantage in the modern business world, and it is likely to become an even more pervasive factor of production in the future. Imagine a global corporate environment in which the key issue facing corporations is not employee relations, due to the achievement of appropriate skill levels by every member of the work force, high work force commitment levels, and their reflection on managerial controls and policies. Leaders are getting better at managing workers, and leadership is now better understood and practised than ever before. Once you have a high performance work culture, what is next and what do you do with it? Further, if a number of the major players in your industry have a high performance work culture, how will they strive for competitive advantage? The answer is through being better at the management of technological innovation.

We all have heard CEOs say things like, "People are our most important resource." That will always be true and is a useful motivational line for CEOs to regularly repeat. But they say that partly because there is still a competitive advantage to be gained by achieving superior motivation and partly because people can listen to them—and their technology resources cannot. In fact, it is reasonable to mount a case that technology resources are very important indeed to many companies. Intellectual property mostly relates to technology, not people. We invest in it, protect it, develop and nurture it, and try to exploit it for commercial advantage.

This clearly applies in spades to high technology industries such as advanced engineering, electronics, biological sciences, aerospace and aviation, hardware, and electronic commerce and software. But it also applies to industries in which the technology does not at first seem nearly so "high." An example is the tire industry, in which the technology of tire design and the design of tire-building technology does not at first appear very sophisticated to those of us who use them on a daily basis. In fact, there are really only three major companies in the world that are capable of making the techno-logical investments necessary to stay independently competitive through tire product and process technology. The many smaller tire companies that exist in the world must acquire this level of technology by licensing it or establishing technical agreements with the big three. This was the case with the South Pacific Tyre Company. Previously a local com-pany in Australia, South Pacific found it needed to join one of the big three groups to keep its products and processes competitive. It investigated more than one of these three major players, ended up with a 50:50 venture with the Goodyear Group, and then was able to get access to its technology and technical support. This joint venture was not about that "most important resource"—people—but about competitiveness and survival of the local firm, which hinged primarily on technological competitiveness.

As we have generally become better at managing our work forces, we have moved on from the paradigm of "management coercion and worker recalcitrance" (Adler, 1993). In the past, the context of technology management often has been that little or no freedom exists to make the changes involved in acquiring, developing, introducing, and exploiting new technology. Managers' attention over the past 50 years has been taken up predominantly with "people problems," which often have stopped them from prop-erly resourcing technological developments. However, all this is changing, and in well-led companies the change is complete. Technology management and innovation in par-ticular are becoming the ultimate battleground for leading companies.

As of the end of the twentieth century, the world's best firms have already achieved this freedom in respect to their human resources—major elements of which are the free-dom to be flexible and responsive, introduce rapid change, and innovate. The rest of the global economy is following slowly but surely and, as this freedom spreads, strong forces of innovation are becoming unleashed. As a result, the importance of competence and indeed excellence in the management of technology (both in product and process) can be expected to increase substantially.

Consider leading international competitors such as Xerox versus Canon, Toyota versus GM, Ford versus Honda, IBM versus Apple, Motorola versus numerous Japan-ese counterparts, and Fuji versus Kodak. The ability of these companies to develop, implement, and achieve speedy returns on technology investments in product and process innovations is their key competitive battleground. The enabling conditions for technological innovation that now exist have permitted major performance improve-ments to occur—to the benefit of all key stakeholders, including customers, suppliers, employees at all levels, shareholders, and the economy. As the new cooperative rela-tionship between the suppliers of capital and labour becomes widespread, opportunities for the improved management of technology will also increase.

As we know from lessons learned by industry, usually the hard way, competence in the technical content of technology is not enough. The key drivers of success or failure are the managerial conditions, systems, and decisions that surround the technology. This is generally true whether one considers new product successes or failures, manufactur-ing processes, or conspicuous examples, such as the space shuttle *Challenger* disaster.

The adoption and implementation of technology can be thought of as one impor-tant aspect of innovation. Innovation is generally considered in terms of new products, new processes, new managerial approaches, and indeed, combinations of these three.

Burgelman and Maidique (1988) provide a synthesis of an innovative capabilities framework composed of the following terms, which can be considered as the variables associated with innovation:

- *Resource availability and allocation.* Considered as the level of research and development funding as well as the breadth and depth of skills in R&D, engineering, and market research. This also includes competencies in terms of technologies relative to the business and the way in which R&D and innovative resources are attracted, developed, distributed, and implemented. This includes new products and process innovations.
- *The organisation's ability to understand its competitors' innovative strategies and industry evolution.* This includes an organisation's data gathering and intelligence systems and its ability to identify and analyse its competitors' innovation strategies and changes to the industry and market structure.
- *The business's technological environment.* What are the technological opportunities and what is the business capacity for technological forecasting? Another variable in this respect is the capacity to assess relevant technologies and to identify and exploit them.
- *The structural and cultural context of the business.* This class of variables includes the mechanisms for managing R&D efforts and transferring technology from research and development to commercial contexts. It also includes the treatment and funding of new product initiatives and ideas from employees as well as the reward system associated with the entrepreneurial behaviour and the values and definitions of success in the business.
- *The business's strategic management capacity in dealing with entrepreneurial behaviour.* What is the business's management capacity to define development strategies, assess priorities, and develop and merge core technical capabilities as well as product and process improvement champions?

Fusfeld (in Burgelman and Maidique) suggests that technology should be considered in the organisational or corporate context, with the following questions being most important:

- How are technological issues recognised by senior management? As a black box? As an input to long-range planning? For meeting short-term objectives?
- How explicit is the recognition of technology in each of these roles?
- How has management used technology to implement strategic objectives?
- How is technology being monitored?
- How are activities relevant to technology recognised and organised in the enterprise?

Fusfeld points to the following seven qualities as determining the success of any technology in industry:

1. Functional performance—an evaluation of the basic function that a device is supposed to perform.

2. Acquisition costs.
3. Ease of use characteristics (i.e., the user interface).
4. Operating costs.
5. Reliability.
6. Serviceability.
7. Compatibility.

Fusfeld's seven points relate to the importance of matching technology and technological push with market pull, which can be considered across the seven dimensions. Technological push can be thought of as the production of technology, coming typically from technical specialists such as scientists and engineers. Market pull means understanding customer requirements, market trends, and competitors' offerings and translating this knowledge into specifications for innovative products and services, which may require technological developments to be fulfilled.

In terms of the management of high technology firms and technologically intensive products and processes, Maidique and Hayes (in Burgelman and Maidique, 1988) have pointed out the existence of a significant paradox:

> Some of the behavioural patterns that these companies displayed seemed to favour promoting disordered informality while others would have us conclude that it was consistency, continuity, integration, and order that were the keys to success. As we grappled with this apparent paradox, we came to realise that continued success in a high-technology environment requires periodic shifts between chaos and continuity.

They suggest that the six major themes of success are business focus, adaptability, organisational cohesion, entrepreneurial culture, a sense of integrity, and hands-on top management. Business focus requires the firm to engage in closely related products and, within that, to apply a very focused R&D strategy as well as maintain a consistent set of priorities across time. 3M is excellent in this regard. 3M applies technical expertise to products based around core technologies, such as adhesives. It invests in knowledge management within its people and uses quite sophisticated information systems.

Organisational cohesion involves good communication, the ability to rotate jobs and integrate roles, long-term employment, and intensive training. The entrepreneurial culture involves having smaller rather than larger divisions. For example, Hewlett Packard is subdivided into many divisions, each of which has less than 1,000 employees. It also requires a variety of funding channels to be available in its businesses and has developed a tolerance for failure.

Technological Innovation: A Framework for Reviewing the Process

Martin (1984) and others have suggested the following multistage model for viewing the introduction of an innovation:

- *Stage 1.* The innovation begins either with a discovery or a new idea or via the development of an understanding of a market need or opportunity.

- *Stage 2.* The proposed idea or design concept emerges, which brings together the existing knowledge and technique of the technical concept.
- *Stage 3.* This stage involves a verification of the theory or design.
- *Stage 4.* The prototyping or laboratory demonstration of the idea takes place.
- *Stage 5.* There is an evaluation and consideration is given to alternative versions of the concept. In some cases, a pilot plant may be built and test markets or clinical trials may occur.
- *Stage 6.* The commercial introduction or initial operation of the innovation takes place.
- *Stage 7.* There is widespread adoption of the innovation.
- *Stage 8.* Proliferation of the innovation leads to extensions for new markets or new applications of the original innovation.

Another important concept in technology management is the emergence of dominant designs. Examples given by Martin (1984) include the Model T Ford and the IBM 360. The IBM PC was also an example of a design that, along with its accompanying software, became an industry standard to be copied, cloned, and adhered to. The management and manipulation of standards by managers and regulators is clearly an important issue in considering the generation and distribution of wealth through technological innovation. A pure knowledge-based product that has also achieved the status of an industry standard is the Windows operating system for PCs.

Technology and the Market

Companies that engage in technical developments that are not aimed squarely at satisfying a known or hidden market requirement are asking for trouble. They are taking the risk that their technical resources and investments may come to nothing in the way of commercial returns. Successful companies aim their technology investments at a known or emerging market requirement. Or, at the very edge of development, they seek to transform the market requirement through their new offerings and the lead they achieve through them. Hence, the ultimate value of technical resources can only be determined in terms of market and marketing variables, volumes, contribution margins, control over costs, and, in the end, profits. However, it is not possible to always "start" with the market in thinking about and planning technical developments. This applies particularly to technologies and technical advances that apply more to processes than products and to early-stage investments in product development, such as more basic scientific work or fundamental research.

Companies must search for portfolios of technical resources and development projects that will reduce the risk of both the individual project and the overall portfolio. For individual projects, it is about balancing the forces of market requirements with those of technological push. For the firm as a whole, it is about constructing and implementing a set of technical efforts that will collectively ensure the future competitiveness of the company's offerings, even though it is usually impossible to predict with certainty which technical effort will be the ultimate commercial success.

Hewlett Packard—The Role of Technology in Organisation

The case of Hewlett Packard (HP) describes the implementation of surface mount technology at the company's Andover Surface Mount Centre (ASMC). ASMC makes digital and analogue boards for HP's Medical Products Group (MPG) as well as other HP companies. By all measures, the surface mount technology (SMT) implementation at ASMC was a major success. In the 1980s, ASMC was widely acknowledged as one of the best surface mount manufacturing facilities inside HP. The case highlights how ASMC adopted new SMT technology to replace old technology in manufacturing high quality ultrasound imaging products.

Through-hole (TH) technology emerged in the 1960s and 1970s as a relatively cheap, flexible, and robust way to produce printed wiring boards (PWBs) for ultrasound machines, which almost all other electronic scientific and medical equipment required. By the early 1980s, TH was a very mature technology. Insertion machines for placing components on boards and wave-soldering allowed for relatively low-cost production. Unfortunately for ultrasound manufacturers, an increased number of transducer channels and features were starting to push TH to the limits of its capabilities. Board complexity not only added to engineering design costs but also increased manufacturing labour costs. HP began to realise that 100 percent TH technology was starting to constrain new products and it was interested in pursuing SMT. Whereas SMT was a capital-intensive advanced manufacturing technology that conceptually had been around since the early 1960s, it had only matured as a viable technology in the early 1980s. SMT typically offered major reductions in board size, improved system performance, and significant direct labour savings over boards made with through-hole technology.

In considering the balance required between technology push and market pull, one core element of the managerial challenge is to make successful new technology development and innovation happen (proactively), as opposed to waiting for random events to occur. This relates to the paradox referred to above because there are always significant uncertainties associated with new technical developments. In addition, as Hayes and Maidique have suggested, periods of stability and normality are usually interspersed with periods of dramatic change and organisational excitement.

The criteria by which firms evaluate innovations are also of interest. Martin (1984) suggests that new technological inventions must be demonstrably feasible both technologically and commercially. In addition, health, safety, and environmental impacts must be socially acceptable and relevant government policies must be supportive and adhered to.

Finally, Martin argues that an innovation must be congruent with corporate objectives and goals. In this regard each one of these areas of evaluation is a vexed issue in itself, since no method is straightforward. For example, demonstrating commercial feasibility raises several issues, including return on investment criteria, net present value techniques and other financial measures, as well as marketing measures. In each of these cases there is a lot of uncertainty and complexity associated with technological invention and innovation, which makes evaluation problematic for organisations. In essence, it is hard to estimate costs associated with new technology, and it is even harder to assess revenue streams! New technology also often brings unanticipated consequences in terms of societal effects, environmental impacts, and the like. Consider the impact of the Internet. Originally associated with achieving redundancy and security through a distributed computing environment, who could have imagined the revolution it would become, sweeping the world that is now the World Wide Web? The quality and reach of information available through the Internet was unimaginable just a couple of decades ago. The Internet is even much more than just a business and consumer tool. In some countries, where governments practise the censorship of information, this technology is threatening government policies and controls. In fact, it is a major factor enhancing globalisation and international trade.

A General Manager's Perspective on Managing Technology

A number of frameworks and open questions exist in the field of technology management, providing both research questions and practical insights and challenges for technology managers. Ramasesh and Jayakumar (1993) have suggested that the following questions are important to consider:

- How should the limitations and potential misapplications of DCF (discounted cash flow) analysis be overcome when applying these principles to the justification of advanced manufacturing technology? The same question should be considered for any technology.
- How should cost accounting systems be modified to provide reliable product cost information and assess values such as reduced inventory, reduced scrap, and lower floor space requirements associated with new technology?
- How should strategic but largely nonquantifiable benefits be incorporated into technology justification processes?
- How should long-term benefits such as technological breakthroughs, which cannot be foreseen, be valued?
- What are the implications of organisational decision making and behavioural, social, and political characteristics of the firm on new technology?

Samson (1991) has summarised much of the literature that applies to advanced technologies. One example that relates to one of the points listed above is an analogy from Hayes, who argues that the introduction of advanced technologies is more like changing from a car to a helicopter than changing from an old car to a newer model of car. The implications of new technology when viewed as a helicopter are that new opportunities will arise that previously were impossible with the car. On the other hand, some capabilities of the old technology will now be more difficult or more expensive. However, without investing in the new technology infrastructure, it will be impossible for a firm to advance into these areas of new opportunity.

Technology, being a necessary tool of advanced manufacturing systems, has provided a new opportunity to achieve new heights of performance in respect to simultaneously high levels of flexibility and efficiency (Vesey, 1991). Tacit in this observation is the implication that the previous tradeoffs between flexibility and efficiency can be substantially reduced or even eliminated using new advanced technologies. Vesey also points out the advantages of being an early adopter of new technology and of relating new technology to time-based management, including the use of concurrent engineering designs and processes so that new product and process developments can be integrated.

In a study of computer aided design/computer aided manufacturing (CAD/CAM) implementations, Beatty (1992) concludes that the "rules of the road" are:

- New technology requires a skilled champion.
- New technology requires a plan for systems integration.
- New technology requires more organisational integration.

Barriers to success are clearly the failure of a champion, the lack of systems integration, possibly the existence of incompatible systems, and the lack of a team structure across the organisation involved in the new technology.

New advanced manufacturing technology allows for a high degree of flexibility in product variants as well as a minimisation of time wasted by switching between production runs. This delivers obvious marketing advantages. Product costs become less dependent on the size of the production run, which may influence stock and distribution policies as well as other commercial arrangements. Hence changes in manufacturing technology may well change the optimal market position and orientation.

In the British textile industry (Baker, 1993), large firms have much more readily adopted new technology than have smaller firms. Very few small firms in the textile industry can afford to make heavy investments in relatively sophisticated technology. This may be generalisable across manufacturing sectors. Hence an important open question is whether and how to encourage and assist small firms in new technology development and adoption.

Zairi et al. (1993) have conducted a field study examining the links between new technology and total quality management (TQM). Their principal findings are that new technology has been successfully used in the United Kingdom, both as a reactive and a proactive element of competitive strategy, and that its use can be enhanced when combined with TQM methods. Conversely, it can be argued that if new technology were to be used with old structures and business methods, its significance and benefits would be substantially less.

Technology Management in Particular Countries or Companies

In this section we cite the findings of specific studies that have considered technology and its management in particular organisational or cultural/national contexts. This perspective reveals some key international trends.

Alic (1993) has examined U.S. policy and identified a need to shift policy in order to help U.S. firms apply knowledge and technology as well as produce it. Alic points to an imbalance between technology generation and technology diffusion and suggests that federal agencies need to do a better job of encouraging the application of existing technical knowledge.

An article on investing in China by Woodward and Liu (1993) raises the issue of technology transfer from foreign partners to operations in China. The broader issue regards the selection of China versus other destinations as a potential location for international companies to use as a base for manufacturing and, therefore, technology transfer. Hence one element of research and policy should perhaps be the consideration of international facility location and technology transfer. This is because the technology infrastructure of a country or region is an important element in such decisions made by international firms.

Two recent studies have commented on technology in manufacturing competitiveness issues in the United Kingdom. Bentley (1991) has found that the U.K. industrial sector is generally inferior to its Japanese counterpart in the application of simultaneous engineering, exploitation of design technologies, application of value engineering, and design simplification principles. The KPMG survey in the U.K. revealed that only 10 percent of CAD/CAM installations were realising the true potential of those systems. Bentley points out the "latent power" of CAD/CAM technology, which is only released when changes occur in the way people use such technology. He points to Matsushita Electric as a leading implementer exemplar of "common first stage/customised second stage" design and production, which provides both customer flexibility and manufacturing efficiency through the use of CAD/CAM.

Bentley asked whether any British or European companies can match the Canon organisation, which registered 847 patents in the U.S. in 1987 and spent 200 billion yen on R&D in 1989, with 30 percent of its total employees qualified as engineers. In the U.K., total R&D spending was 10 percent less in 1991 than in the previous year, and in electronics the drop was 14 percent. The only British companies that made it to the top 50 worldwide in regard to investment in R&D were ICI and Glaxo.

This raises the next question of R&D expenditure both by individual companies and in aggregate terms in the global context, and whether anything should and can be usefully done about it in respect to government interventions. Are domestic economies getting the most "bang for their buck" in terms of the public investment in science and technology/R&D? Is enough or too much science and technology being generated? Should less be done in terms of technology generation and more be done along the lines of the Japanese model of 20 years ago, which demonstrated excellence in technology adoption, adaptation, and exploitation prior to major investment in new technology generation?

A study by Ogbuehi and Bullas (1991) highlights the benefits of establishing research and development facilities and efforts in a dispersed manner rather than having a single central R&D facility. By moving R&D activities closer to the market, wherever that may be, new product development as well as process capabilities are likely to be a closer match to the requirements of that marketplace, although there may be some scale disadvantage effects. These authors suggest that the benefits of dispersing R&D far outweigh the risks in an international context. They also point to the need for companies to extend their capability beyond internally generated R&D to include a variety of licensing and related arrangements.

In a study of Australian engineering firms, Atuahene-Gima (1993) found that the propensity among these firms to adopt inward technology licensing was positively affected by previous experiences and by the awareness of such licensing opportunities.

Inward technology licensing can be just like financing decisions, whereby it rarely makes sense for a company to financially position itself such that its balance sheet carries 100 percent equity and zero debt. Similarly, the purely internally generated technology portfolio is unlikely to be optimal relative to that which draws upon available technology sources from international markets. This suggests a set of skills and some questions that need to be tested about best practise in technology management from the perspective of technology importation and diffusion.

Using the detailed case study of an Italian packaging machine manufacturer, Bonaccorsi and Lipparini (1994) have suggested that the early and close involvement of major suppliers in new product development is a critical factor in influencing the likelihood of new product development success. They suggest that the critical factors are:

- Partner selection and evaluation.
- Proximity of the supplier network.
- Mutual support between the manufacturer and suppliers.
- Continuity and stability of the relationship.
- Synchronisation of the technical dimension of the firms involved in the development process.

Bonaccorsi and Lipparini suggest that this model of supplier involvement is substantially superior to the arm's-length purchasing agreement that has previously been the traditional way of managing suppliers. The advantages of such partnering relationships include the following:

- Reduced development costs.
- Early availability of prototypes.
- Standardisation of components.
- Consistency between design and supplier's process capabilities.
- Reduced engineering changes.
- Better contractual arrangements.
- Consistency between product tolerance and process capabilities.
- Refinement of supplier's processors and availability of detailed process data.
- Concurrent engineering.
- Reduction in cycle time and development time and reduced adoption risks.

Ali and Zahra (1994) point out that once a company loses its technological advantage, gross margins shrink. They illustrate this by comparing Japanese electronic manufacturers such as Fujitsu, Hitachi, Matsushita, and Sony with IBM. These companies have discovered that protecting established lines of business rather than promptly embracing new technology ultimately becomes a "dead end" strategy. Leading companies such as Hewlett Packard consciously and continually strive to bring out streams of new products that make even their own existing profitable models redundant, in the knowledge that it is much better to compete with yourself than to have others compete your products and advantages away.

In respect to the German model for technology development and promotion, Lay (1993) discusses the history of government support and programs for computer integrated manufacturing (CIM). He points to the experience of 1,200 firms that implemented CIM projects with an average planned project cost of DM 700,000, of which approximately one-third was covered by public subsidies. He notes that after the initial euphoria, there has been disillusionment about the role of CIM. Previously seen as a spearhead for maintaining competitiveness, it has not always proven so. CIM has focused on time-based improvements, as opposed to product flexibility and increasing quality in Germany. It could be that CIM was seen by many of these firms as a narrow technical solution rather than part of a broader organisational initiative and this may have limited its impact.

The approach of the Boeing Company has achieved and maintained nearly 60 percent of the world market for commercial planes (Comdit, 1994) over many decades. The president of the Boeing Company in Seattle suggests that the Boeing approach is "technology pull" and "customer driven" rather than "technology push." To achieve technology pull in the new Boeing 777, customers were brought into the design process and participated actively in design reviews. Comdit cites Lester Thurow of MIT, who points out that while U.S. firms typically spend two-thirds of their R&D on new products and one-third on new processes, the Japanese have done exactly the opposite—spending one-third on new products and two-thirds on new processes. The history of video cameras and recorders, fax machines, and CD players has been that the Japanese have taken the lion's share of these markets away from their original inventors, which underscores Thurow's point that, "Those who can make a product cheaper can take it away from the inventor." This point is best illustrated by the recent example of Gillette, which spent 10 years and $1 billion developing its new Mach 3 shaving razor, only to see a British supermarket chain produce a reasonable imitation within one year.

Industry associations can act to facilitate partnering and technology transfer, as exemplified by the Textile Clothing Technology Corporation (TCTC) in North Carolina (Sheridan, 1994). This is a not-for-profit consortium spanning the fibre, textile, apparel, and sewn product industries as well as representing retailers, labour, government, and academic institutions. This organisation has set up a quick response manufacturing technique demonstration that is on display at a teaching factory in its national apparel technology centre. It also boasts R&D laboratory facilities for creating process simulation software and interactive training. From an external perspective, the TCTC is enabling the U.S. industry to increase its flexibility and agility, which is a useful way to compete with the lower cost offshore manufacturers. It is also clearly involved in helping to diffuse and integrate technology across the whole logistic chain. The organisation is spearheading the development of radio frequency for identification processes, the use of scanning devices in retailing, and an optical body scanner that can be linked to a single-ply computer numerically controlled cutter.

In a large study of small- and medium-size manufacturers in western New York, MacPherson (1994) provided evidence that innovators exhibit better market and financial performance than non-innovators. New process development was associated with growth of sales, increases in value added, and pretax profits. MacPherson found that process innovators fell into two groups: (1) those that aimed primarily to use new technology to cut unit costs and (2) those that aspired toward greater production flexibility.

Implied in this analysis is the managerial insight that relates competitive position to the motivation for implementing such new technologies.

In two studies of small manufacturing firms, Francis and Young (1992) demonstrated that innovativeness, the use of computerised technology, and the flexibility of firm responsiveness can be observed as being three separable and possibly unrelated concepts. Therefore an important question from both the policy and managerial perspective relates to which of these concepts is being encouraged by a particular strategy or policy. If it is flexibility, then the benefits of flexibility need to be considered not just in terms of product range or speed of responsiveness to changing market needs but, as Chang (1993) has illustrated, also in terms of the additional benefit of entry-deterrence. Chang points to the classic example of the highly successful Model T Ford, which used highly dedicated technology aimed at producing a large volume at a low cost with a very limited product range. Shifting consumer requirements, coupled with the Chevrolet entry into that market, required extensive retooling from the Model T Ford to the Model A, during which time the manufacturing plant had to be closed down for over 12 months. Clearly, flexibility was not used by Ford in those early days to deter entry. Chang suggests that a benefit of excess flexibility can be considered as the "zone of strategic flexibility," which is a barrier to entry.

Achieving real flexibility in manufacturing involves overcoming two fundamental difficulties (Goldhar, 1991). The first is a failure to understand fully the strategic and organisational changes that must accompany the new technology, such as CIM or FMS. The second is a failure to understand the essential new role of information technology in integrating engineering, manufacturing, and marketing in systems design. Goldhar suggests that acceptable returns to investments in flexible technologies will occur only if flexibility exists throughout the organisation, embracing engineering, marketing, and distribution as well as manufacturing.

Flexibility and Technology

Consider the effect of flexible technology on plant size (Carlsson, Audretsch, and Acs, 1994). To begin with, for over a hundred years—until the early 1970s—technology was generally applied throughout mass manufacturing industries such as metalworking to lower costs and produce standardised products. Numerically controlled (NC) machines in the late 1940s and then computer numerically controlled (CNC) machines in the 1970s started to reduce the minimum economic scale for manufacturing. By 1984, NC/CNC machine tools accounted for over 40 percent of all U.S. machine tool investment. Small plants responded much more strongly than large plants to the later reductions of cost in this equipment. In small plants, the number of NC machine tools grew much faster than in large plants during the period of 1983 to 1989—300 percent as against 40 percent! Hence the cost of small scale production was reduced relative to large scale production; otherwise, one is tempted to ask how small plants could have survived relative to the large scale production facilities with which they compete. So, while there has been some flexibility increase in large plants, small plants have become both more flexible and lower in their relative cost base.

Meredith and Vineyard (1993) have studied the role of manufacturing technology in business strategy and point out that the performance of manufacturing organisations is significantly affected by the following:

- The higher the manufacturing flexibility, the better the performance.
- The greater the role of manufacturing managers in strategic decision making, the better the performance.
- The higher the environmental uncertainty, the lower the role of manufacturing managers in strategic decision making.

The case study research employed in their study has led to the following propositions:

- Firms do not directly employ their manufacturing technologies for Porter's generic strategies of low cost, high differentiation, or focus.
- Firms do not directly employ their manufacturing technologies to address the five basic competitive priorities: cost, quality, delivery, flexibility, and innovativeness.
- Firms do consider the following eight decision categories in their manufacturing technology strategies: (1) capacity, (2) facilities, (3) technology, (4) production planning and control, (5) organisation, (6) work force, (7) new product development, and (8) performance measurement systems.
- High manufacturing technology flexibility does not necessarily lead to improved performance.
- The lower the firm's performance, the lesser will be the role of manufacturing managers in strategic decisions.
- A technology's operating characteristics of batch size, number of active plants, lead time, and capacity utilisation are relatively independent of the firm's business strategy.
- Capacity and image are basic competitive priorities in manufacturing's mission.
- Manufacturing technology strategies are dynamic, changing over short periods of time as the environment and markets change.

Meredith and Vineyard's study indicates the great extent of complexity involved in business strategic and manufacturing technology decisions. We conclude that straightforward or "linear" models are unlikely to capture the richness and complexity associated with such decision processes. Applying some of this thinking to the textile industry, Wood (1993) has suggested that in the textile industry, competitive forces have changed from a manufacturing orientation and domination in the 1950s and 1960s. In the 1970s, the industry went through a period of diversification, and in the 1980s, it embarked upon a period of consolidation through mergers and buyouts. In the 1990s, it reached globalisation and the application of best practise. Wood claims that technology will play a key role in this industry, which has been spending about 3 percent of sales and 1.3 times depreciation on capital investment. He forecasts that these numbers will have to increase through the 1990s and thereafter, and that flexibility will be added to the traditional investment criteria of return on investment, quality of output, and reliability.

Whereas the major cost base in the textile industry used to be direct labour, fixed costs are now a greater element. This is consistent with the theme introduced at the start of this chapter, that technological resources are becoming more important than human resources in determining competitive outcomes. Many questions and challenges still face the textile industry when considered from a global perspective:

- As flexibility and speed become important elements of a textile firm's competitive arsenal, will the Western textile industry be able to compete via capital and brain-based methods despite its labour cost disadvantages with countries such as Thailand and China?
- Is there an alternative view to thinking of the textile industry as a sunset industry?
- Will Western textile manufacturers be able to alter their strategies to capitalise on globalisation, quality, and differentiation?

McCrary (1994) cites the case of a U.S. firm, Cygne Designs, which sources its fabric from Italy, designs it in New York, cuts the cloth in Miami, sews the fabrics in Guatemala, and ships to its U.S. customers all within a 60-day window. This company has enjoyed a 74 percent annual growth rate over four consecutive years. It is highly flexible in providing clothing to The Limited and other leading retailers. With gross sales of about $500 million, this company credits most of its success to flexibility and timely investments in technology. Computer aided design has allowed Cygne to continually upgrade its speed as has most of the textile industry. Cygne produces only what customers order, carries no inventory or distribution centre, and doesn't even buy fabric until it is sold. There are many lessons for other industries in terms of moving closer to a market pull production system. By focusing its strategy on quickness, the firm has been forced to consider issues of quality, flexibility, and productivity. This focus on speed is a very important point to consider in terms of technology strategy and indeed in the broader context of manufacturing/competitive strategy.

In studying the benefits of new technology, Zammuto and O'Connor (1992) have suggested that flexible manufacturing systems report an average 40 percent reduction in lead time, 30 percent increase in machine utilisation, 12 percent reduction in unit costs, and 30 percent reduction in labour costs, as well as product quality and work-in-process improvements. Other studies, for example by Voss in the U.K., have shown that there have been many instances where flexible manufacturing systems and CIM implementation have led to productivity improvement only, and not to improvements in flexibility and responsiveness. Does this have something to do with the systems, processes, and culture that surround the new technology, including the product designs themselves? This leads to hypotheses (Zammuto and O'Connor) such as:

- The greater an organisation's emphasis on control-oriented values (as against those values that are flexibility oriented), the more likely it will experience implementation failure.
- The greater an organisation's emphasis on flexibility-oriented values, the more likely it will gain productivity and flexibility benefits.

- Organisations emphasising control-oriented values can decrease the likelihood of implementation failure by increasing cultural and structural flexibility prior to technology implementation.
- The implementation process prior to gaining significant benefits will be longer for organisations emphasising control-oriented values than for organisations emphasising flexibility-oriented values.
- The greater the emphasis on control-oriented values, the greater the cost of the organisational changes necessary to gain new technology flexibility benefits.
- The less new technology is integrated across functions and subunit boundaries, the more likely a control-oriented organisation will gain productivity benefits.

Technology Forecasting

To consider technology forecasting in its context, we draw on Gerybadze (1994), who has suggested that R&D management can be characterised into three phases:

1. The first generation, 1950–1975, was input-oriented and involved the setting up of many of our modern R&D labs as well as the establishment of research teams and processes.
2. The second stage of R&D management involved the decentralisation of research and development and usually a more rigid coupling of business needs and development activities. Better project management, planning, and monitoring systems were implemented. This second stage generally lasted from 1975 to 1990.
3. The third generation or stage of R&D management is one in which R&D strategy is an integral and vital element of corporate strategy. In this stage, greater emphasis on balancing basic research and generic technologies with applied developments and the needs of the business units is achieved.

In a manner similar to the three stages of industry R&D management described above, in the first stage, technology forecasting can be characterised as being a mere sub-task of project planning. It is tactical, isolated, and not a pervasive part of organisational/strategic planning.

In the second stage, technology forecasting is seen as a data-gathering exercise and as a process of environmental scanning. Technology forecasting is an output, either to be believed or to be dismissed, and it is also considered as something for technical specialists. It is an isolated subtask of the key organisational strategic decision processes.

The new forecasting paradigm for technology integrates it as a part of organisational intelligence. It is business driven. This new approach to technology forecasting is echoed by Tschirky (1994), who views the firm as a sociotechnical productive system, with technology being one of the "potentials," along with marketing, information, logistics, financial, and human potentials.

The tools of technology forecasting are detailed in a number of books, including Burgelman and Maidique and Martin. They also have been widely applied in recent years. For example, Breiner, Cuhls, and Grupp (1994) report on a major study that analysed long-range Delphi forecasts (group forecasting methods aimed at effectively using and combining the knowledge of independent experts) of over 3,000 Japanese technical experts and over 1,000 German experts. They were able to successfully use Delphi methods to forecast future technical trends covering 16 major technical contexts and looking forward 20–30 years.

Coates (1993) has suggested that forecasts fail because forecasters often overestimate the speed with which new developments will penetrate society or marketplaces, or they overestimate the speed with which such trends will become important and pervasive. This is especially the case with advocates and enthusiasts such as inventors and marketeers, says Coates. He points to pitfalls of forecasting such as:

- Unexamined assumptions.
- Limited or misplaced expertise.
- Lack of imagination.
- Neglect of constraints.
- Excessive optimism.
- Mechanical extrapolation of trends.
- Overspecification.

Thomas (1994) provides an outline of "scenario planning," which attempts to find products and services that will be robust to changes in future markets and economic trends. Scenario planning usually does not have the same type of structure as Delphi methods, which are aimed at tapping into individual as well as combined views of experts in a relatively unbiased manner. Mitchell (1992) espouses the benefits of the Delphi method, especially for industries or situations involving a significant amount of instability or uncertainty. He points out that the anonymity and independence of estimates made during Delphi rounds using semistructured questions can provide superior benefits to other forecasting methods.

Kim and Whang (1994) have used one of a large number of alternative methods, the analytic hierarchy method (which allows for the evaluation of decision makers' preferences), to examine the different technological features associated with a particular industry's technical capability (the aircraft industry). This method also enabled them to forecast the pace and state of development of technology in that industry in order to help their local (Korean) producers to identify and understand their most advantageous technical strategies. Using the analytic hierarchy process, Kim and Whang were able to develop a structure of technology classification with weights given to the importance of technological subsets, and they developed forecasts for the pace and extent of future development in that industry.

Bowonder and Miyake (1993) provide an overview of technological forecasting techniques in Japan. They claim that in the 1960s, MITI (the Japanese Government Ministry for Industry Development) began preparing long-term visions of the future for whole industries looking over a 10-year plus period. In the 1970s, for example, electronics industries were identified as the focus for that decade, and in the 1980s knowledge-intensive industries were identified. The Japanese Institute for Future Technology, which is part of Japan's Science and Technology Agency, conducts planning and forecasting exercises and surveys. Delphi techniques have been extensively used. The results of these forecasts have been used for ongoing development within the institution of Exploratory Research for Advanced Technology, which is working on innovative technologies for the 21st century. Some of these include:

- Ultra-fine particles.
- Amorphous compounds.
- Fine polymers.
- Perfect crystals.
- Bioinformation transfer.
- Super bugs.
- Nanomechanisms.
- Quantum flux logic.
- Molecular dynamic assembly.
- Biophotonics.
- Morphogenetics.
- Molecular architecture.

The Japanese planners also have indicated strong interests in lasers, robots, and fuzzy logic as ongoing. Whole industries and combinations of multi-industry partners are involved in integrated projects in Japan. For example, the fuzzy logic project involves 77 distinct organisations. MITI is involved in preparing the broad document highlighting the directions for the future and bringing together interested organisations while establishing their commitment for financial support. For example, MITI began the laboratory for international fuzzy engineering research and, having planted the seed, is fostering large amounts of industry-based development work. There are a large number of institutes and agencies that are coordinating what are sometimes massive multi-industry efforts.

In the Japanese power industry, for example, 14 power companies, electrical machine manufacturers, and cable manufacturers have formed a development association that plans on developing a 70-megawatt superconducting generator. Another industry-based consortium has formed a petroleum energy centre involved in developing a diesel engine that will have less than one-fifth of present nitrogen oxide emissions. There are dozens of similar examples of multifirm collaborations forming the technological infrastructure that characterises Japan.

The Japanese system is summarised by Bowonder and Miyake as having close linkages of technological intelligence, forecasting, planning, and development. In addition, it has the following characteristics:

- Strong involvement of industry associations.
- Focused strategies on three or four areas of superiority.
- Strong interfirm and research institute strategic alliances.
- Good project management.
- Interlinking of many existing projects.

- Continuous extension of core competencies.
- Balance on creating innovations and simultaneous diffusion.
- Willingness to learn from earlier mistakes through a "learning to learn" approach.

Summary

The management of technology and related decisions regarding the investment in and development of new technical resources that will lead to innovation and new forms of commercial value is a key challenge for managers in all industries and countries. Balancing market forces with technical opportunities and thrusts, assembling a portfolio of future technical assets, and staying competitive in terms of both product and service offerings and process outcomes such as cost, quality delivery, and flexibility are key concerns. These elements of competitiveness, which drive business profitability, mean that technology issues and technical prowess are integral to a company's business strategy. As more and more companies increasingly manage their work forces well, this factor will tend to lessen as a competitive battleground, until it becomes a "qualifier" for survival. On the other hand, there is virtually no limit to where technical progress can go. Products can become increasingly better in meeting customer requirements, becoming more flexible and customised to particular needs, more feature-laden, and cheaper. Organisational processes are also amenable to major technical progress. These relate to production, distribution, service, sales, and indeed, all other value-adding and support activities.

It is not possible to completely disentangle the technical and human resources of an organisation, for they must work in an integral manner. However, some consideration of the big picture, regarding which domain has provided and will continue to provide the most progress in taking businesses forward, is instructive from a managerial perspective. One century ago, when a farmer was able to feed his or her family and perhaps a few other people through growing grain, human resources were working hard and technology input was low. The introduction of technical breakthroughs, such as the combine harvester, led to massive increases in productivity. People have changed relatively little in their design and abilities over the past century or two, but their tools and technologies have changed dramatically. This will generally continue to be the case, with people being about the same in their abilities. The rate of technological progress in industries such as manufacturing and services, however, will continue to increase.

In the global economy of the new millennium, leaders must have a strong knowledge and capability in new technology management in order to keep their companies in the game. The technological battleground will increasingly become the dominant field of competition for companies.

Recommended Cases

Case 4: Biotechnol

Case 9: EKATO Ruhrwerke

Case 15: Peters and Brownes Group

CHAPTER 2 Technology Strategy

Technology strategy refers to the choices that companies make in acquiring, developing, and deploying technology in order to achieve their business goals. It involves the acquisition, management, and exploitation of product and process technologies that are consistent and supportive of a firm's business strategies and can ultimately drive its business competitiveness by providing technologically based advantages (Samson, 1991). As companies increase their adoption of advanced technologies and develop more technologically sophisticated products, their need for effective technology strategies is enhanced.

To summarise, technology strategy involves:

- The technological choices that firms make.
- The criteria by which technologies are embodied into new products and production processes.
- The organisational practices and managerial processes for the deployment of technological resources.

Betz (1993) has articulated the objectives of a technology strategy as:

- Maintaining technological capabilities in existing businesses through the incremental improvement of products and processes.
- Expanding markets in existing businesses or launching new businesses through product and/or process innovation.
- Securing distinctive technological capabilities from external sources (i.e., strategic sourcing).

Duct Manufacturing Centre (A)— Focusing on Organisational Rebuilding

The Turbine Systems Corporation has been one of the most successful manufacturers of turbine systems in the industry, consistently maintaining more than half of the market share. Turbine Systems's primary products include turbine jet engines and turbine power generators. The Duct Manufacturing Centre (DMC) is within the Manufacturing Division of the Turbine Systems Corporation. DMC manufactures precision welded metal duct assemblies for use in Turbine Systems's primary products. Specialised tooling, equipment, and skills are needed to build over 3,000 duct models, and on-time delivery is critical to customers. Furthermore, many of the ducts are also critical for turbine safety and reliability and they must satisfy exacting quality standards.

    The general manager, Lipscomb, and other members of the management team realised that designing and constructing a new facility from the ground up offered an opportunity to build a state-of-the-art manufacturing facility. They decided to use the move to a new facility as a catalyst for process improvement. They also realised that, in order to achieve world-class excellence, a radical change would be needed in dealing with their employees, customers, suppliers, and support personnel. Since a new corporate strategy was required to create semi-autonomous business units, senior management created an organisational objective of bringing all aspects of manufacturing ducts into one focused organisation.

Guy Birkin—Developing Technology with the Supplier

Guy Birkin, in the beginning of 1990, was using three different machines—the Leavers, Raschel, and Jacquardtronic—for the manufacture of lace. The different machines target the same end users, but different customers prefer different types of lace. Two important parameters for the lace customer are the texture and price of the lace, both of which are affected by the type of technology that is chosen for manufacturing the lace.

    The first machine technology used to produce lace was the Leavers machine, which was invented in 1813 and subsequently developed. Much of this development was done by the Birkin family. The next development in machinery was the Raschel machine, which was introduced in the late 1950s. This machine uses a knitting principle, which is basic and simple. The knitting principle is different from the twisting principle that is used by the Leavers machine. The advantage with Raschel is its speed and the possibility for each employee to operate up to four machines simultaneously. The next development in lace machinery took place at the initiative of four key players in the lace industry and Karl Mayer of Germany— the only manufacturer of lace machines in the world. Of the four lace manufacturers, Guy Birkin was the one that contributed to this new machine's conception and development. The basic rationale for developing this machine—called the Jacquardtronic—was to combine the advantages of Leavers and Raschel machines in order to produce more intricate and complex lace in wider designs with the cheaper and faster knitting technology.

With the benefit of hindsight, the development and implementation of Textronic machines with Karl Mayer again in 1990 does seem like a well-thought-out strategy. There were four sets of factors that triggered the initiation of the development of new technology. First was the market-driven view of the needs for new products. Second, the cross-functional collaboration and knowledge that this developed led to these market needs being seen in terms of required capability from manufacturing technology. Third, the routine forward- and external-looking activities of the management team led to a detailed understanding of current and potentially available technology. Finally, Guy Birkin's close relationship with Karl Mayer, and the experiences of the Jacquardtronic, led the company to realise that it could be proactive in driving the development of new technologies by its suppliers.

When defining technology strategy, it is important for the core systems of a firm to go beyond products offered and markets served and to relate more to core competencies and abilities. Therefore, business-related and technological knowledge and the ability to translate that knowledge into effective processes are both at the heart of a sound technology strategy. Technology strategy is more than mere research and development policy, since technology can be both internally developed and also acquired from outside the company.

The conceptual and empirical content of technology strategy has tended to be concerned with the concept of "fit," which has been defined (Adler, 1989) in respect to three different and interrelated perspectives:

- Business strategy and technology strategy.
- Technology posture and functional decision-making practices.
- Synergy between decision-making practices.

Conceptual technology strategy frameworks typically have been developed to analyse these dimensions of fit. Therefore, two key structural taxonomies have been developed:

1. Those that relate the overall positioning of the firm's technological effort to business needs.
2. Those that define the technological decision-making elements.

Despite the widespread recognition of the importance of fit, there is currently no general agreement on the form and structure of technology strategy constructs. This makes it extremely difficult to analyse their value. Consequently, fit, as defined above, has not been well documented (Adler, 1989; Capon and Glazer, 1987) and there is little statistical evidence to relate technology strategy to business strategy and, ultimately, firm performance.

The field of technology strategy can be classified into a series of elements that make up this body of knowledge:

1. Particular dimensions of technology policy that are normatively related to one or more dimensions of business strategy (e.g., the firm's technological

resources, technology make versus buy, and organisational policies for the development and use of technology). Betz (1993) has considered the relationship between technology and business strategy. He concludes that in commodity-type businesses where products are undifferentiated, technology should be focused on the cost and quality of production. In a specialty-type business, there is a small but focused market and technology should be focused on expanding the market by improving performance while preparing for competition by lowering production costs.

2. Integrative models that prescribe fit between the different dimensions of technology policy and business strategy. Maidique and Patch (1988) provide an example that is frequently cited in the literature. They define technology strategy as consisting of six dimensions:

   a. Type of technology.
   b. Desired level of competence.
   c. Technology make versus buy (internal/external sourcing).
   d. R&D investment.
   e. Timing of technology introductions.
   f. R&D organisation.

   Classifying business strategy as first-to-market, second-to-market, late-to-market, or market segmentation, they propose technology strategies that are compatible with a firm's business strategy.

3. Empirical links between particular dimensions of technology strategy and business strategy. An example is the study by Hambrick et al. (1983) of the fit between the intensity of product innovation activity and business strategy. The study concluded that "prospectors" emphasise product innovation more than "defenders."

Hewlett Packard—Technology Strategy on New Technology Adoption

Although surface mount technology (SMT) was available to Hewlett Packard (HP) in the early 1980s, the relatively high costs of SMT equipment made it prohibitively expensive for each of HP's 45 divisions to develop surface mount manufacturing capabilities. Most HP divisions initially adopted a strategy to extend the current technology (through-hole technology). However, TH technology was starting to constrain the design and production of new products. Later, the decision to adopt SMT was made mainly based upon strategic considerations and without formal investment justifications.

   In the mid-1980s, HP's Medical Product Group (MPG) was the market leader in ultrasound systems, especially in high-performance systems suitable for cardiac diagnosis. MPG's technology strategy was to continually evolve the high-performance ultrasound system as soon as each new technological innovation became practical. The strategy included adding colour flow processing, installing a larger imaging aperture, and expanding disk storage space. As health care came under further pressure to reduce the costs of delivering medical services, MPG's management grew concerned that the company might be too vulnerable to lower-cost, acceptable performance competition.

Business Competitiveness and Technology Strategy

The changing features of competition include the fragmentation of mass markets, the growing global dissemination of technological knowledge, and the proliferation of technologies that are relevant to any given product (Clark, 1989). In light of these trends, Clark has proposed five precepts for firm strategy that impact the management of technology. According to Clark, managers should:

1. Understand their technological base and envision that base as a strategic advantage.
2. Take an international perspective in regard to technology and seek out the best technology, wherever it can be found.
3. Discipline their business function around the function of production. Therefore, technical knowledge should be focused on value adding to the customer.
4. Integrate all business functions through the information system of the firm.
5. Focus on time as the critical factor in using innovation for competitive advantage.

Iva Manufacturing—
Defining New Technology Strategies

Iva Manufacturing Company has an open policy of exchanging intellectual information and does not believe in keeping its intellectual information secret. Iva interacts extensively with other industries and participates in industry-related shows and conferences. It has a close association with Clemson University's Apparel Centre (CAR). CAR is a demonstration centre sponsored by the state and federal governments and has all the latest technology available in apparel manufacture. It provides investment advice on advanced manufacturing technologies (AMTs) and holds workshops and seminars.

The four key elements of Iva's strategy include:

1. Corporate structuring to enhance technology uptake and exploit Iva's relative technological advantage.
2. The innovative application of technology and automation to work in an environment of small production runs.
3. Developing a marketing scheme that focuses on exploiting technological strength.
4. Focusing on developing technical competence from within.

Clark emphasises that, with respect to an organisation's technical competence, management's fundamental responsibility is to deliberately build such a competence. Eschenbach and Geistauts (1987) have offered precepts for engineers and argue that in order for firms to be able to manage technology effectively, engineers should be broadened to view companies as sociotechnical systems. Specifically, they argue that engineers need to (1) provide explicit value judgments in technology assessments and R & D cost/benefit analysis, (2) articulate a philosophy of management that reflects a commitment to integrative, systematic long-term planning, and (3) focus on the interaction between the firm and its environment.

Steele (1989) also offers a set of core principles embraced by organisations that are adept at the strategic management of technology. They include taking a systems view of technology, being aware of the dynamics of the maturation of technology, knowing who the firm's customers are, and being effective in dealing with ambiguity and uncertainty.

The Strategic Technology Management Process

The strategic technology management process focuses on three key areas (Betz, 1993):

1. The identification and development of a firm's technological capabilities.
2. Products/processes that provide a competitive advantage.
3. The integration of areas one and two.

The technology management field contains tools and techniques to assist in the accomplishment of the above. These include technology S curves, technology by industrial sector matrix, technology systems, product development maps, product improvement planning techniques, concurrent engineering practices, the formulation of technological competencies, long-range research plans, and competitive benchmarking.

Technology strategy is actually a quite complex field. It involves connecting business goals to market requirements and business/market strategy and then considering how technology decisions and investments will enable and drive the business to be successful within its environment.

The evolutionary, integrative, and synergistic nature of technical decision practices has been widely acknowledged (Jones et al., 1994). That is why it is certainly not enough to competently analyse the technical content of any technology strategy, for such an evaluation would be far too narrow in scope and likely to lead to poor decisions. Technology needs to be considered in terms of how it drives the competitiveness of the product or process that it contributes to, and, ultimately, this can be valued only in terms of business and/or market outcomes.

Conceptual constructs focus heavily on the content of technology strategy but generally ignore the processes and practices with which strategies are formulated and implemented (Erickson et al., 1990). The implementation of a technical strategy is just as important as its definition and should be considered an integral part of it (Pavitt, 1990). Many firms have well-articulated strategy sets but are unable to implement them effectively.

Technology as Critical to Business Outcomes

Many strategists (Porter, 1983; Adler, 1989) indicate that the future fortunes of firms are often decided at technological turning points. The interplay between technology and firm strategy—and thus between technical strategy and product/process development and design processes—is therefore a key issue.

In the past, the relationship between technology and strategy often has been treated in a narrow and static way in many firms, with technology being treated as a constraining factor in respect to the strategic opportunities open to firms—rather than an opportunity (Itami et al., 1992). In the future, the same authors argue that technology will become more of an explicit factor in strategy formulation than it is in most firms today. Consequently, the feedback loop between firm strategy and technology strategy will become a key determinant of firm success in the future.

Boeing—A Commitment to Carry Out Technological Changes

In early 1995, decisions about technology and structure would prove critical to Boeing's future in light of the changing context of the commercial airplane industry. In response to customer demand that the firm deliver more value in less time, Boeing implemented two significant innovations in a new airplane design program. The first change involved technology—the company purchased a state-of-the-art digital design computer system for the development of the new 777 commercial jet family. The second change influenced interactions among people and disciplines—Boeing created a cross-functional or "design-build" team structure for the 777 development program. The goal of these innovations was to reduce costly "change, errors, and rework," which historically had added cost and delayed delivery to airline customers.

As noted by Adler, technology strategy decisions should be evaluated in terms of their collective fit with business strategy rather than as independent decisions (1989). Business strategy moderates the relationship between technology strategy and firm performance. This suggests a need to align business strategy and technological choices as a precondition for superior firm performance (Zahra et al., 1993).

Firms whose strategies are built on technological competencies alone run the risk of technological myopia and possible overinvestment in these competencies (Zahra et al., 1993). However, an emphasis on strategic fit does not ensure superior performance. For example, the MIT study (1989) observes that to thrive in mature industries, companies need to pursue strategic options that will complement their technological imperatives, including developing new lines of business.

The strategic deployment of technological resources on a global basis has increasingly become a key determinant for success in many firms. A critical variable driving firms' abilities to globalise technological capabilities is their ability to effectively integrate technology development and technology deployment. Consequently, technology strategies need to be cross-functional and include input from all the affected functions (Jones et al., 1994).

There is significant interest surrounding technology make versus buy decisions (Adler, 1989; Maidique and Patch, 1988). Reduced product life cycles, the increasing application of technology, a greater variety of technologies, and an increasing recognition of the cost/risk of developing technological capabilities are resulting in an increasing interest in strategic sourcing practices.

An important issue is how firms integrate technical strategies with business requirements, which involves the determination of characteristics that facilitate the effective strategic management of technical functions (Adler, 1992).

Best practice mechanisms for the translation of a firm's competitive thrust into concrete capabilities (for example, see Zahra et al., 1994) indicate that the following characteristics are correlated with superior performance:

- Championship of technology issues by a unit or group that oversees strategic technological decision making.
- Adequate levels of technological competence within a firm's executive management.
- The selection of the structural form of the unit(s) responsible for technology development. These units may be functional, product, process, project, or matrix structures dependent upon the thrust of the technology and competitive strategies.
- The coupling (coordination) between functional technology related units and other functions within the firm. Recent research has highlighted the crucial importance of integrating technology development decisions and activities, especially across R & D, manufacturing, and marketing functions.
- The extent and timing of strategic controls used to ensure progress in achieving the objectives of the technology strategy selected. This task involves selecting the type of controls (formal versus informal), their level (casual versus institutionalised), and timing (concurrent versus post hoc).
- Technology transfer mechanisms. Many companies fail to commercialise the new technologies they develop. This failure may result from issues such as an obsession with the technology to the exclusion of market considerations, organisational bureaucracy, and/or dysfunctional behavior. The technical specialists who are working full time on developing a new technology are often not the best candidates for steering the project. This is simply because they are so close to the detail that they can't look dispassionately at the big picture from a business perspective.

Many successful companies (AT&T, Honda, Microsoft, Nissan, and Toyota) pay special attention to technology transfer in order to ensure the commercialisation of new technologies developed. To ensure that technologists do not dominate decision-making processes and that environmental scans are conducted on a regular basis, they employ mechanisms such as:

- Systematically rotating engineers between functions (e.g., product design and process design, marketing/sales support and design, design and manufacture, etc.).
- Adopting processes to ensure clear links between technology development and commercial goals.

- Making extensive use of information technology.
- Maintaining a fluid and open organisational structure with a minimum of bureaucracy (Zahra et al., 1994).

Technology Strategy and Technology Leadership

In 1999, a study of firms classified as technology leaders in four different industry segments[1] revealed that these firms were not only more profitable than their competitors but also performed better in terms of revenue growth. These firms were able to either price their innovative products higher or produce them at a much lower cost or, in some cases, do both. It was also found that these technology leaders excelled in the four key areas of technology management: technology strategy, technology portfolio management, technology planning, and technology development and transfer processes.

Among these firms, technology strategy played an important role in enabling them to achieve their leadership positions as well as develop substantial and sustainable advantages in the industry that were difficult to replicate. For example, firms such as Intel and Microsoft developed explicit technology strategies in order to gain appropriate contexts for making coherent technology investment decisions and allocating resources into those projects that made the most strategic sense.

Peters and Brownes Group—Strategy to Encourage Technological Change

The technological innovation in Peters and Brownes Group did not occur in discrete steps following any linear format. Rather, the process of technological change, which has over time sustained this firm's competitiveness, can best be described as the interaction of social and cultural, economic, and technical factors driven by effective leadership that foreshadowed the salience of technological change as an integral part of strategy.

Initially, Peters and Brownes established R & D mainly for providing product range extensions and solutions to operational problems. This initial step only provided the company a means to improve its operational capabilities. This evolutionary process began by a change in ownership in the mid-1980s that provoked a dramatic shift in management attitudes toward technological change, a commitment to product innovation, and market expansion beyond Western Australia's borders. The new managing director, Graham Laitt, had the necessary entrepreneurial skills and vision and saw considerable opportunities for Peters. He adopted the strategy that envisaged Western Australia as a major company base for tackling national and international markets. The choice of relocating manufacturing to a Greenfield site offered greater logistical economies of scale and overall improved operational effi-

---

[1]Automotive; chemicals and plastics; computers and electronics; and telecommunications equipment.
Source: Michael Sadowski and Aaron Roth, "Technology Leadership Can Pay Off," *Research Technology Management*, November/December 1999.

Peters and Brownes Group—Strategy to Encourage Technological Change concluded

ciencies. Further expansion in R & D was evidence of the recognised importance that the company was attaching to R & D in product, equipment, and processes operations.

Peters and Brownes managed to integrate the technology strategy into the corporate plan, which provides recognition that technology is the strength of the company and a normal part of the business. In response to the freeing up of the export market, Graham Laitt, with the executive team, managed to align the technological change across product, process, and production coupled with innovative management and marketing strategies. This provided a fundamental boost to future growth both locally and internationally. Entry into the Japanese market was also a milestone in the technological evolution of the company.

Technology Strategy: Superior Performance Characteristics

Best practice, in respect to technology strategy and management processes, is reflected in the following list of characteristics:

- Effective mechanisms are in place to integrate technology and business strategy.
- Effective mechanisms are in place to coordinate the activities of technology-related organisations and work groups.
- All affected functions are involved in the technology strategy formulation process.
- The interconnections between key decision elements and the need to manage these elements as a collective entity are understood.
- The appropriate skill mix is available to develop and implement strategies effectively. This means that the process is not dominated by technocrats and adequate levels of technical competence are found at the executive management level.
- Clear responsibility for technology management is allocated.
- Organisational structures are aligned to support the business and technology strategies identified.
- Effective mechanisms are in place to commercialise new technology.
- There is substantive characterisation of core technologies and posture is defined with respect to each.
- A long-term understanding exists regarding how technology contributes to shaping the business.
- Metrics are tied to strategic objectives and are recognised and accepted both within the technical function and throughout the business.
- Clear criteria exist for make versus buy versus license out decisions.
- Effective dual ladder (technical and generalist management) career progression systems exist.

- A mix of individual and team rewards and incentives for entrepreneurial behaviour exists.
- There are clear links between project selection criteria and business and product line strategy.
- Specialists are multiskilled and there is an awareness and respect of other functions, developed by systematic cross-functional assignments and job rotation.
- There is a regular assessment of technical capabilities and technology management processes via the benchmarking of products and processes.
- There is a proactive long-term management of technology and technical functions.
- Opportunities and threats are actively explored, using a well-developed network of customers, suppliers, universities, government agencies, and rivals.

Summary

Technology is not an end in itself. It is a means to the end of business competitiveness and performance. Critical and highly valuable people in organisations are therefore those who are capable of connecting the technical issues and opportunities to the business strategy and environment. Further, when resources are being allocated, such people are critical for ensuring that the bets taken by the company make sense in respect to the risk-return position of the company and its marketing and business strategy. An organisation's strategy is the glue that brings together its resources and its market opportunities. Hence, as one of the firm's key resources, technology needs to be planned and exploited within and through this "big picture" context.

Recommended Cases

Case 6: Bosch-Siemens Hausgerate Group
Case 10: Guy Birkin
Case 18: Telstra

CHAPTER 3 Development of Technological Capabilities

In order to accomplish their strategic and operational goals, organisations must develop an adequate technological base—that is, they must develop the technological know-how and the organisational levers for effectively building and deploying that know-how (Adler, 1990). Organisations need to be technologically equipped to meet their strategic objectives and to create new opportunities as well as respond to the threats created by the market environment and competitors' activities (Roberts and Berry, 1985).

Technological capabilities refer to those technological assets possessed by a firm that have strategic significance, as well as the processes and practices by which these assets are developed and exploited. A firm's technological assets may be developed by mechanisms that include:

- Introducing and diffusing a new technology.
- Upgrading the technical skills and knowledge of employees.
- Improving the organisational routines, structures, processes, and values through which work is performed.
- Enhancing relationships with suppliers, customers, company affiliates, and other organisations.

A firm's core technological capabilities are composed of a set of differentiated skills (which reside in human capital), organisational routines (which operate at firm level), and specific assets (advanced manufacturing technologies, information systems, computer aided manufacturing, etc.) that underlie competitive advantage (Hamilton, 1992).

Peters and Brownes Group—R & D and Capital Equipment Upgrade

Up until the early 1980s, Peters and Brownes Group's manufacturing was relatively labour intensive and there was little or no R & D into either new product development or capital equipment upgrades. The R & D that did take place locally was confined mainly to providing product range extensions and solutions to operational problems. In 1982, Peters and Brownes first established an R & D department focusing on new product development for the local market. Subsequently, the company set about expanding the role of the fledgling R & D department and encompassing marketing. The appointment of an Asian marketing expert provided the R & D and marketing team valuable insight into Asian markets. These moves allowed the company to diversify both in product and market portfolios and ultimately gave it the technological capability to compete in a global market setting.

A series of incremental improvements in previous capital equipment over time and the subsequent strategy of relocating manufacturing to a Greenfield site offered greater logistical economies of scale and overall improved operational efficiencies. Completion of the new manufacturing facility in 1987 dramatically increased production capacity and provided scope for considerable increases in output coupled with a greater flexibility of operation—thus enabling the company to launch new products and develop new markets.

A significant element that brought about a modernisation of the plant was the computer aided specifications and manufacturing, implemented from around 1987. This effectively provides for constant monitoring of raw material inputs and subsequent warehousing throughout the entire operations of the plant. The computer network is also integrated with the company's financial and accounting systems to provide an overall control facility. Furthermore, all aspects of the ice cream manufacturing facility were continuously developed and upgraded.

During the 1970s, many firms developed diverse product portfolios in order to achieve growth and prosperity through differentiated business strategies. As a consequence, the buying and selling of product lines became an integral part of doing business (Meyer and Roberts, 1988). Since then, product variety, technological choice, and product technological complexity have grown exponentially. As a result, many firms can no longer strategically direct their operations based on markets, products, and customer choices alone (Stalk et al., 1992). Today businesses succeed if they "excel" at something that the market values, such as new product development, responsiveness to orders, continuous enhancement of product features, or customer service.

Meyer and Roberts (1988) have noted the benefits for firms that develop a core base of technological assets:

> We observed that companies that attempted to build an overly diverse portfolio of products found themselves over extended periods with technologically mediocre products and diffuse marketing. Companies that concentrated on the internal development of a single or related group of technologies and that focused on related market applications achieved both technological product excellence and a deep understanding of their customers.

This relates technology strategy and the portfolio of technology assets to the business strategy concept of focus—that is, not overly diversifying, but "sticking to the knitting," whether it be market-, technology-, or product-focused.

Concentrating at the level of the product family and, more particularly, on the development and sharing of key components and assets within a product family has become a vital issue (Meyer and Utterback, 1993). Deliberately building product families rather than single products requires management of a firm's core capabilities. Core capabilities are increasingly becoming regarded as a key unit of management in many firms. As Adler and Shenhar (1990) note: "Technical development should follow a capabilities path. Capabilities drive the strategies with which superior products are developed."

Developing Technology-Based Capability

A model describing the various stages that should be involved in an organisation's development of process technologies has been put forward by Jaikumar and Bohn (1986). According to the model, such development should follow three distinct phases, each of which encompasses different stages of development.

The first phase includes the following five stages, which allow for a technology to be developed to the point where it can be implemented and initially controlled but not easily modified or enhanced:

1. Recognition of prototypes. In this stage, the general state of knowledge is quite low and although it is possible to make a distinction between good processes and bad ones, intuitive judgments are relied upon, rather than scientific or analytical understanding.

2. Recognition of attributes within prototypes. In stage 2, common properties and qualitative characteristics of processes are identified, and a distinction between processes based on these criteria can be made.

3. Discrimination across attributes. In stage 3, it becomes possible to distinguish between attributes, and a more scientific approach to these distinguishing features emerges. It is also possible to communicate this knowledge, since it can be described in terms of measurable dimensions.

4. Discrimination within attributes. This stage is characterised by the establishment of quantitative measurement and accurate theoretical bases and although full process control has not yet been established, the knowledge for doing so has been generated.

5. Local control of attributes. In stage 5, full control over stable processes has been achieved and process optimisation through experimentation can be undertaken. However, the level of understanding required to solve problems successfully does not exist, although process control has been properly documented.

The second phase, which includes stage 6, involves

6. Fine-tuning the system and developing and considering the reaction of the system to changes. These may be market, technical, or economic changes or

any other forms of change to the input of a system. This stage involves developing the ability to understand and respond adequately to those changes.

The third phase includes stages 7 and 8 as follows:

7. Remaining in control of the process under changing conditions. Computerised process control is an example of stage 7 knowledge, where sophisticated, automated code is able to anticipate and routinely respond in a programmed way to changing conditions. At this stage, automated process control is used to deal with normal contingencies, but people are still required to deal with unanticipated contingencies.
8. Having complete understanding and knowledge of all possible contingencies. Stage 8 knowledge includes having programmed control systems that are able to deal with the fully described set of possible events.

The practical implications of this 8-stage model of technological knowledge allows managers to focus on the ideal nature and direction of efforts in trying to advance knowledge and process control from one stage to the next. Although related to the development of process technology, it is also paralleled in the development of product technology, where the product design process can be described in a very similar manner to that of process control. For example, Taguchi methods are focused on developing a set of design and process control attributes and on understanding the relationships between those attributes and performance.

Samwon—Three Development Programs

The hostile market conditions in the 1980s drove Samwon to adopt a series of distinct development programs to improve its technological capabilities. The 5S program was originally developed in Japan ("5S" refers to the following five "s" goals: (1) *seri*—determine which equipment is necessary and which is not; (2) *seiton*—have the necessary equipment in reach and in the right place; (3) *seiso*—clean; (4) *seiketsu*—maintain the above 3S; and (5) *sitsuke*—mental discipline and readiness). Samwon adopted the 5S techniques to revitalise the work culture within the organisation.

The core part of the change was the new culture of the workers where everyone believed that he/she was the owner of the company. Once management found the 5S project to be mature and the results established, Samwon then introduced the next action program, which assisted the company in increasing its productivity and sophistication by utilising the 5S foundation. The second program, *Cho Kwan Ri* or CKR (*cho* stands for a second of time; *kwan ri* refers to management), was a time-based management system. Unlike the Japanese 5S campaign, CKR was exclusively invented by Samwon. CKR calculated all work activity, including futile team meetings, chatting time, smoking, and coffee breaks, in terms of a monetary value in an attempt to publicly identify the wasted time in the company.

As part of the company's "continuous improvement" program, Samwon then adopted the *Saryuk* 0.01 campaign after the CKR and 5S programs had been successfully implemented. The *Saryuk* 0.01 (*saryuk* means to make a desperate or frantic effort for the ultimate goal) was a goal-oriented campaign to improve by even 1 percent. The idea of *Saryuk* 0.01 was to continue to seek out any waste in the company in order to meet the competitive situation. In other words, whereas the principle of CKR was to reduce waste that was invisible, the principle of *Saryuk* 0.01 was to reduce waste that was visible.

Jaikumar and Bohn's model is recognisable as being accurate and powerful in describing generically how technological capability often develops. This can be considered in many and varied contexts, such as:

- The way that Hewlett Packard brings new models of laser printers to market, attempting to achieve efficiency and speed in its product development cycles both by starting further down the stages by using existing knowledge and by moving consciously and quickly through the stages.

Hewlett Packard—Introduction of New Technology

Hewlett Packard–Medical Products Group's surface mount technology (HP–MPG's SMT) journey took much of the 1980s. Before SMT was introduced at Andover, engineering always took the lead in product and process changes. Since the SMT implementation, manufacturing had led engineering in process changes. During this time period, manufacturing also spent a lot of time refining its existing through-hole (TH) board production capabilities and vendor base in anticipation of someday migrating to SMT.

SMT equipment was bought at Andover in three distinct phases starting in 1986. In the transition from TH to SMT at Andover Surface Mount Centre, the shopfloor was reconfigured into a smaller area with a classic U-shaped flow. One of the most fundamental changes involved reversing the shopfloor from a batch operation with massive work-in-process (WIP) under TH to a continuous flow with as little WIP as possible using SMT.

A major administrative adaptation was made in MPG's "above-the-shopfloor" information systems. A sophisticated product information management (PIM) system was developed so that board designs from inside MPG's engineering groups, as well as any other company on HP's worldwide network, could be downloaded to Andover Surface Mount Centre (ASMC). An MRPII system was also used by manufacturing to help control and procure inventory. The PIM system has allowed the ASMC to complete prototype boards in less than 24 hours, and it also has helped minimise the number of component misloads (incorrect insertions of components onto boards) in regular production boards. A final technical adaptation was in the area of quality control. With TH, MPG relied upon 100 percent in-process and final inspection. With SMT and flow manufacturing, in-process inspection was gradually phased out in favour of statistical process control (SPC).

Hewlett Packard—Introduction of New Technology concluded

ASMC promoted a multiskilling culture. With TH manufacturing, workers were assigned to a workstation and batches of materials came to them in boxes. With SMT, assigned workstations were removed and people now moved to where the work was in the process. Similarly, Andover's manufacturing management dramatically changed with the arrival of SMT. These managers were strongly oriented toward batch production and none made the transition to SMT flow production. New supervisors, willing to give flow manufacturing a try, were quickly promoted from within to lead Andover's SMT.

Three other areas were changed as part of the transition from TH to SMT. First, performance measures were radically modified. A second change involved shopfloor control and scheduling. Finally, Andover implemented an activity-based cost accounting system to help evaluate and control total product costs. Four key cost drivers were identified by manufacturing: (1) number of auto-loaded parts; (2) number of hand-loaded parts; (3) number of discrete tests; and (4) number of components purchased. This information is widely shared with engineering to help minimise the costs of new board designs for existing systems.

- The way that banks all over the world have tried to develop capability in Internet banking, beginning with only a strategic intent and a loose understanding of the economics of the Internet, and then experimenting and honing skills and knowledge until they have control over the process and its technical aspects. Some banks have become stuck in the various stages, possibly because of their conservatism or their lack of allocated resources, while others have pursued leadership positions in terms of Internet capabilities in the hope that they will obtain cost or market advantages. Others still have misjudged where the leading edge is and have either overinvested or invested poorly in technical capability and hence found themselves not at the leading edge but at the "bleeding edge" of technology.

It is possible to view certain technologies generically in terms of their position or stage of development. For example, technologies such as steel-making, oil-refining, and automobile painting are all in the 7th or 8th stage of Jaikumar and Bohn's framework. These stable, well-known technical processes are also in mature product markets; hence the return on these technical assets is not risky, and expected returns from companies involved in such technologies are relatively low, close to the risk-free rate of return. The price to earnings ratios of such companies are also relatively low as a result of the stability that is associated with the technologies and hence the future prospects of their industries. So-called supernormal returns have been bid away.

At the other end of the scale, consider biotechnology start-up companies, experimenting with pharmaceuticals that might cure diabetes, AIDS, or cancer, or Internet companies such as Amazon.com, which have the potential to revolutionise the sales and distribution of mass markets. These companies are really risking their capital at stages 1 through 3, knowing that the chances of success for any single R & D initiative are low. Interestingly, however, the financial upside of getting it right and coming up with a major biotechnical or Internet-based breakthrough is seen in the capital markets as so positive that, on an expected value basis, the price to earnings ratios of these companies often have been pushed very high.

Whether in the capital market or within a firm, investors usually are looking to invest in a portfolio of technical assets that can be thought of as being appropriately spread across the eight stages. These can involve "bread and butter" technical assets, such as in well-known technologies (in stages 6 through 8) as well as innovative investments in start-up technologies (in stages 1 through 3) or companies in sunrise industries, which are cash flow negative but have higher potential upsides in the medium to long term.

Prahalad and Hamel (1990) have compared the performance of NEC and GTE and have deduced that performance differences can be attributed to executive management's ability to conceive of the organisation as deriving its success from a number of distinctive core competencies in lieu of products.

Sony actively manages its portfolio of technologies. Reviewing Sony's success in technology management, Betz (1993) concludes that a "strategic attitude" on the part of executive management is as important, if not more important, than the strategic capabilities possessed by the firm. As Betz points out, "Strategic attitudes are necessary to planning success because nothing ever really happens as planned and often one learns what are the real goals after a strategic plan has begun." Therefore, it is concluded that a key role for executive management is to create a culture that facilitates a strategic technology attitude.

This strategic approach can be supported by analytic techniques. For example, Clark and Wheelwright (1992a) have developed a project mapping technique to assist firms in rethinking their portfolio of projects in relation to their strategic business intent and the development of their core technological capabilities. They believe the greatest value of any project plan is its ability to shape and build development capabilities, both individual and organisational. Technological and other capabilities can be considered as key assets of the firm.

Quinn et al. (1990) view the firm as an intellectual holding company in which products and services are the application of the firm's technological base. They state: "Core capabilities are the basis of products . . . nondistinctive capabilities lead to nondistinctive products."

Meyer (1993) has identified four inhibitors of technological capability development:

1. Entrenched short-term corporate mindsets.
2. Failure to adapt to generational technological change.
3. Failure to invest in product and process improvement (firm complacency).
4. Disestablishment of design teams (reassigning teams to other tasks).

Clark and Wheelwright (1992) argue that higher levels of core technological capability have tended to precede and then coincide with higher levels of firm performance. Stalk (1992) takes this argument even further. He proposes that the playing field of competitive advantage is shifting from structural attributes such as markets, geography, operating facilities, and cost to capabilities, such as the ability to reduce operating costs and product lead times to market, as well as improve product features and performance. Consequently, the only sustainable source of competitive advantage will become the ability to respond consistently to changing markets with new and improved products and ever improving competitiveness. Clark and Wheelwright (1992) also argue that the development of an effective product development capability unleashes a virtuous cycle in reputation and enthusiasm within and outside the organisation—successful new products energise the organisation's confidence, pride, and morale, and then profits provide for reinvestment in the cycle of success. Microsoft ran such a cycle for over a decade and Hewlett Packard, Toyota, 3M, and Sony have sustained such cycles for some 30-plus years.

Samson and Challis (1996) argue that a capabilities focus will increase the strategic value of a firm's technological base for reasons that include:

- A dependency of key firm capabilities on core technological assets.
- The increased strategic relevance of support activities. Consider Apple, which moved to emphasise "solutions to customers' problems" in lieu of hardware sales. Customer technical support has become a key activity in terms of retaining existing customers and identifying opportunities for future development.
- The complexity and organisational diffuseness of technical processes, which can produce capabilities that are both unique and nonsubstitutable. Consider Siemens, whose reputation in the industrial electrical equipment market is based on the excellence of its top quality engineering and design teams, which is extremely difficult for competitors to either replicate or substitute.

HPM—Methods of Achieving Growth

HPM pursues market growth via two strategies. The first is by acquisition, which is a commercially driven strategic decision. Growth via this strategy involves discreetly acquiring decentralised companies in order to maintain the company culture to achieve tremendous efficiencies. These are parallel independent family-run companies, involving initially 60 percent equity, then 80 percent, and finally 100 percent ownership. Growth is sideways to maintain the family hands-on approach. If HPM were to grow, it would be through a conglomerate of many such small companies. Growth through such acquisition has enabled HPM to enter other product markets such as industrial and commercial street lighting, which is one of the five "pillars" of the business. These ownerships are kept secret to avoid conflicts of interest with major competitors, who in some incidences are also HPM customers for electrical accessories.

The second approach is via internal growth through new product development. Growth via this strategy has achieved 30 percent per annum for the last 20 years, and even through the recession it has maintained at double digits in a shrinking market. The approach is to grow the market, not chase increased market share through entering price wars. A classic example of niche marketing was the introduction of a surge protector for PCs and faxes before these became incorporated into the hardboard. This was extremely profitable until copied by a competitor and then followed by cheap Chinese imports flooding the market. By adding a filter, it was converted for hi-fi systems, giving a profitable extension to its product line. Ultimately, by incorporating a surge protector into a power point and using

> rapid prototyping soft tooling commercial technology to get the product to market in 27 weeks instead of the usual 46, a new market was found with government enterprises having computer-based operations susceptible to electrical storms. Development of a new switchboard with a similar protector is yet another example of how HPM has continued to grow the market.

Technological Capabilities Development: Diffusion and Adaptation

Technology transfer has been defined (Hamilton, 1992) as:

> . . . the process of movement or transfer of information, technical know-how, and people among corporate technical functions such as R & D, engineering, and manufacturing, and nontechnical functions such as marketing and sales in order to yield innovative products and services that meet corporate business goals and fulfill customer needs.

Technology transfer and its role in the development of a firm's technological capabilities was discussed widely during the last quarter of the twentieth century (Hamilton, 1992; Meyer and Roberts, 1988; Meyer, 1993). Much of the discussion focused on the international or interorganisational dimensions of technology transfer.

On an international level, research on technology transfer has focused on the movement or transfer of technology between countries. On an interorganisational level, the emphasis has been on transferring technology from government, academic institutions, and research organisations to private industry. Paradoxically, discussion of intraorganisational transfer has received little attention. The paradox results from the widespread recognition that many countries are adept at developing new technology but poor at its commercialisation and management (Meyer and Utterback, 1993).

Consider product R & D and the commercialisation of new developments. While the U.S. continues to be the world leader in science and new technology development, Japan continues to lead the pack in bringing new or improved products to the marketplace. In 1998, the United States Patent Office granted 32,120 U.S. patents to Japanese firms—a 32 percent increase on Japanese patents for 1997 and well over three times the total for German patents, the next most active foreign applicant.[1] Japan's lead has been attributed to its proficiency in effecting shorter design cycles and its commitment of resources to continuous product improvement (Clark and Fujimoto, 1989), as well as to the role played by research bodies in forecasting technological developments and their commercial application. The Institute for Future Technology, for example, keeps Japanese industry apprised of technological advances and their implications to industry through a survey carried out every four years of 4,000 top Japanese CEOs, scientists, R & D personnel, and engineers.

---

[1]Anthony Paul, "Made in Japan," *Fortune,* December 6, 1999.

A number of models also have been developed to analyse firms' responses to technological opportunities. Consumer research has viewed the technology diffusion process as being conceptualised by an S-shaped logistic pattern, reflecting an exponential growth pattern from innovators and early adopters to majority acceptance in the marketplace (Robertson, 1984). In "Crossing the Chasm" (1991), Moore proposes a revised technology adoption life cycle. The five adopter categories (innovator, early adopter, early majority, late majority, and laggards) can be profiled in terms of their psychographic and behavioural characteristics.

Steele (1989) has divided barriers to effective technology transfer into two types: technical and attitudinal.

- *Technical barriers.* It has been found that it is impossible to transfer technology effectively without "people transfer," through intraorganisational secondments (Betz, 1994). This facilitates understanding, assists in the development of staff, and fosters organisational commitment by overcoming the "not invented here" syndrome that can occur when technologies are introduced from external sources. Additionally, the process of scaling-up product output to the prototype level and beyond almost invariably involves technical design and performance changes. This process can generate "pride of ownership" disputes between R & D staff and production engineers. A related barrier results from attitudinal differences between R & D staff and production managers. To the former a project "works" if it can be produced and can function on a laboratory scale of manufacture, even if it permanently requires an attendant operative or frequent maintenance. To operation managers, a new facility "works" when it can support manufacture at the required level of output and is cost effective in addition to being sufficiently reliable to operate continuously in its intended application.

- *Attitudinal barriers.* As Steele notes, there are significant differences in the attitudes of personnel toward time. Researchers view the outcome as the independent variable and time as the dependent variable. The manager views time as the independent variable and the outcome as the dependent variable. Consequently, because a manager works within defined timeframes, projects are broken into discrete steps to be completed within defined time intervals. Conversely, the researcher produces results through discoveries that are generally unpredictable. Another related difference is the knowledge versus action orientation of researchers as opposed to managers. These and other fundamental differences in attitudes and values underpin, and help define, the basic conflict that exists between the management of innovation and strategic business management. This conflict may inhibit communication between the various groups involved in technology transfer and reduce the likelihood of a successful outcome if not acknowledged and addressed (Badawy, 1991).

Regarding aspects of technology transfer, Badawy (1991) identifies the following as characteristic of American firms:

- A belief that inventing new technology is a necessary and sufficient condition for gaining competitive advantage.

- A lack of appreciation for the importance of speed in delivering products to the marketplace.
- Excessive emphasis on R & D activity at the end of product life cycles rather than developing new areas.
- Lack of balance between research and application.
- Inadequate links between R & D and the marketplace.

Given these characteristics, Badawy (1991) identifies the following common reasons for failure in the transfer of technology:

- Inadequate understanding of the role of technology within business strategy and the dynamic nature of technology.
- The nontechnical backgrounds of executive managers and communication inadequacies between business and technical managers.
- Failure to apply management by integration to effectively integrate business strategy, R & D strategy, and manufacturing and marketing functions.
- Excessive focus on "big bang projects."
- Overemphasis on short-term profitability goals.
- Failure to allocate R & D expenditure effectively.
- Refusal to abandon the "not invented here" syndrome.

Japanese firms are generally held up as exemplars in the practice of effective technology transfer and the structured development of technological capabilities. Analysing the experiences of Japanese firms in technology transfer, Clark and Fujimoto (1989) identify the following as being key to their success:

- Executive management's recognition that technology transfer is essential for long-term industry competitiveness.
- Direct face-to-face contact for transferring technology.
- The capability to commercialise the developments of others and to relate new products and product improvements to specific market needs.
- Managers' broad skills and knowledge in key areas of business activity, ensuring demonstrable levels of technical competence within executive management and fostering the ability to work with others.
- The carefully controlled diffusion of technology along all links in the product realisation chain: from R & D to engineering, engineering to operations, operations to sales and marketing, etc.

Summary

Perhaps the best way to summarise technological capability is to consider both well-known examples and characteristics of companies that have developed such superiority. Consider firms that manufacture essentially physical products, such as Toyota, Sony, Nokia, Boeing, Goodyear, GM, Ford, General Electric, and Dell. These companies invest worldwide in technological assets that will make their products attractive and competitive in marketplaces around the world. Their key challenge is to drive their business competitiveness, expressed in terms of cost, quality, flexibility, and design, through their ability to manage technological innovation.

In the service sector, consider Microsoft, Citigroup, Cisco, AOL, Time Warner, British Telecom, Deutsche Bank, and Diamaru. These companies have the service sector equivalents of the same challenges! Technical leadership is critical in all these firms. Transactional efficiency, customer service, and cost are all driven through the technology that these service firms can develop, acquire, and deploy.

The critical characteristics of these firms' technological capability and consequential business success are:

- A focus on the development of a defined set of technological capabilities.
- An ability to develop a strategic technology culture through routines that facilitate capabilities development and relate technological capabilities to strategic goals.
- The recognition that the contribution of technology and technical functions to competitive advantage derives from superior technological capabilities.
- An ability to balance short-term operating requirements with longer term goals.
- An ability to effectively adapt to generational technological change.
- An ongoing commitment to invest in product and process improvement.
- An ability to institutionalise the learning of design teams in a way that continuously develops essential technological capabilities.
- Adequate levels of technological competence within executive management.

CIG Gas Cylinders—Organisational Restructuring and Performance Improvements

In 1977, five years after its foundation, CIG Gas Cylinders, in response to declining performance and an increasingly hostile and competitive international market, initiated a collaboration with Luxfer Gas Cylinders. This partnership began what has now come to be known in best practice nomenclature as "benchmarking"—and was perhaps the inaugural intercompany example in Australia. Measurement techniques established the basis for comparing individual plants' strengths and weaknesses and setting realistic targets. To improve respective operations, both plants exchanged information regularly and conducted site study tours.

In seeking to maintain its competitiveness and improve productivity and product quality, CIG embarked on a number of reforms. Initially introducing a common interest gain-sharing program (CIP) in 1982 (claimed to be the first in Australia), this was followed by initiatives on total quality control (TQC) in 1985 and then just-in-time (JIT) and value-added management (VAM) in 1987. The outcomes of these innovations included expanded export markets, improved customer focus, and enhanced productivity. Building on these initiatives, a self-managing work team program was introduced at Gas Cylinders in July

1991. The design of these teams was based on socio-technical systems (STS) theory. The STS program comprised two studies. First, an employee survey analysed job satisfaction, communication, individual ambitions, team participation, and sources of dissatisfaction. Second, a technical study closely examined manufacturing processes in the plants. Upon completion of this documentation, all employees were asked to vote on whether to accept the program. A total of 75 percent agreed to proceed.

Recommended Case

Case 17: Samyeong Cable Company

Managing Innovation

Innovation is a field receiving a great deal of attention from companies in today's fast-changing business environment. Realising that most firms and competitors within their industry have acquired the same level of competence in other areas of management, such as operations, human resources, marketing, strategy, and the like, many firms have begun to look to innovation as a key differentiating factor for competitive advantage.

Not surprisingly, the merger and acquisition activity among firms in the last decade was driven primarily by their search for new technologies, ideas, or information that would lead to industry- or market-transforming innovations. Firms are also spending increasingly large amounts of money on licensing and purchasing intellectual property. According to the Patent and License Exchange based in Pasadena, California, trading in intangible assets increased from $15 billion in 1990 to $100 billion in 1998 in the United States. From a corporate perspective, it may be of some concern that an increasing proportion of that amount has been going to individuals and small firms.

While the stars of the American business landscape tend to be innovative companies such as Hewlett Packard, Cisco, Microsoft, Dell, and Amazon, some previously innovative firms are questioning whether their size or culture may be hindering the sort of innovation needed to produce market-transforming products or technologies. As a result, large firms are now devoting more and more time to understanding the key drivers of the innovation process and the environment best suited to fostering it.

There are many definitions of innovation and the innovation process but we have chosen to use the definition by Souder (1987), which summarises the basic concept:

> Innovation is a high risk idea that is new to the sponsoring organisation. The innovation process is any system of organised activities that transforms a technology from idea to commercialisation.

The terms innovation, entrepreneurship, invention, discovery, research and development, and intrapreneurship are often used (and confused) interchangeably. Whereas innovation refers to new products, processes, and services, entrepreneurship involves both the identification and exploitation of opportunities to innovate. Invention and discovery refer to beginnings in the innovation process and we refer to R&D as the formalised process for pursuing innovative ideas and bringing them to fruition. Intrapreneurship usually refers to processes of innovation within the organisation whereas entrepreneurship can include the creation and growth of new enterprises.

Specifically, we can classify innovation into three types (Samson, 1991):

- Product innovation (e.g., new or improved products, new materials).
- Process innovation (e.g., new manufacturing technology, new distribution logistics).
- Managerial and systems innovation (e.g., total quality management, just-in-time).

Our discussion in this chapter will be confined to the first two types of innovation, as they are more often technological rather than purely managerial or systems innovations.

Peters and Brownes Group—Product, Process, and Management and Systems Improvement

Prior to the late 1980s, innovation had not been recognised as part of the culture within Peters and Brownes Group. Manufacturing was relatively labour-intensive and there was little or no R&D into either new product development or capital equipment upgrades. The R&D that did take place locally was confined mainly to providing product range extensions and solutions to operational problems.

Since the mid-1980s, however, Peters and Brownes has seen R&D more in terms of a benefit rather than a cost to the business. During the years between 1985 and 1995, steps were taken to develop such a culture in regard to product development, process development, and management and systems improvement. Roughly 50 percent of the budget for R&D was spent on developing new business and the linkage between marketing and R&D was also developed to provide support in both product innovation and the development of new products for local and overseas markets. The technology team at the Peters and Brownes Group was set up to be responsible for three things: R&D per se, quality, and the laboratories. This team links with four main areas of the company operations: new business, sales, domestic markets, and operations.

Internally, several key performance indicators were identified and used at the ice cream plant, including: consumer complaints, inventory levels, ingredient wastage, absenteeism, compliance to budget, operational efficiencies, and so on. Externally, the benchmarking results between Peters and its competitors were useful in encouraging other organisations to implement new technology in order to remain competitive. Local and international visits were continually used by Peters to examine new technology. Peters benchmarked for process innovation both domestically and internationally. By improving and promoting product innovation, local consumers received an increased choice of products coupled with world standards in quality.

Technological innovation is a key feature in today's manufacturing, services, and information systems environment. As a consequence, it has drawn significant attention from researchers. We will now review what is generically known about the nature of innovation and the various models used to describe the innovation process.

Describing the Nature of Innovation

It has been long recognised by researchers that the attitudes and values of organisations that existed during the 1950s and 1960s were not conducive to innovation. During this period, firms operated in relatively stable environments and adopted product development strategies that were characterised by incremental improvements rather than new directions, a slow pace of change, and functional championing of improvement effort. As economic, market, and technological conditions have become more dynamic, organisations have recognised that to maintain a competitive advantage, different strategies need to be employed and, to be implemented effectively, different organisational characteristics are required. Risk taking, a tolerance for ambiguity, an increased customer and market orientation, a high degree of employee motivation and commitment, teamwork, effective horizontal communication channels, and vesting decision-making authority with entrepreneurs (Betz, 1993) have become hallmarks of the firms that have prospered in this environment. Innovative products and processes have been the outcome.

Conventional wisdom has consistently argued that innovation is fostered by, or at least related to, firm size and industry structure. There are two schools of thought. On the one side are the Schumpeterians, arguing that developing markets and large firms are the driving forces behind innovation (Schumpeter, 1934). Their logic is based on the belief that the more competitive the market structure, the smaller are the gains to innovation. Only by having the carrot of large potential profits can firms be induced to innovate. This logic is the basis of almost all existing patent and copyright law. The opposite view (Robertson, 1984) holds that innovation is fostered by the desire to enter and compete in competitive markets. The driving force to innovate is survival as competitors encroach on one's market. According to this viewpoint it is the stick of annihilation that drives innovation.

Today, we know that both mechanisms are valid under certain conditions. Some organisations have even gone so far as to set up businesses that compete with and threaten to cannibalise their existing businesses in an attempt to aggressively pursue an innovative idea before competitors adopt it. By setting up Internet banking facilities through Wingspan, BancOne has established a business that competes with and threatens to cannibalise its existing branch network. Similarly, at General Electric (GE), Jack Welch's initiatives aimed at the Internet have been very aptly titled, "destroyyourbusiness.com"![1]

Many attempts have been made to identify those organisational characteristics that differentiate an "innovative" firm. Several factors, including continuous and intensive organisational collaboration and interaction, management of uncertainty, a recognition of the cumulative nature of technological capabilities, and the differentiated nature of

---

[1]"Fear of the Unknown," *The Economist*, December 4, 1999.

technological skills, have been identified as characterising superior innovative performance (Betz, 1993; Robertson, 1971; Steele, 1989).

Saleh and Wang (1993) have developed one of the more comprehensive models, which identifies three key organisational attributes for effective innovation:

1. *Entrepreneurial strategies.*

   a. Risk taking. In such a dynamic business environment, risk taking becomes part of doing business, as firms need to make strategic decisions with incomplete information.

   b. Proactive approach. Successful firms are proactive and anticipate, rather than react to, change. Consequently, they regularly scan environments (market, product, and technology) and act accordingly.

   c. Management commitment. Top management is expected to make a sustained commitment to policies and practices that fly in the face of conventional wisdom.

2. *Organisational structure/group functioning.*

   a. Flexible structures. The relationship between innovation and organic structural forms has long been recognised (Burns and Stalker, 1961).

   b. Synthesis. Innovative firms are able to effectively integrate activities across organisational boundaries. Kanter (1985) also has indicated that there is significant evidence that many of the best ideas are interdisciplinary and interfunctional in origin.

   c. Collective orientation. Synthesizing and integrating activities between departments, groups, and individuals is underpinned by a common collective understanding of the goals of the business. A number of authors believe that managing innovation requires an ability to manage interdependence and that this requires common organisational norms and beliefs and not just reward and recognition systems.

3. *Organisational climate.*

   a. Open/promotive climate. Openness in exchanging information facilitates not only effective innovation but also trust and respect between employees. Souder (1987) indicates that promotional climates encourage innovation success and that within these climates growth and innovation are much-talked-about goals.

   b. Collegiality. In a collegial climate, authority and power are shared equally among colleagues. This characteristic has been found to be positively correlated with innovative organisations (Souder, 1987).

   c. Reward systems. Well-planned reward systems have been found to be effective tools for reinforcing expected behaviours and shaping the development of the desired climate (Baulkin, 1988). Kanter (1985) emphasises the importance of what she calls a "culture of pride" that expects and rewards high levels of achievement and assumes that investments in people pay off.

Extensive investigations have been made into a range of innovative firms. For example, many studies have been made of 3M, which spent nearly $4 billion on R&D during the last decade and maintains a staff of over 7,000 scientists. Six attributes have enabled 3M to develop a superior technological capability (Mitsch, 1990):

1. Development of core technical capabilities.
2. Technological differentiation from competitors.

3. Establishment of proprietary positions.
4. Leveraging existing strengths.
5. Entering segments where the company can win.
6. Augmenting the business through acquisitions and licensing.

In a later article, Mitsch (1992) observed that the culture of R&D at 3M had been fostered not only through direction from the CEO but through a number of traditions and practices, including:

- Generating 25 percent of sales from products that are less than five years old (3M has since raised this requirement to 30 percent, from products less than four years old).
- Having the senior R&D executive report to the CEO.
- Recognising and rewarding innovation in tangible ways.

Other authors also have noted that 3M's success has been underpinned by its high level of spending on R&D (18 percent), driving innovation by market demands and developing manufacturing capabilities that support the company's innovative thrust. 3M views manufacturing excellence as an essential ingredient of its innovative success. The mindset through which 3M has achieved its sucess is not necessarily linked to the hype and buzz of electronics or high technology and cutting edge products. In the 3M plant in London, Ontario, for example, in which the major products are sandpaper and duct tape, the same culture, mindset, and reward systems exist as in the advanced technology divisions.

In an international study of innovative practices, Quinn (1985) has found that successful large firms, like many small entrepreneurial companies, accept the chaos that is essential to development. According to Quinn, these firms pay close attention to their users' needs and desires, avoid excessive detail in early technical or marketing plans, and allow entrepreneurial teams to pursue competing alternatives within a clearly conceived framework of goals and limits. Downside risks are minimised not by detailed controls but by spreading risks among multiple projects, keeping early costs low, and gauging the tenacity, flexibility, and capability of the founders. Quinn also notes that entrepreneurial firms adopt different practices than traditional firms for project justification, decision making, and incentive schemes.

Kumar et al. (1994) have studied the innovative practices of American electronics and telecommunications firms. They have found that over half of the respondents in their study do not have a formal process for assessing the strategic value of an innovation to the business nor do they actively involve product personnel during the design stage. They also have found that effective innovation processes reduce the number of iterations in the design cycle. In addition, a moderate correlation seems to exist between those firms that have an effective quality accreditation scheme and those that are innovative.

Ettlie (1990) has studied the innovative practices of 50 manufacturing plants in the U.S. The focus of this work was to discover if the functional experience of general managers had any relationship to the genesis and success of manufacturing innovation. Notable findings included:

- Firms that have CEOs with manufacturing experience are significantly more likely to implement an aggressive manufacturing technology policy.

- A company's commitment to training and work force development is higher during modernisation if senior executives possess manufacturing experience.
- Direct labour savings from modernisation (as distinct from improvements in operating characteristics, efficiencies, etc.) is more likely to be emphasised by traditional senior managers.

In another study, Ettlie (1992) reports on the mechanisms involved in the successful adoption of new process technology. He concludes that, since firms buy most technologies for manufacturing operations, it is difficult for them to use these technologies for competitive advantage because they are readily available to competitors. He suggests, however, that firms can use two types of mechanisms to capture value from process innovations. First, they can make process innovation a unique occasion for organisational restructuring, and second, they can create effective new patterns from the many different options to achieve these changes. Findings support the idea that redesigned organisational structures, improved coordination between design and manufacturing, and greater supplier cooperation have a positive effect on the productivity of new manufacturing systems. Ettlie further posits that forming new customer alliances positively affects new system flexibility.

Boeing—Managing Innovations
(Managing Complementary Innovations)

The 777 design program provided Boeing with an opportunity to rectify many of the problems that had emerged during its product development history. The company implemented two complementary innovations: (1) a digitally based design system and (2) cross-functional design/build teams (DBTs). These programs created many challenges for Boeing. For example, extensive technical training was required for all employees who would be using the digital design systems. Additionally, employees needed assistance in adapting to new reporting relationships and communication patterns. The total cost of implementing and operating the computer aided design technology and related systems was difficult to assess with complete accuracy. Although digital design and the creation of the associated DBT structure had been costly, Boeing officials felt that the system would more than pay for itself over time.

Schewe (1994) has studied the question of whether innovative success is a function of firm-related variables (e.g., innovation experience, market and customer knowledge, distribution channels, etc.) or project-related variables (e.g., technical skills, development costs, development time, etc.). He concludes that, above all, innovation's success is determined by the overall capabilities of the innovative firm. Consequently, firms need to develop approaches that facilitate a cross-functional perspective to the management of innovation. In particular, the impact of key decisions on a firm's innovative capability needs to be considered.

Based on practical case studies, some of the hard-won lessons about risk and success in innovation are (Steele, 1989):

1. Unless a new technology offers real value to the customer in terms of functionality or performance, it will not succeed as an innovation.
2. Technologies are systems and until the total system is managed, success cannot be assured.
3. Although the customer determines the ultimate success or failure of an innovation, the criteria that the customer uses may be multidimensional and may vary with time.
4. Successful new products depend as much on standards and infrastructure (support, etc.) as they do on performance.
5. A radically new technology usually requires a new business organisation for success.

Betz (1993) identifies speed and "correctness" as the essential criteria for evaluating a product development process and indicates that the difficulty in achieving them is due to the uncertainties, variations, and changes that need to be accommodated in the product development cycle. Bower and Hout (1988) have illustrated the importance of these attributes by analysing Toyota's fast product cycle capability. They found that Toyota aims to introduce new products ahead of its competitors. Through constantly trying out new models, Toyota is able to observe customer choices. This enables the company to keep current with changing market trends and simultaneously facilitate the development of a "customer-oriented culture."

HPM—Development of Innovative Ideas

In the case of HPM, the managing director estimates that about 30 percent of input to new ideas comes from "bouncing ideas around and innovating ideas in the think tank environment of the one-hour daily management meeting each morning." This process is supported by site visits by executives to international fairs and exhibitions like those in Hannover and Washington, and talking to other manufacturers worldwide that are producing similar product ranges. Rather than copied, these are used to stimulate thought processes as input to HPM's own innovation. Benchmarking with selected companies is conducted for technology reasons and not for efficiency comparisons, as is the usual basis for competitive benchmarking. Since the Japanese and Chinese situation is fully appreciated, HPM mainly uses European, British, and American firms, with the closest association established with a large, privately owned U.S. firm having an identical philosophy to that of HPM. These exchanges are confirmed by formal benchmarking arrangements to ensure each is a "two-way street." Another key input to HPM's innovation process comes from sharing inventions with various inventors and then developing something different based on the original product, for which the inventor is properly rewarded.

Technological Innovation Process Modeling

For successful technological innovation to occur, the process of innovation needs to be carefully managed. The complex nature of the innovation process has been emphasised by many authors. Tornaski (1983) describes the process of innovation as "a process of many discrete decisions and behaviours that unfold slowly over time," a definition consistent with the observations of Schewe (1994).

The pervasiveness of an innovation also should be considered in terms of the risks and rewards associated with it. Consider the differences between radical, incremental, and systems innovation as suggested by Marquis (1969):

1. Radical innovation provides a new functionality that represents a discontinuity in the existing technology (e.g., transistors, integrated circuits, lasers, etc.).

2. Incremental innovation improves existing functional capabilities, enhances attributes such as quality and reliability, or reduces cost (e.g., doping techniques in transistors and improved memory devices in computers).

3. Systems innovation usually refers to a radical innovation that provides new functional capability based on reconfiguring existing technologies. Consider the automobile, for example, which put together the existing carriage technology with bicycle technology and the gasoline engine.

Iva Manufacturing—Defining Technological Innovation

Iva Manufacturing Company has defined technological innovation as a novel change, application, or rearrangement of equipment. It also includes manufacturing techniques and organisational changes that lead to greater efficiency in terms of cost, quality, and time. Iva's president is the main innovation driver. The driving force for innovation at Iva is the quest for maximising future cash flows.

Iva has ensured that sufficient resources are available to pursue innovation. These include rewarding employees who have innovative ideas through promotion, incentive pay structures, and the opportunity for ownership. Further technical education of employees is encouraged by reimbursing the cost involved and by adjusting work schedules.

An appreciation for the complexity of the innovation process can be gained by reviewing some of the many models that have been developed to help describe it. These models range from simple "pipeline" or "black box" models to more complicated models. Some models focus on consumer product innovation, others are concerned with industrial product innovation, and still others attempt to have a more universal application. It is generally agreed, however, that no model appears to be capable of being utilised as a general model of innovation (Saren, 1984). Models may be catalogued (Forest, 1991) as follows:

- *Stage models.* Innovation is treated principally as a sequential linear activity; that is, the process of innovation is viewed as a series of discrete stages. The unit of analysis within each stage is generally activity or functional responsibility. Examples are offered by Utterback (1971), Mansfield and Wagner (1975), and Saren (1984). Although useful, these models overlook the nonlinearity of the innovation process. Kelly and Krantzberg (1978) have drawn attention to the poor representation that these models provide of the complexity of the innovation process.

- *Conversion models (technology push/market pull models).* Technological innovation has also been described as a conversion process, with inputs being converted into products or processes through a number of steps. Twiss (1980) has developed the simplest form of the conversion model, which is a black box model where the inputs of materials and knowledge are converted into outputs. Twiss (1980) and many others also have developed other models. While a number of models have been developed based on technology push or market pull, pure technology push and market pull models are viewed as extremes of innovation models. Rothwell (1985) has developed an interactive model that addresses the needs of the marketplace and the opportunities presented by new technologies. While such a model provides a more realistic representation, it is still regarded as grossly underrepresenting the complexities of the process.

- *Integrative models.* These models attempt to integrate process and product innovation in respect to the technology life cycle (birth, prosperity, maturity, etc.). In the model developed by Utterback and Abernathy (1978), the dynamic nature of the innovation process was stressed and the process was represented as changing over time as the industry evolved and matured and the initial focus on new product development changed to one where the concentration was on process optimisation and cost reduction. Although extremely useful, the model failed to adequately represent the innovation process when tested over a range of industries (Utterback and Abernathy, 1981).

- *Decision models.* Throughout the process of innovation, many decisions need to be made. Therefore, many models approach the innovation process in terms of these decision points. These decision models offer management a practical approach to the process. The Cooper and More model (1979) points to the evolutionary nature of the decision-making process and also shows that decisions take place between the various activities involved in the process of innovation. Various authors, however, have commented on the lack of generalisability of these models and have indicated that the constructs used and the approaches taken limit their use within particular industry segments.

Many other models that have been developed fall outside these generalised categories. For example, Kanter (1989) conceptualises the innovation process as "newstream" activities that must be autonomous of the mainstream value-adding processes such as production distribution and marketing, as they are fundamentally different in nature and form. Kanter has developed descriptions of the relationships that need to exist between the newstream and mainstream in order for innovation processes to be effective.

Forest makes the following comments in respect to the degree to which these models are representative of the innovation process:

- Most models overlook the complexity of the preinnovation stage: idea generation and screening.
- Although useful in conceptualising the process, most models have not been of use in firm strategic planning processes because they fail to include the dimension of time.
- Environmental considerations (political, economic, sociocultural, etc.), which can have a significant impact on the innovation process, are generally excluded.
- The "human element" has been overlooked. The impact of champions of innovation (organisational agents, governments, trade unions, employer bodies, etc.) has not been considered.
- Strategic alliances, which are generally regarded as a key component in developing an innovative capability, have not been considered.
- Models fail to recognise the cumulative and somewhat chaotic nature of innovation. Any construct or process applied to manage the innovation process needs to have adequate feedback mechanisms and flexibility to address the nature of the innovation process—which is, by its very nature, both evolutionary and revolutionary, deductive and inductive. Einstein once stated that, "I never came upon any of my discoveries through a process of rational thinking."

In summary, it appears that the development of a model that adequately represents the complexity of the innovation process and has general applicability is highly unlikely. Innovation appears to be highly situation-oriented, precluding a single theory or model of innovation. Practitioners might well benefit from considering innovation from a number of these perspectives of decision making, stages of development, and integration of activity.

Characteristics of Innovative Firms

Notwithstanding the fact that success in innovation does not appear to have a recipe, general formula, or prescription, there are some common factors that can be correlated with innovative success:

- Members of top management have technological and business backgrounds and take a hands-on view of technological issues.
- Business issues and technological capabilities are considered simultaneously such that technological capabilities are focused toward supporting and driving business strengths. As is evidenced by successful innovators such as 3M, Texas Instruments, Xerox, Kodak, and Sony, an overemphasis on technological eloquence does not occur but rather there is a nice balance between technical and business forces.

- Among successful innovators, organisational attributes such as culture, infrastructure, coordination mechanisms, organisational structures, and reward systems are supportive of the innovation process. There is a tolerance for failure and an understanding that innovation is accompanied by risk taking, ambiguity, and a certain degree of "organised chaos."

In the same vein, Michael Schrage has asserted that successful innovation is often the result of "creative improvisation," rather than highly risk-averse and carefully laid out strategic plans.[2] By studying companies such as Boeing, Daimler-Chrysler, Disney, and Microsoft, Schrage has concluded that many of the breakthrough innovations achieved by these firms may be attributed to experimentation or "serious play" with models, prototypes, and simulations. Experimentation or serious play with prototyping, which has been made cost effective in recent times by digital technology, may lie at the heart of future innovative strategies by improving communication, collaboration, and collective learning within firms.

As an example, Schrage cites Boeing's "serious play" with modeling technologies in its Catia design program. Desperately needing a communication network within Boeing, design engineers of the 777 deliberately built conflict into the Catia design in order to identify people within the massive Boeing organisation—as well as counterparts in other areas of its design teams—with whom they could work in the future. A flag feature in the design system facilitated the establishment of a network that enabled collaborative interactions between design engineers in different parts of the Boeing organisation, resulting in conditions that were more conducive to innovation.

Summary

Innovation, like other key processes in the field of technology management, is not simple or straightforward to plan and implement. Indeed, even describing innovation and "how to do it" is complex. Some of the characteristics possessed by firms that demonstrate best practice in the field of innovation include:

- A propensity for risk taking.
- A tolerance for ambiguity.
- A customer and market orientation.
- A high degree of employee motivation and commitment.
- Use of flexible team-based work structures.
- Effective horizontal communication mechanisms.
- Decision-making authority vested with entrepreneurs.
- Emphasis on technical skills development.
- Continuous and intensive organisational collaboration and cooperation.

---

[2]Michael Schrage, *Serious Play: How the World's Best Companies Simulate Innovation,* HBR Press, Boston, 1999.

- A recognition of the cumulative nature of technological capabilities.
- An ability to relate technological skills to strategic intent.
- The use of metrics that reflect innovation (e.g., sales from products less than five years old).
- A hierarchy in which the senior R & D executive reports to the CEO.
- A reward system that recognises entrepreneurial behaviour.
- The establishment of proprietary positions in respect to technological achievements.
- The leveraging of existing technological strengths.
- Entering segments in which the company can win.
- Institutionalised environmental scanning.
- Senior management commitment.
- Technological competency among the executive management.
- Openness to sharing information.
- An egalitarian working environment.
- Manufacturing excellence.

These practices tend to "power each other up." They serve to give the organisation creative energy, but there is more to it than that. Creativity is just a spark that often leads to a jump in thinking or an innovative idea. Successful innovators also achieve their success because of the systems that are in place to support and drive innovative thinking and technological development. Further, the company's leadership and organisational climate and culture drive innovation. The organisation's value system and its core purpose for existing are both about innovation. If these elements that support and drive innovativeness are not present in a firm, then it will eventually lose in competitive battles to those firms that do have these properties, systems, values, and cultures. "Role model" companies, such as Hewlett Packard and 3M in the traditional economy and Cisco in the new economy, expend a lot of energy in developing these characteristics—and reap the benefits of the innovation outcomes!

Recommended Cases

Case 11: Hewlett Packard's Medical Products Group

Case 12: HPM

Technology Management, Operational Systems Strategy, and Business Competitiveness Interfaces

In this chapter we review a firm's strategic management processes, which cut across three areas: technology management, operational systems strategy, and business competitiveness interfaces. In addition, we briefly review the relationship between competitiveness and technology.

The work of Adler, McDonald, and McDonald (1992) provides a practical framework for benchmarking the strategic management processes of technical functions. The approach taken by the authors has previously been used extensively by Hayes and Wheelwright (1984) to characterise manufacturing functions. Focusing on the activities of product development functions, Adler et al. have identified four distinct stages or levels of development in strategic management performance:

1. *Stage 1.* Isolated, where the technical function has few links to the rest of the business and makes a minimal contribution.
2. *Stage 2.* Reactive, the classic "firefighting" function that responds to the problems encountered by the rest of the business but never identifies its own long-term strategy.
3. *Stage 3.* Proactive, where the technical function generates lots of new ideas and has a long-term strategy but is not well-tuned to other functions' needs or expectations.
4. *Stage 4.* Integrated, where the function's activities both support the current business priorities and create new opportunities.

Functional characteristics at each stage of technical function development have been defined according to the following elements:

- Mission.
- Objectives.

- Strategic plan.
- Processes (e.g., recruitment, development, rewards, etc.).
- Resources (intellectual property, funding, facilities, etc.).
- Linkages (structure and linkages to other organisations).
- Opportunities/threats.
- Strengths/weaknesses.

This matrix of characteristics and development stages provides a framework for analysing the performance of a technical function and identifying areas for improvement. Although specifically developed for product development functions, it can be modified and adapted to analyse and improve strategic management processes within other technical functions such as manufacturing engineering.

Although this framework can provide useful insights into policy areas such as personnel recruitment and development, it does not identify attributes specific to firm contexts, such as reward systems, project selection, project management, quality assurance, regulatory compliance, and so on. This approach is similar to most best practice frameworks, which identify generic characteristics that are associated with superior performance but fail to define those characteristics at a level that relates to firm-specific competitive factors. Its use as an improvement tool is limited, as it does not provide insights into the relationship between superior performance outcomes and deficiencies in particular strategic management elements. It thus helps managers identify areas for improvement but fails to assist them in developing a roadmap for such improvement.

The MIT study "Made In America" (1989) identifies short-term-oriented management practices, outdated management strategies, inadequate understanding of foreign cultures, inadequate investment in human resources, and a failure to invest in new technology as key deficiencies within American firms. These observations reflect the well-known failure of many U.S. companies to conduct strategic planning with regard to shifts in international technology and manufacturing and to implement responses in a timely manner (Clark, 1986). This failure has been traced to top management practices that view technology as an implementation resource rather than as a factor that shapes business strategy (Berman and Khalil, 1992). This constricts the development and implementation of necessary long-term technology-based competitiveness strategy.

A Booz, Allen, and Hamilton study (1982) of over 700 Fortune 1,000 companies estimated that new products would provide over 30 percent of these firms' profits during the five-year period from 1981 to 1986. For technology-driven industries, the contribution from new products was in excess of 40 percent. In the newer entrepreneurial industries of Internet and biotechnology companies, these figures are even higher.

Technology's Interface with the Market: Customers and Suppliers

Technology for technology's sake has little relevance. As such, the implementation of advanced manufacturing technology or other new technology should always be tied to the needs of the organisation's customers. It is important to check periodically during the implementation of any technological change to see that the needs of the marketplace are capable of being met in case any modifications need to be made.

A strong customer–supplier or producer–user relationship can help considerably in the effective adoption and implementation of new technology. Customers who can support their suppliers with a technology program and implementation skills enable suppliers to implement technology they would not normally have access to.

Market Integration with Technology

The technology that is introduced into any organisation has to satisfy a business need of the organisation or assist to satisfy the needs of a customer. Some of the organisations featured in the case studies in this book reevaluated technology during its introduction to ensure that it was still appropriate. As was discussed in relation to cross-functional teams, some organisations have developed a "gating" process whereby all product and service initiatives from anywhere in the organisation (i.e., sales, marketing, customer service, production, logistics, and finance) are put forward to a "gating committee" with representation from all areas of the organisation. This greatly assists these organisations in ensuring that their new technology is still relevant to their customers' needs.

Customer–Supplier and Producer–User Relationships

The effective adoption and implementation of new technology often depend on having strong customer–supplier or producer–user relationships. Small organisations especially are dependent on the support of a large organisation to identify the appropriate performance standards, the necessary technology, and the implementation method. Automobile manufacturers seem to have almost perfected this art; the industry leader appears to be Toyota, and other manufacturers have adopted Toyota's approach.

Franchising is another alternative for small organisations to keep abreast of industry standards and new technology. Mayekawa's doppos[1] are a good example, as are the institutes that comprise the Fraunhofer Institute. The subsidiary plants, which are partly owned by plant managers in the Iva Manufacturing group, are also run on a franchise-like basis. If franchising is not appropriate, then industry organisations or government technology arms are necessary to drive and disseminate new technology.

The introduction of technology always involves a customer–supplier or producer–user relationship, especially in cases where the technology is customised. The need for an open and trusting environment in which both parties can take risks is important under such circumstances. It is also beneficial if the two parties do their strategic planning together and involve key employees in the information sharing, so that each organisation understands the other's processes.

---

[1]"Doppos" are autonomous business units focusing on a market segment or customer.

Guy Birkin—Interfacing with Technology Supplier and Potential Customers

As a customer, Guy Birkin is seen as "more than a customer and more of a family member" to the machine maker Karl Mayer. Parties from the two companies meet several times per year, and once a year the people of Karl Mayer visit Guy Birkin to talk about future issues. The close collaboration that followed the development of the Jacquardtronic machine meant that, from the perspective of both parties, the relationship was of great commercial advantage. This interaction basically meant that Guy Birkin repeatedly asked Karl Mayer to develop a machine that could combine the benefits of Leavers with those of Jacquardtronic—eventually called the Textronic machine.

The development of the Textronic machine began in 1990. Karl Mayer, in late 1990, advised key lace makers that a new machine was being developed and a prototype would be available in 1991. Guy Birkin immediately decided to take the first prototype. It also made a number of visits to Karl Mayer, to see the machine being built, discuss needs, and get an idea of how the new machine would be configured (size, height, floor space needed, and so on).

As a lace supplier, Guy Birkin managed to launch its new products very quickly after the adoption of the new Textronic machine. The objective of the launch was to generate enough publicity to bring customers to its stand in the trade show. Trade magazines with which Guy Birkin had good relationships featured editorials on key issues. Guy Birkin cooperated with its contacts at these magazines to print articles on the nature and advantages of the new lace.

Having arrived at Guy Birkin's stand in the trade show, the ambition was to show customers the new machine, to stimulate their interest and let them know Guy Birkin was the only manufacturer of Textronic lace—an important message to communicate to customers. Furthermore, Guy Birkin had a clear view of the capabilities of the Textronic machine and its products and was able to tailor its message to suit each individual customer.

In almost all the case studies in this book, a strong relationship between the organisation introducing the new technology and the supplier of the technology can be observed. Both often work together for a long time through a prototyping and piloting program to perfect the technology before its introduction.

Hyundai has a permanent department that works with suppliers such as Samyeong. Development activities are triggered by the regular evaluation of the supplier or as part of the ongoing development objectives for the supplier. High quality suppliers are supported through financing, management aid, and purchases. Hyundai has a long-term strategy for product improvement and cost reduction, which is passed on to its suppliers. Bimonthly meetings are held with supplier CEOs and program managers to share information and progress updates. The assistance even extends to designing new factory premises to ensure that the output will meet Hyundai's future requirements. Toyota also works closely with its suppliers to ensure that they effectively embrace its technology, such as JIT.

Bosch-Siemens Hausgerate Group—Environmental Protection Program

The Bosch-Siemens Hausgerate Group (BSHG) is one of Europe's leading manufacturers of electrical and electronic consumer goods. Environmental protection has been a major focus of the company's activities since 1989. BSHG believes that only by seeing the environmental protection problem as a whole and covering all phases of product life with their many and varied interfaces can the environment be effectively protected. Consequently, BSHG has developed an integrated environmental plan supported by wide-ranging management practices.

Below is presented the total design/use/recycling system related to BSHG's environmental protection program and the integrated interfaces.

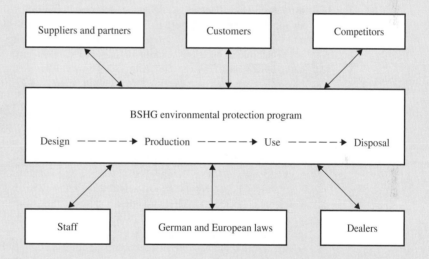

The management of those interfaces has largely contributed to BSGH's successful implementation of its environmental protection program:

- *German government and European laws.* Due to the growing concern regarding environmental protection, legislation to protect the environment is continually being introduced and passed. BSHG is regularly affected by regulations issued by the European Union and by various levels of government in Germany. Thus, BSHG is committed to conform to all environmental laws and regulations. But instead of waiting for new laws to come into effect, BSHG voluntarily adheres to regulations not yet enacted and its environmental standards frequently exceed the legal requirements. By seeing itself as a leader in its field, at least in Germany, BSHG is acting proactively, not reacting to what the competition and the legislature do. To reinforce this approach, BSHG introduces its own voluntary recycling procedures and environmental protection standards. For example, BSHG designers strictly adhere to company guidelines intended to make their products more recyclable and less polluting, right from the start.

- *Improving the standards of its suppliers.* Environmental standards are part of the selection criteria for suppliers. BSHG works only with certified subcontractors, whose practices are also regularly checked by BSHG. An audit program is in place to ensure that suppliers and other partners follow as strict an environmental policy as the company itself. BSHG has developed incentive schemes to encourage its suppliers to be more environmentally friendly. BSHG strives to close the loop, so that no residual waste remains as a result of the manufacturing process or the recycling of old appliances and packaging materials.

- *Informing customers.* Interested members of the public are kept informed about the company's environmental measures and performance in the environmental area through an annual environmental report. In addition, customers are supplied with instructions about how to use appliances in an environmentally friendly way. But environmental protection from the consumer's point of view sometimes can conflict with the company's business interest. Thus, costs to the company can play a significant role in decisions regarding issues such as whether to produce a machine that uses less electricity or water. Although the overall environment might benefit, the cost savings may actually flow to the consumer and not to the company, thus complicating decision making.

- *Involving dealers.* Dealers are closely involved in the disposal of used appliances. BSHG introduced a system to take back old appliances from other manufacturers for disposal. At the last owner-dealer's expense (about US $25), BSHG picks up the old appliances from the dealer and takes full responsibility for disposing of them in an environmentally friendly way. BSHG was the first manufacturer to make this offer, although competitors immediately followed. On average, 4,000 appliances per month are collected by BSHG through this system. BSHG claims (Sirch, 1994) that it is the only manufacturer that puts its full name behind the disposal process and that competitor-manufacturers simply pass the responsibility for correct disposal on to their disposal partners. BSHG also combines picking up the old devices with delivering new appliances to the dealers, thereby using spare capacity in its delivery trucks (which otherwise would return to the BSHG base empty).

- *Customer service responsibility.* Following a repair, all replaced parts are removed by the customer service people and disposed of at a customer's request. At the customer service premises, returned parts are sorted for recycling, and higher grade parts are reconditioned for reuse (to be sold at a lower price than new parts). Unrepairable parts are then given to selected recycling contractors, who arrange for final safe disposal of the part.

- *Transport.* Often left out of consideration, transporting goods is environmentally damaging. BSHG tries to use rail as much as possible (currently 70 percent) and to reduce road transportation. But in 1994 BSHG was forced to send more appliances by road than intended because the railways did not have sufficient capacity. As a result, BSHG put in place a new policy: Delivery companies working with BSHG that use or change to low-emission vehicles are now paid more for their deliveries.

Bosch-Siemens Hausgerate Group—Environmental Protection Program concluded

- *Applying environmental protection measures in all the company's departments.* BSHG not only promotes an environmentally friendly approach in its production area but spreads the spirit throughout the organisation. For example, office employees are encouraged to separate their rubbish and environmentally friendly heating substances are used in the central heating system. Since BSHG relies completely on its employees to implement the firm's environmental goals, it strengthens the motivation and qualifications of its employees in the area of environmental protection through extensive further education and personal development courses. Environmentally conscious behaviour is required as part of each worker's job. Managers have the explicit responsibility for extending and supporting environmental programs at all levels.
- *Disposal subcontractor.* At BSHG premises, unusable components are collected in containers that are picked up by the firm's regional disposal partners when the containers are full. These disposal partners are required to demonstrate that they then dispose of the waste in appropriate ways.

In cooperation with selected partners, BSHG has incorporated ways of recycling packaging materials in its environmental protection plan. For instance, used polyethylene materials are melted down and turned into plastic carrying bags, garbage bags, or plastic wrapping. Old paper is recycled into cardboard or paper. BSHG also buys primarily recycled paper, to close the loop.

To ensure the best-possible harmony between its business objectives and protection of the environment, BSHG has chosen a total approach, integrating the many interfaces into its environmental protection program.

Accountability to Shareholders/Performance Measurements

Most organisations that successfully manage technology benchmark themselves in the areas of productivity, cost, profit, waste, and so on, continuously, and do so both within their own organisation and externally against their competitors and organisations with similar technologies. Some also benchmark their use of technology as compared to their competitors.

Organisations that benchmark extensively are aware of the need to introduce new technology in order to cover shortfalls in product and process performance and technology utilisation that are exposed by the benchmarking process. Benchmarking is therefore often the main catalyst for the evaluation and implementation of technology. If not carried out, it may be too late to recover the situation by the time the loss of relative performance is noticed.

Benchmarking with competitors encourages organisations to implement new technology to remain competitive. The best companies have an ongoing benchmarking program whereby the component parts of the organisation's process are benchmarked against similar organisations for industry comparison and against best-in-class organisations for each part of the process. Benchmarking carried out after the implementation of new technology also can assist in monitoring its impact.

New technology becomes available continually and has to be assessed in order to understand its applicability to the organisation's processes. Its introduction in other organisations needs to be observed to avoid unforeseen pitfalls. Regular attendance at academic and industry conferences and exhibitions also can help to provide good sources of information. Some industries are benchmarked by their industry associations and some by third parties on a fee-for-service basis; best practice information can generally be obtained by either method.

Procter and Gamble undertakes extensive internal and external benchmarking on a regular basis in order to continually establish its competitive position, whereas HPM carries out benchmarking to determine its technological position rather than its productivity rating. South Pacific Tyre benchmarks over 20 attributes within the Goodyear Group to determine the technology, organisational structure, and practices required to remain competitive. When South Pacific Tyre was formed as a joint venture between the Australian company, Pacific Dunlop, and the Goodyear Group, executives running the company argued that access to the benchmarking information was probably the most valuable resource brought to the new company.

Government and Other Stakeholders

Large organisations are able to sustain their own continuous technology introduction but small organisations usually need the ongoing support of major suppliers or customers, who in turn demand increasingly higher production standards and financial performance. When direction from a large supplier or customer is unlikely to materialise, industry associations or government-sponsored innovation centres can perform similar roles. Innovation support that assists industry with evaluation and implementation of new technology is necessary as very few organisations have the capacity to provide all of their own innovation.

Peters and Brownes Group—Strategic Alliance with Overseas Partners

New product innovations in Peters and Brownes Group were mainly driven by customers— particularly those in overseas markets. The technology division also conducted contract research for government agencies and was involved in the development of new products for other companies such as Japanese ice cream manufacturers. Peters managed to ensure that all aspects of operations, from manufacturing and quality control through to product development and packaging, were developed by all employees working very closely with their counterparts in the Japanese buyer organisation.

Peters organised its activities into new business units that drew on all functional areas of the organisation. In addition to closely interacting with other members of the new business unit, each member was also encouraged to maintain an open dialogue with his or her counterpart in the Japanese buyer organisation. In effect, this producer–user interaction formed the basis for a strategic technical and economic alliance between Peters and its overseas partners and has become a model that is being repeated as the cornerstone of its strategy for international expansion.

Hyundai actively supports suppliers such as Samyeong with an active program in order to achieve its own production and marketing goals. Toyota also supports its suppliers, such as TOKAI-RIKA, for the same reasons. The Fraunhofer-Gesellschaft facilitates innovation through the skills it applies to its research contracts and helps to keep German industry at the forefront of technical excellence.

Examples in Japan include the Japan Key Technology Centre, the Agency of Industrial Science and Technology, the Science and Technology Agency, the Japan Industrial Robot Association, and the Small and Medium Enterprise Agency. While Singapore has established a National Automation Master Plan Committee to promote and develop industrial automation, the Malaysian Technology Development Corporation partners with research institutions and universities in the commercialisation of research. Meanwhile, the U.K. government is establishing "Faraday Centres," which are similar to the Fraunhofer Institute in linking industry and academic institutions to speed the transfer of technology.

It therefore appears that public policy intervention may also be necessary to bring about greater awareness among organisations of technology developments in their respective industries as well as to spur innovation through the increased interaction between research institutions and industry.

Fraunhofer-Gesellschaft—
The Technology Transfer Model

The Fraunhofer-Gesellschaft Institute

The Fraunhofer-Gesellschaft (FhG) is a nonprofit innovation research organisation headquartered in Munich, Germany. The FhG has developed an excellent reputation for its applied research and its close contacts to industry in executing its primary mission: transforming research findings into economically viable and marketable products.

It employs predominantly natural scientists and engineers, who operate as researchers, inventors, and consultants in winning and conducting research projects, primarily from industry. FhG services range from developing inventions to the prototype stage, initiating its own applied research projects into future technologies, advising companies on technology management in producing their products, and assisting with patent registration and feasibility studies. The actual marketing and commercial realisation of innovative products is then handed over to the entrepreneurs. The principal aim of the FhG is to assist industry in developing and realising new technologies through specified projects in applied research. The FhG covers almost all areas of research in engineering and the natural sciences.

The FhG in 1995 employed around 7,900 people in 46 research institutes in 31 locations throughout Germany, with several locations in the U.S. On average, each institute has about 100 employees, with an additional 50–100 students (paid for part-time work), and a DM 17 million annual budget. The FhG conducts a relatively large amount of research for small- and medium-sized businesses, but the bulk of its clients are large enterprises. It operates regionally and has been influential in generating employment in economically depressed regions through its research activities. In 1994, total turnover rose to DM 1.1 billion, of which contract research comprised DM 885 million and defense research about DM 68 million (Behlau, 1994).

The FhG is organised as a "fractal organisation," where employees form self-organising, self-optimising project groups. Each group's task is to win research contracts by competing in the marketplace for projects, against competition from universities, private consultants, and other research institutes. In doing so, the FhG has been very successful, based on its dramatic growth in turnover, the number of scientific awards its researchers have received, the number of registered patents by FhG scientists, and its excellent outside reputation among media and industry.

The Context

The FhG model was developed to respond to the specific innovation context in German industry, which, like most of Europe's industry, is dominated by SMEs (small- and medium-sized enterprises). The problem with the innovation system in Germany is not inventing per se, but bringing those inventions to the marketplace (e.g., the facsimile machine was invented in Germany, but marketed abroad). Moreover, Germany is regarded as an expensive place of production in terms of labour costs. With increasing international competition and increasingly turbulent market conditions, companies in Germany have to incorporate new technologies in their products and processes to keep ahead of the competition and to minimise the costs of labour in production.

Technology Transfer Through People: The FhG Model

A significant contribution to technology diffusion through people transfer can be clearly seen in several of the FhG's activities.

- *Flexibility—Constantly adapting to the market.* The FhG has a clearly defined mission of providing research of direct commercial relevance. Its structure enables it to respond quickly to the needs of industry and to change emphasis and direction as required by the market. The structure is flexible enough to allow the FhG to add or delete or modify institutes that are working in areas that are no longer in demand by industry. Its fractal organisation concentrates experts in a single discipline to work together, while at the same time providing flexibility to configure research teams as needed to meet contract requirements and enhancing the exchange of ideas and cross-disciplinary collaboration.

Fraunhofer-Gesellschaft—The Technology Transfer Model continued

- *FhG-initiated research projects.* FhG has a funding arrangement that generates sufficient funds to support additional research projects in areas of unexploited opportunity. By providing the impetus for new projects and continually looking to the future, the FhG is able to identify and present new concepts for innovative technology to government and industry. In pursuing new areas of technological research at its own risk, the FhG is serving the interests of industry generally. In other words, the FhG is not just a consulting organisation, but it grasps the initiative in fostering at its own risk new technology research that companies alone would find difficult to undertake.

- *Benefits to SMEs.* SMEs are the mainstay of many regional economies in Germany and the FhG focuses a great deal of its effort on research required quickly by SMEs to gain or maintain competitive advantage. It also provides consulting to SMEs on topics such as investment needs, the availability of government funding programs for innovation, information about new patents, and the time scale within which different technologies look like they will be successful in the marketplace. For most SMEs and even for larger companies, investing in the necessary R & D facilities and personnel, which are often needed for only short periods, is beyond their financial and risk-taking capabilities. The FhG makes available special equipment, clean rooms, and other facilities for specific research projects. Companies can then work in these facilities alone or alongside FhG scientists as needed. The FhG sees its role as acting as a catalyst for innovation, often by working on new ideas with SMEs and developing the innovations to the stage where the larger companies are willing to take them over.

- *Demonstration centres.* Industrial users can visit 21 FhG demonstration centres throughout Germany to learn about the latest technologies and inform themselves of FhG services. Through these centres, managers are encouraged to take their first, often small, steps into applied research with the FhG.

- *Role in regional economic development.* The FhG sees itself playing a major role in helping affected regions improve their economic structure. The FhG argues that, for a region to succeed, the efforts of local government, business, and research establishments must be appropriately coordinated. By founding FhG institutes in depressed regions, business and industry are attracted to those regions and benefit from the researchers' know-how.

- *International activities.* Several FhG institutes have taken the step of opening representative offices in the U.S. The first offices are referred to as "Resource Centres," small centres designed to transfer know-how from the German operation to their customers operating in the U.S., in addition to supporting their own developmental activities (Polter, 1994).

  The FhG, through its Institute for Management, is actively assisting countries outside Germany in setting up an efficient R & D structure, e.g., in Hungary. This source of turnover may grow over the next few years if expansion plans to Asia are realised and as the U.S. operation develops.

- *Relationship between universities and the FhG.* A close, interlinking relationship can be identified between the universities, the FhG, and industry. Universities

---

Fraunhofer-Gesellschaft—The Technology Transfer Model concluded

educate the young scientists, who learn to conduct the research and undertake the consulting projects for FhG. Many of the FhG institutes (over half) are headed by university professors who are simultaneously active at their universities. In turn, these professors can identify the brightest university students for the FhG, many of whom use FhG projects as PhD and undergraduate thesis topics. Young researchers constantly bring in new ideas, are highly motivated, and possess state-of-the-art knowledge. The professors can incorporate their research/consulting experience in the education of the next generation of young scientists at the universities. In this way, a strong research/teaching loop is established between the FhG and universities.

- *Transfer of experts and expertise to the industry.* As the FhG charter requires, industry benefits from the FhG activities through the transfer of experts from the FhG to industrial organisations. To maintain a dynamic fit to the market, the FhG needs to continually attract new scientists, often from totally different areas. Using a policy of nonpermanent employment of young scientists, the FhG encourages its scientists to leave after about five years. This benefits industry, where many ex-FhG scientists end up, and reinforces long-term contact with enterprises employing former FhG researchers. Transfer of knowledge is also fostered through training sessions for company employees and the introduction of new technology through demonstration centres.

Conclusion

The FhG fills a vital role in the German research, innovation, and commercial exploitation chain. It is in many respects the essential link between public sector research and commercial application, which creates a constant stimulus for research and technology transfer.

Summary

Technology is not an end in itself. It should be considered in the context of the organisation in which it is deployed or being considered. The value of the technology should ultimately be measured in business terms such as in contribution to revenue, market share, or sales, or in terms of a return to society such as an environmental or "quality of life" benefit. "Intermediate" measures such as operational variables of cost, quality, delivery, and so on are often useful to consider as being constructs that connect technical performance to business and broader measures of performance.

Samyeong—Hyundai's Supplier Development Program

Samyeong, a Korean automotive cable producer, worked very closely with its major customer, Hyundai, to become a preferred supplier. This is a good example of exploiting the customer–supplier relationship. Samyeong was heavily involved in Hyundai's supplier development program to introduce technology, reduce costs by 30 percent, double productivity within two years, and achieve defect rates of less than 100 parts per million. The key to Samyeong's performance improvement was Hyundai's extensive involvement in its development.

Hyundai's capability-based single sourcing strategy provided Samyeong with opportunities to compete with other fellow suppliers in improving its capability on a long-term basis rather than compete in selling specific products. Through this kind of selection criteria, Hyundai managed to disseminate its strategic objectives to its suppliers.

A firm's technology represents an important part of its infrastructure. From a business perspective, key questions are how much should be invested and how should technology be organised in order to maximise business goals such as shareholder wealth creation. Operational variables and marketing performance parameters are usually integral to such considerations.

Recommended Cases

Case 1: Boeing Commercial Airplane Group
Case 5: Commonwealth Industrial Gases (CIG)
Case 13: Iva Manufacturing

6 Decisions and Implementation of New Technology

In the previous chapters, we have covered various approaches to technology management, including management issues arising from the case studies and the development of best practice with regard to the adoption and implementation of new technology. In addition, Noori and Radford (1990) have mentioned further management issues. These include the following:

- *Implementing new technology and managing its hand-over from the technology developer.* The hand-over from the designers of new technology to its users should be planned so that it is almost invisible. That is, before the technology changes hands, the groups should run in parallel for long enough to make the transition a smooth one. There are numerous examples in this book's case studies of the technology developer and the technology adopter working closely for a period of time before the hand-over of the technology (e.g., Guy Birkin in the U.K.). Also, Duct Manufacturing Centre and EKATO Ruhrwerke both establish new cells or team structures in old premises before moving the technology to new premises.

- *Technology ownership.* Users of technology need to develop an ownership of the technology and cannot be passive about its implementation. This generally has been the situation found in the case studies. The two instances of initial failure, which were subsequently corrected, occurred because the workers did not develop an "ownership mindset" over the technology. Generally, workers prefer to be involved with new technology because they see it as a way of increasing their job security and as a means for achieving a sense of job satisfaction. Recognition systems and financial incentives in the form of share options or bonus schemes also can help to facilitate the feeling of worker ownership.

- *User advantage.* Any innovation must offer significant and obvious advantages over the technology it replaces, or potential users will have little incentive to use it. There are many examples of employees embracing new technology because it enhances job security or increases remuneration through bonus schemes or share options, or because they have been involved in its selection and implementation.

- *Hedgers.* The introduction of new technology was not successful at Samwon and TOKAI-RIKA at first, since management and workers were given the option of hedging their participation. And at Hewlett Packard and Bull Electronics, it was initially difficult to convince the product management area to accept new technology because current models were performing well. Product managers have to be convinced that current technology cannot provide the necessary features and production costs that are afforded by the new models.

Noori and Radford's list of variables and decision alternatives, listed in Table 6.1, is useful when adopting new technology, bringing together many of the management issues mentioned above. Their decision flowchart for adopting new technology, shown in Figure 6.1, also assists in best practice analysis prior to launching new technology.

Bessant and Grunt's concept of technical progressiveness is correlated with economic success, which comes from management attitudes and organisational climate. They contend that technically progressive managers actively choose to maintain small firm structures and practices, even after considerable growth. This is often achieved by keeping the operating units as small companies for day-to-day operations but using the holding company umbrella to support R & D, finance, purchasing, and so on.[1]

Hyundai's suppliers, such as Samyeong, provide examples of small operating units remaining focused on only a few products but drawing on Hyundai for financial and managerial support. Procter and Gamble also has a very strong corporate culture that supports local autonomy while providing considerable guidance for product and process development.

Performance Impact of New Technology

New technology can be considered as the single most important differentiating factor that enables firms in today's fast-changing technological environment to achieve competitive advantage within their chosen market or industry. In an era in which most firms have comparable efficiencies in other areas of corporate management, such as human resources, process and product quality, raw materials, and cost management, new technology or innovations can play a decisive role in bestowing firms with sustainable competitive advantage. Technological innovations enable firms to produce new products or deliver new services, adopt new processes and management systems, or continue with their old products, services, processes, and systems at much lower costs.

From an earlier empirical study carried out by the authors, it is apparent that, of the total variation in an organisation's operational performance, a significant part is directly related to technological strength. Technological strength is defined as the aggregate of the use of advanced manufacturing technology and the extent to which the technology is appropriate to the organisation, used to its maximum potential, and competitive in the industry.

---

[1]J. Bessant and M. Grunt, *Management and Manufacturing Innovation in the U.K. and West Germany,* Gower Publishing Co., Ltd., 1985.

TABLE 6.1   A List of Variables and Decision Alternatives to Be Considered When Adopting New Technology (NT)

Decision Area	*Decision Considerations*	*Decision Alternatives*
Why Should NT Be Considered?	Increased technological availability	Seize opportunity; or retain existing processes.
	Degree of NT adoption by competition	Respond to competitors; or maintain current processes.
	Labour cost considerations	Reduce labour costs by seeking to improve existing work force productivity; or substitute NT applications for direct labour requirements.
	Flexibility requirements	Introduce a complete flexible manufacturing system; or supplement existing process with NT applications; or retain existing process.
	Quality level	Utilise recent developments in NT providing precision and consistency; or apply manual statistical quality control; or implement quality circles.
	Degree of operating leverage	Increase application of NT; or decrease greater labour emphasis; or pursue existing policies.
	Dependability	Achieve shorter lead times (resulting from increased efficiency of NT applications); or change inventory policies; or reassess capacity constraint.
	Total system emphasis	Increase integration and interaction (among functional areas within firm utilising NT applications); or apply traditional organisational method.
	Information accessibility requirements	Bridge information gap (traditionally found between upper management and operations function through automation of information systems); or address information requirements via existing organisational structure.
	Engineering and design	Utilise CAD system or traditional manual approach.
	Economies of scale	Achieve similar benefits at lower volumes—with product diversity—by applications of NT; or expand plant capacity with existing processes.
	Distinctive competence	Utilise NT to establish distinctive competence/retain such in face of environmental pressures; or pull strategic levers utilising current process emphasis.
When Should NT Be Introduced?	Competitive pressures	Adopt reactive strategy; or adopt proactive strategy.
	Social pressures/ implications	Coordinate timing (so as to minimise negative social impacts/maximise positive social impacts); or base timing on internal factors to the firm only.
	Market considerations	Time NT acquisitions in response to market demands or independent of market demand.
	Corporate culture	Base timing considerations in adherence to traditional corporate policies or irrespective of past practices.
	Management and technical preparedness	Introduce NT applications at point in time when management and staff have developed capability; or do not postpone acquisition based on such considerations.
	Cash flow considerations	Acquire NT when incoming revenues can accommodate purchase; or base acquisitions on other criteria (debt financing).

(continued)

TABLE 6.1   *(continued)*

Decision Area	Decision Considerations	Decision Alternatives
	New product introductions	Time NT acquisitions in accordance with or irrespective of new product introductions.
	Recency of the technological innovation	Acquire NT applications immediately after market introduction; or postpone acquisition until developed further.
Where Should NT Be Introduced?	Plant and equipment condition	Introduce NT as a means of replacing dated equipment and facilities; or introduce irrespective of existing condition.
	Departmental/functional adaptability	Restrict NT introductions based on suitability of process; or seek to alter given processes to broaden adaptability.
	Impact ramifications	Focus NT introduction on specific processes that hold greatest potential for benefit; or adopt an encompassing approach.
	Product life cycle stage	Introduce NT applications particular to specific products (which display adequate remaining sales potential); or allocate priorities based on other criteria.
	Availability of labour	Introduce NT specifically into areas lacking sufficient labour resource base; or adopt a policy of even dispersion coupled with retraining or redistribution of displaced workers.
How Should NT Be Introduced?	Growth implications	Incorporate NT acquisitions into areas of anticipated growth; or utilise NT applications to maintain consistent and broad support.
	Speed of introduction	Adopt gradual or swift approach.
	Employee/union participation	Involve employees in decision-making process; or conduct decisions independent of employee output.
	Impact on employee levels	Consider whether immediate and long-term effects on employment play a considerable role or insignificant role in implementation decisions.
	Utilisation of support services	Heavy reliance on government/consultant support services during implementation; or reliance on in-house expertise.
	Pregeneration of concept acceptance	Initiate measures to encourage positive disposition among employees regarding NT applications; or allow employee reactions to run their course.
	Degree of prior orientation	Preclude NT implementation with training and orientation of personnel as well as process testing; or implement NT and learn by doing.

Source: H. Noori and R.W. Radford, *Readings and Cases in the Management of New Technology: An Operations Perspective* (Englewood Cliffs, NJ: Prentice-Hall, Inc., 1990), p. 492.

We now look at some of the critical variables surrounding the management of new technology and the factors that enable certain firms to demonstrate the best capabilities in managing advanced technologies.

Technology Management and Organisational Context

Although much has been written about technology management, there are no simple recipes, since organisational context is critical. Organisational context refers to the culture and the extent to which softer management technologies such as just-in-time and

FIGURE 6.1

A decision flowchart for adopting new technology

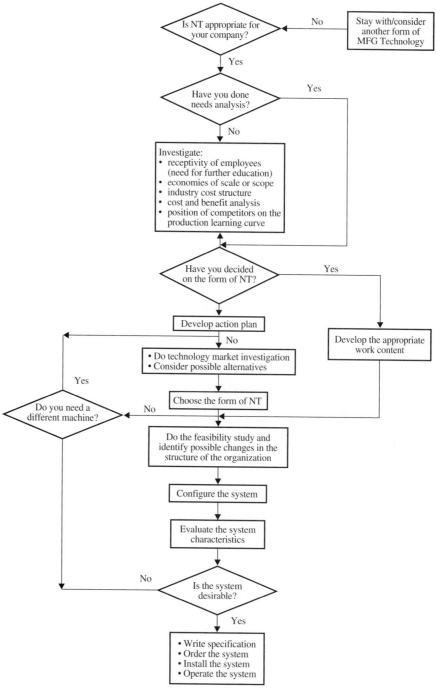

Source: H. Noori and R.W. Radford, *Readings and Cases in the Management of New Technology: An Operations Perspective* (Englewood Cliffs, NJ: Prentice-Hall, Inc., 1990), p. 492.

total quality management are or are not in place, as well as the extent to which there is a unity of purpose within the organisation. Organisational context has a great impact on:

- The extent to which technological strength is developed and exploited.
- How technology itself is managed. Investments in technology hardware clearly need to be considered in the context of organisational change and software.
- The perception of technology both as an opportunity and a threat. In some leading companies, for example, the threat of not engaging in a new process technology is as strong a motivator as the opportunity to lead in the industry. There is a fine line between the leading edge and the bleeding edge in managing technology. Tolerance of failure and risk attitude are important factors, but no company can afford to not have a high success rate.

The best performing organisations, such as 3M and General Electric, manage technology in an extremely competent manner and continue to manage it well. In most cases, the successful implementation of new technology is not a once-only success story but a single step in a continuing journey of new technology implementation. Some organisations have a culture that drives them to maintain and enhance their market position through the appropriate use of technology. They constantly evaluate how to maximise their potential in numerous ways. Other organisations take larger steps less frequently—especially when they are considering a major change in technology rather than a series of incremental steps. Others work very closely with their customers, raw material suppliers, and equipment suppliers to understand best practice in their industry.

Strict financial justification is not an impediment to investment, as most organisations take a long-term strategic view in deciding where they want to be in the future. Only occasionally do they use financial analysis for the comparison of different solutions and equipment suppliers once a project is underway.

A major barrier to introducing new technology in those organisations that do it well is the presence of management and workers who can hedge their acceptance of or involvement in the new technology. If there is a tendency to hedge involvement, it can be overcome by strong and very visible leadership that leaves no uncertainty about where the organisation is going and ties employees' future incomes to the successful introduction of the new technology through bonuses and share schemes.

The introduction of new technology does not generally cause a fundamental change in the underlying processes of organisations, as they continue to produce and sell the same products. More typically, the new technology aids in reducing waste and cost and in increasing productivity and product performance. Benchmarking carried out after the implementation of the technology assists in monitoring its impact. There is little evidence of a formal postimplementation audit just for the technology in question. In each case study, the initial decision to implement the technology is strategic and the organisation is committed to making it work. Where there are strong customer–supplier relationships, customers can monitor the impact of the technology to ensure that necessary improvements are achieved or "enhancement programs" can be initiated.

The specific benefits of implementing new technology vary depending on the actual technology application. However, business benefits usually are achieved via enhanced productivity, reduced production costs and waste and rework, and increased responsiveness and product performance—all of which assist in ensuring firms' continued growth and survival.

Technology implementation also has a diverse impact on the market. In some case studies, market size increases considerably as product features change and an organisation enters markets that were formerly denied to it. In other case studies, the new technology allows an organisation to produce goods for others as well as for itself so that competitors reduce their manufacturing operations in favour of those companies that are at the forefront of new technology. In cases where there is a strong customer–supplier relationship, the customer's market potential is considerably enhanced by the new technology implementation by its suppliers.

Hewlett Packard—Performance Improvement Due to the Adoption of Surface Mount Technology

Hewlett Packard's adoption of surface mount technology (SMT) dramatically changed board complexity. In five to six months, the Andover Surface Mount Centre (ASMC) went from having 100 employees per shift work two shifts to place 200,000 parts per month to having 150 total employees across three balanced shifts place 8.5 million components. In 1995, 250 different kinds of boards with about 12 million components per month were run through the ASMC. Boards were made for the Medical Product Group's product lines as well as other HP divisions. Typical board lot sizes range from 20–2,000 boards. Capacity utilisation at the ASMC was at around 80 percent, which allowed 10 percent capacity for surge demand and also set aside 10 percent of available capacity for prototyping new boards.

In terms of productivity, cycle-time was reduced from six weeks under the old technology (through-hole) to three to four hours for the new technology, SMT. Throughput time was able to guarantee next-day delivery for most orders. Yield was likewise increased from 80 percent up to 97 to 98 percent. In several cases, boards that formerly cost hundreds of dollars are now made for tens of dollars.

Organisational Decision Processes. Who in a firm decides on new technology? Who decides how it is best implemented? New technology begins with ideas, and ideas can be born from opportunities or threats. Ideas can come from customers, suppliers, competitors, or internally, from R & D engineers, marketers, shopfloor operators, or the business leaders of the organisation.

Once an opportunity has been initially identified, good firms recognise that it is very unusual for it to be correctly conceived in the first instance. A process of testing and refinement must be put in place, with multifunctional teams often used to examine the impact of the innovation from a number of perspectives such as engineering, production, marketing, and financial. Continual refinement and testing means that ideas are refined and rejected as they are developed, with more and more details of the potential innovation being fleshed out through the process. The technical innovation needs to be acceptable and feasible in a number of domains, including marketing, financial and economic, production and functional, and strategic. It also must be acceptable from an environmental perspective and must take the company forward in some identifiable and important respects.

Since most large companies have formal processes for the evaluation of new technology, the proponents of a particular innovation must be cognisant of it and able to take it through the formal gates, which are often expressed as return-on-investment hurdles. The difficulty that many firms express is that the costs of a new technology can be estimated fairly accurately, but the benefits cannot. Benefits in terms of market penetration, higher prices, or even cost reduction are only promises at the time of a new technology decision, whereas the capital cost of a new technology or innovative piece of equipment is a firm commitment at the time approval is given by the decision maker or board responsible for the decision.

The immediacy of the expenditure and the delay in achieving the benefits that accrue over time, combined with the uncertainty of those future benefits, mean that decision making about new technological innovations cannot really be boiled down to any sort of science. Even with the best forecasts, there will always be a need for the experience and judgment of wise decision makers.

Summary

Since every organisation is different, there is no single formulaic approach that can specify exactly how, why, when, and where new technology should be introduced. However, new technology generally should be implemented as a matter of strategic business logic, with a strong process focus being given to it. The implementation should be guided by business logic but managed as a tight project, which means that all the project management disciplines of cost, schedule, and outcome quality should be carefully and continuously considered against planned milestones.

Recommended Cases

Case 2: Alan Group

Case 3: Becton Dickinson

Case 7: The Duct Manufacturing Centre (A)

Case 8: The Duct Manufacturing Centre (B & C)

Case 19: TOKAI-RIKA

Organizing for Technology

Clearly, organisational issues need to be addressed in new technology adoption and implementation. Just introducing a major piece of new technology into a manufacturing facility or an office would be organisationally naïve.

Consider an organisation's operating staff. People need to be "managed" in the sense that they want to be informed and to participate in change rather than feel helpless about its onset. Change will be naturally embraced by some people but interpreted as a threat by others if they are not adequately briefed and prepared. In the best of all worlds, a mix or "organisational slice" of opinion leaders—from senior managers through to the shopfloor—would not only be informed about the decision to adopt new technology but also involved early enough to have the organisation prepared and even looking forward to its introduction.

Prior consideration of these factors often leads to good practices and outcomes in technology management. Similarly, new technology implementation usually fails when key organisational issues are overlooked. These issues can be categorised as *internally* and *externally* oriented management issues. Internal issues include management, technical areas, personnel, and the organisation itself. Some of the externally oriented issues are:

- Interface with the market, including the market integration with technology.
- Customer–supplier and producer–user relationships.
- Support for innovative activities from external sources, such as government and stakeholders.
- Accountability to shareholders in terms of new technology investment and benchmarking of performance.

Our main focus in this chapter will be on the internal issues of the organisation, in terms of their influence on the following four specific areas: (1) management, (2) technical aspects, (3) people, and (4) organisation. A categorisation and diagrammatic illustration of these issues is contained in Figure 7.1.

FIGURE 7.1

Management issues in new technology introduction

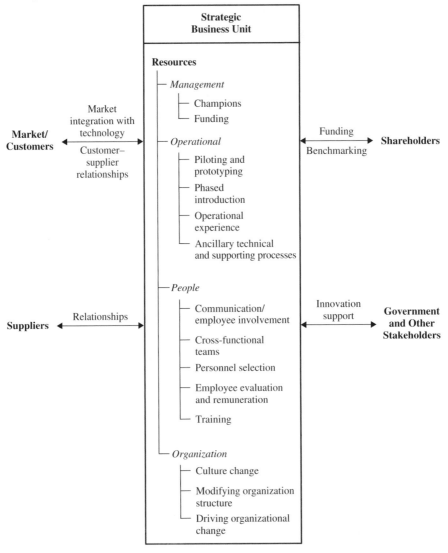

Duct Manufacturing Centre (A)—
Organising the Adoption of New Technology

Several lessons were learned by Duct Manufacturing Centre (DMC) in organising its adoption of new technology:

> First was the importance of top management's commitment to reengineering. DMC's general manager was oriented toward operations. He was not afraid to change or break the rules and viewed his role as one of visionary and motivator. He also successfully persuaded his management team and their subordinates of the need for radical change.
>
> Second, DMC's experience demonstrates the power of communication and training so that everyone in the firm understands the goals and techniques of reengineering. This was accomplished at DMC by forming a special task force. The task force encouraged greater trust between workers, management, and support personnel by collocating and seeking more worker participation in decision making.
>
> Third, DMC made good use of pilots and proofs in order to reduce the risk of proposed changes. Such pilot programs can assist in identifying areas in need of improvement on a relatively smaller scale.

Management Issues

This area essentially relates to the need for champions within the organisation and the criteria used while making funding decisions.

Champions for New Technology

Champions who lead the technology implementation should be at the most senior level possible. They need to be visible and vocal supporters of change and provide a constant emphasis on the direction that the organisation needs to take. Champions also can be external to the organisation in cases where there is a strong and endearing customer–supplier relationship, as between Hyundai and Samyeong.

According to Noori and Radford (1990), if an innovation is to succeed, the organisation needs a sponsor, a champion, a project manager, and an integrator. The roles can be shared or duplicated but the key is that the sponsor has to have organisational power to mobilise the necessary resources. In small organisations the roles tend to be combined to some degree. In large organisations they tend to be separate because senior management in large organisations does not tend to get intimately involved in the project management of new technology.

Where there is strong external involvement, the customer (e.g., Hyundai or Toyota) could be the champion and senior management the sponsor. The integrator role is used at Hewlett Packard, in which process engineers assist the shopfloor to function as a flow and allocate resources to remove excess work-in-progress until the shopfloor is capable of doing it itself.

The executive director of Samwon exhibited very strong leadership in the introduction of its first and subsequent programs. Managers and employees were not given any option of hedging their support for the changes and had to either embrace the changes enthusiastically or seek alternative employment. Samwon's executive director also put his position within the organisation at stake, since he had six months to show the benefits from introducing the changes or leave.

The CEO of South Pacific Tyre met with the multidisciplinary implementation team every two weeks to ensure that necessary resources were always available. TOKAI-RIKA's president realised during discussions with Toyota—after the unsuccessful first attempt at introducing JIT—that he would have to be very heavily involved in subsequent attempts if they were to be successful. When JIT was introduced the second time, the president led the project implementation team and ensured that employee education and information dissemination was carried out.

Funding New Technology

Choosing appropriate evaluation criteria is difficult even for a single case of new technology, especially in scenarios where current processes are working well and profitability is adequate. In such cases, it may be necessary to emphasise likely future scenarios or market situations, as is shown in many of the case studies where strategic issues are more important than purely financial considerations. For example, Hewlett Packard evaluates new technology on strategic grounds and uses new product requirements to justify changes in technology. Company policy in funding new technology also has to be well thought out, so that competing requests for available funds can be readily and consistently prioritised.

Standard capital budgeting and discounted cash flow are financial evaluation models that may have limitations when used for evaluating technology, thus creating the need for other factors to be considered. Purely financial evaluations usually assume the status quo in terms of industry structure and competitive forces—an assumption that is fraught with danger. Decision criteria for investing in new technology generally should not be purely financial and based on marginal "with/without" analysis. The consequences of not implementing new technology may be that the company "disinvests its way out of business."

It is when current production processes are doing well that plans have to be made to secure the future technology. Decisions about new technology should go beyond financial projections and consider changes in market conditions, competitors' likely actions, and technological advances.

HPM—The Company Has the Confidence to Reinvest in Itself

To help facilitate its manufacturing strategy, HPM internalises its profits, reinvesting to enhance production facilities. To remain competitive with overseas manufacturers, a long-term program of acquiring the most modern, automated machinery for its production plants was created as a key competitive capability. "We remain competitive because of our design technology and ongoing automation," confirms Peter Simon. This leading edge capability sets the industry standard, with special emphasis on product design and inventiveness.

> Completion of a $22 million state-of-the-art plastics moulding plant in Sydney is the culmination of more than five years' work and represents the company's continued commitment to Australian-made and Australian-owned products. The plant is one of the most technically advanced in the southern hemisphere for engineering plastics. Located in Sydney's inner industrial suburb of Waterloo, it operates a 24-hour, 3-shift schedule, producing over 1.5 million mouldings each day.

Technical Issues

This area relates to the use of techniques, such as piloting and prototyping, phased introduction, and also operational experience in regard to the introduction of new technology. In addition, one should also look at issues relating to ancillary technologies and supporting processes within organisations adopting new technology.

Piloting and Prototyping

Piloting and prototyping should be a part of the formal evaluation process for new technology, with a general acceptance of failure. The best example from the case studies is that of HPM, where many technologies were evaluated and failures at the prototyping stage were welcomed because of the lessons learned from them.

Hard technologies generally are prototyped and then piloted to ensure their appropriateness and to establish their capability to produce products at costs acceptable to the market. For soft technologies, prototyping is difficult but not impossible and may require working with suppliers or partners on different premises to avoid unnecessary disruption to the principal production processes.

The case studies in this book also show that piloting can assist in demonstrating the technical feasibility of the technology to top management and serve as a credible demonstration model for other units in the organisation. Noori and Radford (1990) consider it essential to choose the most appropriate site—neither the easiest nor the most difficult—or the wrong conclusions can too easily be drawn.

Iva Manufacturing piloted new technology in its wholly owned factory and proved its expected benefits before introducing it at a subsidiary, even though the subsidiary may have had a greater need. In most case studies, the decision process of choosing the pilot site is not discussed, probably because the firms have been successful, thus obviating any discussion on choice of sites.

Both Hewlett Packard and Bull Electronics piloted their new technologies to demonstrate to management that they were capable of manufacturing the product that they required and to assist manufacturing personnel in gaining operational experience with each of the steps in the technology so that they could specify their plant configuration.

After identifying a supplier who could provide them with the required technology, South Pacific Tyre installed a prototype as a pilot on its own premises. This gave the firm's employees hands-on experience with the technology and the supplier was able to see how the machinery worked in the customer's environment.

Clearly, piloting and prototyping are common elements in successful technology implementation for both hard and soft technology. When piloting is undertaken, however, the site and the technology have to be chosen carefully to ensure that the desired impact can be demonstrated to management and workers.

Phased Introduction

With any new technology, the transfer of knowledge from the old operations (where people know the materials and product) to the new process has to be planned carefully. Phasing the introduction, especially when multiple installations are involved, assists in keeping continuity with the older, more familiar technology and reducing the possibility of alienating the workers from the new technology and work practices. Soft technologies generally are introduced in familiar surroundings so that the new technology can be proven and workers' commitment gained before the new work situation is launched.

In several of the case studies, a phased introduction of new technology assisted in preventing worker alienation by keeping continuity with the older, more familiar technology at the same time as the new technology was introduced. With the continual introduction of new technology, the phased introduction has to be shared so that all sections of the organisation can be seen as embracing corporate goals and no sections are left to bear all the upside and downside risks.

Both Bull Electronics and Hewlett Packard optimised their old technology and all of the supporting processes before introducing new technology. Bull Electronics made the transition to the new technology only when it could be justified by either performance or production improvements.

Operational Experience

One of the best ways to introduce new technology is to build on a successful history of older technology. A successful history of technology introduction also gives an organisation and its employees the confidence to embark on new technology projects.

Experience with the introduction of new technology assists in the subsequent introduction of further technology upgrades as the organisation learns that it can introduce new technology and profit from the benefits to workers, management, and the organisation as a whole.

While the case studies generally concentrate on one successful implementation, the two Korean companies Samwon and Samyeong have ongoing programs of new technology, with each phase becoming easier and more successful because of the experience gained from the earlier parts of their programs. Similarly, Guy Birkin's experience from its previous technology introduction helped considerably with the latest development and showed that it could drive its technology supplier to provide the firm with the solution that it needed. Both Hewlett Packard and Bull Electronics optimised all aspects of their old technologies while they were stable before introducing new technology.

Ancillary Technologies and Supporting Processes

All ancillary technologies and supporting processes needed for the introduction of new technology should be identified, introduced, and optimised in familiar surroundings prior to new technology introduction. Both should be in place in order to enable those investigating the new technology to focus on the main issues without diverting attention toward peripheral but often critical side issues.

However, ancillary technologies should be kept in perspective and not be allowed to distract organisations from their core business. If they aid the process of new technology introduction, ancillary technologies and supporting processes should be considered for outsourcing, either temporarily or permanently.

At Bull Electronics, major product and process changes are carefully coordinated because products are totally dependent on the processes chosen. Procter and Gamble has a strong focus on recruitment, training, new product development, business acquisition, distribution network, new computer systems, and a new manufacturing capability to dramatically increase its profitably. It perseveres through continuous improvement to get the product, cost, and pricing right in the long term.

HPM has a workplace agreement that allows for flexible starting and stopping times, covering of additional machines during absences, employees taking responsibility for quality at their workstations, a consultative committee to monitor and review training, and operational staff carrying out their own work planning. Rapid prototyping and tooling have been introduced to significantly reduce the lead-time to create new products.

At Hewlett Packard, the culture of quality management, JIT, cross-functional teams, continuous change, and upgrading allows for the easy introduction of new technology. At CIG, a Best Practice Demonstration Program for total quality and continuous improvement addresses quality, customer service, and administrative issues.

People Issues

This area covers communication and employee involvement, the use of cross-functional teams, the selection of personnel, employee evaluation and remuneration, and training aspects.

Communication and Employee Involvement

Constant communication at all levels of the organisation and employee involvement are necessary ingredients in successful new technology implementation, since employees need to understand the reasons for the new technology introduction, its expected benefits, and the impact that it will have on them. Shopfloor representation in the evaluation process assists in anticipating problems before they arise, and two-way communication helps resolve them as they arise.

Most employees understand and accept a single disruption to their working environment but find it much harder to accept continual change. Thus, the quality of communication and degree of involvement need to be much higher and it is desirable that employees drive both aspects as part of their contribution to the ongoing evaluation and introduction of new technology.

In some organisations, employee involvement with technology introduction is part of the culture. For example, HPM holds a weekly meeting to discuss new product development, project management issues, and the implementation of new product technology. Duct Manufacturing Centre and EKATO Ruhrwerke involve their employees in designing plant layouts and, at DMC, workers who are to use the new equipment test it with vendors in order to be familiar with its use and committed to making it work upon its introduction.

Cross-Functional Teams

Cross-functional teams are necessary in order for affected areas to work together on resolving problems rather than pushing them to other areas. Such teams should come together before the project starts and should see it through implementation and satisfactory completion. In large organisations, it is useful to have separate teams covering all of the affected areas at senior management, middle management, supervisor, and shopfloor levels.

Cross-functional teams are effective in ensuring that (1) all the affected areas have the same view of the new technology project and (2) problems are not resolved at the expense of any particular group. Best practice organisations require each section in the organisation to provide a minimum percentage of its time to participation on cross-functional teams or be seconded to projects away from their functional area.

For ongoing technology introduction, cross-functional teams may come together in a "gating" process.[1] These teams evaluate each project for each level in the gating process so that, by the time a project is finally approved, each affected part of the organisation has some knowledge of the project and its implications. To evaluate the proposals it receives, the company board needs to be technically competent and, ideally, should be submitting its own initiatives to the gating committee, especially for high-level research projects. Organisations that have adopted variations of this process include Peters and Brownes, HPM, Hewlett-Packard, and Bull Electronics.

Procter and Gamble has product category teams that bring branding, sales, finance, and manufacturing together. Guy Birkin has regular development meetings that involve design, draughting, manufacturing, marketing, and raw material suppliers, and there is strong cross-functional collaboration between technical and marketing personnel at all levels from senior management to the shopfloor. Hewlett Packard establishes technol-

---

[1] A process whereby all product and service initiatives from anywhere in the organisation (i.e., sales, marketing, customer service, production, logistics, and finance) put forward ideas to a "gating committee" with representation from all areas of the organisation. As the ideas are screened and approved, they are allocated to the most appropriate section to develop, before going to the next gating level for further evaluation or rejection. If the committee meets regularly and insists on a quick turnaround for all ideas in the system, then initiatives move through to adoption relatively quickly.

ogy management and process management teams at the corporate level to help determine companywide design and equipment standards.

For the actual introduction of new technology, VDO has established a team that is comprised of marketing, product engineering, production engineering and planning, quality, R & D, logistics, materials, and human resources management who oversee all the implications of the technology.

Personnel Selection for New Technology

To give the new technology the best chance of being implemented successfully, it is important to select personnel with the necessary attributes and skills. With the introduction of new technology, personnel who will enhance its success should be selected to work on its introduction. However, when the introduction of new technology is essentially continuous, then all personnel are eventually involved in the new technology introduction and become crucial for its success. This requires very careful personnel selection over a long period of time or intensive training within an appropriate organisational climate so that employees thrive on change and the challenges that it provides. Numerous psychological tests are available to assist human resource managers in selecting personnel who will seek out change and thrive on it rather than be threatened by it.

To facilitate its technology program, Procter and Gamble specifically aims for higher educational and qualification levels when moving to new premises, even starting a graduate intake program to attract future managerial personnel. South Pacific Tyre realises that its new technology and the self-managed work teams that would work with it require operators different from those traditionally employed. The necessary personnel are chosen from the existing work force but only after a substantial screening process. Bull Electronics also moves its best operators onto the new technology to increase its chances of success and keeps the bulk of the work force with tried and proven technology until the new technology is firmly entrenched.

Mayekawa has found that while its doppos[2] have a very high degree of customer focus, there are still some activities that have to be executed centrally because the doppos have neither the skills nor the size to carry them out efficiently. One of these activities is personnel recruitment, since the success of each doppo depends on having the right personnel. Once the personnel have been recruited and trained, the Zensha arrange for their transfer between doppos depending on workload and ability.

Employee Evaluation and Remuneration

Where management and workers have financial stakes in the success of the new technology through share options or bonus schemes, they strive to ensure its success. If workers recognise that the new technology is their best option for future job security, they will be more supportive of its introduction.

---

[2]Recall from Chapter 5 that "doppos" are autonomous business units focusing on a market segment or customer.

The evaluation and remuneration of employees has to be directed toward supporting the ongoing introduction of technology. It must reward creativity, intelligent risk taking, entrepreneurship, preparedness to work with change, and the necessary external values such as customer service. The introduction of new technology is a team effort and the evaluation and remuneration system should be structured to recognise this.

Performance-based pay is common to many organisations that introduce new technology, but at Samwon, the employees set the wage levels and they also enjoy other benefits such as paid external training and children's education. Productivity gains at CIG are shared equally between the company and its workers. Iva's employees have stock options and a bonus program, which encourages them to make new technology work because they immediately share in its economic benefits. While the bonus system at EKATO Ruhrwerke considers group productivity and the improved qualifications and skills of the workers, Hyundai and its suppliers measure value-added and productivity by sales per hour per worker.

Training

Social and technical training before the actual introduction of new technology is important to ensure its smooth implementation. If hard technology is being implemented, then familiarisation with the equipment at the vendor's premises or at another installation is important.

Continual technology introduction requires a highly trained work force with training on the social aspects of change to understand its impact on both the organisation and the work force. Training in the technology itself is also required for those working directly with it or for those who have to explain it to other employees, customers, or suppliers. Training can never be considered as an afterthought when the work force or management has opposed the new technology. It should be an integral part of the introduction and delivered at the appropriate time and as professionally as possible.

Samwon has introduced education and training for all its employees to keep them informed of the corporate vision and target and to update their skills. CIG provides training in social, technical, and business areas, enabling workers to adjust to the self-managed work team environment.

Organisational Issues

Organisational aspects of the introduction of new technology are essentially related to cultural and structural changes, both as a consequence of new technology introduction as well as to facilitate its implementation. New technology often requires a different organisational structure and different work environment to capture its full potential.

Becton Dickinson—The Importance of Human Resources Management and Technology to Facilitate Organisational Change

Key human resources and technology factors were employed in the implementation of supply chain management (SCM) at Becton Dickinson (see the case for more details) in order to facilitate the transition to the new system.

- *A cross-functional team approach with well-defined objectives.* Probably the single most important aspect of Becton Dickinson's approach to the implementation of new technology was its reliance on a highly developed project implementation team. A steering committee comprised of members from each major product division gave overall guidance. The implementation team, responsible for the day-to-day development of the new approach, was also comprised of members from all affected organisations as well as members from external agencies (e.g., representatives from software suppliers and independent consultants hired to provide particular expertise). Furthermore, each member of the implementation team also served as a team manager or member of one of the seven identified project teams. Each project team had very well-developed objectives. Membership in the project team was decided based on the personal capabilities of the available employee pool and was deliberated to assure mixed representation from all the various divisions affected.

- *Extensive training.* Training was deemed a critical element in the implementation of the new SCM system. In addition to the usual development of training materials, a number of additional steps were taken by Becton Dickinson to assure effective training of affected employees would take place. These included the development of a certification program, acknowledging a level of achieved expertise on the part of the participating employee, the establishment of a technical reference library to house the relevant body of knowledge needed to effectively operate a DRP/CRP (distribution requirements planning/continuous replenishment process) system, a PC-equipped training facility enabling hands-on learning of the new system procedures and theory, as well as the design of materials for advertising and promotion of the system to all corners of the Becton Dickinson organisation.

- *Using technology to facilitate organisational change.* The three-stage process of unfreezing, moving, and refreezing is a well-known concept within the literature of organisational change and development.[3] Only after the need for change is well recognised throughout the organisation can a change have a chance for acceptance. Although necessary, it is simply not enough to have a single visionary or champion

---

[3] The original concept was developed in K. Lewin, *Field Theory in Social Science* (New York: Harper & Row, 1951).

for change—the entire organisational membership must feel and understand the need for change (i.e., to unfreeze). Facilitating this important unfreezing was one of the major objectives of the DRP/CRP project team (see the aforementioned objectives for Project Team #5 in the case).

The experience of Becton Dickinson shows that new technology can play an important role in the process of organisational change. In attempting to change its organisation toward becoming more customer-responsive, the implementation of a new software system (only a part of the total change) served as a focal or rallying point. Proper use of the new software system in fact *required* a different organisational structure to truly reap its intended benefits. The lesson is that technical change itself can serve as a change agent and can be used to *lead* organisational change.

- *Not underestimating the importance of technical support.* Particularly for situations where it is critical that the technology uptake process be accomplished in minimum time, it is important to assure adequate technical support. For the case of Becton Dickinson's DRP/CRP project, part of this technical support took the form of technical programming capability for making "on the fly" system revisions as the implementation process proceeded. The costs for this kind of support usually represent a small fraction of the total technology investment, but the benefits can be significant in terms of keeping the project on pace to a predetermined implementation schedule.

Culture Change

New technology often requires a culture change to accommodate it, which cannot be carried out by a single person. The whole organisation has to embrace the need for change, but it has to be driven and directed by senior management.

While organisational culture must change to allow for the successful implementation of new technology, rather than merely rely on a single visionary to continually adopt new technology, culture also cannot change continually or change in different directions at the same time. Organisational culture should be such that it willingly embraces new technology, accepts failure readily, and can accommodate several new technologies simultaneously.

Samwon has established a culture in which everyone is considered an owner, with the profits either reinvested or paid to the workers. On the other hand, workers at Samyeong operate and maintain their own machines under the "my machine" program and have two meetings per week to discuss problems and results.

Introduction of the MRPII program at Procter and Gamble forced each section to focus on divisional results rather than sectional results, which improved its overall performance. Procter and Gamble is a large organisation but because corporate culture drives the need for change, its bureaucracy does not present obstacles.

As a smaller organisation, HPM is very receptive to change and has a company-wide focus on implementing it quickly across the whole organisation. It has deliberately kept its vision, mission, goals, and strategic objectives fuzzy, resulting in a free culture that encourages experimentation without penalties for mistakes.

Guy Birkin is a division of a large organisation that concentrates solely on lace production. It is very aware of innovations in its industry but is able to use the financial strength of its parent to initiate new technology without being unduly constrained.

In the Peters and Brownes Group, safety, quality, and productivity programs lead to a culture of continuous improvement, employee participation, improved skills, and job redesign.

HPM—Creating a Culture of Innovation by Emphasising Results and Performance and Minimising Bureaucratic Red Tape

HPM's "free" culture encourages experimentation without penalties for mistakes, with everybody at all levels encouraged to experiment with innovation. There is minimum paperwork and memos, and no informal meeting lasts more than 10 to 15 minutes. Problem tasks are tackled with the attitude that, whatever it takes to get the job done will be done, irrespective of time, cost, commitment, etc. Results are the key objective. In this environment remuneration is graded, with executives highly paid and tradespersons drawing 30 to 40 percent over the Metal Trades Industry Association (MTIA) award. Design and engineering staff are given necessary resources, freedom of action, full responsibility, and the opportunity to exhibit initiative and creativity—there are no rules to inhibit performance. Technological capability was not part of this early company culture of product innovation, but now it is a total precondition of its existence. The two things the company has are "brains and capital," and it uses these to win markets against cheap-labour-structured competitors based on time-to-market.

A 14-tier wage classification structure has been adopted commencing at engineering production employee level, progressing through engineering tradesperson, engineering associate, and topping at both professional engineer and professional scientist level IV, respectively. Under the agreement, no extra claims, either award or over-award, are permitted. Industrial disputes should be avoided under the Metal Industry Award of 1994, and in the event of unresolved disputes, the matter shall be referred to the Australian Industrial Relations Commission, with no work stoppage or lockouts during the procedures of negotiation and conciliation.

These enterprise agreement conditions are of particular importance to the company's introduction and implementation of rapid prototype development (RPD) technology, where both management and staff strive to achieve manufacturing improvements through industry-recognised production management systems. As the background to the case study emphasises, HPM's competitive advantage rests on its ability to innovate and release new products, plus service its existing customer requirements on a 24-hour turnaround basis. This strategy depends on a number of key operational practices being incorporated into the enterprise agreement to guarantee workplace efficiencies essential for RPD to succeed.

HPM—Creating a Culture of Innovation by Emphasising Results and Performance and Minimising Bureaucratic Red Tape concluded

These cover: workplace flexibility, related to "flexible starting and stopping times for specified periods," "staggering start and finish times for auxiliary staff," "continuity of operation," and "coverage of additional machines due to absences"; quality assurance for continuous improvement, with future progress achieved by employees taking responsibility for quality within their workstations, diversifying the responsibility of quality to each employee rather than to inspectors only; responsibility for control and work planning, taken by operational staff for their own stock at their workstation, instead of relying upon auxiliary or indirect labour; and a consultative committee to continuously monitor and review training for "new technology, multiskilling and job sharing," "shopfloor training for new/transferred staff," "English in the workplace," and "shopfloor training for QA procedures and requirements." And, through productivity enhancement, new technology, job redesign, and skills training, employees will be flexible and capable of accepting change. Other conditions relating to EFT for wages and sick leave provisions also form part of the agreement.

Modifying the Organisational Structure

Organisational structures often require changes so that they are aligned with the operating processes for the new technology. Any new structure should be piloted in the familiar surroundings of the older technology before the launch of new technology.

While the successful introduction of new technology often requires a revised organisational structure that aligns with the necessary operating processes, it is neither practical nor desirable to be modifying the structure constantly. What is required is a structure that allows for the continual introduction of new technology. A project structure whereby people come together for a period of time to work on a particular project and move on to the next project when it is complete is probably best. People's status in the organisation therefore should be tied to skill levels rather than to titles, the occupation of particular offices, or membership in key teams. Major construction companies are a long way down this track and assemble construction teams with varying membership to carry out projects involving technology that may be completely new to them.

As a result of a new technology introduction, many organisations also flatten their structure and rotate managers to facilitate communication and overall operational knowledge. At Samwon, for example, all line managers are rotated as superintendents, and at Samyeong, the line managers are rotated every month.

There also has been a move toward team-based operations or cells. For example, at Mayekawa, each doppo looks after one customer or an industry sector based on one key customer. Self-managed work teams require former hierarchical management to move toward team-based support as well as access to substantial information regarding the performance of teams.

Team-based operations require workers to assume greater responsibility and control and as such, a rigorous screening process is required, such as the one applied by South Pacific Tyre. Modifying the organisational structure is never easy, so Duct Manufacturing Centre tries the new layout in existing premises to form work cells. When each cell becomes functional, it is moved to new premises. The remaining employees are grouped into cells and moved when they are ready. The Alan Group forms virtual cells that only survive for each order so as to enable the movement of employees from cell to cell on the completion of each order. This approach is appropriate when each order is unique and when its completion requires the selection of various skilled operators.

In some of the case studies, the organisational structure is changed to improve customer focus. For example, Becton Dickinson introduces a supply chain services division whereby all the separate customer contact avenues based on product lines are brought into one area to enhance customer responsiveness.

New Technology Driving Organisational Change

The introduction of new technology can be used to facilitate organisational change but, for continuous or ongoing technology introduction, organisational change has to be in place first. Prior exposure to the introduction of new technology can initiate organisational change, allowing for future technology implementation without significant organisational change.

Noori and Radford (1990) have considered the effects of both organisational structure and culture on the ability to recognise the need for new technology and then successfully implement it. In best practice organisations, the strengths from one aspect need to offset the weaknesses from the other. Loosely structured or decentralised organisations tend to be more receptive to innovations, since decentralisation of authority demands more lateral communication and opportunities are investigated more rapidly. On the other hand, centralised organisations are slower to generate innovations but are better able to implement them. This applies to both technological (product) and administrative (process) innovations. Purely structural solutions to the dilemma are either inadequate or compound the problem.

At the Alan Group, for example, the firm's virtual cells call for cell leaders who are different from the supervisors of the process departments, since they have to be comfortable with the responsibility for meeting customer deadlines. In addition, the cell only exists for one order so the members may have other tasks to complete for different cells at the same time.

Peters and Brownes Group—Organisational Change to Adopt New Technology

Several lessons are learned by Peters and Brownes Group in organising the adoption of new technology:

The managing director of Peters initially played a dominant central role at the most senior level by exerting an entrepreneurial style of management. This helped the company to better focus on export markets. Peters also valued inputs from employees and encouraged cross-functional teams during the transformation process for the new Greenfield site.

Peters and Brownes Group—Organisational Change to Adopt New Technology concluded

In March 1992, the company and four unions signed a Memorandum of Understanding that established the Safety, Quality, and Productivity (SQP) program. This led to the removal of some demarcation barriers and the establishment of a single bargaining unit. It allowed general managers greater responsibility for the management of people. The SQP program was commenced in July 1992 and subsequently managed to win funding from the federal government of $A450,000 as part of the best practice initiative. The objectives of the program included:

1. To create a culture of continuous improvement.
2. To foster employee participation.
3. To improve employee skills.
4. To provide an opportunity for job redesign.
5. To link remuneration with productivity.

We thus see that the introduction of new technology often forces organisational change in order to accommodate the operational requirements of the new technology. It is therefore important that management recognises the impact of any new technology on its organisation before introducing the technology.

Summary

The internal management issues identified as recurring themes in the above cases are probably not exhaustive when applied to all examples of technology management. However, they do cover the bulk of the internal issues that should be addressed by any organisation contemplating technological change. There was little evidence of organisations, as a whole, having a clear grasp of the issues before they started on the course of technological change, but in each of these cases, the hurdles that arose were eventually successfully dealt with, although in some cases, this took a long period.

Technology introduction is much easier when organisations consider the management issues that are uncovered and develop solutions to anticipated problems before they occur. If some of these concerns cannot be addressed successfully, then organisations are well advised to search for an alternative advanced manufacturing technology to adopt.

Finally, it is clear from the case studies that, once organisations have learned to cope with technological change, it becomes much easier for them to introduce technological change in the future.

Recommended Cases

Case 9: EKATO Ruhrwerke

Case 14: Mayekawa

Case 16: Samwon Precision Machines Company

Case 20: Decorative Glass

CHAPTER 8

E-Business Technology Developments

In the previous chapters, we have noted that changes in technology can have far-reaching effects—not merely on individual firms, but also on the entire industry within which the firm operates. In recent times, no other technology has had a wider impact on the fundamental way in which firms do business than the Internet. By radically changing the nature and economics of transactions in almost all industries in a manner that provides substantial benefits to both consumers and producers, the Internet has become the most important technology at the beginning of the twenty-first century in terms of business opportunities, threats, and impacts.

An increasingly large number of industry supply chains are deploying e-business to link producers, suppliers, retailers, and customers in a seamless network and harness its potential to enhance revenues, reduce costs and production cycle times, increase process efficiencies, and improve customer service. E-business also is lowering costs and increasing service levels between people and departments within businesses.

E-business can be defined as the use of the Internet and other forms of information technology to facilitate communication and transactions between buyers and sellers involving the transfer of goods, services, or information, normally conducted over open or dedicated networks. PriceWaterhouseCoopers's definition of e-business is:

> An enterprise designed for success in the Information Economy. E-business brings into play an organisation's resources and partners in new and innovative ways to create clear strategic advantage. The potential of e-business goes far beyond new technologies—to impact and engage all aspects of a business—strategy, process, organisation, and systems—to extend the business beyond its boundaries.

E-Business: Making Inroads at Wall Street

Wall Street, the bastion for trading of financial instruments such as stocks and bonds, also has been affected by the Internet revolution. Old, well-established brokerage houses such as Merrill Lynch, Morgan Stanley, and Goldman Sachs felt threatened when hitherto unknown rivals such as Waterhouse Securities, Ameritrade, and E*Trade took the lead in the Internet broking sector and started to capture a share of the market that had been their preserve.

Having earlier dismissed the competition from Internet stockbroking firms as insignificant, Wall Street's big brokerage houses have been forced to acknowledge the radical impact of Internet technology on their business and recognize the potential available in the new technology. For example, Merrill Lynch now hosts web sites such as MerrillAuctions.com and ShopMerrill.com.

Securities are now increasingly traded over the Internet, and the online securities market, which did not exist in 1995, now accounts for about 30 percent of all retail equity trades in the United States. Apart from the benefits that can be expected to follow from the reduced transaction costs to customers, one of the likely outcomes could be the conflict between existing channels, such as firms' brokers, and the online channel. Brokers may see their commissions shrinking as lower transaction costs attract customers away from high-cost channels and toward the Internet.

The Evolution of E-Business

While the use of Internet technology for conducting business between corporations has started only since the mid-1990s, the concept of conducting business over other forms of electronic networks has been around since the early 1980s. Examples of earlier forms of electronic commerce include the electronic data interchange (EDI) system used between businesses for point-to-point data transactions and the Sabre system developed jointly by IBM and American Airlines in the early 1960s.

Electronic Data Interchange Systems

EDI systems enabled the automation of several complex and time-consuming functions that were previously handled manually along the chain of business-to-business transactions. These systems provide enormous benefits to businesses, most notably those whose business processes require a large number of daily transactions with customers or suppliers. Apart from the dramatic reduction in costs, EDI systems also *may* provide the following benefits:

- Reduced inventory requirements.
- Shortened cycle time via the speeding up of business processes.
- Increased productivity.

- Enabling or even empowering the work force.
- Increased customer satisfaction.
- Reduced errors and waste arising from manual handling.

An example of EDI's application is in the automotive industry, where EDI systems are implemented across the entire supply chain. Auto dealers can place their orders directly with distributors on the EDI system, which relays the data automatically through the assemblers and manufacturers to the different component suppliers. Although the savings per transaction are not huge, when multiplied by the millions of transactions involved in the placement of orders from the dealers to the component suppliers, the aggregate savings are big enough to justify investments in EDI by large firms. Savings have occurred not in the actual cost of the transactions alone but in much "tighter" supply relationships as well, meaning that inventory savings in the whole supply chain have been very significant.

The Sabre System

The Sabre system, on the other hand, allows for centralised data aggregation among all airlines in order to provide information regarding ticket pricing and seat availability. It enables travel agents to save valuable time and costs by avoiding the more expensive and inefficient use of phones and faxes to access the same information from airlines for their customers.

Despite the benefits offered by both of these systems, they also have several disadvantages that limit their use to a relatively small subsegment of the total population of businesses as compared to the subsegment that has the need and is able to use Internet technology for business transactions. Both systems are essentially proprietary systems, costly and time-consuming to implement, since they require special hardware and software that has to be customised according to the needs of the individual organisation adopting them. EDI systems between different organisations also are connected through dedicated networks, called value added networks (VAN), which are costly to set up and maintain. As a result, the benefits of these technologies are reaped mostly by very large companies, where the number of transactions and the frequency of use are very high, thus providing the scale for the cost benefits from the implementation of expensive solutions. In the period of 1997–1998, it was estimated that less than 2 percent of the United States' six million businesses used EDI.

The Internet

The Internet and its supporting technologies, such as personal computers (PCs) and telecommunications and content technologies, have converged in recent times to provide the same benefits and more to a larger segment of businesses. Since no customised software or hardware is required, the costs of access and implementation are relatively cheap and affordable for almost all businesses. Table 8.1 provides a quick comparison of the relative benefits of EDI and Internet technology and explains why the latter has grown so phenomenally to replace the supply chain optimisation tasks previously handled by

TABLE 8.1   Relative Benefits of EDI and the Internet

	EDI	Internet	
Electronic transactions	✓	✓	
Aggregated information	✗	✓	
Speedy installation	✗	✓	
Low-cost access	✗	✓	✓ Yes ✗ No

EDI. In a survey carried out by Deloitte Consulting in 1999, more than 80 percent of the companies surveyed indicated that they would implement an Internet-based procurement strategy by 2002. Table 8.1 clearly shows the dominance of the functionality of the Internet over EDI.

In order to gain an idea of the speed with which Internet technology has been adopted, we can compare the time taken from its introduction to its use by 50 million consumers, versus other technologies such as radio and television (see Figure 8.1).

Three distinct phases can be identified in the use of Internet technology or e-business by firms:

1. *Providing information.* The first phase began when usage was initially limited to providing customers with information on products or services through channels such as e-mail, browsers, and shared databases. The development of sophisticated applications and their increasing adoption by a rapidly growing number of firms has enabled barriers, such as security and privacy issues, to be overcome, thus ensuring the continued growth of this function over the years.

FIGURE 8.1

Adoption rate: number of years from introduction to 50 million users

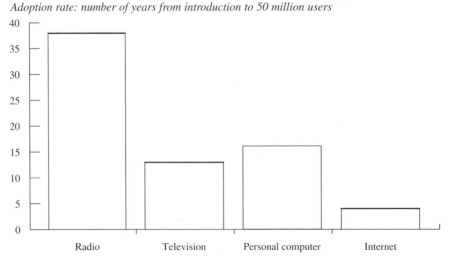

2. *Business to consumer.* This phase started with the adoption of the Internet by firms seeking to offer products and services to customers, reaching out to the growing community of Internet users willing to make purchases online. The most common form of e-business, business-to-consumer e-business, consists of what are essentially electronic shopfronts that allow businesses to sell goods and services via the Internet. Some of the more successful sellers of physical goods over the Internet include Amazon.com, Dell Computers, eToys, and Wal-Mart.

Amazon.com, in particular, has had probably the largest impact internationally on the online business-to-consumer industry, in terms of serving the largest number of customers. It began selling books over the Internet in 1995 using the mail-order system as its business model and, by 1997, it became the first online retailer to serve 1 million customers. Expanding its services to include a calendar and reminder service, an Internet movie database, and a live-event auction site, Amazon.com went on to become the first e-business site to serve 10 million customers in 1999. By selling over the web, firms like Amazon.com are able to cut costs related to physical infrastructure, such as warehouses and bookstores and the employees required to maintain them. Amazon's strategy is an example of how firms can adopt new technologies to reduce transaction costs and, therefore, also reduce the price of their offerings to offer better value to their customers. Amazon has invested a lot of its money into its brand, as recognition is critical to traffic and transaction/sales volume.

However, because of the scale of Amazon.com's operation, the start-up costs have been very high and the payback to this investment has not been realised. Even though the transaction costs are competitive, the company is not yet at a stage where cash flow from operations can cover the start-up costs. The question is, can it move to profitability fast enough to service its debts by the end of 2000 or soon after? Again, with the falling share prices in mid-2000, it will be difficult to obtain additional funding. Traditional competitors like Barnes and Noble (booksellers) are now building their own e-business systems and, by end of 2000, this firm will be in a position to be a strong competitor, but with an already profitable base.

3. *Business to business.* Realising the enormous potential of e-business technology to reduce transaction costs and improve both service and process efficiencies, many large businesses are undertaking initiatives to implement their own e-business models. This requires the complete transformation of processes, organizational structures, and management practices in order to capture the benefits of speed, efficiency, and geographic independence allowed by the new e-business system. Often, the impact of the e-business model can go well beyond the enterprise level, bringing about far-reaching effects in the entire industry as all firms struggle to reach newly established thresholds of competency.

One example is the creation of an electronic platform by automobile manufacturers General Motors and Ford, which enables them to establish an electronic relationship with their suppliers. Since the two firms together are such a vital part of the automobile industry environment, this initiative can be expected to redefine the way business is carried out between them and their suppliers. Over a period of time, their endeavour could also result in the creation of a model for how business will be conducted in the future for the entire automotive industry, given its volume and scope.

WW Grainger—From Bricks and Mortar to Virtual Selling

An example of a well-established firm adopting a new strategy based on an e-business model is WW Grainger, founded in 1927 and now one of the largest distributors of maintenance and repair equipment in the United States. Selling a range of 78,000 different products, worth $4.3 billion in 1998, it also owned 351 "bricks and mortar" branches all over the United States and prided itself on the fact that 70 percent of American businesses were within 20 minutes of at least one of its branches.

In 1998, WW Grainger decided that it was a prime candidate for the high-growth business-to-business e-commerce sector, since its business could come under serious threat if competitors or new entrants used the Internet to offer the same products that it was supplying to its business customers. Risking cannibalisation of its existing business and web site, WW Grainger formed an alliance with its suppliers to form a web site called OrderZone.com. The purpose of the new web site was to offer its customers the alternative of buying directly over the Internet and harvesting cost and process efficiency benefits that conventional purchasing methods did not allow. Its entire product catalogue, which also includes products offered by its business partners, is offered online and is updated regularly to offer its customers a wide range of products and also make the site large enough to deter newer entrants.

OrderZone's success can be measured by the steep increase in sales revenue in the first half of 1999 to $29.2 million. While this constitutes merely 1.31 percent of WW Grainger's overall sales revenues, the company expects this share to grow larger. The added benefit to WW Grainger is that it has gained a first-mover advantage and is moving down the learning curve quickly, knowing that its sales have not been lost to an up-start rival and are also less likely to be lost in the future.

The Internet Economy

For the United States alone, estimates by Forrester Research on the volume of business-to-business transactions over the Internet have indicated that trade in hard goods alone will increase at a compound annual growth rate of 99 percent, from $251 billion in 2000 to $1.3 trillion in 2003. If business-to-business trade in services over the Internet is included, then the overall value of business-to-business transactions over the Internet is expected to reach $1.5 trillion in 2003, up from $131 billion in 1999.

Forrester Research also has estimated that by the year 2003, business-to-business Internet-based trade in hard goods will constitute approximately 10 percent of total trade in hard goods in the United States. As tends to be the case with most new technologies, absorption of Internet technology all over the world has not been balanced, with the United States accounting for more than two-thirds of the global e-business activity between 1998 and 2000. However, its share is expected to recede to 45 percent of the global Internet economy as other industrialised nations catch up. Figure 8.2 shows the growth of e-business in the United States, both overall and industrywide.

FIGURE 8.2

Estimated e-business revenue growth in the U.S. (2000–2003)

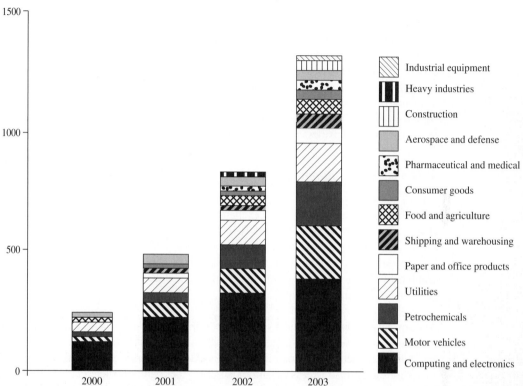

The shift in sales from conventional channels to the Internet will affect distribution-intensive industries the most, since the low-cost method of selling over the Internet provides a valuable alternative for manufacturers to deliver products to customers without incurring distributors' margins. However, other industry-specific factors, such as the level of information technology (IT) sophistication, innovation, and adoption rates of new technologies, as well as demand for Internet buying from customers, will determine the pattern and speed of the adoption of Internet technology within each industry. Supply chain–specific factors, such as the percentage of products sold through distribution channels as a proportion of total sales and the level of customisation of the product, also ensure that adoption rates will vary from industry to industry.

Industries in which distributors traditionally play a key role in delivering the final product to customers, such as computing and electronics and motor vehicles, were once expected to experience the highest degree of change and e-business pervasiveness in their supply and value chains. These industries have been early adopters, with innovative firms such as Dell and Cisco setting the trend in the computing industry, where the software expertise and the need arising from successively shorter technology life cycles has led to the adoption of new selling practices. Many service sectors also have experienced a very high penetration of the Internet. The computing and electronics industry has experienced the largest shift in its supply chain from conventional channels to the Internet, with almost all players in the industry adopting Internet order processing and customer service.

Sophisticated supply chain needs in the motor vehicles industry are also pushing more and more participants in the value chain toward the Internet, as the consolidation and streamlining of supply chains threaten to eliminate inefficient suppliers. Extranets between manufacturers and suppliers have grown in importance and account for an increasingly large share of in-production supplies in the industry. In addition, pressure from large manufacturers like Ford, aimed at persuading suppliers to offer frequently purchased goods over the Internet, ensures the adoption of the Internet as a selling medium—or the risk of lost business by an increasingly large number of suppliers.

Auctions and Exchanges

A large share of the business-to-business transaction volume is expected to increasingly come from Internet auctions and exchanges, which have emerged in recent years to challenge traditional business models in fragmented markets. Auction and exchange sites on the Internet are essentially intermediaries and market-makers where buyers and sellers converge to conduct real-time business transactions in order to overcome geographical boundaries and information asymmetry, thus making the market more efficient and increasing its liquidity.

Auction Sites. One of the most successful examples of a business-to-consumer auction site is eBay, whose market valuation at $1.88 billion in 1999 was greater than the market value of Sotheby's at $1.02 billion. From a business perspective, auction sites enable companies to offload excess inventory, surplus stock, and obsolete equipment into the marketplace at real-time, market-clearing rates. From an economic perspective, this benefits both buyers and suppliers, since the transaction is concluded at a value that is considered optimal at that particular time by both parties. Priceline.com has made effective use of the auction model in the travel industry. Its site enables airlines to auction unsold seats on their flights to customers who bid for them until the ticket is sold at a price that is valued highest by a particular bidder—over and above a reserve price fixed by the airline. In the computing and electronics industry, USBid.com is focusing on the original equipment manufacturers (OEM) segment to auction surplus products from manufacturers and distributors that are still under warranty.

Exchanges. Exchanges consist of sites that act as market-makers to facilitate trading between buyers and sellers, in much the same way as stock exchanges, such as the New York Stock Exchange (NYSE), or metal exchanges, such as the London Metal Exchange (LME). Industries in which exchanges are likely to make the maximum impact to existing supply chains and procurement practices include commodity markets and heavy industries, such as steel and mining.

In commodity markets, access to energy exchanges previously required the acquisition of expensive proprietary systems, such as Bloomberg's terminals, for participation in the market. Internet-based exchanges for commodities such as wheat, soybeans, natural gas, and liquid fuels now enable buyers and sellers by providing a system for price discovery, the posting of bids and offers, and trading at prices that reflect real-time supply and demand conditions. By reducing search and transaction costs and providing a central point for price comparison, exchange sites enhance liquidity in these markets.

In the energy industry, intermediaries such as HoustonStreet.com and Altranet.com have reduced inefficiencies resulting from fragmented supply chains and high search and information costs. Fragmentation along each stage of the supply chain, starting from supply, storage, and delivery, had resulted in a large number of participants within each of these segments and had created multiple marketplaces, adding to the complexity and inefficiencies in transaction processing. By enabling the buyers and sellers to coordinate and consummate transactions in a transparent, frictionless environment, exchanges have changed the structure of supply chains in the energy industry.

Cisco Systems

Networking giant Cisco Systems receives 70 percent of all its orders, worth approximately $5.5 billion in 1999, over the Internet. The San Jose, California, based company has integrated its online customer service with its overall e-commerce strategy by using its web site to augment its customer service and support strategy over the following three aspects:

1. *Marketing.* Cisco ensures that visitors to its web site are able to find information regarding its products by providing brochures, technical information, and white papers on its web site. In order to facilitate the customer's search, Cisco provides a comprehensive search engine and a number of indexes, including a list of topics arranged alphabetically and a list of all its products. A site map helps visitors to navigate through the site and access the information they are searching for.

2. *E-commerce.* Cisco began its e-commerce initiative in 1995 by providing an ordering system on its web site. Customers could fill in and send their orders electronically to Cisco and also check the status of the order on Cisco's web site. This provided various benefits to both Cisco and the customer, including:

   - Reduction of order processing time and the elimination of errors in the orders, thus enabling Cisco to reduce its response time to customers' orders.

   - Improved communication and coordination at the customer organisation by enabling different departments to process the details of the order on the Internet before sending it to Cisco.

   - Savings in terms of both costs and valuable staff time, achieved via the Internet order status and checking system, which moved resources away from conventional customer inquiry systems such as phones and faxes.

3. *Technical support.* Technical support to customers was improved by providing information on easy-to-solve problems on the web site, while the more complex and difficult technical problems were attended to by technical support staff members.

Summary

Internet technology is causing revolutionary changes in business practices and reshaping industries and economic landscapes. By offering firms multiple benefits, such as greater speed and efficiency, closer relationships with suppliers and customers, and various cost benefits, e-business provides firms with compelling reasons to either adopt it or risk being overtaken by competitors who adopt it. Some of the benefits offered by e-business are as follows:

- *Increased penetration by reaching out to more customers.* Due to its adoption by a large number of individual and business users, Internet technology enables firms to access far more customers than they could previously. The high personal computer and Internet penetration in countries such as the United States, Australia, and Western Europe has enabled the rapid growth of business-to-consumer transactions over the Internet by online retailers such as Amazon.com, CDNow.com, and eToys.

- *Improved customer service.* By allowing closer interaction with customers, Internet technology enables firms to tailor their offerings to meet individual customers' preferences. Firms thus are able to offer their customers a greater choice of products and also respond to queries at costs that would not have been affordable without Internet technology.

- *Reduced costs.* Internet technology allows firms to reduce overhead costs related to physical infrastructure and yet still fulfill customer demands by obviating the need for warehouses, showrooms, and staff. The shift from "bricks-and-mortar" to "clicks-and-mortar" or "virtual" selling over the Internet has been more pronounced in some industries, such as computing and electronics. Notable examples are Dell and egghead.com.

- *Reduced cycle time.* By speeding up processes and reducing the lead-time for responses to customers' or business partners' orders or queries, the Internet allows firms to save valuable time and money through the higher utilisation of existing resources. Combined with improvements in the sharing of information allowed through the Internet, the result is better management of inventories and reduced inventory costs.

- *Reduced information-based disadvantages.* The Internet allows buyers and sellers to access market information regarding various products and to view their comparative prices, thus reducing information asymmetry. By facilitating price comparison and transparency, the Internet makes markets more efficient and competitive, which results in redistribution of value in markets that are fragmented and inefficient. The success of Internet-based auction and exchange sites, such as altraenergy.com, priceline.com, and metalsite.com, is largely a result of this phenomenon.

We conclude this portion of the text with some of the insights we have gained by visiting companies that have successfully transformed their businesses in order to be either partly or fully web-based. These visits have led to the following conclusions, which can be treated as guiding principles common to all successful Internet implementers:

1. E-business is not a fad! It is fundamentally transforming business processes, relationships, and value creation. There will be major winners and losers.

2. E-business is mainly about business models and opportunities, such that technical issues are an important subset.

3. Done well, e-business offers cost reduction/productivity improvement *and* service improvement *and* speed *and* broader, deeper market reach.

4. Successful companies implement incrementally, in 30- to 90-day project chunks, ensuring scalability and secure, stable standards.

5. The "service profit chain" still applies: We can do great things in business-to-business (B2B) and the marketplace, but we must bring employees with us (training, intranet, e-mail, templates, etc.).

6. The implementation team and process should integrate technical people with champions from the business in a service relationship, led by the CEO.

7. As routine processing becomes commoditised, with cost and price approaching zero, it is a case of "add value or die." Disintermediation is a threat to all players.

8. Straight-through processing implying automated self-service for business-to-consumer (B2C) and no-touch procurement and payment for B2B should be core to e-business models, driving cost, speed, and service.

9. Web infrastructure will increase bandwidth and reliability and become secure, so it should be central to the model; but web pages should be kept simple enough so as not to slow access.

10. E-mail and telephone back-up are an important part of the mix.

11. Implement projects and solutions before they are perfected (i.e., the 80:20 rule).

12. E-business style involves collaboration, partnering, and big and small firms working together—not just pure competition.

13. Intellectual property issues are important, and it takes hard work to get business partnerships, B2B relationships, and incentives structured correctly.

14. The e-business activities must be considered matters of strategy, not tactics. The integration of e-business thinking with business strategy is essential.

Recommended Case

Case 21: Barnes and Noble

1
The Boeing Commercial Airplane Group: Design Process Evolution[1]

Our successful history has been characterized by an entrepreneurial spirit, fueled by a passion for producing jet aircraft that safely fly higher, farther, and faster. We have been able to effectively translate that passion into integrated product designs and production processes. Our focus on activities that ultimately benefit our customers has allowed us to hold the lead position in the industry, but we cannot take our market prominence for granted.

In the recent past we adopted several innovations in order to ensure that we stay focused on the customer, that we design and build with a shared vision using lean processes, that we function as a set of smaller integrated businesses rather than as isolated bureaucracies, and that our employees innovate on the job continuously. As you know, we are meeting this morning to review two of these innovations in particular, namely, (1) computer aided design and (2) design-build teams.

> —Ron Woodard, president of The Boeing Commercial Airplane Group, during a 1995 strategic review of organizational innovations in the Boeing Company.

In early 1995, senior officials at The Boeing Commercial Airplane Group's headquarters in Seattle, Washington, found themselves engaged in a strategic review regarding design technology and organization structure. The upcoming delivery of the first 777 commercial jet provided an opportune time to review lessons learned regarding innovative efforts and how to make them an integral part of the Boeing organization. These decisions about technology and structure would be critical to Boeing's future in light of the changing context of the commercial airplane industry. It was clear that the pressure from customers to deliver more value in less time would be a permanent characteristic of the market. In response to these pressures, the company had implemented two significant innovations in a new airplane design program and now needed to determine how these ought to be adopted throughout the corporation. The first change involved technology—the company had purchased a state-of-the-art digital design computer system for the development of the new 777 commercial jet family. The second change influenced interactions among people and disciplines—Boeing had created a cross-functional or "design-build" team structure for the 777 development program. The goal for these innovations had been to reduce costly "change, errors, and rework," which historically had added cost and delayed delivery to airline customers. Boeing officials felt that this goal had been accomplished on the 777, but were left with four important questions:

---

[1]This case was developed for use in classroom discussion and is not intended to necessarily illustrate appropriate or inappropriate management practices. Its general purpose is to stimulate critical thinking about new product development strategies. Case information was gathered through interviews with Boeing executives, visits to several Boeing sites, and reviews of various documents provided by the Boeing Company. Case authors were: Karen A. Brown, Seattle University; Kavasseri V. Ramanathan, University of Washington; and Thomas G. Schmitt, University of Washington. Mark McKay, a doctoral student in the management science department at the University of Washington, was the research associate on the project. The authors are indebted to many individuals who provided information and ideas for the case. In particular, we wish to thank George Broady, Donald Fudge, Peter Odabashian, Larry Olson, Elizabeth Otis, Tamara Reid, John Schmit, Bill Selby, Henry Shomber, and John Swihart for their contributions.

1. Had these two innovations truly placed Boeing at a higher level in terms of design effectiveness?

2. Could these two innovations serve as stepping stones for Boeing to reinvent itself as a learning organization?

3. Reductions in "change, errors, and rework" had been the primary performance metric for the two innovations. Were these good surrogates for overall program success, or should other measures be considered, as well?

4. To what extent and how should these two innovations be adopted companywide?

The 777 Commercial Jetliner

In 1990, Boeing began to work toward the introduction of a new jetliner product family. It had been nine years since the company had introduced a new product—there was a need within the company, and in the global market, for a new model. The company's largest competitors, Airbus and McDonnell Douglas, had launched new design programs that had the potential to threaten Boeing's market share. These competing design programs had begun three years previously, placing Boeing in an uncertain competitive position.

Market research indicated that the greatest unmet need in the passenger jetliner market was for a medium- to large-capacity (300 to 400 passengers) airplane with a medium- to long-range distance (5,000 to 8,000 miles) capability. By 1990, Boeing Company officials knew that they were behind in the race to win customers in this market. McDonnell Douglas had targeted the MD11 for this niche and already had planes in production. Airbus was soon to come out with two planes in this category, as well—the A330 and the A340.

The Business Environment for Commercial Airframe Manufacturers.   Deregulation of the commercial airline industry had created a highly competitive environment, and airlines struggled to stay profitable as competition forced extensive cost-cutting in the late 1980s and early 1990s. Airline companies with long histories disappeared entirely (Pan Am, Western, Braniff), and some newcomers such as People Express experienced extremely short lives. With the commercial air transportation industry in a financial slump, many airlines had delayed airplane purchases and were hanging on to their older planes. According to Phil Condit, the Boeing Company president, "Our biggest competition is not from other airframe manufacturers but from the planes we sold 20 years ago."

Cost as an Order-Winner.   The airline industry had become extremely sensitive to cost, and the product life cycle had moved commercial airplanes from a differentiated market toward a price-sensitive commodity market. As a consequence, Boeing needed to offer a product that was available at an attractive price, and that was less expensive to operate and maintain than the planes the airlines currently had in operation. In response to these pressures, Boeing designed the 777 with only two engines instead of the previously more typical three or four. (Boeing suppliers sold their engines on the basis of pounds of thrust, so two larger engines cost roughly the same as four smaller ones. However, the long-term maintenance of two engines would be less expensive than that of three or four engines.) Additionally, the 777 cockpit was designed to require only two pilot operators, further reducing operating cost. Airlines flying both 747-400s and 777s would have a training cost advantage because the cockpits for these two planes were similar. This commonality also increased staffing flexibility for flight crews. An extrawide wing-span promoted fuel economy, adding to the plane's attractiveness in a cost-based market. Based on these design features, Boeing officials felt that they had a plane that would be in a class by itself. They anticipated that its range, flexibility, efficiency, and comfort would attract customers away from models made by Airbus and McDonnell Douglas.

The evolution toward the 777, and the design approach that supported it, had developed from a long Boeing history, which is worthy of consideration in light of the questions that were being addressed in 1995.

Product Background

The Boeing Commercial Airplane Group, a division of the Boeing Company, was the world's largest airframe manufacturer in 1995. The enterprise held 60 percent of the global market for commercial jets in 1994, with annual sales averaging $19 billion between 1988 and 1993. Selected financial and employment data for the years 1977 through 1994 are shown in Table 1.

Boeing held an important competitive advantage in the commercial airplane market: its ability to effectively orchestrate a large-scale, globally-dispersed development and manufacturing system. This was an important capability, given that the design and production of commercial jet aircraft required cooperation among thousands of people located in all 50 of the United States and in 23 countries. For example, parts for the 767 were produced by 3,000 domestic suppliers and 300 for-

TABLE 1   Summary of Financial and Employment Data for the Boeing Commercial Airplane Group: 1977–1994

Year	Sales ($) (millions)	Operational Profit (millions)	Return on Assets (%)	Number of Employees*	R & D Expense* (millions)
1977	$ 3,423	$ 269	15%**	66,900	$ 222
1978	3,827	417	41	81,200	276
1979	6,395	611	37	98,300	525
1980	7,665	678	21	106,300	768
1981	7,004	308	4	105,300	844
1982	5,135	16	0	95,700	691
1983	6,998	98	2	84,600	429
1984	5,457	17	0	86,600	506
1985	8,024	376	10	98,700	409
1986	9,820	411	12	118,500	757
1987	9,827	352	7	136,100	824
1988	11,369	585	13	147,300	751
1989	14,305	1,165	17	159,200	754
1990	21,230	2,189	35	161,700	827
1991	22,970	2,246	29	159,100	1,417
1992	24,133	1,990	20	148,600	1,846
1993	20,568	1,646	13	134,400	1,661
1994	16,851	1,022	7	119,400	1,704

Source: Boeing Annual Report Documents.
*These are corporate-level data. Data for R & D expenses and number of employees at the Commercial Airplane Group level were not available for release by the company.
**ROA for 1977 is based on corporate-level data; all others are for The Boeing Commercial Airplane Group. Note: None of these figures are adjusted for inflation. The reader should bear in mind the rapid rate of inflation in the U.S. during the early 1980s.

eign suppliers, then shipped to the company's Everett, Washington, facility for final assembly. The number of unique part numbers in an airplane averaged about 100,000 and the record-keeping for such a monumental inventory presented a major challenge. All of this activity had to be coordinated to ensure that materials arrived on time and within the appropriate specification and quality levels.

During the company's nearly 80-year history it had produced a successful series of commercial jet families, including the 707, 727, 737, 747, 757, and 767. The 777 was the most recent addition to the company's product mix. A range of configuration types was offered within each of these families. For example, the 767 was available in 200 and 250 passenger models and offered flight-range capabilities extending from 3,000 to 6,500 nautical miles. This strategy allowed the company to meet the needs of a wide variety of customers while also maintaining design integrity and standardization within each family. The family strategy was considered to be highly successful, based on the company's profitability and continuing domination of the market. The date of introduction for each commercial jet family, and the number of planes ordered and sold as of June of 1995, are shown in Table 2.

Boeing's series of airplane families had been a commercial success. The 737, with its orientation toward small, short-haul markets, was the company's most popular model. The 747 jumbo jet, which could accommodate up to 400 passengers, had become Boeing's most profitable model. This history of market achievement had put Boeing in a strong cash position, allowing it the financial capability to embark upon the development of the new 777 jetliner family in the early 1990s.

Historical Perspective on the Design Process at Boeing.   Prior to its entry into the commercial jet market in 1957, the Boeing Company was small enough to operate substantially at one location on East Marginal Way in Seattle. During the late 1940s, the company's entire engineering staff worked in the old Engineering Building, a facility that was housed under the same roof as the hangar where all commercial and military planes were manufactured. Given this proximity, engineers interacted regularly with personnel on the shop floor, and potential manufacturing problems often were averted before they became serious. Design engineers worked in large "bull-pen" rooms, with desks crowded closely together. Drawing boards were located in numerous places throughout the work area. Primary engineering specialties at that time included: preliminary design, structures, aerodynamics, propulsion, weights, systems, and crew station. Employees within each of these design functions clustered together on a single floor. For example, the

---

TABLE 2   The Boeing Commercial Airplane Group: Product Family Data Status as of June 1995

Family	Date of First Rollout	Number of Planes Ordered	Number of Planes Delivered	Current Status
707	1957	1,010	1,010	Retired, 1973
727	1963	1,831	1,831	Retired, 1983
737	1968	3,203	2,730	In production
747	1969	1,167	1,062	In production
757	1982	838	678	In production
767	1981	702	575	In production
777	1994	167	2	In production

Source: Boeing Company Archives.

aerodynamic engineers all occupied part of the third floor of the Engineering Building, and all were within easy visual range of each other.

Some long-time Boeing employees and retirees looked back fondly at the bull-pen engineering days because of the communication and quick problem-solving that were facilitated by these arrangements. Although each engineer's desk was usually equipped with a telephone, nearly all interaction within and among engineering disciplines occurred on a face-to-face basis. These interactions most often took the form of impromptu gatherings around drawing boards and occurred several times each day as questions and problems arose. Formal meetings to resolve design questions were rare.

The bull-pen arrangement continued through the 1950s, and was accompanied by relative fluidity of work assignments. Engineers moved fairly freely among disciplines, across airplanes, and between military and commercial work. They often were assigned temporarily to work with designers outside their reporting function to satisfy needs for cross-functional representation. This diversity of activity allowed most employees to develop expertise beyond their core specialties. According to John Swihart, who retired in 1989 as corporate vice president for International Affairs and had been involved in many of Boeing's design programs: "We didn't really need to label a working group as a 'cross-functional team'—people just pitched in and went where their expertise was needed."

Mock-ups.   The company used physical mock-ups to assess geometric relationships between the systems and structures components of an airplane. This was an essential step that preceded the completion of final design. Mock-ups were full-scale or smaller models of airplane components, and in the 1950s they were produced in the factory that adjoined the Engineering Building. A typical mock-up was made from inexpensive materials such as wood, metal, and plastic, and did not necessarily involve materials that would be used in the final product. Design engineers from all disciplines worked in close relationships with manufacturing personnel during mock-up construction.

Although the engineering groups had worked together frequently during the initial design phase, design conflicts and opportunities for improvement became apparent when a three-dimensional model was available for analysis. The mock-up provided engineers with their first three-dimensional views of the designs that had been created two-dimensionally on drafting boards.[2] The most significant outcome of the mock-up process was in the resolution of incompatibilities between structures and systems. For example, systems engineers might have created a design that required a large wiring bundle or pneumatic duct to pass through an essential structural component. When such an interference was discovered during the mock-up phase, engineers would work in an interdisciplinary mode to eliminate it. Solutions might involve reconfiguring the structure, rerouting the systems apparatus, modifying the structure to allow systems passage, or a combination of the three.

The Beginning of Specialization.   As the company expanded its sales and employment base, it outgrew its facilities on Seattle's East Marginal Way. Company officials sought ways to create locational splits that could allow for a continuation of high-quality communication and effective decision making. In the late 1950s, engineering, marketing, and sales personnel were moved from the Boeing corporate headquarters location on East Marginal Way in Seattle to the company's Renton facility, located about 10 miles away. Final assembly of the 707 product line was performed in Renton, as well, but some subassembly and fabrication work continued at the Seattle plant. At approximately the same time as these moves took place, military engineering and production were

---

[2]A key skill for these engineers was known as "descriptive geometry"—it was essential that they be able to visualize three-dimensional objects based on two-dimensional drawings.

moved to Wichita, Kansas, where Boeing had acquired the Stearman Corporation in 1939. Wichita was a primary site for B-29, B-47, and B-52 production.[3]

As Boeing's product mix and sales volumes grew in the 1960s and 1970s, it became necessary to further diversify the engineering function. Separate engineering organizations were created for each airplane family. Additionally, space limitations sometimes made it impossible to house the engineering staff for an airplane within a single location. The seven basic engineering functions that had existed for the Boeing 707 (preliminary design, structures, aerodynamics, propulsion, weights, systems, and crew station) had long since grown because of the increasing complexity of the products being designed. For example, the systems staff had been partitioned into air conditioning, pneumatics, electrical, and hydraulics. These new specialties were further subdivided, and the total number of subspecialties on an airplane could be as high as 100.

The dispersion of the engineering functions within product families led to scheduling and coordination challenges for Boeing. Components that had been designed collectively and concurrently in the old bull-pen days now had to be designed sequentially. Elaborate barchart schedules dictated temporal relationships among design tasks. Because each engineering function designed its components in relative isolation from other functional groups, drawings that were passed forward often did not meet the requirements of the recipients.[4] The mock-up provided one of the few available opportunities for disparate design functions to convene for joint problem-solving. The sequential process, along with the physical distancing of engineering and manufacturing functions, led to continued reductions in the level of involvement from the manufacturing organization. Designs were locked-in early by designers from the engineering function, and this meant that potential cost savings associated with design for manufacturability often were left unrealized. As the company grew, and as airplanes became technologically more complex, these deficiencies led to increasing numbers of errors and resulting change orders. Change orders could require substantial rework and were viewed as major contributors to schedule delays and cost escalations.

Product Development Time.   Development times and human resource hours varied across airplane families and had grown over the years. Table 3, drawn from Boeing Company archives, shows

---

TABLE 3   **Initial Development Times for Boeing Commercial Airplane Product Families**

Product	Calendar Months for Initial Design
707	36
727	39
737	34
747	44
757	45
767	48
777	54

Source: Boeing Company Archives.

---

[3]The B-52 had previously been assembled at the East Marginal Way facility.

[4]This process was often referred to within the company as "throwing it over the fence."

the figures for the planes that were in production through 1994. These data represent the elapsed time for initial development for each model, and do not include time spent on design extensions. Data on human resource hours per plane were not available, but data on Boeing employment levels and R & D expenditures from Table 1 provide some insights into general trends.

Innovations Supporting the 777 Development Process.   The 777 design program provided Boeing with an opportunity to rectify many of the problems that had emerged during its product development history. In response to the need for change, the company implemented two complementary innovations: a digitally-based design system and cross-functional design/build teams known as "DBTs." According to George Broady, who had been chief engineer for Airframe Design and Integration on the 777 design program, "We brought together people who had never met before and gave them tools that previously had not been available." The goal of these two innovations was captured in the Boeing DBT operations manual:

> Major parts of the strategy for improving our method of operation involve incorporating information relative to producibility, reliability, and maintainability into our designs earlier in the program, thereby releasing more accurate, more complete, and more integrated designs.

Digital Design.   Several computing tools were acquired and developed to support the 777 digital design effort. The centerpiece of the system, known as CATIA,[5] was developed by Dassault Systemes of France, a firm with significant presence in the European defense industry. Boeing had reviewed several computer aided design (CAD) systems, but chose CATIA because it had been used successfully in several pilot programs, and because of its superior capabilities in three-dimensional design. In 1989, Boeing entered into a joint venture with the IBM Corporation, which licensed CATIA in the U.S., to develop a software system for commercial airplane design processes.[6]

CATIA and its supporting systems delivered several potential advantages to the 777 design program. Drawings shown in three dimensions permitted the early identification of physical interferences among parts and systems. Without digital design, structural incompatibilities often went unnoticed until the mock-up stage, or, in some cases, until the plane was in production. Boeing developed in-house several extensions of CATIA which aided the digital design process. Three of these, EPIC, CLASH, and FLYTHRU, enhanced the visibility of interferences by allowing the designer to take a virtual "ride" through a three-dimensional image of the interior of a design component. Additionally, the introduction of computer-generated human images enabled designers to assess the ergonomics and capacity of a manufacturing operator's workspace within an airplane section.

Digital design tools also had the ability to support information exchange across geographically dispersed design locations in the U.S., Canada, Europe, and Japan. Previously, engineers often had been left in the dark with respect to the decisions made within other disciplines. The Mylar sheets historically used for initial drawings required that all decision makers be present in the same room to view them. With CATIA, the Mylar sheets and drawing boards no longer were

---

[5]CATIA is an acronym for Computer Aided Three-Dimensional Application. It was not actually the company's first application of digital design technology. For example, the Boeing Defense and Space Group, which had been created as a Boeing division in 1990, had employed digital technologies as early as 1985 in the design of military aircraft such as the B-2.

[6]IBM had used CATIA in the early 1980s to design high-end printers and brought this experience to the joint venture.

seen as being necessary because designers located at multiple sites could simultaneously view the same drawing on their own computer screens.[7] Another outcome of the digital design process was in the elimination of the physical mock-up phase in the new product development cycle. When interferences could be managed digitally, a physical mock-up added no perceived value. In comparison to previous design experiences, Boeing officials expected the digital design system to reduce the number of changes and errors by 50 percent.

Boeing used the phrase "Digital Product Definition" to describe its new design technology. The word "digital" captured the essence of CATIA and the extension programs that supported it—as drawings were rendered on the computer screen, the system automatically translated them into numerical descriptions through the use of coordinate point indicators. The advantage of such a system was that it enabled an engineer to readily merge drawings of two interdependent parts, and to determine if the two designs were compatible. Under the predigital system, the joining of two drawings required special expertise in descriptive geometry and careful measurement of all drawing dimensions. Computers were sometimes used to support this process, but much of the work was done by hand. Depending on the level of knowledge of the engineer, the process could be subject to translation error. Additionally, changes in one drawing would require the time-consuming reassessment of geometric dimensions for all drawings that needed to intersect with it. Thus, the digital design system was seen as a real advancement because of its potential to save time and reduce errors.

Design-Build Teams.   In parallel with the adoption of 100 percent digital design, Boeing made another significant change: the implementation of a cross-functional team structure for the 777 development program. The Boeing engineering community had long recognized the limitations of its functional specialization—the 777 seemed to provide the opportunity they needed for testing an integrative, concurrent approach that would link designers, builders, and tooling specialists. In 1990, a massive effort was undertaken to form these design teams, most of which were co-located. Initial co-location was at the company's Renton facility, but in 1992 the group was moved to the Everett facility.[8] Although functions had been intermixed at the Renton site, the move to the Everett site brought about a return to a greater segregation of functions. In the words of one participant, "People who could shout to each other across a partition in Renton had to go to another floor to see each other in Everett." Still, cross-functional teams continued to meet on a formal basis as the design proceeded. The official company label attached to these groups was Design-Build Team or DBT.

A schematic depiction of the 777 DBT structure is shown in Figure 1. The figure does not show the full extent of the team organization structure, but illustrates the general nature of the hierarchy. The structure shown here existed in addition to the company's regular organization chart, which was organized by function and specialty. DBT #1, shown at the top of the chart, was composed of representatives from all major functions and was responsible for overseeing the entire process. Its role was focused primarily on monitoring the scheduling of time-dependent events. As with other teams in the structure, DBT #1 was co-led by a representative from design engineering and a representative from manufacturing engineering. In spite of the co-leadership, many individuals who had been close to the process observed that the balance of the power was often oriented toward design engineering.

---

[7]This led Boeing to a full-scale dismantling and removal of nearly all drawing boards in company facilities.

[8]This was also the location of the 747 and 767 final assembly plants and was the future home of the 777 final assembly plant.

FIGURE 1

The 777 design-build team structure (simplified)

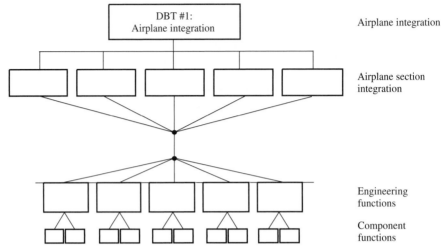

Airplane Section Integration Teams, which operated just below DBT #1, were responsible for major components of the 777 such as wings or landing gear. This group of teams represented the biggest departure from Boeing's historical design structure. Members included representatives from various engineering functions as well as individuals from lower-level DBTs who brought in design perspectives related to safety, environmental management, material, quality assurance, tooling engineering, customer support, and the like. Team membership and attendance evolved over time based on the need for inputs from various functions. Although these teams featured a shared leadership role between design engineering and manufacturing engineering, it was generally recognized that design engineering held the greater power in this relationship. The functional organizations played the role of ultimate arbiter in cases of design conflict, and also reserved the right to reverse design decisions made by their DBT representatives.

At the lowest levels of the organization's network of DBTs, each team included a core group of designers who worked on CATIA stations and interacted on a daily basis. These teams were functionally specialized, did most of their work independently, and did not include significant cross-disciplinary representation.

Although the digital design workstations allowed for links among teams designing interdependent parts, team meetings at all levels were an essential part of the communication process. During DBT and Section Integration Team meetings, participants made frequent use of digital design images, shown on large computer screens, as the basis of discussions regarding design conflicts and challenges. In the early stages of the design process, some integration teams met as often as once per week. As the design neared completion, some integration teams disbanded altogether and others reduced their meeting frequency considerably (e.g., once every four to six weeks). The teams most likely to deactivate were those for basic components that were viewed as unlikely to change in future derivations of the 777. According to one estimate, the total number of teams declined from 268 at the beginning of the project to 150 at the end of the project. However, there was a flurry of team activity at the end of the project. Just prior to the delivery of the first 777 to United Airlines, DBT #1 met frequently (several times per week) to ensure that all systems were working together to meet the scheduled delivery date.

DBTs extended beyond Boeing Company boundaries to include customers and suppliers. Because of their high level of involvement in the design process, major airlines brought in representatives to be housed, full-time, within the design facility. Each of these individuals participated in several of the design teams and reported frequently to his or her home organization—pilots from United Airlines worked with the 777 cockpit design team. Major suppliers represented another set of participants in the new team structure. For example, a Japanese company produced the lavatories for Boeing commercial jets and was heavily involved in the 777 design process— a representative of the company flew from Tokyo to Seattle twice monthly to participate in DBT meetings. More significantly, Boeing teams worked with Japanese partners who had been contracted to produce major portions of the 777 fuselage—these teams did much of their work on-site in Japan but communicated frequently with design teams in the U.S.

Putting It All Together.   The simultaneous development of a new product, employment of a new computer aided design technology, and conversion to a team structure created many challenges for Boeing. For example, extensive technical training was required for all employees who would be using the digital design systems. Additionally, employees needed assistance in adapting to new reporting relationships and communication patterns. The total cost of implementing and operating CATIA and related systems was difficult to assess with complete accuracy, but hardware, software, and training expenses exceeded the company's original estimates by a fairly large margin.

Although digital design and the creation of the associated DBT structure had been costly, Boeing officials felt that the system would more than pay for itself over time. Some of the payoff would be realized in the longer term because the digital design technology would permit Boeing engineers to continue to be geographically dispersed, and to quickly create error-free customized configurations as new orders came in. Additionally, "lessons learned" on the 777 would reduce start-up costs as the design technology was transferred to existing and new airplane families.

Was It Worth It?   As the first commercially available 777[9] rolled out onto the runway and soared into the sky on its way to customer delivery in May of 1995, Boeing officials were in the midst of an analysis of lessons learned from this complex new undertaking. The process had involved tremendous risks—a new product, a new method of organizing work, and a complex new design technology. The design of the new plane had taken 54 months. According to Larry Olson, director of computing, change, errors, and rework—the preeminent measure of success—had shown a 60 to 90 percent improvement over previous design efforts. In spite of this success, the company had concerns about the process and felt that the lessons from the effort would require serious review prior to the extension of 777 methods to other airplane programs. Major problem areas were described as follows:

- *Career path issues.* Some managers expressed concerns about career path issues for employees. Under the company's traditional functional structure, an entry-level employee could clearly envision the route to the top of his or her organizational unit. With the cross-functional orientation, lateral moves between teams provided employees with valuable developmental experiences, but did not always give them the vertical exposure they needed to advance in the organization. As a result of these concerns, one employee remarked to her manager at the end of a very successful one-year cross-functional project: "That was a great experience, but don't ask me to do anything like that again."

---

[9]The first plane to be delivered to a customer was actually the seventh plane built. The first plane was Boeing-owned and numbers two through six were used for various testing purposes before being refurbished for customers.

- *Performance evaluation and incentives.* Members of some teams were uncertain about how their performance would be evaluated. Generally, though, functional managers had responsibility for evaluating those who reported to them, even when an employee did most of his or her work away from the functional unit. As one member noted: "I'm making some important contributions to my DBT, but my functional boss really doesn't know what I'm doing over there."
- *Learning to work together.* Under the company's traditional work system, people had generally worked with others who shared the mindset, training, and language of a particular discipline. The DBT approach required them to work with a diversity of perspectives, and some employees did not feel adequately prepared for such a change. This led to frustrations for some employees because of the delays in decision making that seemed to occur in functionally diverse teams.

  Company officials noted that some teams were more effective than others. It appeared that the most successful teams viewed themselves as being collectively responsible for their design component. Other teams adhered to the requirement that they have regular meetings, but there was no synergy among the disciplines represented. These teams were most likely to unofficially disband and stop meeting as the project wore on.

  Elizabeth Otis, director of Production and Tool Engineering for the 777, summed up the challenge:

  > A successful Design Build Team is much more than a cross-functional, co-located group of individuals. In the truly successful DBT, members behave in a collaborative manner, addressing the total product entity rather than simply representing their functional interests.

  It was clear that not all 777 DBTs had met this expectation.
- *Discontinuities in team membership.* As the 777 program grew, human resource needs became clarified or changed, often resulting in the movement of personnel across team assignments. Team leaders found it difficult to keep group members focused on their objectives and working harmoniously through an established group culture. Disruptions in team membership were viewed as contributors to some design performance problems. As one employee remarked: "We just got started working together—really developing a rhythm—when two team members were reassigned and three more came in. It was like starting over again."
- *Manufacturing input.* Another problem stemmed from DBT affiliations with manufacturing. Although most design teams were co-led by design engineering and manufacturing engineering representatives, members of the manufacturing engineering community sometimes felt that their ideas took a back seat to those of design engineering. Additionally, manufacturing engineers were not always in touch with the actual needs of manufacturing personnel on the shop floor. Because of this gap in understanding, their input regarding design for manufacturability did not always result in ease of assembly for airplane mechanics. Even when shop floor representatives were involved in DBTs, they felt that their influence on the design process was minimal, at best. As a consequence, design for manufacturability was not given the consideration that had been anticipated. As one engineer remarked: "We didn't plan the 'Build' part of DBT as well as we could have."

  Differences in organization structure and assumptions about CATIA may have contributed to deficiencies in the interactions between design and manufacturing. Design engineering was organized by function (e.g., structures) whereas operations personnel were organized by task (e.g., assembly). Because of this difference, it was difficult to find points of intersection where these two parts of the organization could work in meaningful ways on DBTs. The problem of insufficient manufacturing involvement may actually have been compounded by one of the perceived strengths of digital design—one experienced engineer speculated that the software's ability to identify design interferences may have led to assumptions that manufacturing input was unnecessary. The issue may have been further magnified because of the lack of digital integration between manufacturing and design. Although the entire airplane had been defined digitally on the CATIA system, manufacturing personnel noted that these definitions could not be translated directly to the company's numerically controlled machinery. As a consequence, factory programmers had to completely reenter digital data for use in manufacturing equipment. Further development work would be necessary to link the design system with software used in Boeing's manufacturing facilities.

- *Design rework.* A major goal of the 777 development process had been to reduce the amount of design rework. However, some design teams continued to struggle with interferences between structures and systems. This sometimes resulted in the need for three to four design iterations before the two entities could be integrated in a satisfactory manner. The problem seemed to stem from insufficient integration in the lowest levels of DBTs, and also from the challenges associated with learning a new system.

- *Tool engineering.* Tooling issues compounded the disassociation of manufacturing and design. Although tool design representatives participated during the early stages of the 777 design program, most of them were withdrawn from team activity and pulled back into their functional organization when the design was nearly 25 percent complete. The shift was made in response to cost and schedule pressures—designers were needed in their functional areas to produce 777 tool designs, and time spent in meetings was time spent away from the task at hand. This focus on short-term scheduling optimization led later to the need for rework of tool designs, lengthening development time and hindering product manufacturability in some cases. Although product quality was not affected, cost and time to market did suffer somewhat as a consequence of these setbacks.

- *Proliferation of teams.* Another concern focused on the proliferation of teams, sometimes in cases where they were unnecessary. In fact, this problem extended beyond the 777 program to include many areas of The Boeing Commercial Airplane Group. In the words of Bill Selby, vice president and general manager of the 737 and 757 programs: "We have too many teams. We've been using teams for issues and problems that could have been handled more quickly and effectively by an individual." Others seemed to agree that the company had perhaps become too enamored with teams—they felt that individuals or ad hoc groups would have been more appropriate for some kinds of assignments.

- *Limitations of digital design.* CATIA had fulfilled company expectations in general, although some issues still remained to be resolved. Some experienced engineers questioned whether it was possible to develop "big picture" conceptual designs on a small computer screen and suggested that drawing boards were still needed to support innovative team activity in early design stages. They wondered if design elegance and innovation were being sacrificed for the sake of digital definition.

Some design engineers noted that although CATIA and its supporting design programs provided excellent tools for identifying interferences (i.e., spaces where two or more parts would need to occupy the same physical space), they were not as effective in highlighting gaps (i.e., places where parts are supposed to meet but don't). Additionally, training several thousand employees to effectively use the CATIA hardware and software was a bigger challenge than the company had expected—in order to become literate in the use of the design technology, individual employees averaged 100 hours of CATIA training, and some required up to 250 hours. Moreover, unless an employee used the software nearly every day, it was easy to slip back down the learning curve. Modifications to the digital programs occurred frequently as the company gained experience with its features, identified bugs, and saw the need for enhancements or corrections. These changes often resulted in experience setbacks for designers. Although no figures were available regarding the total cost of CATIA and related programs, it was apparent to all involved that hardware, software, and training/learning costs had been very high.

Moving Forward

An analysis of digital design and cross-functional teams on the 777 revealed both strengths and weaknesses. In the words of Don Fudge, 777 manufacturing engineering manager, "Although the 777 design process did not achieve all that it could have, it still was the most effective and efficient production definition endeavor that the Boeing Company has ever undertaken." However, it was clear that if the company were to elect to expand these innovations into other product lines it would benefit from an evaluation of the 777 program. Companywide adoption would be a major undertaking and top-level decision makers felt a need to carefully consider several important questions:

1. Looking back over five decades, what lessons can Boeing learn from the evolution of its design process?
2. What were the outcomes of the 777 program? Highlight both the positive aspects and areas for improvement.
3. Can the use of digital design and cross-functional teams ensure Boeing's ability to meet the challenges of the future? Would one be sufficient without the other? If you had to choose one, which would you choose, and why?
4. If the company did engage in full-scale implementation of these two innovations, how would it measure the success? Beyond "change, errors, and rework," what metrics are appropriate?
5. If digital design technology and cross-functional teams were adopted companywide, what would be the key elements of the implementation plan?

2

A CASE STUDY OF MANUFACTURING ORGANISATION RECONFIGURATION FOR ORGANISATIONAL DEVELOPMENT AT ALAN GROUP, U.K.[1]

Synopsis

Following a turbulent history of rapid growth followed by restructuring over the past 20 years the Company, now employing 57 people, is stable and successful. It is recognised as a "world class" operation in high precision engineer-to-order products and in high volume component manufacturing. It enjoys an outstanding employee skills/loyalty profile.

However, it is not meeting certain business goals nor generating the opportunity to grow both the business and the employees, which it desires. Organisational development through the introduction of a special form of cellular operation was proposed.

The challenge is to introduce a self-sustaining culture of organisational development alongside established technical excellence. The cellular working processes threaten established methods, certain employees, and have far-reaching consequences that cannot easily be tested in an incremental way before widespread introduction or perhaps total rejection. This case study describes the processes adopted by this small company in the crucial pilot phases of a special form of cellular operation.

The Company

Alan Group has 57 employees, all based in the U.K. The Company specialises in the design and manufacture of precision mould tools for the plastic injection moulding industry. Alan Group has the production capability to carry out high volume injection moulding; its main customers are in the communications and IT (information technology) sectors.

The Group has been identified as "world class" in surveys carried out by IBM Consultants and by the London Business School. They were presented with the Queen's Award for Export Achievement in 1994, and were competing in the 1995 Sussex Business Awards.

The Company's statement of purpose is:

> The Alan Group is dedicated to the design and manufacture of "World Class" precision engineered products and, through its commitment to continuous improvement and unsurpassed quality, to providing lifetime support, superior value, and competitive advantage.

[1]This case was developed for use in classroom discussion and is not intended to necessarily illustrate appropriate or inappropriate management practices. The case author was Peter J. Sackett, Cranfield University, October 1995. The funding for this case production was provided by the Australian federal government's Department of Industry, Science and Resources. The authors would like to thank the Alan Group for its help in compiling the data for this exciting case study, in particular, Alan Mason, the board of directors, and the cell members.

History

1973	Founded by Alan Mason and a partner, they were initially involved in the manufacture of interchangeable spare parts for die tools. Customers suggested that they should make complete tools. The Company was split into two divisions, with spares having five employees and the tooling division having one.
1980/1981	The Company bought its first injection moulding machine and started to concentrate on tooling for the plastics industry, alongside the production die side.
Mid-1980s	Embarked on rapid growth via a venture into Scotland, taking advantage of regional financial incentives. Initially, it was successful, but when a major customer reneged on a gentleman's agreement to place a very large order, they faced potentially enormous losses. Alan Group spent the next two years rebuilding the Scottish operation, and eventually sold it to an American company.
1988	The Company was bought out by venture capitalists, who were in the process of building a portfolio of companies. In addition to being given cash and shares in the Group, the partners were allowed to run the Company without outside interference. However, due to business practices by the venture capitalist, the Group went into receivership. With the help of the Receiver, Alan Mason was able to secure temporary financial backing to allow the preparation of a management buyout scheme.
	It was at this time that Alan Mason's partner of 19 years wanted to end the partnership. The Company was bought back with the help of money from directors and employees of the firm. Eighty percent of the current employees are also shareholders, many with a significant vested interest in seeing the firm do well. These employees have had to wait until 1995 to see the first dividends being paid out.

Structure. The Company comprises three divisions:

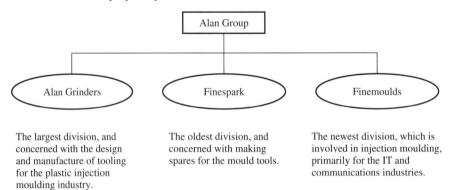

The largest division, and concerned with the design and manufacture of tooling for the plastic injection moulding industry.

The oldest division, and concerned with making spares for the mould tools.

The newest division, which is involved in injection moulding, primarily for the IT and communications industries.

Alan Grinders and Finespark are further subdivided into sections, which cover each of the processes involved in their operations. These sections can have up to seven people, or as few as one. In charge of each section is a section leader, who besides normal duties as an operator, allocates particular jobs to others in the section. The main criteria used are the ability of the particular operator and the difficulty of the job. The section leader must sequence jobs to get them through their own section on time for final customer delivery. The section leaders do not deal directly with the customers.

Employee Skill Levels/Training.   Everyone in the Company, with the exception of three office staff, is an apprentice-trained engineer. Therefore, all have a full appreciation of the work carried out on the shop floor, and indeed the directors are sometimes to be found working on the machines.

It is a point of pride that the Company trains its own apprentices, and operators' skills continue to be updated and added to long after their apprenticeship is finished. The labour turnover in the Alan Group is virtually zero.

The directors are engineers first, and managers second, largely due to their lack of formal management education. This is in the process of being addressed and all of the directors have now undergone a training course in basic management theory.

Business Plan.   In 1995, the Board devised an updated business plan. It covers their high-level plans for the growth of the business up to the year 2000, during which time they intend to increase turnover. They undertook a SWOT (Strengths, Weaknesses, Opportunities, and Threats) analysis of their current position, and identified issues that need to be addressed. These included:

- *Space for expansion.* The current premises are already cramped.
- *The availability of a skilled work force.* The planned rate of expansion is too fast for the Company to fill all of the vacancies with its own apprentices—and suitably skilled labour is scarce.
- *Management.* All levels in the Company will need education and training to manage the projected growth.

The Need to Change

Realisation of the need for change was the result of increasing awareness of influence, internally within the Company, and externally in the marketplace in which it operates. Alan Mason was the driving force. The catalyst was the formal recognition of the Company's status through the Queen's Award. This led to exposure to alternative practice and new business structures from government agencies, practitioners, and academics. The Company engaged The CIM Institute, Cranfield, U.K., to review its strategy options.[2]

Internal Influences.   The primary internal indication of the need for change was the profit performance of the Company. Although Alan Group enjoys World Class status, a happy work force, and satisfied customers, it has not reaped the level of profit it could be reasonably expected to.

Alan Mason is, by his own admission, a perfectionist. As a result, the priority of the Company has always been quality. Prior to starting the Alan Group, he had established a reputation for excellence, and his initial customers were looking for the quality of work that they knew he could produce. As the group grew, the unwritten technical strategy has always been the need to maintain the technical capability required to cater to the increasingly exacting demands of the customer. Consequently the Company has invested in new machinery and computer systems and updated the skills of the operators working in the plant ahead of market demand.

---

[2]P. West. "Manufacturing Strategy Review in a Specialised Application," CIM Institute, Cranfield University, Bedford, U.K., 1994.

Company strategy appraisal carried out in 1994 for the Alan Group recognised the basis of competition and envisioned a development path. It identified that operational efficiency, talent, and the energy in the work force were not being properly utilised. The work force is fully committed, heavily loaded, highly trained, and proud to work for the Company. A need was identified for a method of harnessing latent human potential and channeling it toward making more money for the Company and for its owners, many of whom are the employees. This potential could be realised through organisational development.

A need was identified therefore for something alongside "hard" technology to provide the platform the Company needed to improve its profit performance and maximise employee development. Directors of the Group recently devised a five-year Business Plan, part of which is a financial objective. The main aims of this are:

> A 10 percent profit margin
>
> Turnover to grow at 25 percent per annum

To attain this, there will need to be a radical restructuring of the Company. One of the biggest changes will be in the work force. The Company trains its own apprentices, and most people working for the Company were trained there. In 1994, for example, there were eight apprentices at varying levels of training, out of a total work force of 57. (This is an exceptional statistic, way outside normal U.K. practice.) To achieve the 25 percent growth target, however, they will need to look outside of the Company for personnel, which will inevitably impact the Company's culture.

Current informal communication channels work reasonably well in the present setup, but as the Company grows, there will be a need for more formalised methods of information transfer.

The Company is thought of, by most of those within it, as one big team. It would be highly unlikely, however, that this could be maintained with the expected influx of new employees without special attention to this issue.

External Influences. The study carried out into the Alan Group's business strategy in 1994 also examined the Company's customer base, and identified the major customer demands. It was found that the main customers were delighted with the quality of product and the quality of service they received. Although the procurement pricing was not considered to be competitive, the initial cost of the tooling was justified by the total life cycle costs and realised product performance. The major complaint was the customer perception of unreliability in quoted delivery dates.

In late 1994 at the invitation of the U.K. government but at the cost of Alan Group, Alan Mason went on a trade mission to Japan. This was organised by the U.K. Department of Trade and Industry, and included a number of other British companies involved in the electronics industry. As a result Alan has initiated a major drive to supply certain of the European subsidiaries of the Japanese multinationals he visited. This represents a change in the marketplace. The demands of these customers differ from the established client base. These companies demand exceptional delivery performance from their suppliers, and are unforgiving of those that let them down. If Alan Group is to be successful in this environment, it will have to improve its delivery performance beyond what may be traditionally regarded as good in this industry sector.

Directors see organisational development affecting every member of the work force as a strategic priority. The introduction of cellular working is a part of an empowerment initiative and a way of highlighting the importance of delivery performance to all the employees.

The Context of Change

Factors that determined the Company's decision to move toward cellular manufacturing methods are grouped under two headings.

External.   Until recently the Company has adopted a very low profile. The media attention resulting from the presentation of the Queen's Award for Export Achievement, and the acknowledgment of its World Class status, have put pressure on the Company to live up to its reputation and even exceed it.

The Company's marketplace is truly international, but the majority of its work is for a handful of major customers. This relatively small client base enables the Company to establish and maintain a collaborative learning relationship with each customer over a long period.

The drive to improve delivery dependability results from the demands of new customers. However, a successful outcome should also be increasingly valued by Alan Group's existing customers, both domestic and international. The opportunity exists to extend the breadth of the company's existing business through a more integrated role in the product development process of its customers.

Internal.   Engineers at Alan Group are some of the best in their trade, and they are rewarded accordingly.

Human resource issues do not centre around unions, and strikes are an unknown phenomenon at Alan Group. Issues do arise and there was some minor discontent recently over the decision to limit overtime payments and provide a better quality of life for employees. Traditionally the Company has worked very high levels of overtime and this became a cultural issue not always related to best operational practice. The issue was resolved through discussion focusing on achieving corporate and business goals.

Organisational culture is one of mutual respect. Around 80 percent of the work force are shareholders in the Company, and there is a widespread culture of pride. It is also a point of pride that Alan Group trains its own apprentices who can and do progress to the highest levels in the organisation. The lack of visible hierarchy within the Company adds to the informality within the organisation, and the operators are allowed to do a job in the way they see fit, another sign of the respect accorded to the work force.

The Company's products, mould tools, mould tool spares, and moulded components have to fulfill the demanding specifications of the communications and IT industries, so the machinery and the operator training need to be and are of a very high standard. The technology used is the best available. Due to the tolerances required, leading-edge technologies, such as wire erosion and spark erosion, are used alongside the more common precision tool shop processes.

In the U.K., a major study was undertaken during 1995 on the technology issues affecting Small and Medium Sized Manufacturing Enterprises. Opportunities for growth and the characteristics of SMEs with manageable risk growth potential were examined.[3] These findings suggest that Alan Group is well positioned to use AMT in the process of business growth.

The Process of Transition

Planning and implementation of the proof-of-concept at Alan Group followed a logical sequence of steps over a period of more than a year.

First, the specific strategic objectives that needed to be addressed were identified. There were two such objectives for the Alan Grinders tooling business:

- Improvement of delivery performance.
- Improvement of profit performance.

---

[3]Sackett, P.J., and G. Nelder. "Managing Manufacturing Change in SMEs: a United Kingdom Position Study," Proceedings Autofact '95, Chicago, Nov. 14, 1995, pp. 129–144.

The next stage was concerned with reviewing the type of change required to accomplish the strategic objectives. The main influences on the choice of cellular working were:

- The Strategy Review carried out in 1994, which identified cellular working as a way of tapping and developing the potential of the work force. This gave operator teams the opportunity to take responsibility for a complete order—including delivery, eventually with the potential to interface directly with customers operating in an Extended Enterprise mode.
- Alan Mason attended a seminar on the subject of Kaizen. He came away with the conviction that cells were the way to empower the work force at Alan Group, and that it was the best way to improve the firm's delivery performance.

Alan Mason set about justifying organisational development through cells to the other directors of the firm. Justification is concerned solely with how empowerment through manufacturing cells would help the firm to achieve the strategic objectives: delivery and profit performance.

Cells might achieve the first objective, of improving delivery performance, by giving responsibility for complete orders to cross-functional teams. Each team would have a particular interest in getting their tool to the customer on time, rather than the present objective of getting work done to be passed on to the next section. It would then be a matter of pride for the team to meet the customer delivery date. It might also be reasonable to expect this increased motivation to translate into increased productivity and more importantly enhanced customer perception of values. This would help the Company achieve the objective of improving profit performance by further reducing the significance of first cost as an order winning criterion.

There was some scepticism about whether cells were appropriate to the Alan Group, and this is examined more deeply in the section on the politics of change. The majority board decision, however, was to go ahead and evaluate the cellular method of working in a pilot study.

In most companies that have introduced cellular working, the machinery has been physically moved to form distinct cells. The reason for this is that families of products can flow around the cell, without excessive work in progress, or the need for minimum batch sizes.

In the Alan Group, however, no two tools produced are identical, and there are hundreds of man-hours spent on machine stations. The transport time between different tool processes is the minutes it takes to carry the part to the next room, or down the stairs. Since the tools cannot be split into distinct families, each requiring similar processing times on the same machines, it would not make sense to form distinct physical cells of machinery.

Manufacturing Cells in the Alan Group are order-based virtual cells. Fully implemented, each cell would be a group of people in different sections all working on the same order. There are no product families; as such, the cell would last for the duration of a particular order, and then disband. Operators would then be assigned to new cells. This is a virtual transient cell system. The time frame for the introduction of cells would therefore have to be long, with a gradual introduction into the factory.

It was decided that there would be great danger in going for the "big bang" approach, and introducing multiple virtual cells all at once. Initially, there would be one cell running at a time, so that:

- Its degree of success could be measured.
- Lessons learned from problems encountered by the first one could be passed on to subsequent cells in a continuous improvement process.
- Sceptics within the work force could be won over by being able to see the difference made by cellular working.

Planning.   Planning of the implementation was recognised as crucial, as the success of the project would largely depend on how well the pilot was planned. To increase the chances of success, the Company waited until a suitable order came along. The main criteria for suitability were:

- The job should not be particularly complicated, although none of the tools the Company makes could be described as simple.
- There should be plenty of time to make the product; there should not be an unrealistically tight deadline.

Once a suitable order was identified, the technical director selected a team of people to form the cell. Personalities were chosen with the hope that the sceptics among them would adjust their views once they saw the cell was working. It did not comprise a group of cell "enthusiasts." There was an initial briefing meeting where the cell members were given the design of the tool and the delivery date. It was not known at that stage what exactly the cell would make of the opportunity, because none of the firm's employees had worked in a cellular environment before. The work force knew in outline the theory about how virtual cells were supposed to function, but there was no formal training as such.

Possibly the most crucial function was that of cell leader. The operator chosen had no real leadership experience within the firm. He was chosen because it was felt that he could make a good attempt at the job, even though nobody knew exactly what that role would be. It was hoped that he would take hold of the opportunity and develop the leadership needed to get the job done. This risk-taking illustrates the level of trust placed on all employees in Alan Group.

Although the cell changed the way in which the order progressed through the factory, the jobs done by the cell members did not really alter. As one cell member put it:

> Everyone knows what they are doing anyway, so it is not as if somebody's started something new. It is a job we do every day, we are all fairly good at it, so we all know what we are doing.

So implementing the changes affected how the tool progressed within the Company, rather than what individuals did while working on the tool. The usual method of getting tools through the factory depends on the supervisor in each section getting work through the section in order of priority. They assign a job to a particular operator primarily because of the operator's abilities and the difficulty of the job. Some orders need the involvement of several operators, and this would also be organised by the supervisor.

The virtual cell processes the job without the supervisor deciding who in their section would work on it. This might be seen as threatening to the supervisors, but no resistance was met once it was realised that they were working on the cell job.

There were difficulties encountered and issues that needed to be resolved. One mentioned by the cell concerned noncell members trying to work on the cell job.

> Two people decided they were going to pick up the job to work on, so it had to be pointed out basically, "keep your nose out"—politely, because it would disrupt what was happening within the cell. (quoted from a cell member)

Another problem that it was anticipated could have occurred was with the section leaders. These supervisors have their list of priorities, which are the Company's priorities. If a cell member works on the cell job while there is more pressing work to be done, the section fails to meet its targets. It had to be pointed out, therefore, both to cell members and to section leaders, that the Company priorities were more important than the cell priorities. It was clear that if the section leader asked a cell member to work on another, more urgent job, it would be done. To date no problems have arisen with this issue.

Implementation Cell 01.   At the time of writing this case study, the first cell order has been delivered and the second cell order is nearing completion, so the process has been trialed but it is still novel.

At launch, the cell members were called together for an initial meeting, at which they were given the design for the tool, and a deadline. The major change from normal working, therefore, was that people knew which individual in the sections would be working on the job. Usually, nobody would know or be concerned with who would end up working on a specific order, as scheduling in each section is done by that section's leader. It is interesting to note that, because the design was completed before the cell was assembled, it only consisted of the operators who would work on it. The tool designer was outside of the virtual cell system.

Roles for the cell members were not predefined, and it was not known or preplanned how they would work. It was hoped that the cell leader would take advantage of the opportunity. The operator chosen for the position was not the leader in his section, so this was his first real leadership role within the Company. He made it his business to know where the job was at any point in time, and kept in touch with the other cell members. He greatly enjoyed the extra responsibility, and found it to be a very good motivator and process for personal development.

> Because I have got no real position here . . . it does generate for the like of me, a little bit more responsibility. You are not just "the man upstairs that did that," you are a little bit more. It gives you a sense of achievement as well. (virtual cell leader)

While the tool was making its way through the various processes, the work carried out by the cell members did not differ from what they would normally do. One significant change, however, was that the section leaders (as opposed to the team leaders) played no part in scheduling the progress of the order through the factory. The section leader still has the overriding authority, however, and if there is a conflict between the cell's needs and those of the Company, they can ensure that the Company comes first.

The pilot job went through smoothly, and the cell members were all anxious to see how good the first mouldings would be. There was a serious problem with the finished tool, which would require a significant amount of rework. It was a bitter disappointment to the virtual cell team, who had taken particular pride in the fact that the order had progressed so well. It became apparent that the root cause of the problem was a fundamental design fault, and the cell members were concerned that their work would be remembered as a failure, even though the error was outside of the cell's control. The consensus of opinion is that the problem would also have occurred if the order had been processed normally, and that it would not have been identified any earlier than it was.

Significant amounts of remedial action were required to rectify the problems in the tool's performance. There has been discussion, both inside and outside the cell, about the need to prevent such errors in future. Currently, there is no formal checking of designs before they are launched onto the shop floor, because there is no time allocated for this. The problem was there previously, but the cell has highlighted a problem that the Company needs to address.

The Substance of Change

The substance of the change at Alan Group was the introduction of a special form of cellular type working. Giving a small group of individuals the overall responsibility for an order, from inception to delivery, is seen as an effective way of improving delivery performance, while also tapping the reservoir of talent on the shop floor. It is crucial to realising the company's strategic plan.

Cells have proven very successful in other industry sectors. In the tooling engineer-to-order industry, all orders are unique, processes are measured in 10s or 100s of hours, and there is negligible "idle" work in progress. So the formation of physical cells might be expected to have minimal positive influence on performance.

A cell in the Alan Group sense is a group of operators from each of the major process sections, a virtual cell. They are made "owners" of a complete order from design to the first moulds being made. The Company is taking a step-by-step approach to this project seeking to learn cellurisation from the cells themselves.

The Politics of Change

The Company's CEO Alan Mason is the kingpin of the operation, and although he is not by any means dictatorial, he commands respect from all levels in the Company. The Alan Group has pulled through several major crises in recent years, and much of this is attributed to the CEO. The work force has faith in his abilities. It was Alan who suggested that the Company move toward cellular manufacture, and although there was scepticism from some quarters, the Board decided to back the idea.

There were conflicts at various stages in the planning, running, and reflection stages of the cell's operation:

- One director was sceptical about the applicability of cellular working to the Alan Group. In particular, he saw the Company as one big cell anyway, and did not believe that using cells would bring any significant extra benefit to the firm. This is a view shared with some others at Alan Group, but as one cell member said:

  . . . It is only true if everybody was to work the same way. They do not. If everybody communicated and everybody [was] motivated in the same way, then that would be perfectly true. We would have one big cell.

- Once, two people picked up the cell job to work on it. It was pointed out to them that it was the cell job, and that they should leave it alone.
- When the problems with the tool became apparent toward the end of the project, there was disappointment within the cell, as they believed they had done a good job. As a result, there is some resentment felt toward the designer.

  It is unfortunate that this has happened because you are going to get a situation, as is possibly happening at the moment, in that everybody that worked on it, worked hard on it and achieved the delivery date. And when something goes wrong, you want to blame somebody, it's human nature. (cell member)

There is also a possibility that the section leaders might start to suspect a hidden agenda, because cellular working removes the need for them to allocate and sequence jobs in their section. There was no evidence of this during the running of this particular cell, but if cells are to become more numerous, the worries of the section leaders must be addressed.

The majority of the board were in agreement with the cells idea so the sceptical director went along with their decision. Although he still maintains that cells, even virtual ones, are not designed to work in the Alan Group's environment, his objections were not so forceful as to cause any major rifts.

Employees within the firm know that the Board is not unanimously in support of the cells idea, and they might, as a result, have reservations themselves. To have the best chance of success, any change effort needs the full support of the work force. So, if the sceptical director could be persuaded that cells can work, it would send a very strong positive signal to the work force. The Company is considering trying to identify small companies who have successfully implemented virtual cells, and arrange to visit them. They could also be good sources of advice about how to overcome implementation problems.

Some cell members have identified feelings of resentment directed at the designer of the tool, because had there been no design errors, the cell would probably have been seen as a great success by others within the Company. Now, however, there is a danger that it will be seen to have failed as an idea. They also realise, however, that it is destructive to point the finger of blame at an individual, without analysing the root causes of the problem.

> The cell has shown a weakness, which is very basic tool design. That is not incriminating, that is showing a weakness, because it is a problem that we had. (cell member)

The designer himself feels that he would have benefited from being in the cell, and having direct feedback from the cell members during the project. He would particularly have liked to have had input from the cell at the start, before the designs were finished.

> The buck stops here, but it would be nice to get some feedback, which doesn't always happen. (designer)

How the Company deals with the present situation is important to the chances of successful organisational development. If blame is allotted, without addressing the fundamental causes of the problem, it will:

- Be repeated.
- Serve to back up the perception that cells do not work in Alan Group.

There have been difficulties in the introduction of cells into Alan Group. Problems originating from scepticism will only be really solved by proving the success of cellularisation. The perception that "cells do not work," arising from the difficulties that occurred because of a design error, might be even more difficult to overcome if left unchallenged and unresolved.

The Operation of New Practices

Major rework required on the job, as a result of the design fault, was an unexpected outcome. This particular job had been chosen because it was simple in comparison to the majority of the work they undertake. Possibly because it was considered to be simple, it was assumed that design errors were inconceivable. The cell team was understandably disappointed to find that all of its hard work, in producing the tool to tight time estimates, came to nothing because of a problem that was outside of its control. There is some bitterness felt toward the designer, and the issue was confronted.

A review meeting was planned and set to take place after the job had successfully been completed. Its purpose was to resolve the issues arising. The interviews conducted with cell members indicate agreement on the major point: that the designer should have been in the cell from the start. There was some difference of opinion as to how the problems of design faults are tackled. The two schools of thought were:

1. Have the design reviewed by a toolmaker and/or fitter prior to launching it onto the shop floor. They would not pick up all the errors, but since there isn't the time to get the designs fully checked, they would at least be able to correct the most obvious problems.

   > It's much better to spend an hour at the beginning of it, because if there are any mistakes on the job and they aren't picked up until the end, the job is already late at that stage. (designer)

2. Develop a comprehensive feedback channel to the designers, so that errors made on the job will not be made again.

> Obvious problems, design faults or things which have actually physically changed, usually get marked on the drawings and get back. But a lot of things don't. (designer)

It was expected that at this meeting, the cell will suggest a number of refinements to the cell structure. These will help to form the template for subsequent cells. The cellularisation of Alan Group is still in the initial stages: there has been no stable state reached, although a feedback loop in the form of a review meeting at the end of the cell is in place.

Evaluation of the degree of success of the cell would depend greatly upon who was asked. Those people outside of the cell could come to the conclusion that the project was less than a resounding success:

- There were problems when the tool was tested.
- There has been a significant amount of rework.
- There has been criticism of individuals, from people within the team, which might be seen as scapegoating to those not directly involved.

Cell members found the cell to be a good motivator:

> Giving somebody ownership of an idea, helping them, encourage them to get on and do it, they have a goal. It's great. I like that idea. (cell member)

There is also a willingness to take part in future cells:

> I've enjoyed it . . . To generate that throughout the firm, it gives people that little bit of responsibility that they did not have before. Rather than being just an operator on a machine, it does generate a bit more interest. (cell member)

Virtual Cell Review Meeting

When the tool had been completed, and rework virtually finished, the cell members held an end-of-project meeting to:

- Identify the problems encountered by individuals.
- Identify successes during the project.
- Devise a list of recommended actions for solving the problems encountered.

This meeting used external guidance from The CIM Institute, Cranfield University, on its process of working. All the cell members were invited to the meeting, along with others who had expressed an interest in attending. Among these were the designers of the tool, and the fitter who had been working with the tool in the mould shop.

Problems were initially brainstormed and formed a list that was visible to all participants. The problems were discussed in some detail, and suggested actions were put forward by various individuals.

Outputs from the meeting were in the form of three lists:

- *Stops.* Actions and practices that hindered the work of the cell and should therefore be discontinued.
- *Starts.* Actions that the cell believes would have helped them attain their objective, and that they would like to see started.
- *Continues.* Actions and practices that the cell found useful and helpful and that they believe should be continued.

Main problems identified by the cell were:

- The initial cell meeting was held too late, drawings had already been finalised, and not everyone who would be involved had been invited.

- The cell members were not aware of some important information from the customer, regarding technical difficulties they might face.
- With the need for early planning, problems can arise due to the large number of jobs, which management needs to consider simultaneously.
- Some major decisions were taken out of the hands of the cell.
- In estimating the time to do a job, no allowance is made for any difficulties that may be encountered.
- Inflexible values of estimated working hours at each process might hinder the smooth progress of the tool.
- There is some conflict between sections, which results in a breakdown in communications, and individuals passing the buck when decisions need to be made.
- Trying to cut corners at an early stage leads to more time being spent in total.

Main improvements suggested were:

- The initial cell meeting needs to be held much earlier in the process, with all cell members present, including someone from the mould shop.
- Rather than leave all of the important technical decisions to management, they should be made by the cell as a whole, and discussed with management.
- There is a need for a more flexible attitude throughout the production of the tool, and there should be a willingness to listen to ideas that might prove beneficial.
- More time needs to be allowed at the initial planning stage, where discussions within the cell may save time and money later in the process.
- There needs to be an allowance in the time estimates for some rework and adjustment, which are almost inevitable when producing such high precision tooling.
- Cell members need to be supportive of their team mates and be open to constructive criticism as individuals.

Plus points were mentioned by cell members, the main ones of which were:

- The hours spent in the initial production of the tool were within budget, and the tool was finished by the due date.
- "The few problems which we came across, we solved together and with better results."
- There was greater cooperation, and a real willingness to work as a team.
- Working as a cell, the members found that their personal interest had increased, and that involvement extended to cover the whole production process.

Conclusion

The virtual cell-based organisational development pilot at Alan Group primarily served as a test-bed for the empowerment process idea. Lessons that the Company learned are:

- The Alan Group is atypical of companies that introduce cellularisation. They are not an assembly operation, they do not have multiple batch sizes, and they do not have product families that would justify physical cells. This does not mean that special virtual cells are inappropriate to the Company, but it does mean that issues need to be confronted and addressed through a clear process.
- The work force needs more education about the idea of organisational development via cells and how they are supposed to work. This could serve to dispel any feelings of mistrust, or any misunderstanding there may be about why cells are being implemented.
- Section leaders might lose from cellularisation; it removes some of their authority. The question of what exactly their role will be needs to be addressed. They are a vital resource to the Company, especially in enabling growth through their expertise.

- Cells have delivered organisational development. Those benefits identified by the cell members include:
  - Greater responsibility.
  - Increased motivation.
  - More "ownership" of the project.
  - Team spirit.
  - Sense of achievement.
  - Job satisfaction and enjoyment.

  By increasing the involvement and ownership felt by the cell members, the resulting positive attitude benefits delivery performance on other jobs, as well as the particular cell order.

- There needs to be a recognition of the need for flexibility in the design and implementation of cells.

  > . . . Some of the management have looked into these cells, and they have read one book on it, got this one idea of it. I don't think they realise that you should tailor the cell to the way we work a little bit, as well as trying to make our work fit this one cellular system. They are trying to stick to the letter of the law, and you need a bit more flexibility. They should go and see the way other firms work it. (cell member)

- Cell members suggested a number of possible solutions to the problems they encountered during this project. They also identified possible improvements to the cell structure as it currently stands. Team members understand cells within the Alan Group; they are the best people to design the framework of operation for the next phase in cell implementation.

- The cell served to highlight a problem within the Company by focusing attention on shortcomings in the design process. Responsibility for the order had been given to a group of people, and when an error was detected, they wanted to know what had gone wrong. In the normal mode of working, no individual has the overall responsibility for a particular order, so there is nobody to ask questions when something goes awry. If these difficulties are not fully investigated, they may be repeated.

Following the pilot the cell leader wrote a report and presented it to the Board of Directors. This direct data capture of ideas from the cell members influenced the future working of AMT in the Alan Group. It was made possible by the organisational development achieved during the period of the case study. The tremendous potential business performance improvements available through this organisational change were directly illustrated by this single action.

In 1998 the Company has significantly advanced its strategy of becoming a World Class, worldwide supplier to international players. A key support element in this process has been the further adoption of the cell-based product system described.

The Company is approaching the 21st century with confidence. Global operation is being achieved and staff development needed to support the growth is being sustained through a widening of the cell-based operation to all aspects of the business. According to Alan Mason it's just common sense!

3
A CASE STUDY OF THE IMPLEMENTATION AND MANAGEMENT OF SUPPLY CHAIN MANAGEMENT AT BECTON DICKINSON[1]

Supply Chain Management (SCM)

Recent developments in computer technology in the field of materials handling and communication (e.g., optical scanning, electronic data interchange [EDI], microcomputers) have given rise to an entirely new era in logistics management in many industries. Point of sale transaction processing, for example, through optical scanning of bar-coded product, along with computer networking are enabling fast and efficient electronic data handling of material movement and inventory records from retailers to distributors to manufacturers. This capability has brought about the need to redesign logistics management systems and associated software in order to fully harness the benefits this new hardware offers. This case study describes the implementation of the supply chain management (SCM) elements of distribution requirements planning (DRP) and continuous replenishment process (CRP) at Becton Dickinson. One of the goals of supply chain management (SCM) is to move beyond company boundaries to integrate business processes between successive members of a supply chain. The benefits include drastic reduction in required inventories, shorter cycle times, and lower distribution costs to each member of a given set of industries who interact on a customer–supplier basis.

Becton Dickinson: Background

Becton Dickinson is a major supplier to the health care industry. Table 1 provides a brief overview of the sales and profits over the five-year period (1990–1994).

End users of their products include physicians, hospital clinics and laboratories, public health laboratories, blood banks, and university and government research institutions.

Becton Dickinson has divided its business into two major business *segments,* each accounting for roughly one-half of total revenues: diagnostic systems, and medical supplies and devices. Products in the **diagnostic systems segment** are further divided into two *sectors*: infectious disease diagnostics and cellular analysis diagnostics. Diagnostic sector products focus on providing timely and accurate diagnostic information to target the use of drugs and other therapy in the treatment of infectious disease and in the analysis and control of cell functions. Typical products

[1]This case was developed for use in classroom discussion and is not intended to necessarily illustrate appropriate or inappropriate management practices. The case author was John J. Kanet, Clemson University, 1996. The funding for this case production was provided by the Australian federal government's Department of Industry, Science and Resources. The author wishes to thank Mr. Joe Bakunas, Ms. Judy Zarra, and Mr. Jeff Gora of Becton Dickinson for their cooperation in assembling the information pertinent to this case study. Mr. Bakunas was the key contact person at Becton Dickinson and it is largely his thoughts and perspectives that are chronicled here. Thanks are also extended to Mr. Devar Burbage of Manugistics. It was his suggestion to develop the case study as presented in its present form and it was he who suggested Becton Dickinson as a prime example for outlining the implementation of DRP/CRP technology. Thanks go also to Ms. Carol Ann Hardy and Ms. Kristan De La Rosa of Manugistics for their cooperation in providing background materials on Manugistics and supply chain management technology as well as providing the initial contact to Becton Dickinson management.

TABLE 1   Becton Dickinson Sales and Profit for the Period 1990–1994
(millions of dollars)

	1994	1993	1992	1991	1990
Revenues	2,559	2,465	2,365	2,172	2,013
Net Income	227.1	212.8	200.8	189.8	182.3

Source: Becton Dickinson 1994 Annual Report.

include a variety of devices for blood and cell analysis, including blood sample collection and automated culturing systems, cell sorters and analyzers, and cell image analysis systems.

The second major business segment, **medical supplies and devices,** is also divided into two sectors: technique products and drug delivery. Products from these business sectors focus on facilitating safe intravenous delivery of medication and specialty surgical equipment. This business segment contains over 1,000 active inventory items, selling millions of units with unit prices ranging from $0.12 (for disposable syringes) to $50 (for wall-mounted used syringe collector units). Table 2 provides a summary of the latest three years of operation for Becton Dickinson's two major business segments.

The market for Becton Dickinson's products is worldwide with somewhat over half of corporate sales going to U.S. markets and the remaining portion abroad.

Factors Setting the Context of Change

External Influences

The Call for Total Quality.   Within the medical supply industry Becton Dickinson is the clear leader for the quality and technical superiority of its products. But in the early 1990, as the health industry continued to change, Becton Dickinson began to realize that the concept of quality goes far beyond technical product characteristics and specifications. Total quality encompasses product delivery and customer service as well. Technical superiority was giving rise to a type of complacency at Becton Dickinson. Listening to customers revealed that although Becton Dickinson's products were deemed technically superior, their total customer satisfaction was wanting in the area of timely delivery of the right mix of product to the marketplace.

TABLE 2   Summary of Operations by Business Segment for 1992–1994
(millions of dollars)

	1994	1993	1992
Segment Revenues:			
Diagnostic systems	1,138	1,106	1,050
Medical supplies and devices	1,421	1,360	1,316
Segment Operating Income:			
Diagnostic systems	111.0	111.5	130.7
Medical supplies and devices	274.5	228.3	246.1

Source: Becton Dickinson 1994 Annual Report.

The Development of Supply Chain Management Systems.   Outside the medical supply industry a revolution has been underway in logistics management systems development. Integrated decision support systems where a single demand plan drives inventory, distribution, and production plans for each member of an industry supply chain have already been successfully implemented in a number of industries (e.g., over-the-counter drug, grocery, and apparel). Such systems link historical sales figures, market intelligence, and new customer orders to create a statement of total product demand, which is used to drive all distribution and production decisions. One of the first industries to adapt in this way has been the U.S. grocery industry. Here the clear trend is toward intracompany integrated supply management systems, which serve to squeeze the response time throughout the distribution chain. In a study conducted by Mercer Management Consulting Co.,[2] four broad initiatives that improve inventory and communication systems, distribution operations, organizational management, and performance measurement were identified. Table 3 summarizes their findings for the grocery industry.

The food industry among others has been responding to the call from the market for more efficient consumer response (ECR). Efficient Health Care Customer Response (EHCR) was quickly becoming the "industry version" of this swelling trend. Becton Dickinson, along with other key manufacturers, in conjunction with the industry's distribution association, was supporting this movement.

Internal Influences

Becton Dickinson's Distribution Network.   The distribution of Becton Dickinson products follows a three-step process.[3] Finished products first flow from manufacturing plants to company-owned warehouses, then to medical supply distributors, and finally to end users (typically hospitals, laboratories, and physicians). Customer replenishment orders flow in the opposite direction, emanating first from the end user and culminating at the manufacturing plant after first going through consolidation at the distributor, and then the company warehouse. The end result is that the manufacturing plants are two steps removed from the ultimate customer, causing the information they receive about end customers to be delayed.

A Heritage of Innovation and Quality.   From the time of its founding in 1897, the name Becton-Dickinson has always been associated with high quality medical products. Their reputation for innovation in health care products dates back to these early years of the company with their development and sale of fever thermometers and hypodermic units. During World War I, the company developed high quality all-glass syringes, representing a significant improvement over the previous all-metal design. Becton Dickinson also developed the ACE™ brand bandage, originally identified as an acronym for "all cotton elastic." Since the early part of this century the company has continuously developed numerous inventions that have dramatically improved the quality of health care. They were the first to develop an accurate instrument to measure blood pressure and to modernise the stethoscope, and during World War II they produced the first glass syringe with interchangeable parts. Their development of the disposable hypodermic syringe and needle in 1961 marked a major breakthrough for the company. The needle had to be permanently bonded to the syringe and along with the plastic barrels had to be manufactured in extremely large volumes. The large capital investment required that the company go public and in 1963 the company became listed on the New York Stock Exchange. Sales of this single product helped skyrocket the company to its present size of over $2.5 billion sales, and some 20,000 employees worldwide.

---

[2]"New Ways to Take Costs Out of the Retail Food Pipeline," a study conducted for the Coca-Cola™ Retailing Research Council by Mercer Management Consulting, Atlanta, GA, 1995.

[3]This is the base case. B-D also direct ships to a subset of customers.

TABLE 3   Four Directions for Replenishment Logistics

Directions	Objective	Key Programs
Continuous replenishment inventory	To bring supply more in line with the rhythm of demand.	Automated systems that enable distributors to stock and reorder based on actual consumer demand.
Flow-through distribution systems	To remove wasted space, handling activities, time, and therefore costs out of the process.	New methods that increase the speed of product flow by reducing inventory, relying on timely, coordinated, and dependable transportation and material handling.
Pipeline logistics organizations	To institutionalize key product flow processes, cultivate "total pipeline view," and coordinate operations.	New responsibilities and roles that remove barriers to communication, promote coordination, and provide incentives for aggressive distribution management.
Pipeline performance measures	To establish objective tools for improving management control of processes and motivating appropriate decision making ("You can't manage what you can't measure").	Precise criteria, accurate decision rules, and consistent procedures that support management objectives and take into account total pipeline performance.

Adapted from Mercer Management Consulting, "New Ways to Take Costs Out of the Retail Food Pipeline."

Recognition of the Need to Change

External Drivers

The Threat.   For the last several decades Becton Dickinson has been in the enviable position as market leader in its industry. This has been largely due to its focus on product innovation and quality. Over the last several years, however, new pressures have developed. The modern concept of total quality is a more broadly based concept, expanded beyond simply innovation and quality of the physical product and its design. The word "quality" is now generally accepted to include all utility that a customer perceives. Quality of customer service in terms of the utility of delivery timeliness and required inventory investment has become a major issue in the health care industry. Along with the new emphasis on quality of service, the emergence of so-called "group purchasing organizations" (GPOs) has had a major effect on the industry. With GPOs, a group of customers pool their buying power in order to strengthen their negotiating position.

These factors have brought about a major re-thinking on the part of Becton Dickinson's management to totally review and revise its logistics systems and organization. Although direct competitors were no better in this regard, management became increasingly convinced that unless they acted first, someone else surely would. Competition, in terms of logistics efficiency, was perceived to come from somewhere outside the industry (e.g., through a firm excelling in distribution expertise who would purchase a medical supply company). It was from these pockets of excellence (not necessarily within its own industry) that Becton Dickinson benchmarked itself against.

Internal Drivers

Organizational Inefficiencies.   The existing organizations and systems in place at Becton Dickinson were organized according to product lines with several divisions often selling and distributing product to the same set or subset of customers. Because of differing brand names, end customers were often unaware that a division of Becton Dickinson had responsibility for servicing a particular product. There was a need, in the words of Mr. Joe Bakunas, manager of Logistics and

Supply Chain Management at Becton Dickinson's Drug Delivery Systems division, "to present one face to the customer." The existing divisional organization further caused duplication of effort in terms of demand planning, deployment, order fulfillment, and transportation. Separately running forecasting models were in use by the divisions to plan product requirements.

This disjointed organizational approach to logistics management was also proving to be costly in terms of unnecessarily larger numbers of inventory transactions. For example, rather than sending one consolidated purchase order to replenish all Becton Dickinson products, a distributor would have to place separate orders to each of the responsible Becton Dickinson divisions. In the field of health care, the public outcry for cost containment was exerting great pressure on hospitals and other medical service deliverers to become more efficient in their operation. In the words of Becton Dickinson's chairman, Mr. Clateo Castellini, "The progress and direction of health care reform may be different from market to market, but there is one fundamental characteristic that is the driving force in all our markets: health care reform is increasing the pressure on our customers to raise the quality of patient care and lower the total cost of health care delivery."[4] Since Becton Dickinson's sales growth is based primarily on volume and not price and its profit growth depends more on productivity, not price, the emphasis on logistics management was rife with opportunity to help improve overall corporate performance.

Technological Inefficiencies.   The software systems in place to monitor and manage the distribution process from manufacturing plant to warehouse, and from warehouse to distributor, were not integrated and added to the supply chain inefficiency. The software systems were separate and not connected to one another (if they existed at all). Demand visibility at the production sites (the manufacturing plants) was only so far as the warehouses. When a warehouse placed an order on a plant for a given product there was no way of discerning whether the order was in response to an end customer's urgent request or simply to replenish warehouse safety stock levels; both carried the same priority. Moreover, the distribution process gave rise to situations where the manufacturing plants would either have to respond unnecessarily or carry more inventory to compensate for the lack of coordination between warehouse facilities. One warehouse might unnecessarily place an urgent replenishment order on the manufacturing plant when in fact there was already enough product existing at other locations within the distribution system. There was a clear need for a unified software systems approach to more closely link Becton Dickinson's production facilities with end customer demand.

Context and Substance of Change

The Development of a Technology Strategy.   Given the clear customer call for total quality of product (including service), the well-defined trend in new supply chain management systems developments in other industries, the looming external threat that the competition would act first, the known strengths (Becton Dickinson's market lead in product quality and technical superiority), and the identified weaknesses (the organizational and technically deficient logistics management), a technology strategy evolved. The cornerstone of this strategy was to develop a system (comprised of an organization, software, hardware, and procedures) for:

- Communicating quickly and efficiently with distributors.
- Keeping pace with world class competition.
- Formalizing the planning and inventory management process.
- Responding efficiently to customer demand and inventory management.

---

[4]Becton Dickinson 1994 Annual Report, p. 2.

To achieve these goals two key ingredients were identified: the founding of a new organizational unit, the Supply Chain Services Division (BDSCS), and the development and installation of a new companywide logistics planning system.

Organizational Change: The New Division.   The first part of the new strategy, the forming of Becton Dickinson's Supply Chain Services Division, served as an organizational consolidation, allowing all order processing from customers to be accomplished by a single divisional unit—allowing Becton Dickinson "to present one face to the customer." The mission statement for this new division is straightforward: "to be a leader in providing quality services and promoting supply chain integration with all of Becton Dickinson's distributors/channel partners and shared customers."[5] The scope of responsibilities for BDSCS includes the functions of customer service, traffic and transportation, credit/accounts receivable, logistics planning, EDI, and information systems management.

Technological Change: Supply Chain Management Integration Software.   The essence of the technological change was to implement an integrated logistics planning system, moving responsibility for logistics planning back up the supply chain to BDSCS, where the information can be consolidated. This change enables the scope of control for BDSCS to span from procurement to production. To accomplish this the new system (comprised of software packages and management procedures) provided several new features, including:

1. Distribution requirements planning (DRP) to enable forecasting of individual product demand, efficient allocation and deployment of existing stocks between warehouses, as well as inventory planning software for calculating order points and appropriate safety stock levels.

2. Electronic data interchange (EDI) to allow electronic communication of supply and demand transactions between Becton Dickinson and its network of distributors.

3. Order management and shipment consolidation capability, linked via EDI to allow efficient creation and handling of new orders as well as cost-efficient shipments to distribution centers.

The Process of Transition

Steering Committee and Project Team Formation.   In order to facilitate the transition to the new system, Becton Dickinson employed a cross-functional team approach. A DRP steering committee and a DRP implementation team were established. The steering committee was comprised of managers from each of Becton Dickinson's major product divisions, with a mix of representation from both staff and line responsibility (e.g., representatives from information technology, as well as sales, customer service, inventory planning). The objectives of this committee were to keep the project on a timely schedule, and to provide support, guidance, and direction to the implementation team.

The implementation team, also a cross-functional group comprised of individuals from each product division, had direct responsibility for designing the overall system, selecting the appropriate software, and putting the system into operation. After software selection was completed, representatives from the chosen software vendor (Manugistics) were added to the membership of the implementation team.

---

[5]Notes from Becton Dickinson DRP Steering Committee Meeting, December 5, 1995.

Members of the implementation team were in fact either leaders or members of one or more of seven different project teams, each with very specific responsibilities. The objectives of each of these teams are briefly summarized below.

Team #1: Implement demand management (DM)/distribution requirements planning (DRP) *Team objectives:* To implement the DRP and demand management capability with the Drug Delivery Division as a pilot using the Manugistics software on a UNIX/RS6000 client-server platform. At the completion of this pilot all necessary processes will be designed and interfaces completed to enable Becton Dickinson to expand DRP to all divisions.	**Team #2: Implement continuous replenishment process (CRP)** *Team objectives:* To design and implement the concepts of vendor managed inventory replenishment, including the appropriate EDI transactions to manage the business with major distributors. Deploy this capability with one distributor using the IBM RS/6000 Manugistics platform. This milestone is complete when Becton Dickinson has the capability to expand continuous replenishment to additional distributors and divisions.
Team #3: Design and implement DM, DRP, and CRP system interfaces *Team objectives:* To design and implement the necessary systems interfaces to subsidiary software systems such as EDI and Becton Dickinson's legacy tracking system or new subsystems to drive DM, DRP, and CRP using Manugistics on the IBM RS/6000 platform according to the published timeline.	**Team #4: Install the UNIX/Oracle client-server platform** *Team objectives:* To install the IBM RS/6000 and Oracle database management system in workable development and production environments. Install the UNIX Manugistics application, including user enrollment. Establish access via client PCs configured with necessary software to enable both local and remote access, query/reporting tool execution. Identify appropriate communications requirements and put into place. Ensure that adequate AS/400 hardware capability exists or act to have it established.
Team #5: Develop training and roll out to other divisions *Team objectives:* To publish formal procedures that conform to ISO/9000 requirements and document processes being implemented. The primary source document will be the Manugistics Procedure Packs customized to define Becton Dickinson's DRP/ CRP system. Develop ancillary documentation, including a project plan and roll out training schedule, training, and presentation materials.	**Team #6: Implement a management database** *Team objectives:* To develop a database containing management level reporting information in a relational database SQL environment. This database should be able to be accessed by the reporting tool chosen for the Manugistics application. Additionally, it should become the focal point for all reporting data.

Team #7: Develop metrics
Team objectives: To develop service performance measurements of the effectiveness of the DRP platform enabling the system to be compared with "best in class" or "world class" performance. This includes monitoring the performance standards set by our trading partners as well as results achieved by the various Becton Dickinson divisions and manufacturing plants. To utilize existing measurement systems wherever possible and to create new measurements where necessary focusing on the accomplishments and effectiveness of BDSCS. To design index-type metrics for executive feedback that are motivational as well as informational by creating a foundation for recognition and reward systems.

The Implementation

Piloting First in Single Division.   The new DRP/CRP system at Becton Dickinson was designed and intended to serve all production divisions within the company. The implementation and debugging of the software system, however, was first carried out in a single division. The Drug Delivery Division was chosen deliberately for this pilot process for good reason. This division serves a variety of different market channels with a large array of product offerings. If the system worked in this division with its variety of transaction types it would facilitate rollout to the remaining divisions. But even on a more micro level, the system was first planned for piloting with a single delivery partner for the division. This partner was chosen because of its already existing technical capabilities, and its experience in CRP and the Manugistics software product.

A Focus on the Business Result.   The phrase "piloting the business process" carries significantly more meaning than simply assuring that the software works as intended. What must be assured is that the technology helps produce the intended *business* result. In the case of Becton Dickinson and their implementation of Manugistics DRP/CRP software this means that the new system (comprised of software, people, and work procedures) accomplishes the objective of reducing and streamlining the logistics process between Becton Dickinson and its distributors. To assure this focus on business results, Becton Dickinson has employed a method referred to as "script" or "user test plan process" to create realistic scenarios for testing the new system.

Issues Surrounding the Change

The Effects of the Reorganization.   The formation of the new BDSCS division has given rise to a number of organizational issues. The primary task of the division, that of providing logistics services to Becton Dickinson's entire customer base, represents a consolidation of those tasks that were formerly divided and provided separately to customers by the different product divisions. Consequently, this has involved budget reallocations and transfers of people formerly from each of the existing divisions. The existing product division managers are now in a position in concert with the new BDSCS to provide logistics services that meet emerging customer needs.

Acceptance.   Naturally, this reorganization is not without its share of organizational issues. Predictably, product division managers are asking: "What is the real cost to my division?" "Can we depend on the new BDSCS to service our customers?" "Are the benefits of the change worth the effort?" "Are we getting our money's worth out of this change?"

   In anticipation of these problems, a major task of the DRP steering committee is education— education of the entire Becton Dickinson organization of the benefits of the change, and importantly, this educational process is planned to be ongoing. But on a more fundamental level, the decision to use an extensive cross-functional team approach to introduce the new system was largely motivated to head off these types of political problems.

Operation of New Practices

Performance Measures.   One of the most interesting issues with respect to logistics management is in the area of performance measurement. In order to measure the performance of its DRP/CRP system, Becton Dickinson plans on using a variety of related indicators. An obvious measure, which has direct implication to bottom-line profits, is system inventory. Aside from the obvious financial benefits of lower inventory investment, keeping inventory to lean levels assures efficient allocation of production to the right products (the ones the customers want). Since the new

DRP/CRP system tracks inventory at various points along the supply chain, it is possible to predict with greater accuracy the upcoming production requirements, allowing more stability in the production planning process. In addition to various measures of inventory performance, Becton Dickinson will track total logistic cycle times (from time to end customer order all the way through to delivery of product to his doorstep). This is extremely important to this industry as it is a direct measure of customer service, i.e., the firm's ability to respond to a given customer order.

Conclusions

The experience of Becton Dickinson's implementation process for DRP/CRP has led to the development of the EDI: computer-to-computer transmission of business information. EDI is the driving force for supply chain efficiency at Becton Dickinson. It has been at the forefront of providing support and commitment to industry standards in all forms of electronic commerce and has consequently provided a higher level of customer service and assisted its channel partners in becoming more efficient.

4
BIOTECNOL LDA PHARMACEUTICAL: A CASE STUDY[1]

The Biopharmaceutical Market for Therapeutic Proteins

The biopharmaceutical industry specializes in studying mechanisms of diseases and finding and developing new drugs for their treatment. The rate of progress of these developments in medicine has been enormous. This has enabled the characterization of pathological states and diseases, which subsequently have led to the development of certain drugs aimed at combating previously untreatable diseases. We have seen in the 1980s the appearance of the first drugs produced using recombinant DNA technology.

Genes specifying the synthesis of human proteins—proteins once hardly accessible because of their scarcity or instability—could be cloned, amplified, and expressed in host microorganisms. Proteins like insulin and human growth hormone were the first examples of this successful and profitable technology. Soon, this new industry was able to provide other therapeutic proteins (tissue plasminogen activators, interleukins, interferons, and erythropoietin) that had also been almost impossible to obtain by isolation procedures.

These biopharmaceutical agents were shown to offer effective potential treatments for acute and chronic clinical diseases like diabetes, cancer, anemia, hemophilia, AIDS, and hepatitis B infection. Due to the growth pattern of the world's population, drugs for treating these types of diseases offer high gross margins and a very high return-on-investment, compared with conventional pharmaceuticals. The main reasons are the long commercial patent life (15–20 years) and higher selling prices ($400–$2,500,000/gm) of the biopharmaceutical drugs. These costs are driven by the fact that biopharmaceuticals are more potent, require less drug mass, and are usually employed for treating diseases where costs of alternative therapies are higher or do not exist. A recent study estimated that an average of 5–8 novel proteins will become available each year in the future. In the early 1990s, biopharmaceuticals produced by rDNA technology accounted for $1 billion worldwide. In 2003 the total pharmaceutical market is expected to reach $250 billion worldwide and recombinant proteins are expected to account for at least 10 percent of this market. This indicates that the market for biopharmaceutical recombinant proteins will grow significantly.

The forecast of the growth trend of the biopharmaceutical industry is based on the increasing demand for complex and selective therapeutics to treat AIDS, autoimmune diseases, Alzheimer's disease, cancer, and anemia, to name just a few examples. Although the biopharmaceutical business started virtually in the U.S. during the 1980s, which set the example for an increasingly strong home market, the access to public financing markets in Europe has stimulated the development of new start-ups in biotechnology-based industries elsewhere. In addition, the regulatory processes for the production of biopharmaceutical drugs in Europe have recently been reviewed.

---

[1]This case was prepared by Dr. Michael Bommer, professor of management at Clarkson University, Potsdam, NY, 13699, while a Fulbright-FLAD Visiting Professor at Instituto Superior Tecnico (IST), Lisbon, Portugal, in collaboration with Dr. Manuel V. Heitor, professor and chair, Department of Mechanical Engineering at IST, Dr. Conceicao Vedovello, researcher at IST, and Dr. Pedro de Noronha Pissarra, president and founder of BIOTECNOL.

Note: All financial data are expressed in Euro dollars and some data have been altered to protect the financial confidentiality of the company.

In response to a White Paper in 1994, the European Commission reviewed regulatory guidelines in order to lighten the regulatory load of directives concerning contained use and the deliberate release of genetically modified organisms (GMOs), classification of GMOs, and requirements for administration, notification, and consent of use thereof. Also many European governments have abandoned previously obstructionist attitudes, replacing them with supportive and consistent legislation favoring biotechnological-based processes. Finally, Europe has a large and aging population, and as such it represents an enormous potential market for biotechnology-based products.

The Generic Drug Industry and Market

In the mid-1980s, market forces favouring the use of generic drugs in the United States began a trend that has continued to gain strength into the present and is expected to continue in the future. Such philosophy has since then extended to other countries in the world, including Japan and European countries.

Newly discovered drugs are patented, resulting in exclusive rights to the patentee for the lifetime of the patent. Following patent expiry, other companies are free to replicate these drugs and manufacture "generic" versions without the burden and expense of initial research and development. These companies must still develop the technology necessary to manufacture the drugs, as well as apply for and obtain regulatory certification for the process and generic product.

The passage of the 1984 Waxman-Hatch Act in the U.S. simplified the generic drug approval process and led to a dramatic increase in the number of abbreviated new drug applications (ANDA) approvals. The large number of major branded drugs coming off-patent during this time period added to the increase in availability of generics.

In the early 1990s, heightened pressure to control health care costs all over the world further added to the momentum of the generic drug industry. As the influence of managed care increased and the threat of national health care reform intensified, lowering the cost of drugs became a priority.

The use of generic substitution, which many practitioners had previously viewed with skepticism, began to be widely accepted. The influx of generics into a marketplace that was seeking low-cost alternatives led to an impressive rise in the use of generic drug products. The major factors responsible for the growth of the generic drug industry are as follows:

- Over the 1995 to 2005 period, more than 65 leading drugs lose patent protection in the United States, Japan, and Europe. These drugs have, in the U.S. alone, sales totaling more than $22.5 billion per year, leaving a substantial portion of the pharmaceutical market open to generic competition.
- The growing influence of managed care and the availability of generic versions of some of the most popular drugs will sharply increase both generic and therapeutic substitutions. It is estimated that 60 percent of all new prescriptions dispensed in the U.S. alone will be generics by 2000.
- Generic penetration of new markets will be deep and swift. In most cases, generics will gain up to 75 percent of the market for the product within the first few months of generic competition. At the same time, price differentials between generic and off-patent branded drugs will erode, leading to declining profits.

As these forces continue to act on the U.S. and major worldwide markets, generic drug use will continue to increase rapidly.

Estimated Sales of U.S. and European Generic Pharmaceutical Market from 1995 to 2005 ($ millions)

	1995	*2000*	*2005*
U.S. Generic Drug Market	7,620	14,260	20,089
European Generic Drug Market	4,000	5,877	8,243

No significant generic market currently exists in Asia, Africa, and South America. These countries have limited patent protection laws and multiple copies of drugs are sold under different brand names. A sizeable generic market may emerge after 2005 in these countries after the transition period for the enforcement of GATT patent laws expires.

Biotechnology drugs require extensive technology and expensive manufacturing and fermentation facilities that are not familiar to generic drug companies. These technological and production barriers will limit the competition to few companies with major resources to efficiently manufacture biotechnology drugs. In the challenging pharmaceutical environment, research-based pharmaceutical companies will try to protect the market share of drugs losing patent protection to remain competitive.

There is a direct linear relationship between sales/earnings growth and the number of new ANDA drug approvals. As more than 65 major drugs with a value of $22.5 billion lose patent protection between 1995 and 2005, generic drug companies will need to develop a continuous pipeline of new products to generate sales growth. A full pipeline will also provide a generic company with a broad product portfolio that it can leverage to generate sales from hospitals and managed care organisations. In such a portfolio biotechnology generics should be included as their price is significantly higher than most chemically produced products obtained by fermentation.

The timing of new drug approvals is also a key to sales and earnings growth, just like new drug approvals. The first companies to reach the market have the benefit of filling the distributors' pipeline as well as capturing initial sales after patent expiration at much higher price levels than subsequent participants. The discounts for generics in comparison to brand products offered by generic companies to capture market share are a function of the number of generic competitors.

Since all generic products are inherently similar, a major strategy is to lower the price to make the sale. The more the competitors, the higher the price discount. Typically, the first generic products are priced at 30 percent to 40 percent of the price of the brand product. Depending on the number of competitors, the price can drop by as much as 60 percent in the first 12 months and by as much as 80 percent by the end of 24 months. A generic company stands to make a healthy profit if it introduces the generic product soon after the brand product loses patent protection. The generic companies generally look to maintain prices at 15 percent to 25 percent below brand products when price levels have stabilised. The price erosion is likely to end at a price at which the generic makes about 30 percent to 40 percent gross margin.

The Company: BIOTECNOL LDA Pharmaceutical

The company, BIOTECNOL LDA, was founded by Dr. Pedro de Noronha Pissarra, who studied biotechnology as his undergraduate degree. During his PhD, Dr. Pissarra carried out research work at several research institutions in biochemical/metabolic engineering. Dr. Pissarra was the founder and now is the chairman of the Portuguese Bioindustries Association (APBio), a member of The European Bioindustries Association (EuropaBio), and a member of the advisory board of the European Union Biotechnology & Finance Forum.

It was in 1996 while doing postdoctoral work at the Centre for Biological & Chemical Engineering–Instituto Superior Técnico (CEBQ), on metabolic flux analysis of recombinant proteins production, that Dr. Pissarra developed the idea behind BIOTECNOL LDA and its philosophy. The official start-up was in November 1996. Dr. Andrew Kelly joined BIOTECNOL LDA in December 1996. Dr. Kelly has a strong molecular biology background, which complemented Dr. Pissarra's skills.

During the year of 1997 both Pedro de Noronha Pissarra and Andrew Kelly earned the first seed capital for the company by providing consultancy to a Portuguese pharma group. They were responsible for the emergence of rDNA biotechnology at a classic antibiotic company. During that consultancy contract, Pedro de Noronha Pissarra and Andrew Kelly selected and analysed several key patents and evaluated key molecules for production as generic recombinant proteins.

Upon identification of one target molecule, they established contacts with a German company, who already had the mature technology for production of that particular protein. They then established a second consultancy contract with the German company for technology transfer into the Portuguese pharma group. The contract allowed them to raise enough money to set up their company at a well-established modern science park near Lisbon. Throughout the project they acquired significant know-how and experience in the field for strengthening BIOTECNOL LDA's position.

In addition, Pedro de Noronha Pissarra and Andrew Kelly applied for funding from Agência da Inovação under the aegis of the PRAXIS XXI program—a research consortium between universities and SMEs [small- and medium-sized enterprises]. For that purpose, BIOTECNOL LDA (as project leader) established a consortium contract with the Centre for Biological & Chemical Engineering–Instituto Superior Técnico (CEBQ) and the Biological Engineering Department of the Universidade do Minho. The project was partially funded and the consortium received $355,000 for research and development in late 1997. BIOTECNOL LDA was making the most out of its idea by using laboratory space at the university and having access to academic experts in the field.

The initial organization of BIOTECNOL was a small team, consisting of enthusiastic but inexperienced young scientists. The team did a tremendous job in setting up the company core strategy, acquisition of funds for R & D, strategic partners, development of ideas, and maturing its market and orientation. BIOTECNOL LDA is now in the process of identifying additional personnel to augment the scientific development-based team, with multidisciplinary backgrounds that complement each other. The company also recognizes the need to establish a management team parallel to the R & D efforts. Without sound managerial skills a company, despite its technology, will not have the capacity for taking its technology to the market in the first place.

BIOTECNOL LDA Pharmaceutical Strategy

In such an emerging field, most companies were formed by academic people spawning out from the university scenario. As academics, they started from pure science, then planned to develop and produce expansive, albeit profitable, products. Although potentially extremely profitable, this approach is associated with huge amounts of investment. BIOTECNOL LDA had a different philosophy for entering the market according to Dr. Pissarra: "We identify the market niche, and quantify the demand for specific products. Then, based on the market needs we develop the technology for producing a specific product, according to the demand, and in order to meet the respective needs."

The primary mission of BIOTECNOL is to provide generic companies, already with a marketing structure in place, with the biotechnology know-how that will allow them to diversify their activity within the generic market. BIOTECNOL LDA aims at gaining immediate access to the market by forging a marketing alliance initially with a generics firm, and then building a broad strategic alliance with additional partners. This project is initially targeted for Portuguese and European pharmaceutical companies, who are aiming at entering the generic biotechnology markets and do not have the necessary in-house expertise.

The advantage of this strategy is that a research-based company like BIOTECNOL LDA can quickly become a major player in the generic drug market without making a significant investment. Four main recombinant human proteins that will come out of patent between 2001–2006 have been targeted. Such an approach identifies BIOTECHNOL as a firm:

1. In the technology development business, demonstrating pilot and preindustrial scale viability of the developed technology.

2. That licenses its technology to production and marketing partners in order to complete the "*technology to marketplace*" pipeline.

The firm is *focused* on the development of a competitive and state-of-the-art technology platform viewed as a *vertical* activity. Nevertheless they also believe in diversifying the applications of their bacterial technology. By building a solid platform they will be able to use its technology in other fields (i.e., gene therapy). Such *horizontal* activities (i.e., using their laboratories and know-how for providing services in areas such as plasmids production for gene therapy applications; providing consultancy services in patent analysis and market search, European Medicinal Evaluation Agency (EMEA) registration processes, genotoxicity testing and genotoxicology) could complement and add value to the *vertical* activity (i.e., technology development). For example, another thrust is to develop plasmovirus vector production for use in human cancer gene therapy. The work focuses on the optimization of metabolic and genetic functioning of the host cell used for plasmid-based vector production and subsequent purification. This technology is being developed within a European consortium and subsequently will be taken to phase I clinical trials within the next 24 months. The market for gene therapy, with a focus on human cancer, is expected to grow significantly within the next five years.

Finally, BIOTECNOL also provides consultancy studies concerning drug patents, markets and commercialization opportunities, biotechnology projects management, and organisation. The company has gained substantial experience in evaluating candidate molecules for commercialisation.

Research and development (R & D) costs are at the moment supported by two grants that, in total, make up $350,000 and that were contractually attributed to BIOTECNOL. Other public funding in the total of $50,000 is attributed to BIOTECNOL LDA by the Portuguese government. Over the next two years the aim is to submit at least two world patent applications. This should attract further public funding from the Portuguese government.

The company running costs and R & D projects shared-costs, which are not supported by the research grants, have so far been met by providing consultancy work to both national and international pharmaceutical companies. A revenue of about $150,000 on consultancy services for the year of 1999 is predicted. By the end of year 2000 BIOTECNOL hopes to have its technology ready for licensing and, as such, long-term growth perspectives and activities look promising, as royalties on production technology should then start to accrue.

Barriers to the Market and Competition

The main market barrier is at the level of intellectual property (IP) infringements, namely infringements of product patents. These usually claim complementary DNA sequences, which code for the drugs in question. The only way to surpass such a barrier is to wait for the expiry of the relevant patents. BIOTECNOL LDA has conducted an extensive IP survey on the subject and on the potential candidates. Although it is well established, there is no process of obtaining 100 percent certainty regarding patent infringement. A well-carried-out survey can, however, reduce the risk very substantially. Process patents in this case are not of utter relevance as BIOTECNOL LDA is developing proprietary technology.

To limit market share erosion, the existing pharmaceutical companies that own or have licensed the product patents in question will adopt bold strategies, including entering the generic drug business. This strategy may entail starting a new business, acquiring an existing company, forging marketing or strategic alliances, or becoming a generics distributor. Other strategies for combating generics will include price reductions, product reformulations (it has already happened with hepatitis B vaccines), over-the-counter switches, and moving patients to newer branded drugs. In the end, companies will have to combine strategies, including partnership with traditional generic companies or technology-based companies with innovative processes, to protect minimum levels of market share.

Entering the market with their own product will only be possible in conjunction with a well-established generics company. A broad market penetration relies on successful negotiations with such companies and respective efforts on behalf of such companies. There is currently only one other company, which is located in Germany, that identifies itself as a biotechnology generics company. There are, however, a number of other companies, that, like BIOTECNOL, are working on developing technology for entering the generics market. Given that the potential generics market segment is so large, it should be capable of supporting several players. In the end the threat of other companies will depend upon (a) developing a cost-efficient production process, (b) creating a partnership(s) with a manufacturing, marketing, and distribution firm(s), and (c) how their marketing territories are defined.

The Entry Product of BIOTECNOL LDA—Interferon Alpha

Interferon alpha is considered to be one of biotechnology's most promising weapons for treating hepatitis, cancers, AIDS, and associated conditions. Interferons are lymphokines, chemicals that tell the immune system how to resist infections and inhibit the reproduction of cancerous or infected cells. These interferons are produced in very small quantities in certain cells in the human body, and protect healthy cells from viral infection. Interferon inhibits cells infected with a virus from multiplying, and "alerts" or increases viral resistance in other, unaffected cells.

The plan calls for developing and licensing the basic technology for producing IFN-α commercially as a generic drug. The patent for IFN-α is due to expire in early 2001. It assumes that BIOTECNOL LDA will enter into a strategic collaboration with a pharmaceutical company in late 2000, with the aim of entering the generic market.

The data used for evaluating market potential for this product were obtained from the World Health Organization. The base year for the values is 1996. Projected sales for 2001 should be 25 percent–35 percent higher than the presented figures.

The following estimates and assumptions were developed by BIOTECNOL.

a. Expressed by weight, 1 mg of interferon alpha (IFN-α) contains 200×10^6 units (i.e., 200 million international units (200 MIU)). In biological terms, an international unit is defined as the amount of interferon needed to protect 50 percent of the cells in an indicator culture from lysis by vesicular stomatitis virus. One dose of IFN-α contains 30 MIU.

b. Price per dose of the branded drug is currently $260, which gives a price of $8.67 per MIU.

c. Incidence is considered as the basis for the epidemic calculations. The incidence value given in the table assumes the average of cases reported per year.

d.   Market potential assumes that the treatment would be available to all individuals and that all would respond to treatment. Market potential is calculated by the incidence number and the required amount of product needed per patient. Based upon 1996 prices, it is expected that 50 percent of the conditions will be treated. This results as resources for treating conditions are not as available in many less-developed countries.

Sales Estimation Worldwide per Condition If 100 Percent of the Cases Were Treated with IFN-α per Year Using 1996 Data

Disease	Production for Estimated Market Demand (MIU)	Doses
Hepatitis B	127,187,486	4,239,583
Hepatitis C	108,580,562	3,619,359
Malignant melanoma	180,369,463	6,012,315
Renal carcinoma	36,773,097	1,225,770
AIDS-related kaposi	73,745,431	2,458,180
Total	535,485,339	17,828,450

e.   In the first year of being generic, it is expected that IFN-α price will be 40 percent of the current branded price, but actual sales will increase by 20 percent; in the second year, IFN-α price will be 60 percent of the first year price, but sales will increase by an additional 20 percent; in the third year, IFN-α price will be 70 percent of the second year price, but sales will increase by an additional 10 percent. In subsequent years the price is expected to drop by 10 percent, while sales are expected to increase by 10 percent.

f.   Estimated production costs for the pharmaceutical company producing and marketing the drug are expected to be between $20 and $25 per unit dose.

g.   Prospective market share for the pharmaceutical company is expected to be between 1 percent and 3 percent of the market.

h.   Licensing revenue for BIOTECNOL is expected to be generated at the rate of 6 percent of sales.

New Proposal

The success of modern biotechnology companies depends to some extent on the capacity to integrate several fields (i.e., technology development, engineering, certification, quality control, production, marketing, and distribution). One of the important missing links in many start-up operations is the process of developing protocols and methods to guarantee the quality of both the process and product to the registration authorities (e.g., Food and Drug Administration [FDA] or European Medicinal Evaluation Agency [EMEA]). The problem is usually lack of financing or core expertise. The opportunity now presents itself to form just such an operation.

BIOTECNOL has just identified an opportunity for entering the certification and quality control field via forming a joint venture with a highly reputed Dutch company, with whom BIOTECNOL already has had contractual agreements. The Dutch company is willing to transfer the necessary technology to assist in starting the new company, QualiGene. The new company will perform such activities as development and validation of analytical methods, quality control during production, final product protocol, and handling product registration. The new company would initially operate in the Portuguese market, then after 12 months expand into the European market. The activities would add value by complementing its current activities and at the same time would generate additional revenues. It will also strengthen the core capabilities of BIOTECNOL as the technology developed will be compliant with the regulatory authorities (EMEA and FDA). The manner in which QualiGene fits in with BIOTECNOL appears as Appendix A.

The new company, QualiGene, would be owned 70 percent by BIOTECNOL and 30 percent by the Dutch company. The equity of the Dutch company would be paid by transferring the technology know-how and an initial contract, which the Dutch company already has, to QualiGene. This will result in a break-even revenue scenario for QualiGene for the first year.

By establishing the quality control and certification lab (QualiGene), BIOTECNOL would increase the competitiveness of its structure by (a) having a registration pipeline for its generic products, (b) cashing in on existing contracts, and (c) creating a new area of business at a European level. The lab would gradually evolve toward new areas such as genomics, gene therapy, and proteonics, by targeting the services segments for these activities. Expectations are that this new lab would grow along with the generic biopharmaceutical industry and margins would be in the 30 percent range.

BIOTECNOL will continue to conduct research to obtain technology processing patents for recombinant proteins such as IFN alpha, IFN beta, G-CSF, and gene therapy. These patents will allow BIOTECNOL to license its technology to worldwide pharmaceutical firms. It will also continue to conduct consulting services, but only for projects within the company.

Venture Capital

To accomplish these goals BIOTECNOL needs an infusion of about $4 million capital to help finance its current projects and grow to meet this new challenge. A venture capital firm is willing to invest $4 million in BIOTECNOL in exchange for a percentage of ownership.

It is late on a beautiful autumn day in October 1999. As the sun begins to set over the Atlantic coastline, Pedro ponders the proposal of the venture capital firm. Up until now he has had 100 percent control of all the strategic and operating decisions regarding the direction of the business. Accepting an offer will mean that he will have to share his control and his company with others.

APPENDIX A
ORGANIZATIONAL STRUCTURE

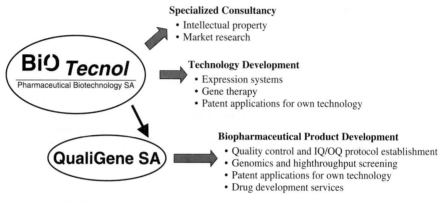

Specialized Consultancy
• Intellectual property
• Market research

Technology Development
• Expression systems
• Gene therapy
• Patent applications for own technology

Biopharmaceutical Product Development
• Quality control and IQ/OQ protocol establishment
• Genomics and highthroughput screening
• Patent applications for own technology
• Drug development services

Source: March 15, 2000.

5

CIG GAS CYLINDERS: A CASE STUDY OF A MANUFACTURING COMPANY'S EXPERIENCE WITH SELF-MANAGED WORK TEAMS (SMWT)[1]

Introduction

This case study explores the "soft" end of advanced manufacturing technology introduced into Australia's leading supplier and manufacturer of high pressure aluminium gas cylinders. Self-managed work teams [SMWT] were introduced in 1991 at CIG Gas Cylinders and over a period of some years have been seen as the organisational arrangement capable of meeting increased international demand for its products and also improved profit performance.

The challenge of attaining global competitiveness required improvements in technology efficiency and related organisational and labour force performance. Reduction in lead times and improved levels of product quality necessitated innovative approaches to plant layout and operations, manufacturing processes, and supplier/vendor management. Coupled with these, production changes were reforms in shopfloor organisation and control, team-based management, common interest incentive programs, and a focus on strategic corporate planning.

The case study traces the genesis of the need for change, the protracted process of preparing the company and its work force for a shift in the "locus of control" implied by SMWT structures. It documents the performance changes compared with targets, and the politics underlying such major organisational restructuring.

Company Background

Commonwealth Industrial Gases (CIG) Pty Ltd was established in 1975. Luxfer Gas Cylinders, a U.K. subsidiary of Alcan, CIG's aluminium supplier, approached CIG Gas wanting to establish a cylinder manufacturing plant in Australia. A 10-year agreement was entered into between the parties where Luxfer would license the technology to CIG for production of the cylinders. The contract covered a 10-year time period and was renewed once.

In 1995, CIG Gas underwent a corporate restructure to become a division of BOC Gases Australia, an international company with diversified gas production interests. This change of ownership placed CIG Gas Cylinders as a minor operation within the total portfolio of BOC Gases worldwide. During the subsequent restructuring program CIG Gas retained the name as CIG for two reasons: to protect the name CIG, and because some customers of CIG were reluctant to buy products from BOC. CIG Gas Cylinders remained an independent profit centre (IPC).

In its "first life," Gas Cylinders supplied a diversified Australian market with state-of-the-art high-pressure aluminium cylinders used for storage of medical, domestic, sports (diving equipment), and

---

[1]This case was developed for use in classroom discussion and is not intended to necessarily illustrate appropriate or inappropriate management practices. Case information was gathered through interviews with personnel of CIG in 1995/96, visits to the CIG site in New South Wales, and reviews of various documents provided by CIG. The author of this case (1996) was Graeme Sheather, University of Technology, Sydney.

industrial gases. Gas Cylinders produced around 250,000 cylinders annually and exported over two-thirds of these to Japan, Southeast Asia, and New Zealand. Later, 50 percent of its cylinder production went to Japan and Southeast Asia. Part of the agreement with Luxfer upon establishing the Australian plant was that Luxfer would not market directly into the Asia Pacific region. Only products that were outside of the CIG Gas Cylinders product range, that is, products it couldn't manufacture, could Luxfer sell to the Asian region.

Gas Cylinders is based at King's Park, Sydney. In 1995 it employed around 110 people. The gas cylinder manufacturing sequence involves some 31 operations, which compress into 11 key stages of: billet saw; lubrication; extrusion; extruder behinder; heading; heat treatment; diedescheim wash; hydro testing; painting; valving; and finally packaging. Composite cylinders, aluminium cylinders, and acetylene cylinders are manufactured in a variety of sizes and are used for beverage gases, medical and industrial gases, as well as fire extinguishers and scuba tanks. Gas Cylinders also distributed parts including valves and accessories.

Factors Affecting the Context of Change

In 1977, five years after its foundation, Gas Cylinders, in response to declining performance and an increasingly hostile and competitive international market, initiated a collaboration with Luxfer Gas Cylinders. This partnership began what has now come to be known in best practice nomenclature as "benchmarking": this was perhaps the inaugural intercompany example in Australia. Benchmarking Luxfer's world class cylinder manufacturing plants in England and the U.S. enabled Gas Cylinders to:

- Compare best practices domestically and outside Australia.
- Begin continuous improvement as the path to world class performance.
- Exchange standards achieved to progressively raise the benchmarks.

Benchmarking with Luxfer was comprehensive, with the two companies identifying the following key areas for potential improvement:

Labour Productivity (measured by):	*Manufacturing Lead Time (measured by):*
Quality	Product cost structure
Organisation structure	Engineering development
Material use	Stock levels
Safety	Marketing techniques
Finance	Maintenance

Measurement techniques established the basis for comparing individual plants' strengths and weaknesses and set realistic targets. To improve respective operations, both plants exchanged information regularly and conducted site study tours.

In seeking to maintain its competitiveness and improve productivity and product quality, the company embarked on a number of reforms. Initially introducing a common interest gain-sharing program (CIP) in 1982 (claimed to be the first in Australia), this was followed by initiatives on total quality control (TQC) in 1985, then just-in-time (JIT) and value-added management (VAM) in 1987. The outcomes of these innovations included expanded export markets, improved customer focus, and enhanced productivity.

The Common Interest Program (CIP).   To overcome the natural skepticism about relative contributions and sharing rewards was an initiative called the "Common Interest Program" (CIP), introduced in 1982. It was seen as the first step in continuous workplace reform. A major objective of the CIG management was to lift production and reduce the likelihood of industrial disputes, thereby reducing unit costs and enhancing export opportunities.

Under CIP, productivity gains were shared equally between the company and its employees. This distribution was based on team work, not individual performance. Furthermore, employees could contribute to any decision made that would affect the company's performance. CIP was designed with three important components in mind: a committee, which included employees from all levels of the company, ground rules, and a mathematical model for allocation of profits.

Between 1984 and 1989, the CIP committee had 10 biannually elected members. These included five shift workers from the aluminium and acetylene cylinder plants: maintenance workers; foremen and supervisors; office staff; management; and a personnel officer. This evolved into a somewhat more informal set of communication devices such as team meetings and fortnightly team coordinator meetings.

Ground rules for the CIP were established. These included guarantees of various employment conditions for employees and specified rules for distributing profits under a new pay structure. The following rules were agreed to by the representative committee:

- Productivity increases will not mean lost jobs.
- Health, safety, and welfare standards will be maintained.
- The gains will be split 50/50 between CIG Gas Cylinders and the employees when there is a profit.
- An equal monthly dividend is paid to all employees.
- Dividends will not be paid to employees on unpaid absences or compensation.
- There will be no pay deductions for productivity losses.
- Plant changes are made only by consensus.
- Productivity gains arising from capital investment are excluded from the agreement.
- A committee representing all company levels will meet monthly to make management decisions.

The mathematical model calculated future gains and losses, based on past performance figures, time to produce a cylinder, and number of rejects. All improvements made to production processes were also measured to ensure that they actually increased productivity, as the model is also used to calculate productivity-related dividends. A number of risks were anticipated, so the model was trailed for six months, with the results assessed against three possible outcomes:

Outcome 1. Continued industrial relations "consultations," which did not achieve too much except to have unsettling effects on both management and the work force.

Outcome 2. Lip service where the right noises were made and documentation was completed, but no real gains were visible.

Outcome 3. A real in-spirit acceptance where "hard" and "soft" (that is, productivity savings and motivation/morale) gains were beginning to show.

The outcome of the trial produced the third possibility. At the end of the six-month period, Gas Cylinders was saving $25,000 per month, retaining half for profit and distributing dividends to employees averaging $100.

The Total Quality Control (TQC) Program.   In an effort to overcome difficulties emerging from historical and current poor performance, the company adopted a comprehensive and continuous improvement philosophy based on total quality control (TQC). This commenced with quality focus at the shop-floor level. The introduction of product-inspection functions using "cylinder technicians" was introduced. To encourage participation, salary restructuring and productivity/quality targets took place. Later, the application of quality principles applied to customer service and administrative functions were seen to be just as important. This change was driven by demands of the customers, particularly the Japanese who demanded exceptional quality.

Main features of total quality management as applied at Gas Cylinders were:

- Training in statistical measurement techniques, to check the quality of production and customer service at every stage and set quantitative goals for improvement.
- Deming's principles, which focus on systems, the theory of variation and statistical thinking, leadership in planning, prediction, learning, measuring, and monitoring.
- Quality circles, where a range of employees are invited to make suggestions for improvements in areas outside their normal fields of work.
- Charting on the shop floor, which is an organised and structured approach to group problem solving.

Value-Added Management.   Gas Cylinders introduced value-added management (VAM) into its operations in 1987. Competition from low-wage countries, such as China and Korea, presented the company a potential threat to its various product markets in Japan. With changes in production technology, Japanese firms were also threatening Gas Cylinders's domestic and international markets. This also presented an opportunity for improved cost and quality performance. Use of just-in-time management improved inventory control and eliminated finished goods stock levels by two-thirds, while tooling changeover times and customisation were improved. Shift from a production push to customer pull philosophy reduced production time from 27 days to 10 days, with comparable reduction in work-in-progress.

Gas Cylinders received government recognition for these programs. In 1986 they received an Australian Export Award for outstanding export achievement from the Australian Trade Commission and the Confederation of Australian Industry. In 1991 the company received an Australian Export Award from Enterprise Australia and a Total Quality Management Encouragement Award by the National Business Bulletin.

Gas Cylinders was used as a testing ground for new practices that were adopted by the parent company if successful.

Recognition of the Need to Change

Management at Gas Cylinders indicated several sensitive and difficult issues that had to be managed over the time of introducing a number of the improvement programs, not the least of which was performance measurement. Arguably, Gas Cylinders was one of the most contentious "old days" management/worker battle zones. Following benchmarking with Luxfer, problems with the introduction of new standards and performance measures arose. These were related to the prevalent "them and us" mentality in the industry, characterised by high levels of industrial dispute and low productivity.

By the 1970s, performance measurement had become a concept that carried "baggage" in the workplace. Introduction of scientific management principles exacerbated the "them and us" control of performance, so that when the jointly designed (Gas Cylinders and Luxfer) measurement techniques were introduced, process workers did not understand why performance was being measured or why changes were necessary. Management recognised that workers did not understand the new performance processes, and therefore it was logical that only management could "own" them.

Two issues arose for Gas Cylinders: First, what is needed to succeed in business? Second, what is needed to demolish the attitudes of "us and them"?

Some important strategic statements set the platform for future reforms. They were:

1. "A business can succeed only if everyone involved works together."
2. "We believe that all employees have a common interest in the success of the company."
3. "Every employee has ability and competence; each person can contribute equally at his/her own level."

In August 1990, the company developed a new vision and philosophy. This reflected significant changes in the relationships between management, the union, and employees. The mission and philosophy, cited below, reflects what Gas Cylinders termed the "true" nature of working life as expressed by all those involved. It emphasised a process of continuous improvement that would provide the focus for the evolutionary development of Gas Cylinders.

Gas Cylinders's mission and philosophy was as follows:

We strive to become a model business through satisfying customer needs, providing a desirable working environment, ensuring a good return for shareholders, and conducting our business in a socially responsible manner.

Operational objectives are the statement that:

- All decisions will be consistent with our mission statement.
- We will use a team-based approach to addressing issues, solving problems, and making decisions.
- Our approach will be one of continual improvement.
- Each employee will have the opportunity to meet individual needs and objectives while meeting organisational needs.
- Applied skill and knowledge of individuals will be recognised.
- All individuals will know how they are performing as team members. They will also know how the business as a whole is performing.
- Safety of employees and the community will be a high priority.
- Each employee will be provided with the necessary tools, information, and training to do the job right the first time.
- Teams have the authority to meet their responsibilities, including stopping to fix quality-related or safety-related problems.
- Job-related mistakes are opportunities for improvement.
- The business will endeavour to offer appropriate personnel and social support services.
- It is an objective that all employees be afforded equal status regarding conditions and opportunities.

Building on the previous initiatives, the company introduced a sociotechnical systems program with the guidance of the Technology Transfer Council to combine its market and technical improvements with social change. A successful application in 1991 to the Australian Best Practice Demonstration Program enabled the company to build on its earlier successes and set the directions for future financial growth and continuous improvements. The six components incorporated in the best practice program application encompassed the following:

- Total quality and continuous improvement—to improve production processes by reducing waste and variation within a workplace culture focused on quality and customer needs.
- Work teams—the development of self-managed work-based teams.

- Training—a fully integrated training program in both technical and social areas based on a training needs assessment and performance audits.
- Production benchmarking—visits to the U.K. to inspect similar plants by a group comprising a manager and manufacturing employees.
- Teams benchmarking—a trip to the U.S. to investigate innovation in the structuring and operating of work teams by a group comprising a manager and manufacturing employees.
- Activity-based costing—the analysis of activities within work-based teams to identify areas of high costs and develop appropriate cost-management plans.

The Substance of Change: Self-Managing Work Teams

A self-managing work team (SMWT) program was introduced at Gas Cylinders in July 1991. The design of these teams was based on sociotechnical systems (STS) theory, which declares: "rather than separate analyses of the social structure and technology, the new [STS] approach examined both, and the relationships between them, as a system in its own right" (Emery 1993:141). The program at CIG had four main features:

- Hierarchical management structures are moved to team-based support.
- An increased focus on customer service.
- Training and multiskilling.
- Salaries and production goals for all employees.

Planning allowed two to three years for introduction of the program. It was designed to give employees more control over operations to improve quality, customer service, productivity, skills, and morale. The sociotechnical system model is illustrated in Figure 1.

The core team processes in the sociotechnical system are illustrated in Figure 2.

The Process of Transition

The implementation process commenced with the introduction of steering and design teams. Employees were asked to volunteer to sit on a "design team" whose brief was to design and implement an appropriate self-managed work teams program. Members included the production manager, personnel superintendent, a maintenance supervisor, a maintenance electrician, and four operators.

A steering team was also established comprising the general manager, engineering manager, union organiser, and a night-shift operator. This team's role was to oversee the design and protect the team from outside influences as much as possible.

Both teams were fully briefed on the theory of sociotechnical systems (STS). The team held workshops to identify a company mission, a set of values, and, most importantly, a list of reasons explaining the change. The Technology Transfer Council and overseas companies that had used the model provided practical advice on applying it to Gas Cylinders's operation.

The STS program comprised two studies. First, an employee survey which analysed job satisfaction, communication, individual ambitions, team participation, and sources of dissatisfaction. Second, a technical study which closely examined manufacturing processes in the plants. Upon completion of this documentation, all employees were asked to vote on whether to accept the program. Seventy-five percent agreed to proceed.

Special interest work teams were then established. These covered the areas of production, finishing, and maintenance. As teams were formed in these manufacturing areas, foremen moved into a team support function role, with their responsibilities assumed by the whole team, who then elected team coordinators. Team coordinators were rotated every six months, so all team members

FIGURE 1

Sociotechnical systems

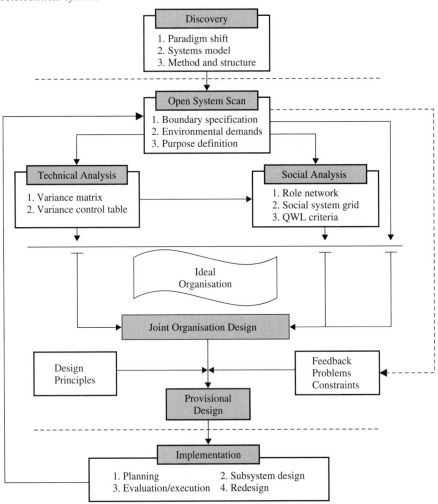

could develop a broad understanding of the entire business. As coordinators became more experienced, they were rotated more frequently.

Because of its responsibility for delivery and quality of cylinder orders, the production team was closest to customer requirements. To perform this function effectively the team required timely and accurate information, resources, and skills provided by other teams. Due to its increased responsibility the team was credited with greater trust, and a deliberate move was made to relax direct supervision.

Training.   Extensive training programs supported the devolution of responsibilities and roles. Three types of training were undertaken: social, technical, and business. Social training included team building, communication, and interpersonal skills. Technical training involved establishing

FIGURE 2

STS core team processes

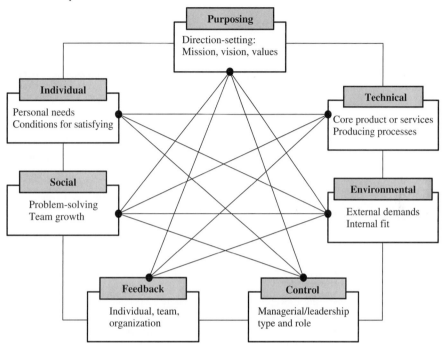

standard operating procedures, maintenance, training methods, and problem-solving techniques. Business training was provided in key areas such as skill upgrading and quality management practices.

Reward for Responsibility: The Bonus Scheme. Increased responsibilities under the new team structures meant all manufacturing employees were to receive salaries based on individual responsibility. Pay was adjusted to reflect these varying levels and no longer based on a fixed wage. An employee appraisal system (implemented in 1995) assists individuals to assess their relative skill status, and provided encouragement for the process improvement. The individual appraisal matrix covers productivity, safety, personal productivity, leadership, and acceptance of responsibility. Adjustments are provided on top of the profit-sharing scheme initiated in 1982. As a productivity offset, teams have to meet specified production and quality goals. If teams meet production targets within normal work hours and without overtime, take-home pay is not altered.

Team and TQM. The TQM framework implemented previously indicated the kinds of activities pertinent to a team leader's role. A program called FADE (Focus, Analyse, Develop, and Execute) was devised as a joint problem-solving tool among teams. The four stages of FADE are:

Focus. First the team must generate a list of problems, and then select one problem and define it in writing.

Analyse. After deciding what further information is needed, statistical data such as measurements and patterns should be collated, and the factors causing the problem defined.

Develop. Alternative solutions are listed, and the team agrees on one solution and develops an implementation plan.

Execute. After gaining management and shop-floor commitment to implement the solution, it can be put into place and its effectiveness measured.

Operation of New Practices

After the introduction of SMWT the following improvements have been realised:

- Productivity has increased by 130 percent.
  - 22 percent through capital investment.
  - 78 percent through teams simplifying work practices.
- Benchmarking against other companies both in Australia and overseas.
- Internal rejects reduced from 4.8 percent in 1989 to 2.1 percent in 1995.
- Teams involved in strategic planning.
- Introduction of appraisal systems for all employees.
- Return on funds increased sevenfold between 1982 and 1992.
- Manufacturing lead-time reduced from 24 days to 6 days. Refer to Figure 3.
- Strategic plan to reduce manufacturing lead-time to three days by year 2000.
- The company has developed an export market with over two-thirds of cylinders produced for export.
- Labour turnover has dropped to less than 5 percent.
- Absenteeism has been reduced to 2.4 percent, from 7.6 percent in 1989.
- Stock levels have been reduced by 72 percent.
- There have been no strikes between 1982 and 1989, and few since.
- Employees receive comparatively high wages plus an average monthly dividend.
- In 1989 the plant produced 150,000 cylinders with 150 employees. In 1995, the plant produced 275,000 cylinders with 100 employees.

The productivity improvement at CIG Gas Cylinders is provided in Figure 4.

FIGURE 3

Lead-time for CIG Gas Cylinders

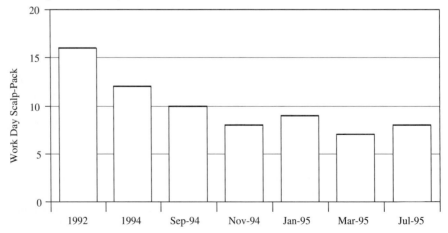

FIGURE 4

Productivity improvement at CIG and Luxfer

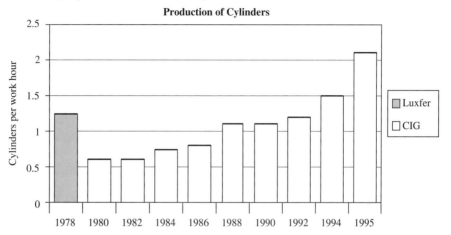

The Politics of Change

With the introduction of self-managed work teams, significant problems emerged between the special interest groups and the design team's role in the whole production process. The problem is described by Peter Lee, a cylinder technician and team coordinator.

> A problem existed right from the first day of the program where it was mooted that this was just a way of getting rid of the foremen. Much false information was spread through the rumour mill. This information was widespread and difficult to combat as people were being exposed to speculation more often than they were to the facts, and because the design team members were busy with their design work. Also, we have three fixed shifts which means that the night shift and to a lesser extent the afternoon shift had limited opportunities to discuss the information with the people in the know.

This perception was countered at the informal organisational level, with members of the design team continuously reassuring colleagues on a one-to-one basis of the facts. Finally, the plant was closed for a day and an off-site public meeting held with senior management, the union organiser, and the design team. Resolution of the issues was endorsed by more than three-quarters of employees finally voting in favour of the changes.

At CIG there was also a need to deal with foremen and managers who perceived themselves as redundant under the new team-based structure. Gas Cylinders described their approach to the problem in the following way for first-line managers, middle management, and supervisors.

First-line supervisors had always been "hands on," so to some degree this supported the new structure. Those who were displaced in the traditional sense were not punished through the new structures by losing out financially; they kept their monetary reward. Of course, some would inevitably feel a loss of status, and in some situations this was the case. The majority of foremen remained. It was essential that there was substantial and continual reassurance about such anxieties as job losses. Internal consultants, together with management, made numerous presentations. Nobody would lose their job, and those affected would be given roles in the new process. Some employees accepted the new roles and some did not, and it has been possible to retain most of the supervisors, and to create new roles for them.

Changes to middle management were more complicated, since their status, in the traditional sense, had disappeared. Two or three who could not accommodate the new directions moved on. The new role for managers/supervisors was clearly defined from the outset. While some disapproval was to be expected, however, with sincere acknowledgment of their personal worth and valued skills to the company, most continued to contribute their managerial and foreman skills.

A more significant impact resulted from changes to the foreman/supervisor role. Gas Cylinders's approach was to begin with these roles by "recognising, respecting, and celebrating" their importance. Senior management would brief managers and those foremen/supervisors whose status and roles were to alter. They would first stress the key role the supervisor would have to play, and how highly valued these skills were.

For those employees who felt directly threatened by the changes it was necessary to create a high-trust environment based on comprehensive and regular communication channels.

A supportive industrial relations climate had to be nurtured to avoid claims of "management exploitation." This was achieved by involving shop-floor employees, unions, and management, especially with respect to future educational expectations. The design team concept effectively achieved this in ways employees could understand. To get "grassroots" support at the union level, Gas Cylinders supported these beliefs by actions:

- Take time to address the question: "What's in it for me?"
- Make sure that both sides of the change equation are balanced when asking people to take on new and different roles and even different values. In particular, the effort-and-reward ratio must be reflected in dollars.
- The dollar is a major tool in breaking down barriers.
- The dollar is a way to show good faith and is a key to common interests.
- The dollar is a tool to start a process and break down barriers in improving productivity.

A fundamental axiom for successful change under the sociotechnical systems approach to organisational change is to base decisions on thorough and rigorous analysis of both the technical and social systems, and the relationship between each system. Gas Cylinders posits that for successful change to occur the organisation needs to approach the process via a three-streamed model, like that outlined in Figure 5.

Communication is the first key driver of change. Once initiated, change must be nurtured and championed continuously, not left "out on a limb." The various types of communication devices are shown in the first "stream," ranging from perhaps the most important personal communication through to consultative and collective dispute resolution mechanisms. A key concept underpinning successful change is "involvement." This must stretch from top management to the shop floor, it must be reciprocal, and the contribution from respective groups must add value to the change process. This cycle of involvement is facilitated by various organisation and managerial arrangements depicted in the third stream under "structures," such as self-managed work teams employed throughout Gas Cylinders's organisation, and the whole model tied together by programs such as VAM, TQM, and CIP.

As mentioned above there are a number of points of potential conflict, unrealised performance objectives, and an overreliance on monetary reward as the principal motivator for job satisfaction and performance targets. Gas Cylinders has particularly recognised the danger of "plateauing," that is, becoming too "comfortable" or complacent with the changes achieved. In the spirit of continuous improvement, if this happens it is the signal to revitalise. Gas Cylinders has approached this threshold by using an annualised pay scheme, plus a mix of weekly hours and overtime, and has "developed the idea of facilitating teams to look at the broader picture beyond the company."

The company has employed numerous techniques and programs to achieve best practice over some 10 years between 1984 and 1995. Perhaps the major criticism of its approach has been that

FIGURE 5

Common interest program

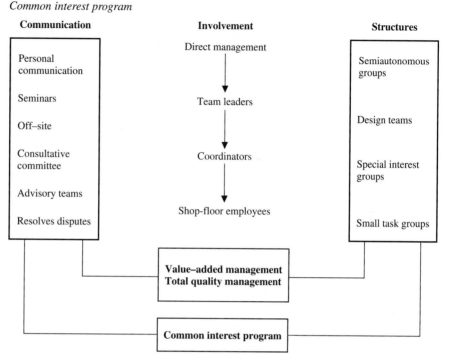

it has not bedded down a single new initiative before introducing a subsequent project. The model outlined above is an internal concept to overcome this characteristic. The company has sought to merge this model with a more integrative approach by adopting world class manufacturing as a strategy for change. In 1995, this has led to carefully constructed five-year business plans covering mission, vision, strategic competitive advantage, values, and business objectives, with detailed action plans covering key issues, milestone actions, and target key performance indicators in marketing, manufacturing, innovation, human resources, finance, loss prevention, and the planning process.

Lesson Learned

- With the commitment of top management, the company has implemented extensive improvements in technical and social conditions at all stages of the production process, resulting in better quality, reduced costs, and more timely delivery of products both within the company and to final customers.
- Sharing the vision for world class performance throughout the company has been encouraged by developing self-managed teams to empower the work force. Reinforcing this are reward systems based on salary, recognition of the value of different skill levels, sharing the benefits of continuous improvement using a gain-sharing model, and comprehensive training to provide technical and social skills.
- Improved attention to health and safety has resulted from devolving responsibility to the teams and creating a special team coordinator to manage safety matters. Equal

FIGURE 6

Best practice at CIG Gas Cylinders

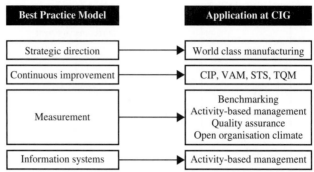

employment opportunities are addressed by new training programs that provide all production employees with the opportunity to train for any shop-floor job.

- Customers and suppliers are now integrated into the work processes. Teams are responsible for dealing with customer complaints and regularly meet with visiting customers. Similarly, team members visit suppliers and discuss their needs for quality materials and timely deliveries.
- Benchmarking of production processes and team development methods has provided valuable insights into improvements and motivated employees to pursue best practice.
- Technology agreements and shared technical knowledge have kept the company at the forefront of process innovations, and closer customer relationships have enabled products to be designed to customer specifications.
- The company has developed an external focus by networking through the best practice demonstration activities, benchmarking visits, customer and supplier relationships, and the use of external consultants.

6

BOSCH-SIEMENS HAUSGERATE GMBH: WORKING FOR THE ENVIRONMENT FROM DESIGN TO DISPOSAL[1]

Introduction

Concern about the effects of human activity on the environment can be heard at all levels—at global conferences, from supranational organisations, e.g., the European Union, and at national, regional, state, and local government levels to varying degrees in individual countries. This case describes the environmental management policy and protection measures adopted by an internationally operating company based in Munich, Germany, which produces household electronic and electrical goods.

Disposal of used appliances is a major environmental problem. For former West Germany alone in 1994, around 1.5 million tons of used electrical and electronic appliances needed to be disposed of. Of this, 600,000 tons were from the commercial and industrial sectors and 900,000 tons from households. Among the household waste, 560,000 tons came from large household appliances (VDMA and ZVEI, 1994). The local municipalities require rubbish to be sorted and currently collect large household appliances separately at no extra cost. Given this background and a growing concern for environmental protection, the electrical and electronic goods manufacturers and their associations felt obliged to introduce their own voluntary recycling procedures and environmental protection standards. They also have to conform to regulations issued by the European Union and by various levels of government in Germany.

The European Context.   In June 1993, the European Union published regulations relating to the voluntary adherence of industrial, commercial, and trade businesses to a common system of environmental management and environmental auditing (in short, the EU-Ecological Audit). At the time of writing, service and professional organisations are not covered by these regulations.

The EU-Ecological Audit places the responsibility for dealing with the environmental consequences of their activities directly in the hands of the businesses concerned, and therefore requires businesses to take an active role in protecting the environment. Businesses are responsible for developing and implementing environmental policies, goals, and programs, in addition to effective environmental management systems. Further, the regulations require that businesses continually improve their environmental protection activities, instruct their employees accordingly, and make information about their environmental protection activities available to the public.

The intention of the EU-Ecological Audit is to provide a standard system to apply to all European Union countries. However, adherence to the regulations at the time of writing is voluntary.

The German Context.   Germany is generally acknowledged as a world leader in environmental protection measures. As part of its environmental protection measures, Germany has introduced

[1]This case was developed for use in classroom discussion and is not intended to necessarily illustrate appropriate or inappropriate management practices. Case author: Gayle Avery, Institute for International Business Studies, Germany, 1996. The funding for this case production was provided by the Australian federal government's Department of Industry, Science and Resources.

laws banning or limiting the use of polluting substances and materials, as well as laws requiring manufacturers and retailers to take back packaging. Local government is required to provide bins for citizens to sort their household rubbish to simplify disposal and promote recycling, which is also supported at the federal level. Now, these recycling requirements are to encompass appliances such as cars, computers, household appliances, and other manufactured products.

The Elektronikschrottverordnung (ESVO) is a new recycling law that came into effect in Germany in 1996. It imposes strict requirements on manufacturers of electronic and electrical goods and other appliances to take back and recycle products at the end of their service life. The responsibility for recycling and/or correct disposal of goods on the part of manufacturers has been reinforced through the federal German courts.

To assist in complying with the new laws and the EU-Ecological Audit, and to help manufacturers identify competent recycling disposal partners, the Federal German Government has drafted a law called "Umweltgutachterzulassungs und Standortregistrierungsgesetz (UZSG)" ("Licensing environmental auditors and site registration law"), which was expected to be enacted late in 1995.

In 1994, in anticipation of the UZSG law and out of a stated concern for the environment, various manufacturing associations in Germany produced a catalogue of criteria for certifying companies involved in the disposal of used electrical and electronic appliances and devices. At present certification is voluntary. The Central Association of the Electrotechnical and Electronic Industry (ZVEI) and the Association of German Machinery and Production Producers (VDMA) have developed this catalogue. The catalogue covers the appropriateness of the organisational structure in the company being audited, availability of skills and expert knowledge among employees, and the complete documentation relating to the materials and methods employed in disposal. In particular, the certification process examines the materials flow and especially how "difficult" parts are to be disposed of.

The Company: BSHGmbH.   The Bosch-Siemens Hausgerate Group (BSHG) is one of Europe's leading manufacturers of electrical and electronic consumer goods. Its share capital is owned 50 percent by Bosch GmbH and 50 percent by Siemens AG since 1967. With a work force of about 34,000 people, BSHG produced around 11 million large household appliances in 1998, with DM 10,283 million in sales. BSHG operates about 37 production sites around the world. It has marketing and customer service companies in all major countries.

The product range includes refrigerators, freezers, cooking appliances, washing machines, dryers, dishwashers, heating appliances, floor-care equipment, small domestic appliances, water heaters, air conditioners and coolers, and home entertainment electronics. The Group's products are sold under several brand names all over the world: Bosch, Siemens, Constructa, Gaggenau, Ufesa, and Neff, as well as 10 brands belonging specifically to the subsidiaries in the U.S., Latin America, Turkey, Spain, and Greece.

All domestic plants, together with customer service and logistics, achieved certification to ISO 9001 (quality management) by 1994 and have since moved toward the ISO 14001 certification.

Research and development expenditure was DM 135 million in 1994, which reflects BSHG's long-term average. Main areas of R & D activity in 1994 were the development of a new range of front-loading washing machines, a dryer with optimised energy consumption, a range of dishwashers with a top basket wash-cycle, and the conversion of refrigerators and freezers to the refrigerant isobutane. This refrigerant is a naturally occurring gas and does not contribute to the global greenhouse effect (BSHG Annual Report, 1994). In addition, the recyclability of products was further improved. In 1998, innovation is still a driving force and BSHG was the first domestic appliance manufacturer in the world to have eliminated CFC/HCF (hydrofluorocarbons) from refrigerators and freezers.

Environmental Protection Background at BSHG

Environmental protection has been a major focus of the company's activities since 1989. BSHG sees itself as responsible for ensuring the best-possible harmony between its business objectives and protecting the environment, even in the midst of a recession such as Germany experienced in the 1990s.

Importance of Environmental Protection.   Environmental protection plays a significant role in all corporate activities at Bosch-Siemens Hausgerate GmbH. It has been firmly anchored in the corporate guidelines since 1989 (BSHG, 1989). The corporate guidelines were created to enable employees to act in accordance with corporate goals and philosophies while carrying out their daily tasks. BSHG's top management sees implementing these guidelines as an essential and important challenge.

Achieving environmental protection has led to the development of new technologies that have made environmental progress not only possible but also economically feasible. Although the environmental protection policies originally only affected the German subsidiaries, they now also bind the company's subsidiaries Europewide.

BSHG believes that only by seeing the environmental protection problem as a whole and covering all phases of product life with their many and varied links, can the environment be effectively protected. Important aspects of BSHG's environmental protection program include conserving natural resources, minimising environmental pollution during production and the useful life of an appliance, as well as ensuring an environmentally friendly disposal of old appliances. Progress in the environmental protection area is documented in regular environmental reports that inform readers about the Group's integrated environmental protection policies and the results of its environmental programs.

Environmental Protection Organisation

To implement the above policy in practical ways, clear organisational and environmental management structures have been introduced. This requires all departments and employees to play their part in environmental protection.

Environmental Protection Management Structure.   The environmental protection management structure at BSHG continues to be refined and developed, but a clear characteristic of the structure is that each task is clearly defined and assigned to a responsible person or persons.

Chairman's Role.   Senior management is responsible for overall environmental protection, thereby demonstrating that the company is fully behind the environmental programs. The chairman of BSHG has overall responsibility for environmental protection at BSHG. The chairman delegates the organisation and supervision of environmental programs to the individual departments and production sites, each of which is assigned an environmental expert(s) to provide assistance and support on the ground.

Steering Committee.   A steering committee advises top management on developing overall strategic goals for environmental protection and evaluates implementation alternatives critically and directs the special environmental protection working groups. Membership of the steering committee includes senior personnel from the following departments: environmental protection, organisational development, product planning, production, communication, and logistics. The head of the central department for environmental protection chairs the steering committee.

Working Groups.   At the heart of the environmental management structure is a system of expert working groups made up of people from the factories and different sectors of the company. The members of the working groups are considered the "environmental experts" at their places of work and these groups develop interdepartmental strategies, concepts, and guidelines for the entire company. Originally, the working groups were established to cover recyclable product design, product characteristics, production, packaging, and recycling old appliances (BSHG, Umwelt-bericht, 1993/4). More recently, the expert working groups have been put together in terms of four key areas: product issues, production issues, logistic issues, and communication issues.

Environmental Department.   A centralised department for environmental protection coordinates the overall environmental protection programs at BSHG. This department reports directly to the chairman of the company and works closely with environmental divisions located at the individual production sites. The environmental department also conducts random inspections and internal environmental audits at the various locations.

Employees' Commitment

Qualification and Communication.   Since BSHG relies completely on its employees to implement the environmental goals, it strengthens the motivation and qualifications of its employees in the area of environmental protection through extensive further education and personal development courses.

Communication of environmental goals and achievements is also a top priority at BSHG. Through special courses, employees learn about the achievements and goals of the company in various areas, including environmental protection. In addition, BSHG produces an in-house magazine that reports on environmental activities. Noticeboards, memoranda, and information stands also inform employees about environmental topics.

Suggestions from employees about improving environmental protection have been stimulated via competitions as well as emerging from regular employee information sessions and meetings. For instance, the monthly group meetings designed as part of the continuous improvement process also discuss environmental topics, as do the daily information sessions at the workplace.

Employee Acceptance.   Acceptance of the environmental policy has been very strong among employees. All employees are made aware of the corporate guidelines and therefore of the corporate environmental protection policy and their role in maintaining and improving it. The strong acceptance has been attributed to the strong feelings among the German population generally about the need to protect the environment. Because employees belong to this population and share this widespread value, the environmental policy at BSHG has been positively embraced by unions and the work force. It may well be that employee support is stronger than support among managers with responsibility for profit and loss. Sometimes conflicts arise between the need to make profits and the need to introduce environmental protection measures. These conflicts do not normally arise for employees at the production level.

Employees tend to resent environmental measures if they have to be adopted because of external laws, which could lead to a competitive disadvantage for the company—for instance, if appliances produced in Germany had to meet certain standards that foreign manufacturers did not have to meet.

Like all behavioral changes, these do not always take place as fast as managers would like to see and so, despite the willingness of the workers to protect the environment, changing long-standing procedures takes a while.

The Environmental Protection Process at BSHG

Recycling Starts with Design.   The design stage offers the greatest opportunities to minimise damage to the environment. BSHG designers adhere strictly to guidelines intended to make their products more recyclable and less polluting. Explicit guidelines are aimed at ensuring that no materials used in the production process contain any hazardous materials. This includes both hazardous materials forbidden by European or German laws and materials that BSHG itself has banned from its products, e.g., bromide flame-retardant additives for plastics (Criens, 1995).

Reducing Internal Waste.   Residual materials "wasted" during the production process are treated as valuable raw materials. BSHG tries to reduce waste by sorting the material residues at the point of production. Large amounts of reuseable materials are collected before being channeled to an appropriate site for recycling. In 1993, around 90 percent of residual materials were able to be reused (Criens, 1995).

Packaging.   BSHG tries to use only environmentally friendly packaging materials for its products. Polyvinyl chloride (PVC) is not used. By delivering refrigerators in reusable packaging to large customers, BSHG was able to save 23 tons of cardboard and 4 tons of polystyrene in 1993. The goal is to reduce the number of materials used in packaging, wherever possible, to only one kind of material. In cooperation with selected partners, BSHG has incorporated ways of recycling packaging materials in its environmental protection plan. For instance, used polyethylene materials are melted down and turned into plastic carrying bags, garbage bags, or plastic wrapping. Old paper is recycled into cardboard or paper. BSHG also buys primarily recycled paper, to close the loop.

Working Life.   During the 15-year or so life of an appliance, running the device places burdens on the environment. Therefore, BSHG focuses on reducing the consumption of energy, and where appropriate, water and detergents. BSHG reports (BSHG, Umweltbericht, 1994/5) that compared with 1970, energy requirements of their modern appliances have sunk by 40 percent.

Reusing and Disposal of Returned Parts.   Following a repair, all replaced parts are removed by the customer service people and disposed of at a customer's request. At the customer service premises, returned parts are sorted for recycling, and higher grade parts are reconditioned for reuse (to be sold at a lower price than new parts). Unrepairable parts are then given to selected recycling contractors who arrange for final safe disposal of the part.

Product Return.   Manufacturers who really want to make environmentally friendly product require an ecologically friendly way of disposing of these products once they have reached the end of their service life. In July 1994, BSHG introduced a system to take back old appliances from other manufacturers for disposal. At the last owner-dealer's expense (about AUD $50), BSHG picks up the old appliances from the dealer and takes full responsibility for disposing of them in an environmentally friendly way. BSHG was the first manufacturer to make this offer, although competitors immediately followed, using various methods and prices. BSHG claims (Sirch, 1994) that it is the only manufacturer that puts its full name behind the disposal process and that competitor-manufacturers simply pass the responsibility for correct disposal onto their disposal partners.

  BSHG also combines picking up the old devices with delivering new appliances to the dealers, thereby using spare capacity in their delivery trucks (which otherwise would return to the BSHG base empty). Thus, no additional burden is placed on the environment through transportation trips. In fact, given that around 50 percent of all truck trips carry empty loads, BSHG claims that around 40 percent in emissions have been saved by this system (Sirch, 1994).

At BSHG premises, unusable components are collected in containers, which are picked up by their regional disposal partners when the containers are full. These disposal partners are required to demonstrate that they then dispose of the waste in appropriate ways.

Product Recycle.   Environmentally friendly appliances have to be constructed so that they can be dismantled easily and their various materials and components easily sorted and—where feasible—reincorporated in the production of new appliances. To learn more about demounting old appliances, BSHG has introduced a pilot project for disassembling old appliances at its Berlin plant.

As a concrete example, take an old refrigerator. Within three minutes, BSHG has sucked out the ozone-damaging fluorocarbon substance and liquidised it. Reuseable or valuable parts such as the compressor, glass and wire shelving, etc., are taken out before the refrigerator is put onto a conveyor belt that transports it into a special vacuumed area. There the fluorocarbon substance is carefully removed from the insulation and useful materials such as iron and plastic are reduced and separated. The latter materials are then recycled in the production of new appliances.

However, recycling has to be both environmentally and economically feasible. The level of recyclability—the percentage of recovered reuseable material in relation to the total weight of the appliance—must be compatible with the cost and effort involved in recovering the reuseable materials and components. Today's old appliances are costly to recycle because they were not designed with this in mind. Depending on the product, up to 85 percent of the old appliances are reused (BSHG, Umweltbericht, 1994/5), with the intention being to raise this to 100 percent by 1996.

Transport Pollution.   Often left out of consideration, transporting goods is environmentally damaging. BSHG tries to use rail as much as possible (currently 70 percent) and to reduce road transportation. But in 1994 BSHG was forced to send more appliances by road than intended because the railways did not have sufficient capacity. In 1994, it also started to require that delivery companies working with BSHG that used or changed to low-emission vehicles would be paid more for the delivery. In the meantime, about 40 percent of the long-distance trucks fulfill this requirement. Currently, BSHG is experimenting with gas-driven vehicles to reduce the use of petrochemicals.

Improving the Environmental Standards of Suppliers. Environmental standards are part of the selection criteria for suppliers to BSHG. BSHG works only with certified subcontractors, whose practices are also regularly checked by BSHG.

Applying Environmental Protection Measures in All the Company's Departments. BSHG not only promotes an environmentally friendly approach in the production area but spreads the spirit and actions throughout the organisation. For example, office employees are encouraged to separate their rubbish and environmentally friendly heating substances are used in the central heating system.

Stability.   Environmental measures are continually being developed at BSHG and to that extent, stability will never be achieved. However, what is stable is that environmental protection is an integral part of the company's philosophy and policies.

Environmental Protection Decisions and Costs

There are investment decisions in environmentally friendly measures being made at Bosch-Siemens all the time. Some of these are to comply with the increasing number of environmental laws in Germany; others are made to improve the ecological balance of the company and so fit with company policy, while others are made to improve products. Profit and loss considerations enter into a decision wherever there is a choice, i.e., where the decision is not prescribed by law or company policy decisions. For financial viability reasons, environmental benefits enjoyed by the consumer of an appliance and not by the company may not be implemented unless the law requires it. Initiatives for new technology can come from the production level up or from the steering committee and/or environmental protection department down.

BSHG distinguishes between two levels of environmental protection in making environmental protection decisions:

- Environmental protection in production. Here the costs are not usually as important in deciding whether to introduce an environmental protection measure as the duty to the environment.
- Environmental protection from the consumer's point of view. Here costs to the company can play a significant role in making decisions about, e.g., whether to produce a machine that uses less electricity or water. Although the overall environment would benefit, the cost savings actually flow to the consumer and not the company, and this complicates decision making. Factors that influence this decision include whether the company is the first one to the market with the benefit or is following competitors who have already introduced it.

Cost of Environmental Protection.   Environmental protection actually costs BSHG money because it now has to cover newly introduced responsibilities, e.g., taking back packaging, disposing of old appliances, avoiding certain materials and substances in production. By improving its expertise in these tasks, these additional costs can be, and have been in some areas, reduced.

Investment in facilities especially for environmental protection cost the BSHG group in Germany in 1994 around DM 10 million, almost the same as in the previous year. In particular, money was invested in emission protection and in water protection. When costs for environmental management and services such as waste disposal are taken into account, a total of approximately DM 40 million was spent by BSHG in 1994 on environmental protection (around 10 percent less than in the previous year). A saving over the year before of about DM 2 million was achieved in the packaging and product disposal area—the result of optimising product packaging and increasing the capacity for recycling of the BSHG appliances. However, the responsibility for disposing of packaging and production has brought new costs to appliance manufacturers, and BSHG does not cover its costs of environmental protection through any such savings.

However, overall environmental protection is regarded as costing the company money, notwithstanding a reduction in energy costs, etc. These "losses" may well be offset by various intangible benefits to the company such as the company gaining a positive image through its concern for the environment, improved employee morale through more open communication within the company, and prevention of damage claims for environmental pollution. It may also have marketing advantages in being seen as environmentally friendly.

Although BSHG has not directly promoted itself under environmental friendliness, indirectly, there might well have been a marketing benefit through BSHG's environmental policies. Given environmentally conscious consumers in the German marketplace, BSHG may well have lost business had it not been a leader in environmental protection. Certainly, in the current recession-dominated marketplace, BSHG appliance sales are above the industry average, according to the 1994 annual report. To what extent this successful performance in the marketplace is attributable to BSHG's environmental leadership cannot currently be determined.

Evaluation of Environmental Protection Policy.   The effectiveness of the environmental protection measures is monitored by the central environmental department, by the local environmental advisors, and audited by externally certified evaluators. The innovation is monitored constantly and measures and benchmarks have been established within the company to quantify this progress. Unfortunately other manufacturers in this industry do not yet publish detailed information about their environmental efforts, making industry comparisons impossible.

For its domestic sites, BSHG has produced an input-output statement, comparing various environmental criteria. The input-output statement measures factors such as the amount of built- and unbuilt-upon areas of company land, emissions, raw materials, other production substances, water consumption, energy consumption, rubbish, packaging, drainage, and noxious pollutants. This report shows environmental improvements from year to year within BSHG. All employees are aware of the measurement process and take pride in the results they are achieving. The culture of owning the processes, which were taking place, has worked very well in this instance.

Measurable success in designing new products, in saving energy, in reducing and improving packaging, and in incorporating recycled materials into new products has been clearly demonstrated by BSHG since the beginnings in 1989. Their ecological balance shows a demonstrable and substantial improvement each year.

Conclusion

BSHG shows how environmental protection can be successfully introduced and "lived" by a major manufacturing company that seriously believes in environmental protection. It can be considered as a model for putting into place environmental policies and procedures.

BSHG has developed environmental management structures, incorporated environmental protection as a quality requirement in quality management procedures, and has developed incentive schemes to encourage suppliers to be more environmentally friendly. BSHG strives to close the loop, so that no residual waste remains as a result of the manufacturing process or recycling old appliances and packaging materials.

BSHG appears to be a leader in the environmental protection field among manufacturers in Germany. Public recognition of BSHG's endeavours has come, for instance, from the U.S. Environmental Protection Agency in the form of an award for protecting the ozone layer through the introduction of fluorocarbon-free polyurethane foam into household appliances. The state of Bavaria has awarded BSHG its Environmental Award for BSHG's long-term achievements in environmental protection.

References

More information on BSHG can be found on the web at: *www.bosch.de/*
Also see: BSHG, Annual Report, 1994.
BSHG, Environmental Report, 1994/1995.
BSHG, Environmental Report, 1998/1999.
BSHG, Umweltbericht, 1993/1994.
BSHG, Umweltbericht, 1994/1995.
BSHG, Unternehmensleitbild, 1989.
Bundesministerium fur Umwelt, Naturschutz und Reaktorsicherheit, "Entwurf eines Gesetzes—
        Umweltgutachterzulassungs—und Standortregistrierun/gs gesetz, 1995.
Criens, R.M. Umweltgerechte Gestaltung von Elektro-Hausgeraten, internal paper, 1995.
European Council, Regulations No.1836/93, 29. June 1993.

Samson, D., and D. Challis. "Technology Management: A Review of Issues and Literature," written for the Review of International Best Practice in the Adoption and Management of Technology, 1995.

Sirch, R. "UberdasBSHG-Entsorgungskonzept fur gebrauchte Hausgerate," speech to the press, August 1994.

VDMA and ZVEI, Kriterien von ZVEI und VDMA zur Zertifizierung von Verwertungsunternehmen fur elektronische und elektronsiche Produkte, March 1994.

ZVEI, "Losungskonzept der deutschen Elektroindustrie fur die Verwertungund and Entsorgung elektrotechnischer und elektronischer Gerate," Frankfurt, September 1993.

7
THE DUCT MANUFACTURING CENTRE (A)[1]

Embarking on Reengineering

Company Background

The Turbine Systems Corporation has been the most successful manufacturer of turbine systems in the industry, consistently maintaining more than half of the market share. Turbine Systems's primary products include turbine jet engines and turbine power generators. The Duct Manufacturing Centre (DMC) is within the Manufacturing Division of the Turbine Systems Corporation. DMC manufactures precision-welded metal duct assemblies for use in Turbine Systems's primary products. Specialised tooling, equipment, and skills are needed to build over 3,000 duct models produced at DMC. For most of the ducts, on-time delivery is critical to DMC's customers. Many of the ducts are also critical for turbine safety and reliability and they must satisfy exacting quality standards. In 1989 DMC produced 38,000 ducts, ranging from a few inches to 10 feet in length. DMC also manufactured a small number of other precision-welded turbine parts.

DMC Production Process

The DMC shop consists of three areas: detail, hard metals, and soft metals. Assembling a duct is a labour-intensive process, comparable to putting together a three-dimensional, snake-shaped jig-saw puzzle. Duct parts are formed in the detail fabrication area prior to assembly either in the hard metals area (for titanium, stainless steel, hastelloy, or inconel), or in the soft metals area (primarily for aluminum). In the detail area, duct stock and other raw materials are formed (precise bending and stretching operations) before fitting. Examples include forming a 90° bend, enlarging one end so that its inside diameter is 1 inch larger than the other end, and tapering (drilling a hole in the duct and forming a flange by pulling a hot, oversized ball through the hole). The finished duct parts are assembled on a "tool," a frame that holds the component parts in position. Each duct model is built on a specific tool that has the exact dimensions for that duct.

In assembly, the mechanic places the finished duct parts into the appropriate tool and marks them for cutting and grinding. (A flowchart for hard metal assembly is shown in Exhibit 1.) After cutting and grinding, he again places them in the tool, fits them together, and holds them in position with tack clamps. He removes the clamped assembly from the tool and takes it to a booth where a welder makes small temporary welds (called tack welds). The mechanic removes the provisional tack clamps and leaves the assembly at the weld booth for a permanent fusion weld. In many cases it is not possible to weld all the joints at once, so the mechanic may repeat the fitting and welding process several times. Some ducts have over 20 weld joints, requiring many iterations of the process. The ducts are also cleaned several times during this circuitous process. Prior to completion, the ducts must pass final inspection using X-ray, pressure test, or other testing procedures.

[1]This case was developed for use in classroom discussion and is not intended to necessarily illustrate appropriate or inappropriate management practices. Case author: Thomas G. Schmitt, University of Washington, 1996. The funding for this case production was provided by the Australian federal government's Department of Industry, Science and Resources.

EXHIBIT 1

Duct Manufacturing Centre Station 1—Flowchart

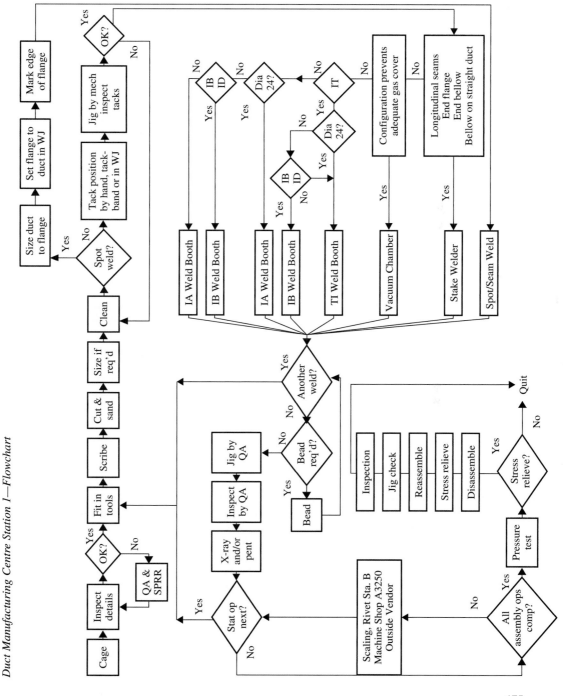

Factors Setting the Context of Change

Reflecting rapid growth in sales of Turbine Systems's products, the DMC hourly work force more than quadrupled from fewer than 100 workers in 1983 to over 450 workers in 1988. By 1989 the 168,000 square foot manufacturing plant was packed with people, equipment, and inventory. Efficiency fell as the building became more crowded and additional workers were added to compensate, further compounding the problem. Also, the current building was constructed during the Second World War to temporarily store fatalities. In early 1989 senior management at Turbine Systems evaluated DMC's operation relative to outside vendors and the senior management was not pleased with the performance of DMC. Also, as part of a corporate strategy to create semiautonomous business units, senior management attempted to create the Duct Manufacturing Centre with the objective of bringing all aspects of manufacturing ducts into one focused organization.

Recognition of the Need to Change

In 1990, the new management team found a building filled with people and materials. Storage areas holding over $5 million of work-in-process inventory overflowed into the aisles. Missing tools, defective parts, and other problems interrupted orders, which were put aside and often lost or forgotten until they became critically late. Thirty employees were needed just to store and track inventory. The labour hours required to build a single duct had on average increased by over 50 percent since 1983. As additional hourly workers were added to compensate for the growth and inefficiency, critical support functions were moved out of the building, often to distant locations. Many of DMC's key support personnel had never been to the factory; some did not even know its location.

The management team concluded that DMC's delivery, cost, and quality problems could be attributed to layout, procedures, and morale. The layout required shuttling parts throughout the shop. The average order took 57 days to get through the shop, of which only two days were value-added time.

The layout also required duplication of equipment and support tooling (dies, clamps, chill rings, tack dams, purge plugs, etc.). Building ducts requires a large number of support tools that are specific to metal type, metal thickness, and duct diameter. For example, one of the many types of equipment used by the mechanics is an expander, which shapes the ends of ducts. The mechanics set up this air-powered machine with dies and spindles specific to part size, metal, and shape of the duct. The "hard metals" station was divided into four substations, each substation assembling ducts for specific turbine models. Since each of the DMC's four substations produced ducts of varying lengths (a few inches to 10 feet), widths (less than one inch to more than five inches), and materials (titanium, hastelloy, inconel, stainless steel), each required a full complement of equipment and tooling. However, the tooling was not effectively tracked. Despite the duplicate tooling across different work areas within the building, the mechanics often wasted time searching for tools. The most commonly used tool sizes were the most difficult to find. Furthermore, numerous incomplete jobs and stacks of inventory in the area made locating tools even more difficult.

The layout contributed to long setup times, and consequently to large batch sizes. In addition, welders had their own procedures for reducing the time spent on setups. Although there was little commonality between the jobs (a job is a batch of identical ducts), the welders could treat different jobs within a given diameter range with one setup on their part rotation and welding equipment. The welders would store jobs until they had accumulated several within the same range. If a job had an unusual duct diameter, it could take several days for them to accumulate a sufficiently large quantity of similar jobs. The welder's system reduced the number of setups, but contributed to high work-in-process (WIP) inventories, late deliveries, and exacerbated the quality problems.

Staffing policies also contributed to these problems. Welders rotated between the weld booths in Station 1 on a daily basis. If a job was brought to the weld booth that required difficult welds or had some other characteristic unpopular with the welders, they could avoid working on it by leaving it for someone else to do the next day.

The large number of part diameters, metal types, and metal thicknesses also contributed to rework and scrap costs. For example, when switching from one type of metal to another, the welders needed to change the tension on their rotating equipment that holds and rotates parts during welding. If they forgot, the rollers could damage the part. Another common welding mistake was to use the wrong type of weld rod (each metal type must be welded with a weld rod of the same material). When such errors were made in changing the setup, the damaged part had to be reworked or scrapped.

Because jobs took so long to get through welding, mechanics typically worked on several jobs concurrently. Mechanics and welders are members of different unions and cannot be cross-trained. After leaving a job at the weld booth, a mechanic would start another job or continue one started by other workers. If there was a problem with a job, perhaps even the mechanic's mistake, he could put it under the bench and move on to another job. The problem job would sit under the bench until it became so "hot" (late) that it came to the attention of the lead man, who would then reassign it, possibly to a different mechanic.

Mechanics sometimes used partially completed jobs under the benches as a source of replacement parts. For example, if a part was damaged, a mechanic might avoid ordering a replacement by exchanging it with a good part from a job stored under the bench. When work resumed on the job under the bench, which may be late, it would need its own replacement parts, causing further delays.

In addition, there was lack of trust between shifts. Workers did not like to work on jobs started on another shift. Consequently, each shift would disassemble the equipment setups from the previous shift and reset the equipment for the jobs they were working on. Also fueling this mistrust was a tendency for workers to cannibalise parts from jobs being worked on by other shifts.

Inspection was the final step in the manufacturing process. If X-rays or other inspections revealed cracks or defective welds, the inspectors tagged the parts for rework and returned them to the beginning of the process. Because of the odd shape of many of the ducts, repairs frequently required expensive, time-consuming disassembly to reach the defect. Defective ducts, particularly late ones, often were not reworked by the worker who produced the defect, so workers didn't learn from their mistakes. Frequently, defects were not detected until a large batch had been produced, occasionally necessitating the scrappage of batches of parts, valued at thousands of dollars.

Employees averaged over eight hours of overtime per week. But even with overtime, DMC was unable to handle its workload and was off-loading orders to outside vendors. This frenzied schedule allowed little time for worker training or process improvements. Late deliveries from DMC caused significant problems for customers (primarily Turbine System final assembly operations). DMC's delivery problems were well known throughout Turbine Systems—in fact, DMC's customer divisions made special note of delivery problems from DMC in their quarterly reports.

Content and Substance of Change

While not pleased with the performance of DMC, senior management approved construction of a $50 million, 280,000 square foot replacement facility. Lance Lipscomb was chosen to lead the new unit. He selected a group of individuals for his management team and in April 1990, this team took responsibility for the management of operations, plus design and construction of the new facility.

Lipscomb and other members of the management team realized that designing and constructing a new facility from the ground up offered an opportunity to build a state-of-the-art manufacturing facility. They decided to use the move to a new facility as a catalyst for process improvement. To achieve world-class excellence, they would need to radically change the way they dealt with their employees, customers, suppliers, and support personnel. They had 18 months while the new facility was under construction to develop the skills, values, behaviours, and management policies they would need for the transition to the new building. Lipscomb recognized the problems in achieving these improvements at DMC:

> The Duct Manufacturing Centre would have been one of the last places I would have chosen for just-in-time manufacturing. The assemblies were so complex and the obstacles so great from a quality standpoint. The tools and the manufacturing plans were terrible. Not only were the processes not under control, they weren't even understood. There was open hostility between the workers and the managers, between support organizations and factory people, and between factory workers on different shifts. It was the worst of all worlds.
>
> What we need to succeed with just-in-time manufacturing is a reliable process, excellent quality and the ability to go from one value-added step to the next. Employees and managers must be empowered through education. There must be an obsession with quality.

Lipscomb advocated just-in-time concepts because of the positive effects that flow-time reductions have on delivery, cost, and quality. With help from a local consulting firm, Lipscomb began the transition by guiding his management team through an intensive reading program on JIT and its implications for quality, process reliability, material handling, setup times, vendors, and customers. Not all of the managers initially shared Lipscomb's enthusiasm for JIT. Jenifer Jacobs, industrial engineering manager, reflects:

> In my case JIT was a bad word, so much of it was counterintuitive to what I had always believed. It was because of my lack of education and my misunderstanding of what JIT is all about. Once I began to understand it, I became enthusiastic and wanted to make changes. We shared what we knew and talked with anyone who would listen. That alone started to cause changes in the shop.

Process of Transition

After six months of learning and discussion within the management team, Lipscomb formed a management steering council to lead the transition to improved manufacturing. The council named itself "Deltaforce," after the invincible U.S. military squad, which had overcome great obstacles. Deltaforce developed a vision that reflected how DMC would look and feel and a plan for achieving that vision. Major elements of this plan included:

- Focusing the product line and facilities. This step would allow DMC to concentrate its improvement efforts on those products and processes where it has distinctive competencies: manufacturing high quality, complex welded metal ducts and reservoirs.
- Orienting DMC to customer needs. DMC decided to work directly with its customers (primarily other Turbine Systems divisions) to determine what was critical to the customer's success, and then to focus on satisfying those needs.
- Moving to a pull system that produces parts only as needed. This step would eliminate the waste involved in storing and tracking excess inventories and also help highlight deficiencies in the production system.
- Developing reliable processes. A pull system requires reliable methods and processes for quick response. Workers would receive education and tools for ongoing process improvement. As processes improved, check points and control points would lock in improvements and ensure consistency.
- Bringing support personnel into the factory to work directly with their DMC customers.
- Building trust and cooperation within the entire DMC Manufacturing Business Unit. This element would be facilitated by improving communication between workers, management, and support personnel.

Deltaforce immediately began focusing on the product line by off-loading nonduct work (about 5 percent of the total) to outside vendors. Besides allowing them to concentrate their efforts on improving duct manufacturing processes, this strategy gave Deltaforce time not only to clear the backlog of work, but also to complete previously neglected activities such as housekeeping, training, and process improvement.

Housekeeping.   A starting point for process improvement was to reduce congestion and confusion. Lipscomb told workers to throw out everything that was not absolutely needed. Much of the material thrown out was scrap and obsolete inventory that had accumulated over the past 20 years. Jenifer Jacobs, the industrial engineering manager, describes the workers' enthusiasm for the cleanup:

> People really got into the spirit of things. If it wasn't bolted down, there was probably someone who was going to throw it away. As it turns out, little that was needed was thrown away. I think you have to attribute that to the fact that people on the floor really knew what they needed.

Part of the cleanup effort involved controlling the flow of work into the shop. Previously, the MRP (materials requirements planning system) pushed work without regard to the shop's capacity to accomplish it. Deltaforce assigned and trained a scheduler to stop the flow of low priority orders until the shop completed its backlog. After that, the scheduler released only those orders that he felt could go directly into production. Removing excess inventory from the floor eliminated several nonvalue-added material handling steps and retrieved floor space for productive uses. Over three months, the housekeeping efforts recovered 40,000 square feet of floor space (25 percent of the total floor space of the old building).

Training.   While Deltaforce team members were excited by the vision of DMC as a world-class manufacturing facility, they realized that accomplishing this dream meant educating and motivating their employees. To achieve this goal, Deltaforce used a top-down teaching system known as "cascade education," where employees are taught by their supervisors. Marshall Atherton, assembly general supervisor and a member of Deltaforce, explains:

> If you expect the work force to improve, you have to teach them more skills. You can't assume that people have skills. Our people had on-the-job training but no formal training. Besides skill training, you have to give them an exhaustive training program on JIT. If they don't understand the premise behind JIT, they'll never buy into it.

Deltaforce began cascade education by organizing self-directed study groups, with five supervisors in each group, facilitated by Lipscomb and Atherton. Roy Doctor, a first-line supervisor and participant in one of the initial groups, said of the cascade education approach, "When my boss is training me and he believes in it, it makes me believe in it. I can't wait until we start training all the people on the floor." Deltaforce more than tripled the training budget to supply workers with the tools they needed to improve the way they did their jobs.

Communication, Morale, and Ownership.   While it took almost a year for the training to "cascade" down to the shop floor, management's enthusiasm had immediate effects on morale throughout the shop. Atherton comments:

> The work force has to see management enthused about something. I believe the work force emulates the management. When we have our feet on the desk and are apathetic about our jobs, they're going to have the same attitude. When we're out there on the floor talking with them, our enthusiasm inoculates the place.

Managers' offices, including Lipscomb's, were relocated directly off the shop floor, and workers were encouraged to bring problems and suggestions directly to managers. To gain ownership of their processes, management needed the dedicated support functions. While proving difficult, the support units were moved into the building. Management encouraged workers on the shop floor to interact directly with support personnel. Doctor describes the effect on the work force:

> We are able to work out problems a lot faster than we have in the past. The supporting groups such as production control, IE, planning, engineering, and tool design are accessible. We have broken down a lot of the barriers between organizations. Now if one of the mechanics on the floor needs something, he knows he can get a planner to come out there and work with him. We don't have this: "Well, I'm a planner and I know how it should be and you're a mechanic." There is more of a teamwork approach to try to solve problems.
>
> For example, tool design is now located in the building. The mechanics can work with them on a tool, as far as improvements or whatever needs to be done. Another big thing is Quality Assurance, there's more of a "work with" type of attitude. Before it was just, write the part up and throw it back over the fence. Now we talk about what the problem is. You see a lot more of the problems being solved that way. I think that when the people see that the problems are getting worked and their opinions are being addressed, this does tremendous things for morale.

Process Improvement.   Because the workers on the shop floor understand their processes better than anyone else, the key to process improvement is empowering them to make constructive changes. Atherton says, "Management's job is to provide them the skills, motivation and freedom to do their jobs better. Many of the improvements they come up with are simple and inexpensive." He cites the following example:

> For years we have had a water pressure test that used a 3/8-inch water line to fill up these big ducts. The workers said, "Why don't we have a 1-1/2-inch line in here; it will fill it up six times faster." For a $27 investment they made an 80 percent reduction in the time needed to fill the ducts. Now they want to find a way to recycle the water.

To increase the workers' flexibility, wheels were installed on work benches and other shop equipment. Previously, workers could not move benches without a fork lift, and consequently layout improvements were rarely made. But with the wheels on benches, workers could change layouts, experiment with different layouts, and even relocate entire operations to improve efficiency.

Putting the work benches on wheels also reduced setup times. Each duct model is assembled on a unique weld jig that can weigh up to 300 pounds. When the benches were stationary, the narrow aisles required either that the larger jigs be moved by overhead crane or that the workers manhandle them in and out of the work areas. With the benches on wheels, workers loaded the jigs onto carts at the loading dock and wheeled them into the work areas.

The Blue Cell—A Pilot Project.   Deltaforce set up a self-contained manufacturing cell, called the Blue Cell, to experiment with cellular manufacturing. The cell, with five mechanics and three welders per shift, included all the resources needed to build a family of duct models, significantly cutting down on part travel and flow time. With the work benches on wheels, workers could reconfigure the cell to accommodate each order. Defective parts were returned to the person who made them, rather than the normal practice of sending them to someone else to fix. Greater worker responsibility and control not only increased efficiency but also improved morale. Doctor, who supervises the area that includes the Blue Cell, comments,

> I've noticed quite a difference in attitudes between the Blue Cell and the other areas. There is more bonding between the people in the cell; they want to get more involved. They take more ownership for things that they do than people in other areas of the shop.

Operation of New Practices

After reviewing facility documents prepared by design engineers outside the DMC business unit in November 1991, a group of workers from the Blue Cell were not satisfied with the proposed layout for their area. They formed a team and, using their new knowledge of the manufacturing process, designed a cellular layout based on entirely different criteria than the one proposed. Besides developing a more effective layout, the team took "ownership" for their design. They presented their design to the rest of the workers in the DMC and sold them on both the process and the layout. Encouraged by the response, the team suggested testing the new layout in their present building. This would allow them to refine the layout before setting it up in the new building. Management agreed that there was no reason to wait, and in July of 1991 the cellular layout was adopted in the old building as a test site for the new building. By November 1991 DMC was midway through its move to the new building.

The changes at DMC have made workers' jobs more interesting. Education, a clean work environment, greater responsibility, participation, and the ability to improve the way they do their jobs have had a tremendous effect on morale. Doctor describes his reaction to the changes:

> I think it's exciting. I've been with Turbine Systems for 25 years and this is the first time I've been really excited about coming to work. Every day is different. I like working more closely with people. I don't know why it wasn't there before, but it wasn't.

An attitude of ownership and responsibility has taken hold throughout the DMC. Asked which changes he thought contributed the most to productivity improvements, Doctor gives his perspective from the shop floor:

> I would say morale has been the single greatest factor, based on what I feel out on the floor. The training and the participation both contributed to improving morale. I think it's great because people are getting hungry to improve things. They are starting to figure out they own their processes.

The attitude of ownership that Doctor perceives on the shop floor pervades the entire organization. Lipscomb observes from his perspective as manufacturing business unit manager:

> Many things have changed, but what it comes down to is one central theme, and that theme is ownership. We have taken ownership for everything: technology, scheduling, suppliers, tooling, communications, and customer satisfaction.

During the first 18 months, overtime dropped from 17 percent of total hours worked to 5 percent. The turn rate increased 50 percent from 0.8 to 1.2, and the cost of rework dropped from $5 per direct labour hour to $2. In addition, delivery performance improved, and work-in-process inventories (WIP) have been reduced. As of November 1991, DMC has not yet been able to implement a pull system for controlling the work flow.

Conclusion

In assessing the reengineering effort of the company, DMC has made a good start toward radical change. The experience offers the company three lessons. First is the importance of top management's commitment to reengineering. Senior corporate management sanctioned at DMC new plant, new equipment, and much more training support. DMC's general manager, Lance Lipscomb, was oriented toward operations and was not afraid to change or break the rules. Lance viewed his role as a visionary and motivator. Reengineering became his personal project. He successfully persuaded his management team and their subordinates of the need for radical change. This was accomplished by articulating a case for action (i.e., here is where we are as a company and this is why we can't stay here), and by forming Deltaforce with some of DMC's best and brightest people.

Second, the experience demonstrates the power of communication and training so that everyone at DMC understands the goals and techniques of reengineering. Deltaforce encouraged greater trust between workers, management, and support personnel by collocating and seeking more worker participation in decision making. Deltaforce developed cascade education where team members taught the class to supervisors, who are now instructing the shop-floor workers. Deltaforce also prepared a vision statement with measurable objectives and metrics. The vision statement is intended to describe in sufficiently clear terms to paint a picture as to what DMC as a business unit will become. Deltaforce believes that the efforts to construct architectural drawings and layout charts for the new building have facilitated this process.

Third, DMC made good use of pilots and proofs in order to reduce the risk of proposed changes. The housekeeping and "wheels on work benches" projects were easy to accomplish and provided noticeable value. The Blue Cell was chosen as a pilot because it was small in scale relative to the rest of the activity at DMC, and it represented a problem area with great potential for visible improvement. The Blue Cell project was followed by several others that were planned and directed by focused problem-solving teams.

8
THE DUCT MANUFACTURING CENTRE (B & C)[1]

TQM and the New Layout for Hard Metal Processes (B) and
The Implementation of a New Pull System (C)

Summary of Part (A)

The Duct Manufacturing Centre (DMC) is within the Manufacturing Division of the Turbine Systems Corporation. DMC assembles precision-welded metal ducts for use in Turbine Systems's primary products: turbine jet engines and turbine power generators. Turbine Systems has been the most successful manufacturer of turbine systems in the industry, consistently maintaining more than half of the market share.

The DMC shop consists of three areas: detail, hard metals, and soft metals. Assembling a duct is a labour-intensive process, comparable to putting together a three-dimensional, snake-shaped jigsaw puzzle. Duct parts are formed in the detail fabrication area prior to assembly either in the hard metals area (for titanium, stainless steel, hastelloy, and inconel), or in the soft metals area (primarily for aluminum). In the detail area, duct stock and other raw materials are formed (precise bending and stretching operations) before fitting. The detail area typically performs tasks on duct parts such as forming a 90° bend, enlarging one end so that its inside diameter is 1 inch larger than the other end, or tapering (drilling a hole in the duct and shaping a flange pattern by pulling a hot, oversized ball through the hole). In assembly, the mechanic places the finished duct parts into the appropriate tool and marks them for cutting and grinding. After cutting and grinding, he again places them in the tool, fits them together, and holds them in position with tack clamps. He removes the clamped assembly from the tool and takes it to a booth where a welder makes small temporary welds (called tack welds). The mechanic removes the provisional tack clamps and returns the assembly to the weld booth for a permanent fusion weld. In many cases it is not possible to weld all the joints at once, so the mechanic may repeat the fitting and welding process several times. Some ducts have over 20 weld joints, requiring many iterations of the process. The ducts are also cleaned several times during this circuitous process. Prior to completion, the ducts must pass final inspection using X-ray, pressure test, or other testing procedures.

In April 1990 top management at Turbine Systems Corporation decided to build a new $50 million, 280,000 square foot manufacturing facility to replace DMC's antiquated, overcrowded building. To oversee the transition and take responsibility for operations in the facility they formed a new management team for the DMC, headed by Lance Lipscomb. Since the team felt that the new building would be poorly served using current management practices, they initiated a reengineering program. They called their reengineering team "Deltaforce." During the 18 months while the new building was under construction Deltaforce began to prune the product line, raise housekeeping standards, reduce work-in-process inventories, enhance management and worker training, and improve the manufacturing layout. Deltaforce also encouraged greater trust between workers, management, and support personnel by collocating and seeking more worker participation in decision making. Deltaforce adopted a top-down training system known as "cascade education." The Deltaforce team members taught the class to supervisors, who are now instructing the shop-floor workers.

[1]This case was developed for use in classroom discussion and is not intended to necessarily illustrate appropriate or inappropriate management practices. Case author: Thomas G. Schmitt, University of Washington, 1996. The funding for this case production was provided by the Australian federal government's Department of Industry, Science and Resources.

THE DUCT MANUFACTURING CENTRE (B)

TQM and the New Layout for Hard Metal Processes

Introduction

In April 1991 approximately 150 welders and mechanics were employed in an area of the old building called Station 1. They assembled over 1,600 different duct models from "hard metals": inconel (an alloy), titanium, hastelloy, and stainless steel. Station 1 was divided into four substations, each substation assembling ducts for specific turbine models (Exhibit B1). The origins of the layout were unknown; its primary advantage was that part delivery clerks would know where to deliver parts for the ducts.

Since each of the DMC's four substations produced ducts of all sizes and materials, each required a full complement of equipment and tooling. However, because the support tooling was spread among all four substations, the mechanics often wasted time searching for the needed tooling. The most commonly used tool sizes were the most difficult to find. Furthermore, numerous incomplete jobs and stacks of inventory in the area made locating tools even more difficult. To reduce time spent looking for tooling, management ordered $70,000 of additional support tooling in early 1991. They also planned to purchase an additional $3 million of tooling for the new building.

Content and Substance of Change

A design for the new building was initially proposed by support personnel whereby Station 1 would be organized into five manufacturing cells based upon part volume. In March 1991 a group of mechanics and welders informed their supervisor, Roy Doctor, that they did not think that the proposed layout addressed many of the problems in Station 1. Encouraged by the spirit of "glasnost" that was spreading throughout DMC, the group offered to design a better layout. Doctor,

EXHIBIT B1

The old layout at Station 1

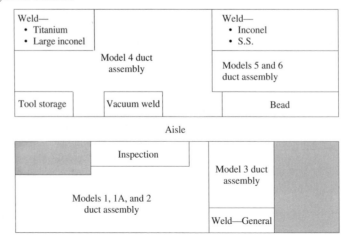

Exhibit B2

The Seven Management and Planning Tools

Workers and management alike at DMC have found the Seven Management and Planning (MP) Tools an effective means to help them structure and solve problems. Deltaforce used these tools to develop the transition management plan, and the worker team from Station 1 used them to design the shop-floor layout. The tools are useful for arranging ill-structured ideas and information into a meaningful form so that an intelligent decision can be made. The tools are particularly useful for describing problems that cannot be described with numerical data, and for helping a diverse group of people reach a consensus.

The seven MP tools were developed in Japan by the Society for QC Technique Development within the context of the Deming Cycle and Total Quality Control. The tools were published in Japanese in 1979 and translated into English in 1983. The Seven MP Tools should not be confused with the Seven Statistical Tools, which are used to describe and analyze numerical data. The Seven Statistical Tools are frequently used for analyzing production and maintaining process control. The following table lists these two sets of tools.

Seven Statistical Tools	*Seven MP Tools*
1. Pareto diagrams	1. Relations diagrams
2. Cause-and-effect diagrams	2. Affinity diagrams
3. Histograms	3. Tree diagrams
4. Control charts	4. Matrix diagrams
5. Scatter diagrams	5. Matrix data-analysis diagram
6. Graphs	6. Product decision program chart
7. Check sheets	7. Arrow diagram

who was currently participating in one of the initial cascade education groups, suggested that they form a team and offered to facilitate it. They established a team of six shop-floor workers and one industrial engineer.

Doctor, having just learned about the Seven Management Tools (listed in Exhibit B2), suggested that they use TQM to structure their ideas. Several of the team members expressed concerns that they were "hocus pocus." One team member commented, "We didn't want to use the tools, but just to prove they were a waste of time, we agreed to go through the process." But in the learning process they found that the tools helped them understand the critical elements of duct assembly as well as reach a consensus on a design for a new layout.

Process of Transaction

The team applied four of the Seven Management Tools: (1) affinity diagram, (2) interrelationship digraph, (3) tree diagram, and (4) T-shaped matrix. First they used an affinity diagram to organize their ideas. In their first one-hour session, they came up with 111 suggestions for defining a cell and put each suggestion on a Post-It note. In their second one-hour session, they organized the Post-It notes into nine categories, with the following headings: safety, training, preventive maintenance, housekeeping, tooling, equipment, shop support, people needs, and material. The resulting affinity diagram is shown in Exhibit B3.

EXHIBIT B3

Safety
- Aisle width
- Flammable storage cabinets
- Chemical & solvent storage
- Air pollution
- Rag cans
- Hazardous waste management (rags)
- First aid kits & supplies
- Eye wash kits

Training
- Tour or visit customer facility
- Part design on tool or order
- Incentives for training
- Standard operating procedure
- Clarify W.O. for welder stamp
- Part-building techniques
- Sample part for demonstration
- Notebook of photos of parts
- Voluntary rotation for cross-training
- Machinery training
- Safety training
- Progressive training & pay for knowledge

Preventive Maintenance
- Maintenance availability in cell
- Machinery maintenance
- Machinery downtime
- Machinery improvements
- In-house Mss support for mechanics
- Preventive maintenance schedule (housekeeping)
- Preventive maintenance of machines by mechanics
- Preventive maintenance on air motors

Housekeeping
- Cabinets, shelves, storage equipment
- Air hose storage
- Air tool accessory storage
- Storage (stones, bits)
- Cleaning equipment storage
- Tool box inventory min/max
- Tool box size
- Storage locker for personal items
- Blueprint storage
- Storage of personal toll boxes
- Cardboard containers
- Paper recycle
- Scrap containers
- Trash can size/location

Tooling
- Ordering STs
- Storing WJs
- Storage availability of STs
- Receiving STs
- Order WJs
- Receiving WJs
- Repairing STs
- Inventory STs
- Purge diffusers
- Purge equipment (availability & storage)
- Better system for lack bands
- Color coding area sizes mail ST tooling
- Repairing WJs
- Tool handling equip. crane, cherry picker
- Welder positioner (STs)

Equipment
- Wand station locations & PM
- Floor fans
- Mechanic push carts
- Adjustable height work tables
- Platforms for short people
- Ratio of tables to mechanics
- Ratio of equipment to mechanics
- Tack tables
- Spray to prevent titanium lines
- Slow sanders for titanium
- Enclosed room for saws
- Machinery quantities
- Automated print machine (blueprints)
- Automated print machine for sketches
- Air motors
- Table layout
- Large sanders for large ducts
- Grinding table alternatives
- Grinding benches
- Grinders in one room
- Milling machines
- Enclosed grinding tables
- Straightening equipment

Shop Support
- Management communication w/employees
- Performance measurement
- Order completion targets for employ (ECD)
- Production measurement
- Engineer availability
- Planning availability
- Welder availability
- Employee recognition from management
- Inspection availability
- Nonaccountability stamp for mechanics
- Supervisor communication w/employees
- Quality improvement
- Location systems
- Improved tie-in w/other shifts
- Inspection location
- Management recognition of employees
- Customer communication liaison
- More crew meetings to inform employees
- Band tolerances too wide
- In-cell AD bug

People Needs
- Flex time
- Cell, decorations, décor
- Shift start time staggered
- Lunch & break areas in cell

Material
- Part configuration by material
- Part configuration by size
- Parts routing within cell
- Kit flanges with orders
- Material distribution (inc. TI)
- Incoming/outgoing location
- Part configuration by model
- Storage of flanges/standards

Next, the team developed an interrelationship digraph to define the relationships between the categories. An interrelationship digraph graphically maps the causes and effects among interrelated product and process attributes. The team wrote the category headings from their affinity diagram on a large sheet of paper and drew arrows to show relationships between the headings. The resulting interrelationship digraph is shown in Exhibit B4. Where two headings influenced each other, they drew only a single arrow from the attribute with the greater influence. To determine the dominant interrelationships in cell layout, they tallied up the number of "in" and "out" arrows for each heading. The root or central attribute is the one with the most outward pointing arrows because it influences other attributes. The team concluded that the central attribute was material, with six outward pointing arrows, closely followed by equipment, with five outward arrows. The attribute with the most incoming arrows is also important because it is influenced by so many other attributes. Training had the most inward-pointing arrows, suggesting that regardless of which central attribute was chosen, it was a potential roadblock to implementation.

EXHIBIT B4

Interrelationship digraph

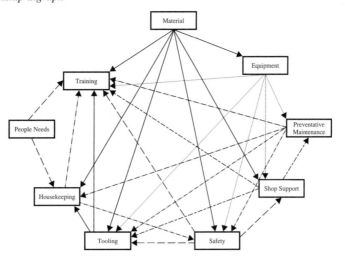

	In	*Out*
Material	0	6
Equipment	1	5
Preventive maintenance	2	4
Shop support	2	3
Safety	4	3
Tooling	4	2
Housekeeping	5	2
People needs	0	2
Training	8	0

The team then developed tree diagrams to further define the central attributes—material, equipment, and tooling (which they considered closely related to equipment)—into subheadings and specific assignable tasks. They differentiated material by size and metal type, and equipment and tooling by task. The tree diagrams are shown in Exhibits B5a to B5c.

To better identify relationships between the central attributes and the strength of their relationships, the team constructed a T-shaped matrix. A T-shaped matrix graphically illustrates the logical connections between items and the relative importance of the connections. The issues with the most and strongest relationships are the most strongly related. Using the subheadings from the tree diagram, the team found that material diameter was the aspect of material that most strongly influenced equipment and tooling. Their T-shaped matrix is shown in Exhibit B6.

The Proposed Layout for Station.   Through this TQM process, the team identified material as the critical attribute in duct assembly, and diameter as the most critical aspect of material. This suggested that they should organize their manufacturing cells by metal type and duct diameter rather than by turbine model.

To develop specific cell definitions, the team also gathered workload data on the material and diameter (the percentages are shown in Exhibit B7). The team proposed dedicating three of the five cells in the new building to titanium, one cell to inconel, and one cell to stainless steel and hastelloy.

The three titanium cells would be further divided by duct diameter: under 2 inches, 2.25 to 4.0 inches, and 4.5 inches and above (shown in Exhibit B8). The divisions between the titanium cells could be adjusted by the workers to accommodate fluctuations in the workload. The team also

EXHIBIT B5A

Tree diagram: Material

EXHIBIT B5B

Tree diagram: Equipment

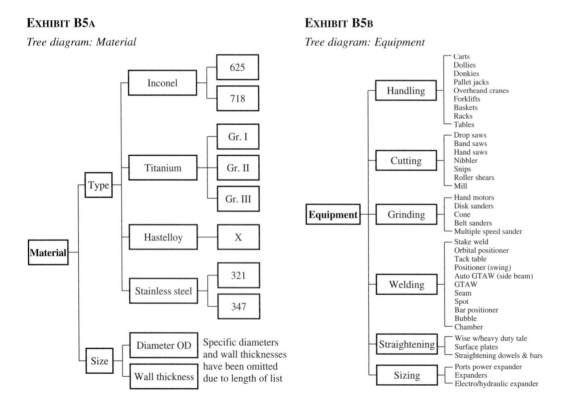

Tree diagram: Tooling

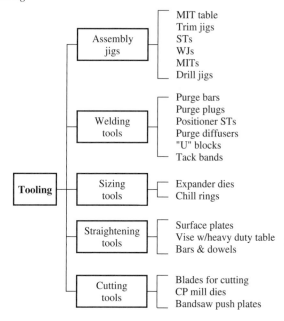

EXHIBIT B6

T-shaped matrix

Strength of relationship: Possible   -
                              Some   –
                              Strong   —

		TI	SS	INC	HAS	Thickness	Diameter
E q u i p m e n t	Handling	-	–	-	-	-	-
	Cutting	–	–	–	–	–	–
	Grinding	—	–	–	—	–	—
	Welding	—	–	–	–	–	—
	Straightening					-	—
	Sizing					-	-
	Material	*TI*	*SS*	*INC*	*HAS*	*Thickness*	*Diameter*
T o o l i n g	Assembly jigs						—
	Weld tools	—	–	–	–	-	—
	Sizing tools						—
	Straightening tools					-	—
	Cutting tools	–	–	—	–	–	—

EXHIBIT B7

Workload breakdown

Duct Manufacturing Centre
Station 1 Workload Breakdown
Percentage of Parts Produced

Diameter	Stainless	Hastelloy	Inconel	Titanium
0.75	0.1			
1.00	1.9			
1.25	0.2			0.1
1.50	0.1		0.1	1.4
1.75	0.1		1.5	1.3
2.00	0.9		4.3	21.5
2.25	0.2			1.3
2.50	0.5		0.9	5.8
3.00	0.4	0.1	5.3	3.1
3.50	1.5		4.7	4.7
4.00	0.5		3.1	6.4
4.50	0.1	0.4	0.6	0.2
5.00	0.2		2.5	1.6
5.50	0.1		0.8	0.1
6.00	0.6		3.5	5.3
6.50	0.1		0.1	3.5
7.00			0.7	6.0
7.50			0.7	
8.00			0.4	
11.50			0.4	
Total	7	1	30	62

EXHIBIT B8

Material distribution

	Diameter			
Material	3/4–2	21/4–4	41/2 +	Total
Titanium	24%	21%	17%	62%
Inconel	6	14	10	30
Stainless steel	3	3	1	7
Hastelloy		1		1

proposed that the three titanium cells be adjacent to each other so that tooling could be easily moved between the cells. The proposed layout is shown in Exhibit B9.

In a series of presentations the team proposed the layout to management and other shop-floor workers. Management recognized the compelling logic of their proposal and agreed to adopt it in the new building. Other shop-floor workers were also impressed; the same workers who didn't trust each other, sometimes pilfering parts and tools from each other and across shifts, applauded their fellow workers' presentation. The workers' enthusiastic response reflected both their approval

Exhibit B9

Proposed layout

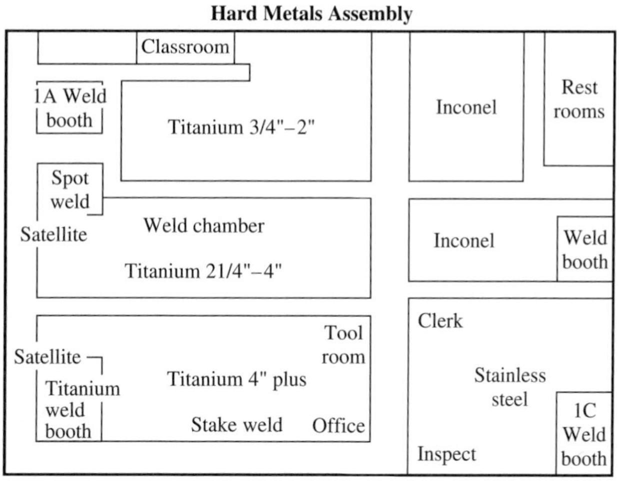

Hard Metals Assembly

	Classroom				Rest rooms
1A Weld booth			Inconel		
	Titanium 3/4"–2"				
Spot weld					
	Weld chamber		Inconel		Weld booth
Satellite	Titanium 21/4"–4"				
Satellite		Tool room	Clerk		
Titanium weld booth	Titanium 4" plus		Stainless steel		1C Weld booth
	Stake weld Office		Inspect		

of the new layout and their appreciations that workers were participating in what were traditionally management decisions.

Encouraged by the response, the team suggested testing the new layout in their present building. This would allow them to refine the layout before setting it up in the new building. They would also benefit immediately from easily accessible support tooling, fewer setups, reduced part travel, and fewer material-related errors.

Management agreed that there was no reason to wait, and in July of 1991 the workers arranged Station 1 into the recommended five cells. Because the workbenches and most of the shop equipment were already on wheels, the change took only a few days. The workers used coloured tape on the floor to designate the new cells and put the equipment that worked best with particular materials into the cells that used those materials.

Workers also redesigned storage for the tooling in the station. They colour-coded the tools by diameter and gave them specific storage locations on wheeled storage racks. The most frequently used tools were now conveniently located near where they were used. After rearranging the station and supplying each cell with the tooling needed to produce its dedicated product line, the workers recovered $450,000 of excess support tooling. Consequently, the $70,000 order for additional tooling was canceled, and the $3 million earmarked for tooling in the new building was no longer needed.

The cellular layout naturally encouraged friendly competition between the cells. Within a few months of forming the cells, the workers were competing to have the "best" work area. They displayed impeccable housekeeping practices: cleaning the floor at the end of each shift, returning tooling to the colour-coded storage racks, and even cleaning equipment that hadn't been cleaned in 15 years. They started their day with a battle cry to show their enthusiasm. One large, deep-voiced mechanic remarked, "Those Japanese sing songs; we yell!"

Operation of New Practices

The successful changes at Station 1 motivated management to form another team to design a new layout for Station 2, the station that assembled parts from "soft" metals, particularly aluminum. This team used the same methods for changing layout with similar results.

In addition to designing the cells for stations 1 and 2, workers also played an important role in deciding which equipment would go into the cells. The people who would use the equipment formed teams to determine their equipment needs. They researched available equipment and then helped to select appropriate vendors. Before making a purchase, management would send workers with test materials to visit the vendor and test the equipment they would be using. If the equipment did not satisfy their requirements, the workers were authorized to order modifications. If necessary, the workers would visit the vendor several times to ensure it met their specifications. Jenifer Jacobs, industrial engineering supervisor, describes the advantages of allowing the workers to select their own equipment:

> First, it gave us a turnkey operation. When the equipment arrived on the shop floor we knew it would perform as expected, and the operator knew how to operate it. Secondly, at minimum cost, it sent a strong message to the workers that we were serious about their input. When we give them an airplane ticket, a hotel room, a rental car, and spending money and tell them to evaluate the equipment, it shows that we respect their judgment and value their input. Thirdly, when the operators select their own equipment, they take ownership for it and make sure that it performs as promised.

Workers and managers have formed teams to examine every stage of manufacturing. For example, a customer satisfaction survey identified part marking as an important process because it was the most common reason for customer rejection tags. Part numbers stamped on the ducts were sometimes incorrect or stamped in the wrong place. A team is now working with the three-part marking areas within DMC to document and improve the reliability of that process.

As another example, new materials will soon be introduced for a new turbine design, and the workers plan to form a team to decide how to modify the cells in Station 1 to handle these materials.

The purchasing division recently established rigorous quality and part variability standards that its outside suppliers must meet. While such certification (commonly known as ISO-9000) is not required for internal suppliers, DMC management felt they could not require higher standards of outside suppliers than of themselves. Therefore DMC sought and was the first internal organization to receive ISO-9000 certification.

DMC teams have found ways to reduce hazardous waste by 67 percent in the past 12 months. This reduction has been achieved by eliminating equipment leaks that resulted in oily cardboard and rags, and by reducing the variety of paints and solvents. Aqueous degrease has now replaced chemical vapour degrease. Furthermore, DMC has reduced nonhazardous wastes by shipping parts in reusable containers and by promoting an employee-recycling program. Protective plastic end-caps are now returned by DMC's customers and are reused.

Accidents are now tracked by process and video analysis on accident-prone processes. In addition, DMC has taken a proactive approach to safety by using Near-Miss forms, which identify dangers so they can be eliminated before an injury occurs.

Progress Achieved in June 1992.   Lipscomb and his managers are proud of the progress they have made toward improving manufacturing performance at DMC. The facilities, policies, and attitudes at DMC bear little resemblance to those of 26 months ago. Cascade education has provided the means for improvement.[2] Managers, shop-floor workers, and support organizations are working together to improve their processes and satisfy the customers. Despite the disruptions caused by moving people and equipment between buildings, DMC has continued to make progress on labour performance, inventory, delivery, and flow time.

---

[2]DMC managers are now completing a self-study course on managing an empowered work force. All shop-floor workers are taking six classes to improve their technical skills in such areas as reading blueprints, understanding technical specifications, and improving mechanical and welding skills.

Labour. Labour performance has improved. Industrial Engineering estimated that the new layout saved 0.5 hour/person/day (or about 75 hours/day).

Inventory. The inventory turn rate at DMC has gone from 0.8 turns/year in the first quarter of 1991, to 4.1 turns/year in the second quarter of 1992. Much of the improvement was achieved by eliminating obsolete and excess inventories in the stockroom. By eliminating obsolete part numbers (some of which dated back to 1969), the number of part numbers stored was reduced from 16,000 to 7,800. One part number had 19,000 parts stored, enough for 1.5 years of production. As Jacobs commented, "If an engineering change comes through next week, we'll have to throw them all away or rework them. What does that cost?" The size of the stock has been reduced by 50 percent, as shown in Exhibit B10.

Delivery. The number of late part deliveries to customers has declined dramatically (see Exhibit B10).

Flow time. Flow time reduction has from the outset been a strategic goal for the division. DMC has reduced the transit and paperwork time but has encountered difficulties in shortening the manufacturing time (see Exhibit B11).

EXHIBIT B10

Performance data

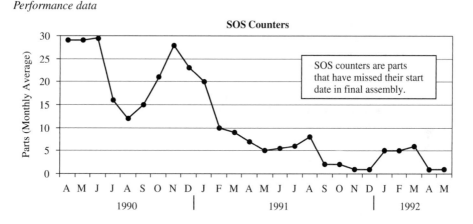

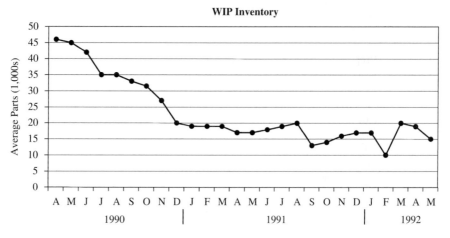

Exhibit B11

Flow time

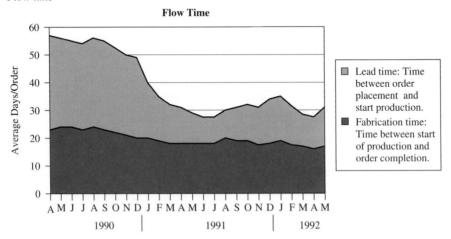

Flow Time

Lead time: Time between order placement and start production.

Fabrication time: Time between start of production and order completion.

y-axis: Average Days/Order

x-axis: A M J J A S O N D J F M A M J J A S O N D J F M A M
1990 | 1991 | 1992

DMC has been able to shorten the transit time to customers and between manufacturing operations. These measures have enabled DMC to reduce its planned lead times on average from 57 days in April 1990 to 31 days in May 1992 (refer to the lightly shaded area in Exhibit B11). Kitting, tool repair, and engineering change processes provide examples where the lead time has been compressed.

The time to customers has been reduced from 20 days to 5 days by delivering the kits directly to the customer the day they are assembled, rather than routing parts individually through the normal transportation system. This eliminates the need for customers to stock individual parts until they could be kitted for assembly. Jobs within the DMC, which were allocated 20 days to move between operations and the stockroom, now take an average of five days.

Support organizations within DMC have also improved response times. For example, it used to take an average of 30 days to get a damaged tool repaired. The paperwork alone averaged 18 days and involved 10 different organizations. DMC constructed a time-line for the process, identifying value-added time and nonvalue-added time. They found that most of the paperwork was for cost accounting, a nonvalue-adding activity. After extensive negotiations with finance and other organizations, they eliminated most of the paperwork and shortened the time from request to repair to 18 hours. As another example, the time to process paperwork for engineering design changes that two years ago took 40 days now takes 1.65 days.

The overall assessment in June 1992 is that the average flow time for jobs has been reduced from 57 days to 31 days, yet much of this time compression can be attributed to less paperwork, transit, and slack time rather than manufacturing time. Efforts have been made to reduce the manufacturing time. For example, a team of workers and engineers meet each morning to look at Station 1's incoming work statement for the next week and, if necessary, adjusts the cell definitions to accommodate work-load fluctuations. The improved order release system, better cell layouts, and wheels on the work benches should have contributed to reduced manufacturing time, but as of July 1992 little improvement has been observed (refer to the dark shaded area in Exhibit B11). However, up to this time, DMC has not yet been able to implement a pull system for controlling the workflow. Many within DMC feel that these difficulties can be attributed to the complexity of the process of making welded ducts. Using cascade education, Deltaforce has prepared by the end of 1992 to train their work force in an advanced course in just-in-time manufacturing.

THE DUCT MANUFACTURING CENTRE (C)

Implementation of a New Pull System

In one summer morning in July 1995, Nancy Wallace, the general manager at that time, was in a conference room with her management team (no longer referred to as Deltaforce), reflecting on the progress at the Duct Manufacturing Centre (DMC) of Turbine Systems Corporation. Nancy had been general manager of DMC for four months. Also attending were general managers of several other business units within Turbine Systems who were interested in DMC's progress. Nancy reviewed:

> With the help of Marshall Atherton, our factory superintendent, I plan first to provide a retrospective on business at DMC. I'm sure that our guests from sister business units can relate to the difficulties of managing during an economic downturn. Since you are particularly interested in our pull system, Pam Petersen, an industrial engineering manager, will then discuss the details of these efforts that have spanned almost four years. Roy Doctor, an area supervisor, will then discuss prospects for process improvement, and I plan to conclude by summarizing the challenges we face over the next several years.
>
> Despite the adversities of an economic downturn and "revolving door" transfers of our general managers, a great deal has been accomplished since we embarked on the re-engineering effort five years ago. Today we are viewed as one of the most progressive business units in the Turbine Systems Corporation. We are in a modern factory, and thanks to our process improvement teams, we have a cellular layout that has facilitated dramatic performance improvements. During the period April 1990 to April 1995, our WIP inventory has been reduced from 46,000 part numbers to 4,500 in (Exhibit C1). Manufacturing flow time has decreased on average from 25 days per part to 6 days (Exhibit C2).
>
> We attribute much of the credit for these improvements to an emphasis on speed. Just-in-time was an initiative started by one of my predecessors, Lance Lipscomb, and supported by the three general managers that followed. Flow time compression was difficult at first, but after a few years we began to make progress. A reduction in flow time of only a few days per part was achieved during the period April 1990 to July 1992. The first pull system was implemented late in 1992, but aborted three months later. Much of the compression in flow time occurred in 1993 when we finally began to realize the benefits of good

EXHIBIT C1

Work-in-process inventory

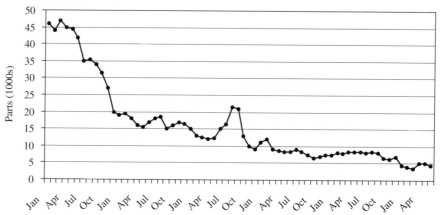

EXHIBIT C2

Flow time

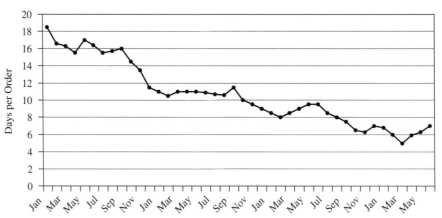

EXHIBIT C3

Cost per part (excludes equipment depreciation, material, and purchased parts)

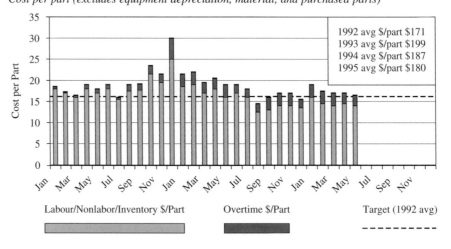

housekeeping, reduced batch sizes, improved quality, staff colocation, and moving the stock room and heat treat into the new building. Another pull system was implemented in January 1995. The second system overcame the blockage difficulties encountered during the first effort. Performance continued to improve because of the effectiveness of this system as well as our program to standardize and simplify the part routings.

Yet we are not satisfied with our progress toward JIT. I share the view with my predecessors that flow time reduction provides the engine for productivity improvement. I sense that we have reached another plateau with respect to flow time, and this, in turn, will limit our ability to improve performance in terms of cost, delivery, and quality. (Refer to Exhibits C3, C4, and C5.) The turnover in leadership hasn't helped, and economic conditions in the turbine business have been poor for several years. There is no question that we are understaffed. Despite these factors, we can continue to improve. We need to fine-tune the

Exhibit C4

Late deliveries

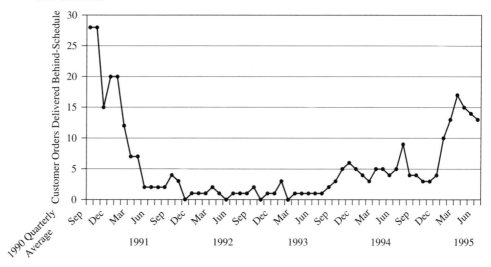

Exhibit C5

Quality

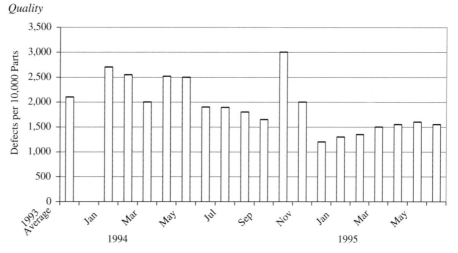

mechanics of the pull system to our complex shop environment and we also must continue to make process and layout improvements. Our "pull team," with some of our best and brightest people, is working on these issues.

I am sure that you share my concern about the effects of the new MRP II system the corporation is installing. I appreciate that DMC has been chosen as the first implementation site within the corporation for a complex manufacturing application, but the scope of activities and the time line for implementation are quite ambitious. The transition will be difficult. Additionally, I am concerned about the compatibility of MRP as a "push system" for order release with our "pull system" for shop-floor control.

A lot has changed since Lance Lipscomb held Nancy's position three years ago. Nancy was the third general manager since Lance was transferred in September 1993; i.e., four in fourteen months.

These leadership changes were due in large part to a corporate directive to share knowledge among business units. The DMC earned the reputation as being progressive and innovative, and the corporation was anxious to share with the other business units the advanced manufacturing techniques, technologies, and management practices they had applied.

Marshall Atherton, the factory superintendent, described some of the difficulties encountered by DMC over the last three years:

> Each general manager had his or her priorities, and it was difficult for the employees to maintain momentum and stability with respect to prior initiatives. This was exacerbated by declining economic conditions during the last three years. Since Lance departed, demand for turbine systems has declined, and corporate responded by requiring each business unit to reduce costs.
>
> Payroll reductions contributed the most to achieving the cost targets since most other line items in our budget, such as depreciation, could not be adjusted. Exhibit C6 depicts the change since 1992 in headcount relative to demand. Note that during this period headcount was reduced by 28 percent while the demand dropped by only 5 percent.

Nancy Wallace (general manager) interjected:

> We feel that the corporation's system for budgeting and accounting is partially responsible for the diminution in the work force. We treat depreciation as an uncontrollable expense much like the federal government treats entitlements. The remaining portion of the budget that is considered controllable must endure large reductions to cover the mandated compression in the overall budget. The problem is compounded by our income-reporting system that overstates the level of depreciation. I appreciate the tax advantages of using a short useful life of five years for our equipment, but most of our equipment has a much longer productive life. This accounting system causes distortions in headcount decisions and it inhibits our

EXHIBIT C6

1995 baseline operating plan: total headcount

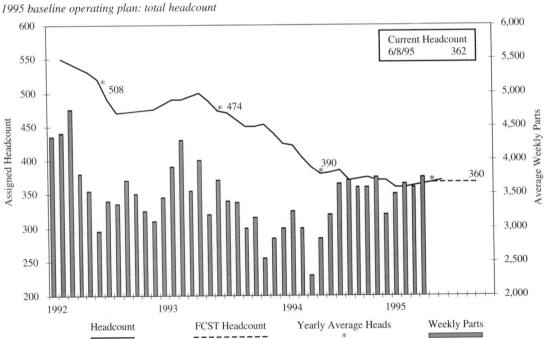

ability to make the capital improvements I believe we need to reach a higher level of productivity. Maybe if we work collectively on this issue we can convince corporate to improve their managerial accounting system.

Unfortunately, reductions in headcount have been offset to a certain extent by rising labour rates. Because of seniority policies and skill levels, many of the people that have remained have the highest paying jobs. Furthermore, our payroll expense has grown to cover salary inflation and extraordinarily large increases in benefits (from 42 percent of direct labour in 1990 to 55 percent today).

Marshall Atherton (factory superintendent) added:

This downsizing has placed a strain on the work force. While our people have become more productive to compensate for the lower headcount and the increased labour rates, there has also been an increased demand for non–work statement activities such as training. With current economic conditions, we cannot afford the level of training and education provided during the tenure of Lance Lipscomb. Yet with the layoffs, the percentage of time spent on non–work statement activities has actually increased.

Product complexity has also increased over the last few years. Some of our new work statements are considerably more complex than prior jobs because of the introduction by our parent company of a new generation of turbine systems.

Balancing cost and delivery has proven difficult in recent months. Because we are undermanned, we have been spending money on overtime to keep up with delivery dates. This has compromised our budget and has been particularly hard on the work force. Some people have been working seven days a week since last fall. Morale could be better and productivity has dropped due to burn-out.

The First Pull System.   To develop pull systems, Deltaforce established separate teams of operators and support people for the three areas within DMC: hard metals, soft metals, and detail. Marshall Atherton explained the history of the effort:

Since the general managers of the sister divisions have expressed particular interest in our just-in-time efforts, we plan to focus on the features of our pull systems. In complex shop environments such as ours and yours, we feel you would benefit most by learning the details.

Pull systems for the three areas were inaugurated late in 1992, but the one in detail was soon abandoned. The two pull systems that remained were essentially the same with the exception of the form of the work authorization document, commonly known as the Kanban. Teams representing hard metals wanted an electronic authorization system while the team for soft metals decided to use Kanban cards as the authorization. The soft metals team reasoned that their physical identification system would be more reliable because it was not subject to computer failure.

Both pull systems departed from traditional JIT practice in two respects: (1) Kanban cards were transferred between some but not all operations, and (2) for those operations governed by Kanban, finished work was stored at the previous operation rather than at the next one. First, Kanban transactions were established between cells but not within them. For example, Kanban cards were not used to control work between operations performed within the titanium cell that makes ducts between 2 1/2 inches and 4 inches in diameter, but were used between titanium and other cells such as cleaning, final assembly, penetrant inspect, and pressure test. The reasoning was as follows. Regulation of the flow between these cells was sufficient to control work-in-process inventory levels. Because of labour substitutions within cells but not across them, the benefits of limiting queues within cells would be more than offset by the disruptive effects from the additional transactions. The idea was to base the intra-cell Kanban limits on historical WIP levels and then to adjust them with experience.

The second departure from conventional JIT discipline was that both of the remaining teams decided to store jobs at the cells where they had just been completed rather than to move them to the next cells in the routings. The finished jobs were placed in containers arranged by destination, although the operator would transport the Kanban cards to the next cell and file them in first-come, first-served order. Only a prescribed number of Kanban cards were allotted between a cell and its destination cells. When all the cards resided at the destination cells (leaving none at the feeder cell to authorize work), this signaled the feeder operation to stop all activity. The teams favoured keeping the work behind because they believed the workers would be less tempted to process work out of order if they pulled a Kanban card in sequence and then asked a dispatcher to retrieve the job for them at the feeder cell.

Unfortunately, the two pull systems that remained were aborted in March 1993 after only three months of use. During the three-month period, jobs began to finish behind-schedule at an alarming rate, and shop personnel began to circumvent the system by increasing the Kanban limits and processing work out of order. Yet it was not clear why the pull systems were ineffective in controlling the workflow. George Stinebuck, the general manager who followed Lance Lipscomb, formed the "pull team" in 1994 to learn from the successes and mistakes of the last pull system and to design a new one.

Efforts by the Pull Team.   What went awry with the pull systems and how to ameliorate them were questions that Pam Petersen (industrial engineering manager) and her fellow pull team members attempted to answer. Pam described the investigation:

> The literature on JIT was not helpful because it covered only very simple flow processes. We traced our difficulties to complexity as manifested in the form of procedural problems, part variety, routing cycles, and workload variability.
>
> We have a complex process, but we added a layer of complexity by operating different systems in each area. Between January and March of 1993, the detail area, the one that feeds the other two areas, continued to use a push system, while hard and soft metals implemented pull systems. And the two pull systems used different types of work authorizations. As the pull team, we viewed standardization of procedures as an important aspect of our mission.
>
> Systems aside, we had a complicated business. In hard metals alone, we had more than 1,100 different part numbers at the time the first pull system was aborted. To illustrate the challenges created by this part variety for our pull systems, consider the two part routings shown in Exhibit C7. Jobs for each part type pass through a titanium cell but then the first job goes to X-ray while the one that follows is routed next to final assembly. With this first pull system, each feeder cell has a Kanban limit. Suppose that at titanium, the second job has not yet been started, but the first job destined for X-ray has just been completed. Also suppose that that there is a backlog of three jobs at X-ray, but final assembly currently has no jobs to process. The system requires that the job just completed be kept behind at titanium, and that the last remaining Kanban authorization card (of a total allotment of four) be filed at X-ray. In this case, the Kanban limit of four has been reached between titanium and its two destination cells, and all four finished titanium jobs are destined for X-ray. This renders the titanium cell idle, thus blocking the second job (waiting at titanium and destined for final assembly). Thus, a bottleneck at X-ray has effectively blocked work at titanium and starved work at final assembly. Workers, conscious of the deadlines on orders, naturally reacted to situations like this by increasing Kanban limits and choosing jobs in an order counter to the first-come, first-served discipline.
>
> Routing cycles and load variability compounded the workflow problems. Many of our parts revisit operations in their routings. The cleaning cell is a good example. We must have the cleanest parts in town because we clean them after every operation. At any rate, because of the merging and diverging flows and the loops in the routings, we cannot consider ourselves a flow shop in the strictest sense.
>
> Workload variability occurs both in the service and arrival processes. Variability in the service times for parts at a particular resource is a function of the plethora of different types of parts that are routed to it.
>
> We attribute the variability in the arrival pattern to routing differences, erratic customer demand, and schedule changes. The demand for our duct parts destined for finished goods is unstable because of lumpiness in customer master schedules, batching in their processes, and new product introductions. The remaining demand, comprised of rush orders for equipment down in the field and of spares for an increasingly aging fleet of turbine systems, is even more volatile.
>
> In addition, we have on average five schedule revisions per order per month. Schedule changes due to internally generated discrepancies such as scrap are minor compared to external changes by our customers and vendors. We suspect that our antiquated MRP [materials requirements planning] system contributes to this problem. We have noticed that with a schedule change, there tends to follow several more changes for the same part. We hope that the new MRP system will dampen these schedule oscillations. Much to our dismay, the current MRP system allows organizations within Turbine Systems but outside the DMC to adjust the lead times for our internal tasks.

EXHIBIT C7

First Kanban card system

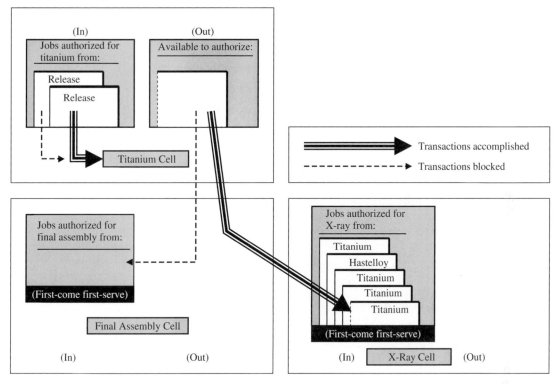

Roy Doctor, an area supervisor and fellow pull team member, commented on the effects of this variability:

> With erratic workloads, we need excess capacity in our pull system to provide good service, but capacity is scarce in these days of downsizing and tight budgets.

Pam Petersen proceeded to summarize the pull team's approach:

> We launched a six-month effort in June 1994 to study and simplify the part flows. After two months we realized that while the DMC produced in excess of 4,000 part types, many followed the same routings through the factory. In numerous cases, parts with quite different configurations had the same sequence. In addition, many of the part routings that differed could be simplified and standardized.
>
> We discovered a great deal of latitude in the planning systems and individual predilections that determined the manner in which ducts were made. Through an extensive effort by our Manufacturing Engineering group, we were able to determine preferred manufacturing methods. For example, the penetrant inspect and X-ray operations could be sequenced either way; some planners chose one sequence while others chose the reverse ordering. These planning variations spawned many unnecessary part routings.
>
> We developed an orientation document called the Planning Convention Book as well as a series of decision trees that formalized the preferred practices. Through training, the planners were able to simplify and condense existing parts, and for new work statements, they knew when the routings for existing families or new families were appropriate.

The New Pull System.   Between December 1994 and June 1995, Manufacturing Engineering at DMC was able to prune the product line from over 4,000 part numbers to 3,526, and to establish a representative set of 1,099 families. This was accomplished despite the introduction of many parts to satisfy new turbine system offerings. (Recall that a family describes a set of part numbers that follows the same routing.) The part numbers and families are identified as of June 1995 by the areas below:

Area	# Part Numbers	# Families
Hard metals	817	325
Soft metals	849	413
Detail	1,860	361
Totals	3,526	1,099

The pull team discovered that although a particular family may contain many part numbers, it might not be very active because the parts it embodied were for turbine systems that were customer unique or obsolete. Conversely, another family may contain one part number but is needed on every turbine system the corporation currently builds. Pam Petersen explained:

> It became clear that to prevent blockage and starvation in our new pull system, we needed to devote special attention to the active families. A Pareto chart (Exhibit C8) reveals that 70 percent of the work processed in the hard metals area is represented by only 60 primary families (of the 325 total). We found similar patterns in the soft metals and detail areas.

EXHIBIT C8

Hard metals families

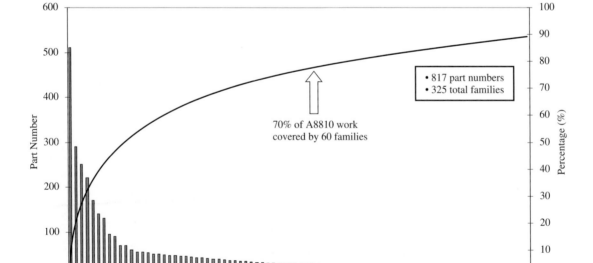

- 817 part numbers
- 325 total families

70% of A8810 work covered by 60 families

Part Number

Percentage (%)

Family Number

Quantity of Orders   % of Work Cumulative

We decided to design the pull system around two types of families: primary and miscellaneous. Primary families represent 70 percent of the volume while the miscellaneous designation covers the remainder. We use separate types of Kanban cards (and associated queue limits) for each primary family plus the miscellaneous category.

Members of the pull team proceeded to explain the pull system discipline. Pam began:

Regardless of the family, the cards associated with jobs destined for a cell are filed in one box according to first-come, first-served discipline. Differences between the families are recognized by a numerical designation on the cards. Primary families are treated slightly differently than the miscellaneous family.

Kanban limits for each primary family are established by allowing only a prescribed number of cards between cells; a job in a primary family cannot be started in a cell without a Kanban card that authorizes the work. Suppose that family A has a prescribed intrastage limit of four and visits three cells, cleaning, titanium, and X-ray, respectively. Four cards for each adjacent pair of cells would be distributed. This limit ensures that there would be at most four jobs for family A: between order release and cleaning, between cleaning and titanium, and between titanium and X-ray. A job for family A that had been released by MRP could not be started at cleaning without an available, family-specific Kanban card that authorizes the work. (A card would not be available at cleaning, for instance, if all four cards for that family were filed in the box at titanium. This indicates that four A jobs were already cleaned, sitting in the container for titanium and thus, not yet started in titanium. When one of the jobs is transferred and finished by titanium, the associated Kanban card would be returned to cleaning and designated as available.)

Roy Doctor described nuances of the pull system:

If we were to make every family in the factory primary, the number of Kanban types and associated WIP would be staggering. Obviously, we needed the miscellaneous category, but changes in the pull system were required to make it work. Since the part types within miscellaneous have different routings, we couldn't create Kanban transfers between all affected cells without experiencing proliferation. The breakthrough came when we recognized that almost all parts within miscellaneous share certain but not all flows between cells. Hence, we were able to gain control over miscellaneous by regulating the common flows and ignoring the unique ones. (Recall that even for primary families, we do not control flows between every operation, just between the cells.)

Pam cited other benefits with the new system:

Let's return to the previous example where two jobs pass through a titanium cell but then the first job goes to X-ray while the one that follows is routed next to final assembly. Suppose the first job is in family A and the one sequenced behind it is in family B. Note that in Exhibit C9 we now have separate Kanban cards and limits governing their flows; the limit reached at X-ray prohibits further flow to X-ray by members of family A but does not stop work on the job in family B destined for final assembly. Hence, the system avoids the previous problems of blockage at the titanium cell and of starvation at the final assembly cell.

Roy Doctor interjected:

Of course, the miscellaneous category with its routing variety could still cause trouble, but because of the infrequent usage, this seldom occurs. Initially, we considered offloading some of the miscellaneous part types, but decided not to do so. Besides being inappropriate in the short term due to declining business, we realized that much of the work classified at the tail of the distribution is bread-and-butter work for us. We have distinctive competencies to perform this work, and we do not wish to create by default these skills in our competitors. Instead, we have had a concentrated effort to define better, more standard manufacturing processes. In August 1994 we had only 1.7 part numbers per family, whereas today we have 4.6. Offload should be a last resort.

As was the case with the first pull systems, Kanban cards within the new system are exchanged between cells, not within them, and we maintain work at the previous cell rather than at the next one in the routing.

However, there are differences between the first and second pull systems. We have already described how the new system treats part families. Another difference is that we now deal with cycling by issuing separate Kanban cards between cells for each pair of operations. Hence, when a job travels between two cells on more than one occasion, separate Kanban cards govern their flow.

Exhibit C9

Revised Kanban card system

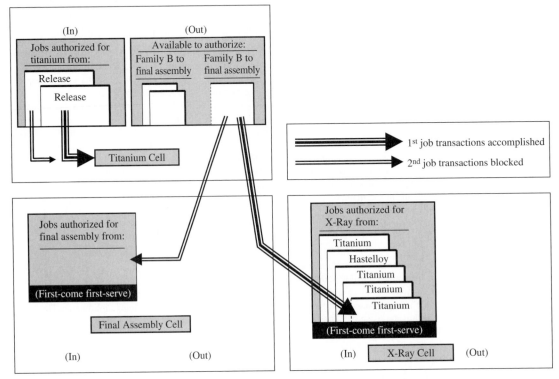

We have also developed a formal means for expediting hot parts through their routings. Kanbans for equipment down in the field are automatically placed at the front of the Kanban boxes at each cell. And in emergencies, the factory superintendent directs parts to be hand-carried through the shop, if necessary interrupting other jobs in process.

Finally, we decided to have the operators retrieve the jobs they intend to work on rather than asking a dispatcher to move the jobs, as was the case with the initial pull systems. This allows the operators to regularly visit their internal suppliers and customers, and this increases awareness of the whole manufacturing chain.

Despite the progress with the new pull system, vexing questions remain as to how to effectively set the Kanban limits. Following the classic reorder point formula, we calculate, for each family, the average usage and the standard deviation; we set the limit as the mean plus one standard deviation times the square root of the lead time at the destination cell.[3] However, this approach for establishing family limits has its weaknesses. It does not recognize the interactions among parts within the same family or across families that are treated by the same resources.[4] The individual limits should have a cascading effect on overall inven-

---

[3]Refer to Vollmann, Berry, and Whybark, *Manufacturing Planning and Control Systems,* Third Edition (Burr Ridge, IL: Irwin), p. 720.

[4]The formula assumes that: (1) the variance of demand for each part type within a family is the same, (2) the covariance in demand between part types within a family is zero, i.e., the demand for each is independent of the others, and (3) the lead time is constant and equal for each part type. The last assumption precludes the consideration of the dynamic queuing effects we would expect to see when part types within or among families are treated by the same resources.

tory levels in the cells. (This is similar in effect to the quality assurance problem of cascading tolerances on an assembly despite tight control of specifications for the individual parts that go into the assembly.)

We have other questions about the limits. For a primary family, should we set the same limits between every adjacent pair of cells in its routing or should the limits differ? How should a bottleneck or nonbottleneck affect these limits?

Informal systems have again emerged. Supervisors regulate the work in their cells because they feel there should be some overall control of WIP. They know from experience how much work the cells need to operate. The supervisors will not permit jobs to be pulled, despite Kanban authorization to do so, if there is insufficient capacity to perform the work.

The operators also have an informal system. Because work is kept at the previous cell rather than at the next one in the routing, bottlenecks at subsequent cells become visible to the workers at the prior cells. They can see the jobs piling up in a container for a particular destination. Even if the Kanban limit has not been reached for the destination with a lot of work in the container, the operator might choose jobs destined for less busy cells where they could soon be processed.

Pam spoke next:

We in the pull team feel that the measures instituted by the supervisors and workers have merit, but we are concerned that they will eventually compromise the pull system. We recognize this as a complex queuing problem, and we are investigating queuing and simulation as a means to resolve it. The appendix [to this case] describes our preliminary findings regarding queuing and simulation. You will note that our research tends to support the merits of the informal approaches practiced by the supervisors and workers.

Process and Layout Challenges.   The layout proposed in 1992 for the new building was significantly better than the previous one, but in many cases the resulting cells were too far apart for workers to help across cells. Roy Doctor commented on the potential for improvement:

I recall a quote from the famous architect, Mies van der Rohe. He said that, "God is in the details." From my perspective, process improvement drives speed; flow time does not drop by itself. In 1992 there were too many routings for the parts to be built within self-contained areas. Yet with the progress we have made on routing simplification and families, we have definite opportunities for process improvements that will have a positive impact on flow time.

I mentioned before that we need more capacity in our pull system to provide good service, but capacity is scarce these days. While worker flexibility would enable us to gain effective capacity, we have encountered several obstacles. The cleaning cell provides an example of how our parts revisit operations in their routings. There is merit to hand-cleaning the parts within self-contained cells rather than transferring them across the shop. Provisions for the space and handling of the special cleaning agents poses difficulties, but I think it can be done. Flow time would benefit in three respects. First, fewer people would be involved since the mechanic would clean the parts. Second, travel distance would be reduced. Finally, more cleaning units would obviate the need with the current cleaning configuration for batching to save setups.

Cooperation across cells often is not practiced even when it is possible. The three titanium cells corresponding to different duct diameters provide a case in point. Operators within the cells have developed a sense of ownership and are reluctant to help elsewhere despite the similarity in tasks. Establishing separate managers for the titanium cells also helped to forge this sense of ownership. In many respects, the workers are so proud of the cells they helped design for the new building that the layout has become somewhat of a sacred cow.

To further complicate matters, many ducts cycle through welding and mechanical operations several times before finishing, yet the two types of operations are governed by different unions. Perhaps we could eventually resolve the need for separate certifications and job classifications.

In retrospect, we would have been better served by designing small versions of the large penetrant inspect and pressure test equipment for which we currently have separate cells. Penetrant inspect involves the examination under ultraviolet light of weld areas on the ducts for inconsistencies in a thin coating of translucent powder. The pressure test forces water into the ducts at twice the prescribed tolerance to uncover leaks in the weld joints. Neither operation is technologically complex, however. Rather than creating separate, centralized cells for this large equipment, we could have replicated and placed the smaller versions in various, self-contained cells.

It would be nice to eliminate a few days of flow time while parts travel from the detail area into stores and then into hard or soft metals. This delay in the storeroom allows us to kit the finished detail parts, thus compensating for variability inherent in the detail process. The bending process is an art, not a science, because of variations in the alloy mix and the temper of the metals. Perhaps with better control of the bending process and better part coordination, we could dispense with our stock room.

Future Direction.   Nancy Wallace closed the session with the following observations:

Improvement is a continuous proposition. The DMC has clearly benefited from the reengineering efforts begun five years ago. We attribute much of the progress at DMC to cascade education, TQM, team decision making, and an emphasis on speed. We even benefited from the endeavour to implement the first pull system in that workers began to understand its mechanics and appreciate how it enforces limits on the inventory. Recognition of the strong work flows through our shop has enabled us to design a better pull system and begin to consider prospects for process improvements.

We could further compress our flow time from six days to two. Our production process is still far too complex, and we need to get people on the shop floor more involved in decision making. There is still a command and control environment at DMC. Management and especially support personnel need to hone their people skills. We need to be more effective in the way we solicit employee suggestions and respond to employee concerns. We have a long way to go in changing the roles of management from fire fighters and expediters to coaches and cheerleaders.

The worst is behind us with respect to layoffs and transfers, but we obviously have a lot of issues with which to contend. The most important task for me is to prioritize these initiatives.

CASE 8 APPENDIX
ANALYSIS OF ALTERNATIVE KANBAN SYSTEMS
USING QUEUING AND SIMULATION

An Alternative Kanban System

We propose a variation of the first and second systems implemented at DMC. We suggest for the proposed system that the Kanban cards be destination-specific rather than family/destination-specific (as is the case with the current system). We illustrate the proposed system in Exhibits C10a, C10b, and C10c. We proposed separate Kanban cards and limits governing the flows between: (1) feeder cells and X-ray, and (2) feeder cells and final assembly. Hence, the proposed system requires an aggregate limit for each cell serving as a destination in the part routings.

EXHIBIT C10A

Proposed Kanban card system

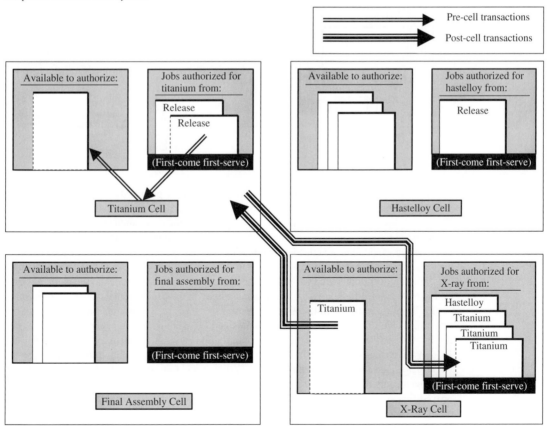

Exhibit C10B

Proposed Kanban card system

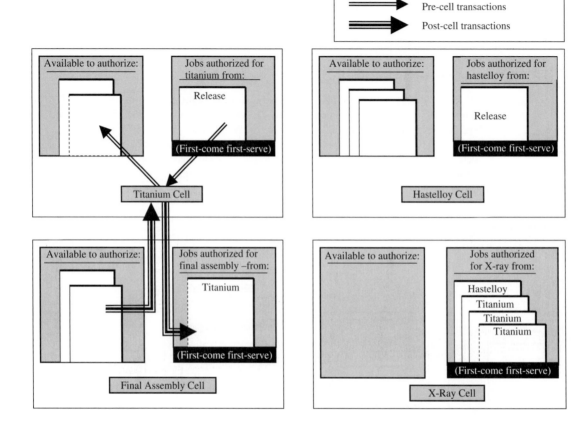

Another departure from the prior pull systems is that in the proposed system, the Kanban card would not be automatically returned to a feeder cell once a job is completed at the destination cell. This is because with multiple feeder cells, the operator at the destination would not know where to return the Kanban without some (most likely, inefficient) allocation system. Instead, the available Kanban would remain at the destination. The operator at a feeder cell would be alerted that at least one Kanban is available at the destination cell, and that he or she should go there to pick up one card as a work authorization. (Perhaps the availability of work authorization(s) could be transmitted by computer, or by a visual signal using a light on the ceiling above the destination cell.)

To illustrate, let us return to the previous example; this time suppose that there are three jobs rather than two. Exhibit C10a indicates that the first job (in family A) goes from titanium to X-ray; Exhibit C10b shows that the second job (in family B) goes from titanium to final assembly; and Exhibit C10c shows that the third job (in family C) is routed from hastelloy to X-ray.

The first event occurs when the operator in titanium is free (see Exhibit C10a). He finds two authorized cards representing jobs waiting to be processed at titanium; he chooses the one that arrived first, a job that is routed to X-ray after titanium. He checks to see that there is an available card at X-ray, he retrieves the card from X-ray, and he gets the parts for the job that are wait-

Exhibit C10C

Proposed Kanban system

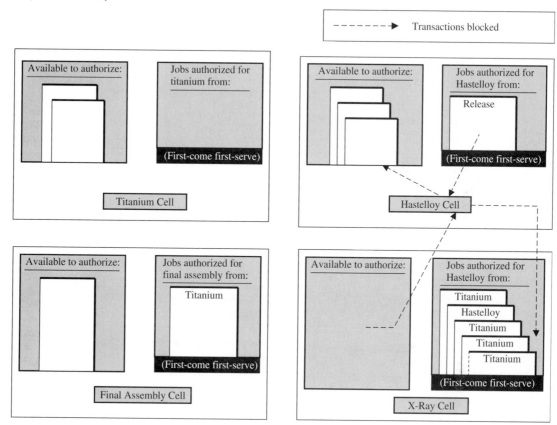

ing to be processed at titanium. After completing that job at titanium, he designates as available in titanium the card that had authorized the work in titanium, and he designates as authorized in X-ray the card that had been identified as available.

The second event occurs when the operator in titanium again becomes free (see Exhibit C10b). He finds one authorized card for a job waiting to be processed at titanium, a job that is routed to final assembly after titanium. He checks to see that there is an available card at final assembly, he retrieves the card from final assembly, and he gets the parts for the job that are waiting to be processed at titanium. After completing that job at titanium, he designates as available in titanium the card that had authorized the work in titanium, and he designates as authorized in final assembly the card that had been identified as available.

The third event occurs when the operator in hastelloy becomes free (see Exhibit C10c). She finds an authorized card for a job waiting to be processed at hastelloy, a job that is routed to X-ray after hastelloy. She checks to see if there is an available card at X-ray. Since there are none available in X-ray, she for the moment abandons the idea of working on that job. She checks for the next job that is authorized in hastelloy. Since there are no others in the box designated as authorized, she has been rendered idle until the next job is authorized in hastelloy or an available card appears at X-ray. Hence, the limit at X-ray has prohibited further flow to X-ray regardless of the feeder cell, but did not block work in feeder cells destined for final assembly.

There are four potential advantages of the proposed system over the current one. First, this system should substantially reduce the number of Kanban limits compared to the current system where a limit is needed for every family and destination. We expect this to ameliorate the problems of cascading inventories due to the multiple limits at each stage. Second, queuing will enable us to derive analytically the queue limits for each cell. Third, the proposed system addresses the concerns of the foremen and operators that have begun to follow informal rules sometimes counter to the rules of the current system. The foremen should be pleased to find that the system is regulating the aggregate flow through the cell, and the operators in feeder cells should find that the limits would keep them from sending too much work to a destination if it is a bottleneck. Finally, queuing analysis permits us to achieve desired flow time allowances by deriving the required capacity levels at the cells. In this respect, queuing analysis could determine headcount as well as appropriate cross-training patterns.

However, these four conjectures may or may not be realized in actual practice because of certain assumptions inherent in queuing analysis (such as independent, homogeneous arrivals and independent services). We next describe an animated simulation program designed to compare under more realistic operating conditions the performance of the current and proposed systems.

Simulation Analysis

We simulate a shop with three families and three cells. Two of the families are primary and the third is classified as miscellaneous. Parts within primary family A are routed from titanium to cleaning to titanium to X-ray. Parts within primary family B are routed from titanium to cleaning to X-ray to titanium to cleaning. Parts in the miscellaneous family M begin at titanium or cleaning, follow a random routing through the remaining cells, and end with a common sequence of tasks, titanium then cleaning. Following standard practice at DMC, parts within titanium cycle between the mechanic and weld booths. In addition, parts within the cleaning cell are batched in lots of four to maintain high utilization of the vats of cleaning solution. (Different part types can be batched together during cleaning. Once submerged, the cleaning cycle is constant at three minutes regardless of the part type.)

To emulate a large number of part types within each family, an exponential distribution (with a mean of three minutes) is used to generate the service times for each operation except cleaning, which has a constant time. The interarrival times of jobs entering the shop are also exponentially distributed with a mean of 12 minutes. Parts and people travel at a fixed rate of 25 feet per minute; the average travel time between operations is less than one minute.

Two alternative Kanban systems are evaluated, the current one with limits for each family/destination and the proposed one with limits for each destination cell. In the current system, the Kanban limits for the families and destinations are derived using the reorder point formula (mean plus standard deviation times the square root of the lead time at the destination cell). In the proposed system, the Kanban limits for the destination cells are derived using queuing analysis. The queuing analysis is based on the mean service and interarrival times.

The results of one replication for the alternative systems are shown in Exhibit C11. The simulation results indicate that for the same level of resources, the proposed system yields on average 58 percent more output, 55 percent less flow time, and 72 percent less inventory than the current system. The proposed system shows promise for improving performance at DMC, although more experimentation is warranted.

Exhibit C11

Promodel Simulation Results

Current System					Proposed System	
Family	*From*	*To*	*Limit*		*Station*	*Limit*
A	Titanium	Clean	20		Titanium	8
A	Clean	Titanium	16		Clean	8
A	Titanium	X-ray	20		X-ray	8
B	Titanium	Clean, first step	20			
B	Clean	X-ray	16			
B	X-ray	Titanium	17			
B	Titanium	Clean, last step	20			
Misc.	Titanium	Clean, last step	20			

Measurement	*Current System*	*Proposed System*	*Improvement*
Average inventory	50	14	72%
Average flow time (hours)	11	5	55
Total three-day output	38	60	58

9
EKATO RUHRWERKE[1]

Introduction

For EKATO, a medium-sized manufacturer of industrial mixing machines in southern Germany, innovation and creativity of its work force were essential to meeting the individual requirements of its customers, and hence to the survival of the company. When the old organisational structure could no longer cope with changes in the marketplace, could not absorb new forms of leadership, and employee morale fell, the company began to completely reexamine not only its organisational practices, but also the physical working environment in which it was then housed. In 1991, EKATO built a new factory complex with the explicit objective of incorporating a new organisational structure and promoting employee innovation and well-being.

1. The Company and Its Problems

EKATO is located in Schopfheim, a small town in the southwestern part of Germany near Basel. It was founded in 1933 and was organised along Taylorist lines. In 1991, it had about 400 employees and produced about 2,500 small and large mixing machines for the chemical and food industries. At the time of the reorganisation, EKATO was the second-largest company in its field and was the market leader in Europe with a turnover of around DM 70 million.

The production is highly oriented to the specific requirements of individual customers, and around 75 percent of all orders need to be customised. Many other mixers are produced as modular machines in small runs. Their core competence is in problem solving and this had led them to adopt a paradigm shift from seeing themselves as manufacturers of agitators to being expert in fluid mixing. This requires constant expertise and innovation on the part of the workers. Around 7,000 working drawings have to be customised annually, and about 2,000 new designs are produced (Hallwachs et al., 1991). The company is ISO-9001 certified.

Like many other firms, EKATO was constantly facing a barrage of new challenges. It soon became clear that the classical division of labour and management which EKATO had traditionally used was unable to meet these new challenges. The traditional methods created serious problems, such as:

- Excessive idle time when skills and experience available in the work force were not being used, due to a highly specialised division of labour between direct and indirect production areas.
- Inadequate information and material flows.
- Unacceptable throughput times, due to the old technical and social communication channels.
- Doubling up on tasks.

[1]This case was developed for use in classroom discussion and is not intended to necessarily illustrate appropriate or inappropriate management practices. Case author: Gayle Avery, Institute for International Business Studies, Germany, 1996. The funding for this case production was provided by the Australian federal government's Department of Industry, Science and Resources.

- Unreliable delivery dates.
- High inventories were necessary, which bound up a great deal of capital.
- It was necessary to outsource large amounts of work in peak periods despite the idle time.
- Plans often had to be redrawn.
- Large amounts of information got lost (Hallwachs et al., 1991).

In dealing with these day-to-day problems, the company was forced to neglect its core business—supplying a wide range of innovative products through improvisation and flexibility on the part of its qualified personnel. This led to additional problems, particularly with the staff, such as a drop in employee morale and difficulty in incorporating cooperative leadership styles and delegating responsibility. This was exacerbated by overcrowded, poorly designed, and generally unsatisfactory working conditions. The lack of space often meant separating areas that in fact should have been located close together to promote cooperation and communication. For instance, production, sales, and assembly were located in physically separate buildings, which made it very difficult to be able to communicate and cooperate, and created high handling and transportation costs.

2. The Reorganisation

In response, EKATO's management decided to completely restructure the organisation and redesign the physical facility, leading to far-reaching personnel, organisational, and technical changes.

Supported by funding from the German Federal Ministry for Research and Technology, EKATO worked in collaboration with the Fraunhofer Institutes, which provide applied research services to German industry, and involved consultants from various disciplines in the reorganisation process:

- Management and operation consultants to recommend new structure and processes.
- Architectural, construction, and production consultants to design the new facility.
- Organisational process consultants to manage communication and the human side of the transition to the new facility.

On the advice of their consultants, the company opted for a "fractal organisation." Essentially, the concept "fractal" comes from modern mathematics, although the word itself derives from the Latin *fractus* = broken. It is used to describe natural phenomena that use similar elements to create multiple, complex, and highly task-specific solutions. The main features of fractals in nature are that they are dynamic, self-organising, and self-optimising systems. A modern market economy can be seen to operate along similar lines to fractals: an economy is self-organising, self-optimising within small loops. Each fractal provides services for some others and receives a benefit in return.

In an organisational context, a fractal is seen as an independently functioning organisational unit such as a work group or team. Each unit has clear goals and functions (Warnecke, 1992). The fractals in an organisation organise and optimise themselves in pursuing the organisation's goals. Fractals are part of an open system and they communicate directly with their counterparts in the client or supplier organisation. The individual employees or groups of employees in fractal arrangements are more challenged than under traditional structures and operate best in networks to set goals and make decisions. The activities of the fractals have fuzzy rather than clear limits, and their activities are not planned ahead in great detail. Rather, a fractal's activities are designed to achieve goals such as providing optimal service to the client. For the fractal organisation to function, it is essential that information is made readily available to all employees, who can call up the information, process it as necessary, and use it to achieve the fractal's goals.

To introduce the fractal model, an organisation has to move away from concepts of defined work tasks and procedures aimed at achieving collective strategic objectives. While fractal organisational structures have helped some companies seeking a way to deal with chaos and turbulence in the business world, they have some limitations (Warnecke, 1994) . For instance, the introduction of fractals assumes certain prerequisite conditions such as the availability of an educated or trainable work force and a stable legal system. These conditions may not operate in some locations but both were fulfilled for EKATO. Fractals also raise new problems such as legal questions when job descriptions are fuzzy and worker responsibility cannot be completely delimited.

New Organisational Structure.   The consultants recommended a complete restructuring of the firm (Schlund, 1995). By delegating responsibility, decision making, and tasks to decentralised work units, the new production structure was designed to create "independent factories within the factory," as close to the customer as possible (Hallwachs, 1992). Production, assembly, and a major part of sales were restructured into production, assembly, planning, and sales groups called "islands" consisting of 5–10 people. The islands were integrated both horizontally (task-orientation) and vertically (e.g., quality control and maintenance came under their control).

The islands assumed complete responsibility for a customer, from bidding for orders and developing proposals, to designing, managing, and executing a client's order. Assembly islands were allocated to regions, and were associated with sales arising from their given region. The islands were responsible for assembling the various components of an order from a client in their region. Construction islands were responsible for customising production and producing working drawings.

For reasons of cost, it was actually not feasible to completely restructure the production area, and the chosen solution was to arrange production into islands grouped around construction groups. The construction islands form the link between sales and the production and assembly islands.

It became clear that this restructuring was to be associated with wide-reaching personnel, organisational, and technical changes.

New Architectural Structure.   It is rare that a building can be designed specifically to accommodate a new factory organisational structure. In the EKATO case, workers and architects developed plans for the new building together. The planning took account of technology, people, society, and the environment. It was no easy task to integrate the needs and requirements of the developer, architect, factory planner, and affected workers in designing the new factory. This was complicated by the fact that various participants spoke different "languages," and had different values and priorities.

The structure of the new building complex was intended to mirror the new corporate philosophy. In the end, production was divided into three halls linked by covered roadways in a low-rise complex. A courtyard served as communications centre. Office and production areas were integrated and distinctive building layouts were provided for the various island units.

Designing such an unconventional factory complex required unconventional planning methods (Hallwachs et al., 1991). In this case, production and building planning were carried out together, with active participation by all levels of affected personnel. Their task was not only to design a flexible and optimal factory at a realistic cost, but also to create an attractive environment to stimulate innovation and creativity. Thus, the main focus of the planning was the personnel who had to work in the new factory.

3. Project Organisation and Implementation

The project of designing the new building complex to reflect organisational structure and corporate values treated the task as a unified planning problem. It involved an integrated and goal-oriented approach, interdisciplinary team work, and a highly participative planning style. Technical, economic, and personnel considerations were treated equally and concurrently. A range of detailed alternatives was considered at all levels in the organisation and the less significant ones were discarded. As the design became more detailed, the role of the workers represented in the planning process changed from that of indirectly representing the interests of others to everyone becoming directly involved.

Planning.   At the beginning of the planning process, task-oriented teams were set up. These teams were interwoven in terms of time, content, and personnel. People could be and were members of more than one team at a time. The number and membership of the teams were generally not prescribed, except for the strategy and production-structure teams. Participation by the project leaders from building and factory areas was mandatory but the other teams evolved out of the planning stages and tasks. Teams from support areas such as salaries, personnel, and training were also involved right from the beginning in the planning process and these teams accompanied the entire process.

The interdisciplinary strategy team provided the backbone for the other teams. The strategic team consisted of the developer, architect, factory planner, specialists, workers' council representatives, and representatives of the affected areas in the company. Their task was to develop goals in the framework of a corporate strategy to guide the subordinated teams. In addition, the strategy team's task was to evaluate detailed alternatives developed by the other teams. Before the planning process could begin, it was essential to develop a common strategy. It is significant to note that at this early stage, the unified approach to planning and the ways of evaluating alternatives were set down. By referring to a clear set of goals, alternatives could be evaluated in terms of how effectively they achieved those goals.

Building upon the work of the strategy team, the production planning team analysed various alternatives for a new corporate structure embodied in the built environment. This team had the responsibility for dividing the company into the fractals, the decentralised island units. The team then assigned responsibilities and production tasks to the various organisational units. At the same time, this was fed back into the building drawings and out of these considerations, the plans began to take shape. Major decisions had to be made at this stage, ranging from whether to have central or localised assembly and/or store rooms, to decisions about transportation, specialisation of parts of the buildings, and size, structure, style, and other aspects of the buildings. These ideas were embodied in rough drawings.

The team responsible for production systems produced a capacity and area requirement for each organisational unit, decided on how automated the various tasks were to be, where cranes were needed, etc. The production system plans had a significant impact on layout and also on the structural requirements of the buildings concerning things like which areas had to be able to support heavy machinery.

The workplace teams were concerned with designing appropriate work spaces, relating the various tasks to one another spatially, and considering factors such as the social environment and work atmosphere. In contrast to the other teams, all affected workers were directly involved in this stage of the planning and their wishes were incorporated into the design.

Complementing these teams was a specialised team for building design and factory planning. Membership of this team included specialists such as structural engineers and architects for the detailed design, as well as organisational, production, and machine planners and designers.

Full information had obviously to be made available to the teams so that they could make informed decisions and suggestions.

Implementing in Stages.   It is seldom realistic to expect to introduce a complete vertical, order-based integration in new physical surroundings in one step. The new structure and the move into the new building complex at EKATO were introduced in stages. First, pilot islands were tested while the new building complex was being developed. Then, the production islands together with some of the independent sales and design areas moved into the new buildings. During this stage, the parts of the company that had remained in the old buildings were divided into islands and given time to get used to the new organisational arrangements. The complete integration of all sections of the company into the new buildings happened in a second step. The purpose behind staging the move was to allow the workers to successively adapt to the new, dramatically changed situation.

This staged implementation was fruitful. The move from the old buildings to the new complex was made in one long weekend. After only two weeks, it was possible to settle down to regular production in the new complex. The entire changeover cost a total of one month's loss in productivity.

Staff training programs were held to smooth the transition and the move and additional on-the-job training was generally well accepted.

4. Human Resources Strategy

From the beginning, workers' participation in the change process played a central role. It became evident to management that this restructuring could only be successfully introduced with the assistance of an integrated, ongoing, and interdisciplinary project-based organisation (Schlund, 1995).

Change Management.   All changes that affected the employees were discussed in the planning groups with participation from workers and representatives of the workers' council (Schlund, 1995). In this process, all personnel strategies were planned and then refined by the individual island groups in terms of their specific needs. Via the personnel team and the islands, a personnel and organisational development concept was developed and implemented.

In introducing the change, a moderator was employed to raise workers' consciousness about the problems and to discuss issues affecting their daily work. The moderated groups eventually developed the capacity to think in terms of the overall system.

Training.   Training has been a key to the success of this radical innovation, and team development and communication training still accompany the process, in addition to task-related skills training. Team skills were being developed in training sessions designed to improve interpersonal communication and encourage cooperation. A continuous process of team coaching was introduced to assist individuals in making the necessary personal adaptations to working in a team on a day-to-day basis. Group members had to learn to deal with conflicts, to solve problems effectively, to improve their people and relationship-building skills, and to understand the roles of other team members. They also had to be aware of the interdependence of the team members, to understand group dynamics and decision-making processes, and to be able to set group goals and priorities. One criticism of the change to the new system is that an in-house training centre was not created. This meant that external trainers had first to be taught about the restructuring, creating delays in training employees during the changeover.

Communication.   To engender acceptance of the proposed changes at EKATO, it was necessary to inform and involve the workers. Information can be seen as a one-way form of communication to bridge knowledge gaps. However, participation is seen as a learning process through which people work in groups to solve common problems. Without as much full access to information as company conditions would permit, it would have been impossible for workers to accept radical changes and to solve the resulting problems in a meaningful way. Information was conveyed through meetings and discussion groups, individual talks, in-house newspapers, or notices.

Most of the obstacles to the new systems could be attributed to fear of the unknown on the part of workers affected, in particular the former production supervisors who thought that they would lose prestige when they became island leaders. These concerns were largely dealt with through information and discussions as well as through special training sessions and involving the workers in designing the new systems. Acceptance of the changes also arose as a result of the training and information efforts.

5. Financial Decision

Since land acquisition and holding costs were relatively low, the developer opted for a low-rise development. Since the ability of the workers to work accurately and to be innovative was very important in this company, investment was made in the quality of the work environment rather than only in automated production technology. The architectural message was deliberately built in: "We believe in the future of our company. Therefore, we are developing our workers and building for our workers. We want to be a good neighbour." The company was not looking for the cheapest solution but for the best value for their investment. The important features had to be right. Falsely investing in unnecessary or useless items was to be avoided.

Building and planning costs (excluding land acquisition costs) were around DM 2,000/sqm gross floor area (including cellar and special building requirements). This is much less than a centrally driven robot factory would have cost (Hallwachs et al., 1991). A "throw-away" building that covered the minimum requirements would have cost about 20 percent less. A higher density solution of the same technical standard would have cost about 6 percent less, assuming that no additional costs were incurred through higher fire safety requirements. In relation to the total costs, these are relatively small differences. The ultimate advantage of the chosen design lies in improved conditions for future production.

6. Outcomes

The first 12 months of operation of the new structure produced such positive results that the new decentralised system amortised itself within the first two years of operation (Schlund, 1995). Throughput times in indirect areas were reduced by over 50 percent and in the direct areas by around 50 percent (Schlund, 1995). Inventories of raw materials and supplies have been virtually halved and stores of spare parts reduced by around one-third. Improvements in using the machinery meant that no more jobs had to be farmed out and this has led to a substantial reduction in machine costs.

The bonus systems led to increases in individual personnel costs, but because the new structure requires less personnel, overall personnel costs fell by approximately 3 percent. The group bonus system has led to high productivity, e.g., new designs and plans only get produced when the island concerned considers it absolutely necessary. Changes to plans have been reduced to about 40 percent. Information is more efficiently available and communication is easier, thereby halving the costs of obtaining information and passing it on. Doubling up on work has been virtually eliminated.

A group identity began to develop among the workers in the various islands, fostered by team development courses and regular group meetings. Integrating workers from the former indirect areas was achieved harmoniously. Of particular interest is that the workers in the various island stations now determine their own further education needs and submit these requests to the centralised personnel department. Island leaders stress the importance of meetings between the different islands and functional areas to exchange know-how and to enlist cooperation. Further, integrating control over production into the islands allows the islands to be self-determining.

Since the islands can determine their own schedules for dealing with orders, crises and emergency situations have been substantially reduced. Orders can be much better planned under the new system (Schlund, 1995). For the individual worker, the quality of the working environment and the task has increased—the worker can largely determine his/her own working pace, thereby reducing stress levels.

The new system is constantly being monitored in group and individual discussions, and adjustments are being made continuously. While the introduction of the new structures is stable, especially as they have been found to be successful, details will probably always be in a state of flux.

In 1997, EKATO's work force had increased to 500 employees and their turnover had doubled since the beginning of the reorganisation to approximately DM 150 million.

References

More information on EKATO can be found on the Web at: www.ekato.com.

Hallwachs, U., H. Kummle, C. Schroedter, G. Steiner, and P. Todtenhaupt. "Integrierte Fabrik- und Industrieplanung: Rahmen fur Wertewandel und Produktionskompetenz," *Industriebau,* 1991, p. 6.

Hallwachs, U. "Dezentrale Verantwortungsbereiche in der Produktion," *Wissenschaft und Technik,* May 1992, pp. 44–48.

Hallwachs, U., P. Todtenhaupt, und M. Schlund. *Mehr Effizienz durch dezentrale Verantwortungsbereiche: Eine praxisnahe Anleitung fur die Reorganisation mittelstandischer Betriebe.* Expert Verlag, 1995.

IPA Tatigkeitsbericht, Fraunhofer-Institut fur Produktionstechnik und Automatisierung, Stuttgart, 1994.

Samson, D. and D. Challis. "Technology Management: A Review of Issues and Literature," written for the Review of International Best Practice in the Adoption and Management of Technology, 1995.

Schlund, M. "Dezentrale Organisationsstrukturen mit Teamarbeit." Paper presented to the AIC Conference, June 29, 1995.

Warnecke, H.-J. *The Fractal Factory—Revolution in Corporate Culture.* Springer, 1992.

Warnecke, H.-J., "Aufbruch zum Fraktalen Unternehmen: Praxisbeispiele fur neues Denken und Handeln," Springer, 1995.

10

GUY BIRKIN—THE DEVELOPMENT AND IMPLEMENTATION OF TEXTRONIC LACE[1]

Introduction

The purpose of apparel lace is basically to add perceived value to a garment. Traditionally lace has been more of a decoration and has been stitched onto the garment. This has changed as a consequence of the technological development in the lace industry, which has made fine lace affordable to more people. Apparel lace is mainly used for lingerie, with bras as the largest market. However, lace is to a larger extent becoming a natural part of garments. It is used for hosiery, swimwear, and outerwear. In fact, some garments are engineered from lace, making it high fashion.

One of the companies that has led the technological development in the lace industry is Guy Birkin, a Nottingham-based lace-making company. Its roots go back to 1827, when Birkin and Co. was founded by Richard Birkin. Over the years, mergers and acquisitions have formed the current company, now a part of the Sherwood Group. Guy Birkin was a key player in the development of the latest technology for lace manufacturing in the apparel lace industry—Textronic. Textronic was developed together with the manufacturer of lace machines, Karl Mayer. Textronic has helped reshape the market for lace and is judged a tremendous success by its customers.

This case illustrates the process by which Textronic lace was developed and subsequently implemented at Guy Birkin. It is based on information collected in a series of interviews with the managing director as well as senior managers and personnel in draughting, design, manufacturing, and technical departments. In addition, plant visits were made in order to observe the technology in operation. Finally, secondary material, for example market data and product information, has been utilised.

Background

This section outlines the background information necessary to understand the process by which Textronic lace was developed and subsequently implemented at Guy Birkin. It starts with a short introduction to the lace business; the products and the market for those products; then, Guy Birkin, the focal company, is described; and finally, the information on technologies that are used to manufacture lace is presented. This history of the technological development in lace is necessary to understand how the company came to recognise the need for developing something new—Textronic lace.

The Lace Business

Products.   The appearance of apparel lace is dominated by textures and threads. However, it is possible to use different kinds of yarn in the same lace, thereby achieving different colours in one pattern. This is possible since different yarns take up colours differently in the dyeing process.

---

[1]This case was developed for use in classroom discussion and is not intended to necessarily illustrate appropriate or inappropriate management practices. Case authors: Christopher A. Voss and Pär Ahlström, from London Business School, 1996. The funding for this case production was provided by the Australian federal government's Department of Industry, Science and Resources.

Consumers are demanding value for money and, in lace terms, this means innovation in luxury yarns, both synthetic and natural fibres, in colour and texture. Comfort is essential, as fashionable and pretty undergarments are worn now by women through their whole life span, which means that the customer profile is much wider. Coming to patterns, it is the imagination of the designer that limits the number of patterns, although there are a few technological limitations. However, the pattern is very important for the success of a piece of lace on the market. The designers, therefore, are crucial for a lace-making company.

Customers.   Lace is sold to the companies that make garments in the lingerie and outerwear business. Marks & Spencer is the major buyer of lace in the U.K. Other companies include British Home Stores, Littlewood, Triumph, Warners, Gossard, and all other brand names. These customers all have in common that they value not only the quality of the product but also the service, where timely and quick deliveries are of utmost importance. Since these garments are to a large extent fashion, it is a seasonal industry. This means that if a delivery is missed, the customer might not be able to launch their garments in due time when the season begins.

In the Far East, although there is strong competition from local manufacturers, there are opportunities for the sale of European styling. These markets are also very diverse in their needs. However, the end consumers—the eventual wearers of the product—do have much in common in their demands. This means that there is more lace used now than 50 years ago, with the Far East being a large potential market.

The Lace Industry.   Lace manufacturing is a highly specialised field that in Europe is dominated by two geographical areas. The first is Nottingham in the U.K., and the second is Calais in France. Said Eileen Measures, managing director and marketing director of Guy Birkin: "lace manufacturing is a small world, we all know each other." Despite this, the lace business is fiercely competitive, since most companies are aiming for the same customers. The technological development has helped reshape the industry toward fewer but larger companies.

One of Guy Birkin's main competitors is Courtaulds, the big U.K. textile group, which has several lace-making companies in the U.K., France, Spain, and in the U.S. Courtaulds owns Desseilles and Societe Dentelles Calaisiennes in France and Galler in Spain. Liberty is their lace and stretch fabric market leader in the U.S. Both Courtaulds and Guy Birkin aim for Marks & Spencer. However, despite this fierce competition, they sometimes cooperate on the production level, sharing production if there should be a lack of capacity for special types of machines. Courtaulds is also just next door to Guy Birkin in the Nottingham area.

Nottingham's name has long been linked to lace. The area has a long tradition of lace manufacturing and other types of textile firms. Today there are 12 lace-making companies in the Nottingham area. The Calais region has companies such as Noyon, which owns the U.K. company Interlace, another major competitor to Guy Birkin.

A third region in lace manufacturing is the Far East. The highest quality comes from Japanese companies. Companies in other countries in that region are considered to have difficulties in making lace of a good quality. They make mostly for the mass market. To achieve sophisticated lace requires investment and creative designs.

Finally, there are some competitors in other regions of the world. Examples are Corvett-Spitzen in Germany, Scanlace in Denmark, Galler, which is the market leader in Spain and Portugal in some segments, as well as companies in Italy and both North and South America.

Guy Birkin. In their own words, Guy Birkin is a company that aims at having: "the highest standards of creativity in both design and technical innovation, a close awareness of the marketplace with the ability to adapt quickly to changes, and flexibility to understand the different needs of the largest and smallest customers and serve both equally well."

History of the Company.   Guy Birkin has a long history. In fact it is the oldest lace manufacturer in the world. It was founded through a merger in 1962 between Birkin and Co., J. Guy & Co., and together with two other companies. However, the history goes back further than that, as we can see from looking at the companies that formed the core of Guy Birkin.

Birkin and Co. was founded in 1827 by Richard Birkin, an entrepreneur aged 22, in the outskirts of Nottingham. He used the lace-making machine that had been created by John Leavers in 1813. From the beginning, the Birkin family worked at improving the technical and the design abilities of the lace machine, and took out several patents, from 1820 to 1880. Many of these are still in use, as of today. Birkin and Co. continued to grow during the 19th century, and over 100 years ago sales representatives went out from Nottingham to travel the world. Furthermore, an office and a warehouse were set up in New York in 1906. Business was also strong in South America and in Eastern Europe. However, in the late 1950s, problems were evident.

Birkin and Co. was good at manufacturing, enjoying the benefits of a good plant and competent technical staff. Their problem was that their traditional markets were in decline. Previously they had aimed for the higher end of the market, a market that had declined drastically after the Second World War.

J. Guy & Co., on the other hand, was good at selling in the high volume middle market. They had no machines and instead were buying and selling lace. The merger of these two companies therefore seemed natural. Along with the other two companies, a group was formed. The objective was to bring together in one group the best resources and expertise in manufacturing, finishing, marketing, and sales of lace.

Eileen Measures, managing director and marketing director of Guy Birkin, characterised the company as having "a culture of change." The merger was an important hallmark in the process of shaping this culture. Birkin and Co. was traditionally a company owned and managed by a family. J. Guy & Co. supplied the entrepreneurial managers. Uniting these two sides proved to be difficult. You were either a "Birkin or a Guy man."

In Derek Allen's, dispatch section leader with 50 years in the company, view the Guy people were the "entrepreneurial," the Birkin company was "Dickensian and formal." "The staff all had to call the family 'Mr.' or 'Mrs.' and almost had to bow or curtsy." To facilitate the process of uniting these two quite diverse cultures, some new people who were neither were brought in. One of them was the current managing director and marketing director, Eileen Measures.

The year 1987 marked the start of the next phase of large changes for the company. That year they were taken over by Debfor Ltd, a major local manufacturer of underwear, at that time a large customer to Guy Birkin. This customer had concentrated on the middle to lower end of the market, whereas Guy Birkin had concentrated on the middle to top end. This meant that Guy Birkin was now owned by a competitor to its customers, a fact that could be sensitive. The takeover by Debfor was the beginning of the creation of Sherwood PLC, now a major international textile group.

The major reason for selling the company was to gain access to the additional capital needed in order to expand the activities. The technological development was an important driver behind this need. Before the takeover the company considered itself a "fiercely private company." Since many shareholders were near retirement, it was convenient for them to sell their stocks. However, all of the key players in the organisation decided to stay even though for some the selling of the company symbolised a "loss of pride." Efforts had to be put in to try to explain why the company was sold. This event has also contributed to what above was termed "the culture of change."

Current Corporate Structure.   Guy Birkin is now a part of the Sherwood Group, an international group in the textile industry with, in total, 14 companies worldwide. In 1994 the group's activities included garments, lingerie, and lace. Its lace-making division consists of Intimate Touch in the U.S. (acquired the 1st of February 1994), Dentex in the Netherlands and Germany, Gustave

FIGURE 1

Organisation of the management team at Guy Birkin

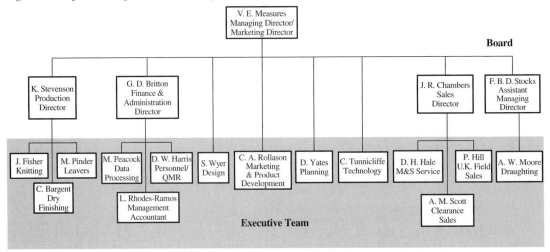

Brunet in France, and Guy Birkin and Floral Textiles in the U.K.. This division is headed by Jim Telfer, who was the previous managing director of Guy Birkin.

Guy Birkin has been described by John Ashton, deputy chairman of the Sherwood Group, as "the jewel in the crown." The company is still based in the Nottingham area. In total, they employ 580 persons. The organisation of the management team is displayed in Figure 1.

Physically, the company is divided between four facilities, located in:

1. *Nottingham*—Head office and administration, as well as the dry finishing process.

2. *Long Eaton*—Leavers machines.

3. *Draycott*—Raschel machines.

4. *Borrowash*—Jacquardtronic and Textronic machines, as well as some Raschel, up to a total of 105 machines (the difference between the machines will be explained shortly).

In total the manufacturing plants cover 17,500 square metres. The factory in Borrowash is the newest site. It was set up in 1978, as a green-field site. The reason for opening it was the growth that had taken place in the company. Now it is used for the latest technology, since it is quite different from the old technology. However, this was not a deliberate strategy when the site was built.

Despite the size, many employees characterise Guy Birkin as a company with family traditions. Many members of the staff have worked there for a great many years, and often members of the same family work side by side. Martin Pinder, factory manager, Long Eaton, explained: "this company is really quite unique because people have worked here so long and know each other really well, it's a good family atmosphere." Mr. Pinder has himself 35 years of service in the company. This is confirmed by Mike Peacock, data processing manager: "although there are lots of different departments within Guy Birkin, there is a great communal feeling—people work for the company, not just their department."

Sales.   Sales at Guy Birkin have increased by 75 percent in the past five years. Sales outside the U.K. have risen from 40 percent of the total to 55 percent. The EC [European Community] takes a very high proportion of the exports, although the fastest growing region is the Far East.

Guy Birkin supplies customers in 33 countries, with France as the biggest export market. Large customers to Guy Birkin are Marks & Spencer, Warners, and Triumph International. Other customers are Ballet, Bertel, Imec, Bugatti's, Selene, Selmark, Lovable, Vanity Fair, Silhoutte, Aristoc Hosiery, Boesch, Marvel, and Le Foglie. Of the exports a proportion continues to go through agents, but increasingly overseas sales are direct. This proportion is growing because of the company's ability to deliver new designs quickly and in volume.

Technologies Used for the Manufacture of Lace.   The whole process of producing lace starts with an idea of a pattern. This idea is converted into a CAD [computer aided design] sketch, which in turn is converted into a format recognisable by the machines and the lace is then manufactured using undyed yarns. The lace is manufactured across the full width of the machines, creating two different types of products, all-overs and lace bands. All-overs have a pattern that is repeated across the width of the machine and is used as a fabric. Lace bands are manufactured in different widths, and are stitched onto the garment. The patterns are balanced from the left and from the right to fit the body. This is crucial for underwear.

The next step in the process is to dye and dry finish the lace and deliver it to the customer, the garment maker. An important part of the dry finishing of lace bands is to separate them from each other, a step in the process known as scalloping. The whole process, from idea until the lace reaches the customer, now takes about three to four weeks. The total process of producing lace is described in more detail in Appendix 1. However, the focus in this case is on the manufacture of lace.

Two important parameters for the lace customer are the texture and price of the lace, both of which are affected by the type of technology that is chosen for manufacturing the lace. The cost is determined by such things as labour intensiveness, speed, and capital costs. Texture, or the "feel" of the lace, is affected by both the technical characteristics of the machine and the type of yarn selected.

In 1990 Guy Birkin was using three different machines for the manufacture of lace. The different machines target the same end users. It is the customers who have the preferences for different types of lace. This section contains a description of the different machines.

Leavers.   The first of the technologies used to produce lace was Leavers, invented in 1813, and subsequently developed. Much of this development was done by the Birkin family. One innovation was the adding of picots and purls to the edge of the lace. This added to the beauty of the product, as well as its commercial desirability. Another important innovation was for the manufacture of wide flounce across the width of the machine.

Despite its age, this technology is still in use, even though its working principles have not changed much since 1880. Some of the machines that are in use today are more than 100 years old. Technically speaking it was the first machine capable of making hexagonal mesh net with twisted instead of looped threads. This was a revolution at that time and still is. What is unique about the Leavers machine is that it uses two sorts of yarn. One is the twisting yarn (wound on a bobbin which is held in a carriage) that twists around the warp, which is static. This means that the lace can be made fine and strong.

The machine actually mimics the motions of a lace-maker's hand, making it quite difficult to distinguish from handmade lace. The way the machine works allows for fine grounds, and the ability to convey a three-dimensional effect. The lace can also be made flexible, which allows for a good fit, moulding the body well in the final product. It is also possible to use both thick and thin threads and it is the best machine for different kinds of natural fibres. When manufacturing lace, pattern capacity is normally expressed in "bars." The more bars, the more intricate the lace patterns that can be made, as a general rule. It is here the Leavers machine has its strength. It has a capacity of more than 400 bars.

The disadvantage with this machine is that it is very labour intensive and slow. It used to be that one person could handle one machine. However, recent technological developments have increased that figure, so now one person can handle two machines. What has been difficult at Guy Birkin is to get the personnel used to this. These machines also require skilled personnel to handle them. This skill is different from that necessary for the newer technologies. The skills needed for Leavers is similar to handicraft and artisan skills.

Despite the continued technological development, the Leavers machine is still slower than the newer machines. Much of this is due to the fact that it is a mechanical machine, weighing 20 tons, with 5,000 moveable parts. The friction involved in its operation puts a limit to the speed that can be achieved.

The labour intensiveness of the machine is still a disadvantage, even though the number of machines per employee has been doubled. This is especially caused by the bobbins. A bobbin is made out of brass and contains one sort of thread. There can be up to 100 metres of thread in each bobbin. There can be 3,600 bobbins on each machine. These last no more than a few days, after which they have to be changed. Assembling and disassembling these bobbins is done manually, a very labour-intensive process. However, the thread is loaded automatically. When the threads have been loaded, the bobbins are cooked under pressure and then cooled down, in order to shrink to fit into the machine. Apart from being labour intensive, this whole process takes time.

However, the machine is relatively easy to set up. A change between different patterns can be done in a few hours. The input for this setup is a sheet with so-called figure sheet numbers, produced by the draughting department (see Appendix 1 for a description of the total process of producing lace). These are manually punched into punch cards, although the possibility of automated punching is being looked at. Changing the pattern is then made by changing these punch cards, which can be done fairly quickly.

The Leavers machines are also robust and easy to modify, should it become necessary. Guy Birkin is still developing these machines, to make them work better. For example, they are trying to incorporate different kinds of plastics in some parts of the machine. Other areas of possible improvement are in lubricants and ways of making the machines stop automatically when threads break.

When lace manufactured on Leavers machines leaves the factory, around 65 percent of the cost is labour, and 35 percent is cost for yarn or material. There are no capital costs for these machines, since they have been written off a long time ago. However, the yarns used in this machine are more expensive than those in other machines, since they have to be specially processed and twisted to be able to be used in the Leavers machine.

Raschel.   The next development in machinery was the Raschel machine, which was introduced in the late 1950s. This machine uses a knitting principle, which is basic and simple. The knitting principle is different from the twisting principle that is used by the Leavers machine.

The early Raschel machines had a capacity of between four and six bars. This was subsequently expanded, so that today up to 56 bars can be used. Still the major disadvantage with this machine is that it is only possible to use one or two very basic types of nets (the "background" to the lace pattern), making the lace flat and quite inflexible. An important restriction here is that the variations in the net take capacity in terms of bars, restricting the sophistication of the patterns that can be produced on this machine. This also means that when manufacturing lace bands, widths are restricted to about seven or eight centimetres if the design is complex.

Another disadvantage is that the change of patterns is difficult. Changing the pattern is done by assembling a chain based on instructions from the draughting team. This chain is for the sideways displacement of the pattern and ground bars. Assembling this chain can take more than two weeks. Thus long production runs are required in order to achieve profit on each order. Furthermore, there is the cost of assembling these chains. Each link in the chain costs around 70 pence. For one pattern, there can be an investment of £8,000 in a chain, not counting the time it takes to assemble it. The individual links can be used again if the chain is disassembled. However, the advantage of this must be weighed against the possibility of the same pattern being ordered again.

The advantage with Raschel is its speed, and the possibility for each employee to operate up to four machines. Raschel lace is therefore low cost to manufacture. Although many of these machines will gradually be phased out, Guy Birkin is still seeking to enhance their operation. One enhancement is to use plastic links instead of metal links in the chains. The upgrading of this technology is also being done by the manufacturer of lace machines. The latest version of this machine has electronic pattern control, which means that the change of patterns is made by inserting diskettes into a computer. This machine is known as the "Binary Raschel" machine.

Jacquardtronic.   The next development in lace machinery took place at an initiative of four key players in the lace industry and Karl Mayer of Germany—the only manufacturer of lace machines in the world. Of the four lace manufacturers, Guy Birkin was one. The others were Norwood Knitting from the U.S., Corvett-Spitzen from Germany, and Siva from Italy. The machine that was developed was called Jacquardtronic, and was launched in 1982.

The basic rationale for developing this machine was to combine the advantages of Leavers and Raschel machines: the ability to produce more intricate and complex lace in wider designs with the cheaper and faster knitting technology. The new machine was a major innovation. It is based on the knitting principle (like Raschel) but is not restricted to simple and basic nets. The machine allows the manipulation of warp threads to any configuration. Important is that only one bar is needed to achieve elaborate nets, the jacquard bar, and the rest can go to patterning, which means that delicate and intricate patterns can be made. The early versions of the machine had 56 bars. The more recent machines have a total capacity of up to 78 bars, which also means that wide lace bands can be attained. Although the lace is not as flexible as that produced with Leavers, it is possible to use elastic warps to increase its flexibility in wear.

The machine also has electronic pattern control, which means that setups are made by inserting different diskettes. The setup times therefore are short, around 10 minutes. However, it is often necessary to change the yarn as well, which means that a change of pattern takes a few hours, including the test of the new pattern. Comparing the speeds of the machine with that of Leavers, the Jacquardtronic is about four times as fast as Leavers. However, Leavers can produce wider lace, so in reality it is only about three times as fast. Finally, a very important characteristic of the Jacquardtronic machine is its cost. It was the first expensive machine, which at the time of its introduction was priced at around £350,000. Today it costs around £500,000. This had a profound effect, as will be seen later on.

Factors Setting the Context of the Change

External Influences.   Perhaps the most important driver of the development and implementation of Textronic machines at Guy Birkin has been the changes that, over the years, have taken place in the market and in the industry. These changes are highly interrelated with the development of the technologies used for the manufacture of lace. In fact, technological development has to a large extent driven the changes in the market and in the industry.

Technology and Changes in the Lace Market.   The changes in the lace industry started with the introduction of Jacquardtronic machines in 1982. This was a huge change for the lace industry; it helped reshape lace fashion in the world. It is important here to notice the difference between allovers (lace used as fabric) and scalloped lace (lace bands). Previously wide scalloped lace with intricate patterns had been produced on Leavers machines, since Raschel was too basic for that type of lace. With Raschel lace bands, up to only 7 or 8 centimetres width could be obtained, after which pattern capacity had run out. With Jacquardtronic, it was possible to produce scalloped lace, with intricate patterns, up to widths of 25 centimetres. This meant that wide scalloped lace became affordable for a wider range of applications.

The other important characteristic of the Jacquardtronic was the capability of high volume output. With 24-hour-a-day operation, one Jacquardtronic machine could produce the equivalent of up to three Leavers machines. Together, these two things marked the beginning of lacy undergarments. For the first time, very intricate wide bands could be made in high-speed production, making it affordable to the middle-market user. Thus, the technology had created a new market. Lace had now changed, from being an added trim, to being an integral part of the garment itself. This meant that the lace had to perform just as any other fabric.

The late 1980s also showed a change in the demand patterns in the underfashion market. In, for example, the United States, sales in all categories of the intimate apparel market grew during the last five years of the 1980s. This can be seen as a result of increasing consumer interest and better retail positioning of underfashion and lingerie departments. Women are also spending more on intimate apparel than before. Young women have also started to wear lingerie as outerwear for evening wear. All this affected the demand pattern for lace.

The increasing importance given to lace as the unique identity of the garment meant that more customers required their own unique designs. Thus, quicker response times became increasingly important as shorter lead times and more frequent new garment collections were being asked for.

Technology and Changes in the Lace Industry.   From the perspective of the manufacturer of lace machines, Karl Mayer, the philosophy is "to innovate machines to produce the finest laces at a cost affordable to all people." This has in turn forced machine development to initiate more complex designs and techniques and has thus opened up a wider market potential. However, it has also reshaped the lace-making industry. Again, the real change started with the development of the Jacquardtronic machine.

The characteristic of Jacquardtronic machines that helped recreate the lace industry was the capital cost of the machine. It was the first machine in recent times with a high capital cost, with an introductory price of around £350,000 (compared to the old Leavers machines, that could be more than 100 years old, and had been written off long since). The introduction of Jacquardtronic machines meant that in order to go ahead in the industry, more capital than before was needed. This was one of the main reasons Guy Birkin agreed to be taken over in 1987. In the industry, this also led to the creation of larger companies, through the merger of smaller players.

Before this development took place, there used to be many small companies in the lace business. In Nottingham alone, there were around 70–80 companies producing lace around the Second World War; now there are only a handful of larger companies. For instance, there are only four manufacturers of Leavers lace left in the Nottingham area.

Internal Influences—Competitive Activities at Guy Birkin.   Needless to say, the introduction of Jacquardtronic machines was a significant change for Guy Birkin as well, having been one of the four players contributing to its conception and development. Each of these four companies got a machine, but Guy Birkin was the first company to use it for commercial production. A major contributing factor to this was the fact that they were the only company of the four that had a wide experience base in Leavers lace. This had given them the experience to work with the jacquard bar technique and a customer base for that product.

The other companies that were adopting this technology early on had their experience in Raschel machines, which is a simpler technology with a product sold at a much cheaper price. At the time of its introduction the price of Jacquardtronic lace was at least two times that of Raschel lace.

At the time of the takeover in 1987, Guy Birkin had 12 Jacquardtronic machines, which made them the first European company to build up a substantial plant of Jacquardtronic machines. This posed a challenge, since it was a machine that was both capable of producing a massive output, and also had to. To be able to recover the high capital costs of the machine, it was necessary to run them 24 hours per day, seven days a week. This meant they had to sell a lot. The high cost of the machines, furthermore, meant they had to charge the customer more than before.

However, the lace still had to be sold to the users of Raschel lace, since they were the high volume users. There was no point in Guy Birkin selling to the users of Leavers lace, since they were using smaller volumes and Guy Birkin had a Leavers plant. Thus, they had to try and upgrade their volume users from Raschel to Jacquardtronic in order to keep the high volumes. At the same time, they had to retain their Leavers customers. This was a different challenge than the one facing the companies who did not have a wide customer base in Leavers lace. The challenge meant that Guy Birkin wanted the middle market volume users to select a more expensive product. Therefore, new markets had to be created. The market had to be moved up to higher value laces.

One of the competitive activities undertaken at Guy Birkin was to try and convince their customers to use wider lace. The width of the machine is 320 centimetres, which can be used to produce all-overs or lace bands up to 25 centimetres wide. For the garment producer, the wider the lace, the more scope there is for innovative garment designs. By trying to convince customers to use wider lace, Guy Birkin were creating a new lace fashion. In doing this, Guy Birkin sought all the help they could. One thing they did was to cooperate with DuPont, one of their suppliers of threads, particularly Lycra. DuPont helped Guy Birkin to promote the new lace on trend shows. In addition, promotional activities were also undertaken by Guy Birkin on their own.

One rather unusual action was to create a video about the Jacquardtronic machine, focusing on its benefits. This video was shown to retail store groups and their garment manufacturers in small parties. This was the first time in the industry that a lace manufacturer had marketed their product to the retailer, to try and persuade them to specify the type of lace to be used in the garments they purchased. Guy Birkin also went onto road shows to show the market how Jacquardtronic lace could alter the market. The whole idea was to make the customers ask for the new product, wide Jacquardtronic lace bands.

Moreover, in 1989 Guy Birkin decided to target the most highly creative European markets (Italy and France) directly, rather than selling through distributors. France is perceived as the gateway to the rest of Europe, apart from being a large and demanding market in itself. Furthermore, some of the major lace manufacturers in the world are situated in the Calais region. Therefore, a subsidiary was set up in Calais with a direct computer link to the office in Nottingham. This meant that French customers could deal with French staff, be invoiced in their own currency, and get quick replies to their queries, making it as easy to buy from Guy Birkin as from the French suppliers in the same region.

These changes coincided with the changes in the underfashion market, mentioned above. Taken together, this meant that responsiveness, both in terms of design and manufacture of lace, became increasingly important. A measure of this is the fact that 70 percent of the company's business comes from development work with individual customers. Another measure is that the lead time, from idea until the lace reaches the customer, has decreased from around three months, 10 years ago, to around four weeks.

Recognition of the Need to Change

With the development discussed above, the management of Guy Birkin could see that something new was needed. By 1989 the number of competitors that had adopted the Jacquardtronic technology had vastly increased, as had the market for its output, but competitive threats were anticipated. The company could see that profits would drop since the market was maturing. Furthermore, having created a market for wide lace, they could foresee a major increase in demand for wider lace bands. Another important change was the importance of shorter setup times. Lace was, to a larger extent, starting to be used to give the garments an identity, by providing an exclusivity to the garment that meant users of them were willing to pay more. To provide even more exclusivity to the designs, shorter runs were being asked for, calling for the ability to change quickly between different patterns.

Shorter runs and more exclusive designs were not suitable for the Raschel machine, due to its inflexible design options and its long setup times. Guy Birkin could also see a point when the simple Jacquardtronic lace would substitute wide Raschel, which meant that they would pull out of wide Raschel. It would instead be used to make narrower lace in larger volumes, utilising the advantages of that particular technology. Raschel is considered very advantageous for lace bands up to 7 or 8 centimetres in width. Thus, simple, high-speed Jacquardtronic would therefore substitute wide Raschel. Therefore, Guy Birkin felt they needed another prestige product to stimulate the market into something new. The competitive reaction was to instigate the development and implementation of a new lace manufacturing technology, which became the Textronic machine.

An important part of the internal discussion on what the next step should look like took place at the regular development meetings held at Guy Birkin. In these meetings participants from design, draughting, manufacturing, and marketing meet to discuss future developments. To these meetings are sometimes invited representatives from suppliers of yarns. Figure 2 summarises the discussion so far. It displays the important changes that have taken place in the technological development, in Guy Birkin, and in the market. The figure also aims at conveying some of the interrelations that exist between these changes. It aims at displaying how Guy Birkin came to recognise the need for continued technological development. Describing the process of this development is the task of the next section.

Process of Transition

With the benefit of hindsight, the development and implementation of Textronic machines does seem like a well-thought-out strategy. However, it is not clear this was the case at the time the development took place. Eileen Measures, managing director and marketing director, said: "I often

FIGURE 2

The interrelation between changes in technology, Guy Birkin, and the market

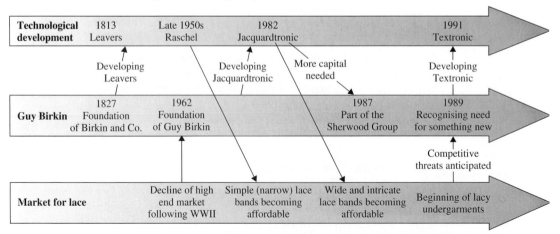

wonder if there was a deliberate strategy from the beginning, it was more of a reaction to market circumstances. The strategy developed accordingly."

Four sets of factors triggered the initiation of the development of new technology. First was the market-driven view of the needs for new products. Second, the cross-functional collaboration and knowledge that this developed led to these market needs being seen in terms of required capability from manufacturing technology. Third, the routine forward- and external-looking activities of the management team led to a detailed understanding of current and potentially available technology. Finally, the close relationship with Karl Mayer, and the experiences of the Jacquardtronic, had led the company to realise that they could be proactive in driving the development of new technologies by their suppliers.

Initiation

Relationship with Karl Mayer, the Lace Machine Manufacturer.   Thus, to understand how the development of Textronic lace took place, the relationship with the machine supplier Karl Mayer is of utmost importance. Karl Mayer has a total world monopoly on the manufacture of lace machines. Therefore, the relationship with them is seen as paramount. Eileen Measures felt that: "without this strong partnership we could not move forward at the pace today's market requires of us."

Guy Birkin has personal relationships with the Mayer family members. This relationship goes back to the late 1970s. To Fritz Mayer, one of three sons of the founder of the company, Guy Birkin is seen as "more than a customer and more of a family member." The parties meet several times per year, and once a year the people of Karl Mayer visit Guy Birkin to talk about future issues. The close collaboration that followed the development of the Jacquardtronic machine meant that, from the perspective of both parties, the relationship was of great commercial advantage. Says Fritz Mayer: "for the future development of lace machinery, it is essential for both companies to work in unison and to have a complete cross-fertilisation of ideas."

This interaction basically meant that Guy Birkin repeatedly asked Karl Mayer to develop a machine that could combine the benefits of Leavers with those of Jacquardtronic. With Leavers it was possible to make flossed lace, which is more like embroidery. Jacquardtronic, on the other hand, produced flat lace with intricate nets with a high speed. The combination wanted was deeply sculptured three-dimensional lace, produced in a high-speed machine with the possibility of quick pattern changes. Guy Birkin knew that Karl Mayer had the capability of producing lace that gave a three-dimensional effect, with top-stitched patterns, on some of their lace machines for curtains. However, curtain lace does not have the same sophistication as apparel lace. Guy Birkin then said to Karl Mayer: "you have a machine that is capable of producing wonderful lace, but on a basic fabric ground. Surely there is a way of combining a fall plate with a jacquard bar?" With a jacquard bar it would be possible to have any intricacy in nets. It is hard to pinpoint a time when this discussion took place. There was a constant dialogue between Guy Birkin and Karl Mayer.

When it came to naming the new machine the relationship between Guy Birkin and Karl Mayer was also important. Since the ambition was to produce lace with texture, on a Jacquardtronic machine, the combination of these two elements were used: Textronic. This name was invented by one of the employees at Guy Birkin. Karl Mayer then agreed to register that name worldwide. This was significant since Guy Birkin did not want anyone with curtain lace to be able to market their lace as this product. Therefore, they wanted to coin a marketing name to distinguish the new product from top-stitched curtain lace. The "-tronic" in Textronic was used to signal to the market that this was a prestigious premium product, by alluding to Jacquardtronic lace.

Producing the First Piece of Lace on the New Machine.   The development of the Textronic machine started in 1990. In late 1990 Karl Mayer advised key lace makers that a new machine was being developed and a prototype would be available in 1991. Guy Birkin immediately decided to take the first prototype. They also made a number of visits to Karl Mayer, to see the machine being built, discussing needs, and getting an idea of how the new machine would be configured (size, height, floor space needed, and so on).

Karl Mayer then had to create some basic designs themselves, in order to sell the potential of the machine to other lace manufacturers. However, since they were machine suppliers and not lace creators operating in the fashion market, the lace that had been produced was very basic. The result was that few lace manufacturers really saw any use for the machine. They thought that the machine did not have enough versatility to be of any value. Not everyone at Guy Birkin saw the new machine's capabilities. Said Alan Moore, draughting executive: "to be fair, there were those among us that were sceptical at the moment." Thus, up until Guy Birkin was able to produce on the new machine, it was looked upon by some "as a white elephant," as Chris Tunnicliffe, technical executive, put it.

However, having had a vision of what the machine might be used for, a few key people at Guy Birkin sat down and discussed what could be done with the new machine. In doing this, they looked at the machine from a broad market point of view rather than a technical point of view. The question they asked themselves was, "what is the potential for creating a different product look by using this machine? Will this machine do what we originally wanted it to do?" Thus, the machine was looked upon from a point of view of producing something that was saleable to customers—something that was different, but yet using the same basic rules as lace from other machines. At this point, a range of more detailed questions started being asked about the market of the product. Guy Birkin looked at parameters such as yarns, widths, costs, output volumes, and target customers to decide on what to produce on the new machine.

In the development of the lace that was produced on the new machine, the experience that existed in the company was crucial. Said Alan Moore, draughting executive: "we have lace making in the blood." This breadth as well as depth of experience is what is seen as differentiating Guy Birkin from their competitors. For instance, they had archives of fabrics, designs, and draughts representing the style and fashion for more than 100 years of lace making. The combination of the experience with the different types of technologies and the new technology was important.

The idea that was put forward was for a piece of lace to be designed and produced especially for the new machine. The archives with the past history of lace were used in this development. In their own words: "it was just a matter of applying this knowledge and, bingo, we got it right on the first try." The long-term experience with lace was combined with knowledge about what the market was demanding. There were some technological changes that had to be made on the drawing to make it suit the new machine. For instance, the lace seemed wider than was anticipated initially. The anticipation was that it would shrink more than it did. The number of stitches per centimetre of lace, the density of the lace, also had to be changed. Finally, the stretch of the lace had to be changed. However, these were only minor modifications.

The installation took place in July 1991, when the new machine arrived at Guy Birkin. Commissioning the machine took another eight weeks, during which drawings and draughts were made. What was developed was a very soft lace, that was made using Tactel micro-fibre. This first piece of lace was produced in September 1991. Immediately, the team at Guy Birkin saw the product, they knew that with good marketing it would be a tremendous success.

In the words of the participants in this development: "it was really a matter of gut reaction, when we developed the lace." The long experience with the different sorts of lace products made them aware of what side effects were going to come all along the production process. This ability to have a grasp of the whole production process, from idea to a finished product, was considered important. Said Barry Stocks, assistant managing director: "a problem you can get when the company grows too much is that the quality drops, since no one is able to grasp the whole operation."

Adoption

A Crucial Investment Decision.   When the samples of lace had been manufactured on the new machine, a crucial investment decision was made. With the samples that were produced in September 1991, Eileen Measures, then marketing director of Guy Birkin, prepared a case to be presented before the board. The aim was to illustrate the versatility of the new machine. Despite the novelty of the technology, the uncertainty of its characteristics, and the fact that it had not been properly tested, the decision to buy six of these machines was taken in October 1991. The ability to move fast is seen as an important asset in the Sherwood culture.

The timing of the investment decision was crucial for the future success of Textronic lace for the company. This was commented upon by Barry Stocks, assistant managing director: "it was also the fact that Sherwood saw the commercial potential and went ahead and ordered six machines. That is something we could not have done by ourselves." It should be kept in mind that these machines at that time cost £450,000.

Since these six machines represented the whole of Karl Mayer's production capacity available for six to eight months, the investment decision meant that no one else could supply the market with Textronic lace. At the time of launch in January 1992 (see below), Guy Birkin had the capacity to supply within weeks. Thus, Guy Birkin was not only first-to-market with Textronic lace, they also captured a significant part of it, by making this preemptive investment. This decision was commented upon by Fritz Mayer as showing a clear vision since they were "swimming against the tide of the lace trade's opposition to this technology."

Installing the New Machines.   With the six new machines due to start arriving in early 1992, the next task was to install them properly and to get them to work on a day-to-day basis. This proved to be an easier task than might have been expected, considering the novelty of the machine. When installing the new Textronic machines, the company decided to keep them separate from the older Leavers machines. Working with Leavers machines was considered a completely different working environment. They felt that it would be difficult to combine the culture of the Leavers environment with that of the newer technologies.

One very important factor contributing to the relative ease by which the new machines could be installed was the experience the company had gained with the Jacquardtronic machine. Although the type of lace that could be produced on the Textronic machine was somewhat of a revolution compared to Jacquardtronic lace, the technologies had many similarities. In fact, one might say that Textronic provided no greater a change than did the Jacquardtronic in this respect. The experience that was gained during the installation of Jacquardtronic therefore was extremely valuable and could be applied to the installation of Textronic.

Said Barry Stocks, assistant managing director: "we were first with Jacquardtronic, which really caused us problems. This machine was much more painful to install and operate than Textronic. We had a long learning curve on that machine." Thus, the extensive experience with Jacquardtronic enhanced the company's staff's skills in working with computer-controlled jacquard machines. In fact, in the early days of the Jacquardtronic machine, they felt that they had to "shield the managing director of Guy Birkin from some of the technical problems" that they had with the machine (this was before the takeover by Sherwood). However, by putting their very best person on the machine, to "treat it as his baby," they managed to get a significant lead over their competitors in working with Jacquardtronic machines.

Looking back, Barry Stocks, assistant managing director, said: "we have been very daring in this development. It would have been easier to have let someone else take the development costs. But it has made us gain experience with the technology, which we have used in the development of the next technology."

Launching Textronic Lace on the Market.   The first piece of lace produced commercially on the new machine was produced in the autumn of 1991; the full market launch of Textronic lace followed in January 1992. It was only then that the company could be confident on the output of the machine, ensuring the ability to meet the anticipated demand. Another factor contributing to the timing of the commercial introduction was that the major trade shows in the industry are in early September and the end of January. Thus, it was natural to launch the product in January. The launch was made at the Spring Interfiliere exhibition in Paris.

The objective of the launch was to generate enough publicity to bring the customers to their stand on the trade show. Since the budget for marketing was not unlimited, advertisements could only be used to a limited extent. What was done was to use trade magazines with which Guy Birkin had good relationships to write editorials on key issues. Guy Birkin cooperated with their contacts at these magazines to print articles on the nature and advantages of the new lace. Among others, articles appeared in "Dessous Mode" and "Clothing World," in the spring of 1992.

Having arrived at Guy Birkin's stand on the trade show, the ambition was to show customers enough to stimulate their interest, not giving them everything. This was because there were not enough patterns at that time to grant exclusivity to all customers. However, Guy Birkin was the only manufacturer of Textronic lace, which was an important message to communicate to the customers. Guy Birkin had a clear view of the capabilities of the Textronic machine and its products and were able to tailor the messages to suit each individual customer.

For example, to a customer that manufactured underwear, in such materials as silk and wool, the message was that they now could have exclusive lace, truly compatible with their fabric. To the middle market high volume users, such as chain stores, it was pointed out that they could have a high impact product in stretch, which could reduce sewing, thereby reducing their cost, enabling them to spend more on the trim. This was at a time when there was a concern in the garment-making industry that there were not enough skilled people to train in sewing. To another customer, a brand house priding itself on its sewing and fitting skills, this message could not be used.

Coming back to what was said earlier: at the time, the way the messages were tailored was not a complex strategy. Said Eileen Measures, managing director and marketing director: "we were simply looking at how we could meet the needs of the individual customers."

Content and Substance of Change

With the development of Textronic lace being outlined, what are the characteristics of the technology making it so unique and different from the other technologies? This section briefly displays its characteristics and thus completes the picture of the different technologies that was initiated earlier. The first thing to notice is that the Textronic machine combines the best of two worlds: the Leavers machine's ability to make flexible, top-stitched or flossed lace, with intricate patterns and nets, is combined with the speedy operation and quick setups that are characteristic of Jacquardtronic machines. The machine is capable of achieving deeply sculptured three-dimensional lace in stretch or rigid. A fall plate, which essentially is an old warp knitting technique, has been combined with weft inlay and a multibar jacquard lace machine. This is what has facilitated the move from flat fashion lace fabrics into those with three-dimensional texture. The machine also has the yarn in front of the machine, compared to the other machines that have it behind or above the machine.

The Textronic machine uses the jacquard principle of making lace. This means that threads are inlayed between the knitting structure. The result is that the threads that make the pattern of the lace almost "float on the surface" (they are top-stitched), like on the Leavers machine, but in fact the threads are "floating" even higher on Textronic lace. The result is that the lace has great richness in texturing and soft handling. The softness means that it provides garments with a lace that is soft to the touch, comfortable, velvety, and offers a three-dimensional look to the products.

However, to achieve this three-dimensional effect, a number of bars have to be sacrificed. The first machines that were developed had 31 bars. Now there is a 53-bar version. The 53-bar machine is basically a mixture between Textronic and Jacquardtronic. On top of that, the machine has been made wider, making it possible to get 15 percent more production.

However, one disadvantage with the machine is that it is not very forgiving with natural fibres, such as cotton. That is because of the "cotton fly" (dust and loose cotton fibres) that is created, which gets inside the machine, making it stop. Therefore it has to be cleaned very often. It also takes about two to three times as long to repair a thread break, compared to for instance the Jacquardtronic machine. That is because the Textronic machine is so inaccessible.

A major advantage is the speed of the machine. One Textronic machine is approximately the same as four Leavers machines in terms of output capacity. It is also quick to set up, due to the ability of electronic pattern control, now the norm of the industry. A Textronic machine can store up to 100 patterns. Changing the pattern is made quickly, but in practice it can take up to one hour. What takes time is the adjustment of the tension of the different threads. All individual threads have different tension. This tension must often be altered when a new pattern is tried.

Table 1 summarises the important characteristics of the different technologies used for producing lace. It is important to note that the aim of the development of new machines has been to make lace more like Leavers lace, but on a machine that is faster, more cost effective, and that can be set up quickly. The appearance/cost ratio is what the technological development is striving to enhance. This ratio is significantly affected by the speed of the machine. Thus, in terms of appearance, Leavers lace is still highly viable, despite its age.

A comment on the item "number of bars" is in place here. Purely technically, a bar is a patterning device. It was mentioned above that pattern capacity is normally expressed in number of bars. The more bars, the more intricate lace patterns can be made. That is not the complete picture. There are other parameters affecting the nature of the lace that can be produced, most importantly the type of yarn that is used.

TABLE 1   Summary of the Characteristics of the Different Technologies

	Leavers	*Raschel*	*Jacquardtronic*	*Textronic*
Basic principle	Twisting threads	Knitting	Knitting	Knitting
Year of launch	1813	Late 1950s	1982	1991
Web intricacy	Intricate	Basic	Intricate	Intricate
Top texturing	Textured	Flat	Flat	Textured
Flexibility of use (give)	Excellent	Moderate	Moderate	Excellent
Number of bars	> 400	56	78	53
Setup time	A few hours	Two weeks	A few hours	A few hours
Speed[1]	1	3	3	4
Labour content	Two machines per person	Four machines per person	Four machines per person	Four machines per person
Cost of machine	N/A	£40–80,000	£500,000	£500,000
Price of lace[2]	£2.10 per meter	£0.90 per meter	£1.30 per meter	£1.80 per meter

[1]The figure gives the relative speed of the machines, using Leavers as a base for comparisons. Thus a Textronic machine is about four times as fast as Leavers, in terms of output capacity.
[2]Comparisons are made using a standard item (14 centimetres stretch lace band), in 1995 prices.

Politics of Change

During the development and implementation of Textronic there was little, if any, functional politics involved, the main reason being that the development was competitive in character. Most of the functions participated in the successful development. However, what can be interpreted in terms of politics is exactly the competitive character of the change, that is, the need for Guy Birkin to stay ahead of competition by developing new technology together with the supplier. Politics here relate to external politics of a competitive nature.

Neither has there been much politics involved on the shop-floor level. The human resource management function has been relatively little involved in the developments that have been described in this case. The main reason for this is again that the changes described were more competitive in character and not seen as foremost relating to personnel issues. There is an active union at Guy Birkin, but it engages only a small percentage of the work force. They did not see the implications of Textronic as being a union issue.

However, as described above, the personnel on the shop floor were crucial for the commissioning and installation of the machines. The effects on employment have also been positive, since the number of employees has increased as an effect of the changes. So even though the technology meant a rationalisation, every new machine created a number of new jobs and Guy Birkin is recruiting for skilled technical personnel.

There are also a lot of hands-on jobs that have to be done, like taking care of yarns. Most of the warps required for the machines are delivered on beams, while pattern beams for the knitting machines are prepared through in-house warping. The number of jobs in this area has increased as a consequence of the new technology.

Guy Birkin also has a tradition in involving personnel that are affected by changes on a "natural" basis. This is something which they pride themselves for. Said Chris Tunnicliffe, technical executive: "here people treat people like people. We work a lot in teams. The whole secret is team work. It is no point for me knowing everything. You should not be frightened of asking people for help. You cannot know everything by yourself. The person who actually does the job is the one with the real expertise."

Operation of New Practices

The Success of Textronic Lace in the Market.   Textronic lace has been a tremendous success in the market, especially among those who value volume, the lace being easy to handle and photogenic (having "hanger appeal" in the store). For instance Marks & Spencer are buying huge series. It has also been a tremendous success among mail order companies, for example French fashion mail order companies.

Looking at volumes between the different machines, it is possible to assess some of this success. Measuring volume in the manufacture of lace is, however, not straightforward. If output is measured in length, one has to take into account the different widths. Therefore, the best way of measuring volume is to look at the value. Looking at shares of the production, in terms of value, the following picture emerges (see Table 2). As can be seen from the table, Textronic has captured a significant part of the market, despite the growth in the total market that has taken place during the time.

As one would expect, a number of factors have been contributing to the market success of Textronic lace. One is that the product allows for elaborate lace designs, which are attractive to those who value "hanger appeal" in the store (the garments should look good in the store). An analysis made by French fashion mail order companies also pointed to the fact that the flexibility in wear of the lace made it comfortable, leading to repeat purchases.

Another important factor is that Textronic lace has similarities with embroidery, which is the competitor in the undergarment business. The drawback of embroidery is that it is expensive in

TABLE 2   Comparison of Output in Value between the Different Types of Machines

	Leavers	*Raschel*	*Jacquardtronic*	*Textronic*	*Others*	*Total Volume[1]*
1990	27%	27%	42%	N/A	4%	100
1994	17	23	21	38%	1	137

[1]Due to reasons of confidentiality, the total volume has been disguised. Using 1990 as the base year for the total volume, these figures are given as percentages.

the market. It is also very difficult, and even more costly, to make embroidery that is able to stretch. With the Textronic machine it is possible to produce lace that is almost like embroidery, but is flexible in wear. This is of great importance to the success of the new lace in the market. Some of the market that Textronic lace has captured was previously held by the embroidery industry, in for instance Austria and Switzerland.

The new technology has also created other new markets, which was one key reason for developing Textronic lace. One important change is that lace continued to be extended to nonunderwear garments, the so-called "worn to be seen" garments. Lingerie looks, previously reserved for the privacy of the bedroom, have now made their way into both outerwear and swimwear. Thus, the dividing lines between different garments, such as underwear, outerwear, and sleepwear, are becoming less marked. This was backed up by the introduction of Textronic lace, since it is possible to produce in volume lace that is beautiful, deeply textured, and affordable. The fashion impact is what has stimulated demand.

Consequently, lace has gained a lot of profile and advertisement for instance in the popular press. Lace has become fashion. The result of this is that everybody keeps asking "what's next?" This means that the development of lace now is going even faster than before.

Current Strategy for Textronic Lace at Guy Birkin.   Currently, Guy Birkin has 31 Leavers, 50 Raschel, 26 Jacquardtronic, and 30 Textronic machines (plus one new one being installed in October this year). Of the total 30 machines, 17 are 31-bar machines and 13 are 53-bar machines. This massive investment in Textronic machines is a reflection of the high hopes the company, and indeed the Sherwood Group, has for the new product. The total investment that has been made amounts to £15 million between 1992 and 1994.

Textronic lace is now selling throughout the world. All together, the policy of purchasing the latest technology has rendered the Sherwood Group world leaders in Textronic lace. It is believed that they have a significant lead over their competitors and that they should be able to maintain this position, due to this policy. The significance of Textronic lace can also be recognised in that at times Guy Birkin has had as many as 15 machines running just to produce one set of lace for Marks & Spencer. No one else has a similar capacity. Courtaulds, Guy Birkin's only competitor in the U.K., has 4 Textronic machines in the U.K., and about 12 in France and Spain.

Other Impacts of the New Machine.   The introduction of Textronic lace has also had other impacts. However, it is important to note that there are no major effects of the new machines in the processes that take place before and after manufacturing. Thus, designs for Textronic are in essence no different from other designs, although the type of machine is taken into consideration in the design stage. The aim is to work with the strengths of the different machines. Dry finishing, the activities that take place in the Nottingham facility, is hardly affected at all by the change to Textronic. Having said that, one effect of the Textronic machine in other areas is that it has challenged the company to think in a new way about old machines. One development that has been made in the Raschel area is to change the gauge to be able to take thicker yarns than before. New design types can therefore be produced on older machines, even increasing their ability to create profit for the company.

Furthermore, Textronic lace is still in short supply. Therefore, the company does not want to produce narrow lace, since that would be just like producing on a Leavers machine, but to use maximum capacity for wide Textronic lace bands. They have therefore used some of the Leavers machines to produce "Textronic narrow lace" cost effectively. This means that although the Leavers machine is over 100 years old in its current configuration, it is still viable. There are those manufacturers that believe the Leavers machine to be a "dying breed." This view is not shared by the people at Guy Birkin.

As a consequence of the development of lace into being a structural part of the garments, the demands on the tolerances have become stricter. Today, garments are engineered using lace. This means that the tolerances have to be strict. It is also important that the lace is stable. However, the problem is that lace is a living thing. Literally, it is a question of making threads go around holes. This makes it very tricky both to manufacture and to design lace with tight tolerances. The size and tolerances of the lace are also affected by the type of dyeing and pattern structure used. Another thing that has come out of the development of Textronic lace is that Guy Birkin is now at the forefront of the technological development in the industry. During the development of Textronic, the "whole world was waiting to see what we came up with and then they followed it," as Chris Tunnicliffe, technical executive, said.

Alan Moore, draughting executive, continued to say: "now we are in the position that everybody is trying to shoot us down. This has led to a big headache for us, since everybody now expects the next development to be a big success." Consequently, there is a need to continuously look ahead to see what the next step in the technological development can be. Or as Barry Stocks, assistant managing director, put it: "we are stuck in a technological race. It would be nice to settle down for six months and just tie up all the loose ends. But we cannot do that. Everybody is chasing us."

Finally, the relationship with Karl Mayer has developed as a consequence of the development of Textronic lace. Since Karl Mayer has the world monopoly on these types of machines they can do pretty much what they feel is right for the market and themselves. However, as Barry Stocks, assistant managing director, put it: "it is in their interest to develop new machines as well." Due to the key role Guy Birkin has played in the development of Textronic and Jacquardtronic lace, the relationships with Karl Mayer have been deepened, putting Guy Birkin in a very good position in the future technological development in the industry.

Conclusion

There are a number of factors contributing to the highly successful development and implementation of Textronic lace at Guy Birkin. The following summarises some of the major lessons that can be gleaned from the case.

Cross-Functional Collaboration.   Vitally important for the whole conception and initiation of the development of Textronic lace is the cross-functional collaboration that existed in the company. There was a constant dialogue between technical and marketing personnel. At the management level, there was a wide and more extensive discussion that took place three to four times per year during major development meetings. Participants at these meetings were the different functional executives, the marketing director, personnel with special technical competence (depending on the matter at hand), and representatives from yarn suppliers.

Furthermore, at a working level, this dialogue took place formally in terms of regular development meetings, often several per week. Informally, cross-functional collaboration took place each time a new piece of lace was produced. Then there was the collaboration between technical and salespeople, often centred on the marketing department, which is the filter between the customer and the design department. A major reason for having the marketing department acting as a filter is that they were knowledgeable both of the customer's needs, his previous purchases, the overall process of lace production, machine situation, plants, and costing.

Thus, the way that the company works, both formally and informally, is geared up to a high degree of cross-functional collaboration, especially between technically and marketing oriented functions. This gives an increased awareness of the technological aspect of the competition in the marketplace. As seen above, technology has to a large extent been the driver of the changes in the lace market.

Close Relationships with Supplier of Machines.   Of vital importance in the development has been the relationship with the machine supplier Karl Mayer. This relationship, which, among other things, includes regular meetings to discuss important technical and competitive issues, is of mutual importance to both parties and has been described in more detail above.

In this case the collaboration basically meant that Guy Birkin repeatedly asked Karl Mayer to develop a machine that could combine the benefits of Leavers with those of Jacquardtronic. Thus, although Karl Mayer supplied the machine, or the hardware if you like, the role of the Guy Birkin people in this development is crucial. They provided the knowledge of how to produce lace, the software, to the incremental development of the machine.

Technical Competence of Personnel.   Despite providing the software expertise to the development of Textronic, it should be kept in mind that Guy Birkin has a skilled technical team able to repair and adapt the machine, although they are not machine builders themselves. An example of the technical skills is the electronic expert who is very good at repairing the computers in the machine, which saves much money. This has proved to be important, since although Karl Mayer has an agent in Loughborough, close to Nottingham, the right spare parts are sometimes not in stock locally. Thus, even though Guy Birkin uses the latest machines, these are constantly refined by the technical staff.

A further indication of the ability of Guy Birkin to handle technical issues on the machines themselves is the fact that other companies have reported problems with the Textronic machine, for instance on how to make rigid lace and how to avoid having the threads going together. These problems have been overcome by the technical team at Guy Birkin.

Barry Stocks, assistant managing director, commented upon this: "of course we do have a few secrets, but the big thing is that we have gained experience by using the Jacquardtronic for so long." Guy Birkin is guarding these "secrets" closely even from Karl Mayer since their competitors could benefit otherwise.

Experience with Older Technologies.   As previously alluded to, one important factor in the development is the long history of lace making at Guy Birkin. One result of this history is that they have all the different technologies in-house. In fact, they are the only company in the industry that has all the different technologies in one unit, with high volume output.

The same creative team has also been used to create designs for all machines. Again, this is not what all other companies did, for instance some of those in the Calais region. The benefit that could be reaped from this was that knowledge and experience could be transferred between the different machines.

The company's long experience in using different types of yarn has also been important. What they did was to work with the suppliers of yarn to develop yarn that could be used on the new machine. Since they wanted a different look, it meant that quality and design, in combination with yarn, led to certain textures and surface effects. There were a number of trials with different kinds of yarn, to have them fit all stages in the production process, from design to dry finishing. What was wanted from the yarn was for it not to snag, to be soft, and to provide comfort in wear.

Team Skills at the Shop-Floor Level.   Crucial to the success of the new machines has also been the competence of the personnel on the shop floor, installing and operating these machines. Teams of these mechanics were sent to Germany to be trained to commission and set up the machines, during the initial stage of the development of the technology. Guy Birkin considers these teams important, since they contain well-trained people. As Chris Tunnicliffe, technical executive, put it: "they are good blokes, simply, there is no magic to it." This view is confirmed by Fritz Mayer, who stated that Guy Birkin built: "teams of people that were capable of keeping abreast of the technology."

Again, a lot of this has to do with the long history of the company and indeed the history of the lace trade in the region. Said Sid Wyer, design executive: "people here are proud of the product. The new people that come in get sucked into it as well. That is the key."

APPENDIX 1
THE PROCESS OF LACE PRODUCTION

To put the manufacturing of lace in perspective, this appendix outlines the total process of producing lace. This process is visualised in Figure 1, which displays the important steps. At Guy Birkin, everything except dyeing is done in-house. Dyeing is done at a sister company, part of the Sherwood Group. The focus in this description will lie on the steps in the process that are a part of Guy Birkin. The examples given below are also from Guy Birkin, although the actual process does look about the same in other companies.

With its hundreds of threads, different nets, plus thick and thin yarns, a lace design is probably the most complex form of textile structure. Therefore, the whole process of making lace, from idea until finished product, is a highly creative one. The creativity of this whole process is what "gives an intense amount of job satisfaction," according to Mr. Alan Moore, draughting executive with 33 years in the company. Mr. Moore continues to say that: "this is why I've been doing it so long."

Idea Generation and Specification of Customer Request

Making lace starts with an idea of pattern. The current range at Guy Birkin consists of around 800 patterns. Around half of these are changed each year. The majority of the patterns are initiated by Guy Birkin themselves. In addition to the designers, the 20 salespeople are an important source of ideas. As they travel the world to sell lace, they constantly run across new ideas. Other important sources of ideas are trade shows and magazines.

FIGURE 1

Lace production

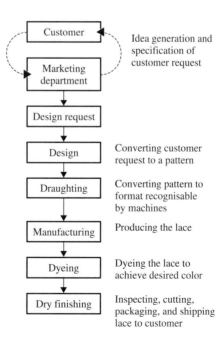

These ideas are already on the market. In addition, Guy Birkin works at least 18 months ahead of time with their lace products, which means that they are relying on input such as fashion trend forecasts and developments in yarn and fabrics to generate ideas for new lace designs. Thus, impetus for new patterns can come from the yarn, or the material. The impact of new yarns is expected to be important during the coming three to five years.

The development of new patterns undertaken by Guy Birkin can be seen as concept development, made with the market in mind, but not a specific customer. These concepts are then shown to all customers. Concept development has been simplified recently, since it now makes it much easier to experiment.

Having been shown the different ideas, the customer orders a range of laces to suit a whole series of garments. Guy Birkin works closely with the customer, via the marketing department, to produce a piece of lace that pleases the customer. The marketing department is the filter between the customer and the design department because marketing personnel are knowledgeable both of the customer's needs, his previous purchases, the overall process of lace production, machine situation, plants, and costing.

Design Request

What the design department receives is a design request from the marketing department. The design request specifies the type of machine that is going to be used. The choice of machine depends on the price of the finished goods and the desired appearance of the product. The aim is to work with the strength of the different machines. From a design point of view the machines have different design capacities. The attributes of the lace are therefore dependent upon the machine that has been chosen.

To ensure that the design request contains the information that is needed to design and produce the lace, a written procedure has been instigated. A contributing factor to the instigation of this procedure is also the fact that Guy Birkin has just achieved ISO 9001 certification. A special form is used for this purpose. The procedures are the same regardless of the type of machine that will be used.

The form is first filled out by the customer together with the salesperson. The form then goes to the product development department in Nottingham (which is a part of the marketing department). They translate the first part of the form into a more technical jargon, since the jargon used by the salespeople is not always usable in a technical sense.

Among other things they add a measure of the width of the lace. This width is kept constant on the different machines, to avoid changes. Thus, different machines are set up for the production of different widths. However, the width can be changed if that is needed, although this takes some time.

The third section on the form is reserved for the design department. If necessary, they can add information on, for instance, reasons why they cannot fulfill the specified requirements, should there be some kinds of technical factors hindering that.

An important development concerning design requests for patterns is that customers are to a larger degree asking for exclusivity. This means that patterns are restricted to one customer only.

The pressure for exclusivity has always existed, but can be said to get really serious as from the development of Jacquardtronic lace in 1982, being able to produce lace quicker and still get intricate patterns. The continued growth of the company has also meant that more and more patterns are exclusive for certain customers. The demand for exclusive patterns has repercussions in the rest of the production process, particularly in the design stage.

Design

Once the design request has been properly handled and filled out, the designer starts with making a drawing of the idea, using pencil and paper. It is important that this sketch portrays as accurately as possible what the final product will look like. To be able to achieve this, the designer must not only be an artist, with fashion awareness. He or she must also know the different technical characteristics of the machines that are used to produce the lace.

Guy Birkin currently employs five designers. Around 400 patterns are produced per year. This means that the actual number of designs is two to three times as great, since all designs are not made into a product.

Having produced a sketch, in the next step the sketch is simulated using a CAD [computer aided design] system. Guy Birkin was the first lace manufacturer to present sketches on a CAD system, back in 1990. This was a large step forward, since each time a new run of lace is produced, it costs up to £10,000, just in start-up costs. The realism that can be achieved with the help of CAD has never before been possible, and gives the ability to make amendments and produce a full new sketch within minutes. This means that the customer can be more confident that the lace will be right, which can save on costs for setting up and manufacturing a sample of the lace.

Before the CAD system was introduced, the sketches were painted by hand on plastic film. The disadvantage with this way of working was that it was too slow, taking up to two days per design, and it was difficult to incorporate customers' alterations. Amendments were impossible or at least very difficult, since the sketch had to be redrawn.

The need for a CAD system basically stemmed from three things. Firstly, there were becoming more and more confinements on the designs (exclusivity), which meant more designs had to be produced. Secondly, the development in manufacturing technology meant there were more machines to be utilised than before, since the development has provided faster and faster machines. Thirdly, the customers were demanding shorter lead times in the whole process.

Draughting

When the design is approved, the sketch goes to the draughting team, who converts it into a format that the lace machines can recognise. Besides the sketch, other types of information that is needed concern the type of yarn and what stretch is allowed to the lace. The draughting process starts with an enlargement of the sketch onto a piece of paper, to work on the details. Then the shapes are checked, since they might alter as the lace is produced. The shapes might collapse or make the lace too rigid. The next step is to convert the drawing into a format recognisable by the machines, different formats depending upon which machine it is meant for, as described above. This often results in up to 200,000 pieces of information for one single pattern.

Although it is possible to imagine the use of a computerised connection between the CAD system and the machines, there is no such connection at the moment. It has been tested, but has not worked properly so far. The problem is seen as being one of a lack of computer language to handle artistic ideas. Making lace is much the work of an artist, since there is a need for imagination, feeling, and creating.

After draughting, the lace is ready for manufacturing, a stage in the process developed above. After manufacturing, the lace goes to the dyeing company. However, the next part of this description concerns the activities that are performed when the lace returns from the dyer, the so-called dry finishing.

Dry Finishing

All dry finishing is done at the Nottingham facility. Upon its arrival to Nottingham from the dyer, the lace is checked in and inspected. The inspection is done to ensure that the lace conforms to specification, in terms of widths, pattern repeat, and skewness. Depending on the type of lace, the inspection is either done manually or by a computer.

The next stage is to separate the lace bands. Knitting machines turn out the lace bands in 3.4 metre-wide webs, with the pattern underlain by a flexible net material that serves to reinforce it. The simpler patterns are separated manually by a thread removal, often on a subcontract basis in people's homes. This gives the flexibility to adjust the production to demand. The separation can also be made automatically, by the cutting out of scalloped edges.

Currently, three different technologies are used for scalloping, all of which uses some form of mechanical cutting. However, Guy Birkin is cooperating with Loughborough University to develop a laser scalloping machine, a vision-controlled cutting machine that would provide the opportunity to cut lace with speed and consistency, having a cleaner edge. Speed is important to Guy Birkin, since they are cutting one million metres of lace per week.

The simple machines with rotating knives that are currently used to cut lace require a lot of supervision. Not only do the rotating knives need careful monitoring, they need a lot of skill to avoid the underlying netting to bunch up in front of them.

Using a laser has several advantages. The beam applies no force to the material, and so causes no bunching. As it cuts, it heat seals the cut ends of the fibres, leaving a smooth surface that does not scratch, tickle, or snag other apparel when used in figure-hugging garments. The laser cuts continuously, never has to be sharpened, and can be used to create finer and more intricate patterns than are feasible with knives. However, the laser-cutting machine is not yet commercially available.

Having been scalloped, the lace ends up in bins to be inspected again. After the second inspection the lace is reeled. The reels are then weigh-checked, to see if there is a shortage, damages, or over recovers. Finally, the lace is delivered to the customer.

11

A CASE STUDY OF THE IMPLEMENTATION AND MANAGEMENT OF SURFACE MOUNT TECHNOLOGY AT HEWLETT PACKARD'S MEDICAL PRODUCTS GROUP: ANDOVER SURFACE MOUNT CENTRE[1]

Introduction

Surface mount technology (SMT) is a capital-intensive advanced manufacturing technology that conceptually has been around since the early 1960s, but only relatively recently matured as a viable technology. Today, surface mount is revolutionizing the production of electronic printed wiring boards (PWB) traditionally done by through-hole (TH) technology. In 1990, U.S. manufacturers spent close to $400 million per year on SMT equipment and this figure was expected to double within the next 10 years. SMT typically offers major reductions in board size, improved system performance, and significant direct labour savings over boards made with through-hole technology.

This case study describes the implementation of SMT at Hewlett Packard's (HP) Andover Surface Mount Centre (ASMC). ASMC makes digital and analogue boards for HP's Medical Products Group (MPG) as well as other HP companies. By all measures, the SMT implementation at ASMC was a major success. Today ASMC is widely acknowledged as one of the best surface mount manufacturing facilities inside HP.

The implementation timeframe for this case stretches from the early 1980s up to the present. Many of the important issues in this case unfolded from 1985 to 1990. Information in this case was collected during a series of interviews with design engineering, printed circuit (PC) layout, manufacturing engineering, and manufacturing personnel. Other secondary reports and memos were also reviewed and incorporated into this case study, along with direct observations made during numerous site visits and two detailed factory tours.

Background

Ultrasound imaging uses high-frequency sound waves to create accurate images of the human body's interior. Sound waves transmitted through the body reflect off of tissues and return an echo to the transducer. The echo contains information about the tissue characteristics, and can be electronically converted by a computer into two-dimensional images for medical analysis. Because high-frequency sound waves cannot penetrate bone or air, ultrasound machines are especially useful for imaging soft tissues to view organs for cardiology and vascular diagnosis. A major advantage of ultrasound machines, over rival techniques such as X-rays or exploratory surgery, is that they are noninvasive (no cuts or injections are required) and there is no exposure to harmful radiation or chemicals. Furthermore, ultrasound's typical system cost of $50,000 to $200,000 compares very favourably to the over $1 million price tag of a computerized axial tomography scanning (Cat-scan) or magnetic resonance imaging (MRI) machine. This modest purchase price in comparison

[1]This case was developed for use in classroom discussion and is not intended to necessarily illustrate appropriate or inappropriate management practices. Case author: Mark Frohlich, Boston University, 1996. Acknowledgement is made to Jeffery Miller and Steve Rosenthal, Manufacturing Roundtable of Boston University. The funding for this case production was provided by the Australian federal government's Department of Industry, Science and Resources.

to Cat-scans and MRIs, in combination with lower training, maintenance, and downtime costs, as well as real-time images, spurred an explosion in ultrasound system sales in the 1980s. As seen in Table 1, dollar shipments in the ultrasound market increased sixfold while the number of units delivered more than tripled from 1980 to 1991.

Until the early 1980s, ultrasound equipment used mechanical transducers to produce two-dimensional black-and-white images. In 1981, Hewlett Packard's Medical Products Group, located in Andover, Massachusetts, revolutionized the industry with a phased array system that offered greatly improved image quality. In 1984, Irex (a subsidiary of Johnson & Johnson) introduced another breakthrough with colour ultrasound equipment. In 1986, MPG once again upped the ante when it successfully combined Doppler technology with colour imaging. This allowed doctors for the first time to monitor both the direction and velocity of blood flow in organs such as the heart. As seen in Table 2, by the mid-1980s MPG had become a market leader for ultrasound systems.

TABLE 1   Ultrasound Industry Dollar and Unit Value Shipments: 1980–1991 ($ value in millions)

Year	Value	Units	Year	Value	Units
1980	$150	2,725	1986	$432	6,950
1981	219	3,785	1987	540	7,475
1982	243	4,660	1988	663	8,380
1983	269	5,350	1989	801	8,975
1984	306	5,760	1990	836	9,510
1985	350	6,550	1991	908	9,950

Source: HBS Case HP Imaging Systems Division.

TABLE 2   U.S. Market Share Positions of Leading Ultrasound Manufacturers: 1983–1991

Company	1991	1990	1989	1988	1987	1986	1985	1984	1983
Acuson	1	1	2	2	2	3	6	6	-
Aloka	6	7	7	6	8	11	-	-	-
ATL	3	3	3	3	3	2	2	1	1
Diasonics	5	5	5	4	4	4	4	2	2
GE	7	6	6	5	5	5	5	5	7
HP-MPG	**2**	**2**	**1**	**1**	**1**	**1**	**1**	**4**	**4**
Hitachi	10	11	11	12	-	-	-	-	-
Interspec	9	9	8	8	7	7	13	-	-
Siemens	8	8	17	15	-	-	-	-	-
Toshiba	4	4	4	7	6	6	10	10	10

Source: HBS Case HP Imaging Systems Division.

Factors Setting the Context of Change

External Influences

Competition.   The most important performance feature all ultrasound manufacturers competed on was image quality. A key driver of image quality was the number of channels in the transducer. Throughout the 1980s transducer channels rapidly grew from 48 or 64 to 96 or 128. By the early 1990s a number of companies were working on 192 or 256 channel systems and even three-dimensional imaging.

Given the "cost-plus" structure of much of the U.S. health care industry, price was for many customers a secondary consideration. In certain markets, however, health care cost containment was becoming more important. In 1983, the U.S. government mandated that all Medicare expenses be part of a prospective payment system (PPS). With PPS, hospitals were reimbursed for tests based on regional costs, not on an individual hospital's costs. In 1991, PPS was extended to capital expenditures. Similarly, by the early 1990s, private health insurance companies began to balk at rising medical costs and HMOs had emerged as a dominant cost control model. Finally, with the rising national concern over health care costs in 1993–1994, capital-intensive diagnostic equipment's price had become an important consideration.

MPG faced aggressive domestic and international competition in the 1980s. As suggested by Table 2, Acuson, a California company founded by a former HP engineer, quickly followed MPG's lead and introduced Doppler colour flow in 1988. Other U.S. companies such as ATL (Advanced Technology Laboratories), Interspec, Biosound, GE, and Siemens likewise offered competitive products in terms of price and performance. Toshiba, the world's leading seller of ultrasound systems, was reported to have the largest R & D budget of any ultrasound company. Other international electronic giants like Hitachi and Philips were likewise attempting to expand their U.S. market shares. Foreign competitors, in particular, were threatening to dominate the low-end/low-cost segment of the ultrasound industry.

Marketplace.   The U.S. ultrasound business consisted of three distinct markets as shown in Table 3. Originally, ultrasound systems were purchased almost exclusively by either large hospitals or imaging clinics. A typical machine in this category could cost anywhere from $150,000 to $250,000. These customers typically bought high-performance systems with the densest available transducer channel capabilities for superior image quality. Large hospitals and imaging clinics also tended to buy "full feature" systems such as Doppler and flow-flow. From the manufacturer's perspective, printed wiring board size or "real estate" was an important consideration with high-performance systems. As more transducer channels and features were added to high-end systems in the mid-1980s, the physical size of systems and board density were starting to reach their limits of manufacturability.

Smaller urban and rural hospitals composed the second customer group. These products had somewhat less imaging performance than high-end systems due to fewer transducer channels and also offered fewer optional "bells and whistles." A typical machine in this segment sold for $100,000 to $150,000. Since electronic components were also relatively densely packaged inside midrange systems, existing technologies and manufacturing methods likewise had trouble accommodating these product lines.

The final market segment was for very small hospitals and private physicians. As cheaper systems became available in the 1980s, independent practitioners and outpatient clinics started buying low-end ultrasound systems. A typical machine in this niche sold for under $100,000. In this market, the price-performance ratio of systems was important. In other words, the closer the performance of a system was to mid- and high-performance systems and the lower the price, the more likely customers were to buy them. Given the limited physical space and technical expertise

TABLE 3   Market Segments and Competing Ultrasound Products

Market	Customer	Competitor	Products	Prices	Features
High Performance	Large urban or teaching hospitals	**HP-MPG**	**Prism 1500 Prism 1000 Enhanced**	>$150K	Phased array 96–128 channels
	Imaging clinics	Acuson	128 XP		Superior image quality
		Toshiba	SSH-140AC		Colour flow, Doppler
Mid Performance	Midsized urban hospitals	**HP-MPG**	**Prism 1000 Basic**	$90–$150K	Annular or phased array
	Rural hospitals	ATL	Ultramark 9		48–64 channels
		Toshiba	140A		Moderate images
					Colour flow, Doppler
Low Performance	Small hospitals	**HP-MPG**	**Sunrise**	$50–$90K	Mechanised, annular, or phased array
	Private practices	Interspec	Apogee		48–64 channels
		Vingmed	CFM750		Acceptable images quality
		Biosound	Genesis		Colour flow, black & white

Source: HBS Case HP Imaging Systems Division.

available to most private physicians and outpatient clinics, the overall size of an ultrasound system, its reliability, and its ease of use were also important considerations.

Internal Influences

Technology.   Ultrasound machines, as with almost all other electronic scientific and medical equipment, originally relied on through-hole technology. TH had emerged in the 1960s and 1970s as a relatively cheap, flexible, and robust way to produce PWBs. By the early 1980s, TH was a very mature technology. Insertion machines for placing components on boards and wave-soldering allowed for relatively low-cost production. Unfortunately for ultrasound manufacturers, an increased number of transducer channels and features were starting to push TH process capabilities to the limits of its capabilities. In some cases the total number of boards required meant that more and more components were being crowded into limited cabinet space. In other situations, features were limited to a single-sided board and relatively costly accommodations had to be made in order to connect options across two or more boards. Board complexity not only added to engineering design costs, but also increased manufacturing labour costs. TH parts were becoming so tightly packed that they exceeded automation capabilities. Finally, since the second most expensive item in PWBs is the board itself, manufacturing material costs were beginning to climb as standard and optional features required more and more board space.

In the early 1980s, many of HP's electronics divisions were facing problems similar to MPG. Customers were demanding greater performance, computers were getting smaller and faster, and finished board costs needed to be reduced. In 1983–1984, HP's CEO, John Young, asked that his 45 manufacturing divisions each take 10 percent out of their board costs for a combined cost savings of $100 million. At the same time HP's top management formed the Manufacturing Engineering Council (MEC) to help make board cost reduction recommendations. Although originally chartered to evaluate existing manufacturing practices, the MEC also took a close look at emerging electronic packaging alternatives. Impressed with the technology in Japanese products such as the Sony Walkman, the MEC recommended that HP begin investing in surface mount technology. Purchasing a new process technology was not the near-term cost solution HP's management was looking for, and the MEC was disbanded. The stage was set, nevertheless, for future adoption of SMT at HP.

Many divisions began to realize that 100 percent TH technology was starting to constrain new products and they were interested in pursuing SMT. Some divisions (like calculators in Corvallis, Oregon) had already switched from TH to SMT in the early 1980s. The corporatewide movement to SMT, however, posed a major cultural dilemma at HP. Traditionally, HP's 45 divisions were highly autonomous. Each division was charted to go after a market segment and always had both its own engineering and manufacturing capabilities. The relatively high costs of SMT equipment made it prohibitively expensive for each of HP's 45 divisions to develop surface mount manufacturing capabilities. Taking manufacturing away from previously self-sufficient divisions ignited a major cultural debate. Some top managers even went so far as to suggest that only a single surface mount manufacturing centre was necessary to supply all of HP's businesses. Hal Edmonson, HP's senior vice president of manufacturing, helped drive the push for SMT while limiting the number of divisions that would develop SMT capabilities. The corporate technology strategy that emerged was that, of the 45 divisions using TH, only a fraction would migrate to SMT manufacturing. Those divisions in which SMT board production was centralized would in turn manufacture PWBs for all of HP's other businesses. To help enforce this policy, Hal Edmonson required that his signature be placed on all major SMT equipment purchases. The stage was set for competition among these 45 divisions to be one of the ones (ultimately 15) that eventually ended up with SMT manufacturing capabilities.

Recognition of Need to Change

External Drivers

Foreign Competition.   By the mid-1980s, Japanese competitors were directly threatening the low end of the ultrasound market. Specifically, there was a niche for machines that cost a quarter to one-third of high-end systems (roughly $40,000 to $50,000) yet offered decent image quality along with flow-flow capability. While lower performance machines only represented 10 to 15 percent of MPG's sales, there was concern that, as with the consumer electronics and automobile industries, once the Japanese controlled the low-cost segment they would next attack HP's more profitable mid- and high-end ultrasound business. The Japanese, in fact, had already made major investments in TH production processes and had a cost advantage over most U.S. competitors. All other foreign and domestic ultrasound manufacturers likewise relied on traditional TH technology. In the mid-1980s none were converting to SMT, although some of MPG's competitors, like ATL, were rumoured to be considering it.

Internal Drivers

Design and Operational Inefficiencies.   In the mid-1980s, MPG's design engineering and manufacturing functions were under growing pressure to accommodate greater ultrasound system capabilities, reduce production costs, and improve quality. In design engineering, even though customers demanded more and more features, the size and weight of ultrasound system carts could not realistically be increased any more. Some of the original through-hole phased array system boards were already very complex: several PWBs had hundreds of TH components and some systems had up to 5,000 electrical components.

Similarly, MPG's manufacturing was under growing pressures. Even though customers were somewhat price insensitive, in the mid-1980s new features quickly drove an average system's cost from approximately $120,000 per unit to well over $200,000. MPG's Andover manufacturing function was expected to help hold down production costs wherever possible so the price of high-performance machines did not spiral hopelessly out of control. MPG's board productivity and quality likewise had room for improvement. Analogue board yield was 80 percent and cycle-time[2] was a relatively long six weeks. System reliability in the field was about average for the industry.

Technology Strategy.   In the mid-1980s MPG was the market leader in ultrasound systems, especially in high-performance systems suitable for cardiac diagnosis. MPG's technology strategy was to continually evolve the high-performance ultrasound system as soon as each new technological innovation became practical. The strategy included adding colour flow processing, installing a larger imaging aperture, and expanding disk storage space. As health care came under further pressure to reduce the costs of delivering medical services, MPG's management grew concerned that the company might be too vulnerable to lower-cost, acceptable performance competition.

In 1985 MPG formed a separate project team at its Andover plant to develop a complementary ultrasound system with similar diagnostic capabilities as the high-end system at a third of the cost. Early on it was decided that the new system would have a mechanical sector scanning "front-end," rather than phased array, and would not include colour flow processing circuitry. In all other specifications, however, the new system was to meet or exceed the high-end ultrasound system.

Process of Transition

Initiation.   MPG's SMT journey took much of the 1980s, and a timeline is shown in Exhibit 1. By the early 1980s, various pieces of Andover's TH equipment were either worn out or obsolete. In 1982, Bert Anderson, manufacturing technology manager for MPG, initiated a study of TH technology to see what changes could be made to the existing PWB production processes in order to improve efficiency and quality. Andover's manufacturing engineering department was chartered, in effect, to do whatever was necessary to overhaul TH. During the course of this analysis it quickly became apparent that, rather than reinvesting in TH, a better strategy might be to move to SMT. Steve Kalenik, a manufacturing engineer hired by Bert to improve TH, visited other companies using SMT and contacted vendors to get component samples. Several trial boards were made after-hours in manufacturing, and hands-on demonstrations were held for design engineers using a makeshift vapour phase SMT process. Based upon what they saw in industry and read in technical journals, Bert and Steve quickly became active champions of SMT. For several years manufacturing, under the leadership of Bert and Steve, formed an SMT "skunk works" and continued to develop and advocate surface mount technology inside MPG until a product line committed to the new technology.

Before SMT was introduced at Andover, engineering always took the lead in product and process changes. Since the SMT implementation, manufacturing has led engineering in process changes.

---

[2]ASMC calls what is typically known as throughput time cycle-time, the elapsed time from when an operator first touches the raw board until it passes final tests.

EXHIBIT 1

Surface Mount Technology Timeline

	1981	1982	1983	1984	1985	1986	1987	1988	1989	1990	1991	1992	1993	1994	1995
First Prism system shipped	*														
Andover manufacturing TH study		*	*												
TH production system improved				*	*										
Andover SMT prototype experiments		*	*	*											
HP corporate implementation teams			*	*											
Sunrise system designed					*	*									
Dynapert system purchased							*								
TH manufacturing phased out							*								
First Fuji system purchased								*							
Second Fuji system purchased									*						
Third Fuji system purchased											*				
First Sunrise systems shipped							*								
Prism system redesigned from TH to SMT							*	*							
First revised Prism systems shipped									*						
Infrared ovens switched to convection														*	

Because the very profitable high-performance product line was originally developed using TH technology, and it was HP's only existing ultrasound system, from 1982 to 1986 there was no new product development project or budget under which Andover's manufacturing could introduce SMT. During the next two years manufacturing informally acted as SMT liaisons with engineering and other departments and educated them on the benefits of SMT. During this time period manufacturing also spent a lot of time refining its existing TH board production capabilities and vendor base in anticipation of someday migrating to SMT. Notably, vendors' raw board interlayer shorts and part delivery problems were solved.

Adoption.   In the mid-1980s the inherent risks of moving the market-leading high-performance system to the relatively unproven SMT process was unacceptable to many managers at MPG. By 1985 growing performance, cost, and quality issues had begun to mildly squeeze the Prism system line, but senior management still declined to convert this profitable product line from TH to SMT. Consequently, Andover's manufacturing managers could do little but continue educating other departments on the potential benefits of SMT, and attempt to recruit engineering project managers responsible for new product development to include surface mount in their plans.

Fortunately for Andover's SMT champions, at about the same time in the mid-1980s, MPG decided to go ahead with a low-cost system later to be named Sunrise. Sunrise was originally partially designed using TH technology, but it quickly became apparent that a low-cost, high-performing "desk-top" system was impossible to produce using TH. Even under the most optimistic assumptions, including a fully automated TH assembly process, the new system still cost $500 over the target number and could not fit in one small desktop package. SMT emerged as the only viable way to achieve the ambitious goals laid out for Sunrise. At first, the Sunrise project manager, Al Langguth, was skeptical about actually using SMT. Faced with no other realistic alternatives, Al checked with engineers at another HP division and heard very good things about SMT. By 1986, Al had become an enthusiastic cochampion along with manufacturing for SMT. Shortly thereafter the surface mount equipment authorization was approved under the budget "umbrella" of the Sunrise project.

The Sunrise product was designed to use almost all SMT components. Engineering and manufacturing contacted component vendors and collected all the existing SMT components they could. In some cases the types of SMT components Sunrise needed either did not exist or were still in the prototype stages at chip manufacturers. Since all its combined businesses made HP a major purchaser of electronic components, the Sunrise project team was able to put strong pressure on manufacturers such as Motorola and Texas Instruments to quickly develop new SMT parts. Several times vendors even developed SMT components on a special hand-made basis for Sunrise. In one case, with the central processing unit (CPU) board, the wait for SMT components was unacceptably long. The Sunrise team went ahead and designed that board using TH technology so that working systems could begin environmental and clinical testing. Later, when SMT CPU components became available, the board was redesigned using surface mount parts.

As SMT components became available, trial boards were hand-assembled by Andover's manufacturing department and driven to the reflow ovens at local equipment vendors and laboratories for soldering. These experiments gave manufacturing's technical people the confidence to convince the nontechnical people that SMT really worked. Manufacturing even developed a portable "SMT kit" (complete with solder paste stencil, squeegee, raw boards, and SMT components) that was taken from equipment vendor to equipment vendor to evaluate SMT process techniques and build trial boards. In the case of some critical new SMT components, Andover only had one or two part samples available on hand that vendors had prereleased to them. In these situations manufacturing was under great pressure to make the process work with the first trial run so the project would not be delayed by ruined components or incorrectly assembled boards.

Once enough trial boards were produced, reliability tests were begun to pass MPG's rigorous quality assurance standards and demonstrate Good Manufacturing Practices to win Food and Drug Administration (FDA) approval of the new technology. Indeed, the ASMC eventually became so good at SMT manufacturing that it later trained over 50 FDA inspectors on how to assess the new board-making process.

Midway through the Sunrise development process a parallel low-cost ultrasound system project in Germany was folded into the Andover project. Although not directly related to SMT, as part of Sunrise, Taguchi methods were widely used to develop robust designs and manufacturing processes. A PhD statistician was even hired to help evaluate Taguchi experiments. In addition to Taguchi experiments, each Sunrise board was subjected to tough analyses involving power consumption and clock speed. In total, unexpected engineering and manufacturing delays, the merger of the Andover and German systems, and problems obtaining SMT components caused the Sunrise project to miss its target launch date by approximately one year.

It is important to note that no formal investment justifications were done for SMT. The decision to adopt SMT was made mainly based upon strategic considerations. In fact, traditional cost-benefit analyses were done and indicated that SMT should not be invested in. Other economic analyses were done using spreadsheets developed by engineering that projected how product material and labour costs would drop if SMT versus TH components were used. Numerous SMT layouts were also simulated and evaluated by Andover's manufacturing engineering until a good shop-floor design was achieved.

The adoption of SMT by the high-performance ultrasound product line was a more difficult process. The procedure lasted from 1987 to 1988, and the original TH high-performance system was completely redesigned using SMT components. The new high-performance system based on SMT was called Prism. MPG's Prism system was, at the time, one of the most sophisticated products any U.S. company had ever developed using SMT. The Prism product line had many complicated boards, and was an order of magnitude more complex than even relatively sophisticated ultrasound systems such as the new Sunrise product. Prism's boards not only had tremendous board density but many were also double-sided. In some cases, Prism's new SMT boards had 1,500 discrete components. In addition to the available features and options of the Prism product line, there were also a greater total number of boards to produce. Using SMT, the number of total components in a Prism system eventually mushroomed to over 27,000. Even after the initial SMT conversion process, it took the design engineering and manufacturing departments nearly another year to work out all of the bugs in the new Prism ultrasound system.

Content and Substance of Change

The Production System.   HP corporate encountered design and equipment standardization problems with SMT. SMT "implementation teams" called the Technology Management Team (TMT) and the Process Management Team (PMT) were therefore set up by corporate to help determine companywide design and equipment standards. From 1983 to 1987, HP's implementation teams developed numerous SMT product and process standards. HP held an SMT "bake-off" among rival oven technologies to determine which vendor to standardize on. Vitronics' oven ultimately won. Similarly, all major SMT placement machines were evaluated before HP decided to standardize on Fuji's equipment. The implementation teams also developed standards for SMT board sizes and pad shapes. Wherever possible, Andover used these corporate standards to guide its own SMT implementation.

SMT equipment was bought at Andover in three distinct phases starting in 1986. In the first phase a Vitronics reflow oven was bought for approximately $25,000. This oven allowed ASMC to more easily produce test boards and further familiarize engineers and operators with SMT manufacturing processes. In the second phase, starting in 1987, a Dynapert MPS 515 picks and place machine was ordered for $400,000. At the same time a corporate Technology Management Team was chartered to determine which SMT equipment was the best and what vendor would become HP's standard. Amid political controversy, Andover's Dynapert order was put on hold until the TMT evaluation was finished. As it turned out, Dynapert won the TMT competition so Andover's originally ordered Dynapert MPS 515 was taken off hold and finally delivered. A second Dynapert machine was leased shortly after the first one. A year later, the TMT was replaced by the Process Management Team. The PMT held a second competition and HP corporate this time standardized on Fuji equipment.

From the beginning stencils were purchased from an out-of-state supplier, and stencilling of solder-paste was done manually. At this point a process engineer was also hired to help perfect the new technology. In the third phase, starting in 1988, a $500,000 Fuji machine was purchased and a second assembly line was set up. Shortly thereafter, another Fuji machine was purchased and a third production line was installed in order to handle growing Prism business and subcontracted board volume from other HP companies. Today Andover's manufacturing department is formally known as the Surface Mount Centre.

Adaptation

Technological Change.   In the transition from TH to SMT, the shop floor underwent substantial change. All the existing TH machines were removed except for the wave soldering line. Any existing TH boards were immediately subcontracted out. The shop floor was reconfigured into a smaller area with a classic U-shaped flow from the stockroom and staging area through the Fuji machines, reflow ovens, manual TH insertion, wave solder, board washing, board separation, final test, and shipping departments (see Figure 1). One of the most fundamental changes involved reversing the shop floor from a batch operation with massive work-in-process (WIP) under TH to a continuous flow with as little WIP as possible using SMT.

No internal changes were made to any of the Fuji machines or reflow ovens, and very few other modifications were made. Operations were purposefully kept as simple as possible. Even the various assembly lines were not connected by any conveyor systems. One significant adapta-

FIGURE 1

Surface Mount Centre layout

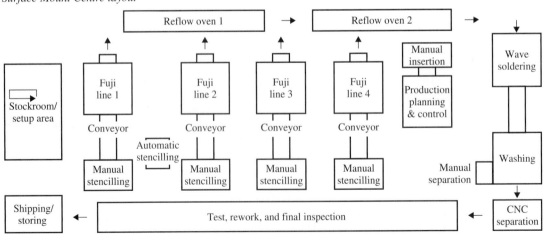

tion, however, was to develop a fixture for prestaging component part reels on a pallet so that it could be quickly exchanged with another pallet during the setup of a Fuji machine.

A major administrative adaptation was made in MPG's "above-the-shop-floor" information systems. A sophisticated Product Information Management (PIM) system was developed so that board designs from inside MPG's engineering groups, as well as any other company on HP's worldwide network, could be downloaded to ASMC. To summarize the PIM, engineering and PC layout [department] design boards using a popular computer aided design (CAD) package. This data is transferred using translators to manufacturing's information system. Manufacturing, in turn, translates these files into a board "recipe." A MRPII system is also used by manufacturing to help control and procure inventory. The PIM system allows the ASMC to complete prototype boards in less than 24 hours and also helps minimize the number of component misloads (incorrect insertions of components onto boards) in regular production boards. It is important to note that the PIM system does not yet interface directly to the Fuji machines in a true computer-integrated-manufacturing (CIM) system. This is in keeping with ASMC's philosophy of "focusing on results, not on tools" and represents a conscious decision to avoid building a costly "information factory."

A final technical adaptation was in the area of quality control. With TH, MPG relied upon 100 percent in-process and final inspection. With SMT and flow manufacturing, in-process inspection was gradually phased out in favour of statistical process control (SPC). Today, Andover's manufacturing managers are firm believers in SPC. SPC has proven particularly beneficial in assuring quality through the soldering process.

Organizational Change.   The transition from TH to SMT affected departments differently. Logical circuit schematic design engineering had almost no trouble converting from TH to SMT. Circuit schematic design on their CAD system was essentially the same for TH and SMT. Design engineers, however, were greatly affected by new demands SMT placed on prototyping boards. With TH, design engineers actually had "laboratory" component stock and would manually build many of their own trial boards. With SMT this was no longer possible due to the much smaller size of discrete components along with the need to solder paste and reflow boards. Design engineers now had to rely on manufacturing to make trial boards. Similarly with TH, design engineers could relatively easily test prototype boards. Because a similar-sized SMT board is typically so much more densely covered with components than a TH board, connecting test equipment to surface mount parts now often became a real challenge for design engineers.

The PC layout department, responsible for translating logical circuit schematic designs into board physical design "blueprints," also struggled during the SMT implementation process. The density of SMT packaging and the greater use of multilayer boards made it difficult for some PC layout designers to make the transition from TH to SMT. SMT dramatically changed board complexity because many more components could now be placed on a PWB. In some cases up to four times more components are placed on SMT boards as compared to a similar-sized TH board. Since SMT components are placed on top of four or six multilayer boards, the number of "vias" (holes connecting different board levels) likewise increased by 30 percent over an identical-sized TH board. SMT component density, in combination with many more vias that had to be carefully positioned, greatly increased PC layout time. With TH the typical layout time was two to four weeks for a new board. When MPG first cut over to surface mount designs layout time skyrocketed to two months. Only recently has SMT board layout time been reduced back to the two to four weeks of the original TH process. On a per-component basis, this represents a major net improvement over through-hole times. In addition to more complicated designs, PC layout also had to develop, from scratch, libraries of standardized symbols and component specifications. PC layout also helped optimize design of pads using Taguchi methods.

Andover's shop-floor workers were likewise called upon to make radical changes in work procedures during the transition from TH to SMT. Andover's manufacturing management made a strategic decision to develop a core competency in SMT. Part of this strategic decision was to immediately eliminate all TH manufacturing at Andover. All TH board-making equipment was replaced by new SMT processes and any remaining TH work was subcontracted out. Employees previously trained to do only one highly skilled manual job such as soldering had to learn how to do multiple tasks on a Fuji line.

This represented a major shop-floor cultural change. With TH, manufacturing workers were assigned to a workstation and batches of materials came to them in boxes. With SMT, assigned workstations were removed and people now moved to where the work was in the process.

Similarly, Andover's manufacturing management dramatically changed with the arrival of SMT. With TH production there were three shop-floor managers covering the major operations of "auto insertion," "hand load," and "test." These managers were strongly oriented toward batch production and none made the transition to SMT flow production. New supervisors, willing to give flow manufacturing a try, were quickly promoted from within to lead Andover's SMC.

Three other areas were changed as part of the transition from TH to SMT. First, performance measures were radically modified. Under TH, in the auto insertion, hand load, and test departments, performance measures were respectively based on the number of component placements per shift, number of hand-loads per shift, and number of boards tested per shift. In effect, each of these departments collectively suboptimized their processes to the detriment of the entire manufacturing function. With SMT, performance measurements were changed to one standard for everybody in ASMC: number of placements shipped. This single performance measure reflected Andover manufacturing management's philosophy of "holding the goal at the highest level." This also helped ensure that the shop would not relapse into its old batch manufacturing habits.

A second change involved shop-floor control and scheduling. Andover's SMC concentrated on reducing cycle-times and keeping WIP moving. A special position—called the "line engineer"—was created to schedule and flow shop-floor production. The line engineer's job was to teach the shop floor how to behave and function as a flow, not a batch, operation. The line engineer constantly moved back and forward through the process and spotted WIP building up. Whenever excess WIP was identified, the line engineer had the authority to immediately reallocate resources to keep things flowing and was empowered to change equipment layouts. The line engineer position was, from the beginning, a temporary assignment. Eventually shop-floor workers began thinking like the line engineer and the ASMC started functioning like a flow shop. When the line engineer position was no longer needed it was eliminated.

The line engineer also helped reduce cycle-times. SMT's greater volume really showed the importance of short cycle-times. The relatively slow pace of TH production, even though it was a batch operation, never piled up nearly as much WIP as SMT was capable of. With SMT's volumes, existing problems were made much worse by long cycle-times. Wherever possible, the line engineer attempted to reduce cycle-times. Principles from the *The Goal* were also used to help motivate employees, identify constraints, and remove bottlenecks.

Finally, with the growing importance of cost in the health care industry, Andover recently implemented an activity-based cost accounting system to help evaluate and control total product costs. Four key cost drivers were identified by manufacturing: (1) number of auto-loaded parts; (2) number of hand-loaded parts; (3) number of discrete tests; and (4) number of components purchased. This information is widely shared with engineering to help minimize the costs of new board designs for existing systems.

Acceptance

Manufacturing.   SMT was a strategic decision that MPG's senior manufacturing management was firmly behind. Manufacturing senior management quickly accepted SMT based upon the significant relative advantages the new technology offered over TH. Manufacturing's workers and supervisors, consequently, had no choice but to accept SMT. As mentioned above, TH manufacturing line managers never accepted SMT and new managers for the ASMC had to be promoted from within. Similarly, some shop-floor workers quickly accepted SMT and some resisted. In general, the more job tenure and the better educated/trained employees were in the existing TH processes, the more eager they were to accept SMT. Typically, the best TH workers were the ones that most successfully transitioned to SMT production. In some cases, workers never made the transition and either retired or transferred to other operations.

Engineering.   After some initial hesitancy Sunrise design engineering quickly accepted SMT based upon its board size and production cost advantages. Indeed, everyone on the project team eagerly anticipated the transition to SMT and the associated growth in their own skill sets. Prism design engineering, on the other hand, was very reluctant to make the changeover from TH to SMT, despite the obvious advantages of SMT. As one person put it, the Prism group had developed a "John Wayne attitude" that they could do whatever they wanted to. As another person described the Prism team, "They didn't care about the process technology, they only concentrated on the technical aspects of design." In fact, it was not until manufacturing ceased TH board production in-house and began subcontracting it out at higher costs that senior management finally convinced the high-performance ultrasound system engineers to design a new product line using SMT.

Finally, some designers in PC layout quickly accepted SMT and some did not. For some PC layout employees, the added board layout task complexity triggered by SMT component density and the routing of vias proved to be an important hurdle to accepting surface mount. Recent college graduation and formal training in complicated multilayer board design along with low job tenure seemed most related to the decision to accept the new technology. Indeed, at least one long-time employee in this department never made the transition from TH to SMT layout.

Politics of Change

Intradepartmental Politics.   During the transition from TH to SMT, there was relatively little "office politics" inside most departments. As mentioned above, the existing manufacturing supervisors were planned out of the new SMT process. Similarly, highly skilled TH workers like the manual solderers resisted the change and shop-floor morale plummeted. To help improve morale, whenever possible TH employees were retrained to perform SMT tasks. At one point temporary workers were even brought in from the outside to help meet the exploding demand for new SMT process work. These temporary workers, by smoothing over peaks and valleys in demand, helped ensure that the ASMC was a success in its critical first few years of operation.

The second "political" problem in manufacturing involved changing people's mind-set from batch to flow production. During the first year of Sunrise, SMT production shop-floor workers continued to produce boards in large batches. Problems became even worse when Prism board production began. At one point the massive Prism volumes choked the shop floor with WIP and nearly brought all production to a halt. It wasn't until the introduction of one standard performance measure for all of manufacturing, "number of parts shipped," and the formalization of the line engineering scheduling job that shop-floor workers were trained and learned to change their perspective from batch to flow.

Interdepartmental Politics.   The major interdepartmental political conflict involved Prism design engineering, PC layout, and manufacturing. As suggested above, the culture of the Prism group was entrepreneurial and the tendency was to do things loosely and "make changes on the fly." Manufacturing's culture, on the other hand, was to tightly control every detail. The PC layout group, in the middle of the process flow between design and production, moderated between these two extremes. Confounding the problem was relatively poor communication among all three groups. Most of the political conflict between the groups was during the prototyping stages. During prototyping, product uncertainty was high and a lot of poorly communicated changes were made by either engineering to designs or manufacturing to processes. A particular focal point of controversy was in the shape and location of pads for placing SMT components.

The political conflicts between Prism design engineering and manufacturing stands in stark contrast to the Sunrise project. Throughout Sunrise, design engineering and manufacturing had excellent communication. Sunrise project management even went so far as to change the compensation structure of its engineers to ensure that they designed boards that could be manufactured using ASMC's Fuji equipment. Key engineering design goals for the Sunrise project team are summarized in Table 4.

A key part of this process was Total Quality Control (TQC) teams. TQC meetings were especially valuable for cleaning up problems with boards. These teams met weekly, strictly to deal with any design or process problems. In these TQC meetings every board failure was evaluated using techniques like Pareto analysis. In addition to TQC meetings, manufacturing engineers were invited to sit in on Sunrise engineering design meetings and design reviews. In 1989, Quality Function Deployment was brought in to facilitate even greater communication between engineering and manufacturing.

Interplant Politics.   In the mid-1980s, there was often fierce competition among plants to become SMT manufacturing centres. Inside MPG the Waltham and Andover plants vied to become the group's sole SMT centre. Waltham manufactured bedside monitors, and some of its employees had originally helped staff the Andover location in the late 1970s. In 1985 Waltham believed that it should become the SMT centre. Andover, meanwhile, had the very profitable high-performance ultrasound product line and was the location for the new Sunrise development project so it thought it should become the SMT centre. In the end, Waltham did a lot of numerical analyses to try and demonstrate that it should be the group's SMT site, while Andover conducted a lot of experiments and built numerous trial boards. Based upon Andover's greater hands-on experience, MPG's senior management decided in December 1986 that the SMT centre should be located in Andover.

As an aside, so bitter was the rivalry between the two MPG divisions for the SMC that after the decision Waltham swore it would never buy boards from Andover. Waltham initially carried through on this threat and sourced all of its boards from an HP plant in Germany instead of Andover (which is just 30 miles away). Andover was counting on Waltham's board volume when it had originally planned for the scheduling and overhead absorption of the ASMC. This loss in volume forced ASMC to cut cost to the bone in order to survive. In effect, this rivalry with Waltham drove Andover to improve its operations much more than it might normally have. Ironically, SMT and Andover's accompanying manufacturing improvements so reduced production costs that when Waltham's German board supplier could not reliably deliver boards, Waltham

---

TABLE 4   **Sunrise Project Team: Engineering Design Goals**

Engineering Design Goals
- No more than 200 unique part numbers.
- No more than 2,500 total electronic parts on all boards.
- No more than 100 part numbers on any boards.
- No manually loaded parts on any boards.
- No temperature rise greater than 10 degrees Celsius on any board.

was eventually "compelled" to buy tens of thousands of boards from Andover. In the long run, ASMC was ultimately in even a stronger competitive position with their hard-won manufacturing improvements along with Waltham's added board volume.

Operation of New Practices

Optimization.   Ramp-up of SMT occurred very rapidly. In five to six months the ASMC went from placing 200,000 components for Sunrise to over 8.5 million parts per month. Before, with TH, 100 employees per shift worked two shifts to place 200,000 parts per month. With SMT, 150 total employees across three balanced shifts placed 8.5 million components. It is worth noting that ASMC's operations always run three shifts per day, five days per week, in order to avoid "cold start-ups" at the beginning of every first shift.

Early in the SMT implementation process, ASMC standardized on board sizes and the number of boards per panels. Today, 250 different kinds of boards with about 12 million components per month are run through the ASMC. Boards are made for MPG's product lines as well as other HP divisions. Typical board lot sizes range from 20–2,000 boards. Capacity utilization at the ASMC is planned for 80 percent. This allows 10 percent capacity for surge demand, and also sets aside 10 percent of available capacity for prototyping new boards.

Infusion.   ASMC currently has four dedicated Fuji SMT lines. Capital costs for the entire SMT project were over $4 million. Approximately 93 percent of the components on a board are SMT and the remainder are TH. TH is mainly used for components that generate heat or take a lot of strain (like board connectors). The Fuji machines are used to place all SMT components and are run on average 24 hours per day, five days per week. Whenever necessary, overtime is worked on Saturday. Most TH components are inserted manually and automatically wave soldered. Some special TH components are manually inserted and hand-soldered by skilled labourers. On a relative scale, manufacturing's cost accounting system charges customers "X" for each SMT component automatically inserted and reflow soldered. TH items with wave solder are charged "10X" per component. Any manually inserted and hand-soldered components are billed at "100X" each. This sharp escalation in the cost for non-SMT board components acts as a strong incentive for engineering to keep the percentage of surface mount components in their new designs as high as possible. Today, because of long component lead times and chip shortages, a relatively large amount of raw inventory is kept on hand. As in many organizations, marketing's forecasts are often imperfect so manufacturing must also carry additional inventory to cover unforeseen demand. Inventory turns are therefore roughly five to six times per year.

In 1994, MPG switched from four infrared ovens to two state-of-the-art ATMOS convection reflow systems purchased from Electrovert. Although they have automated solder-paste capability, Andover continues to rely mostly on manual board stencilling. In keeping with their philosophy of making manufacturing as simple as possible, the SMC still uses manual board stencilling. Manual stencilling is especially practical because the bottleneck on the shop floor continues to be the Fuji pick-and-place machines. Similar to stencilling, many boards are still manually separated. A computer numerical control (CNC) router is used to separate certain high volume boards. As with the rest of Andover's operations, test equipment is kept simple using custom-built fixtures for each board and "pin-tests" for electrical connections. While the in-circuit tests are the same for each board, unique pin-test fixtures are used for each of the 250 different types of boards ASMC makes.

Unexpected Problems.   The only major unexpected problems occurred with the Prism product line. In its first year of production Prism system customer satisfaction suffered. Engineering and manufacturing incorrectly assumed that defect percentage rates for TH and SMT meant the same thing. With TH it is easy to spot an open connector and fix it, but with SMT it is not. A SMT solder junction can look good but "opens" on a pad are very hard to identify. Once Prism's new SMT boards achieved the same defect rates as the old TH boards in test runs, regular production was begun and systems were delivered to customers. Unfortunately, after a substantial number of Prism systems had been shipped, it quickly became apparent that undetected opens were slipping by into the field. Twenty-four machines were brought back from customers and all of them were found to have multiple opens. Over the next six months warranty costs soared and eventually hundreds of $200,000 systems were returned by angry customers. The entire engineering resources of the Prism team were devoted for one year to help solve all the open pad problems. At the end of the process, it became apparent that SMT defect rates need to be an order of magnitude better than TH defect rates before a product is released to customers.

The Sunrise product line, on the other hand, had far fewer problems with opens throughout its entire life cycle. While Sunrise boards were less complicated than Prism boards, lower complexity only accounts for part of the answer. The rich and continual communication between Sunrise engineering and ASMC manufacturing most likely explains the rest of their success in shipping good systems.

Performance Measures.   Once the problem with "opens" was solved, the benefits of SMT met or exceeded all expectations. Cycle-time was reduced from six weeks under TH to three to four hours for SMT. Throughput time, in fact, is so good today that the ASMC guarantees next-day delivery for most orders. Yield was likewise increased from 80 percent up to 97 to 98 percent. The typical SMT PWB uses almost 50 percent less board space, allowing for either much denser boards if features increase while product size stays the same, or much smaller products if the board's functionality is unchanged. In several cases boards that formerly cost hundreds of dollars are now made for tens of dollars. For example, the mother board for Sunrise was quoted by an outside TH board fabricator for "X" dollars each and the ASMC was able to guide the redesign and produce it for almost one-fifth of the outside vendor's price.

In terms of the Sunrise product line, all major objectives were met. The new system in final form was desktop size and cost a third of high-performance models, meeting the original design objectives. Similarly for the Prism product line, after the early issues with opens, there have been no other major problems.

Conclusions

The following summarizes some of the major lessons learned at MPG's Andover location in the course of implementing and managing SMT.

Through-hole technology. Cleaning up process and component supplier problems when the company was still using the old TH technology proved invaluable before the SMT conversion. For over two years, manufacturing conducted experiments and worked with suppliers to remove interlayer shorts in boards, improve yields, remedy on-time delivery problems, and perfect solder paste and plating techniques. If variables like board and component quality had not been removed from the shop floor prior to SMT implementation, it would have been very difficult to implement the new technology. Indeed, if many of these factors were not already controlled it may have been almost impossible for Andover to solve the Prism open pad problem.

Experimentation. Manufacturing conducted numerous experiments with the new SMT technology before actually buying major pieces of equipment and setting up a dedicated assembly line. This experimentation not only allowed manufacturing to learn more about SMT before major capital expenditures were made, but also served as a way to educate other functions such as engineering on the benefits of surface mount. Purchasing its own reflow oven to help accelerate the production of trial boards was another important step. Indeed, it was only after manufacturing had produced numerous good trial boards that many other functions started to begrudgingly accept SMT.

Line management. SMT represented a technological discontinuity, and MPG's senior manufacturing management decided not to transfer the TH line managers to SMT. Manufacturing management recognized that the existing line managers were too steeped in the old batch manufacturing paradigm to quickly and smoothly make the shift to the new flow process. Indeed, even with new line managers, it proved to be very difficult to get workers to change their batch manufacturing habits into a continuous flow mind-set.

Temporary work force. If MPG had to rely only on its own internal work force, then the transition to SMT might have taken much longer. Fortunately, MPG was located in a hi-tech part of the country where major electronic manufacturers such as AT&T, Digital, Raytheon, and Wang had recently laid off numerous skilled shop-floor employees. MPG was able to draw some of this outside talent into the company on a short-term and long-term basis in order to help make the transitions from TH to SMT. These temporary workers helped smooth the changeover to SMT, and allowed the ASMC to more quickly ramp-up production rates.

Matched engineering and manufacturing goals. A major difference between the Sunrise and Prism product lines was that engineering's goals were closely aligned with manufacturing's process capabilities. There was an open and continual dialog between Sunrise engineers and manufacturing that was missing during the Prism conversion process. Notably, the Sunrise design team rejected the classic "throw it over the wall" mentality that so often separates engineering and manufacturing functions.

Worker transfers. The decision to transfer as many TH workers as possible to SMT proved to be a wise choice. A key early step in the SMT implementation project was transferring many of the best TH workers into the new surface mount centre. These workers tended to have the skills, flexibility, and enthusiasm necessary to make the new SMT process work. Transferring key workers from TH to SMT had another benefit. Although some shop-floor workers resisted change, and new hires may have ramped-up production even faster, a valuable precedent for future radical change was made. This has proven important for ASMC today. Shop-floor workers feel that since they survived going from TH to SMT they can now handle any new process changes.

Defects. Based upon the open pad problems for the Prism system, MPG developed a newfound appreciation for quality assurance in conjunction with advanced manufacturing technologies. ASMC, as a philosophy, actively tried to cease dependence on inspection and test. Instead, SPC was implemented to help ensure in-process quality. Finally, processes like the TQC teams were put into place to ensure that action was taken on quality problems as they occurred.

Focus on reducing cycle-time. Introducing the line engineer position and focusing on reduced cycle-time were important steps in unlocking the benefits of SMT. SMT allowed for phenomenally greater productivity, but also set the stage for potentially dramatic growth in WIP. By temporarily instating the line engineer position, complete with authority to move employees and other resources around, the ASMC was able to drive down cycle-times and avoid "drowning" in WIP. The line engineer position also helped educate shop-floor workers and supervisors on how to run as a flow, not a batch, operation.

Relative simplicity. Although SMT represented revolutionary change over TH manufacturing, Andover's manufacturing management insisted that whenever and wherever possible production methods be kept simple. For example, the PIM computer system extends from design engineering to manufacturing but is not electronically linked to the Fuji lines as part of computer integrated manufacturing (CIM). Manufacturing concentrated most of its resources on the physical process, instead of focusing on the information technology side of SMT board production. Similarly, manufacturing has stayed with manual stencils, where an operator can readily tell if solder paste missed a pad by looking at the stencil once it is lifted from the board, instead of introducing more process uncertainty and quality risks by going to automated stencilling. Likewise, Andover's manufacturing has resisted the temptation to introduce elaborate test equipment such as X-ray, ultrasonic wave, or infrared detection systems to catch defects after they are made. Instead, capital is invested in the best production equipment available coupled with carefully documented processes, highly trained workers, and SPC in order to make good boards from the beginning.

12
New Product Development at HPM[1]

Introduction

To compete in today's business environment, HPM Industries must deal with the most competitive and hostile marketplace that it has faced in the company's entire history. Improvements in technology and an increasingly globalised market mean that competitors are now causing severe pressure in markets where HPM has traditionally held dominance.

The company's strategy to overcome this threat is to use innovation and technology to differentiate itself in the marketplace. Over the last two decades HPM has concentrated on developing a strong innovation culture within the organisation, and this is now successfully demonstrated in many areas throughout the company. This, combined with the company's strong focus on using the latest technology in both its products and manufacturing processes, has positioned the company in an excellent position to be able to adapt to market changes.

This case therefore describes how HPM is positioning itself in the marketplace and details some of the ways that the company is utilising technology and innovation to differentiate itself. It also details an example of how the company conducted a comparison between the conventional engineering path from product design to marketing introduction, with two "rapid" development alternatives. One alternative demonstrated the advantages gained by introducing stereolithography models while the other identified the further gains made by utilising the models to produce "rapid tooling" through a cold metal spray process.

Company Background

HPM Industries is a privately owned company established in 1925. Its core business is in the design, manufacture, and distribution of electrical wiring accessories such as electrical power plugs, power outlets, and light switches. HPM has traditionally marketed and sold its products through the electrical wholesale market, and although this area still forms the backbone of the company's success, more recently the company has also been successful in developing and marketing many products for the retail market sector.

For electrical products HPM has been the dominant player in the Australian domestic market for many years, and internationally the company has also managed to break into a number of special niches. Although the company is widely recognised as a leading electrical accessory manufacturer in Australia, the company could not be considered a "household" name. This is despite the fact that almost every home in Australia would contain one or more product lines that HPM manufactures.

---

[1]This case was developed for use in classroom discussion and is not intended to necessarily illustrate appropriate or inappropriate management practices. Case information was gathered through interviews with Stuart Romm, managing director of HPM, visits to the HPM site, and reviews of various documents provided by HPM. The case author of the original case (1996) was Graeme Sheather, University of Technology, Sydney. Scott Cameron was the research associate on the project in the Graduate School of Management at Macquarie University and updated the case in 2000. We wish to thank Stuart Romm and his HPM associates for their contributions. The funding for this case production was provided by the Australian federal government's Department of Industry, Science and Resources.

The company had its origins in button production, when Ruth Simons's parents (Ruth is the wife of the current chief executive officer, Peter Simons) started HPM in the button-moulding business. In 1948 they bought a tool at auction to make plug-tops and started turning out about 20 products.

Today the business employs more than 1,100 employees working in its various factory sites, warehouses, and sales offices around the country, from which it supplies over 3,500 product lines. In Sydney alone, there are approximately 800 employees engaged in manufacturing, with over 200 staff in sales, administration, finance, and distribution around the country.

The Darlinghurst site in Sydney contains the operations of design, engineering, manufacture, and also distribution, while the 500 employees at the newer Waterloo factory are mainly involved in assembly and distribution. There are nine factories in Sydney which supply every part of HPM's manufactured product range. The seven sites average around 200 employees, with each managed by a single engineer plant manager qualified in moulding, materials, processing, and the latest technology.

As an Australian company, HPM has a strong philanthropic ethic and sense of corporate responsibility and each year contributes in various ways to the Australian community. As well as sponsoring the annual HPM Award for Excellence in Design, the company supports a number of Australian community organisations such as the National Trust, the Australian Chamber Orchestra, Kidsafe, and the Lord Mayor's Bush Fire Appeal. In 1994, HPM also committed to fund a three-year scientific research project through the Australian Koala Foundation and James Cook University.

Competing in a Changing Environment

HPM has enjoyed a strong position in the Australian electrical market for almost half a century, and through its attention to quality and strong product development the company still continues to enjoy steady growth. In the pursuit of this growth, however, the company now faces many different challenges to those which existed when the company first began.

One of the most notable changes that has taken place in the market over the last two decades is in the length of product life cycles. In the 1970s and 1980s HPM's products generally had a life cycle of around 8–10 years. However, in today's market the company now must contend with product life cycles of two years and less.

Impact of Technology.   The company's Managing Director Stuart Romm attributes much of the reason for this reduction to the impact of new technology on the market. This is not only because competitors are able to develop alternative products on a much more frequent basis, but also because competitors are now able to reengineer exact duplicates of HPM's products and saturate the market with cheap copies.

In the past, the quality of the cheaper, generally imported, products was very poor, thereby providing HPM with a competitive advantage on quality. However, recent improvements in technology mean that the quality of the imported product coming into Australia is now very good. Competitors can optically scan a product, reverse engineer it, and then produce a product with all the same characteristics as the HPM product.

These products are on the market today, and although they have not been very successful in gaining market share up to now, they are causing severe price pressure in the marketplace. Technology, in this sense, is therefore creating a lot of extra competition in HPM's traditional market areas.

Impact of Cheap Imports.   In contrast to the recent trend for companies to outsource and/or move offshore for their manufacturing requirements, HPM has for many years held a unique "in-house" manufacturing philosophy and sourcing structure. The company has been fully committed to manufacturing in Australia, and this "Australian Made" philosophy has contributed greatly to the company's marketing success. As CEO Peter Simon remarks, "We made a conscious decision a few years ago to continue to manufacture our components locally."

The logic behind this domestic manufacturing strategy was that the company would be able to overcome the cheap labour and the lower setup costs of overseas competitors by investing in more automated manufacturing technology, and by utilising the superior engineering skills that exist within the company.

Today, however, the market pressure facing the company, particularly on standard products, is fast becoming overwhelming. Stuart Romm recognises this and attributes much of the pressure to low-cost Chinese sourcing. He comments that low-cost overseas sourcing has now reached the point where HPM can source a packaged finished product out of China for less than the cost of the raw material in Australia.

This kind of market pressure is no longer forcing HPM to increase its automation; it is forcing the company to totally reposition its manufacturing strategy. Management has come to the realisation that the domestic manufacture of standard, low-technology products has now become uncompetitive against low-cost imports coming from Southeast Asia. In recognition of this, from the year 2000 onward, the company's manufacturing strategy will change dramatically, and the manufacture of high volume, and particularly low-technology, products will probably be forced offshore.

Still concious of its commitment to Australian manufacturing, however, HPM is expanding its manufacturing capability in Australia in higher technology areas, and the company's acquisition of a large electronics factory in Sydney is a good example of this. This factory is larger than currently needed by the company; however, the acquisition forms part of the company's longer term strategy for developing its electronics capabilities.

Strategic Direction: Using Technology and Innovation to Differentiate

To achieve its goals, the company's main strategy is to differentiate itself from low-cost competitors through innovation. Management's aim is to build on the company's strong tradition of product development and to position the company such that the marketplace is constantly looking toward HPM for refreshing new products all the time.

Innovation at HPM.   Similar to the way in which 3M operates, HPM has for many years tried to instill a culture of innovation within the company. This approach is still as strong as ever in the way that the company operates, and it continues to bear fruit.

Developing a Culture of Innovation

Organisational. HPM's culture for innovation has historically been embedded in its free-thinking process. The company structure involves very few rules and regulations, with a deliberate exclusion of set policies, and no job or position descriptions. "We don't like anything formal," comments the managing director, working instead with clear directional indicators and understood limits. There is no formal vision, mission, goals, or strategic objectives set down. They exist in broad terms, but are kept as fuzzy as possible to ensure that necessary changes and resources can be drafted as needed. The only documentation is in the form of a pictorial diagram of the business objectives. This is represented as a roof with five supporting product line pillars. To have a formalised corporate planning process would be too bureaucratic, totally alien to the company, and would destroy its family culture.

Remuneration is highly graded, with executives highly paid and tradespeople drawing 30 to 40 percent over the MTIA award. Design and engineering staff are given the necessary resources, freedom of action, full responsibility, and opportunity to exhibit initiative and creativity—there are no rules to inhibit performance.

The enterprise agreement that HPM has been able to develop with its factory employees over the last five to six years also provides the company with the flexibility it requires and reinforces the company's desire for flexibility, employee contribution, and new ideas. Features of the agreements that have been struck are as follows:

- Workplace flexibility; related to flexible starting and stopping times for specified periods, staggering start and finish times for auxiliary staff, continuity of operation, and coverage of additional machines due to absences.
- Quality assurance for continuous improvement, with future progress motivated by employees taking responsibility for quality within their workstations and diversifying the responsibility of quality to each employee rather than to inspectors only.
- Responsibility for control and work planning taken by operational staff for their own stock at their workstation, rather than relying upon auxiliary or indirect labour.
- A consultative committee to continuously monitor and review training for new technology, multiskilling and job sharing, shop-floor training for new/transferred staff, English in the workplace programs, and shop-floor training for QA procedures and requirements.

To emphasise the importance of innovation and new ideas, the company has also set up a separate research and development organisation that is constantly looking for new product ideas and better ways to progress from concept to marketplace. R & D is given so much credibility in the organisation because it is seen as the key to the future success of the company.

External Influences. Some of the ways in which HPM encourages innovation through its external relationships are as follows:

1. HPM has made a significant commitment to the federal government's Intelligent Manufacturing Systems (IMS) consortium agreement for R & D projects. This program gives the company an insight into tertiary-level research and development and provides it with a network of contacts around the world. Through this program the company has been able to develop strong relationships with other facilitating companies, including Daimler-Benz (Europe), Pratt and Whitney (Canada), and United Technologies in the United States. Participating institutions also include the Fraunhoffer Institute in Germany and MIT in the United States.

   Wherever there is research going on within this international consortium, HPM is in an excellent position to tap into that knowledge and intellectual property. It is the company's strategy to utilise the latest in processing technology, and by maintaining strong links with other leading companies and tertiary institutions the company can be confident that it will have the inside information on any new developments in processing technology.

2. The company is also heavily involved with a number of Australian universities; for example, the company provides the funds for an annual engineering co-op scholarship with the University of NSW, and they are also governors of the Warren Centre, which is Sydney University's commercial arm.

New Product Innovation. The company's approach to product development is very much marketing-led, as Stuart Romm remarks: "The strategy to start with has to be to find the problems in the marketplace, and create the solutions. That's innovation."

At HPM innovation inputs come from four different directions.

1. Management think tank. Every morning there is an executive think tank for 45 minutes to one hour. Executives who know the industry get together to play around with ideas and discuss the progress of different issues. There is also a formal meeting with the R & D executives once per week for about two hours.

2. Inventors. The company encourages these, and there are probably around two to three per week who "knock on the door" with some idea that they are looking to develop. These people are embraced and encouraged.

3. Salespeople. All of the salespeople are strategically aligned with the end user, which is the electrical contractor, rather than the commercial customer, who is the electrical wholesaler. Salespeople are encouraged to spend 70–80 percent of their time with the end installer, the electrician, who actually makes the purchasing decision.

    The issue here is that the user knows the problems with the HPM or competitive products, and he/she knows the problems on installation. This feedback generally provides simple and practical ideas which are then fed back through the salespeople to the designers and engineers.

    This is the area responsible for the majority of the company's new innovation ideas.

4. International study tours. The innovation process is also supported by attendance at a number of the international conferences that are held around the world each year. The idea here is not to copy the products shown at the fairs but to stimulate thought and generate ideas.

Technology in New Products.   HPM's strategy is to concentrate on highly innovative products, particularly focusing on those that hold the following characteristics:

1. Where there is added value.
2. Where the company has some intellectual property in the product.
3. Where the product can't be copied or will take a long time to copy.

In satisfying these criteria the company is increasingly moving toward new electronics technology in an effort to:

1. Increase the product life cycle of their products.
2. Differentiate the HPM product in the marketplace.

Placing electronics into products is allowing the company to do things that could never be done before. A typical example of this is the way in which HPM now offers dimmers and time switches in a lot of its products. This patented technology works off a single wire (there is no neutral required), giving the company an advantage that competitors have as yet been unable to match.

The technology means that an electrical contractor can now take out a light switch (which just has a wire in and a wire out), and without having to bring a neutral wire into it, he/she can replace it with an HPM digital time switch. This allows the user to set the time for whenever he/she wants it to go on or off.

The company is not only using electronics in existing products but is also moving into the area of providing complete electronic systems. The company's "smart house" product, OSCAR, is an example of this. This product is designed for the normal domestic residence, and provides home automation to the consumer for security, light control, power control, and home entertainment.

Management's vision is that tomorrow's consumer will want increased functionality within the home. Consumers will want to be able to plug their computer into any room in the house, to be able to turn on the video downstairs and watch it on the television upstairs. They will also want the ability for remote operation of these facilities, the ability to log in to the network and have total control of the system from anywhere in the world. In a similar style, HPM's continuing focus will be on providing total electronic systems for commercial and industrial applications.

It can clearly be seen that although technology is in one sense causing the company increased competition, on the flip side it is also allowing the company to differentiate itself from the competition and move into other areas.

Increased Market Servicing.   Coinciding with the development of higher technology products, HPM is also looking to increase the number of support services that they offer in the field. In the future the company will offer services such as systems installation, commissioning, and upgrades to support their products.

The premise for this is that the electrical contracting industry tends to be quite conservative, and HPM believes that without this support they will not move at the rate that the company wants to move. The concern therefore is that the momentum of the penetration of electronic systems (like OSCAR) into the marketplace will be limited by a conservative installation industry.

Developing New Distribution Channels. The existing OSCAR system is sold through traditional distribution channels (i.e., the same as powerpoints, etc.). It goes on the shelf of the electrical wholesaler, and is then sold to the electrical contractor.

Future systems will not be sold via this channel, however, as they will need to be programmed on-site by someone with the appropriate programming skills. It is not envisaged that the normal electrical contractor will have these skills and hence new distribution channels and a new style of contractor will be required.

Technology in New Processes.   HPM's main manufacturing strategy in the 1960s, 1970s, and 1980s was vertical integration, and this is clearly shown in the way the company operates today. It makes its own mouldings, screws, pressed metal parts, production tools and equipment, and robots.

The flexibility of designing and making their own equipment gives the company an advantage in creating a fit between the technology it introduces and the goals of the technology introduction. The focus is on the unique requirements of the situation, rather than what is available, and will this work.

New technology flows through the company to all areas, and the direction of the company is for complete computer control. The following describes how technology currently impacts the production of the company's core products, such as powerpoints and light switches.

1. Design is done on CAD [computer aided design] electronically. The tools are made via a direct download from the CAD workstations to either wire-cutting or spark erosion equipment.
2. Component warehousing is computerised with radio frequency control.
3. The components are then all fully automatically made, whether it be metal or plastic, which are all computer controlled.
4. The material handling between these processes is all manual.
5. Assembly and subassembly of products to the lowest common denominator is then done on PLC-controlled robots.
6. Final assembly of these products is then manual or semiautomatic to configure the product to the customer's requirements (e.g., colour).

7. Fully automatic testing.

8. Automatically packaged.

9. Finished goods warehousing is not computerised yet, but will be in the near future.

Adopting New Process Technology

When a new technology is developed or introduced into the marketplace HPM prides itself on being an "early adopter." Introducing new technology when it is early in its life cycle can bring many benefits, as it may let the early adopter get the jump on its competition. However, because decisions must be made without proven evidence of the benefits that the technology can bring, the implementing company must be very thorough in its decision-making process.

Investment decisions at HPM are carefully evaluated, and any major capital purchases must comply with two primary criteria:

- Strategic fit: Investments must be aligned within the company's overall business strategy, which is to satisfy the needs of consumers in terms of their electrical requirements.
- Financial payback: Previously HPM used a two-year payback period as a guide for deciding whether an investment decision was financially viable. This has now changed, however, and financial decisions are made on a more ad-hoc basis. For example, for investment decisions involving a product that has an "electronic" type long-term focus, the company may approve a purchase with a five-plus year payback. However, if it is a copyable product, and especially if it is low-tech, then the company would be looking for well less than one year.

Rapid Product Development

HPM recognises the importance of getting new products to market quickly and therefore pays particular attention to new developments in the area of rapid prototyping technology.

The case that follows is typical of the type of investment decision that the company often finds itself in. It describes how the company was able to evaluate the benefits and costs of using:

1. The stereolithography rapid prototyping technique.

2. A technique to produce rapid tooling for "first off" production samples.

Stereolithography

Stereolithography is a process that has the potential for dramatically reducing product development lead times and their associated costs. Stereolithography was discovered in the early 1980s and patented in 1986.

Traditional prototyping and hard tooling processes rely on the removal of material for the formation of prototype parts and the subsequent manufacture of their tooling for production. Stereolithography and other rapid prototyping techniques are the complete opposite. Using layer-building processes, they deposit only the required material for each particular layer, gradually building an exact replica of the part, regardless of its complexity.

Development of a New Light Switch Product

During mid-1993 HPM perceived a strategic threat to one of its light switch products in the marketplace. It was anticipated that the product could suffer serious damage from inferior but inexpensive import competition by early 1994. The key strategic objective, therefore, was to "fast track" a product development that would produce a new model that was considerably cost reduced and yet maintained the traditional product's superior performance and market appeal.

In developing the new product, HPM also wished to test and quantify the benefits of the rapid product development approach. The decision was therefore made to carry out the product development using three concurrent but different methods, and to monitor the progress of each method. These three product development paths were:

Case 1: Employing conventional engineering.

Case 2: Employing a rapid prototype model.

Case 3: Employing a rapid prototype model plus rapid tooling.

The critical component of the new model light switch to be developed was the switch cover, a highly accurate polycarbonate moulding that would house and locate all the metal components of the product and would be used as an assembly jig during the manufacturing process. The development of this component therefore forms the basis of this case.

Project Management.   For each new product, a project management plan is constructed for the design, tooling, and production stages. Milestones are set to resolve problems and these are continually reviewed in relation to manufacturing processes, functions, and testing requirements.

The company uses the Microsoft Project software to keep track of the various projects that are occurring concurrently at any one time. The main projects and some of the smaller ones are monitored on a weekly basis, against theoretical timescales. Product comparisons and cost estimates are also made at every stage of the project to ensure that the project remains within its boundaries.

At one time there are typically around 40 projects in the pipeline around the company. Of these, around 10 are given priority as they are believed to be the main ones.

Comparative Analysis of RPD Options.   In order to make an accurate comparison between the various methods for developing the new switch cover product, the projects were all measured from a point where the overall product design had been completed and confirmed.

Case 1: In the case of the conventional engineering path, the injection mould tool design was then commenced.

Cases 2 and 3: For both the cases utilising the rapid prototype development technique, the injection moulded component data was processed using INPROTO faceting. These data files, in STL format, were then passed to the Queensland Manufacturing Institute (QMI) for the production of stereolithography models on their SLA 250 machine. For additional security, four complete sets of stereolithography models were produced.

The stereolithography models were produced within a couple of days by QMI and, once received, the components were then assembled to evaluate form and fit. One error and two tolerance problems were discovered when the components were assembled and these changes were incorporated into the design of the production tooling.

The stereolithography models were then measured in all major dimensions and these results are shown in Figure 1.

Once the production of the models was shown to have been successful, no further work was carried out to monitor the conventional engineering path. However, Figure 2 has been extrapolated from results recorded over the last six years to obtain a reasonably accurate comparison with the other two methods.

Cases 2 and 3: For both these cases, the tooling design was completed on the Intergraph CAD/CAM System, and the tool design data transferred to a Sodick A 3CR spark erosion machine for production of the injection mould tool.

FIGURE 1

DIM Number	CAD Dimension	Stereolithography	Cold Metal Spray Tool	Polycarbonate Moulding
1	39.78	39.86	39.89	39.77
2	29.15	29.16	29.01	28.88
3	45.66	46.06	46.09	45.78
4	45.12	45.23	45.26	44.73
5	31.65	31.72	31.50	31.24

FIGURE 2

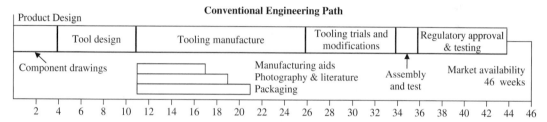

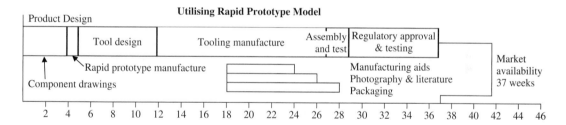

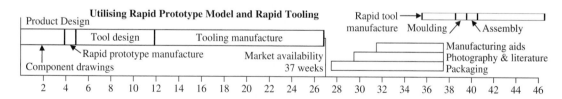

Case 3: For the case utilising rapid tooling, at the same time as the production tooling was being designed and manufactured, one of the four stereolithography models was passed to QMI. The rapid tooling was created using a cold metal spray process known as the HEK process. This process combines the use of zinc alloy wires which are melted under a plasma arc and "blown" by an air blast onto the model. By the time the molten metal reaches the stereolithography model, the metal is almost at room temperature and thus causes no distortion to the photopolymer model. The thickness of the cold metal spray is then built up gradually layer by layer, until a thickness of approximately 4 mm is achieved.

Once this was completed, the stereolithography model was then physically removed from the metal backing. This is a difficult process, as the model must be carefully broken into small parts and removed piece by piece.

The cold metal spray mould was then "backed" in epoxy resin, and with a hand-made metal core, the tool was then inserted into an Engel 150 ton injection moulding machine. The injection moulding was carried out by the Plastics & Rubber Technical Education Centre (PARTEC) in Queensland. Initially, the mould trials were carried out by injecting polypropylene material at the lowest possible clamp pressure, deliberately "flashing" the mould. The clamp pressure was then gradually increased until the flashing was eliminated and the minimum clamp pressure noted. After this trial, the polypropylene was replaced with polycarbonate, this being the engineering plastic required in the final product and essential as part of the Regulatory Approval testing procedures.

For comparison purposes, the cold metal spray tool and the final polycarbonate moulding were both measured and the results are shown in Figure 1. Both were well within the tolerances limits required for prototype performance.

Comparative Improvements.   Figure 2 displays the steps and time taken by each of the different development methods to bring the product to the point where it is ready for release into the marketplace.

Conventional Engineering Model.   With the conventional engineering approach, it can be seen that the market availability (elapsed time) was 46 weeks from the time of confirming the product design until the product was available for mass production and distribution.

The photography and production of literature and brochures is normally conditional on the availability of the finished product, or highly accurate models, and it is therefore shown that, using the conventional development method, this process cannot commence until the product is physically available. It is also conventional practice not to complete manufacture of production jigs and fixtures until the final product or models are available. Packaging design, particularly any blister packaging and drop testing, are also not normally finalised until the product or models are available.

Rapid Prototype Model.   In the second case, where a stereolithography model was used, it can be seen that the minimum time from product design to market availability was reduced to 37 weeks, compared to the 46 weeks for conventional methodology. This reduction of 9 weeks represents a 19.5 percent reduction in development lead time.

The availability of the stereolithography model at week five meant that the production of manufacturing aids and jigs, photography, and product literature, as well as packaging, could commence at week five, although not critically required until week 37. However, even though the stereolithography model was available at week five, the product could not be submitted for the Regulatory Approval tests until week 29, when the product was available in its specified material form. Stereolithography polymers are not suitable for Approval Testing since they are not representative of the final product's electrical insulation, physical strength, and fire retardant properties.

By using RPD processes, a physical appreciation of any redesign to improve functionality or manufacture related to tooling, moulding, or testing can be given early attention.

Rapid Prototype and Rapid Tooling Method.   As can be seen from Figure 2, the major advantage that this approach had on the development project was that it enabled HPM to obtain Government Regulatory Approval for the product prior to the completion of the production moulding tool.

The Approval Testing delay was regarded as one of the obvious strategic areas for improvement, but one that industry generally has little or no control over. The process typically takes eight weeks to meet the requirements for Government Regulatory Approval testing of electrical products in Australia.

Because Regulatory Approval could be carried out in parallel with the manufacture of production tooling, the minimum development lead time was reduced down to 27 weeks. When compared to the conventional engineering path, this methodology saves 19 weeks (or 41.3 percent) compared to the orthodox process.

Cost-Benefit Evaluation.   The development savings from this comparative analysis were clearly identifiable and relatively easy to quantify. Compared to the conventional engineering path, the path employing both the rapid prototype model plus rapid tooling produced an estimated saving of 19 weeks in development time.

An historical analysis conducted by the company's accountants and engineers of the costs incurred in typical tool trials with tooling modifications and rework indicated a saving of approximately A$20,000.

In addition to the operational efficiencies calculated above, the more significant financial gains were achieved through the early introduction of the product into the marketplace. The financial and commercial gains cited below represent the gross profit generated in the first 19 weeks of the product's release onto the market. (N.B.—These figures exclude any commercial overheads associated with the marketing of the product.)

Week	Gross Profit (A$)
1–4	$28,550
5–8	71,375
9–12	99,925
13–16	142,750
17–19	71,275
Total: 19 weeks	$413,975

The direct development costs of the series of experimental trials, excluding management time overviewing and recording the trial, were calculated as:

4 stereolithography models	A$2,000
Cold metal spray cavity and die production	A$2,200
Low pressure injection moulding of 20 components	A$ 500

The relationship between cost savings in development and the cost of the RPD models was found to be typical of case studies reported in the rapid product development literature, that is, savings are approximately 10 times the cost of the models.

It is recognised that there are a number of costs that have not been quantified in this analysis, such as the increased project management costs resulting from the new development method. However, there are also significant additional benefits that have not been specifically valued in this costing. These concern the strategic benefits of bringing a new and unique product into the marketplace, which strengthens both the product range and the company's commercial market presence.

These benefits are of paramount importance to HPM, particularly in HPM's retail market sector, where major retail stores are constantly seeking to reduce the number of suppliers in order to reduce their own administrative costs. Ability to fill orders with new products ahead of competitors is the company's key competitive advantage.

Changes in Operational Processes

The introduction of change initiatives into any organisation is never easy and there are always some difficulties that must be overcome. Listed below are a number of the experiences and insights that HPM was able to gain through the assessment of the new product development process.

Quality Assurance.   The need for a separate and unique quality assurance process for rapid prototype development was evident from the delays caused by the formalities required by the company's adherence to ISO 9002. While every effort was made to gather all the required approvals and signatures as the product design progressed from research and development through to production engineering, the procedure was far too bureaucratic for "fast tracking" a new product development, and the company lost its agility as it introduced ISO 9002.

Compliance with procedures imposed restrictions, particularly when introducing new technology in days and not as part of a six-month project. "If we find something we do it tomorrow, we don't plan it, we get it in, let's try it," says the GM. Following ISO documentation meant the company couldn't short-circuit the design, the R & D, the production engineering, and manufacture of the product, if they were to gain compliance. A form of short-circuit documentation was trialed to avoid these restrictions, finally resulting in a ". . . controlled short-circuit, quick control mechanism that works within ISO 9002" and is mutually acceptable.

Politics of Change.   The need for the company's senior executives and management to support the cultural change necessary to successfully implement rapid product development was certainly one of the key issues. Changing the way of thinking of traditional engineers and designers was a difficult but rewarding process. It was necessary to convince the company engineers and tool designers that an entirely new set of rules and standards for simple rapid tool design was required, where tool longevity and short moulding cycles are no longer acceptable. Prototype tooling design only has a requirement for 1,000–2,000 shots, and if components have to be removed by hand for expediency, then this is perfectly acceptable.

Project Management Resources.   The experiment confirmed current experience of a heavy demand on management resources when introducing rapid product development projects. In this particular case study, involving extensive use of subcontractors, the amount of project management resources virtually had to be doubled for the short period of implementation. Without any doubt, one of the most crucial factors in the implementation of successful rapid product development is the allocation of dedicated project management resources.

Skills Acquisition.   Before RPD was introduced, the CAD skills of the design group were used to incorporate tool-making skills into the drawing office as tool quality was believed to be the way to ensure a quality product. The company now employs highly skilled industrial design engineers with design and tool-making skills, supported by electronic technology and quality engineers. A wide range of new skills have been added to support RPD, where those long-time middle managers who could not accept the changes or reorient themselves to the new process responsibilities were relocated or retrenched.

Current Use of Rapid Prototyping

The success of this and other projects has reinforced the company's commitment to using rapid prototype techniques in order to improve product development. The company today uses the latest technology in this area, working in 3-D CAD with direct connection to computerised spark erosion and wire-cutting equipment.

The company now almost always produces rapid prototypes for a wide variety of products:

- For metal products, these are created directly from the CAD screen, downloaded, and produced by the wire cutter.
- For plastic products, prototypes are generally produced using the stereolithography process with QMI. Numerous other alternatives are also available depending on the requirements of the prototype.
- Once the product is designed, the company uses the latest technology to produce rapid tooling. In conjunction with IMS (intelligent manufacturing systems), HPM shares technology on an international basis (mainly in R & D) and hence it has access to leading edge developments in this area.

APPENDIX 1
THE PROCESS OF STEREOLITHOGRAPHY

The first stage in the stereolithography process is to convert the CAD data into a format that is readable by the stereolithography machine. The most common method is to transfer the CAD data into a stereolithographic (STL) file that breaks down the CAD model into a series of triangles that can be interpreted by the SL machine.

The information is then downloaded to another computer that controls an ultraviolet laser. The STL file is now sliced into layers as fine as 0.012 mm, so the 3-D image of the model is now represented by thousands of 2-D slices. If the component requires the aid of any supports during the forming process, they are added to the file and will be built along with the part to be removed at a later stage.

The first of these 2-D images is then traced onto a vat of liquid photopolymer resin by an ultraviolet laser. Exposure to the UV light causes the liquid resin to solidify, leaving an image of that particular cross-section of the original CAD model. After solidification, the work area, which is on a table within the vat of resin, lowers slightly, allowing new resin to flow in over the hardened surface. The table then rises to a height that remains one-layer thickness below the surface where a blade wipes across the part to break the surface tension and assure a level surface and even coating. This process is repeated many times until the part is fully built.

When finished, the table raises the part to the surface where it stands allowing any excess resin to drain from the part. Any support structures or excess material are then removed and the part is placed in an oven for a final cure. This is required because the SL process does not cure the part 100 percent, and it also ensures no liquid material remains in the component. The SLA-250 units (from 3-D systems) have a work envelope of 250mm × 250mm × 250mm. The larger SLA-500 unit has a work envelope of 500mm × 500mm × 600mm (Vasilash, 1995).

13
IVA MANUFACTURING:

A Case of Implementing and Exploiting Advanced Technology
for Strategic Advantage[1]

1. Introduction

This document provides a review of the assumptions, practices, and philosophies of Iva Manufacturing Co., Iva, SC, USA, with respect to the uptake of advanced technology. It traces the processes adopted at Iva for managing advanced technology and the transition of change necessary for its uptake of advanced manufacturing technology. The document chronicles what Iva does; its focus is on the managerial processes and not on the details of the adopted technology per se. It serves as a "how to" type of manual whereby other similar organizations might learn from the practices and philosophies embraced by Iva's president, Mr. William (Bill) Epstein, and the members of his organization. Wherever possible, illustrative examples of the way these processes are carried out at Iva are provided. The research was completed through in-depth interviews and informal discussions with Mr. Epstein, observations of work practices and procedures made at plant visits to Iva, conversations with various members of the Iva organization and members of the staff of Clemson Apparel Research centre, review of company documents, apparel industry journals, and government publications.

The following chapter, "The U.S. Apparel Industry," provides background information on the nature of the industry, how it compares with other U.S. industries, and gives a feel for the important events occurring on the international scene. It describes the external influences that define the constraining environment in which Iva has had to operate. The chapter thereafter, "Advanced Technology in Apparel Manufacturing," provides a brief description of the types of advanced technology that exist in the industry and are employed at Iva. Chapter 4 provides a brief history of Iva, its internal situation, and describes the external and internal "drivers" that have led to the development of Iva's business strategy or "grand scheme." The content and substance of Iva's technology-oriented business strategy is presented in Chapter 5, "Technology's Central Role in Iva's Business Strategy." Chapter 6, "How Transition and Operation of Advanced Manufacturing Technology (AMT) Is Managed," explains, from conception to operation, the ways in which the strategy is being carried out. Chapter 7, "The Politics of Change," furnishes a sense of the special political issues that exist in a smaller family-run manufacturing firm like Iva and how they influence the motivation for change and the formulation of the company's technology strategy. Chapter 8 concludes the report by summarizing the critical role played by Iva's technology champion—Mr. Bill Epstein.

---

[1]This case was developed for use in classroom discussion and is not intended to necessarily illustrate appropriate or inappropriate management practices. The case author was John J. Kanet, Clemson University, 1996. The funding for this case production was provided by the Australian federal government's Department of Industry, Science and Resources.

2. The U.S. Apparel Industry

The U.S. apparel and fabricated textile products industry consists of producers of a diverse range of textile-based products, mostly garments. In 1992, about 74 percent of total SIC 23[2] production was wearing apparel (garments). Fabricated textile products such as home furnishings, canvas products, etc., accounted for 26 percent [*U.S. Industrial Outlook,* 1994].

Trade and Competition.   Figure 1 shows four indicators of apparel trade in the U.S. from 1972 through 1991: total shipments by all U.S. apparel manufacturers, total sales by apparel retailers, imports, and exports of apparel.[3] While total apparel retail sales[4] increased steadily (roughly by $100 billion over 19 years), shipments by U.S. apparel manufacturers began to grow more slowly after 1981 and even started to decline in 1988. Until 1984 both retail sales and manufacturers' shipments followed similar growth patterns, but beginning in 1985 increasing retail sales did not translate into growing output by domestic apparel manufacturers. The early 1980s also mark the time when imports began to gain an increasingly larger share of the U.S. apparel market. Exports from the U.S. are low over the analysed period but show a slow incline after 1985. With imports growing at a much faster pace than exports, the U.S. apparel trade deficit (shown by the area between the export and import lines) grew over the whole period.

After five years of steady decline, the industry increased real dollar shipments in 1993 by 1 percent. Shipment increases have been largely explained by higher consumer spending on apparel. Consumption of apparel products expanded by the end of 1992 after declines during the two previous years. The U.S. Department of Commerce recorded spending on clothes of $189.5 billion in 1992. Retail sales in mid-1993 were about 5 percent higher than in 1992; the total growth was about 2.9 percent. The trade deficit in apparel and fabricated textile products has been growing

FIGURE 1

Shipments, retail sales, exports, and imports in the apparel industry 1972–1991

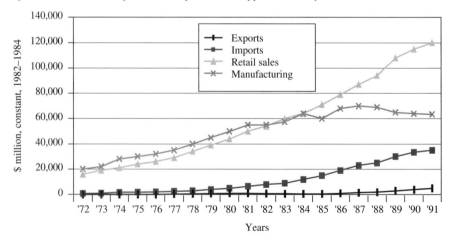

²The U.S. Department of Commerce's standard industry code (SIC) classifies the apparel industry in group 23, "Apparel and Other Finished Products Made from Fabrics and Similar Materials."
³In constant dollars, with the change 1982–1984 as the basis.
⁴The figures for retail sales include retailers' margins.

continuously. Reaching $28 billion in 1992, it increased to $30 billion in 1993 despite a 20 percent gain in exports and only a 9 percent increase in imports compared to 1992. While the historic focus of the apparel industry has been domestic, exports[5] accounted for 9 percent of shipments in 1993 compared to 4 percent in 1989. This growth is attributed to the dollar's depreciation and the revitalization of U.S. manufacturers' reputation for quality products. Table 1 shows exports and imports for the top five countries in 1992.

The 1987 Census of Manufacturers counted 23,168 establishments in the apparel industry (SIC 23), employing a total of 1,080,600 employees; 13,648 companies employed less than 20 employees. Table 2 provides an overview of the 20 major manufacturers' sales in 1992. These companies account for $23,265,424, or roughly 3 percent of the total industry's sales.

TABLE 1   Apparel Trade for the Top 5 Countries During 1992

	Exports			Imports	
Country	*Value ($mm)*	*Share (%)*	*Country*	*Value ($mm)*	*Share (%)*
Mexico	662	17.8	China	4,823	16.2
Dominican Republic	556	14.9	Hong Kong	4,301	14.4
Japan	490	13.2	South Korea	2,619	8.8
Costa Rica	275	7.4	Taiwan	2,302	7.7
Canada	247	6.6	Dominican Republic	1,233	4.1
Total	3,723		Total	29,765	

TABLE 2   1992 Sales for the Top 20 American Apparel Firms

No.	Company	Sales ($000s)	No.	Company	Sales ($000s)
1	VF Corp.	$4,320,404	11	Hartmarx	
2	Liz Claiborne	2,204,297	12	NIKE	
3	Fruit of the Loom	1,884,400	13	Delta Woodside	686,239
4	INTERCO	1,656,814	14	Leslie Fay	
5	WestPoint Stevens	1,500,982	15	Oxford	
6	Collins & Aikman	1,305,517	16	Genesco	572,860
7	Actava Group	1,241,111	17	Jones Apparel	541,152
8	Kellwood	1,203,086	18	Tultex	533,611
9	Phillips-Van Heusen	1,152,398	19	Crystal Brands	444,302
10	Russell Co.	930,787	20	Salant	407,236

---

[5]Export figures include shipments of garment parts for assembly abroad and subsequent reimport (so-called "807 contracting").

Figure 2 shows the CPI-U[6] (solid line) and that for apparel products (dotted line) over the 28-year period 1963–1991. The basis for the indexes is the 1982–1984 price change. Least-square regression reveals an average yearly increase of 3 percent for apparel products and 4 percent for the CPI-U.[7] This means that apparel prices were rising about 25 percent slower than those for all products included in the CPI-U.

The Labour Force.   Figure 3 compares the changes in the number of production workers employed by the U.S. apparel industry (dotted line) and all U.S. manufacturing companies (solid line). While both experienced a decline over this 25-year period, the evolution in the apparel industry shows much less variation than that for total manufacturing.[8]

The number of production workers in the apparel industry declined from 1,246,000 in 1966 to 856,000 in 1991 (a loss of 390,000 jobs). The yearly loss in jobs averaged 15,600. Since then the decline in the number of production workers has continued. In comparison, all U.S. manufacturing industries lost about 2,000,000 jobs over these 25 years. In 1993, 38,000 apparel jobs were lost, so that 84 percent of the work force was made up of production workers, compared to 68 percent for all U.S. manufacturing industries [Ramey, 1994].

Figure 4 shows average hourly earnings of production workers in all U.S. manufacturing industries (solid line) and in the U.S. apparel industry (dotted line). Amounts are in constant (1982–1984) dollars. Apparel workers have always been earning less than the average U.S. production worker. But the gap increasingly widened in the late 1980s and early 1990s, reflecting the fact that many jobs in the apparel industry are relatively low-skilled and often performed by women, whose earnings tend to be lower than those of men. Also, the major pad of the U.S. apparel

FIGURE 2

Consumer price indexes

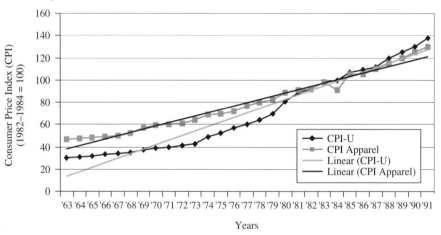

[6]The consumer price index for urban environments.

[7]$R^2 = 0.987$ for the apparel products price index and $R^2 = 0.9556$ for the CPI-U.

[8]This might be explained by the commodity character of apparel. Consumption, and hence production, of commodities is less influenced by business cycles than consumption and production of luxury and capital goods. As demand and production levels are more stable over time, employment in commodity industries shows less variance than that in noncommodity industries.

FIGURE 3

Changing employment: Production workers 1966–1991

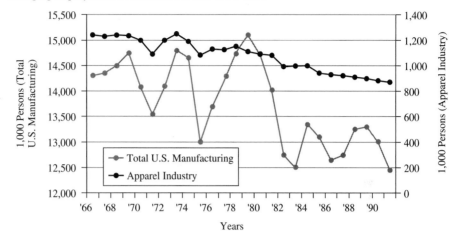

FIGURE 4

Average hourly earnings 1966–1991

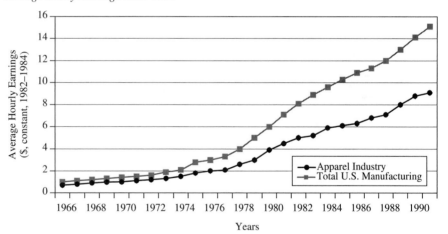

industry's manufacturing facilities is located in the Southeast (e.g., North Carolina, South Carolina, or Georgia), where wages are lower than the national average. Moreover, the apparel industry is subject to heavy competition from countries (e.g., CBI,[9] Latin American, and Far East countries) where wages are significantly lower than in the U.S. Additionally, weekly earnings of the apparel worker are lower because of a shorter work week. While the average work week for a U.S. manufacturing worker ranged between 39.8 and 41.4 hours, his colleague in the apparel

---

[9]The Caribbean Basin Initiative (CBI) includes the countries of the Caribbean islands, e.g., the Dominican Republic, Trinidad and Tobago, Jamaica, etc.

industry spent only a weekly average of 34.7 to 37 hours on the job. Hourly compensation was $7.10 in 1993, 2 percent more than in 1992. Workers employed in the fabrication of men's coats earned the highest wages, while children's wear workers earned the least [*U.S. Industrial Outlook,* 1994].

In Figure 5, output per man-hour for all U.S. manufacturing companies (solid line) and apparel manufacturers (dotted line) are compared. Over this 20-year period, hourly productivity in constant dollars increased for the apparel industry as well as for all U.S. manufacturing. However, since 1970 the gap in productivity between manufacturing and apparel has grown steadily. This is perhaps another reason for the lower hourly wages.[10]

Capital Investment.   Figure 6 shows the ratio of annual sales dollars that are reinvested by the average U.S. manufacturing company (solid line) and the average apparel manufacturer (dotted line). This reinvestment ratio is lower for the apparel industry than for all manufacturing. But whereas the ratio steadily declined[11] for the average manufacturing company, it remained virtually stable for apparel manufacturers.[12]

The International Operating Environment.   American textile and apparel manufacturers are justifiably concerned about the impact of the recently signed North American Free Trade Agreement (NAFTA), the General Agreement on Tariffs and Trade (GATT), and the establishment of the Free Trade Area of the Americas (FTAA). While the latter is an agreement to eliminate tariffs in the Americas starting January 1, 2005, GATT and NAFTA are already having an impact on the domestic apparel and textile industry. The industry is in great flux.

FIGURE 5

Worker productivity 1967–1987

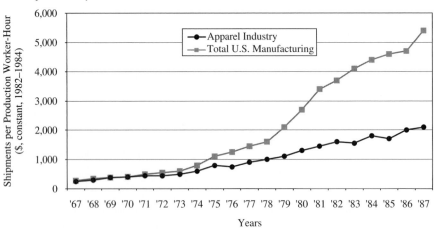

---

[10]These curves provide clear evidence for the notion that apparel manufacturing is labour-intensive. As the curve for all U.S. manufacturing describes the average labour intensity of all manufacturing activities in the U.S., all points below this curve are relatively more labour- (and less capital-) intensive and those above the curve more capital- (and less labour-) intensive. As the slope of all manufacturing companies is steeper than that of the apparel industry, this relative labour intensity increased over the analyzed period.

[11]−0.4 percent per year under regression.

[12]−0.05 percent per year under regression.

FIGURE 6

New capital spending/sales

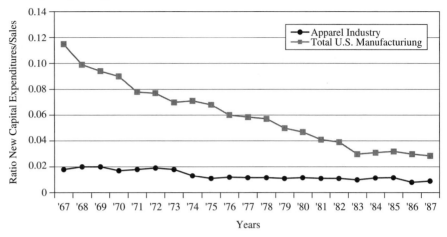

Implications of NAFTA.   NAFTA (enacted on January 1, 1994) ensures a mostly free market throughout North America together with protectionism against outside competitors. It provides strict rules about the origin of apparel and textile products. If these rules are met, tariffs are lifted immediately or are guaranteed to be lifted over a period of no more than 10 years. All quotas are immediately eliminated. To comply with the so-called "yarn-forward rule" most apparel must be produced from yarn made in a NAFTA country and also cut and sewn in a NAFTA country. The "fiber-forward rule" states that cotton and synthetic fiber spun yarn must be produced in a NAFTA country and the product also cut and sewn in a NAFTA country. These rules ensure that only a very small fraction of value is added in non-NAFTA countries. However, products still comply with the yarn- and fiber-forward rules if no more than 7 percent of the combined weight in non-NAFTA yarn is used. Certain fabrics that are short in supply in North America (e.g., silk) are exempt from the yarn- and fiber-forward rules. Both rules are far stricter than those previously applied in U.S.–Canadian trade. However, NAFTA is the first attempt by the U.S. and Canada to open the highly protected apparel and textiles markets to a developing country (Mexico). Simultaneously, fourth countries such as those of the CBI and Latin America are likely to suffer from NAFTA and will try to enter multilateral agreements for liberalization of their trade with the U.S. Apparel that is made from non-NAFTA fabric and cut and sewn in a NAFTA country may qualify for a tariff reduction under restricting regulation.

NAFTA provides special rules when shortages and other emergencies may result, such as tariffs to protect domestic industries when under threat of serious damage or extinction. Particularly in the trade between the U.S. and Mexico the importing country can exclude textiles and apparel that do not meet the yarn- and fiber-forward rules. Such emergency actions are allowed to be taken only once for a maximum of three years until 2004. Thereafter they will be prohibited.

All three NAFTA countries expect their industries to benefit. During the first eight months of NAFTA (January–August, 1994), U.S. textile and apparel exports to Mexico rose by 39 percent and exports to Canada by 10 percent. As several U.S. companies had been transferring labour-intensive operations to Mexico, imports from Mexico to the U.S. increased by 17 percent. But 85 percent of Mexican apparel contained U.S. fiber [*Textile World,* December 1994]. Advantages for U.S. manufacturers consist mainly of increased market access to Mexico and Canada. Mexico expects apparel exports to continue to grow both to the U.S. and Canada, while the Canadian industry is likely to benefit from increasing competitiveness in exports to the U.S. For further details see Ledermann and Hirsh [1994] and Hufbauer and Schoff [1993].

Some manufacturers such as Kellwood are finding relief through the establishment of efficient relationships and joint ventures with foreign manufacturers. Manufacturers will have to restructure their operations to accommodate shorter lead times and improved quality. Many hope that increased computerization of operations will allow them to compete with and work more efficiently than foreign manufacturers. Despite the concerns of the impact of trade agreements, some manufacturers argue that it is essential to think globally as a global economy is inevitable in the long run [Lee, 1993]. Early adaptation to the changing environment will prove to be crucial to the long-run success of the U.S. apparel industry.

"807 Contracting."   Despite NAFTA, apparel still is partly sourced from non-NAFTA countries.[13] The term "807" refers to a tariff paragraph in Schedule 8 of the U.S. Tariff Code. It allows U.S. manufacturers to perform parts of their operations abroad. They benefit from lower cost abroad while keeping part of the value chain in the United States. Under 807, fabric cut in the United States may be exported for assembly into a specific garment. Upon reimportation of the assembled product, tariff duty is assessed only on the full value of the imported garment less the cost or value of U.S. components. Sixty-three percent of 1989's $1.54 billion 807 imports were U.S. component value. In 1990, U.S. apparel imports under 807 regulation were about 10 percent of the dollar value of imports. Sixty-six percent of these imports originated from CBI countries.

The major advantage of 807 contracting is lower labour cost. In 1989, an apparel worker in the Dominican Republic earned $0.40, in Jamaica $0.57, and in Costa Rica $0.69 per hour compared to $6.59 in the United States. This difference in direct labour cost is especially important as garment assembly either requires expensive automation or labour-intensive manual work. 807 contracting in CBI countries and Latin America is more attractive than contracting in the Far East where lead times are longer and quality often poor. An extension of the 807 code, the so-called "Super 807," guarantees both reduction on tariffs and access to U.S. markets. This extension of the 807 code is the major cause for the increase of CBI apparel imports from $954 million in 1989 to $1.7 billion in 1992 [*Journal of Commerce and Commercial,* November 29, 1993]. On the other hand, 807 contracting opens new market niches for U.S. apparel companies who specialize in providing services to manufacturers sourcing abroad [Lee, 1993].

3. Advanced Technology in Apparel Manufacturing

Recent technological advancements include computer aided design, production, and communications as well as ergonomics and modular (team-based) manufacturing systems. Advanced technology applications in the apparel industry can be classified in the following major categories: cutting and marker making, unit production systems (UPS), and quick response (QR) planning and scheduling systems.

Advanced Technology in Cutting and Marker Making.   A marker is a diagram or an arrangement of pattern pieces for a garment. Computerized marker making greatly improves the efficiency of the process by allowing pattern manipulation, storage and reuse of markers, and electronic data interchange (EDI) with other production units. Advanced marker making systems are also capa-

---

[13]Such as Far Eastern and CBI countries.

ble of pattern design and include marking software that allows for connections and data exchange between different production stages of the production process.

During the spreading process, predetermined lengths of fabric are superimposed on a spreading or cutting table. Spreading can be done manually, by operator-controlled machines, or automatically. During the cutting process the fabric is cut into garment pieces that are identical to the pattern pieces of a marker. More and more high-volume cutting is done with automated, computerized cutting systems.

In the area of marker making, spreading, and cutting, state-of-the-art machinery is being increasingly computer controlled and interconnected. Many suppliers such as Investronica or Gerber Garment Technology offer a full range of products from design through marking, spreading, cutting, and production control. The development of more powerful small computers such as PCs and small workstations has allowed manufacturers to install local or wide area networks to control the whole manufacturing process. Many systems are also capable of performing more than one task.

Quick Response Planning and Scheduling Systems.   Quick response (QR) planning and scheduling systems represent one of the apparel industry's efforts to insure timely delivery of apparel with minimum inventories for both manufacturers and retailers. QR aims at reducing manufacturing and reorder cycle times to make production closer to the time of sale. The primary goal is to reduce those times in the cycles where no value is added to the product (the so-called "waste," e.g., storing, moving, handling, etc.). With these computer-based systems, some segments of the industry have experienced reorder cycle reductions from about nine months to two to three deliveries during a season. The QR concept depends heavily on sophisticated communication systems. Communication takes place via EDI employing interconnected computer systems throughout the entire manufacturing and sales network. Point-of-sale information about sold merchandise is immediately transmitted to the manufacturer, who uses this data to adapt his forecast of product demand and his planned production.[14]

Unit Production Systems.   Unit production systems (UPS) were developed in 1963 by Inge Davidson, production manager and partner of the Swedish Eton Shirt Company. He found that only 20 percent of manufacturing costs were associated with sewing while the other 80 percent represented material handling, which added no value to the final product. To increase the relative share of value-added time on the part of the operator, Davidson developed the first UPS. Today four companies provide UPS to the U.S. apparel manufacturers: Eton Systems, Gerber Garment Technology, Iva, and Investronica.

A UPS is basically an overhead transporter that moves a single garment between workstations. In addition to easy pickup and free disposal of the garment at workstations, a UPS acts to minimize the idle time between workstations. One advantage of UPS is that they address the major weakness of imported garments: long delivery and response times. UPS bring about a reduction in work-in-process levels. This, along with increased flexibility, has led to a major shift in management thinking: low (not high) work-in-process inventories allow quick response to customer needs. UPS cause a reduction in direct labour content by presenting the garment directly to the operator and automatically removing it from the workstation upon completion of the sewing cycle. Further, much of the cost associated with garment bundle handling (such as untying and clerical duties) is eliminated. A comprehensive study by the Clemson Apparel Research (CAR) centre on the costs

---

[14]For a more detailed look at the development of QR for the apparel industry, see references Glock and Kunz [1990], *Industry Surveys* [February 3, 1994], and *Training & Development* [June 1995].

and benefits of UPS versus traditional bundle systems found several advantages of UPS, including an 18.4 percent increase in productivity and an 18.7 percent savings in floor space.[15]

4. Iva Manufacturing

Short History, Background.   Iva Manufacturing Company is located in the rural upstate region of South Carolina. It was founded by Mr. William (Bill) Epstein some 42 years ago with an initial investment of $5,000. Epstein's current scope of activity has grown to include a network of six apparel factories throughout the region, as well as two marketing companies, employing some 600 workers and producing some 60,000 garments per week with annual revenues of approximately $20 million. Products include: women's sportswear, pants, robes, and nightgowns; home furnishings; and automotive interiors.

The two marketing organizations New Fashion and Third Generation sell to a variety of outlets, including mail order houses, various regional chains, and directly to smaller retailers. Aside from these two sister organizations, orders for garments are also received from other independent marketing organizations outside the Epstein companies. Depending on the product involved, a garment order is produced in one of the six factories (Iva, Sportswear, Amco, Fair Play, Clark Hill, or Honea Path).

The labour pool available in upstate South Carolina consists of simple, rural, relatively uneducated people. There is no union at any of the Epstein apparel companies. Epstein's personal vigor and capability have been the driving influence on the success of his companies. On balance, Epstein views government largely as a constraining environmental factor serving to add to the expense and or complication of operating (e.g., income tax laws, 807 trade policies, Mexican economic support, occupational safety and health regulations, minimum wage laws, plant construction codes and regulations, depreciation rules for capital investment, etc.). He views government social programs as contributing to the deterioration of the "work ethic." He is a strong believer that people, regardless of background, if given the right economic incentive, will respond. He knows the technology of apparel manufacturing inside-out, having started as a sewing operator himself at age 16. He attended Fashion Institute of Technology, New York, receiving an associate's degree in Industrial Engineering in 1953. Prior to 1989 his firm was able to compete on cost, largely to the credit of his genius for work organization and innovative use of technology—in his words, "by working smarter, not harder." With the adoption of 807 legislation he realized the need for his firm to respond in still other creative ways other than just through cost. He has built this response (to be outlined in the next chapter) to a large degree by focusing on technological competence and capability.

5. Technology's Central Role in Iva's Business Strategy

The Four Key Elements.   Given all the aforementioned environmental factors, President Bill Epstein has developed a long-term strategy for his apparel companies. The four key elements of this strategy include:

1. Corporate structuring to enhance technology uptake and to exploit Iva's relative technological advantage.

---

[15]One of the most striking advantages of UPS is the drastic reduction in cycle times. The CAR study showed reduction from 14.9 days to 5.9 days, an improvement of 60 percent. Obviously this approach fits well with the Operations Research (OR) philosophy. UPS also improved quality by reducing the number of defects by 11.1. percent. For further information on UPS see Hill [1994a].

2. Innovative application of technology and automation to work in an environment of small production runs.

3. Developing a marketing scheme that focuses on exploiting technological strength.

4. Focusing on developing technical competence from within.

A Corporate Financial Structure for Enhancing Technology Uptake.   Figures 7 and 8 help explain Epstein's corporate structure and its rationale. Figure 7 illustrates the flow of orders through the Epstein apparel companies. (It will be referred to later in the description of the marketing scheme.) Each Epstein company in this figure is a separate corporate entity. Several of the companies are not separated by geography and are even sometimes located within the same building. Cutters, Inc., for example, is located in the Iva plant. Cutters was formed in 1990 as part of a new marketing plan to provide greater flexibility of services in response to 807 growth. (The details of this plan are explained below.)

Each of the plants of Figure 7 were built after the original Iva facility over a period of years as the business grew. One reason for the separate corporate entities was to enable giving a stake of the ownership of a plant to its management. This scheme is akin to the profit centre idea used in many larger companies, but in this case the idea is carried through to giving management a part ownership. The managers in the respective factories are owners of those factories, sharing directly in the risk and profits of their operation. In each of the additional factories growing out of the original Iva facility, Epstein has retained approximately 70 percent ownership, with the remaining 30 percent going to the respective plant managers. For the Iva facility, Epstein has retained 100 percent

FIGURE 7

Order flows through the Epstein apparel companies

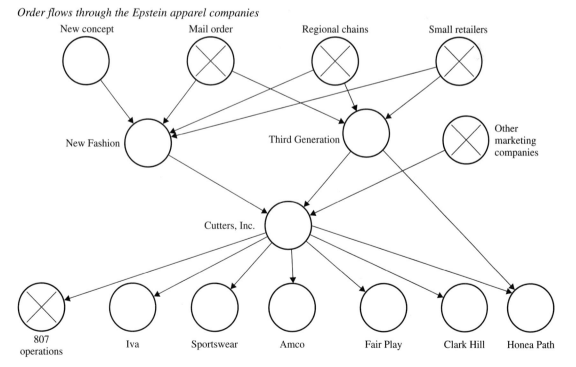

FIGURE 8

Epstein apparel businesses

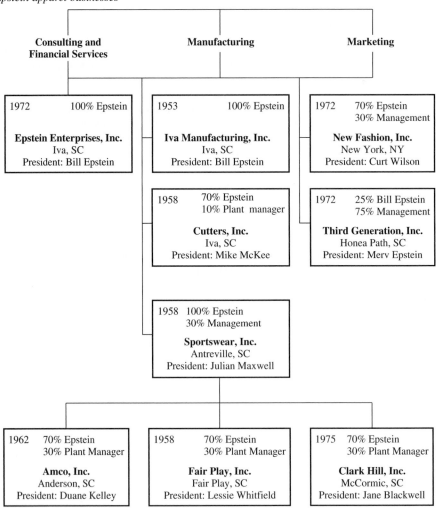

Consulting and Financial Services	Manufacturing	Marketing

1972	100% Epstein
Epstein Enterprises, Inc.	
Iva, SC	
President: Bill Epstein	

1953	100% Epstein
Iva Manufacturing, Inc.	
Iva, SC	
President: Bill Epstein	

1972	70% Epstein
	30% Management
New Fashion, Inc.	
New York, NY	
President: Curt Wilson	

1958	70% Epstein
	10% Plant manager
Cutters, Inc.	
Iva, SC	
President: Mike McKee	

1972	25% Bill Epstein
	75% Management
Third Generation, Inc.	
Honea Path, SC	
President: Merv Epstein	

1958	100% Epstein
	30% Management
Sportswear, Inc.	
Antreville, SC	
President: Julian Maxwell	

1962	70% Epstein
	30% Plant Manager
Amco, Inc.	
Anderson, SC	
President: Duane Kelley	

1958	70% Epstein
	30% Plant Manager
Fair Play, Inc.	
Fair Play, SC	
President: Lessie Whitfield	

1975	70% Epstein
	30% Plant Manager
Clark Hill, Inc.	
McCormic, SC	
President: Jane Blackwell	

ownership. There is a reason for this, which shall be explained in the coming chapter on politics of technology. (Figure 8 provides a breakdown of the corporate ownership in the various Epstein firms.)

Innovation in Process Design to Make Advanced Technology Affordable.   Counter to the argument that high volumes are necessary for the justification of automation, Iva has in fact successfully implemented an innovative scheme for deploying automation efficiently for a market demanding flexibility and short production runs of specialty products. One of the keys to this strategy was to recognize which of all operations performed in garment production are the most repetitious—in this case, pocket setting, fusing, and hemming. Recognizing this, Iva has rearranged its main production facility to group these operations in a single department dubbed by Epstein as "automated preassembly" (APA). This department accomplishes 15 to 18 percent of the value added to a garment. Because the majority of garment types sold by Iva have such features, the department can afford to be furbished with the most advanced automation facilities. The department has state-of-the-art sewing technologies such as Adler automatic pocket setters, Kannegiesser fusing machines with automated fabric stackers, Jet Sew hemming machines with edge alignment capability and automated stackers, as well as ultrasonic welding equipment. The APA department runs round the clock to feed all six of Iva's regional plants. Without this innovative rearrangement of the production process flow, the utilization of the automated equipment would never be cost-justified.

Integrating Technological Capability into the Marketing Strategy.   In response to the increasing cost pressure brought on by the 807 legislation, Epstein has developed a unique marketing strategy that exploits Iva's technological capability and engineering know-how. The capability to offer complete customer service from pattern making, providing production samples, and engineering, all the way through sewing and shipping of final product, has always been a competitive advantage for Iva. Now, as the fashion industry continues to move its orders for sewn garments to inexpensive sewing operations in Central America, Epstein has developed a strategy of "unbundling" Iva's services so as to adjust to the economic reality of cheaper offshore competition. The strategy involves a new marketing approach as well as a new corporate financial restructuring. The new corporation, Cutters, Inc., was created to offer customers a full line of "services for hire" from which garment distributors can "pick and choose." The advantage to the customers is that they can enjoy the benefits of low-cost sewing labour and still receive the needed engineering/technical support and the capital-intensive cutting services that Iva has always been able to offer. Epstein has in fact acted to distinguish his company from a simple "cut and sew" operation. Cutters's niche is in being a highly competent, technically oriented "quick response" service organization. Consider the following list of individual services that are now offered and priced separately:

1. *Engineering.* Here services include production engineering to specify the most efficient processing for the customer's garment. Cutters receives a sample of the desired product and delivers a set of engineered process specifications, including labour standards using MTM analysis.[16] The customer can then take these specifications to a third party and contract production. Also included in engineering services are marker design and grading. From a sample product, Cutters employs its computerized marker making equipment to supply the customer with a plot (layout) as to how the customer might best lay out the pattern so as to maximize material utilization. The customer receives a marker (pattern) used for laying out the garment for cutting.[17]

2. *Cutting.* The customer can supply Iva a sample or a marker and employ Cutters's capital-intensive cutting services. The customer can then plan to have the subsequent sewing done offshore. This option is particularly attractive to those wishing to later deploy the sewing services of an 807 offshore operation that does not have cutting capability.[18]

3. *Sewing.* Complete garment sewing services can be offered as well as preassembly of critical parts for subsequent shipment to a different assembly site. The advantage of this

---

[16]"Methods Time Measurement" using the industry standard "General Sewing Data."

[17]Additionally, they receive a "mini-marker," which is handy to quickly see the material layout and why it is efficient.

[18]For example, a customer may need a total of 1,000 dozen blouses, 200 as soon as possible and 800 later. Iva is contracted to do all the cutting, complete the sewing assembly of the first 200 for quick shipment, and send the remaining material to Costa Rica for sewing of the remaining 800.

option is that the customer reaps the quality benefit of Iva's highly automated APA department for those operations of a garment best performed by highly automated repetitive equipment (e.g., pocket setting, fusing, and hemming).

4. *Shipping.* This service includes drop shipping and invoicing of finished garments to customers' specified destination. Online invoicing is available whereby each package has an enclosed invoice showing the content of the shipment. Aside from just shipping, Iva offers accounts receivable servicing (factoring and/or accounts receivable financing, credit checking, collecting, statements, and reports).

5. *Consulting.* Technical employees and Iva managers are available to visit offshore operations to review problems in sewing, maintenance, quality control, and business systems. In addition to these traditional consulting services, Iva offers a rather unique service to other apparel manufacturers: the opportunity to see how their products would run on the advanced equipment and shop-floor control software systems in place at Iva. The advantage to the customer is that he sees how such advanced technology operates on his own product in a production environment—before having to make a large capital expenditure.

This new marketing approach would not be possible without the variety of technology capabilities and technical know-how in place at Iva to begin with.

Personnel Practices to Facilitate Technical Capability.   Building a technically competent and motivated personnel base is an integral part of Iva's technology strategy. Employee education and training is encouraged and supported. Economic incentives are embedded into the pay and salary structures at all levels of the organization—from floor sweeper to president. Technical capability is exploited to marketing advantage by developing the reputation for being able to do what others cannot. Technical capability is viewed as a tool for revenue generation and new business development. How all this is accomplished is described in the section to follow.

6. How Transition and Operation of AMT Is Managed

Iva's president, Bill Epstein, is clearly the main innovation driver at Iva. His vision of *technological innovation* includes any novel change, application, or rearrangement of equipment (technology), manufacturing techniques, or organizational change which leads to greater efficiency—efficiency in terms of cost, quality, or time. Innovation is not limited to changes on the factory floor but also applies to the corporate structure, the marketing program/plan, and how such a change might be made to mesh with manufacturing technology for improved efficiency. This is clearly a broad, and arguably, an enlightened view of what constitutes "innovation." Epstein views the *driving force* for innovation to be the profit motive.

Remuneration Approaches That Encourage Innovation.   An innovation culture is fostered at Iva that permeates all levels of the corporate structure. One of the bases for this is the remuneration strategy for all employees. Roughly, remuneration at all levels of the organization is always comprised of both straight salary (roughly 70 percent) and some type of bonus program ($\cong$ 30 percent—including equity positions). For example, the plant managers at each of Epstein's plants have a 30 percent ownership position in their operation. Although Iva's stock is not publicly traded, Iva "makes a market" in the stock for its employees. An inventory of treasury stock is available for trading; the trading price is reset each accounting period to the average book value of the four previous reporting periods. Sharing in ownership has related implications to innovation. For example, it enables Iva to carry out a policy of giving employees far more freedom in job design than many comparable firms. Employees are encouraged to exploit their own capabilities and interests in accomplishing the common goal. Epstein credits the policy of providing managers with equity positions with why Iva is free of much of the motivation and work ethic problems that so plague others in American industry. There is little wonder that the *primary resources available for pursuing innovation* are found in the *collective creativity* of all of Iva's employees (i.e., Iva's owners!).

Productivity incentives are embedded in the salary structure at virtually every level of Iva's organization. The floor sweeper, for example, is paid a base rate plus a weekly bonus based on the number of people in attendance at the factory that week. A "discomfort" bonus is paid for some operations. For example, workers in the steaming and pressing room receive a 1 percent bonus for each degree room temperature over 74° Fahrenheit (this can be substantial in summer months). This simple scheme turns a potentially negative situation into a positive one. Rather than complaining about the heat, workers see a warmer day as an opportunity to earn a bonus. A 10 percent bonus for attendance is given each week to a worker who is in the plant for 40 hours and not late more than once during the week. These simple schemes add up to encourage a work ethic among the workers that productivity and good working habits will be directly rewarded.

The Role of "De-Skilling" in Assessing Advanced Technology.   When considering automation and advanced technology Iva always asks:

"Does it reduce costs?"

"Does it enhance quality?"

"Does it add to our capability?"

"Does it de-skill the process?"

Cost, quality, and capability are well known as important issues in the justification of advanced technology. But the question, "Does the technology lower the required skill level?" may be found somewhat surprising. Conventional wisdom has it that advanced technology leads to greater demands on the qualifications of the work force. Epstein sees a different twist. He always looks to see if the technology in some way leads to "de-skilling" the manufacturing process. For apparel manufacturing, operator skill is influenced by both the operator's innate manual dexterity and experience. Operator productivity, in turn, is directly influenced by three factors—skill level, motivation, and technology. As is typical for the apparel industry, Iva's wage structure follows a piece rate system with a guaranteed minimum wage.[19] The operator's pay is thus directly linked to his productivity. As a result, 100 percent of the productivity difference between two operators goes into the more highly productive operator's pocket. The per-piece cost to the firm is the same regardless of who does the operation. So when the firm purchases advanced technology that improves operator productivity, the firm's only option for recouping the capital cost (i.e., the portion of worker productivity caused by improved technology) is to reduce the piece rate paid to the operator (but still allowing the operator to share in the gain!). Figure 9 serves to illustrate these relationships. An operator's skill is determined by his innate dexterity and experience.

Operator skill combined with motivation and technology are what determine operator productivity. It is the operator's productivity and the piece rate that in turn determine the operator's earnings. Examples of technology that have contributed to de-skilling in sewing include: replacement of mechanical clutches with electronic motor control, stitch count control, and optical sensing of fabric edge and ply. When advanced technology de-skills an operation, the firm experiences

---

[19]The U.S. federally mandated minimum wage (currently $4.25/hour).

FIGURE 9

Technology and de-skilling

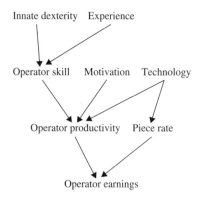

greater flexibility in labour acquisition and scheduling, as well as lower required training time. Looking for this de-skilling property also fits with Epstein's employee selection philosophy. He places greater emphasis in employee selection on an individual's work ethic and motivation than on his skill level or innate dexterity. In the long run, the more motivated, less-skilled operator will prove to be more valuable.[20] Technology clearly affects operator productivity and, in Iva's case, it also affects the piece rate. How Iva manages the relationship (technology versus operator productivity and technology versus piece rate) is discussed in detail in the following section.

Fostering Employee Commitment Through Ownership.   Epstein's straightforward approach is never more evident than in the way he implements employee ownership. The employee gets a two-year option to buy the stock at a fixed price (the average book value of the last three accounting periods).[21] When the employee decides to exercise his option, Bill accompanies him to the local bank. The employee signs a promissory note; the bank gets the stock as collateral; and Epstein personally guarantees the loan. We have to remember the people involved here are not sophisticated Wall Street stock market traders but rather simple rural South Carolina people. But with this procedure they are now also stockholders with a say in the company they work for and with a very good reason for wanting it to be successful.

Developing Technical Competence from Within.   Iva has adopted a policy of training and developing the rank and file, employee ownership, and focus on technical competency. Iva rarely goes outside for higher level management positions. The people of Iva know this and it acts as an effective motivator. A good example of Iva's policy of growing managers from within is the current chief operating officer, Mr. Julian Maxwell. Mr. Maxwell started as floor sweeper at the original Iva factory. He then progressed to sewing operator, mechanic, assistant plant manager, and plant manager before assuming responsibility as chief operating officer. Now his two sons are plant managers and also part owners of the corporation.

---

[20]It also serves to explain the logic of Epstein's practice of extensive employment of the handicapped.

[21]Actually, it is a buy-sell agreement with one condition being should the employee leave the company, then he agrees to sell the stock back to the company.

Consistent with the policy of promotion from within, there is a heavy emphasis placed on cross-training of employees. This has the obvious advantage of providing flexibility to operations, but it also has the effect of cultivating innovation. When an employee knows the technologies involved with the full construction of a garment, he is in a much better position to suggest as well as implement new methods and technological improvements. As an example, customers typically submit samples of what they want when requesting quotes on new products. Because sales personnel are technically capable (and motivated), they are often able to see small changes in the garment construction that could lead to significant customer savings. Often, a sample is submitted back to the customer with two quotes: one for making the garment exactly per the customer's original design, the other incorporating Iva's suggested changes—usually incorporating better quality with no significant effect on style.

Innovative personnel are rewarded in several ways: first, through opportunity to advance; second, through incentive pay structures; and finally, through opportunity for ownership. All educational costs for employees are 100 percent reimbursed at time of successful program/course completion. Moreover, work schedules are adjusted to allow for employee schooling.

An Attitude of Open Exchange.   Unlike many firms in the textile-apparel industry, Iva has a reciprocal open-door policy of exchanging technological information. In the final analysis, the view is that there is far more to be gained through open sharing. Epstein and his management team continuously visit other factories (e.g., contractors) to share technical information and know-how. Iva "networks" extensively with other members of the industry, not only through exchange of visits to/from others, but also through active participation in industry-related shows and conferences, and through association with the regional university's (Clemson) apparel research centre.[22]

An Advanced Approach to Capital Investment Financial Analysis.   One of the tools used by Iva is the Apparel Manufacturing Capital Investment Advisor (AMCIA), a capital budgeting decision support system aimed at the special needs of apparel manufacturing companies in the United States. The AMCIA software assists management of apparel firms in determining the feasibility of planned investments in advanced technology. The software works as an add-in module with popular spreadsheet software such as Microsoft Excel or Lotus 1-2-3. AMCIA includes numerous worksheets that help quantify various cash flows associated with apparel manufacturing technology. The software provides the user with an analysis of its input, including payback, return on investment (ROI), and net present value (NPV) methods. The system has a novel sensitivity analysis feature that allows users to easily change input values and immediately see the impact on payback, ROI, and NPV. It allows the user to specify his level of confidence in each projected cash flow source and automatically adjusts the discount rate up or down depending on the user's degree of confidence in the different cash flows. Another unique feature is that it allows for inclusion of subjective cash flows that might result from the investment (e.g., revenue effects of greater market share due to higher quality, etc.). The appendix provides a more detailed description of how Iva used AMCIA to help with a specific investment decision.

---

[22]Clemson Apparel Research (CAR), founded in 1988, is a federal-state government sponsored demonstration center housing virtually all of the latest technology available to shirt manufacturers. Regional manufacturers are free to visit and see the technology in operation as well as receive technical assistance on how to apply it. The center provides investment advice to help firms with the justification analysis of advanced apparel technology and holds workshops and seminars all for the purpose of supporting the regional apparel industry. Epstein was instrumental in the initiation of CAR and one of its founding directors.

Technology Sourcing Practices: Another Case of Applied Innovation. When unit production systems (UPS) first appeared in Europe, Iva was quickly on the scene to see if this new technology could be put to good use. Epstein saw such systems in Europe but was not satisfied with the level of utilization manufacturers there were achieving with this new concept. In order to increase utilization Epstein altered the system in a number of novel ways. Prior implementations of UPS involved a set of sewing workstations each with one operator and one machine per station. Iva developed a specially constructed carousel table to change to the other machine simply by rotating the table 180 degrees. This not only allows for quick changeover to a different job (minimizing system downtime) but also serves as a backup system, further reducing the distress caused by equipment failure (and further improving system utilization). One of the aforementioned benefits of this type of system is reduced in-system inventory. However, to achieve this in operation, the workstations must be extremely reliable and the work carefully balanced between the stations. Other modifications to the basic system introduced by Iva include elimination of a separate loading station by combining it with operators' hands for productive sewing. These modifications have enabled Iva to improve the system's utilization from the 70 percent (which the Europeans were experiencing) to the 80–85 percent range. The important point here is the little technical things—the attention to engineering details—that are just enough to make new technology work.

Making Technology Generate Revenue and Not Just Reduce Costs. How the unit production system described above is deployed at Iva serves to illustrate another innovative way Iva is able to use technology for strategic purposes. Such systems typically cost over $100,000 to completely install, making them a significant capital outlay for many apparel firms. Iva has three such systems in operation (from three different suppliers: Eton, Investronica, and INA). Iva offers to competing organizations the opportunity to offload work to Iva, enabling the competitor to see his product run on a UPS system that he may be evaluating for purchase. Iva generates revenue from the subcontract work as well as from associated technical consulting services. In this way, advanced technology is used at Iva not just to reduce costs: it serves also as a vehicle for generating additional revenue, dovetailing into Iva's overall marketing strategy of technical service offerings. Using advanced technology not only to reduce costs but also to mesh with a revenue-generating marketing program is a point that many organizations probably lose sight of or at least may realize but do not follow through to implementation.

Compared to many other firms, process technology at Iva plays a far more central role as the cornerstone to providing a competitive advantage. It is central to the firm's business strategy and viewed as an absolute *opportunity*. A carpetmaker in Iva's region received a special order to make 48" round area rugs. (They were to be basketball shaped!) The manufacturer had the technology for continuous weaving and screen printing but had no technology for efficiently cutting round shapes from his continuous-feed carpet weaving machines. Iva had the cutting technology and know-how from its experience in cutting using a plaid matching technique for pinning material in preparation for cutting and thus got the subcontract to cut the rugs to shape, do the serging, pack, and drop ship to the customer's desired destination(s).

Another Example: Technological Capability as a Strategic Advantage. Because of the investment in a variety of advanced technology and the reputation for technical competence, Iva enjoys a competitive advantage in new business development. A good example of this is Iva's current work for the newly constructed BMW automobile assembly factory in nearby Greenville, South Carolina. The automaker was looking for a way to reduce its material handling costs for smaller painted parts (e.g., gas caps, sunroofs, etc.) needed on the assembly line. Their original method was to pack the parts in specialized protective pallets and deliver them "in bulk" to the respective workstations in need of the part. This required considerable space and a constant flow of fork lift traffic. An alternative solution was to install an expensive overhead conveyor system to deliver the respective parts to the line. Iva provided a much more elegant solution. Working with the manufacturing engineers at BMW, Iva developed a special "pouch" made of fabric, quilting, and Styrofoam.™ The pouch could be strapped to the inside of the open trunk of a painted body and loaded with the needed parts at their point of origin—the painting department. Iva now has a contract to keep BMW supplied with these pouches. This is a good example of how Iva is able to generate revenue by innovatively exploiting its *technological expertise*—in Epstein's words "their biggest tool for new business development."

Not Simply a Matter of Cost.   Epstein sees the role of innovation and application of advanced technology as an integral part of a long-term strategy. In his words, "You can't look at ROI and say that unless you get your money back in three years, you're not going to buy a piece of equipment. If you don't buy it, you might not be in business five years from now, so the first decision you have to make is do you want to be in business." In Epstein's view, advanced technology uptake has to fit in the grand scheme of the business. As he puts it, when considering advanced technology, we must always ask, "Does it add to business *capability*?" Having advanced technology and technical competence at all levels fosters a corporate pride in being able to do what others cannot. Technological capability serves to fill an important market niche and is central to new business development.

7. The Politics of Change

Conflicts and Hidden Agendas.   The Epstein apparel companies are not immune to conflicts, hidden agendas, and misunderstandings that can cause difficulties in the uptake of advanced technology. To a large degree, Iva is a family-run organization, with all the special problems associated with any family business. One area where this has an interesting effect is in the perceived relative value placed on advanced technology. For example, the Marketing vice president (with a forte for selling) may well have a much different point of view as to the relative value of marketing expenditures versus expenditures for technology than the Manufacturing vice president whose forte is engineering. When the two are brothers and both are major stockholders in the same company, the possibility of conflict is further heightened. Moreover, there is the problem of authority hierarchy. Consider the conflict that can occur when the younger "kid brother" is higher in the organizational hierarchy. One of the solutions Epstein has adopted to minimize this type of conflict has been to separate family members into different sister corporations. For example, Third Generation was created as a separate corporate entity in part for this reason.

Overcoming Resistance to Change.   One of the age-old problems of introducing any organizational change is resistance on the part of the people involved. Uptake of advanced technology involves organizational change. Technology is and always will be a mesh of man and machine, a combination of procedures, equipment, computers, software, and people. So resistance to change must always be reckoned with and addressed as a fact of life in new technology introduction. How a firm carries this through can make the difference in whether or not the technology is successfully taken up. Iva Manufacturing employs a number of novel approaches for reducing resistance to new technology, including sharing the productivity benefits with operators and managers and allowing people to see the improvement for themselves before asking them to change.

Sharing the Productivity Gains of De-skilling.   As previously mentioned, one of the key properties Iva always watches for in any new technological endeavour is that the technology in some way contributes to the de-skilling of the manufacturing process. The direct monetary effect of de-skilling is a lower labour rate requirement as a result of the technology. Operator pay is based on labour rate per piece times pieces per hour. Iva's costs are the rate per piece. The interests of the two parties are summarized as follows:

Operator's interest: To maximize \$/hours = \$/piece × pieces/hour

Iva's interest: To minimize \$/piece

Suppose the technology permits a 40 percent improvement in the number of pieces an operator can produce per hour. Given the piece-rate pay structure, this would increase an operator's earnings by 40 percent (all else equal), i.e., new earnings per hour would be:

$$\$/hour = \$/piece \times 1.4 \ (pieces/hour)$$

But the de-skilling property of the technology would allow a less-skilled operator and thus a reduction in the required labour rate per piece (Iva's interest). For Iva to reap any benefit from the technology, the rate per piece must be reduced. The operator would receive some benefit as long as the piece-rate reduction were not so great as to decrease his hourly earnings. The policy at Iva is to share some of the productivity increase with the operator. In this example assume Iva shares the productivity increase so that the operator can yield a 2 percent improvement in hourly earnings. To clarify how Iva accomplishes this gain-sharing, consider the following.

Given:

P = Percent improvement in productivity (pieces per hour) caused by the new technology

E = Desired percent improvement in operator earnings per hour

To find:

r = Desired percent reduction in the piece rate (\$/piece)

It can be easily shown that:

$$r = 100 - (100 + E)/(100 + P)$$

In the example above the desired percent reduction in piece rate is thus

$$r = 100 - 100(100 + 2)/(100 + 40) = 27.14 \ percent$$

Giving the desired new *operator* earnings:

$$\$/hour = (1 - .2714)(\$/piece) \times 1.4 \ (pieces/hour) = 102 \ percent$$

As a result, Iva's labour cost per piece is reduced by 27 percent and the operator's earnings per hour are increased by 2 percent. Operators at Iva are motivated to make new technology work because they know they will *directly* and immediately share in the economic benefit when it does. This simple economic concept is so often overlooked in other companies.

Motivated Uptake: "Show Me!"   Aside from providing operators the opportunity to share in the economic benefit of new technology, there may still be resistance to uptake if there is a risk involved. That is, even if Iva believes the technological improvement is substantial, the *operator* must believe it as well. There is always the risk that the engineering estimate of the improvement is too optimistic. In order to minimize this risk, Iva typically introduces new technology on a "pilot" basis, in part to debug the technology, but also in part to prove its benefits to the operators. A tangible example of this occurred with their introduction of electronic motors in some of their sewing machines—replacing the older clutch motors. The technical difference is that the degree of precision in the foot pedal control is increased with the electronic motor technology, allowing the operator to sew faster. But just how much faster was the question. To show the skilled operators the potential output per hour, Iva set up the new machine with an unskilled, lower paid operator. The existing operators could see that the improvement was real, and knowing that they would share in the benefit, resistance to the new technology was eliminated.

"Not So Risky" Capitalism.   In a similar vein as the policy of reducing the risk for operators, Epstein has an innovative approach for reducing the risks of new technology for the management team (his co-owners of his other apparel companies; e.g., Sportswear, Amco, etc.). As mentioned earlier, Iva Manufacturing is the only corporation among Epstein's apparel companies in which he is 100 percent owner. One of the reasons for this is Epstein's desire to assume much of the risk of new technology uptake for all his operations. As a matter of policy the investment in all new advanced technologies is first made by the Iva corporation, then installed and debugged at the Iva facility. The other plant managers can then observe the technology in operation at the Iva facility before deciding to take it up in the factories they manage and co-own.

Keeping Unions a Nonissue.   Clearly one of the simplifying factors at Iva is the absence of organized labour. But this is not accidental. The policies of productivity gain-sharing and co-ownership play a significant role in keeping unions a nonissue at Iva and its sister operations.

8. Summary and Conclusion

There can be no doubt that Iva Manufacturing has a technology champion in its president, Bill Epstein. Epstein is technically innovative but also has a working understanding of economics, finance, and human motivation. He is a risk-taker and doesn't understand the words "can't do." He is tireless. He is a shrewd businessman. But perhaps more importantly, he *has a plan* for his companies and he uses technology to carry out this plan. He knows how to motivate people and remove resistance to change. He employs innovation in all aspects of technology: new products, new processes, new management systems, new corporate structures, and new marketing plans. His business strategy has technological capability as a major element. Technological capability plays a major role in new business development. Epstein has a set of criteria for technology acquisition. He integrates everything, mission, objectives, corporate structure, marketing plan, organizational practices, pay structure, all in a way that facilitates the use of technology. All of this was not developed and carried out in one fell swoop but rather as an evolution over time and always with a grand scheme in mind and a bent for continuous improvement.

9. References

"Apparel Predicted New Top Banana among Exports," *Journal of Commerce and Commercial* 398, no. 28111 (November 29, 1993), p. 5.

Glock, Ruth E., and Kunz, Grace I. *Apparel Manufacturing.* New York: Macmillan, 1990.

Hill, E. "Comparison of Cost and Production Data Between a Traditional Bundle System and a UPS Installation." In *Clemson Apparel Research: Fundamentals of Apparel Manufacturing,* Clemson University, 1994.

Hufbauer, G., and Schon, J. *NAFTA: An Assessment,* Revised edition. Washington, 1993.

Industry Surveys Textiles, Apparel & Home Furnishing. U.S. Department of Commerce, February 3, 1994.

Johns, B. "California Garment Industry Expects to Lose Jobs and Revenue to NAFTA." *Journal of Commerce and Commercial* 398, no. 28085 (October 19, 1993), p. 4a.

Ledermann, A., and Hirsh, B. *The NAFTA Guide.* San Diego, CA, 1994.

Lee, G. "Trim Suppliers Add Services for 807 Users." *Women's Wear Daily* 165, no. 59 (March 29, 1993), p. 6.

Lee, G. "Bobbin Show: Talking NAFTA, Eyeing Globe." *Women's Wear Daily* 6, no. 70 (October 11, 1993), pp. 1+.

"NAFTA Boosts Textile Trade." *Textile World* 144, no. 12 (December 1994), pp. 21+.

Ramey, J. "Textile Jobs Down 6000 in 93; Apparel Industry Loses 38,000." *Women's Wear Daily* 167, no. 6 (January 10, 1994), p. 21.

Ryan, T. J. "Wall Street 95: Big Firms Will Grow, Smaller Ones May Go." *Women's Wear Daily* 169, no. 43 (March 6, 1995), p. 9.

Smarr, S. L. "Iva's Flight to the Top." *Bobbin,* May 1988, pp. 96+.

"High Performance in the Apparel Industry." *Training & Development* 49, no. 6 (June 1995), p. 37.

U.S. Industrial Outlook. U.S. Department of Commerce, 1994.

APPENDIX
THE APPAREL MANUFACTURING CAPITAL INVESTMENT ADVISOR

In 1992 Iva Manufacturing investigated whether investing in new cutting technology would pay off for the company. To do so, Iva used the Apparel Manufacturing Capital Investment Advisor (AMCIA), a spreadsheet-based tool that applies net present value (NPV) analysis to determine the feasibility of capital investments for apparel manufacturers. AMCIA is broken down into 12 worksheets that help the user analyze cash flows associated with a proposed investment. The worksheets address the areas of investment, installation and depreciation, old equipment sale, direct labour, indirect labour, materials, quality-related costs and revenues, inventory, maintenance, fabric utilization, response-time revenues, and miscellaneous items. AMCIA was developed by Clemson Apparel Research, a research facility of Clemson University.

Relevant Background

The feasibility study began with an in-depth analysis of current practices at Iva. A set of 26 questions was developed. (The questions and answers begin on page 298.) The answers to these questions provided some of the input for AMCIA's worksheets. An initial review of the plant's operating practices provided some evidence for increased productivity using a new cutter. Iva also examined whether any major construction would be necessary to provide the space for operating the new cutting equipment. While floor space was sufficient, the study revealed that the factory's layout required the cutter to be able to move laterally across the cutting tables. During the initial phase of the analysis, Iva's president, Bill Epstein, felt that investing in the new cutting technology would not pay off. Especially, he was convinced that there would be no improvements in cutting capacity or capability. Epstein only expected savings in direct labour of $30,000 annually from the elimination of two cutting jobs. He felt that this would not be enough to justify the investment. The next step Iva performed was to gather information about the cutter and how it would impact operations. This was done by consulting with Gerber Garment Technology, a major player in the U.S. cutter industry. Given the special requirements of Iva, the model under consideration was the 593-7, priced at $300,000. Additional operating costs included: $1,500 for a monthly onsite full maintenance contract covering parts and labour or $1,000 for maintenance covering parts and telephone support only; $5.40–$7.35 per hour of operation for replacement of blades and other consumables as well as electricity. The cutter's salvage value was estimated by Gerber to be 50 percent–60 percent of its original value after six years, assuming the machine was well maintained. To guarantee this, Iva used the onsite full maintenance contract for further calculations. However, a salvage value of only $50,000 was assumed, reflecting the current market for used cutters. When reviewing the data collected, Mr. Epstein felt more comfortable about an increase in *sewing* productivity. He estimated yearly savings of $75,000 due to more accurate cutting arising from the time savings required to line up the fabric for button holes and pockets. Iva estimated the machine would provide a higher quality garment due to more accurate cutting, which would translate into increased per-piece revenue of $.37 instead of $.35. Based on an analysis of data provided by the company's tracking system, the time needed to cut a piece of garment (the standard allowed minutes, or SAM) was determined to be .1676 mm/unit.

The Results

In the area of direct labour, the proposed investment would result in changed efficiencies and SAMs. Direct labour efficiency would increase from 87 percent to 90 percent due to less downtime of the automated cutting equipment. This would have allowed Iva to produce 784,260 more units per year. As Iva did not want to take full advantage of its increased capacity, AMCIA's sensitivity analysis on the SAM for the cutter was performed. The SAMs were varied from 0.05 mm/unit to 0.17 mm/unit under two different scenarios. The first scenario assumed Iva would take advantage of the full production capabilities and the second assumed that only 25 percent of the increased capacity would be used. Under full capacity Iva would have been able to break even (i.e., gain an NPV equal to zero) if the cutter cut one piece every 0.141 minutes. A faster pace would have resulted in positive NPV. However, under the second scenario (using only 25 percent of the increased capacity), the cutter's SAM would have to be 0.741 mm/unit. This sensitivity analysis provided some insight into the impact of increased capacity on the feasibility of a capital investment. Other noteworthy results occurred when Iva analyzed the maintenance-associated cash flows with AMCIA. The currently used hand-cutting processes yielded annual maintenance costs of $400. As already mentioned, the Gerber cutter required a much higher annual outlay for maintenance and consumables. The service contract would have amounted to $18,000 a year and consumables for another $10,500 annually. The present value of both costs over six years at 4.1 percent was approximately $115,000. Iva used AMCIA to perform a second sensitivity analysis in the area of sewing productivity. Savings due to increased sewing productivity were difficult to estimate and a sensitivity analysis of the range from $0 to $100,000 showed the breakeven point was at $62,656.

Conclusion

The output of AMCIA's 12 worksheets indicated a net present value of the entire project to be $-24,150, with a payback period of 28 months. As this net present value was negative, Iva decided not to undertake the investment in the new cutting technology. However, the sensitivity analysis suggested that under increased production, the investment might have been worthwhile.

The 26 questions for data collection and Iva's answers:

1. How many annual working weeks does your company have? <u>50</u>
2. What's your company's current tax rate? <u>20%</u>
3. What are the fringe benefits (as a percentage of direct labour payroll) of direct and indirect labour? <u>20%</u>
4. What is the estimated unit sale price of the product over the next six years if you were to continue with the current technology? <u>$0.35, increasing by 5 percent annually</u>
5. What is the estimated number of units you plan to produce over the next six years if you were to continue under the current technology? <u>1,500,000 annually</u>
6. What is the beta (financial risk factor) value of your company and the industry? <u>N/A</u>
7. How many, if any, shares are outstanding in your company? <u>N/A</u>
8. What is the average annual labour cost of repair and reinspection for the products affected by this decision? <u>$3,000</u>
9. What is the average annual cost of scrapped products? <u>$1,000</u>
10. What is the net cost of products that are not of first quality (i.e., seconds)? This cost should include manufacturing costs minus any revenues received for the seconds. <u>$1,000</u>
11. What is the annual excess cost due to repaired, scrapped, or second products? These costs may include overtime or process delays to meet normal production. <u>$500</u>
12. What is the indirect labour pay rate? <u>$9.00 per hour</u>

13. How many regular hours annually does the indirect labour work? <u>800</u>
14. What are the annual overtime costs for direct labour? <u>$0</u>
15. What is the current per unit material cost for products affected by the decision? <u>$2.50</u>
16. What are your annual maintenance expenses for the current technology? <u>$400</u>
17. What is the average inventory level for the products affected by this decision? <u>12,000 units</u>
18. What is your estimate of the percentage change (positive or negative) in inventory levels if the new technology were adopted? <u>+2%</u>
19. With these new estimates of inventory levels, what would the change be in inventory costs? <u>$0</u>
20. What is the estimated number of yards per unit and what is the average cost per yard? <u>1.25 yards</u>
21. What is the standard allowed minutes (SAM) per unit with the present technology? <u>0.1676</u>
22. What is the base rate per minute for direct labour? <u>$0.12</u>
23. What are the excess costs of direct labour as a percentage of the earned pay per unit? <u>25%</u>
24. What is the current total annual workers' compensation as a percentage of the direct labour payroll? <u>minimal</u>
25. What is the current book value of the old equipment? <u>$4,500</u>
26. What is the estimated current value of the old equipment? <u>$3,000</u>

14
RESTRUCTURING AT MAYEKAWA[1]

I. Introduction

In the past, Japanese manufacturers emphasized "Expanding market share" or "Increasing sales volume" as their basic strategy. In order to expand their market share, they have had to withstand some tough competition from many other homogeneous competitors. Usually, their competition has been done through price competition, introducing new products, and diversification of products. This competition caused an increase in investment and also an increase in indirect jobs. The result was an inflated break-even point and a decreased profit.

In order to compensate for lower profits, they have aggressively continued Kaizen activities. But to be successful, at least two requirements are necessary:

- One is high economic growth and continuous growth of the economy generally.
- The other is the existence of a mass market.

However, after the recent economic recession, or after the bubble burst, they could not expect a high growth era, nor the existence of a mass market. In order to cope with these environmental changes, most Japanese manufacturers, especially large and mass production manufacturers, have had to take a similar road.

To cope with decreased sales/product volumes, they have been making desperate efforts to achieve a reduction of BEP (break-even point). As for the methods that can be used to achieve a reduction in the BEP, one is a reduction of the work force, especially reducing indirect workers, white collar people, and managers (the Japanese companies consider personnel expenses as a fixed cost). The other is to cut down all of the investments. It looks like a demassing, as defined by Robert Tomasko, author of "Downsizing," where they do not have any bright vision for the future. In this case, the employees have distrust in and are uneasy with the company and as a result, the company loses many excellent people. This causes a weakness in the competitive advantage of the company because of the loss in human resources power and the business situation of the company gets even worse. As a result, the company declines, and again needs to reduce the BEP.

Today, many Japanese manufacturers are adapting a so-called "demassing" type of downsizing. Their strategic direction is based on an old paradigm under a high economic growth era. The Japanese manufacturers have reached a turning point where they must cast off their old paradigm and find a new way under the new environment, as mentioned above.

Recently, in spite of tough economic stagnation, several vigorous manufacturing companies have arrived as newcomers. These companies not only have high growth but are financially excellent. They also have a high profile, are innovative, and have customer-driven thinking. Some of them are known as 21C companies, which designates vigorous companies operating into the next century.

Mayekawa gained a good reputation as a 21C company in Japan through its managerial innovation.

---

[1]This case was developed for use in classroom discussion and is not intended to necessarily illustrate appropriate or inappropriate management practices. The case author was Jinichiro Nakane, Waseda University, 1996. Frederique Balard, a doctoral student in the Graduate School of Management at Macquarie University, was the research associate who rewrote the case in 2000. The funding for this case production was provided by the Australian federal government's Department of Industry, Science and Resources.

II. Mayekawa: The Company

In order to find a new way to get out of the deadlock, people began to take notice of Mayekawa's management system.

Mayekawa is not a conventional company in Japan. It consists of over 100 small, legally independent companies called doppos. These are all affiliated through the Mayekawa group. Mayekawa has been considered in Japan as a decentralized and autonomous company and has been referred to as a successful reengineering company.

Mayekawa's major product lines are heavy refrigeration systems for commercial and industrial use and almost all are custom-engineered. Conventionally, the company is described as a manufacturer of large compressors and refrigeration systems but the value Mayekawa gives to its customer is primarily problem solving. The doppos consult, install, and operate systems as well as undertake research. They assist customers in identifying and overcoming their problems. Most solutions involve a core competence of thermal engineering but the doppos sometimes develop in other directions with their customers, if a solution takes them there. Each doppo within Mayekawa may focus on a particular customer or it may engage in production or in R & D. As a whole, the Mayekawa group is present in the following business domains and activities:

Products:
- Manufacturing and sales of refrigeration compressors and various kinds of gas compressors.
- Energy generators and reclaimers, steam expanders, very high temperature heat pumps, and steam compressors.
- Associated units, equipment, and packages.
- Helium screw compressors.
- Screw-type high-pressure liquid pumps.

Plant Engineering:
- Automated robot system for processing.
- Energy generation and heat recovery system.
- Large-scale refrigeration plants for agriculture, stock farming, and marine products industries.
- Optimum thermal control system.
- Various automated marine cooling systems.

Consulting Engineering Services:
- Total planning, design, installation, and operation services for agriculture, stock farming, marine products, and distribution industries.
- Thermal engineering R & D programs.

Mayekawa is financially very successful. Most years, the Mayekawa group's ROI [return on investment] exceeds 100 percent. However, the object of each doppo, and therefore of Mayekawa as a whole, is not to maximize profit, the traditional Western objective; nor is it to increase the market share, a traditional Japanese business objective (although Mayekawa has increased its market share). Rather, the objective of each doppo is just the same as any biological organism, i.e., simply to survive in its present form or in an adapted form.

> Mayekawa believes that the purpose of a company does not lie in gaining profit, in increasing market share, in adding large numbers of employees, or in growing just to be growing. Instead, Mayekawa's real purpose is to achieve the ability of all our people to find their own way and to make full use of their talents in harmony with nature under changing circumstances.

Survival is assured by paying very close attention to each customer, trying to make sure that everything done helps that customer to distinguish itself with its own customers. Most doppos are focused on a special market centred on a core customer. Masao Mayekawa, the president, insists that Mayekawa does not sell hardware and compete on price. Instead, Mayekawa complements the capabilities of each customer through a long-term partnership. The trite phrase "Selling solutions" does not quite capture the intent. Mayekawa not only helps its customers to solve a specific problem but assists its customers in overcoming all identified problems (identified by the customers or by Mayekawa).

Most doppos focus on servicing a specific market and consequently have a thorough understanding of it. If the core customer and its dependents must adapt to a new environment, the doppo helps it make the transition. If they die, the doppo must die or transform into something else. Following is an overview of Mayekawa as of 1993.

Capital:	U.S. $21 million (1993)
Gross sales:	U.S. $1.008 billion (1993)
Profit rate:	8–10% of sales/year (1989–1993)
Growth of sales:	8–10%/yen (1989–1993)
Number of employees:	
Japan	1,750 (1993)
Overseas	600
Number of doppos:	100 (1993)
Number of plants:	13 (4 in Japan, 9 overseas)(1993)

III. History of Mayekawa's Challenge

The First Stage.   Mayekawa was established in 1923 as a small, family-run company in the Fukagawa district of Tokyo, a skilled-craft section of the working class area that for centuries Japanese called "shitamachi." In the Edo era (1603–1867), when the shitamachi was at its cultural peak, the pride that skilled craftsmen took in their work was fearsome. This long tradition lives on in Mayekawa and it is the rootstock of the group's culture to this day.

At first, Mayekawa had no formal structure. Every worker had his own skill and function in the factory, but responsibility was never clearly defined. Each person did whatever was needed at the moment if he was capable of doing it and communication was carried out face-to-face. This organization formed naturally, like a growing family. Small, close-knit groups evolved, each overseen by an oyakata, or senior craftsman. No one could separate their personal time from their working time. Everyone's character, foibles, and family background were soon learned by everyone else. Communication was smooth and intimate. A culture evolved that prized thrift, hard work, craft pride, and teamwork.

This free-form organization generated little stress from its own internal politics, so it could flex to respond to the varied demands of customers and to a changing environment. A strong spirit of cooperation developed—"all for one and one for all." The roots of Mayekawa's culture grew in this period, which lasted until about 1960. When later forms of the organization failed to work as expected, the culture rejuvenated from its roots to grow into the much wider network that exists today.

The Second Stage: Bureaucracy Fails.   The 1960s were the era of high growth in Japan, and Mayekawa benefited from it. The company designed standard products for mass production, and volume increased so fast that the informal organization was swamped. Production of large volumes required a more efficient production system. To cope with this increase in production, a more bureaucratic management structure seemed to be necessary throughout the entire company. The fast-growing Mayekawa company split into functional departments: production, sales, development, and administration.

From the beginning, unhappiness clouded the growth of the bureaucratic structure. The assembly of compressors became more efficient with a bureaucratic system, but the process of customizing designs for various applications did not. Departmental separation created friction among former close associates. Worse, the walls between departments inhibited the flexibility to serve the customer.

The Third Stage: How Organic Thinking Began.   During the bureaucratic period from 1960–1969, the Mayekawa organism, too big to live in its old informality, looked for a new form to break free of its bureaucracy. One of the strong influences on its later development was its experience with a new Mexican subsidiary formed in 1964.

Aware that they had entered unknown territory, Mayekawa managers tried some new ideas to understand Mexican society and the nature of the Mexican market. The result was a cycle of concentration and dispersion that two decades later germinated the basic concept for the communication of business plans and other information within the doppo network.

In Mexico, concentration and dispersion evolved through trial and error. To understand the whole market, every Mexican employee (there weren't many in the beginning) was asked to create an overview of the market according to his or her specialty. These varied inputs were integrated into a total market picture and viewed more strategically. This was what was called "concentration." Based on this total market picture, an overall management plan was developed. This basic plan was given to each employee as a guide to their actions but not as a set of strict orders. This is what was called "dispersion."

About the time that this system was becoming established in Mexico, Masao Mayekawa became the company's third president at age 39. Viewing the unhappiness, he met with employees again and again, and asked them to think of ways to change the working style to break the confines of bureaucracy. He began a lifelong search for a better organization himself.

The young president had always been interested in biology, so in the 1960s his managerial philosophy was strongly influenced by reading a book, *The World's Living Things,* by the biologist Kinji Imanishi. According to Imanishi, the closer a living organism approaches its natural state, which is in harmony with its environment, the better are its chances of survival. That is, for any natural organism to live, it must be able to adapt to its surroundings. Organisms that can live in a range of habitats are able to adapt or compensate.

Mayekawa concluded that a company is a type of living organism. Therefore the same principle should apply to the Mayekawa organization, but how could a large organization be flexible enough? After many discussions with employees, a group network system was initiated in 1970. Mayekawa broke into a number of small divisions and flattened the organization, a change that sounds familiar to many companies today. Care was taken to have clear, regular communications between the divisions. Things improved but not enough. Too much bureaucracy still remained. A big organism cannot adapt as quickly as a small one even if they are flexible for their size. Thirteen years passed while Mayekawa struggled to find something better than flattening and decentralizing.

The Fourth Stage: Downscaling into Autonomous Units; The Formation of Doppos.   A mechanical thinker might refer to the formation of small independent companies as downsizing. "Downscaling" is more descriptive because Mayekawa did not lose people. In 1983 it began separating operating divisions into more autonomous "cells"—the smallest possible units that could serve a customer. The doppos, which directly concentrate on customers, have only 10 to 20 persons

FIGURE 1

Relationship between doppos, blocks, and zensha

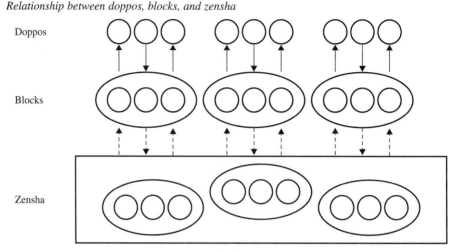

Doppos

Blocks

Zensha

in each. Some of the plant doppos are a little bigger—up to 100 persons. However, each doppo became legally independent—a business responsible for its own survival. The objective was for each doppo to take an imaginative approach to serve its unique market niche environment.

At the outset, downscaling provoked apprehension that the company was destroying itself. Three of the most commonly voiced reservations were:

1. R & D will stagnate because small doppos cannot support it.
2. Communication between many small units will be weak.
3. The doppos will splinter from each other—lose interest in other units or in Mayekawa as a whole.

As it turned out, the fears were unfounded. The pressure for each doppo to meet its own customer needs required them to form different kinds of ties throughout the group. All units relied on a common technology of thermal engineering. The doppos were still dependent on each other, so the patterns of communication grew where communication was really needed, and these linkages eliminated structural blockages or delays. The root culture of the old Mayekawa nourished the growth of a network of doppos, and the new organization began to evolve.

The Fifth Stage: Networking.   Nine years elapsed from the time the doppos were formed until 1992, when the doppo-block-zensha system was formed to better integrate the doppo network (see Figure 1). The details of Mayekawa's network organization as it currently functions can be better appreciated after reviewing the following framework.

IV. Organizational and Managerial System at Mayekawa

Relationship between Doppo, Block, and Zensha within Mayekawa.   From an organizational viewpoint, Mayekawa is composed of many legally independent affiliates (legally chartered companies, legally independent companies), called doppos. Doppo is the smallest business unit of the organization at Mayekawa. Each doppo is an independent company of 10–20 people and has the responsibility of: marketing, sales, engineering, manufacturing, accounting, after service, and general affairs. Each doppo has all the management decisions and responsibilities. Therefore, each doppo has to survive as a co-destiny lot. The leader (president) of each doppo is selected by the general will of all members of each doppo. The total number of doppos in 1993 was 100 (domestic: 78; overseas: 22 companies). Several doppos make a group based on an area and/or a market. This group is called a "block" and its members are the representatives of the several doppos that form this group. Blocks are used to:

- Promote and exchange information between each doppo.
- Complement/support each doppo member as they are mutually complementary.
- Link the doppos to the Mayekawa group.

Zensha (overall Mayekawa group) is the headquarters of Mayekawa. Its functions are limited only to support and act as a consulting service for the doppos and the block, and include the following:

- Basic/long-term R & D.
- Supply funds/capital for the doppo.
- Public relations for doppos as Mayekawa group.
- Solving problems that cannot be solved at block and/or doppo level.

Figure 1 shows the relationship between the doppos, blocks, and zenshas. As mentioned before, these three layers are not bureaucratic layers for the purpose of management but are supporting functions and are mutually complementary with each other, promoting the exchange of information.

Doppos: The Customer Adaptive Units.   The doppo forms the base of the doppo-block-zensha network shown in Figure 1. Note that the diagram is inverted. The blocks and the zensha support the doppos; they do not command them. Within Mayekawa, it is often said that each doppo encapsulates the means and abilities to find one's own way and to use one's special talents in harmony with the doppo's ever-changing environment. This defines what a doppo should be and it is the most important concept in understanding Mayekawa. All doppos are independently chartered within Japanese commercial law; all have a separate P & L statement. Within Mayekawa we more often call these units "LIAs"—the English acronym for legally independent affiliates. Every part of Mayekawa except headquarters has now become a doppo in this sense. Headquarters remains the original rootstock of Mayekawa. It has learned to reproduce itself many times over as a doppo in a different environment but all the parts are linked through the network. For instance, central R & D is attached to headquarters. It is free to contract research programs that do not directly support field doppos but R & D is also highly dependent on the field doppos for intelligence. All the doppos need each other with differing degrees of affinity, so communication links are necessary.

A typical field doppo might be called a sales branch so that those uninitiated to Mayekawa's way of thinking quickly grasp what it does in conventional business terms but rarely with full understanding. These doppos do "sell" relatively standard equipment when that is what the customer needs but they do much more than that. A doppo should be very detailed, comprehensive, and original in approaching each customer. Therefore it should determine its own marketing strategy, "becoming a new mutation of Mayekawa" as the needs of each customer's environment unfold. A doppo is responsible for system design—which may be a combination of relatively standard components, or a truly unique concept. It is also responsible for production of equipment, for obtaining help—and for the manufacturing of quality results.

For example, one of the doppos served a customer that manufactures, markets, and distributes frozen pizza. That doppo conceived a project to give its customer the best-tasting frozen pizza in the Far East. The taste of pizza depends on the ingredients, the recipe, and the thermal cycle from preparation to consumption. The "big equipment" portion of the project was a freeze blaster for pizza. Members of the doppo designed the blaster. Some of them worked at the plant—in a more active role than merely customer representative—to realize the design objectives of the blaster. However, the total project encompassed working with the customer and numerous other parties to assure, as best as possible, the optimum thermal history from preparation to consumption.

Another core customer is a specialized bakery for bread. At first, they saw the need to control the climate of one room in their total process. Discussions and exploration of the total environment for bread continued for about a year. Then the customer discovered for themselves that a controlled climate from raw material to consumption would improve product quality and reduce product waste while also cutting total energy costs. This insight allowed them to reposition themselves in a niche of the bread market.

This kind of work requires individuals to master a broad range of expertise. A rule of thumb is that a newly hired employee at Mayekawa does not begin to pay for himself for at least 10 years. First he must learn the total business and how to use the "Mayekawa human network." Daunting as this is, Japanese graduates are attracted to Mayekawa because they ultimately have more freedom than in a big company.

Significantly, the one area in which the doppos do not have full autonomy is recruitment of the professional staff, a requirement of affiliation in the Mayekawa network. Headquarters hires professionals, one reason being that doppos are too lean for recruiting. About half have work experience and the other half are straight from school. After that, doppos freely transfer professionals between themselves and they hire local staff. Hiring to a common standard preserves the Mayekawa culture by seeing that the key people in each doppo come from Mayekawa rootstock. This practice helps differentiate Mayekawa from a "financial franchise system."

The Doppo-Block Network.   The legally independent affiliates, doppos, all belong to one or more forums called blocks depending on the types of markets they serve or the region in which they operate. Blocks exchange resources and information, either at regular meetings or through other means. Thirteen blocks have been established to date.

Blocks are not incorporated. They have no staff or management. They do not represent a higher level of management. All participants in block activities are representatives of their doppo. The role of a block is not governance but assistance and exchange between legally independent companies.

Block meetings are substantive. The block may decide to exchange personnel between doppos within that block or with other blocks. Most transfers are between doppos. The block may decide how to bail out a member doppo with a problem, technical or otherwise. It may formulate an overall market strategy or even an approach to a specific customer. Blocks are a link between each doppo and the overall company, or zensha.

To make decisions, blocks must judge the performance of each doppo. No block uses a fixed formula but by custom, doppos are judged about half on total financial strength and half on other factors, such as the status of its human talent and technical expertise, its potential to adapt to change, its creativity working with its market, etc. Overall doppo ratings are in five classes: A-B-N-C-D (where "N" stands for neutral). Usually about 15 percent of the doppos get a D rating, and those are deemed to need advice or assistance.

Zensha means the whole company, or the counsel of the entire company. Headquarters is only one part of it. Just as at a block meeting, everyone goes to a zensha meeting as a representative of their doppo, or of their block. The zensha tackles problems too big for blocks and doppos to deal with alone. Typical zensha concerns: overall marketing direction and opportunities (stopping or starting doppos), major geographical business issues, and determining the priorities for R & D. That is, the overall strategic business direction of the army of blocks and doppos is determined collectively by the zensha. No edicts come from headquarters. Functioning according to this method takes a well-honed approach to communication and decision making. The total doppo-block-zensha network is intended to be an integrative mechanism.

A first reaction to this form of "organization" is that decision making must be painfully slow. Some of it is, but not the critical decision making. Each doppo can react to local changes very quickly, and "call the fire department" for help if necessary. Mayekawa does not need to make high-level decisions about mass markets because it doesn't have any. It survives on a large number of very small markets.

The doppo-block-zensha system is called a "heterarchy" rather than a hierarchy. Almost all operating decisions are taken within the doppos themselves or within the blocks, which are creatures of the doppos. The zensha is a means of integrating blocks and doppos, but integration depends on common culture and smooth communication, not on a command and control structure.

Each of the major thrusts of the Mayekawa system cannot be easily understood outside the context of the others. That is, the zensha-block-doppo system supports the market strategy of manufacturing quality results, and vice versa, and neither would be possible in the same way if they were not supported by the basic culture of the company.

Zensha—Functions of Headquarters.   Headquarters consists of President Masao Mayekawa, the staff, and R & D, almost 160 persons in total, whose mission is to support the doppos. Headquarters does not "boss" independent doppos. However, headquarters does have specific duties. It takes care of public relations: it operates the Mayekawa welfare system, retirement funds, insurance, etc. Headquarters also operates the computer network communication system for the entire Mayekawa group. It acts as the bank for all the doppos, receiving funds, disbursing loans, and staking new doppo start-ups, which means that it fertilizes entrepreneurial risk taking from time to time.

However, the most important headquarters function is the care and feeding of the Mayekawa culture—that which makes Mayekawa what it is, and which simplifies the human communication between far-flung doppos. President Mayekawa has occasionally been called the "spiritual adviser." The primary means of culture-feeding is the initial hiring of professionals and the counseling of them. It has become very effective. Most Mayekawa employees identify more with the common culture of Mayekawa than with their local doppo.

The common features of Mayekawa are a core technology and shared respect for the primary values: thrift, hard work, craft pride, teamwork, and local initiative. A "no rules from headquarters" policy reinforces the culture. Management manuals that dictate detailed procedures or rules of corporate behaviour are a no-no. All doppos operate by a recognizably similar pattern but each doppo creates rules to adapt to the environment in which it finds itself.

V. Coordination and Communication at Mayekawa

Doppos are encouraged to communicate with each other but not to report to anyone. Written communications should be few in number and short in length. A large volume of paper is considered a sign of poor communication. Employees in doppos soon learn to keep communications short and simple and to rely heavily on effective informal communications.

Two types of communication exist:

- Standardized data processed by computer.
- Information interpreted by a person.

Human communication is more subjective but more important because experienced people can cut through the routine to determine what is important or different for a specific problem. The most formal communications process within Mayekawa is preparing and sharing business plans among doppos. This process illustrates the principles of concentration, dispersion, and brevity. Each doppo prepares an annual business plan, called a *kigyokakeikaku* in Japanese. All members of a doppo join in preparing an annual *kigyokakeikaku* that expresses what they want to become in the future.

Since the doppos operate in many different environments, no standard format can cover all the cases but in the final form, all business plans are carefully thought out and tightly written on only one or two sheets of paper.

The preparation cycle for the *kigyokakeikaku,* or business plan briefs, begins with a zensha meeting to create a planning guideline for blocks. Block meetings refine and add to the zensha guideline, then disperse it to their doppos to create their own *kigyokakeikaku*. After the doppos' plans are prepared, they become input for developing a block plan at a block meeting, followed by concentration of the block and doppo plans to prepare a zensha plan at a zensha meeting.

After zensha and block plans are finished and dispersed to the doppos, changes to the original doppos' *kigyokakeikaku* are minimal. Block and zensha planning considers a broader strategic perspective than the doppos, although some of the same people consider plans at all three levels.

The doppo-block-zensha network system is intended to further stimulate useful communication by promoting ties between the people of the doppos. The questions the doppos ask of each other during the *kigyokakeikaku* cycle serve as a take-off point for "benchmarking." In this way, each doppo builds relationships directly with other doppos without seniority of hierarchy obstructing the flow of information. The lines of communication thus open where there is interest.

These new ties are forming a new culture within Mayekawa, difficult to explain but evident in people's behavior and thinking. To understand its essence, one must look beyond their patterns of behavior. This new culture is clearly the descendent of the original one formed during the earliest stage of Mayekawa's history. Today's relationships between globally scattered Mayekawa individuals and doppos are somewhat like seeing the seeds of the old Mayekawa culture blown around the world, then taking root in a different environment. The resulting growth is not identical but it has a familiar pattern.

Corporate Culture and Strategic Directions.   A corporate culture at Mayekawa has evolved from its history, many forces of change, and the president's philosophy. Especially, a way of thinking by the president has had a very strong influence on the corporate culture, configuration, and the management systems.

As mentioned before, distinctive features of Mayekawa's culture and strategic directions are:

- Human-oriented thinking.
- Open mindedness.
- Enhancing a "spirit of the enterprise."
- Finding and achieving customers' needs in cooperation with them.
- "Flexible and quick response" to the environmental changes.

In relation to the corporate culture at Mayekawa, people-ware or human resources management (HRM) is at the heart of the management system. The following items are special features of HRM at Mayekawa.

- Almost all decisions at each doppo are done by the general will of all crews of each doppo.
- Every member in each doppo has a kind of multifunctional role and is also one of the executives.
- The president of each doppo is a coordinator to all members of the doppo.

VI. Conclusion

Japanese manufacturers have reached a turning point in casting off their old paradigm to find a new way of understanding the big environmental changes. Many companies are in a deadlock situation but some vigorous companies have set sail for a new way into the next century.

In this case, a field study approach has been adopted on one of the alternatives from the 21C companies. Through the study, the following items as key messages have become evident:

1. A company that is always striving for survival is:

   a. "Agile" to change.

   b. Making full use of "entrepreneurship."

2. In order to increase productivity under the knowledge-based society, the "morale" of people is the key.

3. Fragmented and specialized work rules need rethinking.

4. A holonic management system is one of the tools of tomorrow.

References

Web site: *www.mycomj.co.jp/eenterprise.html*

Nakane, J. "Holonic Manufacturing," Bulletin no. 25, 1995, System Science Institute, Waseda University.

Iwasaki, Y., and Nakane, J. "Downscaling to Adapt Your Environment: Mayekawa Manufacturing Co. Ltd.," Target Vol. 11, no. 4, 1995, AME.

Nakane, J. "Manufacturing in the 21C," Bulletin no. 20, 1989, System Science Institute, Waseda University.

Mayekawa, M. "Mukyoso shakai eno chosen," 1991, Mayekawa shippan.

Vollmaan, T., Oliff, M., Collins, R., and Nakane, J. "Manufacturing Restructuring," Bulletin no. 23, 1992, System Science Institute, Waseda University.

Iwasaki, Y., and Tsuyuki, E. "Management of Mayekawa Manufacturing Company."

Paper titled: Convergence vs. Divergence Co.

15
PETERS AND BROWNES GROUP (WESTERN AUSTRALIA):
Review of Best Practice in the Adoption and Management of Technology[1]

Introduction

This case focuses on the evolution of technological innovation in the Peters and Brownes Group of Western Australia over the period 1985 to 1995. It concentrates on the Peters WA Ltd (Peters) ice cream manufacturing facility and deals with various phenomena relating to innovation and technological uptake within the company. The main features of the evolutionary processes that outline the company's technological transition are the construction of a new ice cream factory in 1987 in association with a commitment to ongoing equipment and product development and management innovation. This has led to a widening and deepening of Peters's product portfolio as well as total market expansion through export. Supporting the company's total growth is the company's SQP (Safety, Quality, and Productivity) program, introduced in 1992 along with an enterprise bargaining agreement.

In specific terms, the Peters case highlights how a company has integrated new technology in manufacturing along with the functional integration of marketing, innovation, and quality. Consequently, the Peters case illustrates how a company has evolved from one with a local market focus and relatively outdated hard and soft technologies to one with a strong export focus underpinned by benchmark standards in the utilisation of leading edge technologies. The fact that this reorientation has been provoked by customer-driven product innovation remains the central thrust of this case.

Affirmation of the events that have transformed Peters from a mature but stagnant enterprise into a dynamic world class competitor stems from a visitation in 1994 by a consortium of ice cream manufacturers from around the world that regarded the company as having world class products and technological facilities.

Company Background

The Peters and Brownes Group has a long history in Western Australia (WA) extending back to the turn of the century. The forerunner to Peters was the Perth Ice and Refrigeration Company, founded in 1887. An American, Mr. Peters had established ice cream manufacturing businesses in almost every capital city in Australia, and in 1929 he bought the ice company and formed the Peters American Delicacy Company. The Peters entity commenced ice cream manufacturing as well as producing dairy products such as milk and cheese. Except for the Perth operations, every other site was consolidated into a single company. These were acquired by a number of corporate owners, which included Adsteam, then Pacific Dunlop, and more recently in 1995, Nestle Adsteam's strategic intent aimed to consolidate the marketing and R & D thrust of the various

[1]This case was developed for use in classroom discussion and is not intended to necessarily illustrate appropriate or inappropriate management practices. Case authors: Alan Brown and Marc Saupin, Edith Cowan University, 1996. The funding for this case production was provided by the Australian federal government's Department of Industry, Science and Resources.

holdings while at the same time corporatising the various entities under the one brand. This strategy was carried on by Pacific Dunlop and has recently been acquired by Nestle.

During that time, Peters (WA) remained largely unaffected by the succession of buyouts, deciding instead to remain independent of events taking shape in the eastern states. The geographical isolation of WA was partly responsible for this. In 1983 Peters in Brisbane was merged with Pauls Ice Cream to form Australian United Foods, while in Perth, Peters acquired Pauls Ice Cream in an endeavour to consolidate their market leadership. Today, the group is the largest producer and distributor of frozen and chilled foods in Western Australia with its base in Perth, the capital city of Western Australia.

While the name Peters is synonymous with ice cream, the Peters and Brownes Group also produce dairy and meat products as well as bulk stock feed. In relation to these products, the main divisions of the group are: Peters Ice Cream, Brownes Dairy, Peters Creamery, Clover Meats, and Milne Feeds. For the most part, this corporate portfolio has some strategic appeal in that Peters is able to control the volume and quality of its raw materials such as fresh milk and cream. Clover Meats adds to the Peters and Brownes product portfolio with a wide array of value-added pre-cooked frozen food products.

Diagram of operating companies structure

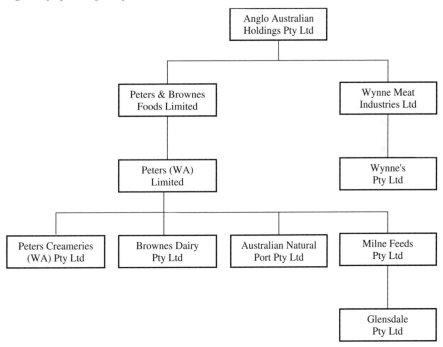

Apart from its own brand products, it is also under license to produce Pauls ice cream and Cadbury ice cream and dairy products. The Balcatta premises also house Peters's distribution centre for its products and for a variety of branded products for other companies, and is effectively the hub of a distribution network spanning some 2.5 million square kilometres in WA alone.

The company has developed overseas markets in a number of Asian countries, including Singapore, Malaysia, Hong Kong, and Japan and is now a major Australian exporter of ice cream.

Much of Peters's international business is conducted with industrial food buyers such as Fujya and Akagi in Japan, who in turn market to the Japanese retail sector.

The Peters and Brownes Group is a privately owned Western Australian company that ranks 51 on the list of Australia's largest 500 private companies (*Business Review Weekly,* 27/7/95). With approximately 60 percent share of the Western Australian ice cream market, sales turnover in 1994 was AUD 300 million.

In 1994, exports were about 25 percent of sales. Such sales are somewhat variable since they depend on the business fortunes of overseas partners. For instance, the Borden Company in Japan who was one of the strategic partners sold their ice cream interests to Lotte in 1994, resulting in the termination of a large contract.

Approximately 1,100 people are employed throughout the entire group with nearly 500 of these in the ice cream plant and distribution centre. A large proportion of the process workers are casual employees due largely to the seasonal demand for the product, although new markets in the northern hemisphere are helping to balance employment throughout the year.

The company mission is "To profitably satisfy customer needs within and outside Australia for food ingredients by utilising our competitive advantages in the production, processing, marketing, and distribution of quality food and food ingredients."

Quality Policy Statement

The Peters and Brownes Group is Western Australia's largest food manufacturer and distributor. We market dairy products statewide, nationally and overseas. The nature of our business demands a high standard of professionalism. We must deliver quality consistently.

Under the Safety, Quality and Productivity programme (SQP), the Group is committed to the quality management systems needed to give us a competitive edge. Our objective is to produce products that meet customer and legislative expectations of quality and safety.

To achieve these objectives, the company will maintain an effective quality assurance programme which integrates with other management functions and complies with AS/NZS ISO 9002. The determination of whether products meet customer and regulatory requirements before release will be made only on objective evidence of quality.

The quality and consistency of our products is the responsibility of every one in the organisation at all times.

This statement is made to underline the board's commitment to the process of continued quality improvement. Properly implemented this will lead to company success and employee satisfaction.

Issue Date 8th June 1995
GS Laitt
Managing Director

Factors Setting the Context of Change

In analysing change within the Peters and Brownes Group, the focus is not on a single event but rather, the process of continuous improvement from around 1985 to the present (1995). This evolutionary process is marked by a change in ownership that provoked a dramatic shift in management attitudes toward technological change, a commitment to product innovation and market expansion beyond WA's borders.

Up until the early 1980s, Peters was producing ice cream using outmoded ice cream making equipment located in a number of old buildings in central Perth. Manufacturing was relatively labour intensive and there was little or no R & D into either new product development or capital equipment upgrade. The R & D that did take place locally was confined mainly to providing product range extensions and solutions to operational problems. As a consequence, the company's product lines had remained relatively narrowly defined for many years. The main factor that enabled

Peters to maintain their market leadership in the local Perth market was the company's name, which had been established solely on the basis of product quality, and the extensive distribution infrastructure.

In 1982 Peters first established the R & D department under Adrian Tutan, focusing on new product development for the local market. In the same year, Dr. Nigel Thomas, a science graduate from Oxford University and a recent employee of industrial R & D at Unilever, was appointed to the newly created position of R & D manager. The company set about expanding the role of the fledgling R & D department and encompassing marketing as the fundamental driving force behind the company's future growth. In the course of events, Mr. A.K. Ching was appointed as export marketing manager and with direct commercial experience in Asia, was able to give the R & D and marketing team the much-needed insight into marketing in Asia. These moves signaled the company's intention to diversify both its product and market portfolios and the tacit recognition of the role that technological change would play in the company's future.

The impetus for this reorientation began to emerge around 1984. With the ownership of Peters slowly undergoing change it was becoming increasingly obvious that product quality along narrow lines was not sufficient to sustain market dominance over the long term. This recognition was mainly derived from Mr. Graham Laitt, a lawyer by profession, who between 1986 and 1990 gradually bought all the shares in Peters and took over the role of managing director in 1988. Over this period, Graham devoted considerable efforts to developing a sustainable export focus, attended to new purchases of capital equipment and the refurbishment of existing equipment, and with the rest of the executive team, set about expanding the number of product lines for export markets.

Thus, prior to the new ownership, the management culture of the company had not been one in which product innovation was a driving force, nor had there been much serious attention focused on technological upgrade. By and large, Peters had for many years seen itself as a Western Australian-based ice cream producer that faced very limited competition from interstate or overseas, due in part to WA's geographic isolation, but also because their name was historically linked to ice cream. In the perceived absence of either market or competitive pressures, sufficient to provoke the need for change, management attitudes had remained complacent by largely ignoring the subtle but perceptible shifts occurring in their company's market, competitive, and technological environments.

Recognition of the Need to Change

Internal Drivers.   Several factors help to explain the new direction that the company took from about the mid-1980s onwards. First, the ownership of the company had changed. The new managing director, Graham Laitt, had the necessary entrepreneurial skills and vision and saw considerable opportunities for Peters. At the time of takeover, the company was seen as a Western Australian-focused company with only about five percent of turnover in Singapore and Hong Kong. Second, a more strategic focus was adopted that envisaged Western Australia as a major company base for tackling national and international markets, in particular, the latter. Third, the existing ice cream manufacturing facilities were underutilised. The company had acquired a large tract of land in 1972 at Balcatta, a northern Perth suburb, and in 1978 built a fully automated frozen food warehouse and distribution centre on the site. The current arrangements between manufacturing and central distribution meant transferring stock some 15 kilometres between factory and warehouse. The choice of relocating manufacturing to a Greenfield site offered greater logistical economies of scale and overall improved operational efficiencies. Moreover, the capital equipment at the previous Perth factory had undergone a series of incremental improvements over time so that production could keep in step with the growing export market. However, production ceilings were achieved quite rapidly due primarily to the lack of space for expansion. The facilities at Balcatta offered expansion possibilities as well as enough incentive to invest other kinds of capital equipment that embodied the latest technology.

The appointment of Nigel Thomas as R & D manager to the company's executive team in 1986 was tangible evidence of the recognised importance that the company was attaching to R & D in product, equipment, and processes operations. The person appointed to this position had a background with a large international company (Unilever) and had joined Peters in 1982. He was later appointed to general manager, ice cream manufacturing and technical divisions. He considered that having a technologically trained and oriented person on the management team helped focus the company to look toward the future rather than maintaining an operational perspective of remaining stable.

Finally, the new managing director felt that the company had an unacceptable profit performance and was seeking to lift performance.

External Factors.   Increased globalisation of companies with international brands creating greater international competition poses a particular threat to medium-sized companies such as the Peters and Brownes Group. These global companies are also restructuring by divesting noncore activities, making them leaner and more competitive. At the same time they are acquiring core businesses outside their geographical location. While the company was not facing any immediate or strong competitive threats within Western Australia, Peters was a mature but stagnant company. It did hold a considerable share of the Western Australian market but to the new owners the opportunities that lay await offshore offered a challenge. Several factors help explain why the export focus came about. First, the globalisation of industry, across the board, meant that international food producers were able to compete on the basis of economies of scale and scope in product offering. It would, therefore, have only been a matter of time before international competitors reached the WA market and outpaced Peters on price and product offering. Streets Ice Cream had started selling in the WA market in 1983 so it could be considered a potential threat. Peters faces the situation of having to decide whether to reduce product range in order to focus resources to face this challenge.

Second, the Western Australian market remains small (1.6 million people in 1995) and therefore had limited expansion opportunities; not so much in scale since Peters had a dominant market position. Moreover, with the brand name history and with the Peters Group under the ownership of Pacific Dunlop in the eastern states market, Peters was unable to take the Peters brand name east.

Third, the inclusion of ice cream and related products in the list of products under GATT [General Agreement on Tariffs and Trade] in 1990 meant a freeing up of export markets in general. The removal of quotas for ice cream in Japan offered a specific opportunity for expansion. Finally, both Graham Laitt and the executive team considered that the need for technological change across product, process, and production, coupled with innovative management and marketing, was fundamental to future growth and such change could only be realised by an internationally oriented company. These factors were sufficient impetus for change that resulted in the first trial shipments to Japan in 1988.

Entry into the Japanese market was a milestone in the technological evolution of Peters. It effectively set the company along a path that depended upon an ongoing effort toward maintaining a sustainable innovative culture that encompasses a continuous process of technological uptake. The Japanese market for ice cream is led by what could only be termed sophisticated industrial buyers who scrutinise all aspects of Peters's production, product quality, packaging, and distribution in very precise terms. This attention to detail has compelled Peters to upgrade every aspect of their operations.

The main conclusion drawn is that the opportunities for expansion and growth arose primarily from recognition of the subtle but important changes taking place external to Peters as opposed to any immediate competitor threats or a sharp move in the tastes and preferences in the local Perth market.

Process (and Content) of Change

The process of transition driven by the adoption and management of new technologies is not one that can be conveniently outlined by a single event that took place within the Peters and Brownes Group. While it commenced in the mid- to late-eighties with the construction of a new factory and the development of an R & D focus, it should be seen as a continuous process that links product innovations and process technology with a sound technological capital base. Management and marketing coupled with effective R & D are much needed and therefore remain fundamental to this process.

The milieu for the management and uptake of new technology in Peters

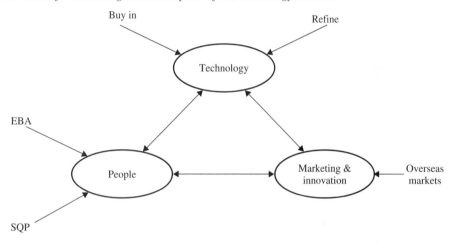

The Milieu for the Management and Uptake of New Technology in Peters

The model describes the milieu for innovation in Peters. Certain aspects between the linkages that exist between these broad functional areas are particularly enlightening and intrinsically innovative. For example, R & D and marketing are coupled together in both a strategic manner and evident in an operational sense.

The following discussion of the process and elements of the transition focuses on the three main elements as outlined in the diagram.

A. New Technology (Technological Capability/Technology Strategy).   Both the engineering manager (Arnold Cooper) and the manager of technology (Nigel Thomas) played a significant role in seeking the most appropriate technology to use in the new factory. This comprised mostly new manufacturing equipment sourced from a variety of suppliers from around the world. It was not exclusively ice cream manufacturing equipment but also came from all areas of the food industry. Some of the equipment such as some freezers and filling equipment came from the old site. However, the new production facility had a significant level of computer control. Employees also had some say in the plant layout, particularly from an operational logistics point of view.

Completion of the new manufacturing facility in 1987 dramatically increased production capacity and provided scope for considerable increases in output coupled with flexibility of operation. Apart from providing a better facility for production in the local marketplace, this new facility was also designed to provide the basis for enabling the company to launch new products and develop new markets. The challenge therefore has been to seek new markets through exports and new product lines. Exports offered an effective means of increasing capacity utilisation.

A significant element that brought about a modernisation of the plant was the computer aided specifications and manufacturing, implemented from around 1987, which effectively provides for constant monitoring of raw material inputs, mixing and dispensing (spraying/pouring), freezing, and subsequent warehousing throughout the entire operations of the plant. The computer network is also integrated with the company's financial and accounting systems to provide an overall control facility.

An important feature of this was the development of computer-controlled processes. Modeled on a system used in breweries, the company wrote its own program that enabled specifications on a program logic controller (computer) to drive the ice cream factory.

While this meant considerable time in development (approximately 5 percent of the factory cost in 1987) since no package was available "off the shelf" and since it required considerable detail, the benefits have been flexibility, integrity, and confidentiality. Factory employees are able to obtain computer printouts of daily production requirements.

The extensive cold storage and distribution centre not only handles Peters's products but also those of other companies. This includes a 7,000 pallets cold store that is fully computerised and uses automated guided vehicles.

Forms of technology employed by the Peters and Brownes Group at its ice cream plant and distribution centre include:

- Automated storage and retrieval.
- Automated guided vehicles.
- Computer aided manufacturing.
- Computer numerically controlled machines.
- Computer integrated manufacturing including computer controlled formulating and mixing and computer aided integrated specification system.

At the most aggregate level of conceptualisation, ice cream manufacturing [see the accompanying diagram] can be described as the intersection of mixing and freezing technologies applied to fluid and semi-fluid mediums under legally enforced and industry-prescribed quality guidelines:

- Mixing of ingredients.
- Pasteurisation and homogenisation.
- Packaging of mixtures or moulding products.
- Freezing of products.
- Testing, weighing of products.
- Storage of final goods.

Diagram of ice cream manufacturing processes

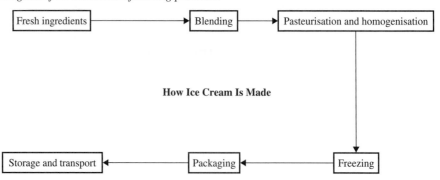

How Ice Cream Is Made

Aspects of the ice cream manufacturing facility have been continuously developed and upgraded since the initial construction. For example, in 1990 a new facility was introduced that has the ability to handle real rather than compound chocolate for ice cream production. A new syrup-manufacturing machine has been introduced along with a strawberry processing plant to enable fresh strawberries to be put into ice cream. These were developed using the company's engineering expertise to modify equipment to suit the company's production requirements.

Technology plays an important role in the Japanese market. As indicated above, new business development in this competitive market usually involves the Japanese making inspections of the company's technological facilities before products are discussed in detail. They tend to regard technological capability as being the first most significant detail to be discussed in any potential contract deal.

While it has been reported that Australian industry sees improved technological capabilities as being only fifth in order of reasons for growth (Pace of Change 103), the case of Peters shows that it was a necessary precondition that then permitted development of export markets and so on. Technology was one of the enablers. Substantial new technology has also been installed at the group's Brownes Dairy operations and the Creamery in the 1990s.

The company has had a technology strategy since 1985. This was considered to be rather rare within Australian food processing companies at this point in time. It is also integrated into the corporate plan, which provides recognition that technology is a strength of the company and a normal part of the business.

B. R & D and Product Innovation (Development of an Innovation Culture).   As indicated above, prior to the late 1980s, innovation had not been recognised as part of the culture within Peters. Since the mid-eighties, R & D has been seen more in terms of a benefit rather than a cost to the business. During the past 10 years, steps have been taken to develop such a culture in aspects of:

- Product development.
- Process development.
- Management and systems improvement.

The technology team at the Peters and Brownes Group is responsible for three things: R & D per se, quality, and the laboratories. They link with four main areas of the company operations: new business, sales, domestic markets, and operations [see accompanying diagram].

Linkages between R & D and other activities

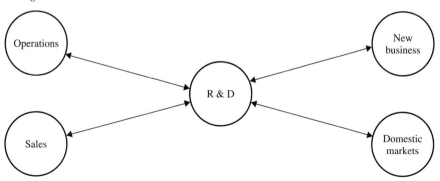

Fifty percent of the budget for R & D is for new business. The technology division also conducts contract research for other food companies and government agencies. The Japanese are also involved in R & D operations at the Balcatta plant. Certification to AS 3902 in 1994 was also largely prompted by the move into the Japanese market. The R & D division is also involved in the development of new products for other companies such as Japanese ice cream manufacturers and also conducts contract R & D for mainly Japanese companies.

Marketing and R & D play an important role in product innovation and developing new products for the local markets and overseas. An export R & D section has been operational since 1988. New product design is often driven by customers, particularly those in overseas markets. There is also R & D that looks at developing new products for the local market.

A second element of the Peters strategy has been product innovation through linking research and development and marketing. The position of general manager, marketing and technology was created in 1994. The incumbent is the previous manager of ice cream manufacturing and technical divisions.

Benchmarking is used to measure/monitor process innovation. Local and international visits are continually used to examine new technology that might be used. In 1995 the operations at some Western Australian breweries have been examined for possible ideas. Overseas companies have generally been happy to allow benchmarking since they don't see a Western Australian company as a competitive threat.

The demands placed on Peters to effect dramatic improvements to their products is best illustrated in preparing the Hazelnut Roll, a chocolate enclosed ice cream confectionary, for the Japanese market. It was the first time a WA company had used real chocolate, which required substantial modifications to chocolate spraying equipment and a measure of training and retraining for some of the company's more experienced equipment operators. It also involved developing a new formulation in the chocolate to stop it cracking since the Japanese buyers would reject the product as opposed to the WA market that seemed to have less fastidious preferences. This required designing and manufacturing new blending tanks incorporating innovative design and assembly compatible with existing manufacturing infrastructure.

Moreover, Japanese buyers were brutal when it came to quality control and hygiene. For example, the legal limit for bacterial content is 100,000 per gram; Australian legal requirement is 50,000 per gram; the Japanese industry code established by the Japanese industry body, JICA, demanded less than 10,000 per gram. While other Australian competitors rejected such standards of quality claiming that it was not feasible or at the very least sustainable, Peters responded and now consistently delivers products with bacterial counts around the 300 per gram mark.

Having painstakingly responded to the Japanese buyers' requests, the lessons drawn and the quality improvements that have followed have been transferred to their domestic WA market. While this has delivered quite considerable benefits to Peters, it also means that the WA consumer has benefited. Furthermore, where Peters's range was some 150 individual products in 1983, by 1995 their product portfolio has increased to around 350. Many of these products are sold to the WA market. Therefore, local consumers have received an increased choice of products coupled with world standards in quality.

Certain details relating to the relationship between Peters and its Japanese buyers are interesting and deserve brief mention. For example, all aspects of Peters's operations, from manufacturing and quality control through to product development and packaging, are developed by Peters's employees working very closely with their counterparts in the Japanese buyer organisation. In the case of new product development and launch, for instance, this has led to a reduction in the time to market (idea to shelf: 3 months), which is fundamental to sustainable competitive advantage in this industry. Peters itself organises its activities into new business units that draw on all functional areas of the organisation. As well as close interaction taking place between the members of the new business unit, each member, depending of course on circumstances, then opens dialogue with his or her counterpart in the Japanese buyer organisation. In effect, this producer-user interaction has formed the basis of a strategic technical and economic alliance between Peters and its overseas partners and is a model being repeated as the cornerstone of their strategy for international expansion.

By 1995, equipment cannot keep in step with the volume of export demand. The allocation of resources for R & D shows product (50–60 percent), process (20–30 percent), and capital equipment (15–20 percent). The heavy emphasis on product R & D is to be expected given the short life cycles of ice cream products in the Japanese market (often less than six months) and that ice cream manufacturing equipment does require upgrade but the time period over which this generally occurs is quite long. In fact some of the equipment utilised by Peters in 1995 was some 20 years old.

C. Work Organisation and Management.   The 1990s has seen a strong focus on improving quality and productivity through improved work processes. These come under two measures, an enterprise agreement and the Safety, Quality, and Productivity (SQP) program. The changing Australian industrial relations context has been one important impetus for this.

In March 1992, the company and four unions represented at the Balcatta site signed a "Memorandum of Understanding," which established the SQP program. This led to removal of some demarcation barriers and the establishment of a single bargaining unit. It also meant that general managers had to take greater responsibility for management of people.

Also in March 1992, the SQP program was commenced and in July 1992 it won funding from the federal government as part of the best practice initiative. The objectives of this program included:

- To create a culture of continuous improvement.
- To foster employee participation.
- To improve employee skills.
- To provide an opportunity for job redesign.
- To link remuneration with productivity.

Responsibility for the overall management of the SQP program is vested in a steering committee and day-to-day management by a consultative committee comprising management, shop stewards, and shop-floor representatives. Teams are established by the committee to work on set projects and usually disband once it has been completed. They are trained in process analysis and improvement, using flowcharts to identify barriers and problems.

Initial teams focused on time and motion activities, which didn't work all that well. Other problems included the fact that many solutions involved expenditure, which were subject to budget constraints. Lists of potential problems were developed, which would then be prioritised by management for action. These included technical ones such as ice cream containers falling over on a conveyor belt or working conditions such as cold air causing discomfort or repetitive work. The teams identify solutions that are then considered for action by the consultative committee.

Under the SQP program several training initiatives were commenced. An induction program was developed that includes occupational health and safety, product quality, microbiology and hygiene, food preservation, plant sanitation, how ice cream is made, and how the SQP program operates.

Other initiatives introduced under this program include a comprehensive induction program, a workplace English language and literacy program, and on-the-job training linked to training manuals developed for the company. Funding was obtained from the government to run a Workplace English Language and Literacy (WELL) program. About 16 different nationalities are represented at the site. Initial participation was moderate. The company has then to conduct much of its own industry-based training in the absence of courses being available at technical and further education institutions and universities.

A specialised food industry training company was engaged to conduct on-the-job training and also assisted in developing job and training manuals. The manuals integrate the national competency standards and AS 3902. The training manual incorporated job descriptions for all factory jobs. Apart from being the basis for consistency in induction and training processes, it provided the basis for developing multiskilled employees. Training of operators in a variety of job skills, based on the training manual, provides for job flexibility. Multiskilling allows rotation among operators on the production line in the ice cream factory. Reclassification for the factory jobs was undertaken in 1993 and other changes mean that production employees can work in the distribution centre.

Casual employees comprise about 60–70 percent of the ice cream factory staff, which would normally pose difficulties with training. However, many are long-serving casuals, the main reason for their employment status being the seasonal nature of demand for the product. However, the impact of this has been reduced somewhat with new markets in the northern hemisphere. Machine operators and leading hands are generally permanent employees.

In May 1994 a facilitator was appointed to the SQP program. Their role was to communicate the program to employees, maintain records for the KPIs [key performance indicators], and organise training. This was seen as an important recognition that the process needs a driver on a full-time basis. A major issue to deal with is communicating to all employees.

While the focus on enterprise agreements started in 1991 in Australia, the Memorandum of Agreement was made in 1992 and an enterprise agreement was negotiated between 1993 and 1994. The enterprise-based agreement was ratified in May 1994 by the Western Australian Industrial Relations Commission. This had taken about 12 months to finalise and covered the factory operators, van drivers, distribution centre employees, and R & D laboratory staff.

An important element of this agreement that has promoted productivity improvements is the use of key performance indicators (KPIs) to determine productivity-based pay increases. Under the agreement, pay increases of up to 6 percent per year over the three-year term of the agreement are possible. Wastage at the ice cream factory was selected as the primary indicator to determine pay increases.

Key performance indicators used at the ice cream plant include consumer complaints, inventory levels, ingredient wastage, absenteeism, compliance to budget, operational efficiencies, and so on. Measurement criteria have been identified for each of these. A housekeeping audit is also included. This comprises some 1,500 items throughout the plant that are audited every month to find a score with nine being regarded as excellent. Indicators are graphed and displayed and monitored and benchmarked.

Some initial difficulties were experienced and the system has required some fine-tuning. One major problem was caused by a storm that damaged the roof of the warehouse, leading to substantial stock wastage and at a similar time, the loss of a Japanese export contract. However, some recent projects have identified useful savings such as AUD$14,000 in chocolate wastage during a three-month period.

Politics of Change

The managing director has played a relatively dominant central role at the most senior level by exerting an entrepreneurial style of management that has forced the company to become focused on export markets. Indications are that he had a major influence on the initial changes back in the 1980s and also during the early 1990s. The manager of the ice cream plant and technology has also taken a leading role in terms of identifying relevant technology and adapting it to the plant.

Most of the significant changes in technology occurred when the new factory was built. The fact that it was a Greenfield site probably helped to create a "fresh start." The new plant was clean, modern, and uncluttered when compared with the old site. The company was also able to draw on some government assistance during this process with the provision of $450,000 under a best practice grant in 1992 and for the English language course. Dissemination of information was an important requirement of the best practice funding. This helped stimulate greater communication between management and employees.

The ice cream factory has been free of any industrial disputation for about 18 years. There were no real barriers or special difficulties with the unions and the employees that would impair the introduction of new technology or the continuous updating of it. On the contrary, the relevant unions appear to have played a supportive role in the transition process, particularly with regard to the new workplace arrangements that have resulted from the enterprise bargaining in recent years. Employees are represented by four unions, the Food Preservers Union, the Transport Workers Union, the Electricians, and the Metal Workers. Most factory employees are members of the FPU and since they are mainly casual, they tend not to be active union members. The union contribution has been greatest in the past three years with enterprise bargaining. There have only been a few "teething problems" that primarily related to machinery breakdowns.

An ex-official from the Food Preservers Union (FPU), representing most process workers on-site, considered that the move to the new plant had been handled relatively well by management. Efforts were made to keep employees informed via a video explaining the new plant and how it would work and workers had been taken to the site by bus. They also had the opportunity to have some input into plant layout and so on. For a transition period of about 18 months, production took place at both the Roe Street and Balcatta sites.

Long-serving employees have not found any major difficulties with the changes resulting from firstly the move to the new plant and then changes due to introduction of new machinery due to new products and new markets. For the leading hands, some felt that they faced more pressure as production had now increased and the increased number of casual employees had to be continually trained, sometimes resulting in production slowdowns. Some had found difficulty adjusting to a fully enclosed air-conditioned environment from the old open factory with windows to the outside. Others noted that the company is now less like a big family than previously. This may be more a reflection of the changes in management and perhaps the physical isolation at the new site. One view espoused was that better preventive maintenance on equipment could be made since machinery did break down and affect production levels.

Operation and Outcomes of the New Practices

It could be said that the change process is ongoing within the Peters and Brownes Group. Refinements and new additions to the technology are constantly being made as new markets are developed. Continuous improvement teams are now operating. Linking operations and research and development is also an important feature of the Peters and Brownes Group. Once the R & D team has developed new products they work with the plant operators and help train them in manufacturing processes for the new product.

Outcomes.   Ice cream exports now account for between 25 and 45 percent of output and have shown steady growth as highlighted in the table below.

Percentage of Ice Cream Sales as Exports

1991	*1992*	*1993*	*1994*
10%	23%	31%	36%

Benefits for the local market have arisen as a result of exports. For example, a number of new products have been developed for the Australian market as a result of involvement in the Japanese market. These include premium quality ice creams and flavoured milk drinks.

Summary

This case demonstrates how a change in company ownership, a new manufacturing facility, and an emphasis on product innovation and development has turned a once mature and stagnant company into a successful exporter with considerable scope for further expansion. The general manager of marketing and technology considers that Australia has a considerable competitive advantage in food processing with its abundant supply of good quality raw materials.

This case highlights several phases in the continuous adoption and management of technology in a food processing company. Considered from time series perspective, the following can be identified:

Late 1980s	Build a new ice cream manufacturing plant on a Greenfield site. Combine this with an existing fully automated warehouse facility.
>1990	Seek new export markets. Combine R & D and technology.
>1992	Develop productivity and quality improvement teams. Achieve ISO 9002.

Key Competitive Advantages.   Key competitive advantages include:

- Customer focused and driven R & D. The major driving force for continuous process and product innovation are customer needs. The company responds to this through R & D, equipment purchase and/or modification, process refinement, and so on. In essence they fit the technology to suit the new markets. An example of this was the need to install a tamper-proof sealing machine on one production line that packages tubs of ice cream for Japan.
- Technology.
  - CAM process.
  - Flexible manufacturing.
  - Cost efficient manufacturing.
  Establishment of the new plant in 1987 (along with the warehouse) provided significant production capacity and flexibility. Additions have been made over the years. While the technology per se is not always new, the company has developed it in a way such as using computerised control of processes. Technology does not drive the company; instead it provides the mechanism for adapting to and developing new markets to achieve production efficiencies. The company's success and competitive advantage are linked to technological excellence and capability and understanding new product development. The company aims to maintain its technological capability and to be the best at this. Technology is seen as customer-driven, both internally and externally, and related to market opportunities.
- Work processes and HR systems. This is an area the company has put considerable effort into during the past three to four years. It is yielding rewards for both the company and the employees.

The Future.   The company has considerable scope for increasing output within its existing plant. The mixing process for various types of ice cream is capable of making an enormous range, and equipment to mould the various products and package them is purchased as required.

Lessons

What lessons might there be in this case for other companies? This case highlights the multifaceted nature of technology and innovation. Apart from introducing new "hard" technology (new plant) and "soft" technology such as work processes, quality, and so on, the strong emphasis on R & D and marketing to develop new products and new markets is a central feature. The technological and quality capabilities are available with the facility, which enables the company to develop new markets, particularly overseas.

- Uses of technological capability and R & D have driven growth for Peters. This is ably supported by training, job redesign, work flexibility, and so on. Quality is also central. The need to integrate HR into operations needs to be acknowledged in order to maximise the benefits of the new technology.
- The main driving force for the adoption of new technology is the market and product development. Where new markets, particularly overseas, are found, the process and hard technologies are found, modified, or designed. One overriding factor here is a "can do" attitude. The managing director is a driver. Faced with significant export markets but with high standards and expectations to be met, the company does not shy away from these challenges.
- Specially allocating one or two people in the organisation who are given responsibility for technology helps maintain constant contact with the latest developments. New hard technologies need not be sourced from your own specific industry. Peters has applied equipment and ideas used in non-ice cream production (such as brewing) to ice cream.
- The physical manufacturing facilities of a company can be an important factor that potential customers take into account before negotiating contracts. With the Japanese market, this seems to be a necessary prerequisite as site inspections usually precede detailed contract negotiations over product and price. Customers want reassurance that the company they will deal with has the technological capability to deliver the product at a quality that they expect. To this end certification to ISO 9000 may also be required.
- Strategic alliances with other companies can provide a cushion for fluctuations in the market for your own products. Peters has developed these for ice cream products for other companies such as Cadbury's.

16
Samwon Precision Machines Company[1]

Introduction

Mr. Yang Yong Sik, age 48, an executive director of Samwon Precision Company who has played an important role in the company's innovative growth, described how he saw the company situation in the business environment in which there are increasing cost and quality demands from buyers, both domestic and overseas. He argued that:

> I can see that Korean products are losing their competitive edge from everywhere, but why is this happening? . . . I have traveled to many countries in Southeast Asia and I see that our products are in good shape, in the matter of design and quality, but the problems lie in their cost. . . . Why is our cost higher compared to other countries?

He then explained:

> In the last few years, our labour and manufacturing overhead cost have been rising constantly, but we are not adding enough value to cope with this rising cost. . . . That is to say, in the past, we worked for 1,000 wons of wages and produced 1,100 wons of value, but we now get paid 3,000 wons but produce only 2,000 wons of value.

He further asked:

> What shall we do now? . . . We must reduce our costs by 2–3 percent a year, and produce more value than our costs. . . . In every part of our company, I can see so many areas of waste where we could be adding value. Our opportunity cost is much higher than before and we cannot afford to waste time and resources when we are working.

He continued:

> Now that I have explained this to my company, we have really seen what we can do, if we just realize what we are doing. . . . It is us who must realize what is in front of us.

According to Mr. Yang, it is going to be two or three years before the Korean economy is going to either prosper again or fall behind other rapidly rising countries. (Appendixes 1 and 2 illustrate some financial data that show the cost increases.)

Background of the Company

The Samwon Precision Machines Company was first established in 1974 producing springs for ballpoint pens, and expanded quietly until 1980. In 1975, the company started to develop auto parts and became a member of the Korea Auto Association. It joined the Korea Metal Industry Association in September 1976. In 1978, the company established a technical coalition with Murada Hatchizo Co. of Japan.

---

[1]This case was developed for use in classroom discussion and is not intended to necessarily illustrate appropriate or inappropriate management practices. Case author: Kee Young Kim, Yonsei University, 1996. Simon Poon, a doctoral student in the Graduate School of Management at Macquarie University, was the research associate who rewrote the case in 2000. The funding for this case production was provided by the Australian federal government's Department of Industry, Science and Resources.

In 1980, Samwon was designated as an auto parts factory by the Korean Ministry of Commerce and Industry and, in 1983, was designated as a supplying company for the Ministry of National Defence. In 1986, Samwon was designated by the government as a promising small to medium company and, in 1987, became a member of the Korea Electronics Association. In 1990, just after Samwon was designated as an outstanding small to medium company, they established a new factory in Kyung Ki Do.

The company now produces about 1,800 different kinds of springs and manufactures 100 million springs per month. From about 2,000 spring makers in Korea, Samwon became one of the largest suppliers after Daewon, which is now the largest company in the industry by size. The organizational structure is shown in Figure 1. However, for cold coil springs, Samwon was the largest in size and supplies various companies ranging from auto to ballpoint pen manufacturers.

Though there had been evidence of growth, it was in the 1980s that the company needed some changes to cope with the hostile business environment. The economic environment of that time was not very pleasant for managers of any industry in Korea. The executive director, Mr. Yang Yong Sik, worked with the owner, Mr. Mun Hak Moo, CEO, who is now 75 years old. Mr. Mun worked in the company from its beginnings as a line foreman. He learned his own managerial skills while managing the growing company with expanding managerial boundaries. It is interesting that Mr. Yang, while he was only a line foreman and never had regular school education beyond the six years of public school and a short term in a vocational institution, could manage to propel the reformation of the company. This is very unusual for Korean companies that traditionally have a top-down management structure.

Factors Setting the Context of Change

Due to the Korean government's growth-oriented policy of that era, Samwon had expanded rapidly to evolve as a well-balanced company, but problems arose as the company expanded. In the 1980s, just like other Korean companies, Samwon faced many problems such as rising wages and worker resistance while their customers' requests for lower costs was the strongest pressure on Samwon.

Recognition of the Need to Change and Content of Change

The hostile conditions of the 1980s were the driving force to adopt the 5S program. Samwon adopted 5S just before the crisis was felt at the company.

FIGURE 1

The organizational structure

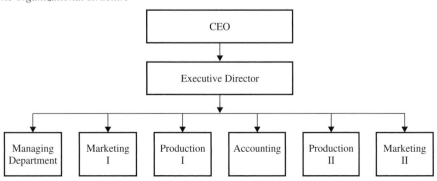

• While Mr. Yang was a line foreman at Samwon, he visited Japan. During his visit, he figured that a crisis would soon come to the Korean industry and he wanted Samwon to be prepared. He met with the licensor of Samwon in Osaka and learned from the Japanese that productivity increases could only be achieved by workers and at the place of production. He felt that his company had to change quickly to compete with the competitors in Japan. Hence, Mr. Yang's mission was to implement the 5S program in Samwon. He took a risk in that he received a six-month window of opportunity from Mr. Mun the CEO, and if the program did not succeed, he was to leave the company. "5S" is Japanese which stands for *seri* (determine which equipment is necessary and which is not), *seiton* (have the necessary equipment in reach and in the right place), *seiso* (clean), *seiketsu* (maintain the above 3S), and *sitsuke* (mental discipline and readiness).

Process of Transition

After his return to Korea, Mr. Yang, with the owner Mr. Mun's permission, launched this 5S project in Samwon without knowing precisely what the consequences would be.

Implementation of the 5S Program.   The adaptation of 5S was the hardest part for the company, just like any other innovation process, reflected in the old Korean aphorism "the start is when half of the work is done." The 5S program was first adopted in 1980 and failed in the first and second attempts because of the resistance of the workers and other managers; however, it finally came to fruition in 1988. When it was fully embraced by the workers, they took six months of pre-educational programs to establish the cultural background before actually adopting the fundamental principles of 5S. This was when Samwon's culture was formed, based on the following forces that drive the culture:

*   "I am the owner of the company"; "Do it myself first."
*   "I get what I earn."
*   "I am evaluated by my work for the company, not by my school diploma."

Senior management were encouraged to take the initiative of setting an example to subordinates and were encouraged to arrive at work earlier than their subordinates. General managers would arrive at 6:30 A.M. 30 minutes earlier than regular workers, and chief executives would arrive at 6:00 A.M. No office meeting would occur during office hours; they would meet before the office hours that normally started at 8:00 A.M.

After Mr. Yang's venture turned out to be successful, Samwon became a lean company with employee support of the new company direction. It took eight years of downsizing to make the company slim and fit enough to cope with the environment. In fact, Samwon was ahead of the downsizing trend that was carried out in Korea. Mr. Yang is proud of the fact that the 5S program was originally adopted from Japan and has been attempted by almost every Korean company, but no other company succeeded in setting up the system.

The core part of the change was the new culture of the workers where everyone believed that he/she was the owner of the company. This is shown in the company's payments, where every increased profit was reinvested or paid to the workers and even more importantly the company kept its word when implementing the project. In order for Samwon to prosper, the 5S program had to be successful. The success was due to many factors peculiar to small companies like Samwon (such as no shift in politics and no changes of CEO). The successful adaptation of 5S from their Japanese licensor company gave Samwon the structure for other campaigns to be successfully implemented.

The Initiation of the Program Cho Kwan Ri.   Once management of the 5S was found to be mature and the results had become well established, Mr. Yang wanted to introduce the next action program to increase the productivity and sophistication of the company by utilizing the 5S foundation. Mr. Yang thought the market pressures on price and quality would increase at a greater rate than they could manage.

The next program was named "cho kwan ri" (CKR: *cho* stands for a second of time; *kwan ri* refers to management), a time-based management system. Unlike the Japanese 5S campaign, CKR was exclusively invented by Samwon. In the process of waste analysis, Mr. Yang wanted to investigate the amount of time wasted during work both on the factory floor and at office desks, and measure these in some monetary terms. In other words, establish how much money the company actually lost due to wasted time.

While Samwon successfully adopted the 5S program after eight years of difficult work, the environment around Samwon had also grown more adversarial than before. Their main problem was with manufacturing cost. Since the material cost was over 80 percent of the manufacturing cost, it was not easy for Samwon to reduce the manufacturing cost while the wages and other overheads increased due to social pressure. They needed something more than just 5S. As was the case with other Korean manufacturers, the material cost as a proportion of the total manufacturing cost actually surpassed the labour cost (which accounted for around 15 percent of total manufacturing cost) in competition with other foreign competing partners. This was in contrast to Korean managers' perceptions that the labour cost was actually the worst factor.

In establishing cho kwan ri, Mr. Yang thought that the 60-minute hour was not accurate enough to measure the wasted time. He took the "second" as the measuring scale to count the time as accurately as possible. Mr. Yang calculated the value of "each second" represented by workers and managers by dividing their average annual salaries by the total number of seconds for the actual annual working days. Hence, one second of floor workers' time and managers' time have a different worth.

Cho kwan ri calculated all work activity, including futile team meetings, chatting time, smoking, coffee breaks, etc., into monetary value in an attempt to publicly identify the wasted time in the company. Figure 2 shows the wage table. For example, if it took 10 seconds to make one spring, then, since it cost 2 wons per second for wages, it has cost 20 wons in wages. It would get more expensive when it is calculated for top managers. If it took 600 seconds to write a report by a manager and it cost 3 wons per second, then it would cost 1,800 wons in wages.[2]

Cho kwan ri initially looked like a way of squeezing time from the workers. On the other hand, it reflected what the workers wanted. The workers would get more days off than at other companies

FIGURE 2

Cho kwan ri

You cannot save time; let's do our best while we have it!

	Managers	*Workers*
1 second	3 wons	2 wons
1 minute	180 wons	120 wons
1 hour	10,800 wons	7,200 wons
8 hours	86,400 wons	57,600 wons
12 hours	129,600 wons	86,400 wons

---

[2]The average working year was assumed to be 250 days, i.e., 7,200,000 seconds. If workers were paid 14 million won per year, then it would cost 2 wons per second and if managers were paid 20 million won per year, then it would cost 3 wons per second.

if the factory was run 359 days a year. The main purpose was to concentrate on working hours and use the saved time to good purpose regardless if it is for personal use or for the company. Samwon started cho kwan ri in 1990 and this time was easier than before, because the new company culture had already been established from the 5S program.

Once the cost measuring system was developed, everyone was equipped in calculating cost information on wasted time and its effect on productivity as well as the value creation by individual workers, departments, and the whole company. This enabled workers to manage their own ways of working in order to be as efficient as possible themselves, without any supervision or direction from the top. Many programs to get rid of wasted time have been automatically created by the employees for themselves. The employees suggested themselves that any business meeting should be called before the workday starts at 8:00 A.M. The company saw that meetings during the working day caused the most waste of working hours and they did not want the company operations being interrupted by workers being called away for the meetings.

As a result of CKR, employees have shifted team meetings to 7:00 A.M. to discuss and find problems that lie ahead. This was quickly supported by everyone. As a result, it encouraged an efficient flow of communication and feedback improvements and the team leaders could then be well aware of what was going on in the company. The information flow between departments was sufficient to ensure that any team leader could answer simple phone calls or questions from external parties.

Some of the effects that cho kwan ri has achieved for the company are listed below:

1. *Wasted time reduction.* A new system for morning meetings usually commenced at 7:00 A.M. in order to reduce wasted time during the day. The best part of this was that all the participants were eager to have the meeting and it was very productive. A suggestion system in fact changed the way R & D efforts were conducted in such a way that workers on the floor supported the work of R & D members, resulting in teamwork between workers and R & D personnel. In an attempt to get rid of the waste, all workers were asked to develop or improve their work, which was very effective in process development. The machines were customized to the workers so that they could run the machines with the knowledge of the processes going on inside the machine. The workers saved a lot of time due to time-based management. They spent this time with the machines and suggested improvements every week. Every worker kept a self-management checksheet by seconds for a month and salaries were set based upon their performance, not by seniority.

   According to Mr. Yang, most of the machines produced four times more springs than when they were imported from Japan and the U.S. Some machines that made long coil springs were redesigned to make short coil springs and replaced the imported machines so that they did not have to import those machines again. They also had a custom-made quality checking machine made by the manufacturing department, which would be very expensive if imported.

2. *Welfare was enhanced.*
   a. Pay was 30 percent more than any other company in Korea.
   b. Bonuses were up to 600 percent–900 percent from 400 percent.
   c. The company paid all the employees' children's educational fees up to college level.
   d. The company supported overseas training.
   e. All the company-owned cars were air-conditioned for efficiency of the work force.
   f. The suggestion system worked without any intervention from upper management.

The CKR system was nationally acknowledged as "best practice" and was also recognized as a benchmark model for other companies. Samsung Group, the national representative business conglomerate, benchmarked Samwon to add the basics of the CKR program to its own operation. Samsung's early office hour system (7:00 A.M. to 4:00 P.M.) started in 1994 after Samwon's CKR system.

Boosting the Phase: Saryuk 0.01 Campaign.   As part of the company's "continuous improvement" program, Samwon then adopted the Saryuk 0.01 campaign after the CKR and 5S programs were successfully implemented. The reason for the Saryuk 0.01 campaign (*saryuk* means to make a desperate or frantic effort for the ultimate goal) was a goal-oriented campaign to improve by even 1 percent. Externally, it was the buyer companies' pressure on price reduction and adversarial economic conditions for small-sized supplying companies. In an effort to reduce cost, they focused on reducing the waste. The principle of cho kwan ri was to reduce waste that is invisible, whereas the principle of Saryuk 0.01 was to reduce waste that is visible. Mr. Yang wished to continue to seek out any waste in the company in order to meet the competitive situation. The Saryuk 0.01 program was introduced into the company in order to get rid of the visible waste in every aspect of the company's operations.

Samwon's motto was:

Saryuk for 0.01 of productivity improvement.

Saryuk for 0.01 of waste.

Saryuk for 0.01 of profit.

Its specific objective was to reach a total of two million wons of waste for the whole corporation. It was calculated that if each member of the company saves 10 thousand wons of waste this would result in 2 million wons of waste for the company. It is natural that this process would be impossible to implement if they did not have 5S and cho kwan ri in place beforehand. Mr. Yang insisted that "a company always has to prepare itself to be a wave rider instead of a victim of environmental change." Buyers always impose their own cost and quality pressures on their suppliers. For the last contract the major automakers wanted a 5 percent price cut while Samwon's profit rate was only about 4 percent. This meant that if Samwon was not prepared for the cost reduction pressures from buyers, there would not be any chance of surviving from such pressure.

Samwon targeted nine waste categories as follows:

1. *Waste from defects.* It is important to keep in mind that quality control is important for all, even in managerial work. In fact, defects in managerial work bring more damage to the company. To prevent these wastes, we must be accurate and sensitive in every operation.

2. *Waste from clumsy work.* We should know that no matter how precise the plan is, there is a chance that it cannot be completed at the right time. It is better to take time in this case, rather than poorly finishing the work.

3. *Waste from inventories.* Inventory is money, whether it is product or material. Any inventories over the minimum required level not only cause stagnation in cash flow, but also a waste in managing the inventories. This can be managed as part of a JIT [just-in-time] program.

4. *Waste of motions.* Every motion of the work can be a process of creating value. We have to keep in mind that we should watch every motion of our work and machines so that it can be improved and add more value.

5. *Waste of waiting.* For example, waiting for service in a bank is a waste of a lot of time. Every member of the company must be organized and information flow should be

comprehensive so that we can reduce the waste of time in places such as the bank or taxation office.

6. *Waste of transporting.* Usage of mass transportation in the company and outside the company can reduce a large waste.

7. *Waste of process.* We should use suggestion systems so that any waste in the process can be found and the improved work situation should be communicated to all workers.

8. *Waste of industrial accident.* This brings most of the waste for the company and for the person, not to mention all of the pain that he or she will suffer. These kinds of accidents are almost always from carelessness of the workers (90 percent of the time). It is only ourselves who can prevent these kinds of wastes.

9. *Waste of managerial work.* This is invisible waste. The most important thing to reduce this kind of waste is to have good information flow in the company, both vertically and horizontally.

The company saved W 49,000,000 and W 59,896,719 for the 24 months from June 1993 when it started the Saryuk 0.01 campaign. There are weekly and monthly schedules in Samwon to reduce waste and keep up the above three campaigns. Mr. Yang asserted that the management systems operate not by order and supervision, issued every time something has to be done as is usually seen in other companies, but by the predesigned "time-work schedule." He says,

> We even care about the waste caused by making schedules about what we do today and this week and who should do this and that every time. . . . Instead, we tried to make ourselves used to the jobs done regularly by whom and by when.

The time-work schedule in Table 1 shows how each department is scheduled to do what at which day of the week and in which week. For instance, on Tuesday, everybody is supposed to carry out the 5S campaign tasks from 7:55 to 8:15 A.M. Specifically, in Week 1 of the month, office cleaning is the work to do. Everyone has to clean up the personal drawers, files, computers, etc., by 5S system rules. Each one has a designated area to clean if it is for a companywide cleaning.

TABLE 1   The Pre-designed "Time-Work" Schedule

Works	Time	Day	Week 1	Week 2	Week 3	Week 4
Presentation: Process, technology	7:55–8:15	Monday	Production I	Process	Marketing	Accounting
5S	7:55–8:15	Tuesday	Cleaning: Office	Cleaning: Factory	Cleaning: Factory	Cleaning: Total
Education, suggestions	7:55–8:15	Wednesday	Education: About the company	Education: Technology	Education: Production, quality	Education: Mental preparation
Organization development	7:55–8:15	Thursday	Related department	Related department	Related department	Related department
Team meeting	7:55–8:15	Friday	Inspection	Education	Inspection	Education
Meeting—Each department	7:55-8:15	Saturday	Meeting—each department		Meeting—each department	

Some of the Achievements of Saryuk 0.01 Campaign.   One of the striking examples of reducing waste was the way in which workers innovated the way of serving meals in the cafeteria. The workers used to be served their meals from a fixed menu and amount by cafeteria workers at the meal stands, which resulted in the workers throwing away any leftover food. That wasted food needed containers and the related activities to abandon the waste and caused workers to be involved in cleaning the containers. The workers' committee recommended a self-service system by which workers select the amount of food to as much as 80 percent that they need at the first trip to the serving stand. This system eventually eliminated 20 percent of cafeteria overhead costs by getting rid of wasted food, waste containers, and the cleaning work. The workers took seats from the first row of tables in arrival sequence so that unoccupied seats were not mixed up with the used dirty seats. They saved cleaning work of the dining room by 20 percent. Trash cans were sorted by items like bottles, metal cans, paper cups, and others. The workers reduced the number of dumping trash cans by crushing the metal cans and piling the paper cups in columns in order to save space in the trash cans. They decided not to put bottled drinks in the vending machines because the empty bottles need more storage room.

Another example was a reduction in the electricity bills by switching the lights in the restroom on and off as needed and indicating the occupancy by using O and X signs on the outside of the door. As such, the ideas were actually suggested by workers themselves. Each worker was committed to report 15 or more cases of removing waste per month. The company called the suggestions a "guaranteed cheque," meaning that the ideas make money by reducing waste. The suggestion system was successfully operated along with an incentive system. The suggesters were paid by a certain ratio of total income gained from the specific ideas plus a compensation reward in terms of promotion and wage increases based on the company evaluation scheme.

Mr. Yang wondered how the office staff determines their workload and identifies the waste in office work. He considered the production workers to be more effectively measurable than the office workers. He finally decided to utilize the CKR technique to analyze their work in seconds for each job for a period of one month. The monthly job analysis sheets gave them important information on which jobs were more important than others in terms of time requirement and then they could easily determine how to improve the way of doing jobs and the kind of jobs that could be eliminated. This process provided the company with very reasonable ways of optimizing the manpower level in the office. As shown in Figure 3, the series of campaigns are depicted as a sand cone.

FIGURE 3

Sand cone of the campaigns

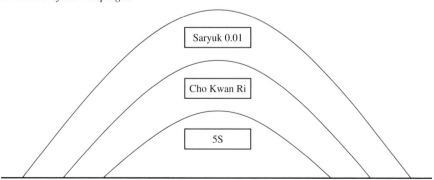

Politics of Change

When the 5S program was first adopted, it seemed that it would be successful. However, just when the work was showing a positive outcome, resistance came not from the workers but from the higher managers. They could not bear to see that this new approach, implemented by only a line foreman, was working out well. They refused to embrace 5S and naturally the workers refused also. Samwon showed its difference from other companies with the owner backing Mr. Yang and supporting him with the power to sack employees, even managers, if they were not embracing this new program. Ten percent of the employees were fired and many of them were managers rather than workers. Consequently, this had a downsizing effect and flattened the organizational structure making it simple, single-pathed, and cross-functional with a lot of power held by Mr. Yang. This was a totally new concept at that time in Korea, as traditionally, there were managers for each department and it became a multiple-path structure.

After eight years of the cultural change within the company, there was little, if any, functional politics during the development and implementation of cho kwan ri programs and the Saryuk 0.01 campaign.

Operations of New Practices

The series of campaigns eventually brought in a broad range of changes in the managerial system assisting to resolve the fundamental operational problems. The typical problems included layoff of people, which was inevitable after downsizing, capital investment that was required for replacing the old equipment and updating the technologies, and wage increases that surpassed productivity increases and the like.

Layoffs were not generally accepted by the public in Korea and were usually subject to very emotional resistance by the labour unions. Unless a natural decrease of manpower exists, the company should depend on some other way of utilizing the excess manpower realized by a reduction of unproductive work time. Samwon Precision Company expanded the plant capacity without extra capital investment by adding a third work shift to the existing two-shift system. The plants were then operated on a 24-hour per day basis, absorbing the excess manpower available from the innovation campaigns. The company also extended the annual working days to as many as 359 days with only six days unutilized per year, which was significantly different from the average working days of 300 or less for other Korean companies. This system utilized the factory at the maximum capacity in such a way as to save extra capital investment otherwise required for increasing production capacity. This maximum machine utilization system, combined with automation of the production process, allowed the company to let their workers free from work for 94 days per capita per year. This holiday benefit was much longer than that of other average Korean companies while keeping the factories working for more days at three full shifts.

The company created its own working calendar with the workers scheduled into two groups, A and B. According to the calendar, employees in group A did not need to work on Sundays while the employees of group B did not work on Tuesdays. The company kept the production lines in full operation throughout the year without shutdowns. It reduced factory overhead by one-fourth and increased overall productivity to four times higher than other similar companies in Korea. This unique operational system coupled with the automation of the process resulted in a reduction of production cost by 30 percent and at the same time, wages increased by 20 percent over the 18 months since the Saryuk 0.01 program was launched. On top of that, the workers benefited by 900 percent of the annual flat bonus instead of 400 percent that used to be the amount a year ago.

The company accelerated the automation of production lines through the innovative activities of the machine workers and R & D staff. Many production processes were automated with the help of the innovative efforts through the Saryuk 0.01 waste banishment program. Nowadays a line consisting of 50 machines is operated by just one worker.

As an example of a typical success story, an automatic sorting machine was designed by Mr. Kim T. S., the operator who wanted to drive out the waste of man-hours required in sorting the oversized springs from the good ones. He spent about one and a half months in developing an electrical sensor to sort the over-sized springs. Mr. Kim won a grade A reward of W 500,000 as one of the "innovative performances of the month," which was an incentive system to encourage the line workers to improve the automation level.

Another was Mr. Lee S. C., who wondered if he could reduce the man-hours to pack the products. He tried to automate the process, by reducing the need for manual packing. He eventually automated the whole process by which the company saved 24 percent of the work time and cut inventory by 20 percent. In the process, 50 machines in that particular line were managed only by one worker. Another example was the simple adjustment of the machine rack that resulted in import substitution of Japanese machines. Mr. Cho C. R. developed it in three weeks and he was subsequently awarded a W 1,500,000 reward.

The main characteristic of these successes was that the R & D activities were cross-functional among the development engineers and line workers who work 24 hours a day on a three-shift system, providing prompt reaction to the floor problems and new product development.

The company motivated its employees to participate in the programs by reinforcing their trust in the company policy. The policy was to reinvest the profits back into the company operations, and for employees' welfare so that the employees were confident that they worked on behalf of themselves, and believed that they could manage their wage increases, not by the CEO. It was not surprising that there was no labour union. The line managers rotated as superintendent every month, so that every line manager and worker had to know about the problems and issues faced in the factories. The company kept its organization exceptionally flat, flexible, and cross-functional so that communication barriers were removed. Training was also considered an important communication device to share the vision, value of the operation, technique, and skill. Management submitted the model to the subordinates and encouraged them to accept the idea "to work for themselves."

Conclusion

This case sheds light on a general proposition that the sustained innovation of a company can only be realized if top management is committed to the vision that everyone in the company shares and is involved in the process of improvement. Mr. Mun, the owner, became a winner of the game by implementing this proposition. He believed in the process by empowering his employees, especially Mr. Yang, initially only a line foreman.

The point of the proposition is to run a company to achieve aggregate effectiveness of the total organization. It encourages the company to integrate all levels of the organization and all functional areas of the company. Motivation, communication, and empowerment are critical foundations for total innovation of the company. This means that production and the process technologies are considered as only part of the total management process. The overall measure of innovation is the aggregate effectiveness of the whole company operation, not the simple sum of the efficiencies of each operation of the individual functions such as production lines, marketing, finance, the information network, etc.

Another point is that the managerial system needs to have a specific prescription rather than a panacea for all companies. This case demonstrates that the Samwon Precision Company discovered their own innovation process and system. Education and training were considered as most important tools for the company in order to keep everyone informed of what their vision and targets were, and also to provide them with updated skills and ideas. The Samwon Precision Company showed how an organization should be oriented for the future, and why the organization should be flexible and motivated to continually improve.

APPENDIX 1

Trends in costs

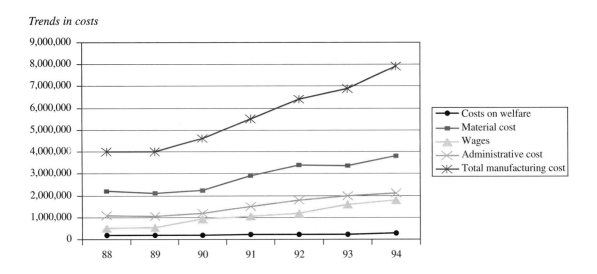

Trends in revenues

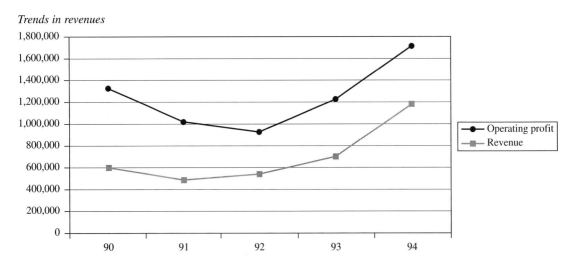

APPENDIX 2

Trends in revenues

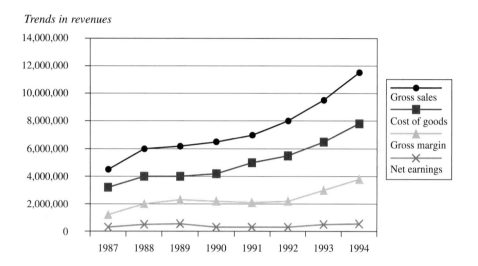

Rates of earnings and cost

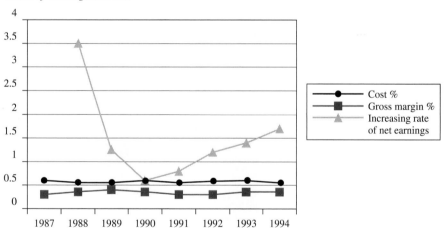

17
SAMYEONG CABLE COMPANY[1]

Introduction

Though it was not the first time for President Choi, Oh Gil of Samyeong Cable Company to attend the annual seminar held for Hyundai's Supplier Cooperation Program, with around 500 suppliers in attendance, there was something in the air that made him feel uneasy. He reasoned that it must be due to the fierce competition between the suppliers that had arisen in the last two or three years.

The uneasiness at the seminar was clarified by the information given by President Park, Byung Jae of Hyundai, who was especially concerned with Hyundai's supplier relationships. Compared to Japan, Korean firms had only half the productivity and were also far behind those of the United States. With regard to quality of supply, the disparity was even worse.

President Park, who had just become the CEO of Hyundai Motor Company, had strongly asserted that to make up for the inferior status of Korean firms in the world market, the suppliers' role was the most important factor and was the key to achieving world class success. The motor vehicle industry is one of the key industries from which to assess the competitiveness of the nation. To improve the competitiveness, it required the whole economic-value chain of suppliers and buyers to improve. It could not be done by just Hyundai, Kia, or another company alone. Figures 1–4 provide some comparative information gathered by Hyundai.

FIGURE 1

Quality—IQS (defect cases for 100 cars in 3 months)

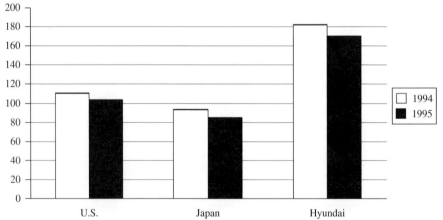

[1]This case was developed for use in classroom discussion and is not intended to necessarily illustrate appropriate or inappropriate management practices. Case author: Kee Young Kim, Yonsei University, 1996. Simon Poon, a doctoral student in the Graduate School of Management at Macquarie University, was the research associate who rewrote the case in 2000. The funding for this case production was provided by the Australian federal government's Department of Industry, Science and Resources.

FIGURE 2

Wage increases

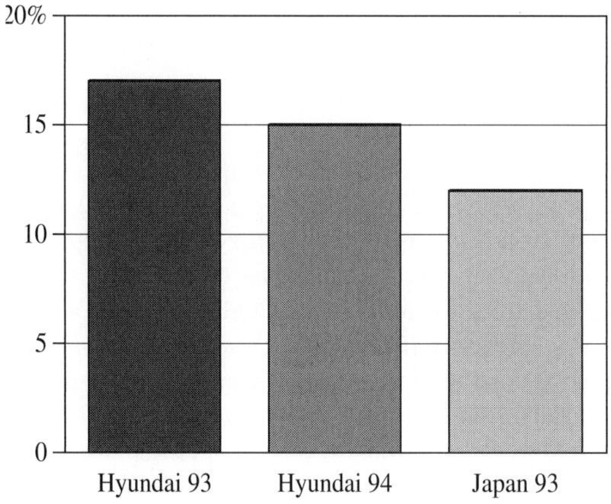

FIGURE 3

Revenue per worker

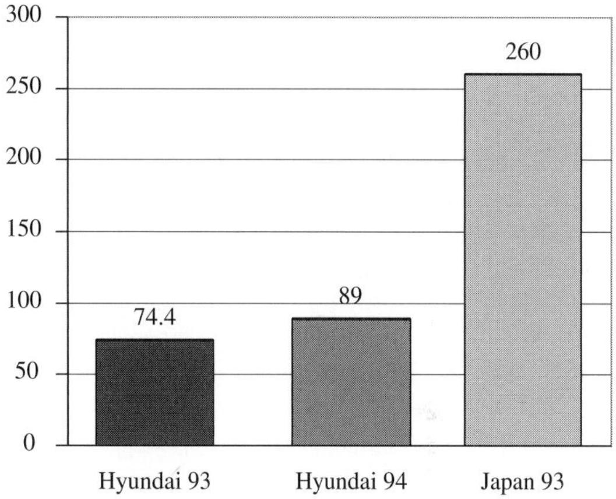

FIGURE 4

Value added per worker

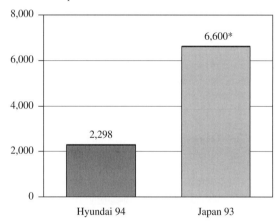

* Japanese data came from 127 Japanese automakers.

After showing these alarming figures, President Park of Hyundai announced that there would be some appraisal of the suppliers. Hyundai would select those few firms that met Hyundai's criteria by their capability and performance to compete in the world market. The manual that showed how this process was to be conducted was distributed to all participants at the seminar.

In the seminar President Park of Hyundai had shown some examples of the world class leaders in the motor vehicle industry such as GM, Toyota, and others in their supplier development program, and announced that Hyundai would adopt some unique programs to cope with the fierce competition.

After the seminar, President Choi of Samyeong returned to his own business to assess its competitiveness. With a careful evaluation of his factory, he found that some major changes were needed at his company. His assessment was conducted in three areas: productivity, quality, and cost, which were the central theme of the seminar and the factors that Hyundai would use in evaluating their suppliers. However, after realising that major changes were necessary, he was at an impasse in trying to understand what to do and where to begin.

Background of the Samyeong Cable Company

Samyeong Cable Company was established in 1969 at Songdong Ku, Seoul, to produce control cables, speedometer cables, and filter elements mostly for motor vehicles, e.g., for Hyundai Motor Co. and other large motor companies such as Kia and Daewoo. A brief history will show how this company has grown and expanded along with the Korean economic boom.

In May 1973, the company name was changed to Samyeong Cable Co., Ltd. It was quite a small company, producing cables largely through manual means. In May 1974, Samyeong was selected by the Consumer Protective Association as a firm that needed encouragement to expand. In July 1978, Samyeong was designated as a specialised manufacturer for automotive cables by the government. This gave Samyeong an opportunity to catch up technologically and to be one of the most technologically competitive firms in the cable industry.

In October 1979, Samyeong moved to a new plant in the Banwol industrial complex, Ansan City, to accommodate the growth in size of the company and in December 1982, it was designated as a "firm of modernisation and rationalisation of medium industry" by the government.

Since March 1987, Chrysler Corporation in the U.S. has approved Samyeong Cable Company as an OEM supplier of hood latch cables. Samyeong has globalised its markets and technological sources. In January 1988, an appreciation medal was awarded to Samyeong by Hyundai Motor Service Co., Ltd., for being an excellent quality supplier. The Industrial Bank of Korea awarded Samyeong Cable Company in December 1989 for being an excellent firm. However, it experienced a major labour dispute in 1989 that severely disappointed the founding president Hahm, Jae Sun who sold his 50 percent share of the Samyeong company to the current President Choi, Oh Gil (age of 52). Subsequently, President Choi took control over the company in 1991.

In April 1990, Samyeong was approved by Rockwell International B.C.S. Australia as an OEM supplier for door regulator cables. In September 1991 a three-year validation of technological aid contract was concluded with YAZAKI Corporation, Japan, for automotive ignition cables. Ignition cables were the only automotive cables where Samyeong did not have their own technology and most of their development efforts have been in this area.

Samyeong Co. established the Technology Research Institute in Chonan in December 1991 with other small–medium firms of about the same size as Samyeong and in the same industry. The new factory for Samyeong was also located in Chonan so that it could take full advantage of the location.

In December 1992, Samyeong established a joint corporation named Shenyan Samyeong Leather Products Co., Ltd., to diversify the company. In February 1993, Samyeong established a trading corporation, Ohsung Korea Co., Ltd., in Seoul to facilitate their exports. In February 1994 it established another joint corporation, named Beijing Samyeong Cable Co., Ltd., with Beijing Cable Co., Ltd., in China. And in November 1994, Samyeong was awarded a prize for excellent trading performance by the South Korean government.

In December 1994 Samyeong constructed a second plant on the site of $13,392m^2$ in Chonan and this was where the case began. The new owner, President Choi, Oh Gil, was a qualified CPA and an MBA graduate. He was previously the president of Dong Shin Pharmaceutical Company. Although it was the first time for President Choi to be the owner of a company, he had experience in senior management positions in other companies. The most important thing in this case was the adoption of new management techniques that he had learned from business school and from his experience in other fields. Unlike the former owner, President Choi had a more rational and innovative management style, which brought many organisational and technological changes to Samyeong. After he had taken over control of Samyeong, it had been continuously expanding in size, in sales volume, and production facilities. With President Choi's new management style, the company changed its culture to a more innovative and challenging one. This organisational change enabled the company to cope with the rapidly changing business environment.

The company's revenue of 8.7 billion won in 1991 grew to 22 billion in 1995; the total number of the workers was 313. Its foreign export was predicted to be $7 million in 1995 and most of that was to Rockwell Co. in Australia and China.

Factors Setting the Context of Change

Supplier Relationship Strategy of Hyundai.　　Since Hyundai was the major purchaser from Samyeong, and Samyeong supplied mostly to Hyundai, it is necessary to carefully look at how Hyundai managed its supplier relationships. Hyundai usually double- or triple-sourced its supply of components to guarantee delivery reliability and had its own measures to evaluate each supplier and assign the amount to be purchased from each supplier. (This was the primary method used to control the suppliers.) So it was important for the suppliers to fit in with Hyundai's evaluation process.

For control cables, Hyundai had two major supplier companies, namely Samyeong and Daedong. This was due to Hyundai's double-sourcing policy that was sometimes varied depending on the items and the level of their suppliers' technological capability. The major characteristic and problem of automotive cables were that, compared to other automotive products, rapid design changes were required as well as worker care. Samyeong was the only source for Hyundai for ignition cables, which were imported from Japan or the U.S. Other than that, most of the products were produced with their own technology.

President Park of Hyundai believed that the basis for supplier selection should be the long-term capability of the suppliers rather than the products being purchased at any one time. The bargaining power of Hyundai as a buyer was actually greater than that of the suppliers as seller, as the buyer purchased through competitive-based sourcing among multiple suppliers. This might guarantee low purchase prices on specific occasions. However, it made the relationship adversarial and short-term with the suppliers, resulting in higher overall costs than would be achieved by taking a long-term view.

Capability-based single-sourcing had been considered as a way of protecting Hyundai from direct conflict with the suppliers who wanted to sell more specific products to Hyundai. This system provided the suppliers with opportunities to compete with their fellow suppliers in improving their capability on a long-term basis rather than compete in selling specific products. Hyundai could also take advantage of this system in eventually selecting the highest capability suppliers from among the multiple suppliers who participated in Hyundai's supplier relationship program. Eventually, the most capable single supplier for each product was selected. This was made possible through the implementation of an appropriate evaluation system.

Figure 5 illustrates a model of the buyer-seller relationship. This is the original model that Hyundai has pursued in its supplier relationships.

Through this kind of relationship, Hyundai aimed to disseminate its strategic objectives to its suppliers. Hyundai's position should be at the lower right corner, which was ideal for Hyundai to project its corporate strategy onto its suppliers. In this kind of partnership-like relationship, continual improvement is crucial to sustain the relationship. It was also advantageous to cope with the constantly changing environment. For Hyundai, the major problem was that the capabilities of their suppliers were far behind that of other world leaders in the industry. Since the parts that were sourced from suppliers would determine the quality of the final products, this implied many important production activities in Hyundai were related to supplier management.

FIGURE 5

A shifting paradigm for the buyer-seller relationship

Basis for Supplier Selection

	Product-/Commodity-Based	*Capability-Based*
Adversarial	Short-term/operational	Long-term/strategic
Bargaining Power	Price-/quality-based	Capability-based
Buyer > Seller	Multiple sourcing	Competitive
		Multiple sourcing
Cooperative	Nonprice based	Strategic emphasis
Partnership-like	Operational emphasis	Single sourcing
Buyer = Seller	Management assistance	Continuous improvement
	Technical advice	Cost, quality, delivery

Supplier Development Program.   In an attempt to develop their suppliers' strategic capability in better responding to changes, Hyundai set up a supplier development program as shown in Figure 6. At the first stage of the supplier development process, they would outline the objectives of the supplier-relationship development program by which they rate the suppliers and determine the areas requiring improvement. Then Hyundai would organise the advisory team to be dispatched to specific suppliers. The development teams would usually stay at the supplier's plant until the problems were solved. Hyundai established three department units: technical assistance, cooperation development, and parts and components development, all of which reported directly to the president.

Hyundai's major difference from Japanese and U.S. firms was that Hyundai had a permanent department that utilised several ad hoc working teams made up of the necessary experts from different functional areas. Also, the developmental activities could be triggered by supplier evaluation results or by the company's long-term development objectives. For the following three campaigns: CR30 overall cost reduction campaign, Productivity "2 by 2" campaign, and Quality Management "100 ppm" campaign (which will be described later), Hyundai supported their suppliers with ad hoc member teams (which consisted of personnel from other departments) and taught their suppliers the operation of the new technology with the necessary support so that they could adopt the campaigns successfully.

Hyundai used delivery reliability as the most important factor, and then cost, quality, and flexibility. Hyundai assigned their suppliers into five groups (A, B1, B2, C, D) with the A and B groups being autonomously managed and supported. The competition among suppliers had encouraged them to improve their capabilities from "D" to "A" grades where an "A" graded supplier would be treated with rewards in terms of financing, purchase volume, management aid, and many other incentives and fringe benefits that are not awarded to lower grade suppliers. (Hyundai's supplier rating report is in Appendix 1.)

Companies in the C and D groups would be kept under tight control but not actively supported by Hyundai. Most of the transactions were normally associated with companies in the A and B groups, where most of the supporting investment was carried out. As shown in Figure 6, the supplier ratings are determined after the evaluation stage and again after the implementation stage of the development action plans. Table 1 shows the rankings of all of Hyundai's suppliers.

Following the process of supplier development, Hyundai would designate their consensus development action plans by acronyms such as CR30, 2 by 2, and 100 ppm. President Park, Hyundai's

FIGURE 6

Supplier development decision process

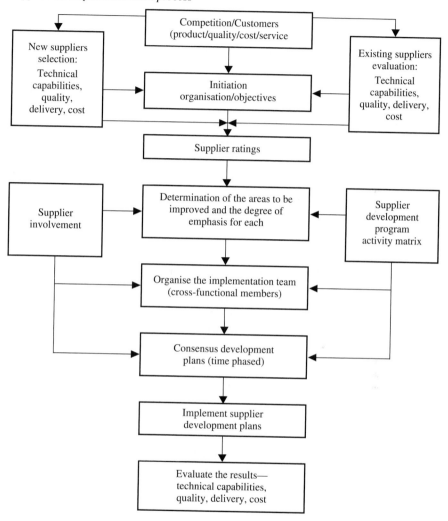

TABLE 1 The Rank Classification of Hyundai Suppliers

	A Class	B Class-1	B Class-2	C Class	D Class
Total Number of 92 Suppliers in Passenger Car Part	14	29 Samyeong	28	14	7

CEO, targeted the cooperative single sourcing system through the capability-based competition among Hyundai's multiple suppliers. Usually, Japanese carmakers could select one supplier relatively easily because the suppliers were already competent, while Korean companies had no reservoir of competent suppliers yet. Basically, grade "A" supplier status was what Hyundai wanted its suppliers to achieve.

Experience in Labour Disputes.   However, single sourcing, in spite of all the expected benefits, had sometimes been found to be vulnerable to unexpected difficulties that caused the suppliers to not be able to supply their parts on time. These difficulties were mainly caused by labour disputes, which were catastrophic to the whole operation of Hyundai. Therefore, the company needed to take protective measures against them. [See Figure 7.] Following are some examples of Hyundai's actual experiences in 1993 and 1994.

The labour dispute was the most serious problem that Hyundai had encountered and was also a major problem where supplier management was concerned. A small labour dispute in a supplier company could damage the whole of Hyundai's process, as had been proved in the case of Apollo Company. The effect was the same as having a dispute in Hyundai since Hyundai could not get the parts to run their production process. It was a big issue in the Korean economy at the time and provided a more realistic view of the supplier chain model. The dispute caused some corrective devices to be added to the supplier relationship program operated by Hyundai.

Contingent Supply Backup System.   Since then, Hyundai has utilised single sourcing but distinguishes it with contingent supply backups. This "contingent supply backup system" stipulates that the suppliers designated to a specific model of car were always kept ready to supply the parts to Hyundai for other models if the designated supplier had difficulty in supplying. This was done by preparing lines, tools, and molds to make parts for other models and keeping them available so that the affected parts could be supplied at short notice.

FIGURE 7

Example of multiple sourcing

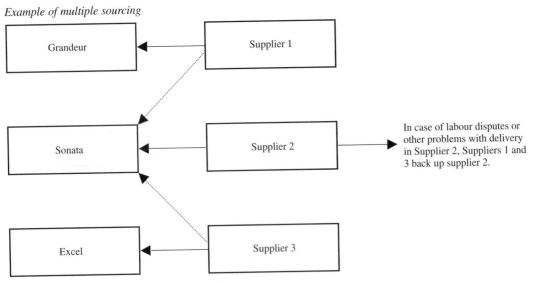

In case of labour disputes or other problems with delivery in Supplier 2, Suppliers 1 and 3 back up supplier 2.

For example, Hyundai had contracts with three different suppliers to acquire seatbelts for the Excel, Sonata, and Grandeur models, but it is still single sourcing from one supplier for each model. In the case of a labour dispute, Hyundai could quickly move to another company and ask them to supply the seatbelts for other vehicle models. It was also easy for the supplier of Excel seatbelts to change its design to supply the Grandeur model since the supplier possessed the capability to produce the other designs. Hyundai had obliged the suppliers to keep the molds, castings, and other necessary items with which they could quickly produce other models.

Content and Substance of Change

Following the supplier rating stage, Hyundai designated the consensus development action plans for their suppliers by the acronyms "CR30," "2 by 2," and "100 ppm"—programs for cost, productivity, and quality, respectively. Hyundai supported their suppliers with seminars, working manuals, and supporting teams that stayed with the supplier company to coach the production personnel.

CR30—An Overall Cost Reduction Campaign.   CR30 was an abbreviation for 30 percent cost reduction. CR30 came into existence in order to countermatch the world leaders like GM, Chrysler, and Toyota, who adopted the "2/3/4" strategy. Here 2 referred to an improvement in the function of the car by 2 times; 3 referred to cost reduction by 1/3 in three years; and 4 aimed for a reduction in weight of the car by 1/4. The objective of CR30 was to identify the parts and components costs that were not competitive with those of the competing companies and help the suppliers of the parts and components to cut down their manufacturing cost by 30 percent. CR30 started in 1987 followed by "2 by 2" in 1991 and "100 ppm" in 1993. CR30 was run in parallel with the other two programs but managed separately. CR30 was utilised by Hyundai Motor Company as an important device for manufacturing cost control of the supplied parts and components. In the supplier relationship, Hyundai was known as a mother company and its suppliers were known as collaboration companies. They exchanged important cost information with each other in order to better control the whole process of manufacturing the cars along the supply chain.

Productivity Campaign: "2 by 2."   The CR30 program was followed by a productivity increase program called "2 by 2," which aimed to double the productivity within two years. This program commenced in July 1994 and targeted to finish in year 1996. The campaign was executed in two phases; the first phase was 1994–1995 and the second, 1995–1996. The year 1993 was to initiate the program to introduce the structure of the campaign and to train people so that the program could begin. The "2 by 2" program was initially introduced by Hyundai in order to absorb the rapid wage increase over productivity increase due to the labour unrest during the 1988–1992 period in Korea. The worker productivity at Hyundai Motor Company then was considered to be only 37 percent of that of Toyota, which had more than one hundred years of experience in car manufacturing. The "2 by 2" campaign was considered beneficial to both Hyundai and its suppliers.

Quality Management by "100 ppm."   President Park, Byung Jae, of Hyundai, who was the founding father of the supplier-relationship development program at Hyundai Motor Company, initiated this campaign in 1990 when he returned to the Ulsan plant for the second time. During that time, he was under pressure because the Hyundai cars were relatively inferior in terms of quality in comparison to their competitors in the world market. The average incoming defect rate of supply parts in Korea was about one thousand times higher than that at Toyota. Hyundai was still using the percentage defect rate as measures instead of parts per million, which had been long adopted by Japanese companies. President Park thought that achieving quality improvements on par with the Japanese levels would provide Hyundai an epoch, an initial turning point in the modernisation of the Hyundai operation. He figured cost, quality, after-sales service, and other competitive priority factors measured by carmakers seemed to be built on a quality foundation. He then decided to launch a "100 ppm" campaign as the cornerstone for innovation in Hyundai's operation along with the CR30 program for cost and the "2 by 2" program for productivity improvement.

At first, "100 parts per million" as a defect rate measure is 10,000 times finer when compared to percent. The "100 ppm" campaign achieved a surprising result, in that Hyundai qualified about 40 suppliers out of 450 by the end of 1995, which was four years after the campaign started. The "100 ppm" campaign was then spread over all industrial companies and the Korean government also promoted this campaign as a national program through public organisations.

Process of Transition

CR30—An Overall Cost Reduction Campaign. Every year during October through March, both parties in the supplier relationship would update the prices of the supplied parts through a bargaining process. Samyeong had to prepare cost data for itself very thoroughly for the price bargaining so that it could convince Hyundai to agree with its price requests.

After the bargaining process and agreement on the price level, Hyundai would decide whether or not they would embark on a managerial and engineering help program with the supplier in order to achieve further cost reductions. After a price bargaining session in March 1995, Hyundai dispatched a three-man advisory team to Samyeong for the CR30 program. Samyeong had already formed a task force and was ready to start working together with the Hyundai staff. The Samyeong CR30 team investigated its manufacturing lines, supply chain from their own vendors, and product structures, etc., as per the Hyundai staff advice. Both teams jointly prepared the CR30 procedure for Samyeong according to the predetermined guideline manual that was recommended by Hyundai. The procedure included the following areas of analysis:

1. *Objective setting.* The target of cost reduction was expanded to the specific areas of material cost (45 percent), labour cost (30 percent), and overhead cost (20 percent) in two years.

2. *Structural and functional analysis of parts.* According to the attributes operationalised in the objective setting, the parts were analysed in a cross-structure and function matrix of value engineering.

3. *Production process analysis.* Manufacturing processes were analysed and motion study techniques were implemented to eliminate inefficient activities.

4. *Aggregate execution plan.* Integrating all the previous stages of analysis enabled an improvement plan to be drawn up. Elimination, combination, change, and simplification were recommended for departments, components, materials, processes, activities, etc., and were detailed in an action program. As a result, the CR30 program came up with some very successful innovations.

The first example was the standardisation of the "Eye End" gear shift cables. These cables used to be designed and produced for different car models so that the production lot sizes were inevitably small, causing higher production costs. The Samyeong CR30 team reduced the number of designs by almost two-thirds, resulting in common intermediate models of cable to fit all kinds of Hyundai cars. This required a lot of change of the related parts and systems of cars. The second example was the change in processing from lathe work to cold forging of metal parts. The forging work was also automated. Ignition cables were also developed by Samyeong's own R & D group in order to replace the imported ignition cables from Japan.

Productivity Campaign: "2 by 2."   In launching the "2 by 2" campaign, Hyundai categorised the "2 by 2" target companies into two groups. The first group was considered as practice models and the best companies. The companies in the second group would receive intensive care to improve their productivity. Hyundai's "2 by 2" promotion centre provided the suppliers with basic guidelines through workshops for the CEOs and the "2 by 2" program managers of the suppliers. In addition, Hyundai operated every other month "mini exchange meetings" that consisted of five to nine supplying companies grouped by item and region. The meetings required the presence of the CEOs and senior managers from the suppliers that were in charge of the "2 by 2" programs. The meetings were designed to provide the managers with an opportunity to exchange their successful experiences in the program. The "2 by 2 circuit study meeting" was another means to promote and encourage the companies to get involved in the program as actively as possible.

The concentrated care program was another major device to help the less successful suppliers by sending Hyundai staff to assist them. Hyundai equipped their "2 by 2" suppliers with a productivity improvement tool with which to increase productivity. The numerator of their productivity definition formula (output/input) consisted of the factors utilisation, yield rate, automation ratio, safety, space utilisation, office automation, information network, etc., each of which was measured and encouraged to increase. The denominator included lead time, set-up time, cycle time, stock level, rework, defect rate, line breakdown, lot size, etc., each of which was, on the other hand, encouraged to decrease.

Like any other suppliers, Samyeong entered the "2 by 2" campaign with seven major action programs. They embraced the above factors and included the following:

1. Worker consciousness of the "2 by 2" productivity improvement program.
2. Layout improvement and line-balancing.
3. Automation.
4. Set-up time reduction.
5. Waste elimination.
6. Value analysis of product design.
7. 5S.

Samyeong adopted a top-down organisation improvement by which the senior management assigned the productivity improvement targets by level and department. The line workers were empowered to make improvements to assist their motivation and the managers applied their own initiatives to set examples for the workers.

President Choi of Samyeong asserted that employee work ethic and consciousness were the most critical elements in order to achieve the "2 by 2" productivity improvement. He also relied heavily on a suggestion system. In 1994 Samyeong solicited around 5,000 suggestions from the workers. "ATTACK100" was the catch phrase for the company to design small group activities, which was equivalent to the Japanese QC Circle. "100" implied "Do it perfectly" on the production line. President Choi often sent middle managers and engineers to Japan to benchmark Samyeong with Japanese companies.

The in-house and outside training programs were also considered important to motivate the employees in Samyeong. The production layout changed from I-shape to U-shape and benefited the company in driving out unnecessary lead time and work in process. The workers could concentrate on their work with much less tension than before. Following are three examples of improvement in processes suggested by Samyeong workers:

1. Simultaneous process of stripping and flaring of the inner wire through automation.
2. Automating the formerly manual process for the parking brake cable conduit.
3. Automation of the inspection process for the parking brake inner wire for the model J-3.

Samyeong identified seven kinds of waste to be removed from the production lines. These included overstocking, moving costs, defects, work methods, waiting time caused by line unbalance, and bottlenecks. The changes in the production layout and automation of production lines had significant contribution in resolving the long-term built-in wastes, especially overstocking and bottlenecks in the production lines. Samyeong controlled the lines by adopting a system called "my machine," which protected the machines and lines as a whole from breakdown and poor operation. The "my machine system" assigned every worker to one machine so that the person could be in charge of the particular machine and be responsible for maintaining his/her machine in the best condition. The company provided the workers about one hour, twice a week, for "my machine day meeting" where they shared their experiences among themselves.

The Japanese 5S technique was incorporated to keep the machines and lines clean and in order. Samyeong rotated the line managers among the different lines once a month so that employees could easily communicate across departments and understand the recent functions operations in the lines and plant as a whole.

A "visual control system" was also imported into Samyeong in motivating the employees to accept changes in the operations and management of the department and the entire plant. All kinds of necessary performance information, such as worker absenteeism, production rate, productivity, defect rates, accidents, and so forth, were measured by date, by department, and even by individual worker. The performance measures were then posted on the walls so that the information was clearly visible to the employees.

The actual performance of the "2 by 2" program was subject to an open evaluation by Hyundai monthly, quarterly, and annually. Hyundai would then compare the actual performances with the plans and targets, and evaluation was measured in terms of the line level, department level, and the whole company. "Productivity" or "value added" was measured in SPH (sales per hour) per worker and per capita monthly sales. Value added was defined as sales less material cost. The calculation of the three measures was based on utilisation factor, production rate, input man-hours (direct or indirect), and material consumption. This new measurement of the organisation became more active and dynamic in the production area.

Quality Management by "100 ppm."   In December 1991, Samyeong adopted the "100 ppm" program in order to improve the quality of its products. According to Hyundai's recommendation, Samyeong started the "100 ppm" program by targeting three quality dimensions: quality in the factory, quality at the supplier level, and quality at the buyer level, which included after-sales service of complete cars. Samyeong made an attempt to be qualified in 1994 but failed. Samyeong continued its effort in the new plant in Chonan City and eventually succeeded in 1995 and was named as the 35th "100 ppm" supplier of Hyundai Motor Company. Hyundai provided very thorough procedures that the supplier should follow to implement their "100 ppm" programs as effectively as possible. Samyeong took advantage of the Hyundai procedure in establishing its brand new plant in Chonan. The company tried to follow the Hyundai procedure as closely as possible because of the potential time saving, especially when compared to the old Samyeong plant located in Ansan. From the beginning of the new plant project, Samyeong requested Hyundai to provide a supplier support team to assist in setting up the lines and management systems. Samyeong's "100 ppm" organisation was under the direct supervision of President Choi and information was reported by the plant superintendents.

The Hyundai "100 ppm" procedure consisted of six major components in sequence. They are as follows:

1st Stage: Initiation and Preparation
- Identify the 100 ppm target items.
- 100 percent inspection for all finished products.

- Set up the organisation and motivate the employees by education and promotion devices such as badge wearing, placards, case study meetings, ceremony award system, and QC circles.
- 3X5S system that is to stabilize the quality by fixing the lot size, containers, and location of operations and the classical Japanese 5S.

2nd Stage: Typology of Defect
- Analyse the causes of defects and identify the types of defect.
- Identify the target processes to improve.
- Set up inspection measures.

3rd Stage: Troubleshooting
- Analyse the parameters for the production lines of the target items.
- Identify the limiting factors causing the trouble from four dimensions such as equipment, materials, working method, and operators. Interviews are recommended for operators.
- Correlative analysis of the tendency of defects and the limiting factors of the four items.
- Draw out the defect causes from the correlation analysis.

4th Stage: Development of the Three-Dimensional Measures
- First measure is to improve the line and then standardise the method by which the line was corrected.
- Second measure is to follow up the corrected process done above.
- Third measure is to audit carefully the quality of the products, so an auditing system is prepared.
- Planning the implementation in terms of ppm for a schedule over a time period.

5th Stage: Implementation onto the Floor
- Put the target lines under control as planned in the 4th stage.
- Set up work method, the procedure to follow the work method, and 3C 5S rules.
- Evaluate and correct the lines until the quality level reaches the target level.

6th Stage: Completion of Improvement
- Self company evaluation and Hyundai Motor Company evaluation are required to get acceptance at completion.
- Follow-up activity is very important to keep the lines under control.

For example, in the case of speedometer cables, they found that the friction between the core pin and the driver gear caused noise. It was due to the attachment of a key joint that was not qualified, and there was too much agitation between the core and core pin recorded on October 10, October 25, and December 10, respectively. They solved the problem by first looking over the design of the driver gear as a related part of the core pin, then adopted CAE (which is NISA reading software for design processes) to improve the process.

Operation of New Practices

CR30—An Overall Cost Reduction Campaign.   Although cost reduction was the most critical item to both Hyundai and its suppliers, the CR30 program was not sufficient to clearly confine its scope and extent. Cost reduction was a long-ranging and comprehensive task to carry out. President Choi of Samyeong thought that even though Hyundai had proved helpful to Samyeong in launching the CR30 program, the time spent between Hyundai staff and Samyeong was not sufficient to cover all of the issues. The problems remained very complex. President Choi of Samyeong remarked that:

> The Hyundai task team members seemed to be overly anxious to dig out some factors as quickly as possible by which they could easily show off their achievement of cost reduction at Samyeong . . . That tendency might cause us just to look at the purchase price of materials from our vendors as a cost reduction source instead of looking at other possible attributes in the overall operation such as waste in production lines, inventory system, physical distribution, inadequate design, wage increases, high overhead cost, physical distribution cost, and so on.

He continued:

> The purchase price of materials from our vendors has a great impact on the relationship we have with our vendors . . . Those second-tier vendors are not so developed technologically and managerially so we have to do something that is helpful to them, but we are not yet ready to help them reduce their cost . . . So we, Samyeong, take the pressure between Hyundai, our buyer, and our vendors.

Productivity Campaign: "2 by 2."   Samyeong's adoption of the programs to achieve "2 by 2" began at the cable manufacturing section. It was because there were more design changes in cable manufacturing than any other automotive products in Samyeong, and the product life cycle of the cable was rather short, about three to four years. In view of this, the rapid design changes and short product life cycle imposed certain limitations when implementing automation. However, Samyeong achieved the automation of 1,000 items out of their total of 2,000 items. Figure 8 shows how rapidly SPH improved over time. Almost 60 percent of SPH measures have been improved.

As shown in Figure 9, the SPH or productivity increased steadily as targeted by Hyundai and Samyeong for the first year after the launch of the program. The result was mainly contributed by process and work analysis and VE techniques, which resulted in increasing the automation of the inner wire flaring, coating, stripping, and flaring processes.

Quality Management by "100 ppm."   To qualify as a "100 ppm" supplier, the identified company had to meet the "100 ppm" level of quality in three areas: (1) the production process, (2) fin-

FIGURE 8

SPH (sales per hour) per person of parking brake cable

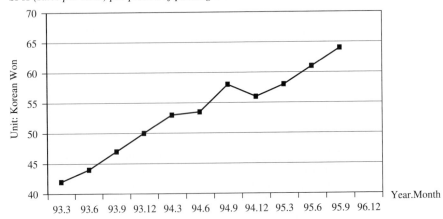

FIGURE 9

SPH of Samyeong (in total)

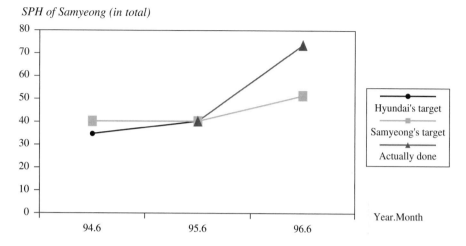

FIGURE 10

Number of after-sales service 3 months after sales for speedometer cable (in 1994)

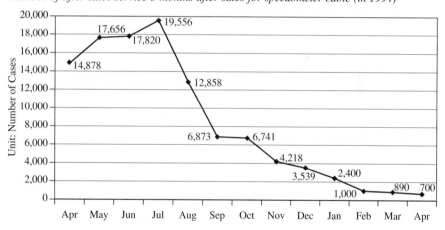

ished products, and (3) outside the company. Requirements (1) and (2) were for a two-month guarantee after improvement. Requirement (3) applied to Hyundai Motor Company incoming inspections for three months after delivery, and to after-service parts for six months after delivery in domestic maintenance, and one year after overseas shipping. The "100 ppm" auditing was a point system, the 100 points achievement was equivalent to 1–20 ppm of finished products and 0–100 ppm of work in process. The lowest score was 55 points, which was equivalent to 10,001 ppm or higher of finished products and 30,001 ppm or higher of work in process.

Samyeong finally passed the 100 ppm completion of improvement evaluation in October 1995, after three consequent internal audits by Hyundai. For instance, the final quality level of speedometer cables improved from 19,556 ppm in July 1994 down to 700 ppm in April 1995. The progression in quality is presented in Figure 10.

Conclusion

This case study has examined three campaigns in an integrated way within Samyeong Cable Company, namely

1. CR30 overall cost reduction campaign.
2. Productivity "2 by 2" campaign.
3. Quality management "100 ppm" campaign.

Surprisingly, there wasn't any significant political battle or resistance from the workers throughout implementation of the new systems. This is due to the following factors.

Firstly, Hyundai placed great effort in working with its supplier companies to achieve its strategic goals through its suppliers. Even though it was a cooperative relationship between Hyundai and Samyeong, Hyundai was the driver of change and Samyeong followed in a cooperative manner. Through a well-designed model of supplier management and strong support, which was delivered by a flexibly manned team, Hyundai was able to aggressively lead the suppliers in the direction that they wanted. This could not have been achieved if there was resistance from the suppliers. Hyundai managed to retain a good relationship with its partners due to this well-designed model. The most unique attribute of Hyundai's supplier development program was that the relationship strived for long-term single sourcing with flexibility. This protected Hyundai from being exposed to inefficient suppliers and helped to develop the supplier's capability without confrontation in any hostile way.

Secondly, even though Hyundai's supplier management program was initially difficult for supplier companies to adopt new and advanced technology such as 100 ppm because of their small size, they could easily get access to the new technology from Hyundai at a low price. This was partly because of Hyundai's supplier management policy, and also because of the suppliers' positive reaction to the programs conducted by Hyundai.

Thirdly, the CEO of the supplier company provided strong support. Samyeong's new owner, President Choi, was a well-educated professional manager who was able to implement new management techniques effectively compared to many Korean companies, especially the small and medium ones, which were managed by their owners with little experience in advanced management styles. In this case, President Choi, who had a strong background in management theory and application experiences, drove the company to adopt a new management style and changed the culture of the firm. Additionally, Samyeong's new factory in Chonan also had the geographic advantage of being close to the co-research centre for the cable industry, which was also established at Chonan.

This case implies that for small and medium companies that cannot afford to develop new technology that requires large capital investment, it would be better to adopt the technology through their buying firm's expense and experience. In the case of Hyundai being the buying firm, it is true that in order to achieve their own strategic goal, it was important to have their supplier companies well managed in a cooperative manner, especially in complex industries like the auto industry.

APPENDIX 1
HYUNDAI'S SUPPLIER RATING REPORT

	Evaluation Parts	*Points*
Managerial (20 %)	Stability	4
	Growth	4
	Activity	4
	Revenue	4
	Productivity	4
	Others	Varies
Technological development (25 %)	A80	5
	Product development capability	15
	Manufacturing capability	5
Production management (25 %)	Production planning	3
	2 by 2	5
	Field management	3
	SS	5
	Task management	3
	Fire prevention	1.5
	Computerised degree	1.5
	Defect rates	3
Quality management (25 %)	Quality insurance	3
	Outsourcing	3
	Process management	3
	Product management	3
	Reliability	3
	Suggestion systems	2
	Domestic A/S	3
	Foreign A/S	5
Incentives (5 %)	Patents	2
	100 ppm	1
	ISO	1
	Exports	1

APPENDIX 2
IMPROVEMENT CASE OF Y3-PARKING BRAKE INNER WIRE

Before:

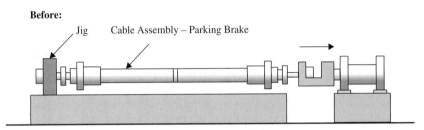

Problem: Inconsistent length of the product due to conduit shrinking.

After:

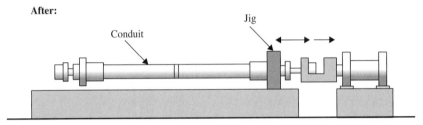

Effects: Saving 162,000 wons a month by low defects and low cost.

Investment: 50,000 wons.

Time taken: 0.3 month.

18
TELSTRA'S NATIONAL TELEMARKETING CENTRE[1]

Telstra—until recently Australia's only telecommunications carrier—is internationally recognised within the industry for providing a world-class telecommunications service to a highly dispersed and isolated population under challenging environmental conditions.

In 1990, the Australian government announced that it would end Telstra's monopoly and move toward a deregulated telecommunications industry. The first step was a competitive duopoly, and in 1991–1992 a private carrier—Optus Communications—became Telstra's first competitor in the Australian marketplace. On July 1, 1997, the industry was fully deregulated. Over this period, Telstra has undergone enormous changes—none of which is more dramatic than the shift from an engineering driven organisation to one with a marketing focus.

The shift in emphasis from engineering to marketing is clearly reflected by the establishment of Telstra's National Telemarketing Centre (NTC). Though originally created in response to deregulation and the threat of its first competitor, the NTC has grown to become a major national marketing channel for Telstra, as well as providing national customer and product support services.

This case examines the function of the National Telemarketing Centre within Telstra, the role of technology at the NTC, and the way call centres affect organisational flexibility and change the relationship between Telstra and its customers.

Telstra's National Telemarketing Centre

Robert Holland, national general manager for Telstra's National Telemarketing Centre (NTC), had just arrived at his office. He retrieved the morning newspaper from his briefcase and started looking through it—he was keen to get the latest news on the booming Australian call centre business. But, before he could find the information technology section, the telephone rang. He put it on speaker:

> Good morning Robert, it's John here, I have a key account manager on the line from our Corporate Division. One of her major customers is a food producer who has just become the victim of an extortion attempt. You may have seen it on the news last night—someone claims to have contaminated a batch of their baby food.
>
> Anyway, they want to know if we can design and run a campaign to call retailers and advise them on the product recall process and generally reassure them that the replacement batch is sound. They also want us to accept incoming enquiries from concerned customers on a 1-800 free call number which they will provide to the news media and place in newspaper advertisements and so on. They are prepared to pay a very nice premium if we start immediately and they are ready to e-mail the list of retailers' names and numbers so we can get underway with the outbound calls.

Robert groaned and leaned back in his chair. With the names and numbers fed into the NTC's various systems, they could have such a campaign designed in half an hour and underway as soon as they could get the additional staff in—probably the next day. He hated to miss an opportunity like this. It was not just the missed revenue. When customers think about telephone calls they naturally turn to their telecommunications provider for help. This was one of those rare opportunities

---

[1]This case was developed for use in classroom discussion and is not intended to necessarily illustrate appropriate or inappropriate management practices. The case authors are Dr. Paul Richardson and Professor Peter Weill from the Centre for Management of Information Technology, Melbourne Business School, The University of Melbourne (revised 19 February 1999).

for Telstra to forge a close relationship with an important customer in a time of need; the cost of turning them away at a time like this was something that he could not place a value on.

> Sorry John, at the moment we are running major inbound and outbound campaigns for the Commercial and Consumer [C & C] group. You can check with Mary if you like, but I very much doubt that we will have enough spare capacity to run or organise a campaign of that size. In any case, we haven't yet formalised the processes for managing and charging external clients. I'm afraid that you will have to refer the client to one of our private industry partners. Oh, by the way, you had better tell the account manager that it doesn't matter how much they are willing to pay—if we interrupt the C & C campaign to take an external client we won't be around tomorrow!

This is exactly what John Hollingsworth, the manager for Business Development at the NTC, had already told the key account manager. She was persistent, but he had turned away others before her for the same reasons. Following telecommunications deregulation in July 1997, the NTC was free to compete in the local telemarketing industry,[2] but external work could not displace that of their internal clients, and various restrictions (especially on personnel numbers) prevented them from increasing capacity.

Furthermore, the NTC was a cost centre in the Commercial & Consumer Business Unit at Telstra—not a profit centre. The NTC must compete with other marketing channels for their budget allocation from the Commercial & Consumer (C & C) Business Unit. Commercial & Consumer also supply nearly 90 percent of the NTC's work, the remainder coming almost entirely from other business units within Telstra on a nonprofit transfer pricing arrangement. Holland flicked through his diary and then continued his conversation with Hollingsworth:

> Thursday week I have to go cap-in-hand to the accountants and justify our budget for the next financial year, which starts in about three months from now. So we need to finalise how many people we need, how much money we want, and provide them with a business plan describing what we are going to do in return—volumes, actions, strategies, and so on. Getting requests like this from major corporate customers proves to me that we have something valuable to offer at a fair price—I'm sure we could be doing more to help important Telstra customers like them while improving service to our internal clients. As things stand, we are bound to end up negotiating on a budget that is one-third of what is required for the marketing our clients would like to do. Why don't you come around to my office now and we will go over the strategic options for the business case again.

Telstra Corporation[3]

For many years, the provision of telecommunications services in Australia was the sole domain of three government-owned instrumentalities—the domestic carrier Telecom, the international carrier OTC,[4] and the national satellite carrier AUSSAT. In 1987, the Commonwealth Government of Australia undertook a fundamental review of the Australian telecommunications industry. This resulted in the announcement of wide-ranging reforms of the basic structural and regulatory framework of the telecommunications sector in November 1990. Reforms focused on the introduction of broad-based competition and a restructuring of the three monopoly carriers. In 1991–1992, a competitive duopoly was established based on a single government-owned carrier (AOTC—formed through the

---

[2]Following concerns expressed by private telemarketing companies, Telstra made an undertaking to Austel (the government telecommunications regulator) that it would not compete in the Australian telemarketing industry while the carrier duopoly arrangement existed.

[3]This section is a revised excerpt from a previous case on Telstra by Carey Butler and Peter Weill, "Standardising the Information Technology Environment at Telecom Australia," Melbourne Business School, 1995.

[4]OTC—Overseas Telecommunications Corporation.

merger of Telecom and OTC)[5] and a private sector carrier (Optus Communications—a private company incorporating AUSSAT). In 1993, the name AOTC was changed to Telstra Corporation Limited. Both companies offered domestic and international services, with Optus initially obtaining a 10 percent market share. On July 1, 1997, the Australian telecommunications market was opened to full, unrestricted competition and shortly thereafter one-third of Telstra Corporation was "privatised" in a public listing in which the Australian public was strongly encouraged to participate.

Telstra provides a full range of telecommunication services and products to domestic and international customers. The corporation is headquartered in Melbourne, Sydney, and Brisbane and owns around 10,000 sites[6] throughout Australia. It also has business offices or joint ventures in 20 countries around the world. The Asia-Pacific region is a particular area of interest and investment.

Telstra owns about 2 percent of telephone lines worldwide, is the third largest owner of submarine cables in the world, and has one of the world's largest digitised terrestrial networks with over 1 million km of fibre optic cable in active service. In Australia, Telstra handles more than 10 million local calls per day. The company's customer base is the largest of any Australian enterprise, with more than 95.5 percent of Australian households connected to its telephone network.

In 1993–1994, Telstra faced its first full year of competition. Despite this, revenues increased by 5 percent on the previous year to A\$13.4b. Three years later, at the time of deregulation on July 1, 1997, Telstra's revenue was A\$16b (a five-year financial summary for Telstra is included in Appendix A). Telstra is one of the largest contributors to Australia's national wealth with a value-added contribution of A\$10.8b in the financial year 1996–1997, representing 2.4 percent of Australia's gross domestic product.

Telstra's organisational structure is shown in Exhibit 1 and the functions of the major business areas are described in Table 1. Each business area is semiautonomous, having its own assets, its own team of employees, and its own culture within the context of the overall organisational culture. Each business area has commercial accountability and a central focus on servicing the needs of a particular customer group, e.g., corporate consumers are handled differently than residential consumers.

TABLE 1   Major Business Unit at Telstra[7]

Network & Technology	• Domestic and international network design, construction, and operation. • Network products and services. • Research and development.	• Information technology. • Mobile networks. • Customer support systems.
Commercial & Consumer	• Sales and service delivery to 7 million residential and SME customers. • Operator-assisted services.	• Payphones. • Telstra Visa card.
Business & International	• Business and government customer sales and service. • Wholesale customers. • Satellite and radio services. • Global business services.	• International carrier business. • International joint ventures. • Mobile sales and service. • Olympic Games Business Unit.

(continued)

---

[5]Of the two entities, Telecom was about 15 times larger than OTC in terms of revenue.

[6]Includes business offices, line depots, major telephone exchanges, and radio terminal stations (1995 figures).

[7]Telstra Annual Report 1997.

TABLE 1 *(concluded)*

Retail Products & Marketing	• Access and local products. • Long distance products. • Customer premises equipment. • Mobile products. • Intelligent network products and services.	• Private networking and data services. • Strategy and pricing. • Marketing communication and advertising. • Internet products.
Regulatory & External Affairs	• Regulatory strategy and operations. • Corporate and public affairs. • Federal government relations.	• Consumer affairs. • Stakeholder and issues management.
Finance & Administration	• Finance. • Treasury. • Audit and risk management. • Legal counsel.	• Corporate secretary. • Strategic planning. • Corporate services. • Investor relations.
Employee Relations	• Personnel. • Industrial relations. • Health and safety.	• Training. • Leadership development. • Organisational effectiveness.
Telstra Multimedia Pty Ltd.	• Broadband network rollout. • Directory services and yellow pages. • Multimedia products.	• Internet platform and access. • FOXTEL.

EXHIBIT 1

Telstra's structure (highlighting position of the NTC)

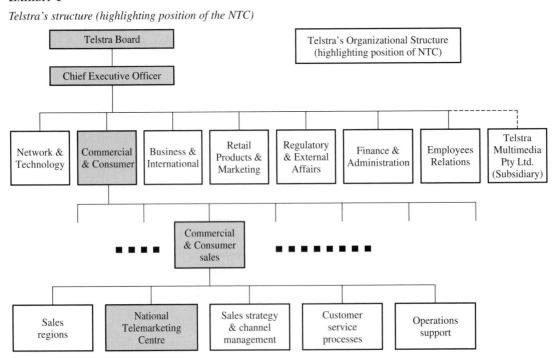

Telstra employs 66,100 full-time staff;[8] hence the sheer size and scope of Telstra's operations means that single business units are often dispersed over multiple geographic locations. Commercial & Consumer is the firm's largest business unit, with nearly 30,000 staff. Telstra intends to reduce staff by approximately 25,500 employees over a four-year period, a process that began in 1996–1997. During 1996–1997 the company reduced full-time staff by approximately 11,900—about 20 percent of which were obtained by outsourcing some activities, by the sale of certain businesses, and the contracting out of some operations.[9] Telstra will continue to reduce staff numbers through a process of natural attrition, outsourcing, and redundancies.

Complete deregulation of telecommunications on July 1, 1997, will be remembered as the beginning of a dramatic change in the telecommunications marketplace in Australia. In preparation for deregulation, Telstra underwent significant changes, and postderegulation will see Telstra continue its transformation from a government-owned monopoly to an independent corporation operating in a highly competitive marketplace.

In recent years, no change in Telstra is more apparent than its shift from a technically focused organisation to one with a strong customer focus. As Frank Blount, CEO of Telstra, writes in the 1997 annual report:

> For decades the "essence of Telstra" was perceived to be primarily technical, built upon its network. In today's environment we now recognise that adding value for our customer base is our driving force, and that the ideal of service and the drive for improvement must be at the core of the culture of the organisation. This shift caused us to rethink our assumptions and attitude at every level of the corporation.

The shift in Telstra's thinking and strategy is reflected throughout Blount's overview in the annual report:

> While we have refined our abilities to win back customers, a higher priority must be placed on retaining them in the first place. The outstanding success of customer loyalty programs such as the Telstra Visa card in no way replaces the fundamental commitment to meet the needs of our customers. . . .
>
> Considerable energy has been devoted during the year to enhancing our understanding of the needs of different kinds of customers, and to tailoring our products and service packages to meet their varied requirements. . . .
>
> We will continue to pursue our existing strategies of growing new markets and increasing volumes in existing markets; improving our productivity and efficiency; adding value to the communications service we provide; and using global and industry-based alliances to leverage new opportunities.

Telstra's vision and strategy is articulated in a poster (based on the corporation's 1996–1999 strategic plan) that was distributed to all staff:

> The Telstra Vision is to be the leading electronic communication and information services company in the Asia-Pacific and among the top 10 globally.

Telstra's key success factors:

- Competitive customer services.
- Best practice financial performance.
- Retain market leadership.
- Efficient and effective investment and infrastructure.
- Growth and business development.
- Employee satisfaction.
- Corporate integrity.
- Political/regulatory environment.

---

[8]Telstra Annual Report 1997.
[9]Telstra Annual Report 1997.

Call Centre Background

Call centres are not an entirely new idea. It is possible for a business to establish a national (indeed international) presence for handling incoming customer enquiries or undertaking outgoing tele-marketing campaigns by ringing customers from a preprepared list of telephone numbers—manually crossing each number off as it is called. As the business demands become more sophisticated, the complexity of the call centre increases with the introduction of real-time access to corporate IT systems, sophisticated computer-telephony integration, and purpose-designed office plans with furniture catering for teams of specially trained call centre staff.

Call centres are a labour-intensive business with staffing costs usually accounting for 65 percent of a call centre's budget.[10] The average Australian Call Centre has 67 seats,[11] with the largest around 800 seats. Research suggests that mid-sized call centres with 200–250 seats (requiring about 2,000–3,000m^2 of office space) are the most efficient.[12] Call centre productivity is highly sensitive to staff-related issues such as turnover, absenteeism, and motivation, and therefore effective human resource management is critical to the call centre. TARP, in its "1997 Teleservice Benchmarking Study," identified a number of characteristics typical of best-in-class call centres. A summary of their report is included in Appendix B.

The call centre industry in Australia is currently undergoing a period of rapid expansion, as is the Asia-Pacific region in general. One estimate[13] suggests the Asia-Pacific call centre business will be worth about U.S.\$187 billion by 2002 and the Gartner Group[14] estimates that the global call centre hardware and software market will exceed U.S.\$10 billion by 2001. Of potential regional competitors, Australian operating costs are significantly lower with an annual cost per seat of approximately U.S.\$48,750. This is compared to U.S.\$64,500 for Singapore and U.S.\$65,250 in Hong Kong.[15] In addition, Australia is perceived as having a mature call centre market with excellent technology infrastructure, skilled and multilingual human resources, and cheap office space. Melbourne rents, already the lowest in the Asia-Pacific region (e.g., Melbourne U.S.\$89m^2 compared to Singapore U.S.\$1018m^2),[16] have been declining over the last few years as a result of an excess in central business district office space.

The Australian call centre industry is growing at l0 percent pa[17] [per annum] to 25 percent pa[18] with the number of Australian businesses using call centres growing at 20 percent pa.[19] Of the 1,200–4,000[20] call centres already in Australia, New South Wales has 60 percent[21] with Victorian, South Australian, and Tasmanian governments keen to increase their states' share. Regional cities, such as Bendigo in Victoria, are also proactive in attracting call centre businesses, offering substantial incentives in addition to their claims that regional cities have lower staff churn rates, absenteeism, and wages than metropolitan areas.

---

[10]In "Growing option for all businesses," *The Age,* 5/1/97.

[11]In "Call centres ring up a new role," *The Australian,* 2/9/97.

[12]In "Revolution on the line, says architect," *The Australian,* 15/8/97.

[13]In "Call advantage 'at risk,'" *The Australian,* 30/9/97.

[14]C. McCormick, "Customer service and support strategies, part 1: The call centre," *Inside Gartner Group* (ISG), 19/2/97.

[15]In "Call advantage 'at risk,'" *The Australian,* 30/9/97.

[16]"Smart call centre Victoria, Australia," State government of Victoria.

[17]In "Call centres ring up a new role," *The Australian,* 2/9/97.

[18]In "Lufthansa plots course for Melbourne," *The Australian,* 15/8/97.

[19]In "Growing option for all businesses," *The Australian,* 5/11/97.

[20]Estimates on the number of call centres vary considerably—presumably because of differing definitions as to what exactly constitutes a call centre.

[21]In "Lufthansa plots course for Melbourne," *The Australian,* 15/8/97.

The industry is believed to employ more than 100,000 people in Australia with forecasts[22] suggesting that there could be as many as 80,000 new jobs in the sector over the next three years. Survey results reported in a recent Victorian government publication[23] designed to promote Victoria's call centre strengths suggest that 66 percent of those working in the sector are female, 47 percent are full-time, and 45 percent are 20–29 years old.

The growth in call centres reflects an increasing recognition in business that they provide a valuable service to customers while lowering the cost of doing business and increasing organisational flexibility. As many goods are becoming highly commoditised, service and support are increasingly becoming the only differentiators between competing products. For example, the National Australia Bank has two national call centres that handle about 50 percent of all customer enquiries—10 years ago, 95 percent of these went through branches.[24] The call centre enables the bank to provide services to customers from any telephone regardless of call centre staff location.

At present Australia has very little in the way of government regulation of telemarketing. The industry has a code of conduct that, for example, discourages outbound campaigns after 9:00 P.M. The level of regulation is much less than in the United States where, in some states, you are not allowed to outbound at all and most states require third-party verification.[25]

The National Telemarketing Centre

Telstra established the National Telemarketing Centre (NTC) as part of its Commercial & Consumer Business Unit in May 1992 in direct response to deregulation and the arrival of its first competitor— Optus Telecommunications. The first service offered by Optus was in the lucrative long distance telephony[26] market, and consumers were to be asked in a "preselection" process to choose by ballot whether they wanted Telstra or Optus to carry their long distance calls. To defend its market share, Telstra set out to contact customers in Australia through direct mail, marketing communications, and outbound and inbound telemarketing.

Background.   At the time the National Telemarketing Centre was established in 1992, Telstra had approximately 150 call centres across the organisation that employed over 5,000 staff. Telstra's existing call centres were almost entirely inbound—i.e., accepting calls from customers[27] for customer service and support functions, such as directory assistance,[28] billing service activation, fault reporting, etc. The NTC was to be the first call centre at Telstra set up for national marketing purposes, intended primarily for sales, with a large component of calls to be outbound (to customers).

The establishment of the NTC also reflected an important underlying change in Telstra as it shifted from being an "engineering-oriented" organisation, with a strong engineering culture and management, to one with more emphasis on the customer. "It is an interesting story in itself," Holland comments, "the shift in perception at Telstra from one where the main asset was the telephone exchanges and cable in the ground to the marketing view that our main asset is the customer

---

[22]As reported in "Call city online," *The Australian Financial Review,* 3/11/97.

[23]"Smart call centre Victoria, Australia," State Government of Victoria.

[24]"Need for speed moved NAB," *The Australian,* 15/8/97.

[25]Where, after a telemarketing sale has been made to a person, another company must telephone that person and basically verify the transaction details are correct.

[26]Often referred to as STD or Subscriber Trunk Dialing.

[27]In the context of the NTC: Customers are the people who the call centre communicates with via telephone on behalf of their client, who is the person or organisation who actually commissions the work.

[28]Directory services receive approximately 400 million calls per annum and billing is the next largest, receiving about 40 million calls per annum.

database." The centralised customer database is fed with customer contact information from most of Telstra's 150 call centres.[29]

The NTC was established in Burwood, in the eastern suburbs of the Victorian state capital of Melbourne. Melbourne was a convenient location because a large proportion of Telstra's business, including its national head office, is located in and around the city.

The National Telemarketing Centre's initial task was to contact customers prior to preselection in their region[30] and create a positive experience with Telstra. In addition to outbound calls to regions about to undergo preselection, the NTC also set up a "free preselection hotline" to answer any questions a customer may have had about choosing a long distance provider. This also gave a representative the opportunity to optimise the customer's account and offer other Telstra services and products. Mary Quinn, group manager for sales at the NTC, explains the nature of the campaign:

> There was a major outbound campaign to customers who were going through preselection. The message was something to the effect of: "Hello. This is Telstra. How are you? We are just ringing you up to see if you are happy with your service . . ." They were quite taken aback! We also had inbound telephone numbers and situations were created where we wanted customers to ring in and complain, since there was not much opportunity for them to do this previously. There was good customer reaction and we were very successful.

Indeed, many believe that the NTC campaign was a major reason why Optus achieved a lower market share from the preselection process than they had expected. On average, 13–14 percent of Australian customers selected Optus as their preferred carrier. The remainder either chose to remain with Telstra or did not return their ballot paper, in which case they remained with Telstra by default.

As the preselection process progressed region by region, the NTC quickly grew to have about 700–1,000 telemarketing representatives (TMRs) distributed over three sites around Melbourne. Quinn remembers this as an interesting time when all NTC staff were extraordinarily motivated by the excitement, importance, and success of what they were doing. However, over the three years following its formation, the NTC started to develop a reputation for not working to normal Telstra processes. In particular, the high use of agency staff (none were permanent Telstra staff) had become a major issue with the unions. As a result of industrial action, the NTC was forced to make many of the agency staff permanent employees. The net result was a drop in size to about 500 TMRs, all of whom were now permanent Telstra staff.

Telemarketing.   Prior to deregulation of the telecommunications industry in Australia, Telstra rarely undertook marketing in any of its forms. When the National Telemarketing Centre was established during deregulation, it became one of several marketing channels available.[31] The client's marketing goals determine what channel is to be used, and which products and what customer segments will be targeted (the people who commission the NTC are referred to as "clients" and the people the NTC telephone, on behalf of the client, are referred to as "customers").

"In general terms," says Holland, "the NTC's current goals are customer retention, win-backs, and product sales." Once per quarter a governance committee consisting of Holland, internal clients, and other stakeholders meet to discuss what client work should be done by the NTC.

---

[29]The directory services call centre being a notable exception.

[30]Preselection occurred at different times for different geographical regions. Customers were required to fill in a "ballot" where they selected either Telstra or Optus as their long distance carrier.

[31]Television advertising, direct sales, and Telstra retail outlets are among the other marketing channels often used by Telstra.

EXHIBIT 2

Source of the NTC's telemarketing work

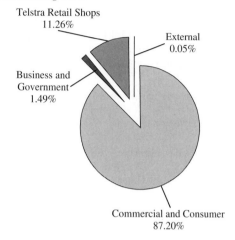

Capacity of the NTC and industry partner(s) is taken into account and decisions are made as to what client's work has the highest priority. Usually internal demand for telemarketing outstrips the NTC's capacity. The NTC's largest client is Commercial and Consumer, followed by Telstra Retail Shops, Business and Government, and external clients as illustrated in Exhibit 2.

When a client has decided to use the NTC as their marketing channel, the Business Development group works through a standard campaign summary (or brief) with the client in order to design a campaign that meets their specific goals. The brief describes the objectives of the campaign, the training requirements, IT and systems requirements, and schedules for training, operational reviews, and so on. Business Development has a lot of experience in running telemarketing campaigns and are often able to add a great deal of value to the client's campaign at this stage. A "campaign coordinator" is assigned to manage all aspects of the campaign for the client, from IT system configuration to execution and campaign reporting. A campaign team meeting is then held where the brief is presented to all of the people involved.

Currently, the NTC's work is split about 50/50 annually between inbound and outbound campaigns. Inbound campaigns are usually conducted in conjunction with some other channel, such as television advertising or mail-outs, because something is required to stimulate the customer to ring in.[32] On the other hand, outbound campaigns can be run independently and are usually much easier and faster to deploy. Outbound campaigns are most useful for things that are not very conducive to mail or television advertising, such as winning back customers, whereas inbound campaigns tend to have much higher sales conversion rates per contact.

It is common for campaigns run by the NTC to involve a mix of inbound and outbound telemarketing. For example, the "Lines #3" campaign ran from August to September 1997. A magazine promoting Telstra products and services was mailed to 840,000 of Telstra's higher spend customers from which the NTC received inbound calls—but the main component of the campaign was a large number of outbound calls to the highest spend customers that did not respond. The campaign objective was to contact 400,000 customers who had received the magazine and sell

---

[32]Usually on a "1-800" (free call) number.

network products such as Easycall, MessageBank, and Faxstream. The sales conversion target was 20 percent and the NTC actually achieved a 47 percent conversion rate for those contacted—equivalent to 129,248 network product sales.

Not all activities undertaken by the NTC are strictly telemarketing to external customers. For example, during the recent Telstra float it came to management's attention at the last moment that about 3,000 Telstra employees had applied for shares but never received their share offer. Quinn explains what happened:

> Concerned employees were ringing [the office responsible] saying that they had not received their offer. There was a lot of concern about this because of the emphasis placed on employee participation in the float, therefore the head of employee relations contacted the NTC at 4:15 P.M. on a Friday afternoon to organise an outbound campaign to contact these employees over the weekend. By 5:00 P.M. the NTC had organised 20 telemarketing representatives for a Saturday campaign and we managed to contact 95 percent of the list by Monday morning.

At 9:00 A.M. Monday morning Quinn got another call. This time it was a request to set up an inbound line to answer staff questions about the float; 2,000 calls were expected. Quinn describes what happened:

> I was on my way to work when they rang on my mobile phone. After they described how they wanted to set up an inbound campaign, I asked when the number was needed—they said "Now!" We didn't have time to put the proper processes in place to get a new number so I looked for one that we were already using that wasn't getting many calls on it. I got the IT guys and voice people to pull the number out of the area it was going to and redirect it to another team. I got the telephone number to them at 10:00 A.M. and five minutes later we had our first call—we only just had time to set up the processes.

A more typical example of the type of campaigns run by the NTC is the "win-back," where ex-Telstra customers are telephoned and encouraged to return to Telstra. The NTC has had huge success with win-back campaigns, a good example being when Telstra exited the "Flybuys" loyalty scheme[33] on June 30, 1997. As Holland explains:

> We recently ran a large-scale outbound campaign where we telephoned all Telstra customers that were in the Flybuys scheme and explained to them why we were exiting. The campaign was expected to be pretty boring—a few hundred thousand calls going something like ". . . I'm just ringing to say that Telstra is no longer going to be part of Flybuys . . . [and explaining why]." So it was not exactly a "feel-good" call and the TMRs were a little apprehensive about that. But as it turned out, the campaign was enormously successful in terms of win-backs and even unexpected product sales.

Some other examples of telemarketing campaigns run by the NTC include:

- The "Frontrunner" campaign, where high spend Telstra analogue mobile customers were targeted with a special offer in order to encourage them to move to Telstra's GSM (digital mobile) service. This was a very difficult campaign because of the technical complexity of explaining to customers why they should be moving to digital.
- Preemptively telephoning areas where competitors are undertaking direct sales activities or offering services. For example, the NTC telephoned Telstra customers in areas where Optus was known to be laying cable at the time.
- The NTC does a large number of customer survey campaigns. In the past, managers had no idea how well a new product would be received prior to its launch. Now they can test the potential market prior to launch using the NTC, e.g., by asking, "What do you think of this particular product idea?"

---

[33]"Flybuys" is a loyalty scheme originally launched by three of Australia's largest marketers in 1994. Telstra jointed Flybuys in 1995. Refer also to the case, "COME BUY WITH US: The Flybuys Story," by Carey Butler and Peter Weill, Melbourne Business School.

- "Feel-good" campaigns—such as ringing customers who have just purchased a Telstra product and checking to make sure everything is okay and that they are happy with the service they have received.
- The NTC has had great success targeting particular ethnic populations such as Greeks, Italians, Cantonese, and Vietnamese. These communities greatly appreciate being able to converse with someone in their own language.

Customer Service and Product Support.   In addition to the NTC's main site at Burwood, which mostly conducts telemarketing activities, the NTC also has two other locations—one in the nearby suburb of Waverley and another at Queen Street in Melbourne's central business district. The other sites cater mostly for incoming customer service and product support calls.

The Queen Street call centre handles national overflow calls from the 39 regional customer service call centres. These calls are initially filtered by an interactive voice response (IVR) system and are diverted to the NTC facilities when operators are not available to take the calls at the regional centres. Services handled include enquiries, fault reporting, and services activation requests. The Queen Street call centre is one of the best in the country—leading many of the regional sites in the full range of customer service performance indicators.

The Waverley site supports nationally just one product—"Telepath"[34]—and its several derivatives. In this case the NTC is essentially contracted to provide customer support for this product (i.e., in contrast to other products where customer support is provided in-house by the group responsible for the product).

The current[35] organisational structure of the National Telemarketing Centre is shown in Exhibit 3.

EXHIBIT 3

National Telemarketing Centre organisational structure

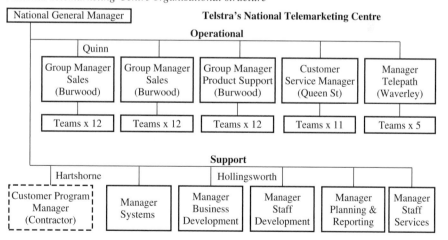

---

[34]"Telepath" is a suite of products and initiatives designed to provide individuals with personalised communication services for anywhere, anyway, anytime communication. One component is a "portable" telephone number where you are issued one number that can be redirected to other numbers—such as work, home, mobile, etc.—as required.

[35]As of January 1998, subsequent changes in March 1998 have added another operational arm, "direct sales," from two sites (Burwood in Melbourne and Grafton in the state of New South Wales).

Telemarketing activities at the NTC are broken into two groups, each managed by a group manager for sales who reports directly to the national general manager. Telemarketing representatives are broken into teams of 15 people each, who report to the group manager through a team leader.

Information Technology at the NTC

ATLAS.   At around the same time as the industrial action, the NTC identified the need for improved systems to support the telemarketing representatives. The existing "pencil and paper" based business process had TMRs manually dialing telephone numbers from paper lists and filling in forms during the call that others would later enter into Telstra's core systems (e.g., to activate the service). Hollingsworth comments:

> In the early days, most of the NTC telemarketing activity was selling Flexi-plans,[36] but the provisioning costs actually outweighed the sales! It was before my time, but apparently there were around 400 back-of-house staff on 24-hour shifts processing orders as opposed to 300–400 actually making the calls!

It was clear that information technology (IT) was required to support and streamline this process. An information system plan developed by the NTC identified and charted the business process shown in Exhibit 4.

Telstra's existing core information systems could not be used as-is within this architecture for several reasons. In particular, five different systems (and screens) would be required in front of each TMR in order to support the full range of marketing campaigns, and the response time of these systems was not fast enough to support the 2–3 minute handling time of a typical telemarketing call.

What the NTC needed was a system that quickly extracted only relevant customer information from the multiple Telstra systems and seamlessly blended this into one screen of information

EXHIBIT 4

Business process at the NTC

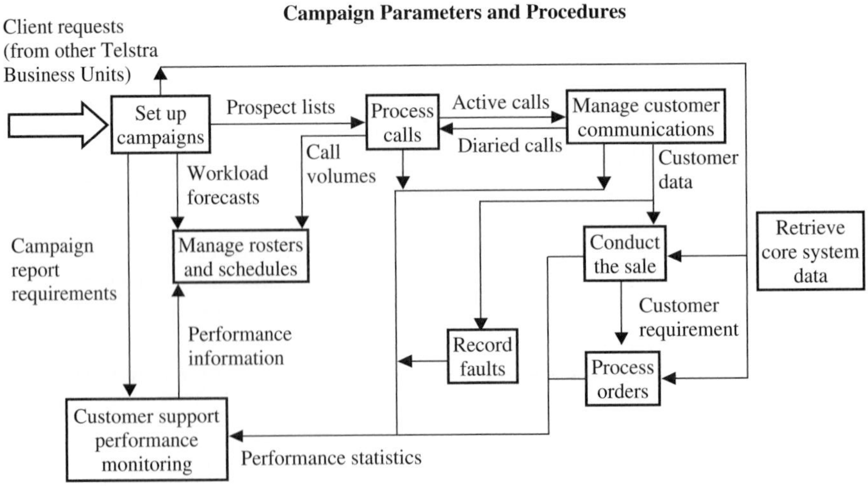

---

[36]Flex-plan discounts are a range of tailored savings plans that discount selected call types, for example, local, long-distance, or international calls.

for display to the TMR as they made the call. The TMR also needed to be able to mark the service for activation from the same screen.

The result was ATLAS-1, a telemarketing IT support system developed in-house. ATLAS—together with the automation of outbound dialing and order entry—were identified as critical success factors to improve the cost effectiveness of the NTC. The business drivers for ATLAS and its architecture are described further in Appendix C.

Peter John Hartshorne, NTC systems manager at the time and a key figure in the development of ATLAS, described its impact:

> ATLAS managed to compress data from multiple core systems down to one or two screens which can be tailored for each campaign so that TMRs have in front of them just the information they need to handle the call. Mostly as a result of this, time per contact decreased from 6 minutes to 4 minutes. Another big advantage is that TMRs need only 10 days' training to use ALTAS—whereas in regional call centres [where they also need access to all of the Telstra core systems] it takes up to 10 weeks to train someone.

The NTC now has a set of standard screen layouts from which the campaign manager can select when designing a new campaign. In addition to a considerable increase in the productivity of the TMRs, ATLAS also enabled a huge improvement in the quality of management information that could be made available to clients. ATLAS is able to produce a comprehensive set of statistics suitable for campaign reporting depending on the clients' particular needs.

Some NTC and ATLAS statistics:

- NTC Telemarketing operates 7:00 A.M. to 12:00 A.M. 6.5 days per week.
- In the financial year 1996–1997, the NTC ran a total of 290 campaigns.
- One new campaign and two changes to existing campaigns are implemented in ATLAS each week.
- Up to 320 people use ATLAS at any one time.
- ATLAS is used for an average of 70,000 contacts per week.
- On average, one in four contacts results in a sale.

Predictive Dialer.   The introduction of ATLAS dramatically reduced the time per contact by providing customer information in a timely and succinct manner, but an issue still limiting the efficiency of the TMR (and an issue to have far-reaching structural implications) was the time spent manually dialing telephone numbers for outbound campaigns. Because of the large number of people who are not at home during the week, TMRs had to manually dial in the order of 30 numbers to get each contact. On a cost-per-contact basis this meant that weekday calls were much higher than evening or weekend calls when people were more likely to be home.

Therefore, most of the NTC's outbound work was conducted in the evenings and on Saturdays. Even with higher labour costs—rates 1.15 times the regular (weekday) rate for evenings and 1.5 times for Saturday—cost-per-contact was lower for evening and Saturday shifts.

The installation of a "predictive dialer" completely changed the situation. A predictive dialer is a computer-based system that can be loaded with a list of telephone numbers that it then proceeds to dial—filtering out no-answers, fax machines, answering machines, and busy signals.[37] The predictive dialer paces itself to the rate at which TMRs are working through calls. The objective is to transfer— without delay—a person who has answered the telephone to a TMR that has

---

[37]Telephone numbers are tried in three different time slots—morning, afternoon, and evening. If there is no answer, the predictive dialer tries the number again in the next time slot and continues to rotate attempts through each slot for a total of nine attempts.

just completed their previous call.[38] The predictive dialer is integrated with ATLAS so that customer information is placed in front of the TMR as the call is transferred.

Installation of the predictive dialer boosted the productivity of TMRs on outbound campaigns by 300 percent. More significantly, by completely eliminating unsuccessful call attempts, it was now more economical to do outbound campaigns through the week and reduce the number of people working the penalty shifts. As a result, the entire outbound staff on Saturday penalty shifts could be moved to normal weekday shifts.

However, changing staff rosters is easier said than done and this is especially true when the change would result in an effective pay reduction. A union requirement that at least six months' notice be given prior to any changes in the rosters meant that some delicate negotiations and trading took place to enable the shift changes to be coordinated with the installation and commissioning of the predictive dialer.

Interactive Voice Response.   Inbound calls to the National Telemarketing Centre are queued and distributed directly to telemarketing representatives by an automatic call distributor (ACD) that is integrated with ATLAS. Hence, the NTC does not use an interactive voice response (IVR) system to filter incoming telemarketing calls as it does for its customer service and product support activities. Holland believes that they could probably make more use of IVR technology in their telemarketing, especially in large campaigns where a very large number of callers are expected. IVR technology, together with the introduction of Caller ID,[39] would allow products to be activated directly by the customer within the IVR system.[40] If a caller is in the IVR and wants to speak to a human, they would dial "0" whereupon information extracted from the customer database and IVR would be placed on a screen in front of a TMR as the call is transferred. Hartshorne described the potential for IVR technology in telemarketing at the NTC:

> IVR would enable us to reduce the cost per contact for inbound calls on certain types of campaigns. For example, depending on the campaign, it may cost around $6.00 per contact to have a human handle the call, whereas with an IVR it would cost about $1.50. We expect that using the World Wide Web to handle such a transaction would cost in the order of 50 cents. But while there are substantial cost advantages associated with using IVR technologies—there is also a downside in that it provides very limited opportunities to cross-sell to customers.

Management Issues

Management Relations.   Telemarketing is very much a people business. Direct labour accounts for 64 percent of the NTC's cost per contact, while IT costs account for 10 percent. Exhibit 5 shows a breakdown of the NTC's cost per contact.

With labour a major component of the call centre operating costs, it is not surprising that industrial relations is critical. The difficulty in changing rosters is one of the issues addressed in a new workplace agreement currently being negotiated on a national level. As described by Quinn:

---

[38]Statistically speaking, the larger the number of TMRs working from the dialer, the more reliably this hand-over can be achieved. Therefore predictive dialers, and the efficiency gains they can provide, are only suitable for relatively large call centre operations.

[39]Caller Identification is a network service where the caller's telephone number is sent to the called party. At the time of writing, Caller ID had just been introduced into Australia.

[40]E.g., callers may ring the IVR in response to a mail-out advertisement for a product—the customer only need say "yes" to a voice prompt and the IVR could activate the service automatically.

Exhibit 5

Breakdown of NTC's cost per contact

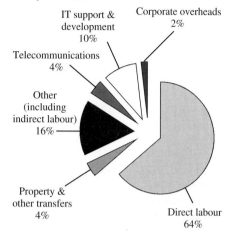

We are still struggling with the rosters, six months' notice is almost impossible to work with. The new enterprise agreement will allow more flexibility in this area. Another restriction we are hoping to address is that, under the current arrangements, no more than 25 percent of our total work force can be casual. Under the new workplace agreement there would be no restriction on the type of staff we can have.

Another key area of interest for NTC management is staff performance. Currently there are major industrial issues that limit the NTC from motivating staff using incentive-based pay or from implementing individual quality monitoring systems. It is a high priority to introduce a pay structure that is more motivating—although commission-based pay may be problematic because of the potential for unethical sales and the fact that many NTC campaigns are not sales campaigns where performance is more easily measured. The need for some form of performance motivation is highlighted by Quinn:

> There was one campaign where we did about 450,000 contacts each lasting approximately 30 seconds. It went something like: "I am just ringing to say thank you for buying [product name], in appreciation we have put you in a draw for a new car. We just need to confirm your address . . . " TMRs were going stir crazy doing 30-second calls like that, one after the other, for six weeks.

TMRs regard outbound campaigns as something akin to punishment—working on inbound campaigns is far more popular. There is some relief from running different types of campaigns; but even so, after 100,000 of any campaign it becomes tedious. Thus careful recruitment of personnel suited to this kind of work is an important activity within the NTC.

In addition to union restrictions on the proportion of casual labour the NTC can use, there are also corporate limits on the headcount. The end result is that the Burwood telemarketing site—with a capacity of 240 TMRs on the phones at any time—is underutilised. Holland has labour and property issues foremost in his mind:

> We have far too many fixed costs, especially in labour and property. There is a very clear shift, we try to move from fixed costs to more variable costs. But at the same time, it's not doing us much good moving to variable cost labour if we still have high fixed property costs and headcount restrictions preventing it from being fully utilised.

Unlike some other call centre organisations, the NTC has stringent occupational health and safety guidelines that translate into high property costs.[41] Quinn remarks about her experience in benchmarking potential outsourcing partners:

> We have state-of-the-art properties, furniture, technologies, the best of everything really. We went to see some of these other operations—they can charge A$1–2 per contact,[42] but they have everyone working manually, and some of them are real backyard operations. You look at us and we have the technology to comfortably power through a few hundred thousand calls in a week if we want to, they simply can't do it. So if you don't look at these other factors you are not comparing apples with apples.

Outsourcing.   As Telstra settles into a more competitive environment, it is taking a serious look at identifying its core business and those areas that could be outsourced. Telstra recently took the corporate decision to outsource[43] its IT systems (including ATLAS) to a joint venture company in what is the largest outsourcing deal in Australia.[44] The call centre outsourcing industry is also booming in Australia as companies contract industry specialists to undertake telemarketing activities and provide corporate help-desk facilities.

In this environment of outsourcing, a major goal of the NTC has been to ensure that it is cost competitive with industry rates. John Hollingsworth, manager for Business Development, described the situation:

> For a number of years I think we didn't clearly know what our main value-add was to Telstra and there was a major threat of outsourcing. It's only in the last six months that we have taken that threat and turned it into an opportunity. We have now established the NTC as a highly competent campaign organiser and manager of external telemarketing firms.

The NTC has forged a close partnership with a number of private telemarketing firms to whom they outsource many marketing campaigns. In particular, the NTC has identified TeleTech as a strategic partner to whom they currently direct 90 percent of their outsourced work (refer to press release included in Appendix D). Hollingsworth explains the advantages of this arrangement:

> Outsourcing has grown our channel enormously. Our restrictions on campaign size are now more funding-related instead of infrastructure- or headcount-related. Now if somebody wants to do a campaign the decision to go ahead is made purely on the overall promotions and advertising budget.

The "Lines #3" campaign is a recent example of where the NTC successfully coordinated a complex campaign across several outsourcing partners. "Lines #3" was also quite complex because it involved multiple products from multiple internal clients. Hollingsworth reflected on some of the lessons learned from this campaign:

> The sales results were good, though we have some work to do on our reporting. We had problems because we were working over multiple sites using multiple outsourcing partners. This is the first time we had done this so we had some system issues and report consolidation issues that surfaced.

---

[41]For example, all NTC telemarketing representatives have ergonomic desks and chairs.

[42]A$1.00 is equal to approximately US$0.70 in 1997.

[43]Under the arrangement, Telstra will outsource all of its data operations and applications maintenance to IBM Global Services Australia (IGSA). Telstra will have a 26 percent stake in IGSA, with the project management group Lend Lease holding 23 percent and IBM 51 percent. The value of the contract has not been disclosed, but *The Australian Financial Review* newspaper estimates it to be around A$4 billion over 10 years. Reported in "Australia—Telstra, IBM, Lend Lease in $29 billion pact," http://www.nb-pacifica.com/headline/australiatelstraibml_1031.html.

[44]Telstra press release: "Telstra, IBM and Lend Lease seal alliance: Agreement creates services joint ventures and largest data centre in southern hemisphere," http://www.telstra.com.au/newsroom/release.cfm.

The strategic partners currently operate their own IT support systems, with data batch-translated between the Telstra and outsourcer's systems in much the same way as ATLAS obtains the data from Telstra systems. The NTC is considering providing strategic partners with ATLAS, and possibly providing access to other Telstra core systems so that they can provide customer support services in addition to telemarketing.

As John Hollingsworth explains, the most valuable lesson learned in selecting an outsourcing partner was just how cost competitive the NTC was:

> In selecting an outsourcing partner we did a pretty comprehensive review of a number of organisations to ensure that they could meet our standards and requirements for the sort of campaigns that we run. We found that our operating costs were about 14 percent more than the operating costs of a comparable private industry operation.
>
> Now consider that our internal clients are paying our cost price—we make no profit—whereas they add about 12 percent profit onto their operating costs. Hence when we compared their price to our clients against the NTC price to our clients, we were only about 2 percent worse.
>
> This was very pleasing for our stakeholders and us. It was a major win because there is no doubt that the general perception was that we were 30–40 percent behind in the price to our clients. Prior to this exercise there was no way to know for sure. Now that we have an apples for apples comparison we have a reasonable target to aim toward.

One of the NTC's operational goals over the next 24 months is to close the gap completely (i.e., the whole 14 percent) so that they are genuinely competitive with external telemarketing firms.

The Future.   While waiting for Hollingsworth to arrive at his office, Holland searched through the newspaper for the information technology section. Sure enough—surrounded by advertisements from new telecommunications companies offering cut-price long distance and overseas telephone calls—there were several articles on call centres. Most were about various multinationals deciding to set up their Asia-Pacific call centres in Melbourne, and the virtues of Melbourne over Singapore, Hong Kong, and other countries in the region. One article in particular caught his attention. In part it read:

> . . . Australian call companies are well placed in such areas as systems integration, consulting, software, training, and carrier services. However, while the technology is an enabler of service delivery, the call centre agents are the delivery mechanism and the greatest asset of the call centre. In this respect Australia's skilled and multilingual work force is a tremendous competitive advantage. The problem facing Australia is that senior management doesn't realise the power it is sitting on. As a result there is a lack of understanding of what call centres can contribute to the organisation and this is reflected in the fact that call centres are often viewed as a cost centre rather than a potential profit centre . . .

Holland put down the paper and thought about what he had just read. On the one hand, there was always the possibility that Telstra would outsource its telemarketing. While on the other hand, another major corporate customer had just approached the NTC looking for some urgent assistance with a telecommunications-related issue, yet he was unable to help them because of restrictions that are beyond his control. Indeed the demand from internal clients alone outstripped the limited resources he had available. Holland wondered, How could the NTC be positioned to best meet the corporation's goals?

APPENDIX A
TELSTRA FIVE-YEAR FINANCIAL SUMMARY

Financial Statement Items ($m)	1992–1993	1993–1994	1994–1995	1995–1996	1996–1997
Sales revenue	12,133	12,788	13,613	14,716	15,436
Operating revenue	12,656	13,363	14,081	15,239	15,983
Profit before tax (after abnormals)	1,994	2,528	2,405	3,447	2,703
Profit after tax and minorities[45]	905	1,699	1,753	2,305	1,617
Dividends	674	738	944	1,368	4,146
Total assets	23,160	21,139	24,083	24,362	25,858
Gross debt	7,470	5,733	5,854	5,143	7,981
Shareholders' equity	10,886	10,755	11,727	12,668	9,938
Operating cash flow	3,961	4,118	5,414	4,478	5,254
Capital expenditure and investments	2,608	2,496	3,282	4,071	4,504

Source: Telstra Annual Report 1997.

Financial Ratios (after abnormals)	1992–1993	1993–1994	1994–1995	1995–1996	1996–1997
Return on average assets	13.3%	15.5%	13.6%	17.5%	10.1%
Return on average equity	8.7	15.7	15.6	18.9	12.7
Interest cover (times)	3.4	4.7	7.0	9.0	5.5
Gross debt to capitalisation	40.7	34.8	33.3	28.9	44.5
Net debt to capitalisation	34.0	30.0	20.7	22.8	41.5

Source: Telstra Annual Report 1997.

---

[45]Operating profit after income tax expense attributed to the shareholder.

APPENDIX B
EXCERPTS FROM THE TARP
"1997 TELESERVICE BENCHMARKING STUDY"

This appendix contains excerpts from the "1997 Teleservice Benchmarking Study" and is used with the permission of TARP Australia. Telephone: +61 3 9650 5055, E-mail: tarpaust@ozemail.com.au.

Study Background

Four studies were conducted by TARP between October 1996 and May 1997:

- Customer Care Call Centres
- Telemarketing Call Centres
- Credit and Collections Call Centres
- Interactive Voice Response Systems

Over 500 companies from more than 30 countries participated in the benchmarking study, including respondents from Australia, New Zealand, North America, and the United Kingdom. TARP identified a group of call centres whose performance is superior to all others, designating them as best-in-class (BIC) and comparing their performance with all other participants who are identified as non best-in-class (non-BIC).

Telemarketing Call Centres

Key Findings:

- BIC call centres demonstrate a more results-focused management style—e.g., emphasis on hiring rather than initial training, specialised staff, results-focused performance measurement.
- BIC call centres optimise due to use of technology—e.g., contact management software that captures both qualitative and quantitative information.
- BIC call centres measure and plan for higher efficiency—e.g., forecasting call volumes and staffing levels, greater outbound activity than non-BIC.

Inbound Findings:

- Research showed that inbound BIC centres stay open longer.
- Inbound BIC centres have a stronger tendency to utilise the services of third-party bureaus.
- The majority of BIC centres had been operating for between three and five years.
- The majority of inbound BIC centres indicated that their staff were capable of handling calls for all products and services offered by the company.
- Inbound BIC centres prefer not to "staff up" to handle large call volumes, instead preferring to utilise the services of third parties to handle extra call volumes.
- 100 percent of BIC centres test for the voice capabilities of new staff, compared with significantly smaller numbers of non-BIC centres.
- Inbound BIC centres have on average nine telemarketing representatives reporting to each team leader.
- Half of the inbound BIC centres reported their average representative tenure at between two and five years. This was almost double the equivalent figure for non-BIC centres.

Outbound Findings:

- Outbound BIC centres are twice as likely to undertake telemarketing to "noncustomers."
- Outbound BIC centres start their calling later in the day than non-BIC centres during the week and on Sundays, and close their calling later in the day during the week and on Saturdays.
- Outbound BIC centres generally prefer to manage their outbound telemarketing themselves rather than use third parties.
- All outbound BIC centres test potential staff for selling skills, and a high proportion also test on their voice.
- Outbound BIC centres have an average of 10 representatives per team leader.
- The majority of outbound BIC centres reported that their average representative tenure was between 6 and 12 months, with the balance being between one and two years.
- Outbound BIC centres have a more rapid staff turnover than non-BIC centres, with a mind to keeping their representatives fresh and motivated to sell the products and services of the company.
- All outbound BIC centres cross- or up-sell during the call.
- Outbound BIC centres, on average, spend 33 more seconds on talk time than non-BIC, but only a total of 59 seconds on after-call work time, compared with 215 seconds in non-BIC centres.

Customer Care Call Centres

Key Findings:

- BIC call centres are more likely than non-BIC centres to optimise the use of technology and use advanced customer interaction technology such as interactive voice response systems and voice data integration.
- BIC call centres are more likely than non-BIC centres to log and analyse customer contacts. BIC centres also have more complex tracking systems to classify call types. This information is more likely to be used to improve processes and increase customer satisfaction.
- BIC call centres measure both representative and management performance with a wider assortment of measures than are used by non-BIC centres. The most frequently used measures are: the number of calls handled, attendance, and talk time.
- BIC call centres operate at a higher cost per contact than non-BIC centres, but this is regarded as the premium paid for delivering higher standards of customer service. Key expenditure areas for BIC call centres are salaries, telecommunications, and benefits.

Other Findings:

- Call answering performance is better for BIC centres than for non-BIC centres, particularly in relation to average speed of answer. In addition, after-call work time is significantly less than for non-BIC centres, with New Zealand currently having the highest after-call work time.
- The management of call volumes is achieved in BIC centres by reducing upstream processing errors and improving advertising communication with the customer. BIC companies are more inclined to analyse the various means available to reduce unnecessary calls.
- BIC call centres are more likely to forecast call volumes and call durations to within 5 percent of their actual call statistics. New Zealand centres were least likely to achieve this level of accuracy overall.
- The future will see BIC centres concentrating on optimising technology as a major priority.

- Australian call centres are significantly less likely to measure customer satisfaction and employee satisfaction than other call centres.
- Satisfaction with contact experience is significantly higher among BIC call centres. In addition, they are more likely to exceed customer expectations of the contact experience.
- BIC centres have a higher percentage of full-time employees than do non-BIC centres.
- Only 15 percent of BIC call centres outsource any of their customer care calls and, of those who do, few outsource more than 25 percent of their call volume.

Interactive Voice Response Systems

Customer satisfaction is impacted most by:
- Customer education—e.g., awareness programs.
- Number of first menu options—e.g., defaults and user errors increase with a higher number of menu options.
- Involvement of human factor experts.
- Systems testing.

Comparison between Australia and North America:
- North American companies receive on average up to one million calls into the IVR system each month, whereas Australian companies receive approximately 273,000.
- Australian respondents identified the top four benefits resulting from IVR implementation as: the ability to handle a higher call volume, a lower cost per call, broader hours of coverage, and increased customer satisfaction.
- North American companies are inclined to use IVR for more complex applications than is the case in Australia.
- North American companies have a higher proportion of calls successfully completed within the IVR system, compared with Australian users of IVR systems, who find that a higher number of customers opt out of the system before completing the call.
- Australian companies are less likely to test the application before going "live."
- Both North American and Australian companies tend to begin the call response with a greeting, and are more likely to use a female rather than a male voice.
- Australian companies have reported a higher increase in call volumes than in North America. However, North American companies reported greater reductions in CSR handling times.
- The average cost per minute of calls handled by North American respondents was lower than in Australia, regardless of whether the call was handled by a CSR or by an IVR.
- North American IVR systems are more likely than those in Australia to offer an "opt out" option and "dial ahead/dial through" options.

APPENDIX C
INFORMATION TECHNOLOGY AT THE NTC

An information system plan (ISP) for the National Telemarketing Centre (approved in March 1994) recommended that the NTC's core system be ATLAS. The business drivers for ATLAS were:

- A fast mechanism of setting up campaigns, including setting up lists, defining call guides, arranging staff and physical resources, defining reporting requirements, and arranging order entry.
- An automated, adaptable, efficient, and effective set of information systems to support the sales representative including: access to accurate and up-to-date customer information and screen procedures that are friendly and fast.
- Automatic production of the byproducts or results of sales activity, especially order fulfillments and statistics.
- Flexible, timely, and lucid performance and management reporting with minimum intervention by information systems personnel.
- Systems to support efficient and effective centre management.

Exhibit 6 illustrates the relationship between ATLAS and other Telstra systems; the nature of their interaction is shown in Table 1. Many of Telstra's core systems are accessed in an "offline" manner, with information batch-transferred to (or from) ATLAS on a periodic basis. Batch transfer is

EXHIBIT 6

System context diagram

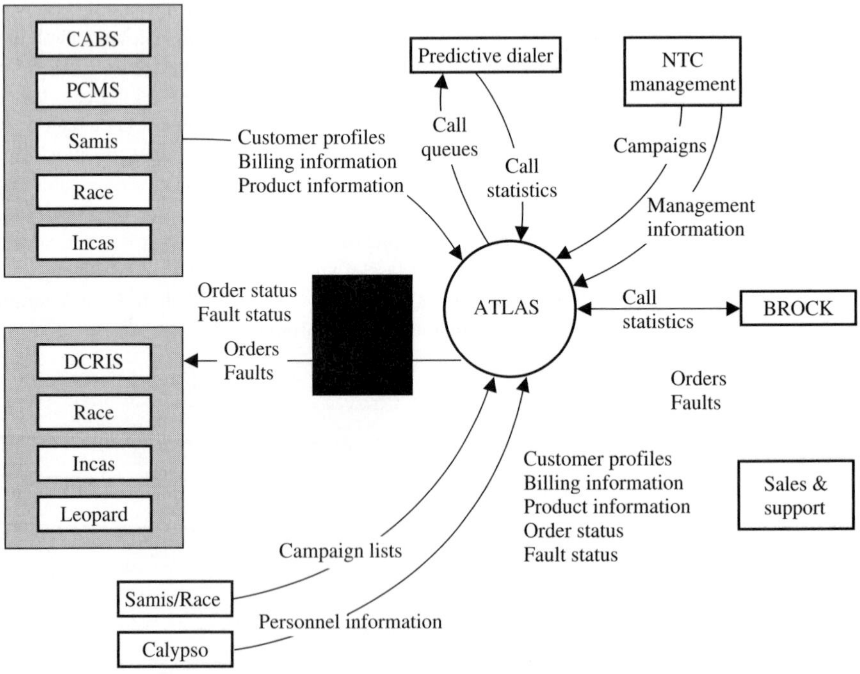

Source: NTC.

TABLE 1   ATLAS Relationship to Other Telstra Systems

System	Flow	Data Type	Frequency	Method
Samis, Race	In	Campaign prospect list	As required	Batch
	In	Value-added core data	Monthly/weekly	Batch
	Out	Customer, contact history	Weekly	Batch
CABS	In	Customer, service & equipment details	As required	Real-time
	Out	Service order provisioning via cabaret	Daily	Batch
FLEXCAB MIS Interim.	In	Customer, service & equipment details	Weekly	Batch
FLEXCAB Final	In	Customer, service & equipment details	As required	Real-time
Predictive	In	Completed campaign lists	Daily	Batch
Dialer	Out	Campaign lists	Daily	Batch
BROCK	Out	Customer contact history	Weekly	Batch
DCRIS	Out	Service order provisioning via brodi	Daily	Batch
AXIS	Out	Service order provisioning via order proc.	Daily	Batch
Printing	Out	Manually entered orders and referrals	As required	Report

typically used where it is more important for the TMR to have a fast response from the system than it is to be guaranteed the information they have in front of them is accurate to the last second.

Information generated from the call, such as service activation requests and customer contact history, is recorded by ATLAS and later output in a format suitable for batch processing by the main Telstra systems.

In addition to a fast response time, changes in function or presentation may be quickly implemented in ATLAS without impacting the core systems, and without undergoing a lengthy change request process to modify the core systems.

APPENDIX D
TELSTRA PRESS RELEASE[46]

Telstra announces telemarketing alliance with TeleTech, 11 September 1997:

Telstra announced today that it has formed an industry alliance with TeleTech to provide additional telemarketing services for its customers.

Telstra managing director, Commercial and Consumer Sales, Peter Frueh, said TeleTech would complement Telstra's own National Telemarketing Centre. The National Telemarketing Centre currently handles over five million contacts a year and manages more than 400 campaigns.

"The alliance will allow Telstra to improve services to its customers by ensuring we are able to handle incoming inquiries from customers and will assist us in the promotion of our products and services," Mr. Frueh said.

"The number of inquiries from customers and the demand for outbound telemarketing is growing at a rapid rate as Telstra introduces a greater range of products and services. TeleTech will help Telstra manage that demand."

Mr. Frueh said TeleTech would perform major, complex campaigns interchangeably with the National Telemarketing Centre and would provide Telstra with the flexibility to respond quickly to peaks in the demand for telemarketing activities.

The alliance would allow the two companies to explore further marketing opportunities together and to develop their technology and expertise, he said.

Regional vice president of TeleTech in Australia and New Zealand, Greg Johnson, said he was delighted with his company's developing relationship with Telstra. TeleTech has been providing telemarketing services for Telstra Multimedia since October 1996.

"This latest development in the strengthening alliance between one of the world's largest customer care providers and Australia's leading telecommunications company is a milestone achievement for TeleTech in Australia," Mr. Johnson said.

"The Australian market is continuing to realise the importance of customer retention and the true value that an alliance brings to leading corporations. In an increasingly competitive and deregulated market, companies that are serious about acquiring and retaining customers can benefit from alliances which help maximise every customer interaction," he said.

TeleTech will provide Telstra's National Telemarketing Centre services from its new 230 seat call centre facility in Melbourne's central business district (CBD). This new centre will become one of the most advanced in the region and follows the recent opening of a new call centre in New Zealand and the expansion of TeleTech's Sydney call centre, Mr. Johnson said. TeleTech also has 14 call centres in the United States, United Kingdom, and Mexico and employs more than 10,000 people worldwide.

---

[46]Telstra press release, http://www.telstra.com.au/Press/yr97/sep97/97091103.htm.

19

TOKAI-RIKA: ADOPTION OF JUST-IN-TIME SYSTEMS[1]

I. Introduction

The JIT system (just-in-time system) was developed at the end of the 1940s by the Toyota Motor Company and has evolved as the Toyota Production System.

Although the number of companies that have adopted the JIT system has increased rapidly, there have been very few success stories. Since the system can be used as a powerful tool for implementing organisational change, this same system is capable of producing a significant harmful effect when used incorrectly. That is a phenomenon that has not only been seen in Japanese companies, but has also been common to companies in all parts of the world.

The company profiled in this case, TOKAI-RIKA, is well known as a company that was successful in meticulously adopting the Toyota Production System (JIT system). It is also known as a component supplier in the automobile industry, which was one of the pioneers in adopting the system. In addition, it has an established position as being a legitimate JIT user. TOKAI-RIKA is one of the organisations that most other companies visit at least once when they are endeavouring to adopt the JIT system. It is also a company that boldly challenges the refinement of the JIT system itself.

The process that TOKAI-RIKA went through when it adopted the JIT system provides us with many lessons to follow when adopting this method.

II. TOKAI-RIKA Company

Founded in 1948, TOKAI-RIKA Co. Ltd. is a major Japanese manufacturer and supplier of auto parts. Its headquarters are located in Nagoya, in central Japan, and it has five factories located in the vicinity. It also owns five overseas factories in the United States, Canada, Taiwan, and Korea. At the time its operation started, the company manufactured switches, locks, and keys for cars. Afterwards, it expanded its automobile-related production to seat belts, air bags, wheel covers, shift levers, cigarette lighters, ornaments, mirrors, steering wheels, and signal combination switches, and expanded further into producing household electrical appliances and electronic devices for medical equipment. It supplies automobile parts and components to large automakers in Japan such as Toyota Motor Company, Honda, and Mitsubishi, and to many overseas automakers beginning with the Big Three in the United States. It had capital assets of 13 billion yen and yearly sales of 200 billion yen in 1994. The total number of employees in 1994 was 6,600.

TOKAI-RIKA is one of the representative independent auto parts manufacturers in Japan, but it is also known as a pioneer in adopting, and an A-class user of, the JIT system.

[1]This case was developed for use in classroom discussion and is not intended to necessarily illustrate appropriate or inappropriate management practices. The case author was Jinichiro Nakane, Waseda University, 1996. Frederique Balard, a doctoral student in the Graduate School of Management at Macquarie University, was the research associate who rewrote the case in 2000. The funding for this case production was provided by the Australian federal government's Department of Industry, Science and Resources.

This case study will focus on TOKAI-RIKA's Otowa plant in Japan, an innovative plant in adopting the JIT system among TOKAI-RIKA's factories, and examine, in particular, its JIT installation.

The Otowa plant is TOKAI-RIKA's main factory. The plant has 2,200 employees and produced products valued at 72 billion yen in 1994. The principal products in 1994 are as listed.

Automobile keys	420,000 units/month
Automobile locks	500,000 units/month
Shift levers	110,000 units/month
Cigarette lighters	1,000,000 units/month
Air bags	60,000 units/month
Neutral safety switches	300,000 units/month
Housing connectors	28,000,000 units/month
Plastic moulds	12,000,000 units/month
Die castings	800,000 units/month
Miscellaneous products	

The Otowa plant began operation in 1966, by producing die castings and key locks. In 1972, the company built a new factory comprising a tool and die plant and began installing and adopting the Toyota Production System (JIT system) in 1975. It received the Deming Prize in Japan in 1978.

The following year, the company built a new plant and began producing plastic parts and cigarette lighters. In addition, the company received the Japanese Preventative Maintenance Award in 1983.

By 1994, the company had expanded its production to include steering wheels, connectors, and air bags and began operation of the Hagi plant branch factory.

III. The Old System in Crisis

As mentioned previously, TOKAI-RIKA continued to grow along with the development of the automobile industry in Japan from its conception in 1948 to the beginning of the 1970s. In a high growth economy, the company displayed the strength of mass production to a significant extent and made plans to further expand its business.

However, with the oil crisis and the Arab oil embargo, the situation changed. The oil crisis sent shock waves through the automobile industry. The market cooled rapidly and demand dropped significantly. The effects of this, of course, extended to TOKAI-RIKA. Orders from the respective automakers fell, and the company's financial position quickly worsened. For TOKAI-RIKA, a company that had continued to expand under the high growth economy, the task of continuing the previous level of production in any manner was made impossible.

Later, the effects of the oil crisis on the manufacturing sector lessened, but the mass market that had supported mass production was no longer there, replaced by a mature market that demanded planning for a change in market strategy.

The increase in customisation of products, product segmentation, the shortening of the production cycle, and the increase in changes in demand (orders) saw TOKAI-RIKA (and also the Otowa plant) change its former small variety, high volume production method and be forced into a many variety, small volume production method that accompanied these changes and variations.

After the oil crisis in 1973, the number of manufactured items increased rapidly. Sales, which had decreased for a time after the oil crisis, recovered, but inventories increased and there was also an increase in missed shipping dates and items that were overdue to customers. In addition, profitability for the company worsened considerably when compared with before the oil crisis.

FIGURE 1

Order launching and expediting system

Monthly Production Plan

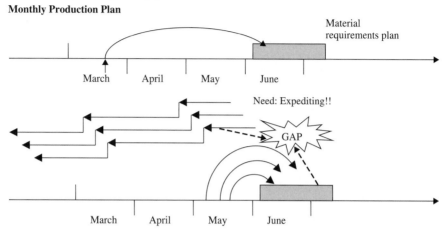

In order to respond to the complaints from and uneasiness of the company's customers, the company conducted a review of the production management system it had been using. Figure 1 indicates an outline of the production management system used at TOKAI-RIKA.

The manufacturing lead-time at TOKAI-RIKA, including the material requirements, was approximately two months. Because of that, at TOKAI-RIKA, the company prepared a production plan for the next three months at the end of each month based on demand estimates from the sales department. With the monthly production plan, the company decides on the products that should be produced in each respective month for the next three months and the volume for those products. Based on that production plan, the company sets the materials requirement and sends planned orders to vendors and suppliers.

On the other hand, a month before the actual production month (in this example, June), the company gives consideration to orders and changes in demand that may occur afterwards and prepares a final assembly schedule (FAS). In principle, the FAS allows confirmation of the production for the following month (June) at the end of the previous month (May), but in reality, even during the active month (June), there are many changes.

The FAS that has been produced in this manner is the substantive production plan at TOKAI-RIKA (the plan that must be carried out regardless of the situation). Accordingly, in order to achieve the production specified in the plan (FAS), the company requests the required materials and parts, at the appropriate time, and in the necessary quantities, and makes appropriation for that material with material that has been distributed based on the monthly production plan produced three months earlier.

However, there are many significant differences that occur between the information in the production plan, decided on three months earlier, and the information decided on in the FAS, with changes in orders and demand during the interval. In order to fill this big gap and somehow carry out the FAS, the people responsible for production management and the factory manager planned to expedite matters with the affected shop floor, purchasing department, or supplier.

Expediting activities at TOKAI-RIKA are not unusual tasks but, rather, have come to be everyday activities. That is, the production management situation does not always occur according to the production plan. Shortages on the shop floor are handled by informal "fire-fighting" efforts based on expedite information.

As described above, production management at TOKAI-RIKA had become the so-called order launching and expediting department. Moreover, to make things worse, in addition to many varieties, large volume production, and increased changes in orders, the company had not been able to go beyond the mass production paradigm and production was, as before, large lot size production, by the old paradigm.

The company's production management gave rise to the following problems:

- Excess inventories.
- Lead-time inflation.
- Indirect, expedited jobs increased.
- Shortages increased.
- Overdue orders increased.

Customer dissatisfaction increased and the situation invited a worsening of the company's financial situation. In addition, company personnel had to frequently expend much effort to correct problems that had occurred, and this led to low morale among employees.

IV. The First Attempt

Production based on the former mass production paradigm and the order launching and expediting production management system put pressure on the company's management system with the rapid changes in the economy and the market brought about by the oil crisis. Customers also lost confidence in the company.

With this in mind, in the spring of 1974, in order to break out of that situation, the company decided to embark on making improvements to its production system. In making improvements to the existing system, the company surveyed the improvements being made at Toyota Motor Company factories, a customer, and at suppliers' facilities and decided to go ahead and improve its system using the JIT system.

The company promptly assembled a project team for the installation of the JIT system. The director of the production planning and control department at the company's headquarters was designated as the project leader and the company gathered plant managers, production managers, staff personnel, and supervisors. The project team consisted of a total of 20 members.

The team decided on the following items:

1. The company would make a change from the order launching and expediting production management system it had used until then to a Kanban pull system based upon a levelized production schedule.
2. In order to install a Kanban pull system effectively, the company would have to be enthusiastic about incorporating the improvements being carried out at JIT user companies, i.e., small lot sizing, setup time minimisation, flow lines, mixed lines, multifunctional workers, etc., and incorporating Jidoka into the former Q-circles and improvement activities. (Jidoka refers to halting an entire process to prevent defective goods production. This is often done automatically by equipment used.)

The project team, giving consideration to keeping a product inventory in the background, started implementing the Kanban system based on a levelized FAS to each respective final assembly line. Instead of the former monthly production plan or expediting instructions, the team leveled and averaged as much as possible the final process using the Kanban system.

However, these efforts produced terrible results due to such things as work errors, quality defects, process imbalances, and equipment trouble. The production flow worsened and production was not possible using the Kanban system. Problems began to occur often in the factories.

In response to those problems, the company tried using production improvement teams that emphasised Q-circles and the improvement efforts of shop-floor managers and staff to solve problems, but the situation did not improve at all. Employees were disappointed with the project and morale sank.

Eight months passed since the beginning of the project (actually 12 months if the preparation period was included) but there were no positive results and the confused situation became worse. Upon looking at the situation, the company president at the time once again asked the project team and the actual managers for their opinions about why the Kaizen (continuous, incremental) improvement efforts were not making any progress. With that, the following points became clear.

1. People understood the JIT system as just a production management system and simply arranged and managed adoption as only a control system that centered around the Kanban system.

2. The manufacturing division believed that the project was an extension of the previous Kaizen effort by small steps.

3. In installing and adopting the JIT system, the company provided for a big finished product inventory in advance as a safety measure. That did not impart a sense of urgency in people, but rather, it caused great fluctuations in production.

4. Strong leadership was lacking.

5. The JIT system was not properly understood.

In response to this, the president decided that to continue the project in the same manner would not produce positive results but, rather, make the situation worse. He ordered the project to be discontinued.

V. Successful Challenge to the JIT System

At the end of 1974, Mr. Ono, a vice president at Toyota Motor Company and the man responsible for the development of the Toyota Production System (JIT), received a visit from Mr. Imura, TOKAI-RIKA's president. At that meeting, Mr. Imura asked Ono for his assistance in adopting the JIT system.

After Ono asked Mr. Imura about his requirements, he answered as follows.

1. In installing and adopting the JIT system, top management themselves must always be in the vanguard and exhibit strong leadership.

2. It must be understood that adopting the JIT system is not simply a Kaizen improvement for the production system, but company innovation that is a companywide structural change.

3. Accordingly, outside support could only be used to understand the thinking behind the system and methodology. The group that would carry out the project must be the personnel at the company and, moreover, top management themselves must take the initiative.

4. Any problems arising from installation and adoption of the JIT system must be dealt with and solved at the time they arise and at the spot where they occur so they do not accumulate afterward.

Mr. Ono mentioned that if Mr. Imura promised to do the things mentioned above, he would not regret the cooperative effort. Mr. Imura pledged that he would put all those policies into practice and with that, he received the overall support of Toyota Motor Company.

Immediately, a team was again formed with the president as its leader. The group was composed of several technical staff members and managers and supervisors from respective departments. The president decided to make the Otowa plant a model plant in adopting the JIT system and designated Mr. Kato (the plant manager at the Otowa plant and an executive director of the company) as the working leader of the pilot project. Mr. Okumura, the manager of the production management department, and Mr. Okada, the manager of the manufacturing engineering department, were appointed as subleaders.

In addition, one or two Toyota Production System (JIT) instructors from Toyota Motor Company participated in the project as support staff. Those instructors, in keeping with the original agreement, gave only guidance on the methodology of adopting the system and system know-how. They adhered to the stipulation that they would not actively participate in the system's installation at TOKAI-RIKA.

The first thing that happened was an announcement, aimed at all employees, of the decision to adopt the JIT system and of the vision of that system by the president himself. The president announced the decision on why the company was introducing the JIT system, what was expected from introducing the system, and what the ideal configuration of the system would be. Afterwards, in conjunction with project progress, the president visited factories and frequently attended JIT management meetings. The mood at the company was that this effort to adopt the system had the survival of the company at stake and that the company was very serious about it this time.

Activities to install and adopt the JIT system began at the end of October 1974. To begin with, they closed warehouses. Using days off, the company even removed the belt conveyor installed on the final assembly line but they did this while having ready the required materials and parts used by the assembly line.

The production control department issued the Kanban received from customers, with a levelized final assembly schedule, to the final assembly line. The assembly line managed product assembly in accordance with the Kanban. Since there was no conveyor belt, handling between each station was done by hand or the following station would go to the last station to pick up the item. If there were shortages or if work-in-progress stopped, work would be stopped and would not commence again until the problem had been dealt with. At the very least, the work that had to be done on that particular day was completed no matter what problems occurred.

In a break with the past, since there were no warehouses, the final assembly line was filled with stress and the work was done carefully. When problems occurred, they were taken care of without delay. Since the production volume that was posted on the Kanban for a particular day would have to be completed that day and any problems that occurred that day would have to be solved that day, there were many instances where not only workers, supervisors, and management staff worked into the night but also where even the project leader and the plant manager did the same.

With this kind of drastic method, the operation began to work by the JIT system, for the interface between the final assembly line and the customer. If, at the very least, the material and parts required for assembly were available, operations, without waste, by the Kanban became possible.

At that point, and as a next step in the adoption of the JIT system, the company took up the JIT system applicability to the materials and parts that were supplied to the assembly line. That is, that assembly line takes the required materials and parts, at the required time, in the required quantities. Consequently the process work center produces only the volume taken.

Firstly, the company took up the challenge of having the JIT system deal with the parts that were produced in-house for the assembly line. This stage, more than the assembly operation up to that point, had been fraught with problems. For example, in conducting JIT production with the Kanban, the company wanted to minimise the lot size and, if possible, carry out piece-by-piece production. To do this, it is necessary to drastically decrease setup time. Minimisation of lot size and setup time was not simply a matter of operation Kaizen. There were many other problems such as revolutionary tool and die equipment, solving engineering-related problems, and quality problems. Moreover, there was a weak point in the paradigm shift from the large lot sizes that had been used before for mass production. In addition, there was the strict understanding that instructions from the Kanban and problems that occur with these instructions would be solved that particular day and not brought forward.

Until then, the company had been accustomed to just producing things in large quantities and quickly. It was their first experience in producing something with a JIT system. Doing things such as producing things when necessary and slowly seemed easy at first glance, but when tried (for example, the plastic injection process), it was more difficult than expected.

However, as a result of everyone gritting their teeth and expending maximum effort to realise the JIT system, the thinking and the methods of the JIT system became clear to those in the factory and positive results became visible. Efforts to adopt the JIT system produced a sense of togetherness in not only the project team, but also among all employees at the Otowa plant. There were signs of a revolution in the method of production. It was the spring of 1976 and it had taken approximately one year to realise that change.

The results of this stage are as follows.

1. Reduction of inventory (excepting raw material stock and parts from vendors/ suppliers):

	Before JIT March 1975	After JIT March 1976
Finished goods	25.0 days	4.5 days
Work in process	24.0 days	5.0 days
Total days on hand	49.0 days	9.5 days

2. Improved productivity (80 percent decrease in man-hours/product).
3. Manufacturing lead times: 1/3 to 1/5.
4. Plant space: down 40 percent.
5. Products/parts defect rate drastically reduced.
6. Decreased setup time/lot size: 1/10 to 1/20.
7. Development of new business and products.

It goes without saying that the company adopted the use of flow lines and mixed lines, fostered multifunctional workers, made thorough efforts at standardisation, and utilised Jidoka.

VI. Expanding the System

The installation and adoption of the JIT system at TOKAI-RIKA was at first limited to an in-plant operation. That was because the company's policy was to first attempt to adopt and use the system at one site, to establish a sound record in using the system, and not cause any inconvenience on their vendors and suppliers.

However, TOKAI-RIKA, the same as many other companies in the assembly industry, obtained many materials and parts from outside sources. Accordingly, Kaizen at the company's suppliers and vendors was an important consideration, even from the standpoint of quality, cost, and delivery. Even with those considerations, it was not appropriate for the company to compel its suppliers and vendors to introduce the JIT system.

With that, in developing the JIT system with its suppliers and vendors, the company had those companies learn about how TOKAI-RIKA dealt with adopting the system and the actual situation at the company. TOKAI-RIKA decided that it would give support to suppliers and vendors that indicated they also had an interest in adopting the system.

At the outset, the company began to pick up materials and parts from suppliers and vendors at their locations, using one truck to pick up material from several suppliers, i.e., mixed loading. If the suppliers would ask for the company's help in regard to the JIT system, the company would send its own support staff, who were experienced in system adoption, to the supplier at no cost.

Several suppliers achieved positive results from the introduction of the JIT system within their companies, and other suppliers, who were apprehensive at first, actually recognised these accomplishments, which led to an increase in the number of suppliers who began to adopt the system.

At the end of 1977, of the company's major suppliers, more than half (about 30) had adopted the JIT system. Together with that, it became possible for the company to be supplied with materials and parts from suppliers who had previously been outside the framework of the JIT system application on a "just-in-time" basis. In addition, at the same time within the plant, plans were made to foster the JIT system and the positive results of these efforts became more significant. Those benefits were as follows.

1. Reduced inventory:

Total Days on Hand

	March 1976	December 1977
Total days on hand:	20 days	4.5 days
Finished goods	4.5 days	1.0 days
Work in process	5.0 days	1.0 days
Raw materials	10.5 days	2.5 days

2. Labor content was reduced by 30 percent from March 1976–December 1977.
3. Plant area decreased by an additional 35 percent from that of March 1976.
4. Manufacturing lead times decreased 50 percent from that of March 1976.
5. Top management, managers, and engineers became fully convinced of the benefits of the system and developed it as a robust source of further innovation.
6. Increased manufacturing and engineering capability.

VII. Fine-Tuning and Consolidating the System

The JIT system installation and adoption at TOKAI-RIKA overcame the failures and setbacks the company experienced in 1974. During the period from 1975 to 1977, the company achieved significant results as an A-class JIT user. Then, the company expanded the JIT system, developed primarily at the Otowa plant, to all its other factories, and together, while competing for positive results, has made efforts to further develop the system. Nevertheless, the strength of the JIT system, as stated at the outset, is in its being a mechanism to promote Kaizen. This aims at producing an ultimate, ideal system and is a mechanism that promotes constant improvement, or Kaizen, to a system that is always in transition. It is a path to utilise the strength of the JIT system to allow for even more effective use of that mechanism, which promotes that improvement.

TOKAI-RIKA has achieved the first step in adopting the JIT system. However, that accomplishment is only the initial step toward an ideal system.

TOKAI-RIKA is promoting the following items for fine-tuning the JIT system:

1. The company will be developing Kaizen activities along with the JIT system on a companywide basis (including both domestic and overseas factories, management, and indirect departments).

2. The company will establish and promote a Kaizen plan and target for the year from both a top-down and a bottom-up effort.

3. The company will create a JIT system that handles large variations in production volume.

4. The company will create a strong corporate structure that can handle changes and transform its corporate culture.

5. The company will show how JIT system thinking can be applied to new product design.

References

Web site: *www.tokai-rika.co.jp/eng/main.html.*

Hall, Robert. *Zero Inventories,* Dow Jones-Irwin, 1983.

Nakane, J. "Paradigm Shift Beyond KAIZEN," *Bulletin,* System Science Institute, Waseda University, No. 24, 1993.

Ono, Taiichi. "Toyota Production System," *Diamond,* Japan, 1978.

Hall, R., and Nakane, J. "The Next Competitive Battle in the 1990s," *AME Research Report,* 1990.

20
International Decorative Glass[1]

In June 1996, Delta, British Columbia, remained overcast and rainy. Frank Lattimer, vice-president operations of International Decorative Glass (IDG), mused that it really didn't matter, as there would be little time for golf this year. Rapidly increasing demand for decorative glass panels by steel door manufacturers in the United States, IDG's primary market, had its two production facilities in Delta and Shuenyi, China, scrambling to keep up.

Lattimer had been asked to develop a recommendation for capacity expansion for consideration by the board of directors. The board had emphasized the need to move quickly as sales were increasing faster than IDG's ability to meet them. Although either existing plant could be expanded, IDG also had recently been approached about considering further off-shore sourcing in the rapidly developing country of Vietnam. Frank knew that any decision would have significant ramifications for the company's long-term positioning and ability to meet its ambitious goals for growth.

The Industry

Decorative glass panels typically are inserted into residential steel doors and were increasingly being used by builders and home renovators to add architectural interest and a customized appearance to doorways. Growth in the industry was being fueled by the general trend away from wooden exterior doors to steel doors. Forestry restrictions, lumber prices, energy efficiency, and increasing criminal activity all contributed to the growing demand for retrofitting wood doors with steel replacements, often with decorative glass panels. In addition, the lower price of steel doors relative to the traditional wood door, with wholesale prices starting as low as C$300, further eroded market share in new home construction. Decorative glass was now being incorporated into 10 percent of new home construction.

The total North American sales for decorative glass panels was conservatively estimated at $2 billion in 1995 (all figures are reported in Canadian dollars), and the market showed signs of continued strong growth. Industry experts predicted that annual sales could reach $4.5 billion in the U.S. alone, within five years. Canada's weighting of the North American market was disproportionately high, at 15 percent, reflecting the somewhat earlier development of the market there for these panels. By 1996, panels were found in approximately 85 percent of steel doors in Western Canadian homes.

Manufacturers in Canada tended to be more vertically integrated than their U.S. counterparts, with plants fabricating both the steel door and the decorative panel. Locally, British Columbia's

[1]Jim Barker prepared this case under the supervision of professors Robert Klassen and Paul Beamish solely to provide material for class discussion. The authors do not intend to illustrate either effective or ineffective handling of a managerial situation. The authors may have disguised certain names and other identifying information to protect confidentiality.

Ivey Management Services prohibits any form of reproduction, storage, or transmittal without its written permission. This material is not covered under authorization from CanCopy or any reproduction rights organization. To order copies or request permission to reproduce materials, contact Ivey Publishing, Ivey Management Services, c/o Richard Ivey School of Business, The University of Western Ontario, London, Ontario, Canada, N6A 3K7; phone (519) 661-3208; fax (519) 661-3882; e-mail cases@ivey.uwo.ca. Copyright © 1997, Ivey Management Services.

The Richard Ivey School of Business gratefully acknowledges the generous support of The Richard and Jean Ivey Fund in the development of this case as part of the Richard and Jean Ivey Fund Asian Case Series.

supply capacity grew well past the sustainable growth rate during the late 1980s and early 1990s as new market entrants scrambled to ramp up production capability to capitalize on the residential construction boom. The result was steadily eroding margins, followed quickly by industry consolidation, with high cost producers closing or being absorbed by more competitive operations. In spite of these changes, Canadian industry continued to be characterized by oversupply, underutilized capacity, and commodity pricing. Lattimer had recently completed a basic competitive assessment of several key Canadian competitors as part of IDG's business plan (Exhibit 1).

By contrast, U.S. manufacturers of decorative glass panels acted as original equipment manufacturers (OEMs) for large residential steel door fabricators and retail chains. The industry was quite fragmented, with the largest three producers in the U.S. each having less than 6 percent of the total

EXHIBIT 1

Summary of Major Canadian Competitors

Company	Accent	JCX Glass	Roseview
Target Market	Small regional distributors	Anyone who calls	Small regional distributors
Supply	Custom—None Volume—Langley, B.C., and Tacoma, WA	Custom—None Volume—New Westminster, B.C., Georgia Buy from China	Custom—None Volume—Surrey, B.C.
Positioning	Good quality	Copy designs of others	Design leader Lower quality
Cost Base	• 2 locations, 38,000 sq. ft. • Heavy overheads • Nonunion • Small orders, but purchase materials in volume; thus very high raw material & finished goods inventory • Efficient production system	• 2 locations, 105,000 sq. ft. • Heavy overheads • 1 year left on collective agreement • Volume purchase • Finished goods inventory of $3.2 million • Efficient production system	• One location, 38,000 sq. ft. • Heavy overheads • Nonunion • High raw material costs • Finished goods inventory of $1.6 million
Sales (est. 1995)	• $11 million • Down, some of their lowest months	• $14 million • Up 39%	• $3 million • Down
Warranty	1 year	10 year	1 year
CAD	Yes	No	No
MRP	Some implementation	Some implementation	No
Reputation/Customer Relations	Very good in Pacific Northwest with the "old boys" network	Generally poor, can let the customer down	Generally poor, always lets customer down
Management	Good, but have lost their spark and desire	Aggressive, but weak in the middle management	Generally weak

EXHIBIT 2

Summary of Major U.S. Competitors

Company	Spanner Door	Western Design	Billings	New England Glass
Target Market	National (U.S.)	National (U.S.)	National (U.S.)	Eastern (U.S.)
Positioning	Good quality Simple, high volume panels	Broad product line	Broad product line; focus on high volume commodities, although some lower volume panels	Fast delivery, high quality
Supply	Good operations in Mexico, with long-term commitment	Plants in Mexico and Thailand	No offshore production	High cost producer; focus on automation
Est. 1995 Sales	$120 million	$85 million	$60 million	$25 million
Reputation/Customer Relations		Extensive distribution system	Product line is narrower than IDG	Strong, dependable supplier
Management		Three top managers have left recently		

market. Unfortunately, information on these producers was limited (Exhibit 2). Manufacturers ship panels to predetermined central warehousing and assembly points where their panels are fitted into the steel doors and distributed by the door fabricators through their retail channels. In general, the U.S. marketplace demanded high quality, fast service, and, increasingly, low price.

At this time, the U.S., unlike Canada, was rapidly growing and underserved. In addition, Canadian manufacturers generally were about three years ahead of their U.S. counterparts in product functionality and design and, thus, able to develop strategic partnerships with steel door manufacturers. An undervalued currency also provided Canadian suppliers, such as IDG, with an initial competitive advantage. Combined, these factors created a significant market opportunity for any Canadian supplier who could meet rigorous quality standards and maintain a high level of customer responsiveness to design customized panels.

Early attempts by Canadian firms to develop their export sales quickly revealed that a customer would pay only so much for quality, service, and product differentiation, and price was becoming an increasingly important driver in the purchase decision. In response, manufacturers on both sides of the border began to source production of the glass panels at lower cost to facilities located abroad. Because labor represented a large portion of cost of goods sold, production was increasingly being moved to countries with low labor costs, such as Mexico, Thailand, and China. At this time, only a few Canadian manufacturers had been able to address all of these challenges successfully.

Production of Decorative Glass Panels

The production process for decorative glass panels was quite standardized, with little variation among firms and plants. As might be expected with a product that until recently was considered a "craft," the process was very labor intensive, with the equivalent of up to two-person days required for each panel. Production equipment was generally quite flexible and could be purchased from several suppliers.

Decorative glass panels consist of multiple glass panes of different sizes, colors, and grades assembled between soldered brass rods to form a decorative picture. The production of the panels used a multistep process that cut and formed the glass and brass components and assembled the parts into sealed decorative glass units that could withstand the harsh exposure needed for exterior doors.

The manufacturing process began with the cutting of raw glass sheets of various colors and finishes into pieces of the precise shape and size needed for the final design. Some of these pieces were then bevelled to give a more attractive final appearance. The specialized cutting and bevelling of the glass pieces were the most capital-intensive steps in the production process.

In a separate area, brass rods were cut and shaped into segments that ultimately serve to hold and separate the glass pieces. The correct set of glass pieces and brass rods were grouped into panel-specific "kits." These kits were assembled and soldered into predetermined patterns that formed semifinished panels. Several cleaning and touch-up steps followed.

Next, clear solid glass panes were added to each side of the inlay, creating a "sandwich" that protected the more delicate decorative inlay. Swizzle, a sealant material, was added around the edge to insulate and protect the panel from water damage. The panel was then put through an automated sealing machine, washed, and inserted into a frame. Finally, the finished panel was labeled and packaged for shipment. These operations typically were performed in small batches of panels.

The Company

Located near Vancouver, British Columbia, IDG was founded in 1984 by Michael Jeffrey, decorative glass designer and entrepreneur. Initially, the company started as an integrated manufacturer of steel doors and decorative glass panels, and IDG enjoyed modest prosperity through the 1980s as the housing market boomed in that province. During this period, numerous firms entered the market, hoping to share in the prosperity of the industry. As real estate development slowed and even stagnated in the early 1990s, and the competitive basis shifted to cost, Jeffrey realized that the company was losing money in their manufacturing of steel doors. He felt that IDG could significantly enhance profitability by concentrating exclusively on decorative glass panels.

Jeffrey also recognized the need for a senior operations and business development person to make the operations more competitive in that market. Lattimer was hired in 1991 with the mandate to grow the international market, to improve cost efficiency, to set up a fully integrated management information system, and to create a corporate structure and culture that would support continued expansion. To meet these objectives, contacts and sales were further developed with several U.S. steel door manufacturers, the largest being Midwest. Lattimer also gained concessions in wage rates and flexibility in staffing requirements during collective bargaining with the union. Finally, a management information system, including materials requirements planning (MRP), was installed and brought on line to improve access to timely information and to raise customer responsiveness.

Historically, IDG's sales had been driven by custom orders for the glass panels. However, with recent efforts to increase sales volume, an increasing number of higher volume orders were being pursued, although often at much lower margins. In spite of labor concessions, high wage rates and limited flexibility continued to make IDG's plant in Delta increasingly less cost competitive. To reduce production costs, Lattimer was forced to explore alternative, off-shore sources of production.

Century Glass

In January 1995, IDG began sourcing some of its high-volume, low-skill production through a strategic partnership with Century Glass, located in Shuenyi, approximately an hour's drive outside of Beijing, China. This manufacturing facility was developed solely to meet the production needs of IDG, although the actual plant was owned and operated by the father of a former employee, Jianwei (Jerry) Lo. Lo had returned to China to set up the joint venture with IDG.

When IDG first arrived, the Shuenyi facility was little more than a deserted warehouse, situated across the highway from the village of 2,000 people where Lo had been born. The Lo family was well respected in the area, even though they came from modest means relative to Canadian standards. There was no electricity, telephone, or plumbing in the village, and fresh water was unavailable.

With minimal infrastructure in place, power requirements, communication, and capital equipment challenges all needed to be addressed. Cogeneration power supplies and inverters were supplied by IDG; satellite and cellular phones were used until Century received a land line (faxes were sent from Beijing in the interim). Basic production equipment needed to cut glass sheets and brass rods were sourced locally; however, one large panel sealing machine was imported from Korea. Practically everything else at the facility was built by the local work force. Approximately one-third of the workers lived in four-person dormitory rooms located on the premises, and the production plant also included space for the workers to grow their own food in the courtyard.

Family ties of the Los facilitated the shipment of goods, as Chinese bureaucracy was legendary. Jerry's uncle was the police chief of the local district and, thus, extremely well connected politically; IDG benefited from the association. The movement of raw materials into China and finished goods out of China, via Tientsin to the Gulf of Chihli, was expedited through Jerry's uncle.

Because of differences in proximity to the market and cost structure, the Chinese production facility concentrated on producing high-volume, low-cost glass panels for IDG. These panels were then shipped in bulk to the Delta production facility for final processing, followed by packaging and shipment to U.S. or Canadian customers. The additional processing in Canada resulted in a change in product classification under the North American Free Trade Agreement (NAFTA), which allowed the finished product to be imported duty-free into the U.S. market. (By contrast, if complete, sealed panels were imported directly from China into the U.S., a 60 percent duty would apply.)

For some customers, the standardized panels produced at Shuenyi were modified and further assembled at Delta to form larger, more complex, customized panels. By necessity, these arrangements required a long lead time, currently 18 to 20 weeks (Exhibit 3), well above that of the Delta plant, where lead times averaged one month.

Initial start-up problems in 1995 centered on logistics and quality. Rather than allow IDG's reputation for excellent customer service to suffer by missing delivery dates, orders of panels were, at times, air freighted to Delta from China, at an extra cost of $250,000 in the first year. These problems were gradually overcome as typical production lead times were reduced to their current levels. Low yields and high waste/breakage also plagued the start-up. However, as the skill levels of the local work force improved, yields increased dramatically. By mid-1996, fin-

Exhibit 3

Order Cycle Time for Production at Shuenyi Plant

Raw materials ordered and received for shipment	2–4 weeks
Components in transit to China facility	5 weeks
Raw materials conversion to WIP and semi-finished goods	4 weeks
Subassemblies shipped to Canada	5 weeks
Final assembly completed at Delta, B.C., facility	2 weeks
Finished goods shipped to customer	1/2 week
Total time	18–20 weeks

ished panel yields consistently surpassed 99 percent, although in-process breakage and other losses remained a problem.

Current Status.   By June 1996, Century Glass produced 80 percent of IDG's panels, representing 60 percent of revenues. The remaining somewhat more specialized, lower volume panels were produced by 70 employees in the Delta plant. The Century plant was operating close to capacity, with approximately 100 employees producing 8,000 panels per month. Dorms were overcrowded and people were elbow-to-elbow in the manufacturing area.

The joint venture agreement specified that IDG purchase all materials, own all inventories, and specify all finished product standards. The production arrangement with Century stipulated a fixed charge per employee and a variable cost per finished panel. Specifically, IDG paid $140 per employee, per month. In addition, IDG also paid Century a product transfer price of $4 for each panel that met IDG's rigorous quality standards for finished panels. Employment levels could be varied as needed to match sales volumes. Employees worked seven eight-hour days per week, every week. This was high by Chinese standards, where the five- or six-day work week was more common.

By comparison, in Canada, unionized employees received $9.75 per hour per 40-hour work week. Combined, these differences in labor translated into a significant cost advantage for Shuenyi, without accounting for the operational advantages of increased labor flexibility. Relative product costs are illustrated in Exhibit 4.

Labor savings were offset to some degree by a higher working capital investment necessary to finance larger inventories and longer payment cycles. For example, inventory turnover at Century Glass was only two turns per year in 1995, whereas Delta averaged six. In addition, banks refused

Exhibit 4

Typical Production Costs

Product	Production Location	
	Shuenyi	*Delta*
#677, Oval-San Marino		
Materials	95.19	92.97
Labor	6.61	69.44
Freight	7.82	1.25
Total direct costs	$109.62	$163.66
#936, 22" × 36" panel		
Materials	44.27	44.27
Labor	3.18	40.27
Freight	7.08	1.25
Total direct costs	$54.53	$85.79
#445, 7-1/2" × 18-1/2" panel		
Materials	15.51	15.51
Labor	1.10	10.13
Freight	1.08	0.50
Total direct costs	$17.69	$26.14

to finance or factor raw material and work-in-process (WIP) inventories located in, or in transit to or from, China as the risk of recouping funds in the case of insolvency was considered too high. This risk varied by country. Some developing countries, such as Mexico, were viewed as less risky, while others, such as India, offered government guarantees for export-oriented manufacturers.

The Lo family was anxious to keep 100 percent of IDG's business at their facility. However, Lattimer was very concerned about having only a single supplier in China, where political risks were perceived to be significant for such a large portion of their production. For example, the repatriation of Hong Kong in 1997, adverse trade tensions, and possible trade restrictions between China, the U.S., and Canada all indicated that a move to establish another production source might have strategic and operational merits.

Financial Results

IDG's revenue growth had been impressive since 1990, increasing from $2.6 million to $5.4 million for fiscal 1995. Financial results for the last two years are summarized in Exhibits 5 and 6. Revenues were projected to reach $10.5 million this year, with 95 percent of sales being made in the U.S. As noted earlier, margins had eroded during the early 1990s as residential construction slowed and competition increased. Sales levels had risen significantly in 1995 as new production

EXHIBIT 5

International Decorative Glass

**Income Statement
as of September 30
(all figures reported as $000s)**

	1995	1994
Sales	$5,404	$3,634
Cost of sales	4,365	2,610
Gross profit	1,039	1,024
Expenses		
Administration and marketing	388	413
Travel and promotion	97	44
Rent and assessment	120	138
Amortization of debt	48	55
Bank charges and interest	141	48
Interest on long-term debt	18	17
Other expenses	182	258
Subtotal	994	973
Income (loss) from operations	45	51
Other income	28	0
Income (loss) before taxes	73	51
Income taxes		
Current	24	0
Deferred	(6)	11
Net income (loss) for the year	$55	$40

EXHIBIT 6

International Decorative Glass

Balance Sheet
as of September 30
(all figures reported as $000s)

	1995	1994
Current		
Cash	$ 1	$ 2
Accounts receivable	1,513	474
Income taxes recoverable	15	22
Inventories	1,422	988
Prepaid expenses	54	28
	3,005	1,514
Capital assets	233	296
	3,238	1,810
Current		
Bank loans	1,435	593
Accounts payable	886	482
Income taxes payable	17	0
Current portion of long-term debt	32	39
	2,370	1,114
Long-term debt	152	177
Deferred income taxes	13	20
Due to (from) affiliated company	522	372
	3,057	1,683
Share capital	0.1	0.1
Contributed surplus	45	45
Retained earnings	136	82
	$3,238	$1,810

capacity became available at Shuenyi. However, profitability fell as a result of poor initial yields and air freight shipment costs at this new plant. Looking forward, Lattimer expected margins to increase as productivity further improved in Shuenyi.

Both Jeffrey and Lattimer strongly felt that the market for strong growth by IDG was there. IDG had already been turning away business as they struggled to meet existing customer commitments from their two production facilities. Current plans called for revenue growth to $30 million by the year 2000. Critical to achieving these long-term results was an increase in production capacity to match the forecasted sales volumes.

This aggressive growth necessitated access to additional capital to finance investment in new capacity and additional working capital. In August 1995, IDG approached a venture capital firm, Working Opportunity Fund, for $2 million of equity financing. The structure of the investment was negotiated, due diligence conducted, and the deal finalized in November of that year. In addition, IDG paid down its line-of-credit from the bank by financing its inventory in China with a guarantee from Canada's Export Development Corporation. This effectively reduced IDG's investment in working capital and made the sourcing of manufacturing to Asian facilities increasingly attractive. Combined, these additional sources of capital enabled IDG to increase its operating flexibility and further develop its presence in the U.S. market.

Capacity Expansion

Lattimer had narrowed the options for expansion of production to three alternatives. Expansion was possible at either existing plant. In addition, another strategic partnership could be developed in another low labor-cost country, similar to IDG's earlier decision to expand into China. After exploring options in other developing nations with low labor costs, Lattimer, in consultation with senior management, had narrowed the candidate list of countries to one: Vietnam. This country offered a critical advantage in Lattimer's mind over other developing nations: a potential local partner, Dan Kim. Kim's firm currently supplied raw glass to IDG, and Kim had approached Lattimer about establishing a manufacturing joint venture.

Expansion in Delta.   At this time, companywide capacity could be doubled by investing a relatively modest amount of capital, $30,000, in the Delta plant. Labor costs would rise based on existing wage levels. Given the close proximity of this plant to the U.S. market, the existing production planning system could be further leveraged and customer responsiveness further improved.

Expansion in Shuenyi.   Because production at the Shuenyi plant was already very tight, any expansion would involve a significant increase of middle management and support staff, and an expanded production planning system, mirroring the earlier MRP investment made in Delta. Existing arrangements for labor would be maintained, where IDG would pay a flat monthly fee per person, plus a variable rate per panel.

Although some of the existing production equipment still had excess capacity, additional equipment would be needed. In total, an estimated capital investment of $30,000 would be needed in new cutting equipment to double companywide capacity. Incremental manufacturing overhead costs would be approximately $150,000 per year. Direct labor costs would increase proportionately with production volumes. These costs did not include either a desperately needed new building or additional inventory carrying charges. Timing for ramp-up to this volume level would be approximately six to eight months.

The most significant concerns with expansion at Shuenyi were related to further dependence on a single supplier and issues related to political risks associated with production in China. Trade uncertainties between China and the U.S. also aggravated long-term planning efforts. Management was apprehensive that existing tensions could escalate over any, or all, of repatriation of Hong Kong in 1997, intellectual property rights (software piracy and patents), dissident protests, strained relations with Taiwan, and a general trade imbalance.

Smaller manufacturers that supply the U.S. market, like IDG, inadvertently have been punished by short-term high tariffs, customs delays, and other nontariff barriers. Although quite unlikely now, the worst case scenario would be a ban on importation from China. Unfortunately, because of the general income levels in China and construction norms, there was little local market for IDG's products at this time, although it did look promising in the longer term.

Foreign Operations in Vietnam.   Vietnam had only recently begun to exhibit the economic growth characteristic of other countries in Asia-Pacific. Like many developing countries, infrastructure at this time was terribly inadequate. Lattimer estimated that development was at least five years behind China, and conditions were even more challenging than those first faced by IDG when they established their joint venture in China.

In recent years, Vietnam had been plagued by internal political problems, and foreign investors were apprehensive to invest. This situation now was beginning to change, as the U.S. had moved to reestablish diplomatic relations with the Socialist Republic of Vietnam in 1995. In turn, this thawing of the political climate had encouraged foreign investment, which had grown rapidly as a result. Vietnam also had a strategic location for reexport to other markets in Asia.

Although a Communist state, the central government had instituted the beginnings of "Doi Moi" or "open door" policy as early as 1986. The objectives of Doi Moi were to develop export-oriented production capabilities that create jobs and generate foreign currency, to develop import substitutes, to stimulate production using natural resources, to acquire foreign technology, and to strengthen Vietnam's infrastructure. Incentives offered included: the option to establish wholly owned foreign subsidiaries; favorable corporate income tax and tax holidays; waivers on import/export duties; and full repatriation of profits and capital.

With 75 million citizens and a labor force of 32 million, Vietnam had the second lowest wage rate in the Pacific Rim. Only about 11 percent of the working population was employed in manufacturing, another 19 percent in the service sector, and the remainder in agriculture. Inflation was high, at 14 percent in 1995, partially because of the devaluation of the "new dong" as the government had allowed the currency to float in world markets for the first time. The primary industries of Vietnam included food processing, textiles, machinery, mining, cement, chemical fertilizers, tires, oil, and glass. Vietnamese companies already supplied some of the standard glass and bevelled glass components used by IDG.

Generally, the labor force was energetic, disciplined, and hard working, although unemployment remained high, at 20 percent. English and French were widely spoken but literacy was relatively low, at 88 percent. Unfortunately, basic human rights and freedoms had received little attention. There was widespread conflict between local and central governing bodies, extensive corruption, and exhaustive bureaucracy at both levels.

Production of Decorative Glass Panels in Vietnam.   The State Committee for Cooperation and Investment (SCCI) identified seven areas of the Vietnam economy where foreign investment would receive preferential tax treatment. Of particular relevance to IDG, labor-intensive manufacturing was one such area. The SCCI would assist the new venture in whatever way they could, typically through the development of contacts with customers and suppliers, as well as guiding the investor through the government bureaucracy that approved any business venture.

The Vietnamese government also had legislated five approaches for establishing a business venture in the country. Of the five, the international business community and the government widely favored the joint venture approach. Under this approach, a foreign firm such as IDG would sign a contract with one or more Vietnamese parties to create a new legal entity with limited liability. Foreign capital had to constitute at least 30 percent of the new entity's total capital. A foreign investor could then leverage the local partner's contacts, knowledge of the local market, and access to land and resources.

The Vietnamese had a saying; "*Nhap gia tuy tuc,*" which means, "When you come into a new country, you have to follow the culture." Clearly, identification of a strong local partner would be critical for meeting the cultural norms in Vietnam and ensuring the success of any investment by IDG; this had been a major obstacle for many other foreign firms.

Lattimer saw many parallels with the earlier joint venture into China. That investment had succeeded largely as a result of IDG's strategic partnership with Century Glass and the Lo family. IDG had been able to limit their investment risk to supplying capital equipment for the facility and inventories. By contrast, other decorative glass suppliers operating in China were paying higher costs and making larger investments in plant and infrastructure. The partnership with Century also had provided IDG with additional political clout and allowed them to bypass much of the Chinese bureaucracy.

EXHIBIT 7

Production Equipment Required for Start-up in Vietnam
(all figures reported as $000s)

Production Equipment	Cost
Electrical back-up generator	$ 13
Air compressor	2
Glass equipment	
Two-shape cutter (pneumatic, from Korea)	7
Shape cutter (CNC, from Canada)	110
Glass washer	60
Brass equipment	
Roll-former	55
Roll-forming dies	22
Circle rollers (large and small)	5
Saws (4)/blades/sharpeners	4
Bevelling equipment	
Straight-line beveller	125
Curved bevelling machines (12)	30
Miscellaneous equipment	
Small forklift	7
Pallet jack	2
Computer, fax, etc.	3
Hand tools, tables, etc.	5
Total capital equipment	$449

One obvious choice for a local partner was IDG's bevelled glass supplier, managed by Dan Kim. Kim operated a glass plant in Da Nang, which was well under capacity and had an oversupply of qualified labor. Kim had approached both IDG and government authorities and essentially paved the way for IDG to begin joint venture operations within a 6- to 12-month time frame. Labor and product transfer prices were likely to be significantly lower than either the Delta or Shuenyi plants, with these costs being approximately half those of Shuenyi. Additional overhead costs were estimated at $50,000 annually. Finally, a significant investment would be needed in new equipment to reach the same, companywide production volume possible with the other options (Exhibit 7). Lattimer wondered whether he might be able to extract more favorable terms for any joint venture relationship, such as shifting responsibilities for financing inventories to Kim.

The Decision

As Lattimer was putting together his proposal for the board, he reflected on a conversation he had with Jerry Lo last month. Lo had indicated that Century would soon expect their piecework compensation to increase from $4 to $7 per finished panel. While seemingly a small fraction of total production costs, Lattimer worried that further requests for increases would follow unless other alternatives were developed. He also was only too aware that with up to $1 million invested in inventory at Century at any given time, IDG was in a very precarious position. Single sourcing had given Century a level of bargaining power that might limit IDG's future options and cost competitiveness.

Lo had become agitated as Lattimer described IDG's exploration of additional manufacture sourcing arrangements, but had to agree it made sense from IDG's perspective. Lattimer reassured Lo that IDG wanted to add capacity, not replace it. This discussion had reinforced the need to delicately handle IDG's existing relationships. Any recommendation for locating new production capacity would have to take into account the skilled Canadian work force, Century Glass and the Lo family, and Dan Kim's offer for an expanded relationship in Vietnam.

21
Advanced Book Exchange, Inc.:
The Barnesandnoble.com Partnership[1]

The principals of Advanced Book Exchange, Inc. (ABE) looked at one another. They had come so far, so fast—and now, in August of 1998, they had an opportunity to partner with a major player in electronic book commerce. There seemed to be no downside to the offer of a relationship with Barnesandnoble.com, but was it really as good as it looked? How would their clients react? Could they make it work? They had to decide, and they had to decide quickly. In the world of the Web, he who hesitated often lost big.

Company Background

In October 1995, Cathy Waters was self-employed as a contract programmer and analyst, as were her husband, Keith Waters, and their future business partner, Rick Pura. Anxious to pursue her interest in bookselling, Cathy gave up computer work to open an antiquarian bookstore in Colwood, British Columbia. She had significant understanding of the rare- and used-book industry, combined with a technical background and grasp of the opportunities presented by the nascent World Wide Web. This combination led her to propose that Keith and Rick develop a database system and sophisticated search technology suited to making her inventory available to dealers and individual book hunters worldwide. Keith and Rick spent their free time from late October 1995 to May 1996 developing the system that would become the heart of ABE's operations. Described in detail later in this case, the system allowed book dealers to list their inventory on a database server, then link to the server via a search engine on the World Wide Web.

In May 1996, Rick quit work on all other programming contracts, and ABE went live on the World Wide Web with 13 booksellers. Its development and launch was, like many start-ups, financed solely out of the personal resources of the four partners (Keith and Cathy Waters and Rick and Vivian Pura). The company began by offering free six-month subscriptions to the first 50 booksellers who joined and free months for successful referrals. ABE signed on its first 100 dealers by August 1996, after only four months in business. In the summer of 1996, Keith wound up his contract work and joined Rick working full-time for ABE.

The company grew rapidly. By October 1996, Cathy was dividing her time between her Colwood bookstore and ABE's offices in Victoria. After a brief hiatus from ABE (spent concentrating on her physical bookstore), Cathy hired a manager for the Colwood operation and joined ABE full-time with responsibility for marketing and office management. Keith and Rick were responsible for systems and operations; Vivian oversaw financial administration. In 1998, the company moved its offices to Victoria's newly developed Selkirk Waterfront, where it occupied 5,000 square

[1]Dr. Rebecca Grant prepared this case solely to provide material for class discussion. The author does not intend to illustrate either effective or ineffective handling of a managerial situation. The author may have disguised certain names and other identifying information to protect confidentiality.

feet on two floors. ABE's staff comprised the four partners (who served as directors), 23 full-time and four part-time administrative staff, technical and support staff, and three co-op student positions.

Competitive Environment

Book prices fluctuated according to taste and trends in the market, similar to antiques and artwork. A single title could vary dramatically in price. Price could depend on the condition of the book, its edition, whether it was signed (which raised the value) or inscribed (which, without the author's autograph, lowered it), had a dust jacket, had the price clipped from the cover, and a host of other factors. For example, a 1951 U.S. edition of *Winnie the Pooh,* by A.A. Milne, in very good condition, but the 204th printing of the book, might list for $15.[2] On the other hand, a 1926 British first edition of the same book, described as "one of 350 numbered copies signed by Milne and Shepard. Slight offsetting on endpaper else fine in a lightly used dust jacket with a few faint traces of foxing," was listed on the ABE inventory at $6,500. Dealing or buying such books was an information-intensive process; the more information one had about the book, the author, the dealer, and comparable books in the market, the more successful one could be in a transaction.

ABE identified three major competitors. The first competitor was Boston-based Bibliofind .com. Bibliofind was noted for its aggressive competitive style. That style was unusual in an industry noted for cooperative efforts among booksellers, who were one another's customers as well as competitors. On its website, Bibliofind allowed customers to search for a particular book by its title, author, price range, and other attributes. Customers could also view a book's selling price in various currencies, register for a search on a particular book,[3] subscribe to mailing lists, and obtain help on buying antiquarian books. Bibliofind charged its dealer members $25 per month plus a set-up fee. Dealers could create their own home pages on Bibliofind's website, and they could submit their list of books in almost any database format. Customers purchased their books directly from each individual bookseller, and the bookseller was responsible for delivering the books to each customer. Bibliofind listed nine million books from thousands of book dealers.

ABE's second major competitor was Alibris.[4] Unlike ABE and Bibliofind, Alibris took physical possession of the books it represented and operated a distribution warehouse in Sparks, Nevada. Rather than operating on a subscription basis, Alibris took a 20 percent consignment fee on the books it sold. Customers could search the Alibris database by author and title. An advanced search engine was available that allowed customers to search by publisher, price range, subject, International Standard Book Number (ISBN), and other attributes. Once an order had been placed, customers received an e-mail to confirm that the order had been shipped or canceled. Customers could check the status of their order through the website. Alibris also highlighted certain books, authors, reviews, and other websites that were of interest to their customers. To be listed, dealers had to have at least 1,000 books or a very specialized collection. Dealers were given a home page on the Alibris website to provide contact information.

The third major competitor, Bibliocity, was based in Australia but it represented booksellers worldwide. As with the other booksellers, Bibliocity offered a search engine on its website that allowed customers to search for books by title, author, range of publication dates, and other attributes. Customers could search for specific book dealers, maintain "wants" lists, and view pictures

---

[2]All amounts in U.S. dollars, unless otherwise indicated. ABE financial data have been disguised.

[3]ABE's "want" function would continue to search the database for matches each day until the customer deleted or modified the "want." Bibliofind's system provided only a one-time search, however.

[4]Formerly Interloc.com, the first of the online services.

TABLE 1   **Listing Characteristics of ABE Dealers**

% of Dealers Using Other Services	
• Bibliofind	41%
• Alibris	18
• Bibliocity	11
Percent listing only with ABE	58
Percent listing with 2 services	23
Percent listing with 3 services	7
Percent listing with 4 services	7
Percent listing with 5 services	3

of the books when available. Bibliocity was opened to all booksellers, and it offered a free three-month trial period. After the three-month period, booksellers were charged $40 per month. Booksellers maintained their own home pages on Bibliocity's website and submitted their book list in any database format. For an additional fee, booksellers could upgrade to Bibliocity's secure ordering system. Purchases were made directly with each bookseller, and the bookseller was responsible for fulfilling the orders that it received.

It was not unusual for ABE clients to list with multiple database services. An informal survey of 122 ABE dealers provided the competitive data shown in Table 1. In addition to listing books with the database services, book dealers often used the same services to buy books from other dealers. Finally, the dealers also used the databases to survey the inventory of competitors and priced their own books accordingly.

Market and Clientele

ABE operated as an infomediary in the rare- and used-book industry. As an infomediary, it straddled two markets. The first market consisted of book dealers, the second of serious collectors and occasional buyers. An individual might have been a bookselling client in one ABE transaction, and a buyer in another.

The bookselling industry was characterized by a wide variety of participants, ranging from large storefront operators, like Barnes and Noble (B & N), to weekend dealers and book scouts who might have handled fewer than 50 books at any one time. The American Book Trade Directory listed some 29,056 booksellers, but this was only a partial list. ABE had concentrated on individual buyers and sellers, garnered through publicity, promotion, and relationships with trade associations. However, libraries also bought and sold used books.

Most booksellers catered to a local clientele and sold their books from small storefronts. Since each store had a unique set of books to sell, it was difficult to match a particular customer with a particular book on their wish list. Customers either visited as many bookstores as they could to find the book that they wanted, or they just hoped to run across it someday. Many collectors would spend years looking for a single book.

Some book dealers printed and mailed catalogues in an attempt to reach more customers. The catalogues were time-consuming to produce, costly, and ineffective. By listing their books with an online service such as ABE, book dealers were able to overcome these problems. Customers searching for a particular book could go to one website and find their book in a matter of sec-

TABLE 2   Listings by ABE Client Dealers

Number of Books Listed	% of ABE Clients
0–200	31%
201–500	14
501–4,000	39
4,001–30,000+	16

onds. Booksellers could then sell their books beyond their physical locations. Since electronic sales created a larger market, booksellers found that they could sell their books at a higher price. Booksellers could also find books for customers who did not have access to the Internet. Many booksellers closed their stores in favor of working out of their homes and selling their books completely online.

ABE's client base was constantly growing. In January 1997, the company had 224 bookseller clients. By August, it had approximately 3,000. Its database served more than 130,000 individuals who had registered for no-fee accounts that allowed them to browse the database and maintain "want" profiles of books they were searching to buy. The database was available to registered users and to unidentified individuals who simply searched its contents without setting up a personal account. Amazon.com's out-of-print book buyers often searched the ABE database for books to fill requests from Amazon.com customers. In fact, when asked in a survey which state or province accounted for the largest number of orders they received, a number of ABE clients replied, "Amazon.com"!

Dealers varied greatly in the number of books they listed on the ABE database (Table 2) and in the activity they generated. Approximately 50 percent of the dealers generated 70 percent of the sales transactions that originated with ABE, and 25 percent generated sales that one could describe as "substantial." There was a group of dealers who regularly adjusted their inventory, to ensure they would stay below the 200-book level and thus remain at the $10 per month level. The amount of support required for dealers was, however, inversely related to their sales activity; the low-volume dealers required the greatest amount of assistance from the "help desk" staff. The average price of books listed on ABE was approximately $40, based on a random sample of the database.

Strategic Focus

ABE competed on customer service. From the industry's only toll-free dealer help line to free "How to Make Money on the Internet" seminars at book and trade shows, the company focused the majority of its attention on the dealers. Cathy defined ABE's role by saying, "We're here to help the dealers sell books." Rick emphasized, "You've *got* to be good to the dealers." A significant portion of Cathy's time was spent preparing press releases about client bookstores as part of ABE's publicity and participation in book fairs and trade shows. Before a trip to a Boston book fair, for example, she sent press releases to Boston area media announcing ABE's participation in the show. The press packets also included company and contact information about Boston area ABE clients who would be available for tie-in interviews or stories about the book fair.

The emphasis on dealer support began at the help desk. ABE had a staff of 12 customer support people who helped dealers with everything from setting up Web pages, to loading inventory, to recovering from data entry errors. The help desk was staffed from 8 A.M. to 4 P.M. PST, and Cathy projected that ABE needed one new customer support staffer for every 500 new dealers who signed up. Dealers had unlimited, free access to this customer support. They could also access helpful brochures and Web pages explaining how to set up inventory, promote their virtual and physical business, how to manage the online inventory, and how to use the database reports ABE provided as part of the subscription.

Dealers who listed with multiple online services sometimes had their inventory in a format specified by one of ABE's competitors or used internally by the dealer. ABE did not do data entry for its dealers. However, it accepted digital inventories in virtually any format and converted them to fit ABE's database at no charge. In addition, if an ABE dealer wanted to sign on with another online service, ABE would help the dealer download their ABE inventory in a format most compatible with the requirements of the other service. This could have served to undermine ABE's strength in the marketplace; it certainly reduced the cost of switching to another service. However, Cathy saw the company's strongest competitive advantage as outstanding customer service. Supporting the dealers, whatever their needs, was the lynchpin of maintaining dealer loyalty and preventing dealers from abandoning ABE entirely.

ABE's sole source of revenue was the dealer subscription fee. ABE prebilled on a monthly basis, charging fees directly to a dealer's Visa or Mastercard credit card. ABE used a four-tier pricing model (Table 3) and gave dealers who prepaid a year's fees 12 months for the price of 10. Fees were extremely low; even so, many cost-conscious dealers regularly adjusted inventory to stay below 200 or 500 books.

ABE earned no commission on the direct sale of books facilitated by its database or search engine; this undoubtedly cost it revenue. However, the flexibility of the searching and ordering system made a commission system extremely difficult to maintain and enforce. There were many ways for a book buyer to order from one of ABE's dealers. Upon finding a book the buyer liked, he or she could do any of the following:

1. Send the dealer an order via ABE's e-mail order system, requesting that the book be held and specifying the preferred method of payment.

2. Send an e-mail directly to the dealer, using the dealer's e-mail address as it appeared in the search output.

3. Link from the search output to the dealer's own website and order electronically at that site.

4. Phone the dealer, using the contact information that appeared in the search output, and place an immediate telephone order.

Only in the first instance was ABE guaranteed to learn of the purchase transaction. ABE's analysis of transaction patterns had led the company to conclude that about one-third to one-half of customers who ordered books from the ABE inventory did so via method 1. The rest went directly to the bookseller, via methods 2, 3, or 4. Even when a buyer used the ABE e-mail link to

---

TABLE 3   ABE Dealer Fees

# of Books Listed	Monthly Fee
0–200	$10
201–500	20
501–1,000	25
1,001+	35

contact a dealer, the transaction may not have ended in a purchase. The book could have been sold by the time the buyer decided to contact the seller, or the parties could have carried on an extended e-mail discussion, which ceased to be mediated by ABE once the initial e-mail went to the dealer.

The difficulty of tracking sales when ABE didn't control the inventory of books was not the only factor that favored a subscription model. Cathy's vision that ABE existed to help dealers sell books drove the company to encourage individuals and services that performed metasearches of the ABE database. Services such as BookFinder provided metasearch engines for book hunters and regularly searched the databases of ABE and its competitors. The metasearches then produced hyperlinks to the database listings, identifying the source of the hit (Exhibit 1). If ABE operated on a commission basis, such searches could have threatened income by making the database available to buyers who might then order outside ABE's e-mail system. Instead, the services strengthened ABE's marketing position by showing dealers that ABE was generating business and "hits" on the inventory even by people who didn't know about ABE specifically (Table 4). In addition, BookFinder actively promoted ABE and other sites whose databases it searched.

EXHIBIT 1

Results of Bookfinder.com Search1

Current Search:

First Name is "Patrick"

Last Name is "O'Brian"

Title is MASTER AND COMMANDER

Advanced Book Exchange
(Shipping costs vary)

Author	Title	Price	Note	Dealer	Action
O'Brian, Patrick	Master and Commander	US$35	Publisher: NY-W.W.Norton & Company 1994; HB-VG+. 1st Edition by Norton. The Aubrey/ Maturin Novels. 412 pgs.	garyandajsbooks	Buy/Info
O'Brian, Patrick	Master and Commander	US$1250	Publisher: London Collins 1970; The first British edition of the first of his acclaimed Jack Aubrey maritime novels (preceded by the American publication of it). Foxing to page edges; a very good copy in a very good edgeworn dust jacket creased along the front spine fold. Extremely scarce. First Edition.	Ken Lopez— Bookseller	Buy/Info
O'Brian, Patrick	Master and Commander	NZ$1600	Publisher: Collins London 1970; first edition 349pp VG+ (slightest cocking, owners inscription inside front board, faint foxing to endpapers) in VG d/w (price clipped, corners rounded with sl surface damage to upper front, spine sl sunned with rubbing and tears to head and foot, minor foxing to flaps).	Hard to Find Books Ltd.	Buy/Info
O'Brian, Patrick	Master and Commander	£650	Publisher: Collins 1970; 1st UK Hard Back Edition. A near fine copy (with a neat name in ink on the front free end-paper) in a very bright and attractive near fine dust wrapper that would be fine except for faint soiling to the very edge of the rear flap.	James M Pickard	Buy/Info

(continued)

EXHIBIT 1 *(concluded)*

Bibliocity
(Shipping costs vary)

Author	Title	Price	Note	Dealer	Action
O'Brian, Patrick	Master and Commander	US$1035	First edition, Collins 1970. The first 'Jack Aubrey' novel. VG+ in slightly rubbed and edge-worn price-clipped dustwrapper, with some creasing to the front panel and a couple of short closed tears to the rear.	Nigel Williams Rare Books	Buy/Info
O'Brian, Patrick	Master and Commander	US$1043	Collins 1970. 1st UK Hard Back Edition. A near fine copy (with a neat name in ink on the front free end-paper) in a very bright and attractive near fine dust wrapper that would be fine except for faint soiling to the very edge of the rear flap.	James M Pickard	Buy/Info

Antiqbook
(Shipping costs vary)

Author	Title	Price	Note	Dealer	Action
O'Brian, Patrick	Master and Commander	US$728	First edition, 8vo, 350 pp, in the original cloth, an excellent copy with the d.w. chipped and creased with some slight staining along lower edge.	Bow Windows Bookshop	Buy/Info

Details:
- No matching titles were found at the following sites: Powell's Books, YourBooks.com.
- Collectible first editions are not available at the following sites: Amazon.com.

Source: http://www.bookfinder.com, May 1999.

[1]Figures were rounded to fit text to page. Not all matching selections were shown.

TABLE 4

One-Day Sample Order Activity Captured by ABE

Transaction Category	Number of Transactions
Books in shopping baskets	958
Orders resulting from ABE "search" requests	2,984
Orders resulting from ABE "browse" requests	24
Orders resulting from ABE match reports	12

Organization of Business Activities/Processes

Internally, ABE looked like a very traditional business, organized around three basic functions. The first was dealer support. Here, ABE employees worked a standard eight-hour business day in a call centre environment. The system used by the support staff was custom-developed by Keith and Rick, and programmed internally.[5] Booksellers could e-mail requests for help or call ABE's toll-free support line. There was a single incoming line, answered by a switchboard operator who routed the call to an available support rep. The support rep had the ability to access the dealer's inventory, website, and various account files on ABE's servers. The rep then used that information to answer questions about database setup and maintenance, inventory management, the Home-Base software operation and features, and general enquiries about ABE and its services. E-mail requests for help received e-mail replies, handled by the same support staff.

The development and internal support staff were responsible for all programming and system development. They designed and maintained the website, as well as the database programs and search routines used to actually support the inventory and want databases. In addition, they did system maintenance and answered internal system-related questions from other ABE staff.

An administrative group managed the daily clerical and financial activities. The most complex of these was the accounting function. The bookkeeping was done by a staff bookkeeper, Carol Barr, with financial advice that came from the firm's auditors. ABE operated in U.S. and Canadian dollars simultaneously, with banks and financial partners in both the United States and Canada. They dealt with four banks and credit card processing organizations. All transactions were recorded as if they involved a single currency, and the ledgers were periodically reconciled. Because of the constant currency fluctuations, the financial position of the company couldn't be easily determined at any point in time.

Advanced Book Exchange operated a small but efficient data centre, which serviced all of their internal and database processes. Multiple independent systems served the centre's various functions: the database of books and client dealers was maintained on one server, running Oracle database software; inventory searches were built around an Alta Vista search engine running on another server; a third machine acted as the company's Web server, linking the database and search engine servers, and housing the Web pages of the clients who used the space provided by ABE; a fourth machine hosted the administrative programs and was used for various batch processes. There were 33 desktop machines used by employees, networked to the server. ABE had T1 Internet access, provided by Shaw Cable and Pacificcoast.net in Victoria. The access cost was approximately Cdn$3,600 per month.

ABE's systems provided the following functions to the dealers:

> *Dealer inventory maintenance.* ABE's internally developed software package, HomeBase, enabled dealers to enter inventory into the dealer database, modify inventory, and upload or download their entries to and from ABE's database server. The software was free to dealers and could be downloaded from the ABE website.
>
> *Inventory activity reporting.* ABE provided dealers with a host of reports analyzing the activity against their inventory.
>
> *Demand analysis.* Dealers could examine outstanding customer "wants," looking at the demand for books that they might have had but didn't list. These wants also alerted dealers to books that could sell profitably if a copy were found.

---

[5] At a cost of approximately Cdn$36,000.

Web presence. A dealer could maintain a custom website, either stored (at no extra charge) on the ABE Web server or housed on another server. ABE provided a Web page template that dealers completed for a simple one-page site; alternatively, dealers could design and program their own elaborate site.

Contact interface with customers. Whenever a customer got a match between a desired book and a title in inventory, ABE provided that customer with direct links in three ways:

- A Web hyperlink that brought up a Web page with a full description of the book, and a preformatted, preaddressed e-mail message to the dealer, indicating the customer's interest in purchasing the book. The customer needed only to complete payment information and click "submit" to send the request to the dealer.
- A "mail to" hyperlink to the dealer's e-mail address opened the customer's e-mail package, enabling them to create their own message.
- Contact information provided by the dealer (such as mailing address, phone number, and hours of operation) appeared in the body of the match report, which allowed the customer to contact the dealer off-line.

Customers and dealers could perform the following functions:

Browse a dealer's inventory. Buyers could specify a country, state, or dealer and browse the inventory available within those parameters.

Search for a book. By providing a title (or portion thereof), author, or publisher, buyers could request a search of all dealers (or a subgroup). The search could be narrowed down further by type of binding (hardcover, paper), presence of a dust jacket, whether or not the book was a first edition, and whether or not it was signed. The system returned a list of matches that met the criteria provided. Searchers could explore the listing in more depth, click on the price to have it converted to another currency, or add the book to their shopping cart.

Build a shopping cart. Customers could add specific items to a pseudo-shopping cart. When they were ready to buy, the system sent e-mail messages to the dealers whose books were in the cart, indicating the customer's desire to buy the book. ABE sent an e-mail message to the customer to confirm that the dealer had been notified. It was then up to the dealer to contact the customer directly to continue the transaction.

Maintain "wants." The three functions described above did not require the customer to have a user account with ABE. However, if an individual registered a free user account, they could then take advantage of the system's automatic searching function. To do this, the customer built a "want"—a record of a title, author, or publisher of interest—by completing a "want" screen. The system maintained this record in a file and regularly queried the inventory database for matches. When matches were found for any or all of a user's wants, the system formatted an e-mail message (Exhibit 2) alerting the customer to the availability of the book(s) and providing the three methods of contact described above. Users could add to, modify, or delete wants over time (Exhibit 3).

The Barnesandnoble.com Partnership

Early in 1998, Tom Simon approached ABE. Simon was involved with MUZE, a firm that installed interactive-order kiosks and supplied information on music, video, and book titles to online retailers. He had been courted by Bibliofind.com's Michael Selzer, who suggested a partnership to

EXHIBIT 2

Want Match E-mail Message

The following wants have been matched by ABE:

***

Your Want: # A1525800

Info:

Author: O'Brian, Patrick; Publisher: Collins; Attributes: First Edition . . . Must have dustjacket.

Has been matched with the following book(s):

————

Master and Commander by O'Brian, Patrick, Collins 1970, 1st UK Hard Back Edition. A fine copy in a near fine dust wrapper with a slight crease at the top right hand corner of both the front flap and the rear cover. An outstanding copy of a rare title seldom seen in this condition. (Keywords: naval)

The price of the book is £695.00

Please reference the seller's book # 00318 when ordering.

The seller is James M Pickard

21, Grenfell Road, Leicester, United Kingdom, LE2 2PA.

JPRAREBOOK@aol.com Ph: 0116 2707169. Fax: 0116 2702010. Terms of sale: Postage at cost. Any book may be returned within 10 days if book does not match given description. We accept payment in US Dollars and GB Pounds.

Source: http://www.abebooks.com, May 1999.

EXHIBIT 3

Want list maintenance screen

 Advanced Book Exchange

Maintain want ... Frames Help Search Browse Signon Menu Stores News Home

✔ Your want has been deleted

Search for a book by author, title, publisher or keyword

Enter new search criteria.

Add new wants to your want inventory.

Author	Title	Publisher	Keywords	Attribs	Want#	Upd	Del	Matches	Delete Matches	Search
.	Lexicon of Intentionally Ambiguous	.	.	.	A4824539	Upd	Del	None	.	Search
Bemelmans, Ludwig	Madeline	.	.	First Edition Hardcover	A4824535	Upd	Del	None	.	Search
Dexter, Colin	.	Macmillan	.	First Edition Hardcover Signed Must have dustjacket	A4824536	Upd	Del	None	.	Search
O'Brien, Patrick	.	Collins	.	First Edition Must have dustjacket	A4824537	Upd	Del	None	.	Search
Thompson, Kay	Eloise	.	.	.	A4824538	Upd	Del	None	.	Search

Total # of want displayed, 5

Source: http://www.abebooks.com, May 1999.

deliver out-of-print database content via kiosks in bookstores. Simon's wife, however, was an ABE client and convinced him that MUZE would be better served by doing business with ABE. Discussions between Simon and ABE began. In the midst of these exchanges, Simon moved to Barnesandnoble.com as vice president of its out-of-print book division. He maintained his connections to ABE, shifting the emphasis to Web, rather than kiosk, delivery.

ABE now had the opportunity to sign a one-year, renewable agreement with Barnesandnoble .com for an exclusive partnership as the latter company's out-of-print book source. Under the agreement, ABE's dealer/members would sign on to provide Barnesandnoble.com exclusive reseller rights to the dealer's ABE inventory over the Web. The dealer would retain the right to sell that inventory online directly (or through database services such as ABE), but could not partner for online sales with competitors such as Amazon.com. The agreement would allow U.S. book dealers who were ABE clients to have their inventory listed and searched by Barnesandnoble.com customers looking for out-of-print books. Under the proposed terms of the agreement, Barnesandnoble.com would be given a 20 percent discount off the price listed on the ABE database.

On a regular basis, ABE would provide the inventory of participating members to Barnesandnoble.com and would act as a clearinghouse for payments to the dealers. Barnesandnoble.com would identify the dealer as the source of the book when a customer searched for out-of-print books at their website, but would not identify abebooks.com as the original source of the data. In return for managing the process on behalf of the dealers and providing Barnesandnoble.com with regular database updates, ABE would receive a percentage commission on all sales generated by the partnership. The commission was based on the discounted dealer's price for each book sold and, as such, couldn't be predicted exactly; however, a review of the books listed on the database suggested that commissions would average somewhere between $2 and $3 per sale.

The Barnesandnoble.com process would be an add-on to ABE's basic systems. The basic flow of information and product would be as shown in Exhibit 4. The process would begin when a dealer participating in the B & N program updated their inventory on the ABE dealer inventory database. ABE would periodically review updates to the database and prepare update files for B & N. That file would then be transmitted to B & N and used to update its out-of-print database. There would be two separate and distinct databases. B & N would use the basic information about the book, its availability, and condition for its own listing. However, B & N could add notations about the cost of shipping and shipping options, and format it to feed the B & N search engines.

When a B & N customer executed a search on the main Barnesandnoble.com site for a book that was out of print (OOP), they would receive a screen telling them that the book was out of print and might be available from B & N's out-of-print services. The customer would then be invited to click through to the OOP search engine and provide the parameters of an OOP search. Next, the B & N engine would be run against B & N's out-of-print database. If a match was not found, the site would convey that information to the customer. If there were one or more matches, the site would display the matches and their descriptions, including the name of the bookseller who holds the book in inventory (Exhibit 4). If the customer indicated the desire to purchase one of the books matched, B & N would then notify ABE by e-mail of the potential transaction. ABE would contact the bookseller, who could then accept or decline the sale. (The book could have been sold since being added to the database, for example, or the dealer may have since agreed to hold it for another customer.)

If the dealer agreed to sell the book, they would ship it to B & N. When B & N received the book, they would pay ABE. The payment would include the dealer's ABE list price (minus B & N's discount), any necessary reimbursement for the dealer's shipping expense, and ABE's commission. ABE would, in turn, remit the discounted selling price and shipping reimbursement to the dealer using the American Clearing House electronic funds transfer network. The dealer payment portion of the transaction could take weeks to be complete.

EXHIBIT 4

Barnesandnoble.com processing flow

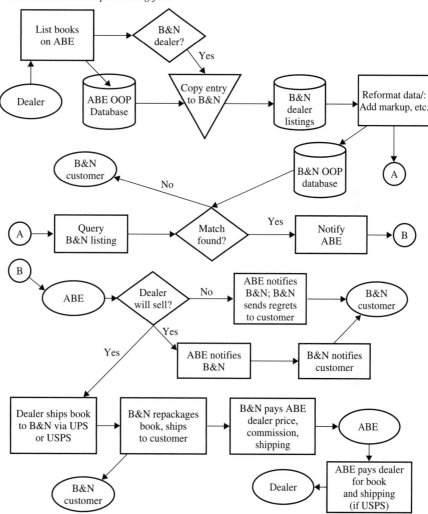

Source: Compiled by author.

The Decision

Competition was fierce in the world of online book retailing, and Barnes and Noble wouldn't wait indefinitely for ABE's decision. If this was a good offer, ABE would want to move quickly. "Well," said Keith to his partners around the table, "what do we do?"

EXHIBIT 5

ABE
Quarterly Income Statement
June to August 1998

Revenue

Dealer subscription fees	$266,350
U.S. dollar exchange income	102,373
Total revenue	**$368,723**

Expenses

Accounting and legal	$ 4,272
Advertising/promotion	3,348
Interest expense	139
Bank fees	370
Casual labor	665
Consulting	45,497
Credit card fees	2,460
Dues and fees	1,607
Entertainment	520
Telephone	7,141
Insurance	281
Internet fees	7,020
Management fees	29,575
Miscellaneous	269
Courier/postage/supplies	2,600
Rent	6,500
Equipment lease expense	17,241
Repairs and maintenance	1,567
Travel	5,144
Software expense	13,967
Building expense	27,922
Utilities	1,169
General operating	13,000
Wages	123,500
Payroll tax expense	7,150
Total expenses	**$322,924**
Net Income	**$ 45,800**

Source: Company financial records.

(continued)

EXHIBIT 5   *(continued)*

ABE
Simplified Balance Sheet
30–Aug–98

Assets			
Current:			
	Petty cash		$ 65
	Canadian banks		13,057
	U.S. banks		23,897
	Accounts receivable		<u>33,752</u>
	Total current		**$ 70,771**
Fixed:			
	Hardware	$65,535	
	Acc. hardware dep.	<u>(5,357)</u>	
	Net hardware		60,178
	Software dep.		(731)
	Furniture/equipment	18,723	
	Acc. dep.	<u>(252)</u>	
	Net furniture/equipment		<u>18,471</u>
	Total fixed		**$ <u>77,918</u>**
Total Assets			**$<u>148,689</u>**
Liabilities			
Current:			
	Software subcontractor fees		$ 18,925
	Accounts payable		64,724
	Vacation payable		11,296
	Taxes payable		16,672
	Goods/services tax payable		<u>(14,163)</u>
	Total current		**$ <u>97,454</u>**
Equity			**$ <u>51,235</u>**
Total Liabilities + Equity			**$<u>148,689</u>**

Source: Company financial records.

(continued)

EXHIBIT 5   *(continued)*

Employee Name	Sheryl Gregson
Department ("x")	IVEY PUBLISHING
	TO BE PAID DIRECTLY TO VISA

Description of Claim: *eg Course/Project Name, General, etc*   monthly Ivey Publishing Visa

Period Covered	From:	02-Feb-01
	To:	12-Feb-01

	Canadian Total	Foreign Currency Total	Total Claim	Account #
Transportation	$ -	$ -	$ -	5360-400
Conference Fees	$ -	$ -	$ -	5280-400
Permission Fees	$ -	$ -	$ -	5148-000
GST	$ 136.45	$ -	$ 136.45	1-0-00-000-2040-007

Other

	Canadian Total	Foreign Currency Total	Total Claim	Account #
Canadian Securities Institute	$ 2,266.69	$ -	$ 2,266.69	5148-000
Annual Card Fee	$ 7.55	$ -	$ 7.55	5121-000
0	$ -	$ -	$ -	
0	$ -	$ -	$ -	
0	$ -	$ -	$ -	
0	$ -	$ -	$ -	
0	$ -	$ -	$ -	
0	$ -	$ -	$ -	
0	$ -	$ -	$ -	
	$ -	$ -	$ -	
	$ -	$ -	$ -	
	$ -	$ -	$ -	
	$ -	$ -	$ -	
	$ -	$ -	$ -	
	$ -	$ -	$ -	
Total	$ 2,410.69	$ -	$ 2,410.69	
Less Cash Advance				1-0-00-000-1022-000
Due to/(from) Employee			$ 2,410.69	

	Signature	Date
Employee		
Approval		
Finance		

(continued)

EXHIBIT 5 *(concluded)*

Canadian

	All Other Provinces		Total	GST	Net

Transportation

Supplier	Location From	To	Departure Date					
					0.0566	$ -	$ -	$ -
					0.0566	$ -	$ -	$ -
					0.0566	$ -	$ -	$ -
					0.0566	$ -	$ -	$ -
					0.0566	$ -	$ -	$ -
					0.0566	$ -	$ -	$ -
					0.0566	$ -	$ -	$ -
					0.0566	$ -	$ -	$ -

Subtotal $ - $ - $ - $ -
GST $ - 0.0566 $ -
Net $ - $ -

Conference Costs

Supplier	Location	Date From	To					
					0.0566	$ -	$ -	$ -
					0.0566	$ -	$ -	$ -
					0.0566	$ -	$ -	$ -
					0.0566	$ -	$ -	$ -

Subtotal $ - $ - $ - $ -
GST $ - 0.0566 $ -
Net $ - $ -

Permission Fees

Description	Date	# of Items					
				0.0566	$ -	$ -	$ -
				0.0566	$ -	$ -	$ -
				0.0566	$ -	$ -	$ -
				0.0566	$ -	$ -	$ -
				0.0566	$ -	$ -	$ -
				0.0566	$ -	$ -	$ -
				0.0566	$ -	$ -	$ -
				0.0566	$ -	$ -	$ -
				0.0566	$ -	$ -	$ -

Subtotal $ - $ - $ - $ -
GST $ - 0.0566 $ -
Net $ - $ -

Other

Description	Date	# of Items*	All Other Provinces		Total	GST	Net
Canadian Securities Ins	05-Feb-01	1	$2,402.69	0.0566	$ 2,402.69	$ 136.00	$ 2,266.69
Annual card fee		1	$ 8.00	0.0566	$ 8.00	$ 0.45	$ 7.55
				0.0566	$ -	$ -	$ -
				0.0566	$ -	$ -	$ -
				0.0566	$ -	$ -	$ -
				0.0566	$ -	$ -	$ -
				0.0566	$ -	$ -	$ -
				0.0566	$ -	$ -	$ -
				0.0566	$ -	$ -	$ -

*Similar items can be added together.

Subtotal $2,410.69 $2,410.69 $136.45 $2,274.24
GST $ 136.45 0.0566 $ 136.45
Net $2,274.24 $2,274.24

$ 2,410.69 $ 136.45 $ 2,274.24

Bibliography

Abernathy W.J. and Utterback J.M., Patterns of Industrial Innovation, Technology
Review, 80, 1978.

Adler P., and Shenhar A., Adapting Your Technological Base: The Organisational
Challenge, Sloan Management Review Fall 1990

Adler P., McDonald D., MacDonald F., Strategic Management Of Technical
Functions, Sloan Management Review, Winter 1992.

Adler P., Technology Strategy: A Guide To The Literatures, Research On
Technological Innovation, Management And Policy, Rosenbloom, Richard S. and
Burgleman, Robert A. (eds) Vol 4, JAI Press 1989.

Adler, P., Time and Motion Regained, Harvard Business Review, January 1993, V71,
N1, pp 97-108

Ali A.J. and Zahra, S.A. Managing Technology in a Changing Global Marketplace,
Journal of Euromarketing, 3 (3) 1994.

Alic J., Technical Knowledge and Technology Diffusion: New Issues for US
Government Policy, Technology Analysis and Strategic Management, 5 (4), 1993.

Arend M., Survey Gauges CIOs' Outsourcing Acumen, ABA Banking Journal, 84 (5),
May 1992.

Armour H. and Teece D., Vertical Integration And Technological Innovation, Review of
Economics and Statistics, 62, 1980.

Atuahene-Gima K., Determinants of Inward Technology Licensing Intentions: An
Empirical Analysis of Australian Engineering Firms, Journal of Product
Innovation Management, 10 (3), June 1993.

Australian Science and Technology Council. Science, Technology and Australia's
Future, Canberra 1990.

Badawy M. Technology and Strategic Advantage: Managing Corporate Technology Transfer In The USA and Japan, Engineering Management Review, Summer 1991.

Bailey J., Job Design and New Technology, Work Study, 41 (2), March/April 1992.

Bailey T., Stuck in the Past, Apparel Industry Magazine, 55 (3), March 1994.

Baker M., Sharpening the Focus of Viewpoints Between Higher Education and Employers of the Expertise Required for Contemporary and Future Technical Managers, IEEE Transactions on Engineering Management, 40 (3), August 1993.

Baker P., Production Restructuring in the Textiles and Clothing Industries, New Technology Work & Employment, 8 (1), March 1993.

Baker T., South Australia Survey: Conservative State Needs Radical Reform, Australian Business Monthly, 13 (7), May 1993.

Baulkin, T., Reward Policies That Support Entrepreneurship. Compensation Benefits Review Vol 20, 1988

Beatty C., Implementing Advanced Manufacturing Technologies: Rules of the Road, Sloan Management Review, 33 (4), Summer 1992.

Bell, S., Resizing On-line Business Trade, 1999, Forrester Research Inc., *www.forrester.com*

Benson B., Sage A. and Cook G., Emerging Technology-Evaluation Methodology: With Application to Micro-Electromechanical Systems, IEEE Transactions on Engineering Management, 40 (2), May 1993.

Bentley J., Integrating Design and manufacturing Strategies for Business Transformation, International Journal of Technology Management, 6 (3-4), 1991.

Berman E. and Khalil T., US Technological Competitiveness In The Global Economy: A Survey, International Journal On Technology Management, V7 No 4/5, 1992.

Bessant J., Burnell J., Harding R and Webb, S., Continuous Improvement in British Manufacturing, Technovation, 13 (4), May 1993.

Betz F. Basic Research And Technology Transfer, International Journal Of Technology Management, V9 No 5/6/7 1994.

Betz F. Strategic Technology Management New York, Mc Graw-Hill 1993.

Boaden R., and Dale B., Total Quality Management in the Construction Industry: A Preliminary Analysis, International Journal of Technology Management, 7 (4-5), 1992.

Bonaccorsi A., and Lipparini, C., Strategic Partnerships in New Product Development: An Italian Case Study, Journal of Product Innovation Management 11 (2) 1994.

Booz, Allen and Hamilton, New Products Management For the 1980's, Booz Allen and Hamilton, New York 1982.

Bower J. and Hout T. Fast Cycle Capability For Competitive Power., Harvard Business Review, Nov/Dec 1988.

Bowonder, B. and Miyake T., Technology Forecasting in Japan, Futures, 25 (7), September 1993.

Breiner S., Cuhls K. and Grupp H., Technology Foresight Using a Delphi Approach: A Japanese- German Co-operation, R&D Management, 24 (2), April 1994.

Bridges E., Coughlan A. and Kalish S., New Technology Adoption in an Innovative Marketplace: Micro- and Macro-Level Decision-Making Models, International Journal of Forecasting, 7 (3), November 1991.

Brownlie D., The Role of Technology Forecasting and Planning: Formulating Business Strategy, Industrial Management and Data Systems, 92 (2), 1992.

Burgelman, R.A. and Maidique, M.A., Strategic Management of Technology, Irwin, 1988, Homewood, Illinois.

Burgleman, R., Intraorganisational Ecology Of Strategy Making And Organisational Adaption: Theory and Field Research., Organisational Science, 2(3), 1991.

Burns T. and Stalker G., The Management Of Innovation. London, Tavistock 1960.

Capon N. and Glazer R., Marketing and Technology: A Strategic Co-Alignment, Journal Of Marketing 51 July 1987.

Carlsson B, Audretsch D.B., Acs Z.J., Flexible Technology and Plant Size U.S. Manufacturing and Metalworking Industries, International Journal of Industrial Organization, 12 (3), September 1994.

Carter, T., Internet Procurement Gains Corporate Support, Knowledgespace, May 26,1999; *www.knowledgespace.com*

Challis, D., and Samson, D., A Strategic Framework for Technical Function Management in Manufacturing, Journal of Operations Management, June 1986, V14, N2, p17

Chang M-H., Flexible Manufacturing, Uncertain Consumer Tastes, and Strategic Entry Deterrence, Journal of Industrial Economics, 41 (1), March 1993.

Choi, M-J., Manufacturing Cell Design, Production and Inventory Management Journal, 33 (2), Second Quarter 1992.

Clark, K., and Fujimoto, T., Lead Time In Automobile Product Development: Explaining The Japanese Advantage. Journal Of Engineering And Technology Management, No 6 1989.

Clark, K., and Wheelwright, S., Competing Through Development Capability In A Manufacturing Based Organisation, Business Horizons, July/August 1992.

Clark, K., and Wheelwright, S., Creating Project Plans To Focus Product Development. Harvard Business Review March/April 1992.

Clark, K., Company Technology Strategy, R&D Management, V19, N3, 1986.

Clark, K., What Strategy Can Do For Technology, Harvard Business Review, Nov/Dec 1989.

Coates, J., Why Forecasts Fail, Research-Technology Management, 36 (4), July/August 1993.

Comdit, P., Focusing on the Customer: How Boeing Does It, Research-Technology Management, 37 (1), January-February 1994.

Conti, R., Work Practice Barriers to Flexible Manufacturing in the US and the UK, New Technology Work and Employment, 7 (1), Spring 1992.

Cooper, R.G., and More, R. A., Modular Risk Management: An Applied Example, R & D Management, Feb 1979, V9, N2, p93

Davis,S., Meyer C.,, Blur–The Speed of Change in the Connected Economy, Reading Massachusetts, 1998.

Dertouzos, M., et al, Made In America., Report by the MIT Commission On Industrial Productivity, MIT Press Cambridge, MA, 1989.

Dini, M., and Guerguil, M., Small Firms, New Technologies and Human Resources Requirements in Chile, International Journal of Technology Management, 9 (3-4), 1994.

DITAC Direction Setting For Science Technology and Engineering: A Strategic Framework , Science and Technology Occasional Paper No 1, 1991

Dubarle, P., The Coalescence of Technology OECD Observer, 185, December 1993/January 1994.

Dubashi, J., Benchmarking: Mastering Customized Manufacturing, Financial World, 161 (19), 1992.

Economic Planning And Advisory Council Science, Technology and Industrial Development. Discussion Paper 91/08 Canberra 1991.

Erickson, T., Magee J., Roussel, P., and Saad, K., Managing Technology as a Business Strategy, Sloan Management Review, Spring 1990.

Eschenbach, T., and Geistauts, G., Strategically Focused Engineering: Design And Management, IEEE Transactions On Engineering Management, EM-34, No 2, 1987.

Ettlie, J., Bridges, W., and O'Keefe, R., Organisational Strategy And Structural Differences For Radical vs Incremental Innovation, Management Science, 30, 1984.

Ettlie, J., Organisational Policy and Innovation among Suppliers In The Food Processing Sector, Academy Of Management Journal, 26, 1983.

Ettlie, J., What makes a Manufacturing Firm Innovative?, Academy Of Management Executive, Vol 4, No 4, 1990.

Ettlie, J.E., High Technology Manufacturing in Low Technology Plants, Interfaces, 23 (6), November/December 1993.

Ford, D., Developing Your Technology Strategy., Long Range Planning, 21, October 1988.

Forest, J., Models For The Process Of Technological Innovation., Technology Analysis And Strategic Management V3, No 4, 1991

Foster, G., The Innovation Imperative, Management Today, April 1993.

Foster, R., Working The S Curve—Assessing Technological Threats, Research Management 29, 1986.

Francis J.D, Young R., and Christopher H., Manufacturing Strategy and Production Systems: An Integrated Framework, Growth and Change, 24 (1), Winter 1993.

Fusfeld, A., Formulating Technology Strategies To Meet The Global Challenges Of The 1990's, International Journal Of Technology Management, 4 (6) 1989.

Gerybadze, A., Technology Forecasting as a Process of Organisational Intelligence, R&D Management, 24 (2), April 1994.

Ghosh, S., Making Business Sense of the Internet, Harvard Business Review, March-April 1998

Goldhar, J., Jelinek, M., and Schlie, T., Flexibility and Competitive Advantage— Manufacturing Becomes a Service Business, International Journal of Technology Management, 6 (3-4), 1991.

Grant, R., Contemporary Strategy Analysis, Concepts, Techniques and Applications, Blackwell, New York, 1991.

Hambrick, D., Business Unit Strategy and Changes In The Product And R&D Budget, Management Science, 29, 1983.

Hamilton, W., and Singh, H., The Evolution of Corporate Capabilities in Emerging Technologies Interfaces July/August 1992.

Hamson, K., Managing the Strategic Fit Between Technical Capabilities and Industry Environment, Fourth International Conference On Engineering Management, Melbourne 10-12 April 1994.

Hayes, R., and Wheelwright, S., Restoring Our Competitive Edge: Competing through Manufacturing., Wiley, NY, 1984.

Hesterbrink, C., E-Business and ERP: Bringing two Paradigms together, October 1999; PricewaterhouseCoopers; *www.pwc.com*

Itami, H., and Numagami, T., Dynamic Interaction Between Strategy And Technology, Strategic Management Journal, 13, 1992.

Jaikumar, R., and Bohn, R., The Development of Intelligent Systems for Industrial Use: A Conceptual Framework, Research on Technological Innovation, Management and Policy, V3, 1986, pp 169-211

Jones, O., Green, K., and Coombs, R., Technology Management: Developing A Critical Perspective, International Journal Of Technology Management, 9 (2), 1994

Kalakota, R., and Robinson, M., E-Business—Roadmap for Success, Reading Massachusetts: Addison-Wesley, 1999

Kanter, R., Swimming in Newstreams: Mastering Innovation Dilemmas, California Management Review, Summer 1989, V31, N4, pp45-70

Kanter, R., The Change Masters, New York, Simon and Schuster, 1983

Kanter, R., The Change Masters: Innovation For Productivity In The American Corporation, New York, Simon and Schuster, 1983.

Kaplan, G. and Jaikumar R., Manufacturing A La Carte; 200 Years to CIM, IEEE Spectrum, 30 (9), September 1993.

Karshenas, M., and Stoneman, P., A Flexible Model of Technological Diffusion Incorporating Economic Factors with an Application to the Spread of Colour Television Ownership in the UK, Journal of Forecasting, 11 (7), November 1992.

Kelley, K., Customer Service Online, Knowledgespace

Kelly, P., and Krantzberg, M., Technological Innovation: A Critical Review Of Current Knowledge San Francisco Press, USA, 1978.

Kim, S-B., and Whang, K-S., Forecasting the Capabilities of the Korean Civil Aircraft Industry, Omega, 21 (1), January 1993.

Kim, Y., and Lee, J., Manufacturing Strategy and Production Systems: An Integrated Framework, Journal of Operations Management, 11 (1), March 1993.

Kjeldsen, J., Tech-Ploitation: The New Manufacturing Credo, Journal of Business Strategy, 14 (4), 1993.

Krupp, J., Core Obsolescence Forecasting in Remanufacturing, Production and Inventory Management Journal, 33 (2), Second Quarter 1992.

Kumar, U., and Kumar, V., Technological Innovation Diffusion: The Proliferation of Substitution Models and Easing the User's Dilemma, IEEE Transactions on Engineering Management, 39 (2), May 1992.

Kumar, V., Mathur S., Kumar, U., An Overview Of The Innovation Process In The Canadian Electronic and Telecommunication Industry, Engineering Management Journal, V6, 1994

Lay, G., Government Support of computer Integrated Manufacturing in Germany: First Results of an Impact Analysis, Technovation, 13 (5), July 1993.

Lee, J., Lu, K. and Horng, S., Technological Forecasting with Nonlinear Models, Journal of Forecasting, 11 (3), April 1992.

Lenz, J., Determine How to Manage a New Manufacturing Technology Before Adopting It, Industrial Engineering, 24 (4), April 1992.

Lester, T., Squeezing the Supply Chain, Management Today, March 1992.

Levary, R., Enhancing Competitive Advantage in Fast-Changing Manufacturing Environments, Industrial Engineering, 24 (12), 1992.

Litvak, I., Winning Strategies for Small Technology-Based Companies, Business Quarterly, 57 (2), Autumn 1992.

MacPherson, A., Industrial Innovation Among Small and Medium-Sized Firms in a Declining Region, Growth and Change, 25(2), Spring 1994.

Magjuka, R., and Schmenner, R., Cellular Manufacturing, Group Technology and Human Resource Management: An International Study, International Journal of Management, 10 (4), December 1993.

Maidique, M., and Patch, P., Corporate Strategy And Technology Policy, in M.L. Tushman's Readings In The Management Of Innovation (2nd ed) Ballinger, Cambridge MA 1988.

Maital, S., Caution: Oracles at Work, Across the Board, 30 (5), June 1993.

Mansfield, E., and Wagner, S., Organisational And Strategic Factors Associated With Probabilities Of Success In Industrial R&D. Journal Of Business, No 48, 1975

Marquis, D., The Anatomy Of Successful Innovations., Innovation, November 1969.

Martin, M., Managing Innovation and New Technology, J Wiley, New York, 1984

Martinez, Sanchez A., Advanced Manufacturing Technologies: An Integrated Model of Diffusion, International Journal of Operations and Production, 11 (9), 1991.

Martino, J., Technological Forecasting: An Introduction, Futurist, 27 (4), July/August 1993.

McCrary, E., Flexible by Design, Apparel Industry Magazine, 55 (7), July 1994.

McDermott, K., The End of Mass Production, D&B Reports, 42 (1), January/February, 1993.

Meredith, J., and Vineyard M., A Longitudinal Study of the Role of Manufacturing Technology in Business Strategy, International Journal of Operations and Production Management, 13 (12), 1993.

Meyer, M., and Roberts, E., Focusing Product Technology For Corporate Growth, Sloan Management Review Summer 1988.

Meyer, M., and Utterback, J., The Product Family and the Dynamics of Core Capability, Sloan Management Review, Spring, 1993.

MIT Commission On Industrial Productivity, The Working Papers Of The MIT
   Commission On Industrial Productivity, 2, MIT {Press, Cambridge, MA, 1989.

Mitchell, V., Using Delphi to Forecast in New Technology Industries, Marketing
   Intelligence and Planning, 10 (2), 1992.

Mitsch, R., R&D at 3M : Continuing To Play A Big Role Research-Technology
   Management, Vol 35, No 5 Sept/Oct 1992

Mitsch, R., Three Roads To Innovation., Journal Of Business Strategy, Sept/Oct 1990

Moore, G., Crossing The Chasm, New York, Free Press, 1991

Morgan, J., Building a World Class Supply Base from Scratch, Purchasing, 115 (2),
   1993.

Neiger, D., E-Commerce in Depth, PC Authority, January 2000

Newman, W., and Hanna, M., Including Equipment Flexibility in Break-Even
   Analysis: Two Examples, Production and Inventory Management Journal, 31 (1),
   First Quarter 1994.

Noori, H., and Radford, R. W., Readings and Cases in the Management of New
   Technology, Prentice Hall, 1990

Ogbuehi, A.O., Bellas, R.A., Decentralized R&D for Global Product Development:
   Strategic Implications for the Multinational Corporation, International Marketing
   Review, 9 (5), 1992.

Ogbuehi, A.O., Decentralised R&D for Global Product Development, International
   Marketing Review, 9 (5), 1992.

Pavitt, K., What we Know About the Strategic Management of Technology, California
   Management Review, Spring 1990.

Porter, M., Competitive Advantage, Free Press, New York 1985.

Porter, M., The Technological Dimension Of Competitive Strategy in R.S.
   Rosenbloom's Research On Technological Innovation, management And Policy,
   JAI Press, Greenwich 1983.

Prahalad, C., and Hamel, G., The Core Competence of The Corporation, Harvard
   Business Review, May/June 1990.

Quinn, J., Doorey, T., and Paquette, P., Technology In Services : Rethinking Strategic
   Focus Sloan Management Review, Winter 1990.

Quinn, J., Managing Innovation: Controlled Chaos., Harvard Business Review,
   May/June 1985.

Ramasesh, R., and Jayakumar, M., Economic Justification of Advanced
   Manufacturing Technology, Omega, 21 (3), May 1993.

Rappa, M., Assessing the Rate of Technological Progress Using Hazard Rate Models
   of R&D Communities, R&D Management, 24 (2), April 1994.

Reddy, N.M., The Institutional Domain of Technology Diffusion, Journal of Product
   Innovation management, Vol 8 No 4, December 1991.

Rhys, D, McNabb, R. and Nieuwenhuis, P., The Significance of Scale in the
   Aftermath of Lean Production, International Motor Business, 153, January 1993.

Rieck, R., and Dickson, K., A Model of Technology Strategy, Technology Analysis
   and Strategic Management, 5 (4), 1993.

Roberts, E., and Berry, C., Entering New Businesses : Selecting Strategies For
   Success. Sloan Management Review, Spring 1985.

Robertson, T., Innovative Behaviour and Communication. New York, Holt, Rinehart and Winston 1971.

Roddy, D., The New Economics of Transactions: Evolution of Unique e-business Internet Market Spaces, Deloitte Consulting, New York, May 1999, *www.dc.com*

Roddy, David J., The Birth of B2B Market, Deloitte Consulting; www.dc.com

Rotella J., Break the Barriers to Innovation, Chemical Engineering, 100 (10), October 1993.

Rothman H., You Need Not Be Big to Benchmark, Nation's Business, 80 (12), December 1992.

Rothwell, R., Project Sappho: A comparative study of Success and Failure in Industrial Innovation, Information Age, October 1985, V7, N4, pp 215-220

Rothwell, R., The Characteristics of Technically Progressive Firms, R & D Management, 1977, V7, N3

Saleh, S., and Wang, C., The Management Of Innovation: Strategy Structure and Organisational Climate IEEE Transactions On Engineering Management, V40, No 1, 1993.

Samson D. and Challis D. A Strategic Effort For Technical Effort In Manufacturing. Melbourne Business School, 1994.

Samson, D., Manufacturing And Operations Strategy. Melbourne, Prentice Hall 1991.

Sandberg, U., Reasons for the Success or Failure of an Automation Project: An Investigation of Small and Medium-Sized Swedish Manufacturing Companies, Integrated Manufacturing Systems, 3 (1), 1992.

Sankaran, S., and Kasilingam, R.G., On Cell Size and Machine Requirements Planning in Group Technology Systems, European Journal of Operational Research, 69 (3), September 1993.

Saren, A., A Classification And Review Of Models Of The Intra Firm Innovation Process, R&D Management, 14, 1984.

Schewe, G., Successful Innovation Management: An Integrative Perspective., Journal Of Engineering and Technology Management, 11, 1994.

Schnaars, S., Chia, S., and Maloles, C., Five Modern Lessons from a 55-Year-Old Technological Forecast, Journal of Product Innovation Management, 10 (1), January 1993.

Schumpeter, J., The Theory Of Economic Development Cambridge MA, Harvard University Press 1934.

Serwach, J., GM Steers Toward E-Commerce with E-GM, Knowledgespace, 27 August 1999, *www.knowledgespace.com*

Shahabuddin, S., The Role of Competition in Economic Dominance, International Journal of Technology Management, 9 (1), 1994.

Sheridan, J., A Vision of Agility, Industry Week, 243 (6), 21 March 1994.

Sillup, G., Forecasting the Adoption of New Medical Technology Using the Bass Model, Journal of Health Care Marketing, 12 (4), December 1992.

Sohal, A., and Singh, M., Implementing Advanced Manufacturing Technology: Factors Critical to Success, Logistics Information Management, 5 (1), 1992.

Souder, W., Managing New Product Innovations, Lexington MA, Lexington Books, 1987

Spira, J.S., and Pine, B.J., Mass Customization, Chief Executive, 83, March 1993.

Sprow, E., Little Lathes Make it Big, Manufacturing Engineering, 113(1), July 1994.

Stalk, G., Evans, P., and Shulman, L., Competing On Capabilities : The New Rules Of Corporate Strategy. Harvard Business Review, March/April 1992

Steele, L., Managing Technology: The Strategic View, New York, McGraw-Hill 1989.

Thomas, C., Learning from Imagining the Years Ahead, Planning Review, 22 (3), May/June 1994.

Tornaski, L., The Process Of Technological Innovation: Reviewing The Literature, Washington, National Science Foundation 1983.

Tranfield, D., Smith, S., Ley, C., Bessant, J., and Levy, P., Changing Organisational Design and Practices for Computer-Integrated Technologies, International Journal of Technology Management, 6 (3), 1991.

Tschirky, H., The Role of Technology Forecasting and Assessment in Technology Management, R&D Management, 24 (2), April 1994.

Twiss, B.C., Managing Technological Innovation 2nd ed., London, Longman Group, 1980.

Utterback, J., The Process Of Technological Innovation Within Firms, Academy Of Management Journal 1972

Utterback, J.M., and Abernathy, W.J., Multivariant Models for Innovation/ Looking at the Abernathy and Utterback Model with Other Data, OMEGA, 9 1981.

Vandstone, A., Create To Compete: Developing New Directions For Australian Industry Policy. Discussion Paper, Canberra, 1994

Vasilash, G.S., GM Truck and Bus: On the Cutting Edge of Laser Cutting Technology, Production, 104 (1), 1992.

Vesey, J., The New Competitors Think in Terms of 'Speed to Market', SAM Advanced Management Journal, 56 (4), Autumn 1992.

Voss, C., A New Spring for Manufacturing, Journal of Business Strategy, 15 (1), January/ February 1994.

Wood, F., Succeeding in Textiles in the Nineties, Textile World, 143 (9), September 1993.

Woodward, D., and Liu, B., Investing in China: Guidelines for Success, Long Range Planning, 26 (2), April 1993.

Youseff, M., Computer-Based Technologies and their Impact on Manufacturing Flexibility, International Journal of Technology Management, 8 (3-5), 1993.

Zahra, S., Sisodia, R. and Das, S., Technological Choices Within Competitive Strategy Types: A Conceptual Integration, International Journal Of Technology Management, 9 (2), 1994.

Zairi, M., Competitive Manufacturing: Combining Total Quality with Advanced Technology, Long Range Planning, 26 (3), 1993.

Zammuto, R., and O'Connor, E., Gaining Advanced manufacturing Technologies' Benefits: The Roles of Organization Design and Culture, Academy of Management Review, 17 (4), October 1992.

Index

Index